Bridal Hair

Pat Dixon and Jacki Wadeson

HAIRDRESSING Training BOARD

First published 2000 by
MACMILLAN PRESS LTD
Houndmills, Basingstoke, Hampshire RG21 6XS
and London
Companies and representatives
throughout the world

ISBN 0–333–77467–1

A catalogue record for this book is available from the British Library.

This book is printed on paper suitable for recycling and made from fully managed and sustained forest sources.

10   9   8   7   6   5   4   3   2   1
09   08   07   06   05   04   03   02   01   00

Printed in Great Britain by
Jarrold Book Printing,
Thetford, Norfolk

Contents

Hairdressing Training Board / Macmillan Series

Start Hairdressing! – The Official Guide to Level 1 Martin Green & Leo
  Palladino
Hairdressing: The Foundations – The Official Guide to Level 2 Leo
  Palladino
Professional Hairdressing – The Official Guide to Level 3 Martin Green,
  Lesley Kimber & Leo Palladino
Patrick Cameron: Dressing Long Hair Patrick Cameron & Jacki Wadeson
Patrick Cameron: Dressing Long Hair Book 2 Patrick Cameron
Mahogany: Steps to Cutting, Colouring and Finishing Hair Martin Gannon
  & Richard Thompson
The World of Hair: A Scientific Companion John Gray
Safety in the Salon Elaine Almond
Trevor Sorbie: Visions in Hair Trevor Sorbie, Kris Sorbie & Jacki Wadeson
The Art of Hair Colouring David Adams & Jacki Wadeson
African-Caribbean Hairdressing Sandra Gittens
Men's Hairdressing Maurice Lister
Bridal Hair Pat Dixon & Jacki Wadeson
The Total Look Ian Mistlin

The Science of Cosmetics John V. Simmons
The Beauty Salon and its Equipment John V. Simmons
Manicure, Pedicure and Advanced Nail Techniques Elaine Almond
The Complete Make-up Artist: Working in Film, Television and Theatre
  Penny Delamar
The World of Skin Care John Gray
Beauty Therapy – The Foundations – The Official Guide to Level 2 Lorraine
  Nordmann
Professional Beauty Therapy – The Official Guide to Level 3 Lorraine
  Nordmann, Lorraine Appleyard & Pamela Linforth

If you would like to receive future titles in the Hairdressing Training Board /
Macmillan series as they are published, you can use our standing order
facility. Contact your bookseller, quoting series standing order ISBN
0–333–69338–8, or write to us with your name and address, the title of
the series and the series ISBN. Customer Services Department, Macmillan
Distribution Ltd, Houndmills, Basingstoke, Hampshire RG21 6XS.

Foreword

Do you create magic?

Can you imagine the perfect style?

A wedding is what you make it. For most people it's a special occasion, an opportunity for celebration. But for a bride it has to be the most special day in her life. And she expects her hair to be part of the magic of her special day.

As a professional hairdresser, you can weave your magic and produce the perfect style. This book contains a range of imaginative and aspirational styles that will widen your repertoire. Your brides will appreciate it.

Alan Goldsbro
Chief Executive
Hairdressing Training Board

Acknowledgements

Hair: Pat Dixon, Classics Hair & Beauty, Kenilworth

Step-by-step make-up: Liz Hoskins and the beauty staff at Classics Hair & Beauty, Kenilworth

Bridal style gallery make-up: Vicki Cameron, Carol Maye and Amanda Lawley

Photography: Simon Donnelly

Still-life photography: Barry Cook

Classics Bridal Hire Collection, 1 High Street, Kenilworth, CV8 1LY.
Tel: + 44 (0) 1926 511246

Cocoa, 9 Clarence Parade, Cheltenham, Gloucestershire, GL50 3NY.
Tel: + 44 (0) 1242 233588

Kesté by Myring Kesterton, Studio 209, The Custard Factory, Gibb Street,
Digbeth, Birmingham, B9 4AA. Tel: + 44 (0) 121 683 5108

Vicki Waring, 53 Wainbody Avenue, Coventry, CV3 6DA.
 Tel: + 44 (0) 1203 410098

The Flower Cellar, The Old Forge, Balsall Street, Balsall Common, Warwickshire,
CV7 7AP. Tel: + 44 (0) 1676 534117

Pauline Worthington at Cobwebs and Creations Jewellery Workshop.
Tel: + 44 (0) 1676 542284

Karen Singleton, 85 Coronation Road, Southville, Bristol, BS3 1AT.
Tel: + 44 (0) 117 9637474

Virgin Bride, The Grand Buildings, Northumberland Avenue, London WC2N 5EJ.
Tel: + 44 (0) 171 766 9112

Heapys Morning Suit Hire, Westgate House, Warwick, CV34 4DH.
Tel: + 44 (0) 1926 400647

H. Samuel, branches nationwide, call Freephone 0800 3894683

With special thanks to: Cara Wagstaff, Myring Kesterton, Vicki Waring, Carol Price, Pauline Worthington, Karen Singleton, Kim Baker, Caroline Neville Associates, Jane Bloxham, and all our beautiful models.

This book is dedicated to the nursing and medical team at the Bone Infection Ward of the Nuffield Orthopaedic Centre in Oxford, who have helped give me the strength of body and determination of mind to overcome the trauma of losing my leg. I would also like to thank my husband, Roy, whose enduring love and support has enabled me to continue my career in hairdressing.

Pat Dixon

Introduction

On the most important day of a bride's life, the only person who can create the hairstyle of her dreams is her hairdresser. This beautiful book explains how to offer a comprehensive bridal hair and beauty service: from helping your bride to choose her dress, head-dress and flowers to co-ordinating these with a style that suits her hair type and texture. Whatever her hair length, you and your bride will find inspiration in our bridal style gallery. Techniques, from the basic to the more complicated, are all illustrated in our easy-to-follow step-by-steps that fulfil many of the NVQ Levels 2 and 3 criteria. There is also a selection of romantic styles for seasonal and themed weddings, plus hints and tips on working with flowers, veils and hats. Everything you need to know to ensure that your bridal clients look magical on their wedding day.

Jacki Wadeson

Consultation

Ideally your bride should visit the salon three months before the wedding for a consultation of at least 30 minutes. It is a good idea if her mother or a friend accompanies her, and essential that she brings along details of the dress she has chosen or is planning to buy. You need to know whether the dress is simple or fussy, slim or full and, most importantly, what type of neckline it has. Hair tone and depth should also be taken into consideration when finalising the fabric and head-dress colour: white is good with ash-blonde, medium brown or black hair; colours from ivory to oyster go well with strawberry blonde, auburn or chestnut hair; gold looks good with warm hair tones such as golden brown, chestnut and red; silver suits dark blondes, blue-black, ash-brown or ash-blonde hair and pastels look best on fair hair.

Ask about the timing and type of wedding: Is it going to have a traditional, modern, classical or medieval theme? Is it going to be in a church or will it be a civil ceremony? Does the bride have definite ideas about whether she wants to wear a tiara, veil, flowers, diamanté clips, slides, pearls or butterflies in her hair?

Assess the bride's face and body shape so you can make sure the finished hairstyle balances perfectly. Check how tall the bridegroom is – you don't want to suggest a head-dress that leaves the bride towering over him. Have to hand a bridal style book containing pictures that show different looks so you can get a general feel of the bride's preferences. Once you have decided on the best style, then check whether the bride's hair type and texture are suitable. A beautiful head of tonged curls may be her romantic dream but if you know the hair will drop, persuade her to opt for something different. If a head-dress or veil is being worn, check its weight – it may not stay in place if the hair is too fine.

Make sure the bride has thought about her outfit as a whole; shoes and jewellery are important elements. The overall look should also be in keeping with her general style. Another consideration is whether the bride is going to change for an evening party. If so, her hair will need to be designed so that it will look good with both outfits.

Once you have decided on the best and most appropriate style, then is the time to draw up a pre-wedding hair and beauty plan, which includes a schedule to get hair healthy and glossy in time for the wedding. Include recommendations for timings of colour, cutting and perms, for facial, body and nail treatments, and for artificial tanning. Draw up a list of home maintenance products so the bride can keep up the good work between salon visits. Book an appointment for a dress rehearsal and find out whether the bride will visit the salon on the day or whether she wants her hair done on site. Don't forget the rest of the wedding party – the bride's mother, the bridesmaids and the bridegroom will also need to book salon appointments at this time.

Hair accessories: Classics Bridal Hire Collection and Virgin Bride

Head-dresses

Head-dresses are a bride's crowning glory, and there are so many beautiful styles to choose from: close-fitting skullcaps, beaded combs, snoods, floral headbands, richly jewelled antique tiaras encrusted with crystals and diamanté or modern tiaras on more minimalist lines.

Many designers will custom-make head-dresses to suit the line and shape of the dress. If this is what your bride wants, then make sure she places her order in plenty of time.

Whichever head-dress is chosen, it is important to have a trial run. Don't rely on the combs or fixings that are already attached to the head-dress. Experiment with additional clips and pins to ensure it stays securely in place.

Snood and beaded comb: Classics Bridal Hire Collection
Headbands: Virgin Bride

Opposite Skullcap and dress: Cocoa

A simple upswept style can be changed by the choice of tiara – see how the purity of pearls gives a clean line, glamorous gems a richer look and glass stones set in gold a more regal air.

Dress and tiaras: Classics Bridal Hire Collection

*Modern tiaras are fashioned in copper and brass,
with simple clean lines.*

Modern tiaras: Cobwebs and Creations Jewellery Workshop

Antique tiaras are often very ornate
with seed pearls, mother of pearl
and an abundance of diamanté.

Antique tiaras and dress: Cocoa

Flowers

Single flowers gripped into a hairstyle make an instant transformation. Keep blooms in a cool place before use and mist with water to freshen up before clipping into hair.

Roses and gypsophila gripped to either side of a low ponytail are simple yet effective.

Flowers: The Flower Cellar

How to fix flowers in place

1 Thread stem of flower through looped end of a hairpin.

———✳———

2 Push hairpin into hair, then further secure flower stem with a hairgrip. Repeat with as many flowers as you wish to use.

———✳———

3 Shows side view.

Veils

Veils add the finishing touch to the bride and give a fairytale aura to the simplest dress. The more layers the veil has, the fuller the look. Pure silk or antique veils have a softer feel and flow better than the stiffer man-made veiling or net. Embroidery, beading, ribboned edges and crystals draw attention to the veil. Opt for a simple veil with an ornate gown, or a more detailed one with a plain dress. Veils always work best when the hairstyle has some height, which gives lift and balance to the look. There are many different styles of veils. Five popular styles are listed opposite.

Bouffant – this just touches the shoulders and is quite fluffy and informal. Fun with shorter hair.

Cathedral – very long, this type of veil finishes six feet after the train. Looks beautiful with almost any hairstyle.

Church – full-length veil that ends about foot beyond the dress. Exquisite with more elaborate hairstyles.

Fingertip – ends where your fingertips touch your legs when you are standing. Perfect with soft curls or ringlets.

Mantilla – a lace-trimmed one-layer veil that frames the face and is attached with pins or a comb. Superb with smoother, dressier hairstyles.

How to secure a veil

1 Attach a hairgrip to each end of tiara and push into place.

———— ✳ ————

2 Insert comb which is attached to veil into hair and slide in until it feels firm.

———— ✳ ————

3 Take veil back over hair and fluff out.

———— ✳ ————

4 Shows veil and tiara in place.

TIP

To remove creases from a veil, hold taut and use the hot air from your hairdryer to smooth over the surface. Modern veils can be stiffened with spray starch but this is not suitable for antique ones as it may damage the fabric.

Opposite Dress, head-dress and hand-embroidered choker: Cocoa

Hats

Hats are often the first choice for thirty-something brides who are having a civil wedding. Whether the design is plain, or swathed with organza, lace, or flowers, it needs a neat hairstyle that balances perfectly. Short hair can be styled behind the ears, while longer locks are best slicked back and formed into a neat, smooth bun at the nape of the neck.

How to dress hair to wear with a hat

1 Smooth hair back into a low ponytail. Divide hair into sections and wind onto heated rollers. Leave rollers in place until hair and rollers are completely cool.

— ✳ —

2 Remove rollers and take a small section of hair from underneath and wrap round base of ponytail. Pin in place.

— ✳ —

3 Shows back of hair completed before positioning hat.

✳ ———————————— ✳

𝒯IP

When a hat is worn with longer hair, it is important that the ponytail is positioned low into the nape of the neck so that the hat sits perfectly.

✳ ———————————— ✳

Opposite Dress and hat: Classics Bridal Hire Collection

Bouquets

A wedding isn't complete without flowers, and these days brides have a wondrous array of blooms to choose from, most of which are available all year round. The key to getting perfect wedding flowers is to talk to the florist, who will be able to advise you as to what shape of bouquet will flatter the wedding gown. Flowers should complement, rather than overpower, the wedding outfit. Whether the bride chooses a trailing shower bouquet or a hand-held posy, it's important to keep things in proportion. As a general rule, the bigger the skirt the bigger the bouquet. Also, a tall bride can carry a larger bouquet than a petite bride.

Dress and jewelled hairband: Virgin Bride
Flowers: The Flower Cellar

Dress and tiara: Kesté by Myring Kesterton

The meaning of flowers

Azalea – true to the end

Cedar leaf – I live for you

Celandine – joys to come

Chervil – sincerity

Forget-me-not – true love

Freesia – fragrant

Geranium – true friendship

Gorse – enduring affection

Heliotrope – devotion

Hyacinth – constancy

Ivy – fidelity

Mudwort – happiness

Pink – pure love

Red rose – love

Sweet pea – bright

Violet – faithfulness

White rose – purity

Accessories

Baubles and beads add that finishing touch and make any bride sparkle. Traditional pearls and diamonds are perfect for formal gowns but many contemporary brides wear modern accessories that feature splashes of colour. Short or slim gowns with very little detailing provide the perfect canvas for a dazzling choker or a necklace, while more ornate gowns look better with a single item such as a drop pearl or a solitaire diamond.

Jewellery from a selection at Classics Bridal Hire Collection and Virgin Bride
Opposite Gloves: Classics Bridal Hire Collection

Antique lace gloves evoke the
romance of a bygone era.

19

Dress rehearsal

Once all the ingredients for the bridal look have been chosen, it is essential to have a dress rehearsal, with the hairstyle, head-dress, tiara, veil and mock-up flowers in place. At this stage there is still time to make adjustments to ensure the look is perfect for the wedding day. It is also the time to ensure that the bride has remembered those little extras, such as a satin or embroidered bag to hold make-up essentials, a garter trimmed with blue ribbon, and something treasured to borrow from a special friend.

Traditional wedding slippers are made in silk or satin to match the dress, but as fabric doesn't give like leather, half a size bigger than normal is a good idea. Heels shouldn't be too high and the shoes should be worn indoors a few times prior to the wedding day to break them in and make sure they are comfortable. The style of the shoe is also important and should be appropriate to the time of year. Whatever style is chosen, the shoes should be worn at the final dress fitting to ensure the length is correct. If they have price stickers on the soles, this is the time to remove them.

Parasol, bag, shoes: Cocoa
Garter: Virgin Bride
Pearls: Classics Bridal Hire Collection

Opposite Dress and head-dress: Cocoa

Bridesmaids

Young misses will love to have their hair blow-dried straight or tonged into soft curls. Floral tiaras should co-ordinate with the bride's bouquet and the overall colour theme.

Dresses: Classics Bridal Hire Collection
Floral head-dresses: The Flower Cellar
Opposite Pageboy outfit and dress: Classics Bridal Hire Collection

Tiny pageboys and little maids need newly washed hair that is simply misted with spray shine for extra gloss.

Maids of honour

Modern maids prefer smooth and sophisticated hairstyles and dresses that can be used for evening wear later on.

Dresses: Kesté by Myring Kesterton
Head-dress: The Flower Cellar

Bride's mother
& bridegroom

The other two most important members of the wedding party should also have a hair and beauty plan to ensure they look good on the day. For the bridegroom, a haircut and nail buffing. The bride's mother deserves a little more pampering, with weekly facials, neck, hand and body treatments during the run up to the wedding, and haircut, colour or perm a week before. Hairstyling on the day should be done in plenty of time and kept simple and neat.

TIP

A distinctive buttonhole is all important. Bridegrooms should choose a single flower to match their bride's bouquet, or try a simple spray of foliage.

Morning suit: Heapys
Dress, jacket and hat: Model's own

The big day

Soft, feminine bridal make-up is the order of the day. Blemishes should be disguised by applying concealer with a small brush, then liquid foundation to match the skin tone applied with a damp sponge. Start with a light covering and build up if necessary to give a flawless finish that will last all day. Set foundation by using a pad of cotton wool to press loose powder over the face and neck, then remove excess using downward strokes of a large powder brush. Blusher should be applied with a large brush to cheekbones and blended so it fades naturally towards hairline. Eyelids should be powdered to give a base, then softly coloured with the lightest of eyeshadows. Accentuate brows with a pencil and slick them into place with a tiny dab of hair gel. Lashes should be curled, then two thin coats of mascara applied. If lashes clog, gently separate with a small comb. Lips should be outlined in pencil and filled in using a lipbrush, then glossed over for a dewy finish.

The perfume the bride chooses will forever recall memories of her wedding day so it is important that she picks wisely. The key to finding the right fragrance is to identify the type of bride. A spring bride who chooses pale pink and peach colours with soft flowing fabrics, tiny garden flowers and ultra-feminine accessories will ruin the effect with a musk-based scent that is more suited to a glamorous evening reception or winter wedding. The romantic bride who wears reams of chiffon or antique lace and carries pastel roses or a wild-flower bouquet needs a gentle floral fragrance. The classic bride with her full veil, simple head-dress and full-skirted gown or corset dress needs a timeless fragrance with rose or lavender, while traditional brides can choose a heavier, more powerful scent. Wacky brides who wear colourful dresses can set the tone with a daring fragrance of amber and a twist of grapefruit, while the young bride should opt for the freshness of a water-based, lighter scent.

Opposite Dress, bag and tiara: Kesté by Myring Kesterton

Head-dress: Karen Singleton
Dress: Classics Bridal Hire Collection

28

Bridal style gallery

34 romantic looks

Our beautiful bridal collection features 34 romantic wedding-day styles. Choose from classic, timeless looks or from alternative styles for the contemporary bride. Take inspiration from the basic shape and line but personalise the looks to suit individual hair type and texture.

Ballet shoes: Cocoa

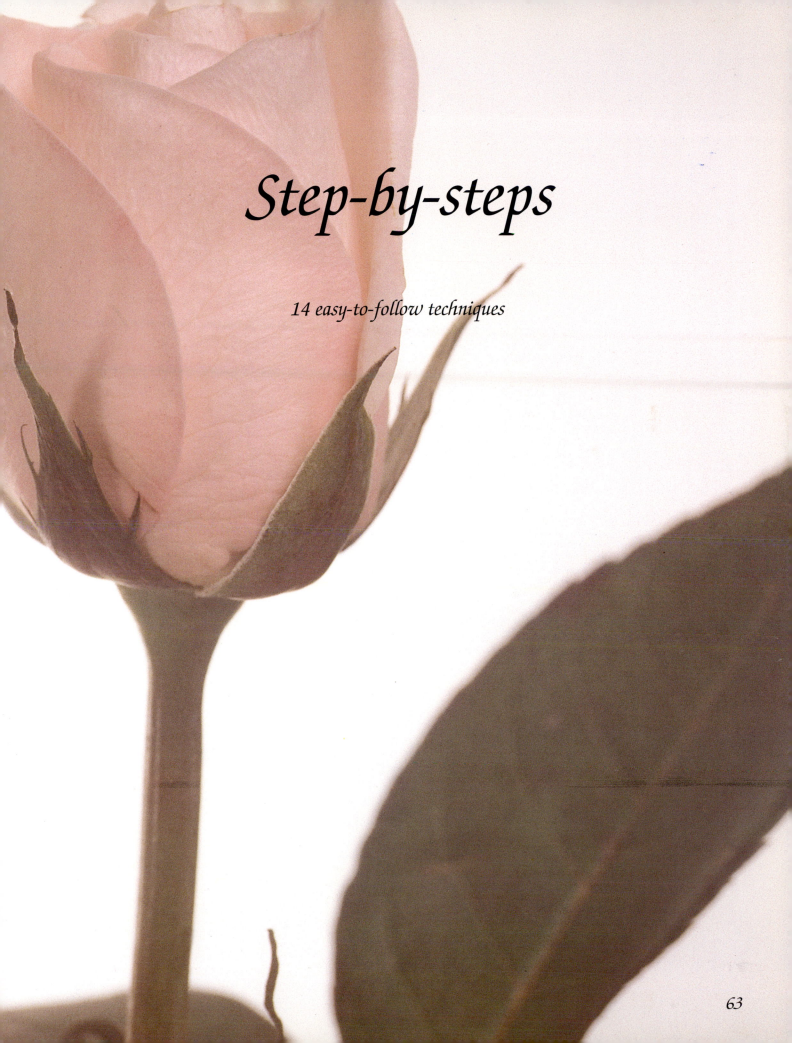

Step-by-steps

14 easy-to-follow techniques

IRIS

1 Section off top hair and clip out of the way. Blow-dry, lifting hair at root level to achieve volume.

———— ✳ ————

2 Unclip top hair and blow-dry in same manner.

———— ✳ ————

3 Use a hot air styler with a large barrel brush to build body and create smoothness.

———— ✳ ————

4 Flick out ends of hair using a hot air styler with a small barrel brush. Backcomb hair lightly at roots before fixing tiara.

TIP

Point the barrel of the hairdryer so that the warm air flows down the hair shaft. This flattens the cuticle of the hair and helps give a greater shine.

Dress and tiara: Cocoa

BLOSSOM

1 Mist hair thoroughly with styling spray. From a side parting, fingerwave front hair and spiral barrel curl back hair. Heat set under a dryer and allow to cool completely.

———— ✳ ————

2 Release barrel curls and allow to fall.

———— ✳ ————

3 Use a bristle brush to gently smooth hair, allowing it to form into gentle waves.

TIP

A bristle brush helps eliminate static and is great for hair that tends to be flyaway.

4 Take a small section of hair from behind ear and loop upwards and pin, curving ends into a curl.

———— ✳ ————

5 Take another small section of hair and twist over first curl, allowing ends to hang temporarily free.

———— ✳ ————

6 Secure end of curl at nape of neck using a grip. Dress remaining lengths of hair in same way.

———— ✳ ————

7 Position then grip head-dress in place.

Opposite Head-dress: Classics Bridal Hire Collection

LAVENDER

1 Section off front hair from a diagonal parting and secure with section clips. For the time being, secure back hair into a low ponytail and leave until you are ready to work on this section.

———— ✳ ————

2 Shows back view of sectioned hair.

———— ✳ ————

3 Take one side section of hair and mist with styling spray. Comb hair and sweep backwards, placing finger under the point you want the twist to start.

———— ✳ ————

4 Twist this section of hair towards the head, holding tension.

5 Continue twisting, smoothing any stray ends with a tail comb.

——— ✳ ———

6 Secure twist with a hairgrip at back of head.

——— ✳ ———

7 Repeat for other side.

——— ✳ ———

8 Fold ends of twists upwards and grip. Mist with hairspray.

✳ TIP ✳

Use a firm hold hairspray for this style to ensure it stays in place all day.

9

12

10

11

9 Release hair from ponytail and lightly backcomb.

———— ✳ ————

10 Use a bristle brush to smooth hair upwards, as if into a high ponytail. Mist with hairspray, making sure all flyaway ends are smoothed into place.

———— ✳ ————

11 Twist hair, allowing ends to fan out.

———— ✳ ————

12 Grip to secure.

LAVENDER

13 Lightly backcomb ends of hair.

———— ✳ ————

14 Mist with hairspray, lifting ends to achieve texture.

———— ✳ ————

15 Take head-dress with a comb attachment. Align teeth of comb centrally on crown of head.

———— ✳ ————

16 Slide comb of head-dress into place.

Opposite Dress and head-dress: Classics Bridal Hire Collection

CRYSTAL

1 Part hair in a zig-zag line, leaving side tendrils free.

———— ✳ ————

2 Blow-dry lower hair, using the minimum amount of styling product, so you maintain the maximum shine on the hair.

———— ✳ ————

3 Use a hot air styler to achieve volume on crown.

4 Lightly backcomb crown hair at roots to give height and provide a good base for attaching the floral head-dress.

———— ✳ ————

5 Grip head-dress in place.

———— ✳ ————

6 Apply a little gel to side tendrils and curve onto face.

TIP

By combining the use of a hot air styler and backcombing hair at the roots you will ensure that the floral head-dress stays in place.

Flowers: The Flower Cellar

Opposite Dress: Kesté by Myring Kesterton

Tulip

1 Part hair in a zig-zag from forehead to crown.

———— ✳ ————

2 Take a section of hair, in a circle, from zig-zag parting and hold with hand.

———— ✳ ————

3 Secure section using dressmaking elastic.

———— ✳ ————

4 Take two more circular sections in same way – picture shows top view.

———— ✳ ————

5 Back view – the central section of hair has been lightly twisted to show partings clearly.

———— ✳ ————

6 Take the central back section and twist half way down length.

———— ✳ ————

7 The twist will begin to double back on itself and form a coil.

———— ✳ ————

8 Grip coil in place, leaving ends to fall free.

———— ✳ ————

9 Twist other two sections of hair in same way – picture shows all three coils completed.

10 Divide free ends of one coiled section into three and randomly curl using tongs. Do not tong the entire section, just part, as shown, to achieve this texture mix.

———— ✳ ————

11 Repeat for other coiled sections.

———— ✳ ————

12 Take a small section of hair from side and tie into a knot just a little way from roots.

———— ✳ ————

13 Shows completed back view.

Opposite Dress: Kesté by Myring Kesterton

Hellena

1 Smooth hair back into a high ponytail and secure with dressmaking elastic. Separate a quarter of the ponytail hair into a separate, smaller section.

———— ✳ ————

2 Tong each section of ponytail hair separately. Clipping one out of the way while you do the other.

———— ✳ ————

3 Take the small section of tonged hair and wrap round base of ponytail. Tuck ends in and grip in place.

———— ✳ ————

4 Take remaining larger section of hair and lightly backcomb. Flip forward and grip as shown.

———— ✳ ————

5 Curve back, allowing ends to form into a curl, and secure with grips.

———— ✳ ————

6 Position and grip flowers in place.

Tip

Try to use grips and pins that match the hair colour.

Opposite Dress: Classic Bridal Hire Collection

Daisy

1 Set crown hair on heated rollers straight back. Set back hair, from ear to ear, on hot sticks, working vertically. At one side, divide hair into three horizontal sections, leaving a tendril of hair to fall free. Start with lowest section and corn weave hair flat to head back towards ear. Secure by tying with cotton, then wind loose ends onto hot stick. Work on second section in same way.

———— ✳ ————

2 Work third section in same way, then repeat for other side.

———— ✳ ————

3 Shows completed pli.

———— ✳ ————

4 Blow-dry smooth the hair that was left out at the back.

———— ✳ ————

5 Unclip top of one hot stick and slide out of hair, keeping ringlet intact.

———— ✳ ————

6 Separate hair of ringlet into tendrils.

———— ✳ ————

7 Shows all hot sticks removed and hair cascading in tendrils.

———— ✳ ————

8 Remove heated rollers, except front one.

———— ✳ ————

9 Lightly backcomb crown hair at roots.

10

12

10 Smooth over and pin at top of ringlets.

———— ✳ ————

11 Remove remaining heated roller, lightly backcomb hair at roots and smooth over and clip in same way.

———— ✳ ————

12 Tong side tendrils.

———— ✳ ————

13 Shows completed front view.

———— ✳ ————

14 Shows completed side view.

11

13

*T*IP

For an even firmer set, use a dryer with a diffuser attachment set on a low heat/speed setting to further dry the hair. Allow hair to cool completely before removing rollers and hot sticks and styling as illustrated.

Opposite Dress: Kesté by Myring Kesterton

14

GYPSY

1 Set partially dried hair on self-fixing rollers – picture shows completed front view.

———— ✳ ————

2 Shows completed side view of pli with fringe and side hair set in barrel pin curls.

✳ ————————————— ✳

TIP

Use self-fixing rollers with a heat-retaining metallic band – they give a firmer, longer-lasting set.

✳ ————————————— ✳

3 Hood dry. When hair is completely cold, remove rollers.

———— ✳ ————

4 Shows all rollers removed.

———— ✳ ————

5 Start smoothing hair from front, using a bristle brush.

———— ✳ ————

6 Brush right through to ends, flicking hair out.

———— ✳ ————

7 Mist with hairspray while lifting with fingers to give volume and texture.

———— ✳ ————

8 Position head-dress and grip in place, then comb fringe.

ARIES

1 Take section from side and slightly twist to centre back.

———— ✳ ————

2 Secure with a grip.

———— ✳ ————

3 Repeat for other side. Divide lower section into three, leaving a few curls out at centre back.

———— ✳ ————

4 Roll one side section of hair from nape and secure at centre back with a grip.

———— ✳ ————

5 Repeat for other side.

———— ✳ ————

6 Scoop up remaining centre section and secure with grips.

———— ✳ ————

7 Gently dress curls to give full and natural movement.

TIP

Mist finished hairstyle with a light hold product so that when hair is let down, it will fall into soft, tumbling waves and won't feel sticky.

Dress and jewellery: Kesté by Myring Kesterton
Tiara: Classics Bridal Hire Collection

MIMOSA

1 Part hair at side and section off back, holding in place with a section clip.

*

2 Shows front view of sectioning.

*

3 Unclip back section and use a bristle brush to smooth hair.

*

4 Twist hair around fingers as if tying a knot.

*

5 Pull knot up ...

*

6 ... and through.

*

7 Pull out ends and twist.

*

8 Secure with grip inserted vertically down twisted section.

*

9 Now grip horizontally.

MIMOSA

10 Bring up one section of side hair and lightly backcomb.

————— ✳ —————

11 Smooth this hair to crown, curving into place and leaving ends free. Grip in place.

————— ✳ —————

12 Take other side, separate out a small section and leave to fall free and curve onto face. Backcomb the main section and smooth over, taking ends to crown, curving into place and allowing ends to form a tuft. Grip into place.

————— ✳ —————

13 Backcomb tuft of hair from the knot, leaving the two ends that were taken from the sides free.

————— ✳ —————

14 Shows back view with ends backcombed.

————— ✳ —————

15 Finally, backcomb ends of curved hair that was left free and fan out.

————— ✳ —————

16 Push tiara into place and secure with a grip.

TIP

This is a versatile style that is suitable for all types of head-dresses.

Opposite Dress and head-dress: Classics Bridal Hire Collection

ROSE

1 Smooth hair back to crown and secure in band.

———— ✳ ————

2 Mist with hairspray to smooth any frizzy ends.

———— ✳ ————

3 Take a small section of hair from underneath ponytail and comb smooth.

———— ✳ ————

4 Wrap this piece of hair round base of ponytail and grip underneath to secure.

———— ✳ ————

5 Take ponytail and backcomb at roots.

———— ✳ ————

6 Smooth top layer of hair.

———— ✳ ————

7 Grip into place.

———— ✳ ————

8 Clasp length of ponytail in one hand and twist slightly to one side, using end of tail comb to achieve shape.

———— ✳ ————

9 Secure with grips positioned vertically as shown.

ROSE

10 Divide remaining hair into two sections, comb one smooth.

───── ✳ ─────

11 Twist this section until hair starts to double back on itself and form a curl.

───── ✳ ─────

12 Secure with grips.

───── ✳ ─────

13 Twist remaining section of hair and grip into place in same way.

───── ✳ ─────

14 Shows back view. Add tiara and grip into place.

✳ ──────────────── ✳

𝒯IP

When smoothing hair over, mist comb with hairspray to help slick in stray ends.

✳ ──────────────── ✳

Opposite Dress, head-dress, and choker: Cocoa

LILY

1 Smooth hair into a ponytail, making sure that base aligns with top of ear.

———— ✳ ————

2 Section off top third of ponytail and clip out of the way.

———— ✳ ————

3 Backcomb remaining hair – firmly at base of ponytail but lightly at ends. Mist with hairspray.

———— ✳ ————

4 Smooth ponytail using a tail comb.

5 Tuck in ends and pin into place.

———— ✳ ————

6 Mist underneath with hairspray, making sure you use sufficient product to ensure a firm hold.

———— ✳ ————

7 Unclip reserved section of hair, then divide into three equal sections.

———— ✳ ————

8 Lightly backcomb centre section.

9 Hold section upwards and insert two grips, crossing them over each other as shown.

———— ✳ ————

10 Smooth this section of hair into a gentle curving curl.

———— ✳ ————

11 Bend back end of fine hair pin. This prevents it falling out when placed into hair.

12

13

14

15

12 Use the bent pin to secure the curl.

———— ✳ ————

13 Take second reserved section of hair and backcomb.

———— ✳ ————

14 Twist into a curl.

———— ✳ ————

15 Tuck in any stray ends using a tail comb, then pin in place. Repeat with last section of reserved hair. Pin flowers in place.

Opposite Dress: Classics Bridal Hire Collection

GENESSA

1 Section off a circle of hair on crown and clip out of the way. Set small tendrils on forehead in pin curls, then set remaining hair in hot sticks. To do this, take horizontal sections from hairline to crown. Place hot stick three inches from end of hair and wind hair over.

———— ✳ ————

2 Continue winding until you run out of hair, tucking end in so hair doesn't unravel.

———— ✳ ————

3 Wind hot stick up to scalp, tucking in any stray ends using a tail comb. Fold over each end of hot stick to secure.

———— ✳ ————

4 Shows completed side view with side tendril left free.

5

5 Continue setting hair in hot sticks in this way until all back hair is wound. Leave a few tendrils free – these will be curled later.

———— ✳ ————

6 Unclip top section of hair and set in heated rollers in the normal way.

———— ✳ ————

7 Tong side and back tendrils using a medium barrel tong.

———— ✳ ————

8 Remove hot sticks by first straightening folded over ends and unwinding a little way.

6

8

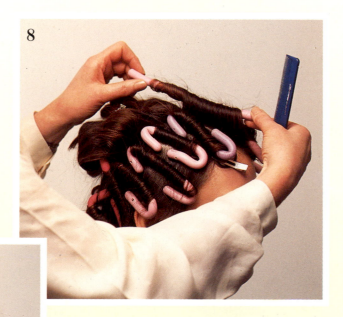

7

✳ ————————————— ✳

𝒯IP

Take care not to buckle ends of hair when using hot sticks or heated rollers.

✳ ————————————— ✳

9 Gently loosen the hot stick and start to remove, allowing coil of hair to stay in place. Encourage coil to stay in place using the end of a tail comb.

———— ✳ ————

10 Carefully pull out hot stick.

———— ✳ ————

11 Tie end of hair into a loose knot.

———— ✳ ————

12 Grip curl in place at base of knot.

13 Remove heated rollers and loop hair into curls.

————— ✳ —————

14 Continue working in same way until all curls are formed and pinned.

————— ✳ —————

15 Tidy any stray ends using a tail comb.

————— ✳ —————

16 Release front pin curls and secure hair at back with pins.

Opposite Dress and head-dress: Kesté by Myring Kesterton

IVY

1 From a side parting, section off front hair. Divide back hair into two ponytails as shown.

———— ✳ ————

2 Working on one section at a time, smooth front hair and drape up to top ponytail, taking ends round base of ponytail. Temporarily clip in place.

———— ✳ ————

3 Backcomb end of lower ponytail, and smooth using a bristle brush.

———— ✳ ————

4 Form hair into a roll and tuck in ends using a tail comb to smooth.

———— ✳ ————

5 Take top ponytail and lightly backcomb. Divide into two sections curving one each side of head.

6 Lightly twist ends of one of these sections round fingers, using a tail comb to tuck in ends, then secure with grips and pins.

———— ✻ ————

7 Repeat for other side, first curving the section of hair ...

———— ✻ ————

8 ... then coiling, tucking ends in and pinning into place.

———— ✻ ————

9 Shows completed back view.

———— ✻ ————

10 Position floral headband and secure with grips.

Seasonal & themed wedding styles

AUTUMN

Dress and head-dress:
Kesté by Myring Kesterton

WINTER

Dress: Classics Bridal Hire Collection
Head-dress: Karen Singleton

MEDIEVAL

Dress and head-dress: Cocoa

Dress, head-dress and ear-rings: Classics Bridal Hire Collection

TRADITIONAL

Dresses: Classics Bridal Hire Collection
Head-dress (this page): Classics Bridal Hire Collection
Head-dress (opposite): Karen Singleton

MODERN

Dress: Kesté by Myring Kesterton
Head-dress: Cobwebs and
Creations Jewellery Workshop

Dress: Virgin Bride
Hair pins: Classics Bridal Hire Collection

Suit and hat: Model's own

The tradition of throwing rice over newly weds goes back to pagan fertility rituals. Little cakes, nuts and biscuits were also sometimes thrown and symbolised good luck. Paper confetti came into use early this century – and these days it comes biodegradable. Many brides are opting for real, scented rose petals, or little pots of bubbles, the twenty-first-century alternative. Embroidered horseshoes add that finishing touch and provide a keepsake that brings back happy memories of the day.

Horseshoes: Cocoa

Scene Design
and Stage Lighting

Scene Design and Stage Lighting

Sixth Edition

W. OREN PARKER

Carnegie-Mellon University

R. CRAIG WOLF

San Diego State University

Holt, Rinehart and Winston, Inc.

Fort Worth • Chicago • San Francisco
Philadelphia • Montreal • Toronto
London • Sydney • Tokyo

Publisher	**Charlyce Jones Owen**
Acquisitions Editor	**Janet Wilhite**
Developmental Editor	**Susan Alkana**
Senior Project Editor	**Charlie Dierker**
Manager of Production	**Tad Gaither**
Manager of Art & Design	**Guy Jacobs**
Text Design	**Marilyn Marcus**
Cover Design	**Pat Sloan**

ON THE COVER: *Starlight Express*, photo courtesy Martha Swope.
PAGES 1, 135, AND 321: *Cats*, photos courtesy Martha Swope.

Library of Congress Cataloging-in-Publication Data
Parker, W. Oren (Wilford Oren)
    Scene design and stage lighting/W. Oren Parker, R. Craig Wolf.—6th ed.
        p. cm.
    Includes bibliographical references.
        1. Theaters—Stage-setting and scenery.   2. Stage lighting.
I. Wolf, R. Craig.   II. Title.
PN2091.S8P3   1990
792′.025—dc20   89-19862
                                                                                  CIP

ISBN: 0-03-028777-4

Address Editorial Correspondence To: 301 Commerce Street, Suite 3700
                                          Fort Worth, TX 76102
                    Address Orders To: 6277 Sea Harbor Drive
                                          Orlando, FL 32887
                                          1-800-782-4479, or 1-800-433-0001 (in Florida)

Printed in the United States of America

0 1 2 3   069   9 8 7 6 5 4 3 2

Holt, Rinehart and Winston, Inc.
The Dryden Press
Saunders College Publishing

To Howard Bay

Preface

During the years since the fifth edition of *SCENE DESIGN AND STAGE LIGHTING* was published, our theatre has witnessed many lavish and perceptive productions on Broadway and touring the countryside, displaying the best of English design and originality. While the spotlight of attention shines on these productions, many fine examples of creative design have been occurring at the periphery. Professional design is increasing in American regional theatres from coast to coast.

The sixth edition of *SCENE DESIGN AND STAGE LIGHTING*, while honoring the innovative designs of England and Canada, also salutes the designers in our own American regional theatre. Part I has been reorganized for better sequence and has been reillustrated with current examples of design; this edition significantly increases its representation of American creativity.

Part II has been revised to include new tools and building techniques. Color in the theatre has been improved and expanded into the stage lighting section for closer reference.

Part III has undergone several major changes, the most obvious of which is the inclusion of a new chapter on sound design and production for the theatre. Recognizing the importance of sound as an element of design in the theatre, this chapter acts as an introduction to this important subject.

Extensive rewriting of the lighting chapters has resulted in greater clarity and readability. The sixth edition emphasizes safety and provides updated information on equipment, technology, and technique.

The total art program has been revised in the sixth edition. The order of the lighting chapter has been altered to present the student with a sense of design before an examination of tools and technique.

This edition, like preceding ones, would not have been possible without the valuable assistance of former students, colleagues, and friends. We wish to acknowledge the technical assistance of James Bakkom and Rod Carter, the artistic contributions of Barbara and Cletus Anderson, John Conklin, June DeCamp, Ming Cho Lee, William Matthews, Susan Tsu and Tony Walton.

The sound chapter would not have been possible without the assistance of Charles Weeks, audio engineer for CBS in Los Angeles. In addition, we wish to recognize Tony Tait of the Old Globe Theatre; Mark Able and Peter Nordyke, sound designers at Cal-State Long Beach and San Diego State; and Annette Lignowski of Audio Services Corporation in North Hollywood. We have the honor of including light plots designed by Tharon Musser and Cindy Limauro in this edition as well as design sketches by Beeb Salzer and Susan Gratch. Additional thanks go to lighting designers Tom Ruzika and Pat Simmonds.

A special thanks is extended for the cooperation and assistance of the Yale Theatre Collection; Museum of the Performing Arts, Lincoln Center; the Harvard Theatre Collection; Shaw Festival Theatre, Canada, and the English National Theatre, London.

Finally, we must acknowledge the valuable comments of our colleagues from around the country who kindly participated in reviews that made the sixth edition a reality. The following individuals reviewed both the fifth edition text and the sixth edition manuscript: William Valle, Central Michigan University; Victor McQuiston, University of Nevada-Las Vegas; Alex Adducci, Northern Illinois University; John Burgess, Memphis State University; Howard Brewer, California State University-Fresno; Bob Schmidt, University of Texas-Austin; David Kriebs, University of Maryland; and Lee Watson, Purdue University. The following individuals reviewed the fifth edition text only: Odia Ball, Pierce College; Allen Cornell, Adelphi University; Jeffrey Fiala, University of Massachusetts-Amherst; David Hale, Temple University; and Larry Sutton, De Pauw University.

W.O.P.
R.C.W.

Contents

Scene Design
and Stage Lighting

PART I

THE DESIGN CONCEPT

Introduction

Although design in the theatre may branch off into various areas of specialization, it primarily materializes in three basic forms: First, as an environmental background, or *scenery*; then as *costumes* for the actor within that setting; and finally, unifying all, as *stage lighting.*

The paths leading to a career designing in the theatre are numerous and varied. They may come from within the theatre itself or from the outside world. An actor or director gifted with a visual sense of theatre can contribute to design just as surely as can the trained visual artist, equipped with the practical ability to draw and paint, who possesses a strong desire to be in the theatre. A student from the latter background standing at the threshold of training for a career in design for the theatre may puzzle over what the future holds. The sudden but transitory flush of excitement involving one's first experiences in the theatre should not obscure the need for a long-range artistic commitment to hard work. Anyone interested in achieving creative and personal fulfillment as a scene, costume, or lighting designer, however, must first thoroughly understand the complexity of theatre as an art form.

Theatre today is undergoing rapid change. In the short interval of this century its literary form, its physical form, and, in some cases, its theatrical form (that is, the basic idea of theatre itself), have undergone changes. Some are natural developments or extensions of traditional theatrical forms; some are self-conscious changes for change's sake; while others, by their obscurity to present-day theatregoers, seem designed for an "audience of the future." All these changes in some measure affect designers and their position in the theatre.

THEATRICAL FORM

Theatrical form in its simplest description is the communication of ideas between two groups: performers and audience. The assembly of audience and performers, or *performance*, is the presentation of ideas by the performers to the audience. These ideas may range from the very ancient to the most topical, from the profound to the absurd, and at the same time be either sentimentally obvious or intellectually obscure. The performance can exist in a number of styles and descriptions and in a variety of physical forms. Theatrical styles will be discussed in detail later; it is more important in an introduction to elaborate on the description of types of theatrical forms and the variety of physical forms, or theatre structures, that make up our sometimes controversial, frequently exciting, but always interesting, contemporary theatre.

The three types of theatrical forms that involve the designer most are the *literary form*, or drama; the *musical form*, including opera and book musicals; and, for want of a better name, the *audio-visual form*, which is nonverbal communication that places emphasis on sound and sight and not on the spoken word (for example, ballet, modern dance, and recent experiments in visual sound). All three types of theatrical form, of course, can be united into *total theatre* or joined in such combinations as dance-drama or choral readings.

Of the three forms, the literary form, or drama, has so dominated theatre historically that the word *drama* has become synonymous with *theatre*. The significance of drama to the designer is evidenced by the fact that the major portion of a designer's training for the theatre is spent in learning to interpret and expand the ideas of the playwright.

In recent years the dominance of the literary form has been challenged in the United States by musical theatre. Characterized for so long by its two extremes of either lighthearted musical comedies or the heavier fare of "grand opera," the new musical theatre has tried to unite these extremes in a concept of "total theatre." The strong book musical such as *West Side Story* becomes near-opera in its musical dimension, while its "book," or libretto, drawing a strong contemporary parallel to the classic *Romeo and Juliet* theme, retains a popular appeal through its more accessible use of dialog than opera's recitative.

At the same time, opera has been undergoing a resurgence that in part reflects the influence of the intricate staging of musicals and the philosophy of modern scenography. Opera scenery of the past was for the most part a background of theatrical realism and painted atmosphere. In contrast, modern stage design's interpretive form, color, and light relate much more closely to the emotion of the music and the theme of the libretto. Today's stagings bring visual unity and nonverbal support to an already powerful theatrical form.

Challenging all three theatrical forms is the recent penchant for *spectacle* exemplified by such productions as *Cats, Starlight Express,* and *Phantom of the Opera.* Here design is in the forefront. The audience is dazzled with innovative style, brilliant pyrotechnics, and, in some cases, overwhelming scale.

The need for the presence of the designer in the literary and musical theatre is obvious, for both place great demand on the visual background to set style and often to make a strong visual comment. The audio-visual theatre, however, is almost entirely a visual show. What the performers wear (or do not wear) and their visual surroundings become extremely important. Technical advances in the handling of lights and the electronic production of sound have opened new vistas in this type of theatrical experience. One of the most novel concepts in the audio-visual theatre is revealed in the performances of *Laterna Magika* in the Czechoslovakian theatre, where the media of dance and pantomime are com-

Figure 1-1
Theatrical Forms

(a) *Ballet.* Movement and music are the means of communicating in this decorative and highly stylized performance technique. Shown is the ballet version of Scott Fitzgerald's novel *The Great Gatsby.* Designer—Peter Farmer, Pittsburgh Ballet Theatre. *Photo courtesy Randy Choura.* (b) *Drama.* An atmospheric moment in *The Madwoman of Chaillot* by Jean Giraudoux. Designer—Cameron Porteous, Shaw Festival Theatre. *Photo courtesy David Cooper.* (c) *Opera.* The last act of Dvorak's *Rusalka.* Designer—Stefanos Lazaridis, English National Opera, London. *Photo courtesy Clive Barda*

a

b

c

bined with moving picture projections to create a new and imaginative theatrical form. The proposed theatre of sound and sight by Jacques Polieri in Paris is an audio-visual theatre form of the future. It promises either to eliminate performers altogether or to lift them to unexperienced dimensions by the use of light projections. Innovations of this type have the potential of developing into an exciting, abstract — though largely sensational — theatrical form of the future, with many opportunities for stage designers and theatre technicians.

PHYSICAL FORM

The various types of theatrical form often determine in a general way their physical form. The size of a theatre for a musical production, with its presentational style and spectacular scale, for example, is the opposite of the needs of a theatre for drama, which is more intimate in nature. Both have clung in the past to the traditional, proscenium theatre arrangement of the audience facing the stage. The physical shape of new theatres, however, has undergone a variety of changes, discussed in detail in Chapter 2. Like the innovations in theatrical form, many new theatres contain either modernized improvements on the conventional proscenium shape or are completely different in form and production concept, while a few try to combine both by converting at will from a conventional to an unconventional seating arrangement.

Over the past few years, a great number of new theatres of all forms have sprung up all over the country. Professional resident companies have grown from coast to coast, bringing live theatre to an ever-expanding audience.

Designed primarily for drama and possibly intimate musicals, many recent theatres have taken on the new-old form of the thrust and arena stage. Prompted by the desire to bring the audience closer to the actor, these variations either partially or completely surround the acting area with seats. Although these shapes invariably reduce the amount of scenery normally found in the conventional proscenium theatre, they in a sense give the theatre back to the actor and the playwright by minimizing the scale of the production.

Some of the unique concepts of theatre shapes are those advanced for audio-visual theatres. Although none have been "built" in a traditional sense, their projected schemes foresee a radically different audience-performer relationship. The audience, for example, may be separated into groups with widely different views of a constantly changing performance area. Aside from these audio-visual theatres of the future, dance and ballet have their own special requirements in the audio-visual theatrical form. While dance can give shape to its performance area by the pattern of its choreography, it is more fully enjoyed if viewed from a slightly steeper angle than is provided in the normal theatre seating arrangement.

The trend toward minimum-production theatres, such as the thrust and arena stages, may be disturbing to the beginning designer because of the extreme limits of the staging. Although minimized, however, the need for design is still present. The emphasis merely has changed from the background to what the actors wear and to what they sit or stand upon. Costumes, properties, and lighting rather than elaborate scenic backgrounds become the major areas of design concentration.

Figure 1-2
Proscenium Theatre

The playhouse at Pennsylvania State University includes many recent improvements of the proscenium form such as an elevator system to provide a flexible apron arrangement, side stages and a steeply graded auditorium for optimum vertical sightlines. *Photo courtesy P.S.U. Photography Studio*

Figure 1-3
Thrust Stage

(a) Midwest: Tyrone Guthrie Theatre, Minneapolis. *Photo courtesy Minnesota Theatre Company.* (b) West Coast: Mark Taper Forum, Los Angeles. *The Dream on Monkey Mountain* by Derek Walcott. Designer—Edward Burbridge, Lighting designer—Tharon Musser. *Photo courtesy Carol Oken.* (c) East Coast: Long Wharf Theatre, New Haven Connecticut. *Photo courtesy M. Edgar Rosenblum, Executive Director*

a

b

c

Figure 1-4
Audio-Visual Theatre

A sketch from Jacques Polieri projected scheme for a *Theatre du Mouvement*, a theatre in which the audience, while being carried on slowly moving platforms, is totally surrounded by an experience of sound and visual effects.

Figure 1-5
Arena Theatre

Arena Stage in Washington D.C., a successful example of theatre-in-the-round. *Photo courtesy Capitol Photo Service, Inc.*

a

Figure 1-6
Extended Apron, Open Staging
(a) The greatly altered and highly mechanized forestage of the Stratford-on-Avon Shakespeare Theatre. Half of the acting area is downstage of the old proscenium line. *Photo courtesy Joe Cooks.*
(b) *Blue Window* by Craig Lucas. Set design by Loy Arcenas.
Photography © 1989 by T. Charles Erickson

b

In spite of the popularity of these current forms there are signs that indicate that the proscenium theatre has far from passed from the scene. Arena stage directors, feeling the strain of continually trying to top themselves on a bare stage, are beginning to use more and more traditional production devices to vary the staging. Similarly, after a number of years of staging plays on a thrust stage, the audience and director are now quietly admitting that not all plays lend themselves to thrust staging and perhaps a proscenium-type theatre could *also* be used.

In an effort to find a form midway between thrust and proscenium staging, unique uses of the proscenium theatre form have evolved. In one

Figure 1-7
Nontheatre Forms

(a) Theatre in an old railroad roundhouse, *The Round House,* outskirts of London. (b) Theatre in a garage. The Performance Group, New York. (c) Shakespeare in the Park, *Richard III.* Set design by Santo Loquastro. *Photography by Susan Cook, © 1989 by Martha Swope*

a

b

such case, the picture-frame feeling is reduced by extending the apron of the stage and doing away with the traditional act curtain. The result gives the illusion of a thrust into the audience and at the same time provides a stage far more flexible for the limited use of scenic elements than the true thrust stage.

Nontheatre Form

Partly as a reaction to the theatre building boom there has been a move toward creating theatre in nontheatre structures. The conventional audience-performer arrangement is altered to fit into an old garage, a deserted warehouse, or a gymnasium or ballroom. The unusual relationship of the seating arrangement and performance area is a part of the theatrical experience and is sometimes more exciting than the show itself. Unconventional arrangements free the audience and the performer from any preconceived notion of what will be seen or what can be done.

No matter what direction the physical form of the modern theatre may take from year to year, however, it is evident that the designer must be trained to work in all types of theatre and with all theatrical forms.

SCENE DESIGN

Theatrical form, of which scene design is a vital part, combines many related arts into the very intricate, sometimes frustrating, but always fascinating, art of the theatre. In the drama, or literary theatre, the written words of the playwright are transformed for an audience by the director and fellow artists into an audible and visible expression of the author's ideas. In the presentation of a play, scene design exists solely to bring visual substance through the stage setting to the dreams of the playwright.

In simplest terms, scene design is the designing, executing, and lighting of a stage setting. It is a very limited and specialized area of design based on a wide background of semirelated knowledge as well as specific training in modern theatre practice.

c

The Total Visual Effect

Scene design in the modern theatre is concerned with the total visual effect of a dramatic production. In any production the total visual effect is the sum of all the elements that depend upon being seen to make their impression on the audience. The scenic background is the largest and most obvious visual element that supports the spoken word of the dramatic form. The designing of a setting, however, is not confined to creating the color and shape of framed pieces of scenery alone. It also includes the planning of the quality and intensity of the lights that reveal the scene; the selection and styling of the furniture and set-dressings; the careful consideration of the actors' costumes to blend or contrast with the background; and, because a dramatic production is not a static form, the easy movement of actors. The combination of all these visual elements represents the total visual effect.

The visual requirements of a script may be as simple as those of Wilder's play *Our Town,* which all but eliminates physical elements of scenery, or as complicated as those of Verdi's opera *Aïda,* which requires vast quantities of spectacular background. In either case the visual elements, simple or complicated, have to be designed, prepared, and lighted by someone.

Scene Designers

The esthetic responsibility of the total visual effect is normally in the hands of scene designers, although their importance and influence may vary with the extent of their talent, experience, and personality in comparison to those of fellow artists. Beginning designers are frequently dominated by more experienced directors until they develop enough ability and confidence to warrant full membership on the production team.

Qualities of Designers • Beginning designers are expected to know so many things almost at once that they may be puzzled where to begin. They will soon find that if they wish to design for the stage they must quickly develop three qualities that are directly related to the specific demands of modern theatre. Anyone who aspires to be a designer will need the vision and imagination of the creative artist, the ingenuity and skills of the stage artisan, and, above all, the knowledge and sense of theatre of the actor, director, and playwright.

To function as creative artists in the theatre, designers must be talented and articulate in line, color, and form. They must be able to bring meaning and visual significance to a stage picture through imaginative and creative qualities developed by training in the nonverbal techniques of design, drawing, and painting.

As stage artisans designers must be able, through the use of unique materials and theatrical techniques, to bring substance to their ideas with skill and dispatch and within the structural limitations of their medium. To create a design that can be wholly realized, they must know the structure of scenery, the limitations of materials, the methods of moving scenery, and lighting techniques.

As a collaborating artist the scene designer makes an important visual contribution to the dramatic form. Through the study of dramatic structure and perception of the playwright's goals the designer is better able to find the author's image and bring a visual interpretation of the theme onto the stage. Awareness of the necessary movements of the actors and directing techniques helps the designer create a proper environment to support the action of the play. This is the designer's theatrical quality. A strong sense of theatre is needed in order to bring a theatrical flair to designs while still keeping them in proportion to the dramatic import of the play and movement of the actors.

Design Collaboration

Within the realm of the total visual effect are several areas of design concentration. In this age of specialization, not all productions are designed by one designer. Frequently, the design of a large production is divided between a scene designer, a costume designer, and a lighting designer. In this case the work of the three is a collaborative effort strongly influenced by the basic ideas of the scene designer. The design of the scenery either directly controls or indirectly influences the total visual effect of any dramatic production. The scenc designer, however, cannot design a setting without considering costumes and lighting, even though their design and supervision may be in the hands of someone else.

A designer also cannot design a scene without thinking of the movement of the actors, although the final action and positioning of the actors is the prerogative of the director. The floor plan of a setting influences the ease or effectiveness of the actors' movements whether the director is aware of this influence or not. The director is, perhaps, more aware of the restrictions of a poor floor plan than of the virtues of a successful one. Nevertheless a good floor plan is a highly important part of the total visual effect.

In theatre forms such as the thrust stage and arena theatre the visual effect often centers on the costume design and lighting rather than the scene design. Conventional scenery is either minimized or eliminated entirely, with greater emphasis placed on the design of properties and small fragments of scenery to help establish locale.

Costume design is an essential part of the total visual effect and, although it directly concerns the actor, it complements or highlights the scene design. But, while deeply engrossed in their own contribution, scene designers must always remember that to see and hear the actor interpret a role is the main reason the audience comes to the theatre. The costume gives meaning to the individual character, and at the same time places each character in proper relationship to the total visual effect. The major role of the scene design and of the lighting design is to supplement and emphasize the costume or actor in the ever-moving stage composition. An audience may leave the theatre with a lasting impression of the costumes. But this does not mean that the scene and lighting designers have been outdone; rather the opposite: They have performed their job well.

Whether the attributes of the artist and artisan are found in one person or separate individuals, the ultimate goal of scene design is the same. Designing for the stage means working within specific time limitations and a predetermined stage space, be it thrust, arena, or conventional proscenium staging. At the same time, the designer must strive to satisfy the visual requirement of each production . . . ballet, opera, or drama.

Scene Design and the Theatre

Materials and techniques that are the bases of scene design must have a direct influence on the final design form. These materials and techniques create a medium through which design is transmitted. Each medium requires a specific handling, which gives it an individual effect. A painting, for example, may be done in an oil, watercolor, or fresco medium. Scene design, however, does not stand alone; it is a part of the overall dramatic form. A scene designer may draw sketches or make models, but final designs do not reach a full state of expression until they are on stage in a theatre. As a result the scene designer is concerned not only with the media of canvas, paint, and wood, but also with theatrical materials or material that can be adapted to theatrical uses and techniques. If new or old materials and techniques are to be used intelligently, the designer must have an awareness of the theatre as a medium of expression.

THE THEATRICAL MEDIUM

The basic communicative qualities of scene design are the same as in any other visual art—color, line, and form create the same emotional response on the stage as they do in a poster or display design. Any differences in the design form are traceable to special materials and stage techniques associated with the functions of scene design. In order to understand, at least in general terms, the extent and limitations of the materials and techniques of this medium, the beginning designer must develop an awareness of the theatre as an organization, a show, a machine.

Theatre as an Organization

The preparation of any production requires the close cooperation of many specialists. The theatrical medium brings together the writer, actor, director, designers, and audience. The ultimate success of a play often rests on the efficiency of the producing organization in: (1) selecting a play; (2) procuring financial backing and establishing a budget; (3) securing a theatre; (4) selecting and rehearsing the actors; (5) designing the scenery, lighting, and costumes; (6) building, painting, and lighting the sets; and (7) promoting an audience. Lack of cooperation or understanding, complicated by faulty planning in any phase of the organization, can weaken the production as a whole (Figure 2–1).

As in any other well-functioning organization, there must be a guiding force. The director or producer is the dean of the production group and the chief interpretive artist for the playwright. The director's basic overall concept of the production brings a unifying control to the visual elements, acting style, and literary interpretation.

The designers' contribution to the production is, of course, a vital part of the visual concept. Designers are, nevertheless, a part of the organization and its collaborative effort, which may mean subordinating personal triumph many times for the good of the whole. Great moments of

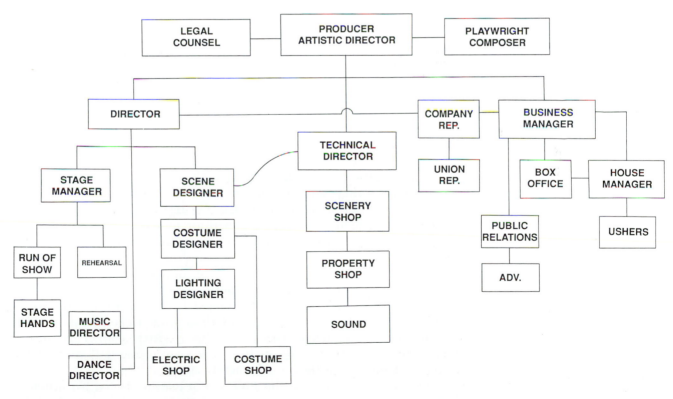

Figure 2-1
A Producing Theatre's Organizational Chart

An average theatre organization. Personnel would vary with size of organization or type of productions.

unified achievement in the theatre are usually experienced when the goal of the production is placed above individual gain.

In addition to being aware of their general relationship to the over-all production plans, designers need to know the specific organization of their own area of theatre—design, technical production, and lighting. A thorough knowledge of backstage and scenery-shop organization often leads to a more efficient production as well as a more faithful reproduction of design ideas. Because of its specialized nature, the personnel organization of designing and technical production is discussed in detail in Chapter 10.

Theatre as a Show

The designer's awareness of the theatre as a show emphasizes the temporal quality of scenery, the dramatic qualities of the visual elements, and above all the sense of joining with an audience to give a performance.

As a performing art the theatre has a feeling of immediacy and audience relationship that does not exist as completely in other art forms. It is true that a painting has an audience, or viewers, too, but the painting remains a painting without viewers. A theatrical performance without an audience, however, is little more than a rehearsal. The audience and its participation are vital parts of the theatrical medium. Consequently, the theatre's almost total dependence upon an audience gives it a temporal quality that becomes an intrinsic part of the medium.

The direct influence of this temporal quality brings about a specific attitude toward scene design and the structure of scenery, for although scenery may look solid for the most part, it must be lightweight and portable to move easily from scene to scene or from audience to audience. And, finally, when the production reaches its last curtain, the usefulness of the scenery ends. It is doomed to storage, rebuilding, or destruction.

The performance aspect of the theatre has a direct bearing on the attitude of designers. There is a tendency to think that the actors are the only performers, which is not the case. *All* the artists and workers in the theatre are performers. A performance is the collaborative effort of all performers. Its success is dependent on the teamwork of its members. Any sense of achievement lies in the reaction of the audience to a good performance. They are more often than not responding to an overall experience rather than to an individual performance. Visual artists working in the theatre are not their own bosses; they are collaborators in a joint venture.

The dramatic qualities of scenery are, of course, mainly achieved through the versatility of the designer's use of the visual art form. A dramatic quality more specifically related to the theatre is the use of proportion or scale. The theatre, more than other art forms, is an overstatement of life. Even a realistic play is drawn a little sharper and greater than real life. Any idea, no matter how significant, will make little impression on an audience if it is merely stated.

The size and distance of the audience in relation to the performance has an influence on the scale of any overstatement in scenery. If, for example, the theatre is large and the audience is at a great distance from the performance, the scenery has to take on an increased scale just to be in proportion to the size of the auditorium and stage. But whether a musical spectacle at a great outdoor arena or a drama of intimate proportions in a vest-pocket theatre, the theatrical medium has the capacity of offering a broad spectrum of electrifying moments.

Theatre as a Machine

The modern stage is a complex machine that promises to become even more complicated in the near future. A practical understanding of this machine is of prime importance to anyone expecting to design in the theatre. The designer's use of the physical stage and its equipment is predicated on a philosophy of scene design. To superimpose a design form without regard for theatrical techniques and the limitations of the physical stage would be as ill conceived as architecture that forces interior planning into a predetermined exterior shape.

THE PHYSICAL STAGE AND ITS AUDITORIUM

The most important step for beginning designers is to learn their new medium by becoming acquainted with the physical stage. They need to know the actual shape and physical make-up of the performance area, for each defines the space in which they must work.

Proscenium Theatre

In the contemporary theatre the stage has various forms based upon the relationship of the audience to the stage area. The most common form is the proscenium type of theatre, where the audience is arranged on one side of a raised stage area. The enclosed stage is open to the audience through the proscenium opening. Early proscenium openings were surrounded by a decorative frame to separate the audience from the play in an artificial and often unrelated manner. Modern theatre structure tries to blend the proscenium opening with the auditorium so that the stage and audience are not so obviously separated. The proscenium wall of the modern stage is merely a masking to hide stage machinery, lights, and scenery storage from view.

Stage Directions

Because actors and audience face each other, directions can become confusing. On the stage all directions are related to the actors' right or left as they face the audience. *Stage left* is to the actors' left and the reverse holds for *stage right*. Because past stage floors used to slope toward the footlights, *down stage* is towards the audience and *up stage* away. *Off stage* refers to the right and left areas out of view, while *back stage* is the entire area behind the proscenium.

The same directions apply to the thrust stage but, of course, do not work for arena staging where directions are established by areas.

Teaser and Tormentors

Because the proscenium opening is a part of the architecture of the theatre, it has fixed proportions. Often the size of the opening must be changed to fit the scale of an individual production or setting. For this reason the teaser and tormentors, which are adjustable framing members, are located immediately upstage of the proscenium opening. The tormentors are the right and left vertical frames that move laterally onstage to reduce the width of the opening. The teaser is the top horizontal frame that is lowered to reduce the height of the opening. While both help shape the proportion of the frame, they also mask, or hide from view, the backstage area of the setting.

The framing of a stage opening is usually accomplished in one of three different ways. The teaser may be a neutral-colored cloth border hung in fullness or pleats accompanied by a corresponding cloth tormentor that can be pulled open or closed on a horizontal traverse track. A second variation is to frame the cloth teaser, thereby forming a continuous flat plane hanging overhead. The matching framed tormentor that sits on the floor can be easily moved on stage or off to narrow or widen the opening.

The most-complicated masking arrangement furnishes the framed teaser and tormentor with a "reveal," or thickness, on the onstage edges. This gives the framing members a heavy look and at the same time provides better masking of the spotlights directly upstage of the opening. The reveal may be attached perpendicularly or beveled at about a 45-degree angle (Figure 2–2).

The downstage edge of the setting usually does not attach directly to the reveal of a framed tormentor. It is held free to allow space for lighting instruments. The free edge of the set is supported by a "return," which turns the set offstage parallel to the tormentor.

Figure 2-2
Tormentor and Teaser

The proportion of the frame for a stage setting is established by the tormentor and teaser, which may have one of several forms. The plan at right shows (1) right wall of setting, (2) right return, (3) stage-right tormentor, (4) house curtain, (5) safety curtain.

a

b

c

Figure 2-2 (cont.)

Three of the more convenient types of tormentor and teaser: (a) Drapery border with legs on short traveler tracks, (b) framed border and wings without reveals, (c) framed border with beveled reveals that include detachable plug to change the height of the reveal (1). Diagram directly above shows (1) position of light bridge or first pipe, (2) framed teaser with beveled reveal, (3) framed tormentor and beveled reveal, (4) house curtain, (5) smoke pocket.

Show Portal

Sometimes, to set the tone of a production, the designer will use a "false proscenium" a little up stage of the proscenium opening. As a show portal, it is a temporary part of the show and not of the theatre structure, hence its name (Figure 2–3).

Figure 2-3
Show Portal

Sometimes called a *false proscenium*, the show portal is located upstage of the fixed proscenium and has two basic functions: (a) The show portal may be decorative to set the tone or style of the production; or, (b) It can be a simple frame to bring unity to a variety of scenes.

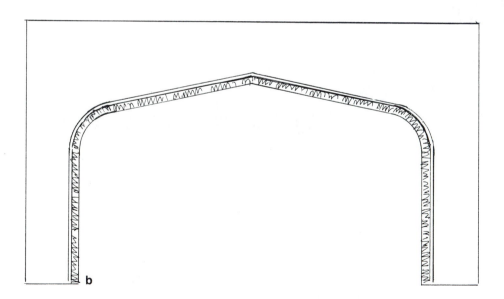

Sightlines

After learning the size and shape of the stage area, the designer is interested in the sightlines of the auditorium to determine how much of the stage is in view. The proscenium theatre has a characteristic sightline problem that varies only slightly with the different patterns of seating arrangement. If the flare of the seating arrangement is very wide, for example, people sitting on the extreme right side of the auditorium see very little of the left side of the stage and vice versa. Similarly, persons sitting in a very steep second balcony see very little of the back wall of the setting. If the auditorium floor is flat without a gradient, or if the stage floor is unusually high, the audience does not see the stage floor and sees very little even of the actors' legs as they walk upstage.

The designer must know these extreme sightline conditions in order to plan a setting that brings the most important areas into the view of all the audience. It is not necessary to find the sightline of every seat in the house but only of the extreme or critical locations.

The extreme vertical sightlines are harder to locate, for they are found on a sectional view of the auditorium and stage that frequently is not available to the designer. The extreme vertical sightlines are drawn from the front row upward and from the last row in the balcony downward. On occasion, when a large balcony overhangs a considerable portion of the orchestra, it is necessary to consider a vertical sightline from the last row of orchestra seats (Figure 2–4a).

Figure 2-4
Sightlines

(a) Sectional view. (b) Plan of auditorium and stage. In each view (1) is the stage area, (2) orchestra pit, (3) front row end seats, (4) widest part of the auditorium, which determines the splay of the seating arrangement, (5) back row of the orchestra, (6) balcony seats.

a

b

The extreme horizontal sightlines are drawn from the seats farthest to the right and left in the audience. The horizontal sightlines are located on the plan of the stage and auditorium (Figure 2–4b).

From the pattern of extreme sightlines, the designer can see how much of the stage is in view to each member of the audience. In Figure 2–4b, for example, the horizontal sightline (4) shows the designer how far onstage a person sitting in this seat can see and how much of the stage-right wall cannot be seen. In this manner, the designer consults the sightlines of an auditorium in order to plan efficiently the use of stage areas for staging the action of the play.

Staging

The designer uses the sightlines of a theatre in two different ways: first, when studying the staging of the play, to develop the design form; and then later, for technical reasons, to check the masking of the nearly completed setting.

When planning the staging, in collaboration with the director, the designer maps out the arrangement of properties, levels, and general floor plan to facilitate the easy flow of the play's action. Because the designer is thinking like a director at this point, the staging is more than a traffic pattern for the actors. Its chief concern is to help bring into focus each scene or moment in the play with the proper degree of relative importance to the other moments.

The designer, through composition of the visual elements, can alter the basic value of any stage area. Due to their position on the bare stage, certain areas are stronger than others. The very nature of the proscenium theatre makes an actor standing downstage nearer the audience more important than an actor in an upstage position. The relative importance of the various positions on a bare stage is shown in Figure 2–5a by first dividing the stage into six equal parts and then numbering the areas in the order of their importance.

Such devices as raking or angling the side walls of a set to force the action in the weak upstage left and right areas toward the center, placing furniture to bring important scenes into good sightlines, and using levels in the upstage areas to increase their importance are just a few examples of staging techniques in scene design.

When the stage is cut, left to right, by a series of portals made up of vertical wings and horizontal borders, as in the wing-and-backdrop type of plan, the staging becomes more two-dimensional. It falls into a series of horizontal planes related to the portals, each traditionally referred to by numbers. Beginning at the apron the downstage strip is number one, the next number two, and so on upstage. The staging can be directed by indicating whether an actor or piece of scenery is to be in "one," "two," or "three," as desired (Figure 2–5b).

Staging in Front of the Proscenium

Two variations of the proscenium theatre are the *extended apron* and the *thrust stage.* Both are outgrowths of the desire to break through the frame of the proscenium in an effort to reduce the distance between the audience and the actor. Each is a part of the contemporary trend or revolt from the romantic theatricality of the past which depended upon a cer-

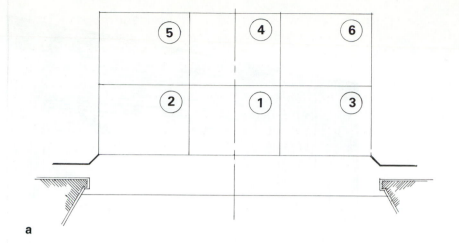

a

Figure 2-5
Stage Area

(a) The stage divided for easy identification into basic areas that are numbered in order of relative importance: (1) downstage center, (2) downstage right; (3) downstage left, (4) upstage center, (5) upstage right, (6) upstage left. (b) A second method of dividing the stage, a series of horizontal planes determined by the location of portals or wings and numbered from downstage to upstage.

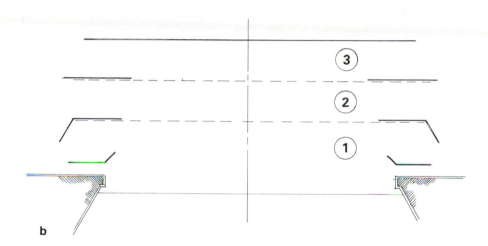

b

tain esthetic distance to complete its illusion. Although the extended apron and thrust stage are not necessarily new forms in the theatre, they are very much a part of present-day staging and represent a space in which today's stage designer must be prepared to work.

Extended Apron

Although somewhat alike in shape, the apron and thrust stages differ in the arrangement of their respective audiences. The extended apron plays to a seating arrangement similar to that of the proscenium theatre with only slight differences in sightlines. The greatest change occurs in the vertical sightlines caused by the increased gradient. The necessity to keep an actor in full view and in a position well ahead of the proscenium results in a steeper rate of rise in each successive row of seats.

The extended apron is usually equipped with access openings or doors within each flanking wall ahead of the proscenium opening. The fore-

Figure 2-6
Flexible Apron

A proscenium-form theatre
equipped with a flexible apron that
when raised or lowered can
assume a number of shapes.
(a) The apron raised to stage level,
providing an extended apron
ahead of the proscenium opening
with entrances from the sides and
through the apron floor. (b) The
apron lowered to orchestra-pit level
for a musical production. (c) The
apron at auditorium level. This
arrangement with the extra seats is
for a proscenium production.

stage area may be used in conjunction with proscenium staging, allowing elements of the scene to spill out onto the side stages, or in a more formalized manner, with all action originating on the apron.

The most flexible form of apron stage is illustrated in Figure 2–6, which shows how the area ahead of the proscenium opening can be modified by the use of elevators or removable platforms and seats to one of three variations: (a) full extended apron; (b) side stages with orchestra pit; (c) regular proscenium staging with additional seats.

NONPROSCENIUM THEATRE

Thrust Stage

The thrust stage, or open stage as it is sometimes called, is as the name suggests a stage thrust out into the audience area. With seats arranged on three sides of the peninsula-shaped acting space the bulk of the audience is closer to the actor than it would be in conventional seating. Semipermanent elements of scenery or an architectural background make up the fourth side of the theatre (Figure 2–7).

Though in appearance the thrust stage is structurally related to the proscenium theatre, its chronological development stems from the arena theatre. The long-felt need in the theatre-in-the-round for greater variety of staging and a stronger axis of visual composition led to a semicircular grouping of seats around the thrust stage. At the same time, the widely diversified sightlines are an obvious improvement over the limited angle of view of the proscenium theatre. Since the upstage portion of the stage is anchored to the structural part of the theatre, a rather important axis is established in the opposite direction.

Figure 2-7
Thrust-Stage Theatre

With seats on three sides of the stage area, the thrust stage and its background can assume a great variety of forms other than the conventional living-room interior in the illustration. Entrances can be made from the audience tunnels, the sides, through the stage floor, and from the back.

Figure 2-8
Arena Theatre

The audience surrounds the stage area, which may or not be raised. Any use of scenic elements is limited to properties and an occasional open set piece.

The strong visual axis, however, has its shortcomings. The people sitting in the end seats of the right and left sides have a radically different compositional view. This is even more in evidence if the seating arc is greater than a semicircle, in which case the audience in the extreme side seats may find themselves enjoying a vista that approaches a rear view. The ideal configuration seems to be slightly less than semicircular, thereby providing a more equitable distribution of seats without losing the sense of close contact with the actor, which is so much a part of both the thrust stage and arena theatre concept.

The features of an ideal thrust stage that influence design are the extreme conditions of both the horizontal and vertical sightlines as well as the basic aim of this theatre type to simplify the amount of scenery needed to establish the locale. The abnormally wide horizontal sightlines force the use of conventional scenery to the back wall, with properties and levels utilized on the stage to set the scene. The sharp vertical sightlines, owing to the steeper gradient, make the floor treatment an important part of the design.

Both the apron and thrust stages, because of their exposed positions, work best with one fixed setting or relatively simple modifications during act changes. Any speedy change of locale is somewhat awkward and depends upon the ingenuity of the director to stage it visually or to resort to the uncertainty of a "blackout" change.

The design limitations of both the apron and thrust stages are offset by the improved flexibility of the staging. The three-quarters facing of the thrust stage plus the presence of actors' entrances from the audience area as well as the unconventionality of the theatre itself continuously encourage a greater use of style and design detail than is called for in the proscenium theatre. Costumes and properties become the center of the visual composition with most of the environment only suggested or defined with light.

Arena Theatre

Another familiar stage form is the arena type of staging where the audience encircles the stage area. The scale of arena staging can vary from an intimate theatre-in-the-round to an arena the size of Madison Square Garden, with many sizes and variations in between (Figure 2–8).

Although the sightlines of arena staging are greatly improved over the proscenium type of theatre the stage form is very limiting to the designer in terms of conventional scenery and techniques. The visual elements have to be confined to small low units or open pieces that can be seen through. Design detail becomes more important because of the intimacy of the theatre and the lack of larger elements of scenery in the composition. This type of staging is intentionally simple, depending upon a suggestion of scenery to set the scene and stimulate the audience's imagination to fill in the rest.

Flexible Staging

Flexible staging is an outgrowth or expansion of arena staging. It is obvious that arena staging has some advantages over proscenium staging, but on the other hand there are many plays that do not lend themselves to arena presentation.

Figure 2-9
Flexible Staging
The seat platforms and stage are movable and thereby able to assume a variety of arrangements. The audience partially surrounds the stage area, which may have a limited amount of scenic background. (a) L-shaped arrangement. (b) Proscenium-type. (c) U-shaped, with the audience on the three sides of the stage. (d) The audience split to produce a number of acting areas.

Flexible staging provides an area for the easy changing of the stage–audience arrangement. Within this flexible space the staging can be altered from arena staging to three-quarters-round, or to proscenium-type staging (Figure 2–9). Ballroom or cabaret staging is a further variation with the audience on two sides and a small stage or bit of scenery at one end, or both. The sightlines vary, of course, depending on the type of staging. When the seats are arranged for proscenium-type staging there is a decided improvement in the sightlines over the conventional proscenium theatre. The seating is usually arranged with a negligible flare, thereby creating good sightlines for the entire house (Figure 2–9b).

Flexible staging offers many exciting designing and directing possibilities. Its main drawback is the relatively small audience capacity, which limits its commercial use. A more serious handicap is the loss of time and energy that occurs during the changing of the theatre from one arrangement to another. It is, however, an excellent staging medium for experimentation in new dramatic forms.

LIGHTING AND THE SCENE DESIGNER

Of all the techniques within the theatrical medium affecting scene design and the structure of scenery, lighting is the most influential. Because lighting technique will be covered in great detail later it will not be necessary here more than to point out its general influence on the materials and structure of scenery.

The use and control of lighting is strictly a theatrical technique, born and developed in the theatre. It is an additional element of design that gives the scene designer a greater flexibility in composition than occurs in any other visual art form.

Light is visible energy. Among its characteristics is the apparent ability to transmit some of its energy onto whatever surface it falls. The energy of light reveals, brightens, and adds color to an inert object, thereby increasing its vitality. By the same token, it might be argued that color also brings life to a painting, but it is not as animated as, for example, light through a stained glass window or a projected color image on the stage.

Of all the components that make up a stage composition, the two most active and vital are the *actor* and *light*. The power of light to animate form makes it a forceful design statement in a stage composition. For a dynamic example of designing for light, refer to Figure 3–6 on page 38.

Aside from its design possibilities, light on the stage has an unavoidable effect on the structure and materials of scenery. The scene designer must consider in advance the relative changes in the intensity of light and the position of the light source, which may determine whether an area of scenery is to be opaque, translucent, or transparent. In the making of transparent or translucent pieces of scenery, the pattern of the framing and the location of the seams have to be carefully considered. Frequently the design is altered slightly to conceal or modify a seam or structural element. Conversely, opaque areas should not be neglected, for a strong backing light may reveal an interesting but unwanted pattern of framing.

Often the design of the lighting comes too late in the planning of a setting, almost as an afterthought. This sometimes reflects an indifference or unawareness of the theatricality and compositional value of light itself. An alarming number of young designers either cannot or do not want to be bothered with lighting their own sets. The continuation of an unfortunate disinterest of this kind can only lead to the surrender of a portion of scene design to specialists who are willing to give the thought, time, and skill necessary to design and supervise the lighting of a stage setting. Lighting is too important a part of the theatrical medium not to be considered in the beginning along with the other theatrical techniques that condition the design and structure of scenery.

CHECK LIST

Before venturing too far into the designing of a production the designer should check the stage or performance area for the following:

- Floor plan—showing offstage space and heights
- Flying system—number of lines and spacing
- Traps—sizes and area
- Overhead obstructions—ducts or vents
- Load-in door—size and access to stage
- Sightlines
- Lighting positions and control
- Local fire code—restrictions and tests

Scene Design as a Visual Art

The exciting interplay of line, color, and form in a vibrant stage setting or the subtle refinements of an inconspicuous scenic background do not happen by chance. The proper integration of color and style of costumes and the dramatic presence of light in the stage scene depends on an understanding on the part of all the designers of the principles of design. To create a setting the scene designer uses, either consciously or intuitively, well-established rules and fundamentals of design common to all the visual arts. The beginning designer should have a knowledge of these fundamentals to aid in the development of final design forms.

DESIGN AND THE DESIGNER

We think of design as a creation of order that is the work of the artist. Artists bring two things to their work: *emotion* and *intellect.* Both are expressed in the feeling and rationale of a work of art. The emotional aspect of creating is individual and introspective. Its intangibility is sometimes called talent. It is hard to quantify and impossible to teach.

The intellectual side of design, however, can be measured and defined in terms of composition. Within emotion or feeling lie desire, imagination, and a sense of theatre which are so necessary to creativity. Intellect, or the mind, on the other hand, cultivates the practical skills as well as the conceptual and interpretive powers of design. The merging of emotion and intellect is the beginning of the creative process that spawns the design form.

Beginning designers may wonder how this abstract definition of design applies to their special interest in the theatre. It means that during the process of designing, for example, there are two forces at work: a personal vision or feeling for the final design form; and the practical realities that are tempered by thoughtful judgment and taste. Both are regulated by the dictates of the playwright, the concepts of the director, and the limits of the performance space. In other words, emotion and feeling become the *ideal,* thought and intellect the *reality;* the first being the *goal* and the second the *realization.* The greater the skill and ability to realize the ideal, the more successful the designer.

COMPOSITION AND THE ELEMENTS OF DESIGN

Composition, in general terms, is the composing or organizing of the elements of design in space into a unified *form.* The result may be a single form or the interaction of several forms acting as a whole. The elements of design are the elemental factors that make up the visual form, whether it be a two-dimensional shape or a three-dimensional sculptural object.

The elements of design can also be thought of as forces that, by manipulation, can singly dominate a composition and help give the form *meaning.* The reason for or meaning of any visual form brings to a composition a unity of purpose that is particularly important when designing in the theatre. The meaning attached to the designing of a visual form may be dictated from the outside, or come from within the artist, often formulated by the simple desire for personal expression.

The major factors that make up a visual form can be listed in the order of their importance to the creative process. They are: line, dimension, movement, light, color, and texture. Of these elements, *line* and *color* are the most forceful; in terms of design, *light* and *movement* are unique to the theatre.

Line

Line, as an element of design, *defines* form. It is a most important force in a composition because it is present in many different ways. Line can enclose space as *outline* and create shape (two-dimensional form), or as *contour lines* suggest three-dimensional form. Line in a composition can appear as *real line* in many different modes (straight, curved, spiral, and so on) or as *suggested line* simulated by the eye as it follows a sequence of related shapes.

Figure 3-1
Real Line and Linear Shapes

(a) Examples of real line. Straight, curved, subtle and strong reverse curves, serpentine and spiral.
(b) Real line can enclose space and create shape. Some shapes are linear, thereby taking on line characteristics by assuming direction and attitude.
(c) Suggested line. The eye will follow a line suggested by repetition of shapes, parallel lines, concentric circles, gradation of size or color, or a shape that points.

a   b   c

Figure 3-2
Linear Form in Composition

Stage compositions dominated by the use of linear forms. (Top) *Iphigenia auf Tauris.* Designer— Ruddi Barch. *Photo courtesy German Information Center.* (Bottom) *Pelléas et Mélisande.* Designer—Robert Edmond Jones. *Courtesy Yale Theatre Collection*

Figure 3-3
Suggested Line in Composition
The eye is led by the repetition of form to the center of interest. *Lohengrin,* Metropolitan Opera, New York. Designer—Charles Elson. *Photo courtesy Sedge Leblang*

Line is a path of action and therefore cannot help but take on a sense of *direction* and become a part of *movement*. This is particularly true when the form is *linear* in shape. It soon becomes apparent that in an arrangement of several linear shapes the lines not only assume a direction but also take on an *attitude* toward each other, be it one of harmony or opposition.

The use of line and shapes with linear characteristics becomes a vital force in any *form* or arrangement of forms. A composition may use line as a dynamic force with a sense of violent action or as a static force with a feeling of strength and stability.

Dimension

Dimension is the *size* or *mass* of form. As an element of design, dimension is not only concerned with the size of a shape or mass of a three-dimensional form, but also with the relationship of the size of one shape to another—large to small, large to large, and so forth. *Real dimension* is always present in a two-dimensional shape, but, of course, becomes *suggested dimension* when a three-dimensional form is represented on a two-dimensional surface.

Dimension, in addition, includes the amount of space between forms in a composition. The size of the interval has a definite effect on the apparent size or mass of the form and its proportional relationship. The prominence or recession of the interval or size of mass is, of course, influenced further by the use of color, light, and texture. The proportional relationship between interval and mass also begins to establish a rhythm or sense of *movement*.

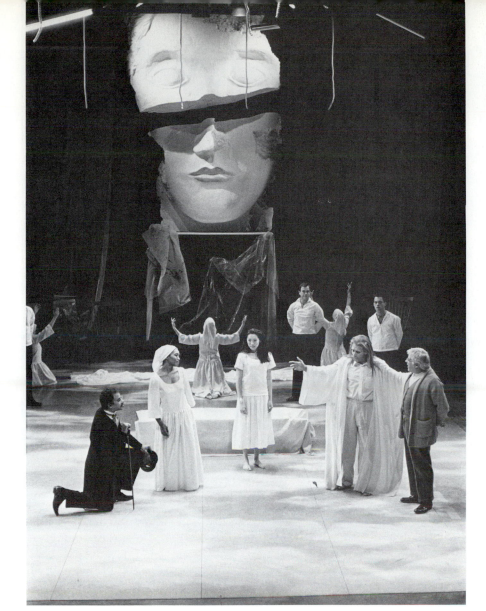

Figure 3-4
Dimensional Relationships
The scale of the form in the
background dominates the
composition in *Pericles* by
Shakespeare. Designer—John
Conklin, Hartford Stage Company.
Photo © T. Charles Erickson

Movement

Movement is the *action* of form. It is the kinetic energy of composition. Motion in design is always present even in a static composition. The pattern of optical signals that touch the retina and then the brain is a continuous flow and hence mobile in character.

The *real movement* of form within a composition is very much a part of stage design. The movement of light, of the actors, and on occasion animated elements of scenery are commonplace in the theatre.

The movement of the eye, or *optical motion*, however, is a type of movement that is present in any fixed arrangement of forms. The use of *suggested line* (one characteristic of *line*) stimulates optical motion as the eye is led from one shape to the next.

Optical motion begins with an intuitive sense of *orientation* that everyone has or has experienced. It provides the basis for an interpretive feeling of movement frequently so subtle the viewer does not distinguish the effect as a product of optical motion. The tendency of the viewer, for

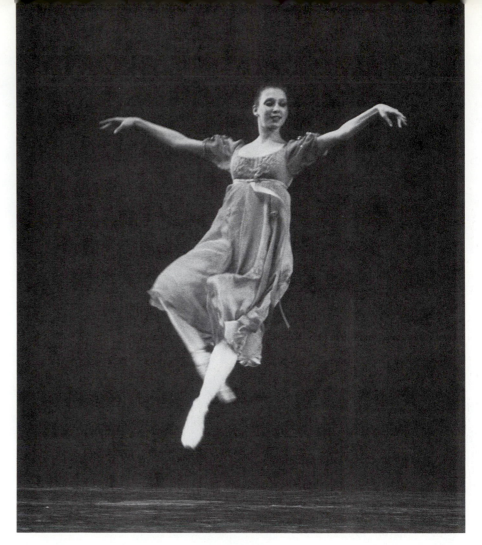

Figure 3-5
Real Movement
The movement of actors and lights is the kinetic energy that brings life to a stage composition. *Photo courtesy Randy Choura*

example, to interpret a diagonal line extending from the lower left to upper right corner of a composition as an upward motion is a product of orientation. It is a part of the *left to rightness* common to us all as well as the fixed association of a *top and bottom* to all compositions.

Movement also involves the fourth dimension—*time*. The interval and size of form relationship (mentioned earlier) cause a kind of movement or rhythm. The interval spacing or *tempo* may be staccato, pulsating, or ponderous in its timing. The vibration of repeated shapes, complementary colors, rapid changes of direction, and high contrasting areas are all visible examples of *optical motion*.

Although orientation brings an instinctive sense of movement to a composition, the designer has many means of controlling optical motion. Strong direction can be countered, reversed, or subtly changed by altering the *position* or *attitude* of the forms in relation to each other. The outline of the form itself can establish a direction, as can the other elements of design such as color and light.

Another interesting phenomenon of movement is its *transferability*. Both real motion and optical motion can be transferred to a static object. A simple figure or shape placed against a busy or pulsating background will appear to dance or vibrate itself. This unwanted optical motion can happen to pictures, for example, if they are hung on a background of vibrant wallpaper. Real motion can also be transferred from a moving background to a fixed object in the foreground. Most everyone, for example, has experienced the sense of motion while sitting in a stationary railroad car or bus when the adjacent vehicle begins to move. The technique of moving the background behind the actor or fixed scene to create the illusion of movement in the scene is frequently used on the stage.

It goes without saying that all movement on the stage has to be carefully controlled and coordinated. Movement catches the eye and can detract from the scene as easily as it can enhance it. Ask any actor who has been "upstaged" by the innocent waving of a handkerchief or scarf of a fellow actor.

Movement and Composition • A stage composition is in a constant state of flux. Actors change position and grouping; elements of scenery change location; or, a static arrangement changes by the movement of light with color and a shift of direction. Figure 3–6 illustrates with four drawings how composition can be changed by the movement of light and the positioning of actors.

Light

Light *reveals* form. Although it has not been traditionally viewed as an element of design, light is a most dominant presence in all areas of stage design. As such, it must be considered a basic influence at the beginning of the creative process and not something to be added later.

Light can be thought of in three different ways: first as *real light* capable of revealing form; second, as light having its *own* design-form; and last, as *simulated light* as it might appear in a two-dimensional representation of a three-dimensional form.

The design potential of light is inherent in its physical characteristics. The three variants of light are *intensity, color,* and *distribution.* By controlling its brightness, color, and direction, light becomes a strong factor in creating a design form.

Intensity is the *actual* or *comparative* brightness of light. The actual brightness of the sun, for example, can be contrasted with the comparative brightness of automobile headlights at night. Spotlights in a darkened theatre offer the designer the same comparative brightness under more controlled conditions.

The ability of light to transmit and reveal *color* is one of its most dramatic qualities. The modification of local color of form by colored light is a design technique unique to the theatre. *Color modification* and the additive mixing of colored light are two basic concepts of color as a quality of light that have to be understood by all designers in the theatre.

Distribution is the energy path of light. The control of the distribution of light gives it *direction* and *texture* as a design feature. The various kinds of distribution begin with the general radiation of direct emanation, through the more specific reshaping of the light rays by reflection

Figure 3-6
Light in Composition

Use of the distribution, color, and movement of light in this production of *Prometheus Bound*, designed by Donald Oenslager, was unique for its time. Produced at Yale in 1939 and conceived much earlier, it represents the kind of innovative use of light we accept as modern practice. Within the simple "gray gauze box" sitting in space, through which light could penetrate, wash with color, project on its surfaces, or make it disappear before our eyes, we watched the anguishes of Prometheus unfold. Lighting—Stanley McCandless. Costumes—Frank Bevan.

and optics, to the parallel rays of the laser beam. The sharp or soft-edged quality of the light beam coupled with its degree of brightness gives *texture* to light.

It is easy to see how a knowledge of the distribution of light can affect the design form by the introduction of *highlight, shade,* and *shadow* into composition. Beside the atmospheric quality that light can add to a composition there is the obvious design character of an exposed light source such as candelabra, chandeliers, or visible lighting instruments.

The final use of *real light* is as its own design form. Patterns of light can be projected over a form as a part of the composition, or the projected image can be the entire composition. Although the use of light as projected scenery can be thought of as a medium in itself, it is, however, still a visual art and therefore draws upon the same fundamentals of design for its realization.

The use of *simulated light* is most often present in the designer's sketch, where it represents the effect of light in the composition. Although *line* is used first to represent three dimensions, the added use of simulated light and its shades and shadows is the designer's most effective way to represent three-dimensional form in a sketch or backdrop. However, the most successful use of *simulated light* in a sketch or painting is based upon a first-hand knowledge of what *real light* can and does do.

Color

Color *modifies* form. As an element of design it is a powerful stimulus that can change the dimension of form, reverse the direction of line, alter the interval between forms, and generate optical motion. Color in the theatre comes from two basic sources: pigment or dye present on the surface of the form; or color transmitted by light.

Color in either light or pigment has three variants: *hue, value,* and *chroma.* A specific color can be thought of in terms of its *hue,* which is the color's wavelength or position in the spectrum; its *value,* signifying the color's black-to-white relationship; and its *chroma,* indicating the color's degree of purity (saturation) or freedom of neutrality.

Value

Although value has been defined as a variant of color, it is an important medium of expression itself. Suggested form can be modeled on paper without color in shades and highlights using various black to white tones.

Value is experienced early in the process of designing scenery. Many preliminary sketches are expressed in black and white with occasional gray tones. For more on *color,* see Chapter 8.

Texture

Texture is the *tactile* aspect of form. As a design feature, it adds interest by embellishing the surface and thereby giving character to the finished form. The composition takes on a temperament partially inspired by the make-up of its texture. Surfaces may vary from the extremes of highly polished to rough/natural in quality. A rough-hewn surface or decorative bas relief, for example, stimulates different emotional responses. Each illustrates the purpose of texture as a design element.

The reason for using texture in the theatre is to catch, interrupt, and reflect light. The irregular shadows and highlights of a textured surface

Figure 3-7
Texture and Light

(a) Rusticated surface emphasized with side lighting. (b) Decorative bas-relief. (c) This small but expressive scene design illustrates the dominance of texture in a composition. Designer—Vladimir Suchanek, Bratislava.

a

b

c

enrich a design form; thus the dependency of texture on light is a crucial component of design.

Texture in the theatre has two different dimensions. First, it may be seen as *real* texture: the various surface treatments just described are examples of real texture. But it may also occur as *simulated* or painted texture. The two-dimensionality of painted texture is used for the same design reasons as real texture, but the surface is mottled with paint to add interest and character.

The earliest concept of the word *texture* was associated with weaving. The size and make-up of the warp and weft had a tactile sense that was smooth or rough to the touch. A tactile image also appeared in the woven pattern and color variation. The same textural trait can be seen in techniques of paint and in surface decoration. The enrichments of a surface with a repeated motif of wallpaper or of geometric patterns are examples of simulated or visual texture, as are mosaic, parquetry, and tiled surfaces.

Light and Texture • Real texture is best revealed by directional side-lighting, while painted texture appears more real under a wash of light without a strong sense of direction. A wash of light is shadowless and therefore does not cast telltale shadows (such as wrinkles) in a drop that may expose the simulated texture as a painted surface. Conversely, a wash of light on a textured detail such as a cornice or molding will deny its three-dimensionality and sometimes require the addition of painted shadows and highlights to create the appearance of reality.

Designing for Light • Since the function of real texture is to divide light into interesting shadows and highlights as a design feature, it is not too difficult to apply the concept of "real texture" to scenic forms as a whole. Although scenic forms are large in scale they, too, should be designed to interact with light.

The successful unity of light and scenic form results most often as a result of the close creative collaboration of the lighting and scene designers. The theatrical value of light to scenic form, first envisioned by Adolphe Appia and Edward Gordon Craig at the beginning of the twentieth century and fully realized later by the inventiveness of Josef Svoboda, is very much a part of present-day scenography. The use of abrupt surface changes, reflective covering, density variations from opaque to transparent, as well as the addition of highly textured areas on scene forms all contribute to the unity of lighting and scenic form.

Figure 3–8 is an excellent example of designing for light. The illustration shows two moments in the National Theatre of London production of *Richard III* on the open stage of the Olivier Theatre. The open stage, or thrust stage, shown lends itself very well to the more dramatic use of light and scenic form.

PRINCIPLES OF COMPOSITION

The elements of design are the raw materials ready to be brought together into some order or purpose. Composition is the organization of these elements into a unified form. The principles of composition are the various ways the designer can control and use the design elements to bring

Figure 3-8
Designing for Light
These two atmospheric drawings are facsimiles of the London National Theatre's production of Shakespeare's *Richard III.* Revolving forms and sliding panels cast shadows and slash the stage with shafts of light in a series of dramatic compositions. A striking example of designing for light. Scene Designer—Ralph Koltai. Lighting Designer—David Hersey. Director—Christopher Morahan.

a fusion of interest and meaning to the stage. A good composition brings into play two controls, *harmony* and *contrast.* The interest or appeal in a stage setting is the direct result of the manipulation of these controls.

Harmony

The simplest act of bringing order to disorder is to sort unrelated objects into groups that have some sequential relationship or continuity. The objects may have in common a similarity of shape, color, or texture. Repetition, then, is a basic control. The repetition of one or more of the elements of design shows the presence of outside control. The repeated use of line or linear forms, for example, can dominate a composition, although other elements of design may be present. In the design shown in Figure 3–2 *real line* dominates the composition in a dramatic way. The repetition of line also affects the overall mood of the design and establishes strong optical motion. Examples of set designs dominated by one or more of the other elements of design are illustrated on the following pages.

Although repetition is one of the easiest and quickest ways to bring harmonious control to a composition, it suffers the danger of becoming monotonous or gauche. The possible monotony of repetition can be relieved with a little contrast or variation.

Contrast

The designer depends upon contrast to create form. Form cannot be revealed without contrast, as is evident in the examples of the absence of contrast occasionally seen in nature. The protective coloration of an animal or bird reduces contrast to the point of making it invisible against the background. But in the theatre, such lack of contrast—an actress in a red gown sitting on a matching red sofa—would be disastrous. Between the two extremes lie infinite variations.

The most visible examples of harmony and contrast are found in the use of color and value tones. A design with a single color scheme would be harmonious. The further colors are apart in the spectrum the greater the contrast. The same thing occurs with value coupling. Black and white, for example, are extreme value contrasts. On the other hand, value tones that are close together are more harmonious. Again, refer to Chapter 8 on color.

Variation

When the repetition of one element produces monotony, a variation of one or more of the other elements can add interest to the composition. It is interesting to note in Donald Oenslager's designs for Aeschylus' *Prometheus Bound* (Figure 3–6) that, although the design is dominated by the use of *light,* the manipulation of the direction, distribution, and intensity of light is the major variation brought to a rather simple form. *Color* of the scenic form in this production was held under strict control. The overall tonality was gray or neutral with moments of color achieved through the use of colored light.

Pattern

The injection of variation into composition to relieve repetition establishes a rhythm as the variation recurs. This is the basis of most pattern

Figure 3-9
Pattern Composition

(a) Border motifs in repetition,
(b) motifs in opposition, (c) motifs in
inversion, and (d) motifs in
alternation. *Overall patterns.* The
same motif is shown in four
variations of the many methods of
creating an overall pattern such as
wallpaper. Inserts indicate the
geometry of the control. (e) Diaper.
(f) Scale. (g) Ogee. (h) Vertical
stripes.

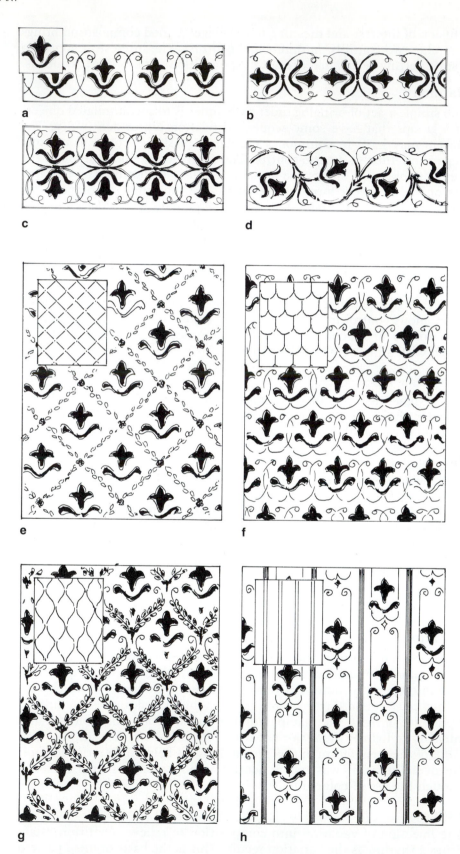

compositions, which exist in two forms: border and overall patterns. Although more obvious, the manipulation of the elements of design is the same in any composition *except* for light. The open or closed qualities of a pattern involve light, particularly if the structure is a grill or lattice designed to let light pass through. The rhythm of the variation repeat (or *motif,* as it is called) is known in terms of its relative positions. That is to say, the motif may be placed in relative positions of alternation, opposition, or inversion.

The motifs may be placed in alternation by alternating their position in relation to a central axis without changing the original direction of the pattern. To place motifs in opposition tends to break the rhythm into a series of static arrangements, creating a feeling of stability. To place the motifs in inversion takes the direction out of the movement, especially if used in an overall pattern. Inversion is frequently used in textile patterns permitting the material to hang either up or down without the motif appearing to be upside down.

These arrangements can be combined and compounded into numerous variations of each element of design, thereby adding interest to the border or pattern composition (Figure 3–9).

An analysis of border designs may seem unrelated to scene design. However, a border or pattern is a type of composition. It has an obvious control that is easy to see and study. The same control appears with a subtler and less restricted handling in the composition of a setting. Besides, pattern composition as found in wallpaper, paneling, and cornice decorations still occupies a large part of the scene designer's time.

Gradation

The variation of motifs within a border composition can, as has been shown, establish a rhythm or feeling of movement. The feeling of movement or change is frequently desired in composition of a stage setting where the controls will be less obvious. The sequential controls of a border composition are sometimes too obvious or abrupt. Sharp contrasts can be reduced by the use of the sequence of gradation, which by transitional steps softens contrasting elements and at the same time brings a feeling of movement into the stage picture. The graded wash of a sky-drop as the dark blue at the top gradually becomes lighter near the bottom is an example of gradation of the value of a color. The use of gradation may occur in line, shape, or in any one or more of the elements of design. The resulting feeling of movement in the composition is free of the repetitive rhythm of the pattern composition (Figure 3–10).

COMPOSITION AND SPACE

Space is to the scene designer what a block of wood or stone is to the sculptor. The space in and around the stage becomes an area to enclose or leave open, to light or leave dark, to flatten out or to create the illusion of even greater depth.

Although undefined space is limitless in scope, it can be defined in two-dimensional terms. Figure 3–11 graphically illustrates the definition of two- and three-dimensional space and solid form by showing the many options a scene designer has to create a space or a form within a space.

If the lines in the drawing that define a space, often referred to as a *space frame*, were considered to be outlining a plane of solid surface, the final arrangement would be known as a *hollow solid*. The hollow solid is a familiar scenic form associated with proscenium theatre. The *sculptural solid*, designed to be viewed from all sides, is more suitable for the thrust and arena stages. The first, like scenery, defines a space that becomes the design form itself. The second creates a form within a space.

Designing within the limits of two-dimensional space begins with a perception of the relationship of *figure* and *ground*. Ground, often background, is a two-dimensional plane. In the simplest example, it can be likened to a sheet of drawing paper. The figure or shape outline has to be in contrast to the ground to be visible. An example of figure is the enclosure of a portion of the ground by an outline. For greater contrast the figure may be filled with a flat tone or color.

The spatial feeling of a composition made up of a single figure and ground is flat. As figures or large shapes are overlapped, one figure becomes the ground for the other and composition begins to take on depth.

The ground may be simple with a textured or patterned figure, or in reverse, with a complicated ground and simple figures (Figure 3–12).

The composition of a wing-and-backdrop type of setting is an example of the use of figure and ground in scene design. The flat plane of each wing when contrasted against the adjacent wing gives an illusion of space that belies their two-dimensionality, especially when other signs of space are used.

Up to now the figure has been thought of as an outline, or outline and flat tone. The figure can also represent a solid with not only height and width but also a depth or thickness. The representation of volume in outline or in solid areas is also an indication of space. The outline itself may be varied in thickness and the ground modeled to accentuate the three-dimensional or plastic qualities (Figure 3–13a).

The figure can be given further plasticity by chiaroscuro modeling, which is shading by means of light and dark tones without regard for a light source. Chiaroscuro modeling combined with a sequence of gradation emphasizes the structure of solids and gives stronger indication of space (Figure 3–13b).

Figure 3-10
The Sequence of Gradation

(a) Gradation of shape from a rectangle to an oval opening.
(b) Gradation of value in the sky and of direction of the steps.

a

b

a

b

c

d

The next step to heighten the three-dimensional quality of the form is to model it in light and shade as if coming from a definite light source. The direction of the light and the cast shadows help to describe the form and place it in space (Figure 3–13c).

The final exploit of space perception is the illusion of literally breaking through the plane of the drawing paper with the use of perspective. Perspective and the shadows of directional lighting are combined to achieve a total effect, a feeling of space in two-dimensional form (Figure 3–13d).

Figure 3-11
Space and Form

(a) Undefined space. (b) Two-dimensional space frame. (c) Three-dimensional space frame.
(d) Hollow solid surrounding a sculptural solid.

COMPOSITION AND UNITY

The composition of a stage setting is expected to bring a unity to the overall arrangements of the visual forms. In addition to the unifying effect of harmony expressed in the sequence of repetition and gradation, scene design needs a greater sense of unity to bring strength to stage composition. The compositional unity of a scene design is first dependent on balance and movement and then on proportion and rhythm. At first glance, balance and movement may seem the same as proportion and rhythm; however, a closer analysis will show that they are related but not the same. Balance and movement are the outward, more obvious expressions of the subtler, more sensitive effects of proportion and rhythm.

Unity suggests balance, a balance of the forces within the composition. These forces are the forces of tension, attraction, attention, and movement that exist between the forms of a stage design. All scenery forms have mass and size (dimension), which means that their proportion must be considered. And lastly, the proportional relationship between

Figure 3-12
Figure and Ground

(a) Ground, undefined space.
(b) Single figure defining a portion of the ground. (c) Several figures.
(d) The upstage figures become the ground for the downstage figures, helping to establish the planes in space. (e) Example of complicated figures against a plain ground with the reverse in the center.

forms cannot help but bring rhythm into the composition, whether it be static or dynamic in feeling.

Balance and Movement

Balance is described as the relationship of forces within a composition. But what is the visual expression of a force? The strong visual pull of attraction and attention are forces. The intense colors of a poster attract the eye. The attention value of the poster contains the interest and meaning that stimulate a response in the viewer.

These two forces, attraction and attention, are of significance to scene design. Many times a setting has to make a telling effect in the opening moments of a play and then have sufficient attention value to sustain interest through two hours of performance.

A visual expression of tension also exists between forms. The degree of tension is dependent upon the interval or space between forms. The space between the finger of God and Adam as God gives life to man in Michelangelo's fresco in the Sistine Chapel is an example of tension. The spark of life can almost be seen. If the fingers were touching, or moved farther apart, the tension would be absent. Tension as a force is found in the composition of a setting in the spacing of scenery masses, the grouping of furniture, or in the relationship of the actor to the scenery and furniture.

Another example of a force in composition is the force of gravity and the viewer's unconscious reaction to it. Gravity has probably the greatest effect on balance. A viewer reacts to visual signs with an organic sense of balance schooled by a lifetime of living with the pull of gravity. Because of this, an unsupported heavy object may seem to be falling, as does a leaning object, unless its center of gravity holds it in balance. Also, a recognizable shape in an unnatural position may cause a feeling of imbalance. The reverse is also true. To abstract a recognizable shape, the designer sometimes consciously uses unnatural position as pure design in an effort to deny reality.

Depth perception is also crucial in the theatre. It allows a viewer to judge whether objects are in the same plane or are receding in proper order. However, it is the same sense of depth on the part of the theatre audience that is fooled, by altering the signs of space perception through perspective foreshortening, into seeing more distance than is actually on the stage.

Movement as a contributor to unity is concerned with *change* and *time.* The harmonious and progressive change of the sequence of gradation is an example of movement as the eye is led, step by step, through the change of color, form, dimension, or direction.

A well-organized form has a firmly established plan of movement. Some arrangements of form stimulate a greater sense of movement than others. Some cause a different kind of movement, such as a precarious balance of tension. The plan of movement within a composition, in any event, is a closed plan, always staying or returning to the overall form.

In the theatre, as has been noted, the inclusion of time in actual movement is quite apparent. The actors move from area to area; the lights dim and brighten; scenery, on occasion, moves in view of the audience. All these are part of the composition of the dramatic form and

a   b

c   d

Figure 3-13
Composition and Space

Composition with the definition of form in space. (a) Simple outline and outline with flat tone. (b) Chiaroscuro or shading to bring out the form within the outline. (c) Cast shadows which establish a light source and increase the feeling of space. (d) Total effect combines perspective with directional lighting to create the illusion of three dimensions.

involve the element of time. The element of time, however, exists in a fixed composition, too.

There is an interval of time as the eye follows the pattern of movement through a composition. The interval is minute, of course, when compared to the broader movements on stage. The visual change can lead the eye, abruptly or gradually in terms of time, over the movement plan of a composition. (See page 44 on movement.)

Proportion and Rhythm

The second portion of obtaining unity in a composition is the use of proportion and rhythm. Proportional judgment is probably one of the initial signs of talent. A certain amount can be acquired by training and sharpened by analysis, but a sense of proportion is largely intuitive.

Proportion is the ratio of something to something else. On stage it is natural to relate proportion to the human figure, for the actor is a part of the total composition. In the theatre this is referred to as *scale*. The designer is constantly checking the size of a form in ratio to human scale (Figure 3–14). Some productions demand a greater scale or an increased ratio of the size of surrounding forms to the actor.

Proportion can also be linked to the reason or function of a visual form. The proportion of a chair as a visual form, for example, depends upon how the chair is to be used. A simple dining-room side chair is small when compared to the scale and the grandeur of a canopied throne chair. Stage settings and even entire productions can differ in scale for similar reasons. The proportions of the ballroom scene in *Romeo and Juliet*, for example, are of more significance than the scale of Friar Laurence's cell; similarly, the pageantry of *Henry VIII* demands greater scale as a production than *The Merchant of Venice*, which is of more intimate proportions.

Many forms and arrangements of forms, however, are not associated with human scale. In addition to the concept of proportion as scale, a proportional relationship exists between one form and another and between the space used between forms. Perhaps more important is the proportional relationship of forms to their surrounding space. The rhythm and proportions of a sculptural arrangement of forms set in an unbound space, for example, may seem different from a similar arrangement of shapes framed or confined within a rectangular shape such as a proscenium opening.

Although scene designing, at least in its formative stages, composes within a rectangular or near-rectangular shape, it is also concerned with

Figure 3-14
Scale

The feeling of scale in a stage setting is linked to the size of the human figure. In these two examples, the design forms are identical in size. Their scale changes in relation to the size of the figure in the composition.

the freer compositions of the nonproscenium stage. Designing for non-proscenium theatre approaches the use of sculptural techniques to create a desirable proportional relationship between scenic forms in a more or less undefined space. Whereas the composition within a proscenium frame is viewed basically from a frontal direction, nonproscenium scenic forms have to be composed satisfactorily for viewers from all directions.

As balance is linked to movement, so proportion is joined with rhythm. The space between forms and the attitude of one shape to another creates a rhythm in the composition. Rhythm is a type of movement that recurs at intervals or completes a cycle. The proportional relationship between forms establishes a rhythm, as does the subdivision of single form.

A conscious inner relation and rhythm is present in stage composition in many ways. It may appear in the quiet dignity of a formal arrangement or in the vigorous movement of a dynamic composition. Or it may be expressed in the rhythmic flow of harmonious forms or in a nervous, staccatolike organization of shapes.

Rhythm as a unifying factor is usually expressed in the lines or linear qualities of a stage composition. The use of actual lines or the feeling of a line caused by the position and direction of one shape to another results in a rhythmic movement that may be as strong or as subdued as the designer desires. Diagonal lines and lines parallel to the diagonals give a greater sense of movement than the use of strong horizontal and vertical lines, which tend to stop movement (Figure 3–15).

Although the rhythm of straight lines is more bold and forceful than curved lines, curved lines have infinitely greater variety. The rhythm of a curved line may have the grace of flowing lines, the turbulence of reverse curves, the whirl of a spiral, as well as the repetition and order of interlaced geometric curves such as circles and ovals.

Whether the rhythm of a stage composition is dominated by straight or curved lines, it eventually becomes a part of the basic movement plan. Likewise, the proportional relationship of forms, which determines the rhythm, forms a balance, resulting in greater feeling of unity, especially when the rhythm is visibly repetitious.

COMPOSITION AND INTEREST

In addition to maintaining unity in a stage composition, the designer tries to bring interest and meaning to the setting. Any meaning attached to the scenic forms of the composition is, of course, a part of the designer's interpretation of the scenic requirements of the play that are a result of an attempt to bring visual substance to the playwright's ideas.

A stage setting, however, can fulfill all the scenic requirements of the play and still not be interesting. Just what makes one setting for a play more interesting than another?

A setting is interesting many times because of a unique and daring design interpretation that stimulates an intellectual response on the part of the audience. This is frequently possible when the play is a classic or one familiar to the audience. European scene designers constantly produce exciting and innovative design approaches to well-established classics. In university and community theatres in the United States, where people are going to see a production or interpretation of a well-known play more often than a new play, the emphasis is also often on the design idea or an exciting production scheme.

Figure 3-15
Rhythm and Movement in Composition
(a) A composition based on diagonal lines has a definite sense of movement.
(b) A composition based on strong horizontals and verticals has a static feeling.

a

b

The designer, unfortunately, cannot take such great liberties with a new play. Here the audience is seeing the play for the first time and will not appreciate too "intellectual" an approach unless it is a part of the production scheme. It is more important to first stimulate the proper emotional response and not to allow a self-conscious design to overwhelm the play.

The way in which a designer achieves balance in composition also accounts for one design being more interesting than another. A mechanical balance of the design forms may bring unity to a composition but still be monotonous and uninteresting. An interesting composition varies or stretches the balance into a more exciting arrangement of forms without losing unity.

Types of Proportional Balance

Several types of arrangements of forms bring a sense of balance or equilibrium to a specific area. These arrangements are classified as axial, radial, and occult balance.

Axial balance is a symmetrical arrangement of forms of equal weight on either side of an axis. The axis may be an actual line or a central-division line. A composition based on such a symmetrical balance may seem dignified and classical in feeling though rather static and severe in effect (Figure 3–16a).

The formality of symmetry can be eased somewhat by using an asymmetrical arrangement wherein the basic forms remain in symmetry but with a variation of color or detail taking place within the overall forms.

A stage setting of a formal or architectural nature frequently employs symmetrical balance, both within the composition (individual wall treatment) and as a whole. Sometimes a near-symmetrical arrangement is used to give the effect of symmetrical balance in a softer, freer manner (Figure 3–16b).

Radial balance is a symmetrical balance around a center, and the movement is always circular. It is most useful in a decorative pattern or ornamental detail, although it may occasionally be seen in the floor plan of a setting (Figure 3–16c).

Occult balance differs from axial balance in the absence of any axis or focal center. It is the balance of unlike elements, the felt balance of mass against space. There are no rules for the achievement or use of occult balance except the judgment of the designer. The result can be a feeling of greater movement and excitement which lends itself readily to dramatic uses (Figure 3–16d).

Because occult balance depends on the interrelationship of elements within the composition, the use of proportion and rhythm aid the designer to arrive at the delicate balance present in an occult arrangement.

Center of Interest

Unless the composition is an overall pattern, it is organized about a center of interest, or focal point. This is a point in the composition (not necessarily the center) to which the eye of the viewer is led by either obvious or subtle means. The leadlines that are present in the movement plan of the composition direct the eye to the center of interest. In addition to the focal center there may also be secondary areas of interest as

a

b

c

d

Figure 3-16
Balance in Composition

(a) Symmetrical balance. *Fidelio.*
Designer—Donald Oenslager. *Photo
courtesy Grimes.* (b) Asymmetrical
balance. *Up in Central Park.*
Designer—Howard Bay. *Photo
courtesy Graphic.* (c) Radial
balance. *Les Troyens.* Designer—
Peter Wexler, Metropolitan Opera.
Photo Copyright © Beth Bergman.
(d) Occult balance. *The Ancient
Mariner.* Designer—Robert Edmond
Jones.

Figure 3-17
Centers of Interest

Designer's sketch for Archibald
Macleish's *JB*. The stage
composition has two well-defined
centers of interest. The shift of
emphasis from one to the other
was accomplished by varying the
intensity and distribution of light.
Designer—Donald Oenslager.
Courtesy Yale School of Drama

well as intriguing bits of detail within the composition that hold attention yet do not detract from the main point of focus.

A stage setting is usually designed around a strong center of interest with important secondary areas. Although the setting as a background has its own center of interest, the true center of interest in the total visual effect is the actor. As was mentioned earlier, a stage composition is a fluid, ever-changing thing with a different center of interest for each scene.

Fortunately, stage lighting, costume colors, and the movement of actors all help to make any change of emphasis rather simple. By dimming most of the lights and brightening one area, stage lighting can easily bring focus to a specific point on the stage, as can the color of a costume in relation to the setting and to other costumes in the scene. The movement of the actor can also be used to change the center of focus, as is so effectively demonstrated in a ballet or group-dance composition. The mobility of the actor allows the director to use groups of actors as a composition tool in order to direct the interest of the audience to any portion of the stage setting. The contributions of stage lighting, costumes, and groupings of actors toward the complete stage composition all serve to emphasize the importance of the visual side of the theatre as well as to underline the function of scene design as a visual art.

The Design Idea

A design idea is concerned first with the function it will perform. A scenic idea may warrant pure decoration as for a beauty pageant; the mood-inducing staging of a ballet; or a realistic environment for a cola commercial. In other words, design serves the story line that is unfolding, defining its very own function.

FUNCTION OF SCENE DESIGN FOR DRAMA

Scene design, like other kinds of creative design, is the creating of a form to fulfill a purpose or function. The function of scene design is obviously linked with the dramatic form it serves. Scene design, in providing a visual support to the dramatic form, is an integral part of the modern theatre. Its function, as a result, is woven into the philosophy of modern theatre practice. The basic concept of present-day theatre, as a playwriting and play-production unity, has brought scenery out of the pretty background class into full partnership in the production of a play. The scene designer brings to the production a visual expression of the author's aim. As a result, scene design becomes a fusing of the visual effect and the basic intent of the play into a single dramatic impression.

The function of scene design can be more clearly revealed by looking at the dramatic form of the play itself. The form of the play should enable the designers to understand the relationship of scenery to action, to dominant mood, to theme, and to the story in general.

Action

If scene design is supposed to bring to the play a visual expression of the author's intent, the designer must first examine the *action* of the play and the kind of people involved in the action. Unless completely abstract, every play (or any other theatrical form, such as ballet or pantomime) presents a conflict. Out of the conflict, whether of heroic proportions or a simple domestic problem, comes the action of the play. The action of the play is the force that moves it forward and makes it a living, breathing form. Dramatic action is a combination of physical or bodily action, visual movement, dialogue, and characterization. Characterization creates sympathy or repulsion on the part of the audience for the figures caught in the action. The characters either create the conflict or are shaped by the conflict in the ensuing action.

The Scene of Action • By incorporating all the elements of the total visual effect, scene design creates in visual terms the scene of the action. At the same time, it is more than just a place; it is an environment for the action. Sometimes the scene or elements of the scene may become a part of the action, which can be seen in the frankly theatrical use of scenery in a farce or musical comedy. The scene, on the other hand, may recede into the background and become a witness to the action, to be more felt than seen.

Characterization

Character development or *characterization* bears an important relationship to the environment of the scene. The people in the action react in accordance with, or in opposition to, their surroundings. The influence of the characters on scene design, sometimes subtle, sometimes symbolic, is, on occasion, more obvious. When the place is an interior, a study of the people living in the house gives the designer many important clues for details. For example, the family of Grandpa Vanderhof and his bizarre friends in Kaufman and Hart's *You Can't Take It with You* certainly contribute a wealth of detail about the kind of house and collection of curios that make up the environment of the play.

The basic function of scene design, then, is to create the appropriate surroundings and environment for the action of the play. The first function of scene design toward creating an appropriate environment is to fix the action of the play in time and place.

Time and Place

The action of the play must occur in a specific *time* and *place*, which are usually calculated, by the author, to establish the proper atmospheric surroundings for the action. Place, even though it may be in limbo, makes a visual impression on the audience. A specific time in the historical past can prepare a state of mind in the audience as much as can the absence of a specific time or place.

Although time and place are linked with the overall atmospherics, the connection is sometimes rather loose and may merely suggest a place that carries connotations of the atmosphere inherent in the play. The first act of Anouilh's *Legend of Lovers*, for example, is set in a French provincial railroad station in the early twentieth century. A closer examination of the play shows that it is not a literal station but a point where travelers pause as they come and go between this life and the life hereafter. Specific time is thus of very little importance except that it is not contemporary.

Establishing the Mood

The second function of scene design is to establish in the visual elements of the surroundings an expression of the dominant atmosphere, or *mood*.

Figure 4-1
Legend of Lovers
*Courtesy Yale School of Drama
Theatre Collection*

Scene design aims to create in this first impression an expression of the mood and its relationship to the action and characters. Mood can be described as the quality of a play that, when properly transmitted, creates a state of mind and emotional response in the audience. It can be expressed in such words as *sparkling, warm, gloomy, violent, earthy, mystic,* and so forth. Some more general expressions of mood are *tragedy, comedy, farce,* and the like, that are also used to define a type of play.

A play, it can be argued, is the dramatization of a mood, a theme, and a story. All three elements are always present in a play, but one may be emphasized over the other two. Hence, a play may be primarily a dramatization of mood with theme and story in a secondary position; the plays with mood dominating seem to be at the extreme ends of the emotional scale. A tragedy is usually a mood-dominated play, as is low comedy or farce. The tragedy *Legend of Lovers,* just mentioned, is an example of dramatization of mood. The Garson Kanin comedy *Born Yesterday* is another example, although it is in the opposite mood.

The relationship of mood to action is stressed, for on occasion a visual atmosphere is established in contrast to the apparent mood of a play. Comedy scenes are sometimes played in the ghostly surroundings of a

a

b

Figure 4-2
Mood

(a) *Drama.* The compositional use of light reinforces the dramatic mood of *Camille.* Designer—Ming Cho Lee. *Photo © T. Charles Erickson.* (b) The dramatic use of movement and light intensify the avalanche scene in Henrik Ibsen's *Brand.* Designer—Richard L. Hay. *Photo courtesy Hank Kranzler.*
(c) *Comedy.* An Art Deco-styled interior in shades of red is the gaudy background for the farce *Lend Me a Tenor.* Designer—Tony Walton. *Photo © 1989 by Martha Swope*

haunted house, or tragedy against the raucous background of a street carnival. The contrasting moods combine into a single dramatic impression. Hence, fun in the haunted house might turn into farce, and murder at the Mardi Gras may become irony.

Tragedy, of course, frequently begins in a lighter mood which may or may not be expressed in the surroundings. A festive scene may have an air of foreboding that anticipates the approaching tragedy.

Reinforcing the Theme

Theme is, of course, closely linked with mood as well as with the story-telling part of the dramatic form. The theme of some plays is clearly apparent, especially if the author is using the dramatic form as a pulpit or soapbox to lampoon society or government. Comedy often carries a message to an unsuspecting audience as effectively as does the more direct approach of the serious play with a strong story line.

An example of an expression of theme in scenery is found in Shaw's *Heartbreak House.* The living room of Captain Shotover's house is designed like the fantail of an ancient sailing ship. The incongruity of this misplaced bit of architecture is a constant visual symbol of the lack of purpose and aimlessness of the cultured, frank, charming, unconventional people who live in it.

The expression of theme in scenery cannot always be easily achieved. More often the theme is treated with subtlety and in symbols known only to the designer and his muse. The most obvious example of a theme-oriented play is found in the documentary theatre. Removed from the fictional format of literary theatre, the documentary theatre is free to move to its objective with dramatic and theatrical directness. The most familiar documentary theatre, stemming from Germany in the 1930s, is that of Bertolt Brecht and Erwin Piscator. Their "theatre of alienation"

a

b

Figure 4-3
Theme

Heartbreak House by Bernard Shaw. (a) The traditional design of the bizarre room in the form of an ancient sailing ship. Designer—James Russel. *Photo courtesy Morris Shapiro.*
(b) Designer Michael Levine chose not to follow Shaw's nautical image. He achieved a disquieting atmosphere by creating an all white room dressed with oversized clutter. A few minutes into the first act, the ceiling begins to rise from a normal level to an absurd, yet droll, height. Shaw Festival Theatre, Canada. *Photo courtesy David Cooper*

had a sociopolitical orientation that was frankly aimed at the elimination of capitalism as a social and political way of life.

Although impact of the message has lessened as audiences have become more sophisticated and tolerant of shock, the documentary theatre remains a vital theatrical form exerting a strong influence on modern theatre practice and design. Light projections using mixed media of film and live actors to express theme have become the hallmark of documentary theatre, as have the conscious efforts to bring real-life objects and true materials to the stage in an attempt to remove scenery (and all of theatre for that matter) from the world of make-believe and playacting. The effect on the young designer is evident in the freedom of present-day stage design from the taboos of illusion and sentimentality that dominated the romantic world of make-believe.

Staging the Story

Story is the connecting thread that holds together the other elements in a complete dramatic form. It is the train of related incidents that brings continuity to the many events in a play. Story is probably more important to the theatre than to other art forms. The expression of an idea in the theatre is dependent upon having and holding the audience's attention every moment. The theatre audience, if confused, cannot turn back the pages, like a novel reader, and reread a passage for clarification. An engrossing story can hold an audience spellbound. A good storyteller, of course, uses mood to create the atmosphere for a story. The storyteller can also use the story to make a point, which is apparent in plays with strong themes. Any good play usually has a good story, but a play that is dominated by the dramatization of story is primarily dedicated to telling an interesting tale, whether it be of love, adventure, intrigue — the list is long and varied.

Because the environment of a story-dominated play is usually real, the designing problem becomes one of selection of realistic details and forms that place the action and establish the mood. This, more often than not, has already been accomplished by the author through the choice of realistic location for the scene of the action. A more important contribution of design in the story-dominated play is the staging of the action. Staging, or fitting the action on the stage, provides the areas, levels, and properties in such a way as to allow the continuous flow of action so necessary to telling a good story.

The many English and French so-called bedroom farces are story-dominated plays that depend heavily on staging. The skillful juxtaposition of hallways, doors, closets, and the ever-present bedroom, all visible to the audience, is necessary to facilitate the fast pace and split-second timing of the nonsensical action of the story. An unusual example of imaginative farce staging is Alan Ayckburn's *Taking Steps*. The three floors of a house are staged on one level. Light helps to define the change of floor levels as well as the actors when they pantomime going up and down nonexistent stairs. Once the audience catches on to the convention, its imagination separates the different levels of the house. The cleverness of the staging adds humor to the performance and develops an interesting production style.

DESIGN AND OTHER THEATRICAL FORMS

The question may be raised whether or not the functions of scenery for a play or any other literary form in the theatre can be applied to other theatrical forms such as mime, ballet, audio-visual, and unstructured theatre. Unless the production is totally abstract or completely unstructured, the guidelines are the same. The absence of a predetermined story line may limit the planning of staging but, eventually, staging is involved even if the action is accidental or improvised.

Theme and mood are both present in any theatrical form. The psychedelic lighting of a rock show imparts a poignant theme through the atmospheric senses of sight and sound. Although classical ballet usually has a story line, its modern counterpart frequently does not. Hence the decorative background of ballet that sets the locale and mood of the dance has given way to the limited use of scenery in the form of stylized properties and arbitrary lighting more expressive of theme than anything else. Mime, both group and solo, is the most absolute of the theatrical forms. Imagination supplies the scenic background and hand props. Although the same thinking is involved, the skill of the performer, rather than the designer, creates the mood of the locale in the minds of the audience. Mime is sometimes incorporated into literary theatre. The pantomimed props and scenery in *Our Town* is an example, as well as the imagined costume in *The Emperor's New Clothes*.

In ballet the miming of dialogue by the dancers is a conscious control or theatrical convention that has little to do with the scenic background except that it establishes a performing style.

In other words, whatever type of theatrical event a designer may be asked to do he or she asks, more or less, the same questions:

1. What is the reason for this event? (commercial, charity function, historical celebration, etc.)
2. What is the atmosphere? (happy, serious, etc.)
3. What is it saying? (How will scenery, costumes, and lights help you say it?)
4. How and where will it be staged? (theatre, stadium, on the street, etc.)
5. What is the style? (entertainment, documentary, pageant, etc.)

HOW TO BEGIN

At this point, beginning designers should be conscious of the importance scene design has in relation to the play. They should be aware of the influences of the theatrical medium and be familiar with the intricacies of the creative process. But, they may ask, how does one get an idea for a design?

It is impossible to set down universal rules for developing a design idea; there are as many methods as designers. And an individual method is often so subjective and intuitive that it is of little value to another designer as a way of working; each must and usually does develop his or her own method of reaching the inner reservoir of creative ideas.

Still, although it is possible to make recommendations and to point to examples of good design, the actual conquest of an idea is the designer's individual struggle.

The design idea, of course, does not exist until the play becomes a production and the written word becomes dialogue and visible action. It is the individual expression of the artistic imagination, theatrical sense, and technical ingenuity of the designer through the visual control of line, color, and form. The design concept is often evident as a visual theme with variations that weave through a complicated setting or series of settings, bringing unity of thought to the whole. Many times the theme is so subtle that only the trained eye of another designer can see and appreciate its presence.

The design idea is aimed at stimulating an intellectual or emotional response in the audience. The control of the design elements may be broad and sensational to arouse primitive emotions, or they may be subtle and refined to stimulate an intellectual response. Good design is the result of logical yet imaginative thinking and intuitive feeling expressed through an idea or central theme.

The ideas for many an inspirational setting have been worked out on the back of an envelope during a coffee break or have been virtually completed before the author has finished the third act. Although this is frequently the pace at which a scene designer is expected to work, it is hardly a practical procedure for an inexperienced designer.

Analysis of the Script

Developing a concept for a setting begins with the study of the play. Ideally, the play is analyzed from three separate readings, assuming that the designer will have the script longer than overnight or for more than two hours on a train. The three separate readings represent the logical steps toward accumulating information that shapes and inspires the design idea.

The designer's first reading of the play is for its *content*. The designer should react as a member of the audience, avoiding any preconceived image of the background other than the author's description. In this way a first impression will serve as an overall response that will help answer these questions: What kind of a play is it? What is the action and where is it taking place? What is the dominant mood? Is the play a comedy? Or is it a tongue-in-cheek satire with political overtones? Is it a tragedy of classical proportions or a domestic misunderstanding?

The scene of the action often suggests or sets the atmosphere of a play. A deserted house on a stormy night for a mystery or a love scene by candlelight are typical examples. The action, however, is not always in harmony with its surroundings but may be in opposition or contrast to its environment.

The mood of a play or scene often suggests *color* to the designer. Out of the mood of the environment comes the overall tonality of the play, which often can be expressed most forcefully in color or even in the absence of color.

The second reading is for the play's *intent*. What is the author saying? It is a more careful reading—between the lines and within parentheses. What is the theme? What is the style? Has the author expressed a point of view through allegorical symbols or in daily-life realism? Has the playwright soared into the realm of epic poetry or dropped into the lusty imagery of sidewalk prose? In the style of the play the designer finds a clue to the degree of reality or unreality of the scenic environment.

From the theme of the play the designer can usually find a visual image that leads to a design concept. And from the style of the play the designer gets an indication of the form of the design. Style and form interact, for style influences form. A realistic style implies realistic forms; a fantasy or dream suggests unreal forms.

The final reading is discussed later in this chapter.

Style, Form, and Concept

Because style in the theatre is felt, heard, and seen in so many different ways, it is difficult to define in specific terms. Literary, acting, directing, and visual styles, as well as period styles, unite to form a single production style. Style is sometimes visually obvious, but more often it will be unnoticed by the audience unless some element of it is jarring or incorrect in terms of the whole.

Style, form, and concept are so closely interrelated that it is hard to distinguish where one begins and the other leaves off. Briefly, style can be defined as the degree of reality expressed in visual forms and the mode of performance. Style (or the degree of reality) influences form. Concept is the *idea* or manner of presenting style and form. In other words, concept is the expression of an idea in a degree of reality (or unreality) that cannot help but affect the form of the design and the manner of performance.

Production Style and Reality • The overall style of a production is expressed in the degree of reality of the performance. There are many kinds of reality in the theatre: the lifelike copy of nature (naturalism), the fantasy of dreams, the make-believe quality of storytelling, the immediacy of documentary or of improvisational style, and the performance reality of the theatrical style. The two extreme realities in a performance are the lifelike quality of naturalism and the theatrical reality of presentional theatre. It might be seen as the difference between the actor and the performer.

The theatrical reality of the performer is something that *is* happening at the moment as opposed to an actor's dramatic re-creation of something that *has* happened but in such a way as to make the audience believe that they are experiencing it for the first time. Each is a different degree of reality to which the audience reacts with contrasting emotions. Although an audience may justly appreciate an actor's convincing performance, the reality is still make-believe. If, for example, a light cue is missed or scenery falls down, the make-believe spell is broken with an unfortunate intrusion of reality. A presentional style, however, might keep technical mishaps and muffed lines in the routine to give the performance an immediate reality.

Occasionally production styles are combined. The docudrama style (documentary and literary styles) is often used to capture the emotion of an actual happening. It has the factual reality of a documentary but is actually a fictional style. The documentary format heightens the reality and holds the audience while the story unfolds.

The docudrama, as a style, is less convincing on the stage than in the more immediate media of radio and television. A classic example of the emotional impact of a docudrama style occurred in 1938. Orson Welles' famous radio adaptation of H. G. Wells' *War of the Worlds* was presented as a newscaster's report of the landing of the Martians. The docudrama was so real that many listeners were on the verge of panic.

Visual Style and Form • The effect of style on form is more easily seen in visual styles than in the performance styles just discussed, although the two are related. Visual styles can be defined in similar degrees of reality.

The representional style, for example, is lifelike. The design form is represented in a painting or sculpture rendered as near to its natural form and color as the technical skill of the artist allows.

The nonrepresentational style, the opposite reality, is ornamental. Because its goal is sensation, the interplay of sheer form and color becomes important. The designer does not attempt to create a form that bears any resemblance to natural or manmade objects.

Between these two extremes lie as many degrees of realism, symbolism, abstraction, or complete nonobjectivity as designers care to define.

The effect of style on form is more apparent as the degree of reality decreases. The form is distorted into an abstract but recognizable shape. The metamorphosis of a tree form on the stage can be used to illustrate the influence of style on form. For example, the realistic apple tree in Osborn's *On Borrowed Time* contrasts with the decorative forest in Gilbert and Sullivan's *Iolanthe* and with the abstract trees in the forest scene of Dürrenmatt's *The Visit*. The trees in the latter production were reduced to pendants of gauze that were slashed with side lighting and projected patterns on the floor.

As a visual art, scenery styles conform to the same degrees of reality as do production styles. Scenery style, in fact, is the most important visual element supporting the overall production style (Figure 4–4).

Reality and Light • It is obvious that the lighting and scene designers must be aware of all styles in the theatre, for they are called upon to visually support (and occasionally contrast) the acting, literary, and directing styles and create a unified production style.

The reality of light on the stage is easily seen in its degree of conformity (or lack of comformity) to light in nature. We are so used to seeing each other under normal angles, distribution, and colors of the sun that when these angles deviate, or when colors change too much, we consider the light "unreal" or "theatrical." The low angle and rich colors of a sunset are frequently so dramatic that they seem to belong on the stage. For the same reason, light on an actor from a low angle seems unnatural or stylized.

Figure 4-4
Visual Styles of Scenery

(a) *Realism.* Real action and materials shape the realistic style of *Distant Fires.* Hartford Stage Company. *Photo © T. Charles Erickson.* (b) *Anti-Illusionary Scenery. Puntila* by Bertolt Brecht. An example of Brecht's aversion to illusionary or "make-believe" scenery. Real, unconventional textures such as the straw-covered portals, unpainted old boards, and a brass sun are used. The result is of course not realism but stylization which, though denying illusion, is still theatrical. *Photo courtesy Nelson.* (c) *Surrealism.* The unnatural juxtaposition of a large, tilted mirror upstage revealing the entrance-way, and a reverse image of the action on stage attempts to express the irrational subject matter in *Right You Are If You Think You Are* by Luigi Pirandello. Designer—William Matthews. *Photo courtesy Feinstein.*
(d) *Fragmentary Scenery.* A view from the wings of a setting for the operatic version of Eugene O'Neill's *Mourning Becomes Electra* at the Metropolitan Opera, New York. The highly stylized interpretation of the stately Classic Revival style is achieved by the imaginative use of textured surfaces and exposed structural members. Designer—Boris Aronson. *Photo courtesy Gary Renaud.* (e) *Suggested Scenery.* Elements of scenery have been manipulated to convey a backstage scene for *Dalliance,* Tom Stoppard's adaptation of Schnitzler's *Liebelei.* Designer—John Conklin. Long Wharf Theatre. *Photo © T. Charles Erickson.* (f) *Concept Based on Period Theatre.* An interesting concept for an opera version of Shakespeare's *Two Gentlemen of Verona.* Designer Henry Haymann developed Victorian Toy Theatre look (above) inspired by a fifteenth century Serlioian Street Scene (below). Three River Shakespeare Festival, Pittsburgh. *Photo courtesy Jeffery Cepull*

a

b

c

d

e

f

Scena Comica.

a

Figure 4-5
Style and Light

(a) Patterns of light increase the tension in a scene from *Morocco*. Designer—Michael Wyergan. *Photo © T. Charles Erickson.* (b) Dramatic use of light and simple scenic forms for Shakespeare's *Love's Labor Lost.* Yale Repertory Theatre. *Photo © T. Charles Erickson*

b

Although much of stage lighting may seem naturalistic in style, there are types of theatrical productions and performances that are more dependent on a style of color, distribution, and movement of light than on general illumination or visibility. Ballet, for example, is a theatrical extension of life into a highly stylized performance technique. Realistic illumination is less important than the theatrical atmosphere, exotic colors, and arbitrary angles of light that make up this style of production.

The theatrical reality of Brecht, on the other hand, strips away atmosphere and illusion. Lighting instruments are exposed and uncolored to reinforce the feeling that what we are seeing is happening *now*, on the stage in the reality of the performance.

Historical Style and Concept • Historical styles, both period and national, are significant in their own right. The effect of each period on form is quite clear. The geometric and flamboyant tracery of Gothic, for example, is distinct from the reverse curve of the baroque and the whiplash of art nouveau. The same is true of national styles. There is a difference, for example, in the forms of the rococo in France, Germany, and Austria.

When a historical style is used on the stage, however, it becomes a *concept*, for it is not *the* period that is being demonstrated but a conceptualization of the historical style. The historical scenes in Miller's *The Crucible*, for example, are conceptual versions of seventeenth-century America. It is not too difficult to see that period style can take on many degrees of reality. A historical period can be authentically reproduced, suggested, or even spoofed.

Historical moments in theatre frequently serve as a framework for a contemporary idea. The Shevelove/Gilbart/Sondheim musical *A Funny Thing Happened on the Way to the Forum*, for example, is a burlesque of Roman comedy with a present-day message. *Girl Friend* is a nostalgic spoof of life and the theatre of the 1920s. The melodramatic revival of such plays as *Under the Gaslights* is an exaggeration of period mannerism as a concept.

Finding a Concept • The search for a concept cannot help but be influenced by personal taste, background, and experience. An experienced designer falls into the habit of mentally storing ideas and then waiting for the opportunity to use them. By observing people, nature, and unusual happenings, the designer develops an eye to see and record.

Ideas in one art medium can be transposed into another. To work, for example, in the manner of a famous painter—colors from the palette of Cézanne, the light of Rembrandt, and the forms of Picasso—can suggest a compositional control of light and form within a stage production. Similarly, the dramatic colors and the compositional use of light by Turner are another example of elements that are very adaptable to a stage color concept.

In Chapter 3 we mentioned that the strong emphasis of a single element such as line, color, or light in a composition becomes a design control leading to a concept. *Carmen Jones*, a black musical version of Bizet's opera *Carmen*, keyed each act to a single color. This progression of color and intensity reinforced the emotional climax.

Movement as an element of design is frequently used in a lighting concept. It can be expressed in the movement of color and the distribution of light in dance, or to interpret the rhythm of music in color and form.

Light can also dominate a composition and become a concept. Patterns of exposed sources, specific distribution, or projected images can become a visual style with light as the central force. Natural light and colors can also be an inspiration. The crushing intensity of the sun, the dampness of a forest, or the fog of a river can be lighting concepts that give the designer a control or way of thinking and creating.

A thematic image can lead to a variety of uses of symbolic form, color, or atmosphere. Symbolism in scenery and light can be extremely subtle, serving basically as a control for the director and the designers. Obvious symbolism could cause a negative response on the part of the audience and should be used with caution. Too much symbolism in scenic forms can be so overwhelming that the actor and playwright's words are anti-climactic.

Style and Theatre Forms • Today's theatre is moving away from naturalism toward a more imaginative use of style. The stage, rather than trying to compete with the photographic realism of the movies and television, has turned to more abstract, stylized, and sometimes expressionistic styles in both writing and staging. However, an interesting contrast

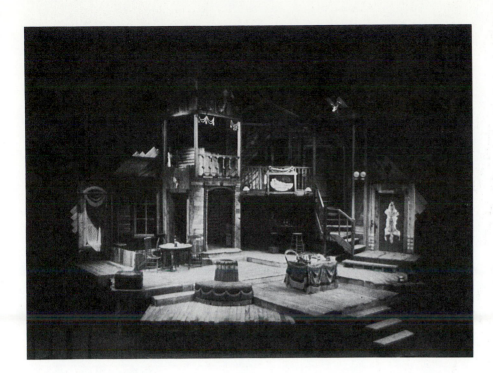

Figure 4-7
Concept and Style
An interesting concept for Ben Jonson's *The Alchemist.* The Elizabethan comedy was set in the time of the California Gold Rush, when a similar preoccupation with gold prevailed. Designer—Richard L. Hay. Oregon Shakespearean Festival. *Photo courtesy Hank Kranzler*

Figure 4-8
Style and the Theatre Form
The thrust and arena stage often force the designer into theatrical convention or stylization that would be optional in the proscenium theatre. An intimate staging of O'Neill's *A Moon for the Misbegotten.* Designer—Richard L. Hay, Oregon Shakespearean Festival. *Photo courtesy Hank Kranzler*

of styles has developed in the production concepts of the two nonproscenium theatre forms, the thrust and arena stage. Where the emphasis of the proscenium theatre was on *production*, we find the thrust and arena theatres concentrating on *performance*.

The lack of scenic elements on the thrust and arena stages calls on the imagination of the audience to complete the scene. Invisible walls and doors, different locales indicated by levels on the floor, hanging fragments overhead, and the color of light are common theatrical conventions on thrust and arena stages. They establish an abstract degree of reality the audience is asked to accept as a mode of production. On the other hand, furniture and hand properties are painstakingly real, and the actor's costumes are fully detailed in a contrast of styles. Because the audience is physically closer to the action, it is virtually in the scene and a part of the action. There is a more subjective or intimate alliance of audience and performer when the proscenium wall is removed, although the reality is very much a theatrical reality.

The proscenium theatre, on the other hand, depends on esthetic distance and a more objective relationship with its audience. There is, however, a great latitude of expression from bare stage to full stage productions in a variety of styles, and on occasion, a thrust through the proscenium for closer contact with the audience.

Acting and Literary Styles • Dramatic form combines the literary and acting styles. With scenery style, they all have an effect on each other and must have some degree of unity in order to create a strong dramatic form.

The literary style reveals through dialogue the degree of ideality represented in the play. The style of a play may capture a cross-section of life, such as Elmer Rice's *Street Scene*, or it may be as expressionistic as the treatment of Mr. Zero's problems in Rice's *The Adding Machine*.

The epic style of Brecht and his attempts to denude the stage of illusion or any visual make-believe obviously has had its influence on scenery style. By appealing to the intellectual side of the members of his audience, and denying them any escape into sentimentality, Brecht forces them to listen, and perhaps more important, to react. The belief that any reaction, even the shock of unconventionality, is better than having a passive, hypnotized audience is reflected in elements of scenery. Thus, a barren stage, the presence of *real* materials and textures, exposed lighting instruments, and clear unatmospheric lighting create the essence of his scenes.

Paradoxically, this opposition to the fakery of illusionary scenery and the effort to free the theatre of conventionality actually imposes a new system of theatrical hocus-pocus. The result is almost a scenic stylization that is in tune with present-day junk sculpture and pop art and which the audience responds to in vicarious recognition of its unconventional cleverness.

The acting style of today, for the most part, is believably real when compared to the highly mannered period examples of the seventeenth, eighteenth, and nineteenth centuries. Acting style, however, may vary from naturalism to conform with the style of a specific drama. It takes its cue, as does scenery, from the literary style of the play.

The theatre contains many examples of conflicting literary and acting styles: one illustration is the nineteenth-century conception of opera. A stilted literary style was combined with a presentational acting style of singing dialogue—both set against a conflicting background of painted realism. Today, the style of the scenery has been brought closer to the less realistic acting and writing styles to form a more unified and convincing art form.

Scene design, as a visual art, can reinforce and heighten literary and acting styles. Strangely enough, it can on occasion be a contrast to the acting style without breaking the unity of the production. The designer has always felt that stylized scenery does not necessarily call for stylized acting, as was demonstrated so expertly in Jo Mielziner's setting for Miller's *Death of a Salesman*. The reverse, however, is not true. If the acting is stylized, the scenery must be, too. The important thing is that the audience will accept any degree of departure from the real in scenery as long as it is consistent and in good taste.

WORKING WITH THE DIRECTOR

During this formative stage there is only so much a designer can do alone. From the beginning there is a need for close communication with the

Figure 4-9
The Unit Setting

The production scheme for Anouilh's *Colombe* as produced by the Yale Dramatic Association. The repetition of the theatre proscenium form brings a visual and thematic unity to the production.

director, especially if a strong directorial concept is considered in the design. Directorial influence on design can vary from a complete "hands-off-solve-it-yourself" attitude to a "this-is-what-I-want" directive. A more-equally balanced collaboration is, naturally, ideal. One-sided domination can lead to personality clashes that abort the creative process. The most successful and unified productions are usually the result of the mutual respect and openmindedness on the part of both the designer and the director.

The collaboration, of course, begins with talking. Preliminary discussions can lead to agreement about the nature of the play, the dramatic image, and general atmosphere (colors, style, staging, and directorial concept). Talk, however, has its limits. Words have a way of triggering a different image in each individual. At some point the designer must put visual impressions on paper. Only then can the designer and director really begin to communicate.

An understanding and agreement about *style* is probably the most important part of the designer-director collaboration, especially if other designers are involved in the production (costume and lighting). Although the impact of a style confusion appears later in the execution of the design, it is significant enough to be mentioned now at the formative stage.

The theatre, as we have seen, brings together many styles. During production, the director is the only one with an overall view and therefore must be responsible for coordinating the various styles as the show is being put together. The lack of immediate communication to the designer or designers of directorial changes or style adjustments in other areas of design can lead to conflicts at a time in the production schedule when it is too late to make changes. The best-laid plans can go astray without constant supervision and communication on the part of the director. An experienced designer soon learns to not take anything for granted and makes frequent checks with the director and other areas of design.

Final Reading

After reaching a mutual understanding with the director on theme, style, and general interpretation of the play, the designer returns to the script for a third reading.

This reading of the play is for its technique. Close attention is paid to the physical requirements of the plot structure and, if there are many scenes, to the changes of locale. The action and staging requirements are examined to determine the number of people in a scene, the types of entrances and exits, references in the dialogue to the scene, bits of action hidden from one actor but visible to the audience, and so on—all leading to the development of a basic idea and scheme of production.

Scheme of Production

The design solution of a multiscene play, which is known as a *scheme of production,* brings scenery-handling techniques into the design concept. The design idea is developed around a method of handling the numerous changes of scene. The kinds of changes and the methods of handling scenery, such as wagons and turntables, are discussed fully in

Figure 4-10
Simultaneous Scene
Several locales are placed in
juxtaposition in the drama *The
Down Side* allowing simultaneous
action. Long Wharf Theatre. *Photo
© T. Charles Erickson*

Chapter 10 and indicate the necessity of designing a large production around at least a basic scheme for moving the scenery.

Although discussed separately, a scheme of production is, of course, closely related to *style*. Many times the designer, through a scheme of production, establishes certain conventions that the audience is expected to accept and which, consequently, create a scenery style. Conversely, a scenery style may dictate how the scenery is to be handled, thereby becoming a scheme of production.

Unit Setting • The movement of scenery may be reduced by the various uses of a unit setting. This form of setting is based upon the retention or reuse of certain elements of scenery to stimulate a change of scene. This is usually accomplished by repeating either the plan, design shape, or color in the various settings. The design shapes and colors, for example, may be varied in each setting although they are placed in identical floor plans, or the same shape can be moved to a variety of positions.

A unit setting can be used in two different ways, either as a cleverly camouflaged method of reusing scenery unbeknown to the audience, or as an obvious device that becomes a unifying force for the production, as well as a means of simplifying scene changes (Figure 4–9).

Simultaneous-Scene Setting • Sometimes a production scheme can eliminate all movement of scenery by placing two or more locales on

a

b

Figure 4-11
Projected Scenery

(a) Two of the fifteen variations of *The Turn of the Screw* by Benjamin Britten are set in a gloomy Victorian country house. The eerie mood of the opera lends itself to the effective use of projections. Two basic screens are backed by a third upstage, creating a three-dimensional effect. Designer—Patrick Robertson. Lighting Designer—David Hersey. *Courtesy Noel Staunton, English National Opera, London.* (b) The documentary use of projections in Bertolt Brecht's *The Measures Taken.* The screen is used as a visual support of the play's theme, rather than to establish environment. Designer—Frederic Youens. *Photo courtesy Nelson* the stage at the same time. The action moves from one area to the other without a break. The only movement is in the changing of lights. The areas, which retain their initial identity throughout the show, may be different rooms in a house, different houses in the same town, or remotely located scenes (Figure 4–10).

Although the simultaneous-scene setting is mentioned here as one of the many schemes of production, it was, of course, discussed earlier as a kind of production that emphasized the important design function of staging the story (see page 63). Even though the scenic elements and furniture in the simultaneous-scene setting may appear as extreme realism, the style of the setting is, in the final analysis, unrealistic. The audience is asked to accept theatrical conventions such as *cut-away walls* and *strange locale juxtapositions* to facilitate the staging of the story.

Formal Setting • A freer example of the simultaneous-scene setting is the use of an arrangement of abstract or architectural forms in such a way as to allow a flow of action over the set, relying on lights to change the composition. Three or four basic areas may be established, but they do not take on the connotation of a specific locale. A formal setting locates the action only in a very general way. It is contingent upon the actors, properties, and dialogue to establish the specific locale of the scene. Occasionally a formal setting is dressed with a minimum of moving set pieces to add variety.

Projected Scenery • Light projections as scenery are included with many production schemes for handling multiscene shows. The rear projection of a design onto a translucent screen makes the shifting of a scene as simple as the changing of a slide.

Because projected scenery is *light* and not *paint* it has a strong dramatic quality which tends to dominate the scene. It becomes in a sense an actor rather than scenery. Projected scenery, when used correctly as an integral part of the play, functions best in a nonrealistic or abstract production where the scenery is acting and not just background.

Brecht, for example, used the screen as an actor. He frequently projected instructive messages or illustrative images on the screen more as an instrument of propaganda or idea than as a visual background to set the scene. It is a classroom or documentary technique which when used in dramatic surroundings serves to heighten his epic theatre.

In spite of its limitations and dominating characteristics, projected scenery can be used as a highly dramatic and exciting production scheme. Many production designs have been based on projected scenery with successful results (Figure 4–11).

Preliminary Studies

The designer's first impression of a design concept may have been formed as early as the first reading of the play, only to be substantially revised or rejected after a closer study of the script in the second and third readings. A first impression is often correct, but sometimes it is wrong, and the designer may find it difficult to change this early impression. For this reason the beginning designer may be wise during the first reading of a new play to keep an open mind free of preconceptions until all the

a

b

Figure 4-12
Projections On Scenery and Dancers
The Nikolais Dance Theatre. (a) *The Tent. Photo courtesy Brynn Manley.* (b) *Grotto. Photo courtesy Caravaglia*

facts are accumulated. At that time everything usually falls into place with little or no effort.

An idea may first appear to the designer in the form of an interesting floor plan to be developed later into a related elevational drawing, or the reverse—as a decorative shape or historical form that must be adjusted to a workable floor plan.

Preliminary studies usually consist of small, freehand thumbnail sketches and rough floor plans. After consultation with the director, the tentative ideas of the designer are ready to be expanded into a more complete form of presentation.

PRESENTATION OF THE DESIGN IDEA

The designer's presentation communicates his or her ideas to the other members of the design and production team. The designer usually presents a color sketch, floor plan, and model. The importance placed on each form of presentation can vary with the type of theatre company and the scale of a production. The sketch, for example, might be a collage expressing the atmosphere and visual impact of the setting while placing more emphasis on a larger scaled model with more detail. On the other hand, a single setting with many changes of scenic elements and lighting might be best presented with a series of photographs.

An unsubsidized theatre company often makes a presentation to encourage backers. On such occasions slides or videotapes are used along with live scenes or readings from the script.

The Sketch

Although scene design is essentially a three-dimensional art form, the two-dimensional sketch medium is used to present the design idea. The sketch can be rendered in color and perspective to show atmosphere that would be difficult to accomplish in a model. Many sketches can be made to show changes in lighting, scenery, and composition of the actors. The sketch is lightweight, easy to carry around, and therefore adaptable to the selling of an idea.

What is represented in the sketch depends somewhat on the working arrangement of the designer. For example, it may be an established designer working with a new producer, an established producer working with a new designer, or a producing team experienced in working together for some time.

The producer views the sketches of an established designer more with a knowledge of what the designer has done in past settings than for what is actually shown in the sketch. The producer knows that after an agreement on the general concept the experienced designer will fill in the details and create a setting to a high standard of excellence.

Because a new designer does not have past examples of work, his or her ideas are bought or rejected on the strength of a sketch. In addition, of course, the young designer must be able to back up all ideas with faithful execution.

Under either condition, the sketch tries to catch a significant moment in the play. The designer usually picks a moment that will best show the setting and still express the dominant mood of the play. The sketch

Figure 4-13
Designers' Sketches

(Above) The preliminary sketch: a designer's first thoughts. Sometimes in color, more often in black and white. Shown here is a preliminary ink-and-wash sketch for *Grand Hotel*. Designer—Anon Adar, Tel Aviv. (Below) A more finished sketch of the barn scene from Dürrenmatt's *The Visit*. The director insisted on a detailed, atmospheric sketch to set the tonality of the scene for everyone concerned with the production.

is an idealized drawing of the total visual effect which serves as a goal for the execution and guide for the lighting. Supplementary sketches are sometimes needed to show what would happen at another dramatic moment with different lighting and actor grouping.

In the purest sense, however, the sketch is only a means of presenting an idea. It is not the final design and therefore should not be displayed or judged as a complete art form. A stage setting is not complete until it is on the stage, lighted and viewed in the context of the action of the play and the actors' movements. The judgment of the success or failure of a design in the final analysis is based on how it functions under finished performance conditions rather than as a beautiful sketch.

The sketch is not meant to be a working drawing. Although it maintains a consistent proportion to show the actor-scenery relationship, it is not necessarily drawn to an accurate scale. It is possible, however, to execute a design from a carefully proportioned sketch if large portions of the set are parallel to the footlights as in a wing-and-backdrop setting. The colors in the sketch are not intended to be the scenery colors, but represent the color as it would appear under the stage lights in the total visual effect.

If the designer is a member of an established producing group, such as summer stock or television, the sketch may take on a different character. The designer, director, builder, and painter may be so used to working with each other that much will be understood without being set down on paper. The designer's sketch becomes schematic, with marginal notes. It is carried just as far as necessary to convey the idea and is drawn for the designer's *professional colleagues.* The designer will resort to a full sketch or model only when trying something experimental which needs careful explanation.

The sketch is always accompanied by a floor plan. If the floor plan is drawn to scale and the sketch is in good proportion, the director and others concerned with the production can form an accurate opinion as to how the actual setting will look.

The Model

Although the sketch has been pictured as the prime means of presenting an idea, it is frequently backed up by a model. Because of the three-dimensionality of scenery, some designers prefer to work directly in the model form of presentation. The model gives a true indication of the space relationships of scenery and actors and is, therefore, of interest to the director when planning the staging.

Within the model, each piece of scenery is constructed to an accurate scale, thus giving the designer a miniature preview of how the setting is going to look. Because the model is three-dimensional, composition and sightlines can be checked from all the extreme angles of view.

In addition to being a means of presentation, the model also can be used to check construction and effects before making a sketch. In this way the new designer is assured that all sketches can be reproduced in full-scale scenery without technical difficulties.

The scale of the model varies with the designer. Some like to work at the scale of one inch equal to one foot, while others prefer a smaller scale. The ¼-inch scale model is a convenient size for fast execution,

Figure 4-14
Sketch, Model, and Set
(Top to bottom) Designer's sketch, designer's model, and completed setting for *He Who Must Die,* a translation and adaptation of Nikos Kazantazakis' *The Greek Passion.* Designer— Rolf Beyer. *Photo courtesy Street*

which sometimes is important. The smaller scale is also convenient because it is easier to make changes and experiment with than a larger scale.

The sketch and model are the designer's means of presenting or selling a design concept. Once the director and designer have reached an area of agreement and the idea has been bought, the designer has to prepare another type of presentation; this time for the people who will build, paint, and light the design.

a

b

Figure 4-15
Model and Production Setting
Scenery for the thrust stage.
(a) Model for *Incident at Vichy.*
Photo courtesy Myren Walken.
(b) Production photograph.
Designer—Darwin Reid Payne.
Photo courtesy Elliot Mendleson.
Reprinted from *Theory and Craft of the Scenographic Model* by Darwin Reid Payne, Southern Illinois University Press, publisher.

Drafting the Design

Although scene design is three-dimensional in final form, most of the presentation of the design idea in preparation for construction is two-dimensional in character. The graphics of presentation are the visual language or fundamental means of communication between the designer, stage technicians, and director. The planning of a show throughout all its phases relies upon a common knowledge of simple drafting techniques to communicate technical and artistic information. The designer must give simple, clear, and accurate information so that all ideas may be carried out efficiently and accurately.

DRAFTING EQUIPMENT

The young student designer will need to become acquainted with certain tools and materials. Drafting for the theatre is similar to architectural drafting and engineering drawing but is not as elaborate.

A good *drawing board* is made of clear white pine, cleated to prevent warping, and for most purposes is about 24 inches by 30 inches in size. A *drafting table,* the top of which is a drawing board, should be a little larger. A top of about 30 inches by 42 inches gives additional work space around the drawing.

Drawing boards need to be padded to prevent the pencil from following the grain of the wood. The best surface is a vinyl plastic cover that is tinted pale green on one side and an off white on the other. Although expensive, it is an excellent drafting surface and will last a lifetime.

The *T-square* guides off one side of the drawing board to establish the horizontal lines in the drawing. Its accuracy depends upon the straightness of the working edge and the squareness of the head and blade. A

For the beginner, a list of basic drafting equipment should include:

1. A drawing board or drafting table
2. Drawing board padding
3. T-square or parallel rule
4. Set of triangles or set-square
5. Small set of drafting instruments
    a. Compass
    b. Lengthening bar
    c. Inking attachments
    d. Dividers
    e. Bow compass and bow dividers
    f. Ruling pen
6. Scale rule
7. Pencils and leads
8. Tracing paper
9. Accessories
    a. Erasers
    b. Erasing shield
    c. Drafting tape
    d. Lead pointer
    e. Drawing cleaning powder
    f. Rapidograph pen

30-inch T-square made of hardwood with a transparent-edge blade and fixed head is best for all-around service. A traveling parallel straight edge which serves the same function as a T-square is attached permanently to the top of a drafting table. Its length, of course, is determined by the longest dimension of the top.

Two transparent celluloid *triangles* give the customary set of angles as well as perpendicular lines when they are guided off of the T-square. A 6-inch 45-degree and an 8- or 10-inch 30–60-degree triangle are the most convenient sizes.

An instrument that lends itself to drawing the many odd angles so frequently found in a stage setting is the *set-square.* It is a combination triangle and protractor with an adjustable edge that allows the selection of any angle between 45 degrees and perpendicular.

When assembling drawing instruments for the first time, it is wise to invest in a good set. The accuracy and clarity of the work depends on the quality of the instruments. Buying a cheap, low-grade set is a nuisance from the beginning and will prove worthless in a short while. It is better to economize on the number or size of the set and buy good instruments.

The basic drafting instrument is the *compass.* It is necessary to draw a circle or swing an arc. Many small drafting sets consist only of a compass with lengthening bar and inking attachments. Extra points are also provided to turn the compass into dividers.

Figure 5-1
Drafting Equipment
(a) Drawing board and tools.
(1) Cleated white-pine drawing
board. (2) Tinted-vinyl padding for
drawing-board surface. (3) T-square.
(4) 45-degree triangle. (5) 30–60-
degree triangle. (b) Drafting table
with adjustable tilt and height.
(6) Parallel straight edge attached
to the top of the drawing table by
a cable system that allows it to
travel from top to bottom and
remain parallel. (7) Set-triangle that
is able to adjust to many different
angles. (c) Detail of set-triangle.

The *lengthening bar* is an attachment that increases the length of one arm of the compass, making it possible to swing a larger radius to make an arc or circle. An *inking attachment* can be fitted to the same arm of the compass or to the end of the lengthening bar. The inking attachment, like the *ruling pen,* has a double-blade tip that holds ink and is adjustable to a thick or thin line.

Although the ruling pen is still issued in the more complete set of drafting instruments, its use has diminished since the advent of the popular *Rapidograph,* a technical fountain pen. However, it has other uses for the designer. The pen can be filled with thin watercolor paint to indicate small-scale lining in the designer's elevation for the painters.

Dividers are used to hold or transfer a dimension. The compass can perform the same operation but with less accuracy. Bow instruments such as the *bow compass* and *bow dividers* are better for small circles and measurements and for retaining a recurring dimension or arc.

A set of drafting instruments containing a 4-inch compass and dividers with lengthening bar and inking attachments plus a bow compass and bow dividers would fulfill the average drafting requirements.

Most scenery is too large to be represented in a drawing at actual size, so it is necessary to reduce the size in regular proportions. The *scale rule* is devised to make the change in proportion as painless as possible. The most-useful scale rule is the triangular form, which provides twelve different graduations (Figure 5–2). To the beginner, a confusing factor is the discovery that there are two types of scale rules: the Architect's scale, which divides the proportional foot into twelfths or inches, and the Engineer's scale, which divides the inch into decimals or tenths, with divisions from ten to sixty. The names are trade names, not an indication of the profession using them. Engineers have as much use for the Architect's scale as do architects. Inasmuch as stage sets, like houses, are built in feet and inches, the planning of scenery is done with the Architect's scale rule.

Figure 5-2
Drafting Instruments

(a) The minimum set of drafting instruments. (1) Compass. (2) Dividers. (3) Combination bow compass and bow dividers with inking tip and divider points to replace pencil lead. (4) Extension arm for compass. (5) Ruling pen. (6) Inking tip for compass. (7) Divider point. (b) Architect's scale rule, triangular form, three edges, six faces, and twelve scales. (c) Drawing of one face to demonstrate the method of reading a scale rule. The face shown contains two scales: 1" = 1'0" to the left and ½" = 1'0" to the right. To read the 1-inch scale, for example, inches are read to the left of zero while foot divisions are read to the right. (d) Drawing showing a sample reading of a surface 2'8" in dimension at the scale of 1" = 1'0". (e) Compass with extension arm attached to increase radius.

The Scale Rule and the Metric System • In the near future the United States may join the majority of nations and convert to the metric system of measurement. Until that moment the theatre draftsman may be required to know and use both systems. Plans and construction drawings for European and British imports are usually in the metric system and have to be transposed or executed according to metric rules without converting to feet and inches.

There is a conversion scale rule from Britain designed to convert metric ratio to imperial dimensions. It is an open divided-scale similar to the Architect's scale. Figure 5–3a shows the ratio 1:24 as being nearly equal to ½-inch scale (½″ = 1′0″). This odd ratio is formulated by the division of the imperial inch into twenty-fourths. Hence 1:12 equals 1-inch scale, 1:24 equals ½-inch scale, and so on.

The metric drafting-scale rule (Figure 5–3b) uses two basic divisions: the millimeter (mm) and the meter (m), which is 1,000mm. Although not indicated on the rule, the centimeter (cm) can be determined by noting every 100mm or by moving the decimal point of the reading. Small measurements are dimensioned in millimeters (450mm), whereas greater distances are indicated in meters and centimeters (20.52m). As a present-day point of reference it will be noted that 25mm is approximately equal to one inch, which is an easy number to remember if it is necessary to convert or refer to feet and inches. Hence the ratios: 1:12.5m is approximately one-inch scale; 1:25m = one-half-inch scale; 1:50m = one-quarter-inch scale, and so on.

Although the centimeter does not appear on the drafting scale, it is used on the measuring tape (Figure 5–3c). The tape is numbered in centimeters (cm), each being divided into tenths (mm) with, of course, 100cm equaling one meter.

Drawing pencils and *leads* for lead-holders have varying degrees of hardness and softness. Soft lead produces a blacker line than hard lead. The leads are graded by letters from 6B, which is very soft, through HB and H, which are medium soft to firm, to 6H, the hardest lead. The combination of H, 2H, and 4H leads gives the variety in line quality necessary for a good blueprint.

The choice of drafting paper depends, of course, on what type of drafting is planned. An ink drawing, a pencil drawing, or a preliminary study each requires different *tracing papers.* There are many kinds of paper and no standardization of the numbering system, so the beginner is wise to seek the advice of a competent dealer. The supplier can recommend the proper density of tracing paper to ensure a clear, good-contrast print.

The accessories that complete the draftsman's list of equipment are made up of such items as a *lead pointer* for pointing the leads of the draftsman's mechanical pencils; a *ruby eraser* and *erasing shield* for erasing pencil-line mistakes and an art gum eraser or *drawing cleaning powder* to help keep the drawing paper clean; and *drafting tape,* which is used to fasten the tracing paper to the drawing board.

Drafting in Ink • Although most scene designers draft in pencil, some technical drawings are done in ink. The *Rapidograph* is excellent for this purpose. It has a long point for working against a straight edge and provides a nonclogging flow of ink. The pen uses India ink, which is opaque for clear reproduction, dries quickly, and does not smear from erasing. The most useful points for normal drafting are sizes zero and one.

THE GRAPHICS OF DRAFTING

Drafting practices in the theatre are so numerous and loosely defined that they cannot easily be categorized. There are as many ways to draft

Figure 5-3
Metric-scale Rules and Measuring Tapes

(a) *Metric-conversion scale rule.* The metric scale 1:24 is shown in direct comparison to the scale of ½ inch equals 1 foot. (b) *Metric-scale rules.* (1) The open divided-scale rule. This example has two scales on each edge. Centimeter divisions are shown outside the zero mark, while meter divisions are indicated toward the center of the rule. Draftsmen in the theatre will find this the easiest rule to use. (2) Use of the open divided rule for dimensioning. (3) The fully divided scale rule shows centimeter and millimeter divisions the full length of the rule. (c) *Metric measuring tapes.* (1) The 3-meter tape. Numbers note centimeters; the smallest divisions are millimeters. (2) The 30-meter tape. The major divisions are at 10-centimeter intervals, with the millimeter the smallest division.

a show as there are designers. A close inspection, however, reveals that each designer differs only in the amount of information given and in the way the material is organized. All have in common a background of engineering drawing and its basic principle—orthographic projection.

Orthographic Projection

In spite of its academic sound, the orthographic projection is a simple drawing. Orthographic means straight line. A straight-line projection is a method of representing the exact shape of an object in a line drawing on a plane perpendicular to the lines of projection from the object. It is easier to understand when it is compared to the converging line projection inherent in the foreshortening of a perspective drawing or photograph. A perspective of a three-dimensional object is very descriptive and easy to visualize. The object, however, is not represented in true dimension because of the foreshortening of some surfaces. Problem sheets one and two give the reader an opportunity to supply missing lines in orthographic projections.

For example, it is easy to recognize the familiar three-step unit from a perspective drawing (Figure 5–4a). The carpenter, however, who needs more information than a pretty sketch, wants to know height, width, and depth. An orthographic projection is a draftsman's way of drawing the three steps to give this information. It reveals the object one view at a time and from all angles. The observer is free to move around the object to view it from front to rear and from top to bottom. Each view is seen in true dimension by straight-line projection.

View Alignment

Obviously, a series of unrelated views of an object are of little value unless they are organized in a connective manner to show the position of the object in space. Hence, a conventional arrangement of views is the basis of all drafting techniques.

To understand the method of transposing the views of the object in space onto the drawing board requires some visual imagination. Imagine, for example, the three-step unit in the center of a transparent cube. Projected on each side of the cube is a line drawing of the object as it appears in each view. With the side containing the front view as the center, the other faces of the cube are unfolded to either side, to the top, and to the bottom (Figure 5–4b).

The front view is always the most recognizable one, showing the main characteristics of the object. It is the key view that gives the carpenter a bearing for visualizing the three-step unit in three dimensions. The top and side views are shown above and to the side of the front view, providing the three principal views of the object. Borrowing architectural terminology, some views are referred to as elevations, a term that is applied to all views seen in a horizontal direction. The horizontal views include the front elevations, side elevations, and rear elevations. An academic (and less frequently used) expression refers to the views as projections. The front, top, and side views become respectively the vertical, horizontal, and profile projections.

Of course the carpenter does not refer to the drawings as orthographic projections; they are working drawings, for with the simple addition of a few dimensions and material specifications to the orthographic projection of the three-step unit, the carpenter is ready to start building (Figure 5–5).

Figure 5-4
The Orthographic Projection

(a) Pictorial of a three-step unit.
(b) Three-step surrounded by transparent cube with projection of each side. (c) Cube unfolded. (d) View alignment.

VIEW ALIGNMENT

Figure 5-5
**Scaled and Dimensioned
Drawings, Problems**

Designers' working drawings
(a) generally show three views of
the object, drawn to scale and
dimensioned. Occasionally one
view may be omitted or an
additional view (such as a section)
included, depending upon the
complexity of the subject.
Orthographic Projection Problems.
(b) Supply missing line. (c) Construct
missing view.

TOP

FRONT

SIDE

DESIGNER'S WORKING DRAWINGS

As the designer begins to make working drawings, which are flat and less descriptive than the original sketch, he or she soon discovers that the draftsman has a way of making the lines speak for themselves. In the draftsman's language, symbols and conventions are words. The vocabulary has lines of all types. There are thick lines, thin lines, dotted lines, dashed lines, straight lines, and curved lines. Each has a different meaning and function. The draftsman's language, like any language, depends on a mutual knowledge of the symbols to read correctly a set of working drawings.

Drafting Conventions and Line Symbols

The first and simplest convention is the drawing of lines in different weights or thickness. The scene designer drafts with three weights of line. (Occasionally for speed, or because of the simplicity of the drawing, two weights of line are used. The goal is clarity of presentation and accuracy of representation.) The three different weights—light, medium, and heavy—are relative in thickness from one drawing to another. Because the scene designer drafts in so many scales, standardization of thickness or number of weights is impossible. A floor plan may need three weights of line, a mechanical or decorative detail two weights, and a full-scale pattern only one.

A line is made heavy or light depending on its eye-catching importance on the blueprint. Obviously, heavy lines are going to be seen first, medium-weight lines second, and lightweight lines last. The use of different-weight lines gives the blueprint a feeling of depth. It is a very slight third dimension, but it is enough to make the print easier to read. Beyond the slight descriptive quality of the weight of a line there is the meaning or symbol of the function implied in the use of certain lines that needs to be explained.

Medium-Weight Lines • It is easiest to begin with medium-weight lines, for they are used the most and have already been seen in the orthographic projection of the three-step unit (Figure 5–5). They are the *outline lines* that represent the shape of the object, showing visible edges of all surfaces as they appear at the angle of view. The visible outline is a solid, medium-weight line. Occasionally a view will cover or hide a surface outline. It then becomes a *hidden outline* and is drawn as a dotted line or series of small dashes.

Frequently a draftsman will want to show where an adjoining element of scenery touches a surface or show an alternate position of the same object. The *phantom line* symbolizes the removed object by outlining its position in the view. The designer has a choice of two symbols: a dashed line or the repetition of an elongated dash and two dots. Because a phantom line should always carry a label, the choice of line depends on the complexity of the outline of the removed part. Whichever symbol is chosen should be used consistently throughout the drawing.

Lightweight Lines • Lightweight lines are many and have a variety of uses. Their function is to give additional information about the object and still not detract from the overall picture created by the outlines.

Figure 5-6
Line Symbols

(a) Lightweight lines. (b) Medium-weight lines. (c) Heavy-weight lines.

Dimension lines, with arrowheads at the ends, mark the extent of the surface that is being dimensioned. Figures, set into the line, show exact distance. If dimension lines are set too close to the drawing, or within the drawing, they may become confused with outlines. To keep the dimension line away from the object, the *extension line* is used. These lines are solid and are drawn perpendicular to the surface of the object. As the name implies, they extend the surface to the dimension line. Although the arrowheads of the dimension line touch the extension line, the extension line itself is held clear of the object, about 1/16-inch, wherever possible (Figure 5–6).

Leaders, relatives of dimension lines, are made with one-sided arrowheads that touch the surface where a note or dimension applies. If the leader is always drawn slanted or curved, there is less chance for anyone to confuse it with the dimension line.

Break lines are space savers that denote a shortening of length or height. Occasionally, the draftsman wants to draw a unit of scenery that is too long to fit on the paper. A reduction of length is accomplished by taking a piece out of the center and using a break line to show that the piece is not represented in full length. The break line can also be used to indicate that the outer surface of an object has been cut away to show inner structure. The *long break line* is a straight line with spasmodic eruptions occurring at intervals, while the *short break line* is a more subtle curve with less regularity.

The *center line,* symbolized by an alternating long dash and dot, is used to establish the center of circles and to show the dividing line of symmetrical parts. The center line is also a familiar symbol in the floor plan of a stage setting, where it marks the center of the stage or proscenium opening. It is an important reference line for the location of scenery on the stage.

The final lightweight line is the *hidden construction* line. It is a dashed line used to indicate rear construction such as bracing, picture battens, or covered hinging not visible in the view.

Heavy-Weight Lines • Heavy-weight lines are used solely to indicate the cross section of an object or the cutting away and removing of a portion to reveal the inside. The *cutting-plane line,* drawn over an adjoining view to locate the position of the cut, consists of a repeating dash and a double dot. The arrowheads point the direction seen in the sectional view (Figure 5–6c).

The other heavy-weight line is the *section outline,* which appears in the sectional view. It is a heavy solid line that outlines the cut surface to emphasize it over the uncut surfaces. The cut surface is further set apart by the use of *section lines,* which are lightweight crosshatched lines drawn within the cut-surface outline.

Scaled Drawings

The most important part of a set of working drawings is the dimension. A carpenter cannot begin to build without some indication of size. Scaled or dimensioned drawings are crucial for such information. Most misunderstandings that occur between the drawing board and the finished setting are over dimensions, such as the wall that is too small for the sideboard or the door that is too large for the door opening.

Many errors can be avoided if the designer uses a scaled drawing. If it is carefully drawn, it not only provides the carpenter a way to figure sizes, it also gives the designer a fairly accurate basis for studying the proportional relationship of various elements of the set.

The usual scale of a working drawing is ½-inch equals one foot (½″ = 1′0″), which means that every half inch on the drawing is equal to one foot at full-scale or actual size. Decorative details which might not be clear at the small scale are frequently increased to the scale of 1″ = 1′0″ or larger. Any important bits of detail that the designer wants accurately reproduced, such as wallpaper patterns, scrolls, brackets, railings, and the like, are presented at full scale.

Figure 5-7
Sectional Views

(a) Revolved section, drawn directly on the elevation to indicate contour. (b) Removed section, a revolved section that has been removed and set to one side of the elevation. Each section is labeled A–F. (c) Cross section B–B is a vertical section and A–A is a horizontal section, frequently called a *plan*. (d) Half section, used on a symmetrical object combining the cross-section and elevational views.

Dimensions

An unscaled drawing needs some indication of size before the carpenter can begin building. The placing of dimensions opposite a surface is done in a matter to show its exact limit and measure. Dimensions, however, are not reserved strictly for unscaled drawings. It is common practice to place dimensions on a scaled drawing to save time in the shop. A properly given dimension includes the dimension line, measurement, and extension lines.

Sections

On many occasions the designer feels the need of supplementing the working drawings with another view that will add information to the normal top, front, and side views. The additional view most frequently used is the *section*. A designer often finds it easier to explain a three-dimensional piece of scenery by cutting it open to show the inner structure or exact contour. Because the section offers a more descriptive view, it is sometimes used in place of a side or top view.

Figure 5-8
Floor Plan Symbols

FLOOR PLAN SYMBOLS

There are many types of sectional views and a variety of uses (Figure 5–7), but the two sectional views used consistently in the theatre are the floor plan and the hanging section. Of the two drawings the floor plan is more important to the designer, although the hanging section, to check technical details and vertical sightlines, is also used.

FLOOR PLAN

Long before starting the working drawings of a set, the designer must realize the importance of the floor plan. A designer continually thinks of the plan while the idea of the setting is being developed. The plan grows with the design, pushed one way for esthetic reasons, altered another way for practical reasons, modified for staging reasons and, finally, solidified into the key working drawing and information center, the floor plan.

All phases of production seek information from the floor plan. To explain the design of the set adequately, the designer finds it necessary

FLOOR PLAN SYMBOLS

to refer often to the plan. The carpenter consults it to lay out the construction. The director and stage manager are unable to map out the staging without understanding and studying it. The setup, rigging, and lighting depend on information in the floor plan to complete the final assembly of the set on the stage.

The floor plan is a horizontal section with the cutting plane passed at a level that shows (when the upper portion of the set is removed) the most characteristic view of the shape of the set. Because a stage set is made up of many small units of scenery, the floor plan is also an assembled view. The floor plan, then, reveals the horizontal shape of the set, locates it on the stage, shows the scenery assembled, and identifies with labels the units and pieces that make up the complete setting.

Symbols

The floor plan is usually drawn at the scale of $\frac{1}{2}'' = 1'0''$ or smaller. At this scale, it is necessary to use symbols and conventions to help explain the set with a limited amount of detailed drafting. Most of the symbols shown in Figure 5–8 are familiar ones; their use and meanings are logical enough if one keeps in mind that a plan is a sectional view.

Dimensioning the Floor Plan

The floor plan is dimensioned from two reference lines: the center line of proscenium opening and the set line, the second a dashed line drawn from the right return to the left return of the set to mark the downstage extremity of the set. It is not necessary to dimension the plan in great detail because all the scenery will appear in separate elevational views with complete dimensions. Remember that the floor plan is also an assembled view; it will help to determine what dimension the stage carpenter needs to know to locate and assemble the set on the stage.

How wide are tormentors? How deep is the back corner of the set? Distances to the left and right use the center line as a base line, while all depth measurements are taken directly or indirectly from the set line. Any point on the stage is located by its distance right or left of the center line and its measurement upstage from the set line. After all important corners and backings are located, a few additional dimensions may be needed, such as overall dimensions of a wall or unit of scenery and radius dimensions of circles or arcs that may be in the floor plan.

Labeling

Part of the function of an assembled view is to identify and label the parts that make up the whole. The floor plan gives this information in varying degrees of completeness depending upon the working conditions and the nature of the show. Summer stock or university and community theatres, where the bulk of the structural planning falls on the designer's shoulders, may require a more specific labeling of each piece of scenery. The label becomes an easy, accurate means of identification for a single piece of scenery or assembled units of a setting.

As in the theatre, the floor plan of a television show contains a careful notation of each piece of scenery. Television scenery is almost entirely of stock units and standard sizes. The designer's labels and notes on the plan are a catalog, or index guide, for assembling the set in the studio.

Figure 5-9
The Designer's Floor Plan

A horizontal section taken through all wall openings and above all steps and levels. The section's cutting plane is taken at a height that will give the most information. A check with the *Floor Plan Symbols* (Figure 5-8) will help the reader to understand the plan. The dark solid lines represent a cross-section of the wall of the setting. The medium-weight lines outline the steps and levels as seen in a top view. The dotted medium-weight lines indicate openings and headers. The lightweight dimension lines locate the set on the stage as it relates to the references lines, the center line, set line and plaster line. All units of scenery are numbered for cross-reference with the elevations on page 105.

DESIGNER'S ELEVATIONS

Of almost equal importance to the floor plan, as a working drawing, are the designer's elevations. Compared to the floor plan, which is an assembled section showing the relationship of many parts, the elevational drawings are, in a sense, a disassembled or dismantled view of the individual parts. Because the elevation of an assembled set as it would appear in a normal front view has little value as a working drawing, the scene designer uses another technique. The set is taken apart, flattened out, and each piece of scenery is shown in front view at a scale of ½″ = 1′0″. Starting with the right return, the setting is drafted to show all pieces of scenery laid out in order, piece by piece, to the left return. All pieces are represented at ½-inch scale in true size and shape.

Each flat wall surface or unit of scenery is outlined. A solid line or space between units marks an open joint. For special reasons, it may be necessary to indicate a covered joint on the line where two or more wings are hinged together to make up a flat wall surface. The covered joint is indicated with a dotted line and a note to hinge and to dutchman, or cover, the joint. Normally, this is not necessary because the carpenter decides just how an oversized surface will be subdivided. The decision as to how it is to be made is guided by such technical considerations as the size of the stage, the method of handling the sets, and, if the scenery

Figure 5-10
Floor Plan Showing a Change-of-Level

A lot of information has been worked into a single drawing. A floor plan with several levels and a moving unit is explained, with over and under cut-aways, enlarged details and elevations of risers and levels. The numbers of each unit of scenery are the same in both views.

Figure 5-11
Schematic Floor Plan

Floor plan showing three positions of an off-center revolving unit. The positions are numbered 1, 2, and 3.

has to be transported, the nature of the transportation. The standard maximum wing width of 5 feet 9 inches is based on the height of a baggage-car door through which all the scenery of a road show must be able to pass if it is traveling by train. If the scenery is moving by truck, or not traveling at all, the maximum standard width can vary accordingly. The designer will do well, however, to keep in mind these technical considerations, for they are the limiting features that often control the size and shape of the design.

Applied Detail

Designers vary in the amount of detail they show at ½-inch scale. Although the decorative trim and other details are best shown at a larger scale, it is sometimes wise to at least sketch a portion of the detail on the ½-inch elevations. It not only shows the trim in assembled view but also gives the carpenter some idea of any special construction that may be needed. Because of the light wood frame and canvas construction of scenery, pictures, valance boxes, or lighting fixtures cannot be placed in the middle of a wall without providing extra structural support from behind. If the applied details are partially sketched in the elevation, or indicated with the dashed-line symbol of an adjacent part, the carpenter will know where to supply the additional construction (Figure 5–12).

Figure 5-12
Designer's Elevation

The front elevation of every element of scenery is shown in a flattened-out view. The basic outside dimensions and interior openings are indicated. Attached details and parts removed (stairs) are shown. The numbered-labels correspond to the identifying numbers in the plan (Figure 5-9). The carpenter can build from this drawing.

Obviously, the labels of the elevation must agree with the labels of the corresponding units in the floor plan. The accuracy of cross-labeling is especially important when stock scenery is being used, for unless the set is extremely simple, it is the carpenter's only guide as to how the pieces assemble. On occasion, for clarification, a portion of a floor plan may be repeated near the elevation drawings of a complicated unit of scenery. If there is still a possibility of misunderstanding, a pictorial drawing can be included.

COMPUTER-AIDED DRAFTING

The adaptation of computer graphics as a drafting aid is a rapidly advancing technique. The various software systems are designated as: CAD (computer-aided design); CADD (computer-aided design and drafting); the most sophisticated AutoCAD, with a *digitized tablet* that serves as a drawing surface; and a *word processor*, with several fonts and letter sizes—all used in conjunction with a *laser printer* to produce excellent line quality.

AutoCAD is, of course, very expensive and out of reach for most theatre groups. However, this was not a limiting factor in the printout illustrated in Figure 5–14. To solve their design problem, the English National Opera of London turned to an outside computer specialist—and at a minimum of cost and time.

The use of a computer, however, does not replace the need for knowledge and skill in drafting. It is still necessary to study drafting techniques and to be familiar with its symbols and conventions as well as the special requirements of the theatre.

Figures 5–13a and 5–13b are examples of computer drafting from the Department of Theatre and Dance, University of Alabama. They are drawings aided by AutoCAD of a floor plan and one sheet of elevations.

Drafting Three-Dimensional Scenery

Architectural forms such as columns, step units, or a fireplace mantel are usually presented with at least three views: a front view, a top view, and a side or vertical section. Most of the time, a sectional view gives more information than the traditional side view.

With the addition of dimensions all the three-dimensional forms in Figure 5–7 are suitable drafting presentations.

An irregular three-dimension, however, is more difficult to draft. The form is segmented into a series of contour pieces that will be fastened together and covered to create the three-dimensional form. The tree trunk shown in Figure 5–7b is a typical example. The designer will get the best results if he or she also submits a scaled model sculptured in modeling clay. The carpenter can then cut horizontal sections at intervals to get an accurate contour (Figure 5–15).

TECHNICAL PLANNING

For the most part, the scene designer is not concerned with technical planning unless to indicate the best place to divide an oversized element of scenery or to hinge two units. There may be occasions, however, when the scenery is built by unskilled hands, in which case the designer becomes the chief guardian of construction. To avoid being tied down by shop supervision when countless other details are pressing, the wise designer will provide construction drawings.

The simplest way to lay out the framed construction of scenery is to use rear elevations. A view from this direction looks at the scenery as it appears under construction in the shop. A rear elevation shows the framing and profiling, explains the assembly, locates the hinges, and indicates bracing and stiffening. The detail and completeness of the rear elevations must be determined by the aptitude of the shop help. An experienced carpenter might need a construction drawing for the occasional unusual piece of scenery, while inexperienced help would need every piece of scenery detailed (Figure 5–16). As can be seen, rear elevations employ many symbols to indicate joining hardware and hinging and bracing techniques, all of which are a part of technical planning. The symbols illustrated in Figure 5–17 will mean more after a study of scenery construction and tools in Chapters 6 and 7.

Three-dimensional pieces such as fireplaces, doors, steps, and rocks are not clearly explained in a rear elevation. They are built by combining sectional views with designer's front and side elevations. The sectional view not only shows the internal structure but helps to explain the contour of the object. Irregular forms, of course, may require many sections. Very special shapes or profiles are often drawn at full scale to serve as a pattern.

TECHNICAL DRAFTING SYMBOLS

Line weights and symbols used in technical drafting are slightly different from those used by the scene designer. The need for accuracy and detailed information leads to precise drafting and uniform standards. In an effort to conform more closely to ANSI* standards for engineering drafting, technical drafting for the theatre is limited to two line weights, *thin* and *thick*. These thicknesses are fixed for all drawings. USITT's† Graphic Standard Board recommends the following thicknesses:

pen	thin, .010" to .0125"	
	thick, .020" to .025"	
pencil	thin, .3mm	
	thick, .5mm	

A concession is made for the possible need of a heavy-weight line by supplying an *extra-thick* or double-thick line for section outline.

A comparison of line thicknesses and symbols can be seen in Figure 5–6. The thin and thick line specified for the pen are comparable to the medium and heavy line symbols in the illustration.

Other technical drafting symbols more specifically related to the planning of the construction and joining of scenery can be seen in Figure 5–17.

*American National Standards Institute
†United States Institute for Theatre Technology

Figure 5-13
Computer Aided Drafting

Drawings assisted by AutoCAD.
(a) Plan. (b) Elevation. *Printouts courtesy William Teague, Department of Theatre and Dance, University of Alabama. Drafted by John Wolf.*

a

Figure 5-14
Computer Aid to Drafting

Elevation of a stair railing descending through the stage floor to a lower level. The computer was supplied with a scale drawing of a balustrade (A). The number of balustrades, overall distance, and vanishing point were also specified. The computer spaced and reduced the image of (A) into this foreshortened elevation. Each balustrade was then photo-enlarged to full scale to serve as a pattern for the carpenter. *Courtesy Noel Stanton, Technical Director English National Opera, Coliseum, London*

WINDOWS
BACKED WITH
SHUTTERS
SEE PLATE 6.

FOR CORNICE
DETAIL SEE
PLATE 6.

SECTION A—A

(A)

(B)

FILL WITH
SCREEN
MATERIAL.

TRANSOM
FILL WITH
1/4" ACRYLIC.

CLOSET POLE

CURTAIN

3/4"X1/2" BASESHOE

SECTION B—B

(C)

(D)

THE UNIVERSITY OF ALABAMA
DEPARTMENT OF THEATRE & DANCE

STREETCAR
FRONT ELEVATIONS

DIR:	SET DES: J. WOLF
LT DES:	DWN BY: J. WOLF
DATE: 10/3/87	APRV BY:	REV:
SHEET: 2 of 5	SCALE: 1/2"=1'

b

Figure 5-15
Drafting an Irregular Three-Dimensional Form

The three-dimensional form shown of a tree trunk. The designer's elevation provides an accurate outline of the trunk and a clay scale model shows the contours of the trunk. (1) The outline of the tree trunk is framed. (2) The clay model is segmented at intervals that reflect the dimensions of the covering material. Each cut is a scale cross-section or contour of that interval. (3) The contour pieces are framed and placed at the measured intervals on the framed outline of the trunk. The rest is easy. Contour pieces are cross-braced, then covered with screen or chicken wire and shaped to the contour of the tree trunk to be covered, textured and painted.

① **ELEVATION** **②** **SEGMENTED CLAY MODEL** **③** **CONTOUR PIECES**

a

b

c

d

Figure 5-17
Technical Drafting Symbols

The drafting symbols are grouped into four areas related to the (a) framing, (b) joining, (c) stiffening and bracing, and (d) the rigging of framed scenery to fly. Flat scenery framing or rear elevations symbols include (1) framing layout, (2) keystone and corner blocks, (3) brace and toggle rail, and (4) change of material. Framed scenery joining techniques and hardware symbols include (5) tight pin hinge, (6) loose pin hinge, (7) stop block, (8) stop cleat, (9) lashline in corner block, (10) lashline eye, and (11) lash cleat. Stiffening and bracing framed scenery symbols are (12) loose pin stiffener (horizontal 1 × 3 on edge), (13) stage brace cleat, (14) keeper hook, and (15) vertical LPH brace or folding jack. Rigging framed scenery to hang symbols include (16) top hanger iron, (17) bottom hanger iron, (18) hinged foot iron, (19) rigid foot iron, (20) ceiling plate, and (21) picture hook and socket.

Figure 5-16
Rear Elevations

Detailed construction drawings show the framing of each piece of scenery and indicate how each is assembled. Note the use of vertical and horizontal sections as assembled views. The numbers cross-relate units of scenery to either of the assembled views.

Figure 5-18
Hanging Section and Plan

(a) Drawing shows the relationship of the floor plan to a section. Section cutting plane line, A–A, is taken on the center line. Sectional view is from stage right looking stage left. (b) A typical hanging section for a musical. The section is a necessary view for the lighting designer to establish lighting angles.

SECTION AA'

PLAN

a

b

The Hanging Section and Plan

The hanging section is another important part of technical planning. A drawing of hanging scenery is necessary to the designer in planning a multiscene production or a heavy hanging show. The designer soon discovers that flying space is filled very quickly with lighting equipment, traveler tracks, masking curtains, and the like. To avoid a hopeless tangle in the flies, the hanging plot of a heavy show is carefully studied first in plan and section.

The hanging section, which is a sectional view taken vertically through the stage on the center line, is not a working drawing in itself. It provides information that can be used in the floor plan and elevations as working drawings. In addition to taking the guesswork out of vertical masking by checking the extreme vertical sightlines, the hanging section gives an accurate picture of floor-space problems. It shows the up- and downstage space requirements more clearly than the floor plan that becomes the working drawing (Figure 5–18).

If a show is extremely heavy it may require a separate hanging plan to indicate the disposition of all scenery that is to be flown. To keep the plan from becoming confusing, most of the scenery on the floor is not shown. The hanging plan may be very general and schematic or quite detailed, depending on the proportion of the rigging, the theatre, and the type of show. For a wing-and-backdrop type of production, for example, it is little more than a listing of drops in the order they will hang and the numbering of the act and scene in which they will work. A more-complicated hanging plan would indicate the exact positions of spot lines and extra rigging.

Recent engineering developments in a more-flexible flying system and gridiron design than the existing pin-and-rail and counterweight methods indicate a time in the future when the hanging plan will be a required drawing for every show.

PLANNING PROPERTIES

The designer is responsible for the selection of properties, for the design of specially built pieces of furniture, and for the furniture plot or general arrangement of properties in the setting.

In planning the properties, the designer's chief concern is to coordinate design needs with those of the director. A meeting of minds can be achieved easily if the designer can show by sketches, clippings, or photographs what is planned and indicate by means of a scale furniture plot the size and position of set properties as they appear in the setting plan.

Figure 5-19
The Furniture Plot

A schematic floor plan locating the position of furniture or any movable properties in the set. The plan is overlaid with a grid of 1-foot or 2-foot squares so the reader can figure distances by counting squares. This kind of plan is of value to the director and stage manager as well as the property head.

Figure 5-20
Free-hand Pictorial Drawings

Dimensioned free-hand isometric drawings of simple furniture. If an object is simple in form, a pictorial drawing with dimensions can serve as a working drawing. There is enough information provided in this type of drawing to allow the carpenter to begin building immediately. A more complicated object would need additional views.

The furniture plot is a schematic plan locating the position of the set properties in each scene. It is generally drawn at ¼-inch scale with all furniture in position. The furniture plot is not dimensioned unless there is need to call attention to a certain measurement. It is drawn on a grid of 1-foot or 2-foot squares, so anyone can figure distances by counting squares. Such a plan is useful to the director and stage manager for laying out rehearsal space and studying the staging. It is valuable to the property person as a visual reference list of the set props. And the designer will find it useful in planning the lighting of the production (Figure 5–19).

The floor plan of a television show is handled in essentially the same way. Drawn at ¼-inch scale over a grid of 1-foot squares, it shows the set props in place, notes and numbers each piece of scenery.

The construction of a special prop, like any three-dimensional piece of scenery, would require some sort of working drawing. The usual plan, front and side views, can be used, or, if the piece is not too complicated, a dimensioned pictorial drawing will serve as a working drawing (Figure 5–20). Again, the designer will find it wise to study out all the important details at full scale.

PICTORIAL DRAWINGS

The designer's sketch is a type of pictorial drawing, but because of the foreshortening it cannot be used as a working drawing. But imagine a pictorial drawing with the edges of the receding surfaces not converging and the sides not foreshortened. Such a drawing can be drawn to scale and used as a supplementary view to the working drawings. The lack of perspective makes it possible to draw to scale, although the view may have a distorted mechanical appearance.

The two basic kinds of pictorials are the isometric and the oblique drawings. Their difference is dependent upon the angle of the view. The isometric drawing represents an object seen from one corner and slightly above (Figure 5–21a). An oblique drawing shows the object as seen opposite one face with the side angled off to the right or left (Figure 5–21c).

The term *isometric*, meaning equal measure (as compared to the foreshortened distances or unequal measure of perspective), accurately describes its appearance. An isometric drawing has three axes to represent the principal planes of the object. The first is a vertical line to indicate all the upright edges; second, a slanted line to the right, 30 degrees to the horizontal, for the horizontal edges of the right plane; and third, a 30-degree line slanted to the left to represent the horizontal edges of the planes to the left. These lines, and all lines parallel to them, are known as isometric lines. Conversely, lines that are not parallel to any of the three axes are nonisometric lines. Heights and distances can be measured on isometric lines but a nonisometric line cannot be drawn to scale (Figure 5–22).

Because irregular edges, curves, and angles are distorted in an isometric view, it may be desirable to change the direction of the view to show them at a better vantage. By moving around the object until the complicated surface is parallel to the plane of the paper, or frontal position, it is possible to see the irregular edge or curve without distortion. A view from this direction is an oblique drawing.

The same general pictorial characteristics are present in the oblique drawing as in the isometric with the exception of a more pronounced distortion in appearance. Because of the frontal position of one of the principal planes, two of the oblique axes are at right angles to each other.

The angle of the third axis, representing the plane of the sides, may vary from 30 to 45 degrees to the horizontal. It can be drawn either to the right or left, and slanted either up or down (Figure 5–23). By placing the side that contains the irregular outlines, angles, or curves in the frontal position drafting time can be saved and the appearance of the view made more attractive.

To reduce the distortion and improve the looks of the oblique drawing, the draftsman sometimes uses a cabinet drawing. It is constructed with the complicated face parallel to the picture plane—like the oblique—but distances measured parallel to the angled axis are reduced in scale. A ratio of two to three or three to four between the frontal planes and the angled axis produces a pleasing proportion. By always labeling the cabinet drawing and giving the ratio of the measurements on the angled axis, the possibility of it being mistaken for an oblique drawing is avoided (Figure 5–23[4]).

Pictorial drawings may be dimensioned like a working drawing. The technique, however, is slightly different. Instead of being perpendicular to the surface, the extension lines are drawn as extensions of one of the isometric planes, and the dimension line is parallel to the object rather than perpendicular to the extension line. To help give the feeling that the dimension is in one of the isometric planes, the figures are slanted with the extension lines. If the object is not too complicated, a dimensioned pictorial drawing can be used as a working drawing.

Besides their use as working drawings, pictorials are frequently used as supplementary views to explain bits of complicated assembly or mechanical detail.

THE PERSPECTIVE DRAWING

A perspective drawing, as has been mentioned, is not a working drawing because of the converging of horizontal lines in the sides of the object. It is, however, a more representational view, and, in its two-dimensional concept, it is more closely related to the designer's sketch than to a working drawing.

The laws of perspective become part of the designer's drawing skill either by observation of normal foreshortening in nature or by knowing the mechanics or graphics of perspective drawing. Figure 5–24 illustrates the basic perspective views of an object in space and orientation to the

**ISOMETRIC
MECHANICAL DETAIL**

**ISOMETRIC
EXPLODED VIEW**

a

OBLIQUE

c

b

HORIZONTAL MAIN AXIS

d

**Figure 5-21
Pictorial Drawings**

(a) An exploded isometric drawing to show how certain pieces of scenery fit together. (b) Isometric drawing used to explain a complicated pivoting movement. (c) An oblique drawing of a decorative bracket. (d) An isometric drawing using a horizontal axis instead of the usual vertical axis.

horizon line (HL). Shown are a combination of views of a cube in simple perspective drawing. "A" represents the cube in a frontal position parallel to the picture plane or plane of the paper. The cube in this position has only one *vanishing point* (VP-C) on the horizon line. "A-1" represents the cube above HL, "A-2" on HL, and "A-3" below HL.

In "B" the position of the cube is angled to the picture plane and therefore has two vanishing points, VP-R to the right and VP-L to the left. The side walls of the cube converge to their respective vanishing points on the horizon line.

The Graphics of Perspective • The initial concept in the graphics of perspective is *foreshortening.* To understand foreshortening is the first step toward being able to visualize the graphics of perspective. Foreshortening is present, for example, in the converging lines of a fence or railroad where parallel lines appear to meet in the distance. To transpose the visual foreshortening of nature into *graphic* foreshortening on the drawing board, two assumptions have to be made.

Figure 5-22
Construction of the Isometric Drawing

The object is a 2-inch cube. (1) Vertical axis, the nearest corner of the cube. (2) Slanted axes, right and left. (3) Slanted lines and uprights drawn to scale. (4) The completed isometric drawing of the cube.

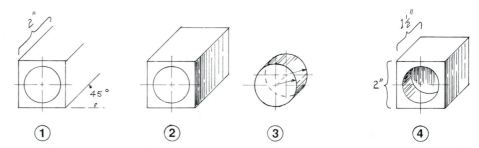

Figure 5-23
Construction of the Oblique Drawing

(1) The principal face with slant line drawn to right or left. All the lines are drawn to a scale. (2) The completed oblique drawing. (3) An oblique drawing of a circular disk. The center of the circle of the thickness is set to the right on an oblique line. (4) A cabinet drawing. All slanted lines are drawn at a reduced scale to minimize the distorted look of a regular oblique drawing.

Figure 5-24
Graphic Perspective

The front face of box A is parallel to the picture plane. In this position the sides, top, and bottom of the box have a single vanishing point (VP-C). A-1 represents the box above the horizon line (HL), A-2 at HL, and A-3 below HL. The corner of box B is facing the picture plane. In this position the sides have corresponding right (VP-R) and left (VP-L) vanishing points. B-1 represents the box above HL, B-2 at HL, and B-3 below HL.

Because the eye, through peripheral vision, is able to see more than is practical to draw, the first assumption is that all verticals are perpendicular to the ground. This is true in the center of the eye's vision but not true of the extreme right or left areas. The vertical lines seem to converge or diverge depending upon whether the observer is on the ground or high above the ground. The second assumption is that the horizon line is straight and parallel to the ground. This is not true of visual foreshortening, in which the horizon seems to curve around the observer in a gentle arc.

Added to these basic assumptions is the positioning of the observer at the *observation point* (OP), which is the most desirable or ideal location. To capture an approximation or illusion of the visual foreshortening on paper, the best location for the OP would be a distance from the stage or major portion of the stage that provides a cone of vision of not greater than 30 degrees. In other words, the angle between lines drawn from the extreme right and left sides of the object to OP should approximate 30 degrees. It is possible, of course, to set up a graphic perspective system with an OP closer to the stage or with a greater cone of vision than 30 degrees, but the resulting graphic foreshortening is distorted and unnatural. The designer, however, can on occasion use this distorted foreshortening to exaggerate the perspective for design reasons.

Figure 5–25 is a pictorial representation of the components that make up a perspective system. In addition to the components already mentioned, HL and OP, the illustration also shows the *picture plane* (PP) and

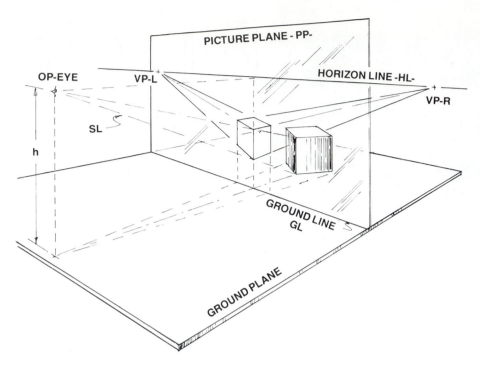

Figure 5-25
A Perspective System

A pictorial arrangement of the components that make up a perspective system. The picture plane (PP) intersects the ground plane forming the ground line (GL). The height (h) of the observation point (OP) determines the distance the horizon line (HL) is above GL. The object is projected into the picture plane by the use of sightlines (SL) from OP. The sides of the cube in PP converge to right and left vanishing points (VP-R and VP-L).

the *ground plane* (G), which is usually the stage floor. The picture plane is an imaginary transparent plane placed between OP and the object. It is usually perpendicular to the ground and its line of intersection with the ground plane forms the *ground line* (GL). The ability to visualize the picture plane is an important step toward understanding the process of developing the perspective drawing on this plane after it is folded into the plane of the drawing board. In the theatre, PP is normally considered to be at the proscenium opening or slightly upstage at the front edge of the setting.

Our description of the perspective system is almost complete except for designating the location of the horizon line. The height of OP off the ground determines the height of HL, which is drawn parallel to GL on the picture plane. The location of OP is arbitrary. It can be placed in a position to reveal the object either in a favorable or a distorted view, whichever is desired. The normal position for a perspective sketch is a little above ground and on the center line.

It will be noted that all vanishing points fall on the horizon line. This is true of all planes parallel or perpendicular to the ground plane. The shape and vanishing points of an askew (slanted) plane can be plotted by using the floor and perpendicular walls as reference planes.

PERSPECTIVE SKETCHING TECHNIQUE

The particular perspective method a designer may choose in preparing a sketch is influenced by individual sketching techniques and personal methods of working. Individual sketching techniques vary primarily with the angle at which the setting is viewed. Whereas most designers prefer to show, for example, a little of the stage floor in their sketch, some prefer to show no floor at all. Others take an elevated viewpoint showing more floor than is necessary.

There are occasions, however, when a designer may choose an extreme viewpoint in order to fit the form of the particular theatre. A high ballroom stage, for instance, with the audience seated on a flat, ungraded ballroom floor, creates a situation in which no one is able to see the stage floor. The opposite might occur in an amphitheatre with a rather steep seating arrangement in which the majority of the audience sees a great expanse of the stage floor.

The three basic angles of view are illustrated in Figure 5–26. Using the conventional vanishing-point method, the perspective sketch of a simple unit of scenery is shown under three different conditions. The first is the minimum floor view (a), followed by the extreme no-floor view (b), and, finally, a sketch from a high vantage point (c). In the first condition (5–26a), OP is at a proper distance from the object, determined by keeping an angle of 30 degrees or less between sightlines (SH) drawn from the outside edges of the object to OP. The horizon line is established

Figure 5-26
Perspective Viewpoints

The three basic angles of view that may appear in a perspective sketch for the theatre. (a) Minimum floor view. HL at about 6 feet above GL. (b) No floor view. HL is on the floor (GL). (c) Maximum floor view. HL is abnormally high, giving the set the look of being viewed from a high vantage point.

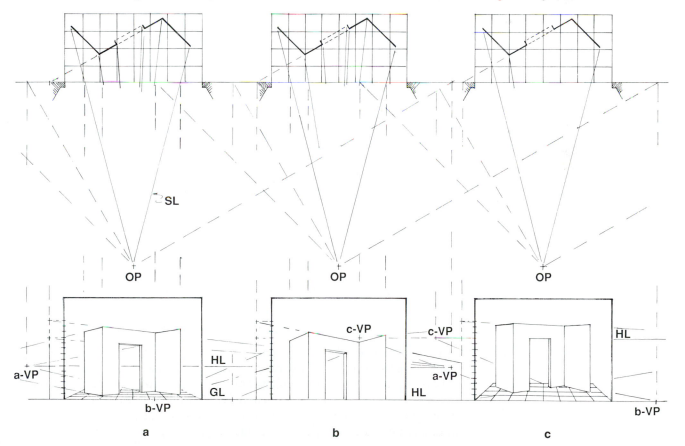

a

b

c

at a height of about five or six feet above ground or stage floor. As a result the perspective drawing shows a little stage floor and appears normal.

The vanishing point for each wall is located by drawing a line from OP parallel to the angle of the specific wall until it intersects the picture plane. It is then projected downward until it crosses HL. The point of intersection with HL is the vanishing point for that wall. The vanishing point for each wall was found in this manner (some of which fall out of view in Figure 5–26b).

The conditions in Figure 5–26b and Figure 5–26c are the same except for the position of HL. The second view has located the horizon line in the floor or on GL, while the third view has raised HL above the normal view to show more of the floor.

The application of normal perspective techniques to the sketch of a stage setting does have one disadvantage. Because the walls of a setting, especially an interior, are frequently raked to bring them into better sightlines, they tend to appear more exaggerated than right angles. To a certain extent this also happens in the real set, for the raked side walls of a box set tend to make the setting look deeper than it really is. This is not so apparent until the set is placed within the two-dimensional form of a sketch. As a result, adjustments either in the sketch or floor plan are sometimes required to bring the elements of the composition into a desirable proportional arrangement. It is important to remember that if the sketch is being developed with the observation point at the conventional distance so as to form a cone of vision of 30 degrees or less, the result does give the designer some clue as to how the set is going to look before the scaled model is made.

Perspective-Grid Method • Because of the many angled walls that may occur in a setting, the designer seeks to avoid the space-consuming method of a full graphic perspective system involving the location of vanishing points from a sprawling observation point and the precisely aligned floor plan. Instead, the designer looks for an easier way or short-cut to produce an approximation of the perspective drawing. The perspective grid is an aid in simplifying the graphics of perspective.

The use of a perspective grid of the stage floor as a guide under the sketch is helpful to the beginning designer in the development of a perspective view of a setting from the floor plan. Like most shortcuts, the grid method is an approximation and therefore less than accurate. The inaccuracies, however, are not alarming and are offset by the time and space saved.

As a technique, the perspective-grid method does not employ either the use of an observation point (other than the initial setup) or the cross-reference of sightline points from an aligned floor plan. It does use, however, the traditional horizon line and vanishing points in addition to measuring points.

The grid, which can be prepared in advance and reused indefinitely, is developed in one of two ways (Figure 5–27). Both begin with a scaled grid of the stage floor. The upstage and downstage lines of the grid appear in true dimension along the picture plane, or downstage, edge of the plan. All vertical lines converge to a common vanishing point at the center (VPC) because they are perpendicular to PP.

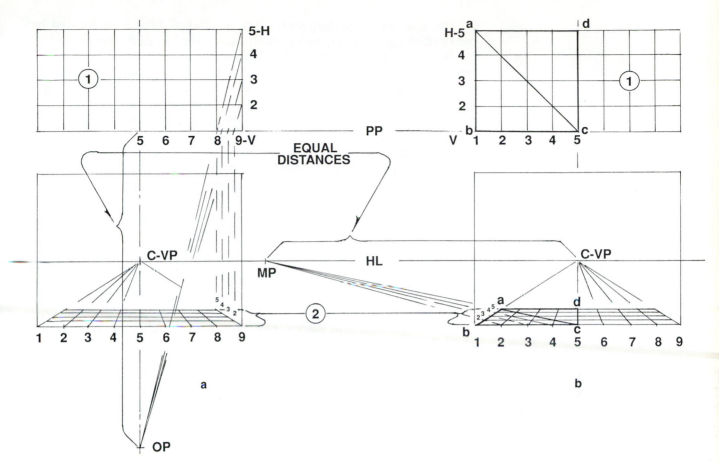

Figure 5-27
Developing the Perspective Grid, Two Methods

The two methods of developing a perspective of the stage floor are shown. (a) The observation-point method: (1) The stage floor is marked in a grid of equally spaced horizontal and vertical lines. The vertical lines are numbered from 1 to 9 and the horizontal lines are numbered on the right from 1 to 5. Because all the vertical lines are perpendicular to the picture plane (PP) they all vanish or converge to a single vanishing point in the center (C-VP). The location of the depth in perspective of each horizontal line is accomplished by sighting a line from OP to the intersection point of a horizontal line and one of the vertical lines (for example, 5-H on line 9-V). The point where the sightline crosses PP (at 8-V) is projected downward until it intersects perspective line 9-V as it is converging toward C-VP. As the horizontal lines are parallel to PP, it can be drawn through this point to the left, terminating at line 1-V. (2) Each of the horizontal lines is located in this manner to complete the perspective grid. (b) The measuring-point method: (1) The gridded stage floor as in (a). The measuring point (MP) is measured on HL the same distance from the center line (C-VP) as OP was from PP in (a). The perspective position of each horizontal grid line is located on 1-V by sighting a line from MP to a series of points on PP representing the true distances each horizontal line is apart. As the true grid is made up of squares, vertical lines 1, 2, 3, 4, and 5 are the same distances. The points where the sightlines from MP cross line 1-V (2) locates the perspective spacing of the horizontal lines. The perspective grid is then completed in the same manner as in (a).

The spacing of the horizontal line parallel to PP can be located by conventional perspective methods shown to the left of the center in Figure 5–27a. Sightlines are projected from the observation point to each position on the outside edge of the grid. The corresponding positions in perspective are located by projecting downward the point of intersection of the respective sightlines and the picture plane. Once the grid has been developed in perspective the observation point is no longer needed.

Measuring-Point Method • The measuring-point method which is demonstrated in Figure 5–27b dates back to the theatre of the Renaissance. Originally known as the *distance-point method*, it was developed in 1435 by Leone Battista Alberti. The system's basic difference from the perspective-grid method is that it does not use an observation point, needing only to know the distance OP would be from the picture plane.

The formula for the method is based upon the reality that in a perspective plan the diagonal of a square, if extended, will fall upon the horizon line at a point the same distance from the center line as OP is from PP. Figure 5–27b shows how the *measuring point* (MP) is used to locate the position of the horizontal lines of the grid in perspective. True dimension intervals on PP are projected back to MP, and where they cross the outside edge of the grid locates the respective spacing of each line. If accurately drawn, the right side should match the spacing to the left of the center line.

It is important to remember that to be accurate the measuring-point method is based upon the square or subdivision of the square and its diagonal. If the stage is deeper than the side of the square, the grid should be expanded offstage to make the proper double-square proportion. Although only the floor grid will be used in the perspective method of sketching, the measuring-point system can be used as a measured-perspective technique by establishing an MP to the right and left.

Perspective Floor Plan

Figure 5–28 illustrates with a simplified example of scenery the steps taken to use the perspective grid as a guide for a sketching technique. Figure 5–28a is a scaled floor plan of the set drawn over a grid of squares. For the sake of clarity in a small drawing, the squares shown are 3 feet in dimension. Because their size is optional it might be desirable in a larger drawing to use 2-foot squares for more dependable accuracy. If the sketch is developed on tracing paper over the perspective grid, as is suggested in Figure 5–27b it can be saved for future use.

The first step toward the sketch is the transference of the floor plan onto the perspective grid by locating each element in its corresponding square (Figure 5–28c). Vertical lines representing corners and edges are extended upward, for the moment, to undetermined heights. Before individual heights can be found, the vanishing points of key walls must be located. The VP of the right and left walls are the easiest to locate because of their sharp angle to PP. As their faces are parallel to each other, the same VP will serve both. To locate this important vanishing point the base line of each outside wall is carefully produced from its position on the perspective grid until it intersects HL. This is the approximate VP for the base of both walls and for any line parallel to the respective base lines.

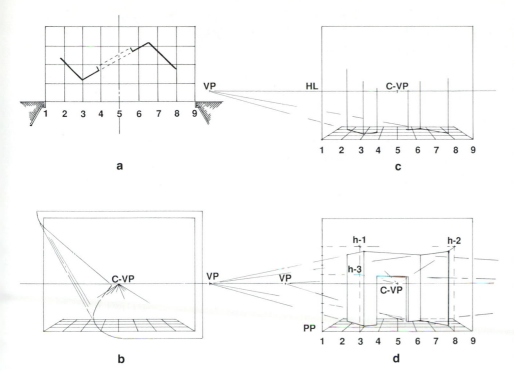

Figure 5-28
Using the Perspective Grid

(a) The floor plan of a simple element of scenery drawn on a gridded stage floor. (b) A perspective grid predeveloped by either the observation-point or measuring-point method is covered with tracing paper to preserve the grid for future uses. (c) By referring to the floor plan on the true grid (a), it is reconstructed, point by point, onto the perspective grid. The corners, edges, and vertical sides of openings are extended upward but not terminated. The vanishing point of the two parallel walls is located by projecting the base line in the perspective plan until it intersects HL (VP). (d) The height of the scenery is found by extending one of the corners to PP. The downstage corner resting on V-3 is projected to PP along line V-3. The height is then measured directly above and projected back to C-VP. Where it intersects the vertical of the corner from the plan (c) is the height in perspective. Other heights are located the same way: h-2 is off line V-8; h-3 is the height of the door opening. With the heights all located, the sketch is completed by drawing the tops and all lines parallel to them to their related vanishing points.

The final step to complete the drawing is to find the height of the doorway and scenic unit. One method is to use the center vanishing point (VP-C), which is the VP for the grid. Figure 5–28d shows how h–1 and h–2 are taken in true dimension from PP back along a perspective line on the grid to VP-C, passing through a corner to the critical point of measurement. The point of intersection of the vertical raised from the corner in plan and perspective line h–1, for example, VP-C, determines the height. The height of the doorway and other verticals can be found by the same method.

Furniture, platforms, and set dressing can be located by using the perspective grid and approximate VP in the same manner. The ceiling or overhead area may also be gridded and constructed in perspective to the same HL and OP system to provide a more inclusive guide for the designer's sketch.

Figures 5–29, 5–30, and 5–31 show three different uses of the perspective grid as a sketch technique. The first is the conventional interior setting, showing the steps that were taken to develop the final sketch: (a) the scaled floor plan with a grid overlay; (b) the grid in perspective with the walls blocked in and the vanishing points located; (c) the addition of set dressings and furniture; (d) the final sketch with the grid removed.

The second example brings together some unusual conditions. The setting not only thrusts ahead or through the picture plane but also has a ramped floor and slanted ceiling. The floor plan (a) is gridded and shows the location of PP. In the split view (b) the stage left center portion shows the perspective grid and the method of determining the ramp of the floor. It will be noted that a reflected perspective grid was used overhead to plot the slant of the ceiling piece. The final sketch (c) is completed with the grid and construction lines removed.

Figure 5-29
Perspective Sketch Technique—Conventional Interior
(a) The scaled floorplan with a grid overlay. (b) The grid in perspective with wall blocked in and the vanishing points located. (c) The addition of set dressings and furniture. (d) The final sketch, with grid and construction lines removed.

c

10 9 8 7 6 5 4 3 2 1 2 3 4 5 6 7 8 9 10

d

The most difficult form to represent in perspective sketch is the thrust stage. The third illustration presents an adaptation of the perspective grid technique for a thrust-stage setting. The perspective grid is developed from an off-center view rather than on the centerline: (a) the floor plan with grid; (b) the perspective grid which, if drawn on tracing paper, can be reversed to present a view from the opposite side; (c) the final sketch.

Any perspective technique in the final analysis should *guide* but not control the drawing. It should *free* rather than restrict the creative style of the designer. The mechanics of the technique should not be used as a means to the end but more as a check when, to the eye of the designer, "something doesn't look just right."

Figure 5-30
Perspective Sketch—Sloping Floor and Ceiling
(a) Floor plan with grid overlay. Note position of PP with scenery ahead of proscenium. (b) Split view showing on stage-left side the perspective grid and the method of determining the ramp of the floor in perspective. (1) Perspective grid. (2) A second perspective grid overhead to locate slope of the ceiling. (3) Position of PP as it cuts ramped floor and sloped ceiling. (4) Center line. (c) Finished sketch. It should be noted in this example that the grid has been expanded to 3-foot squares. Some designers prefer a rectangular grid two feet across and three feet deep (up stage) which looks more nearly square in perspective.

b

c

Figure 5-31
**Perspective Sketch Technique—
The Thrust Stage**

An adaptation of the perspective
grid technique to a thrust-stage
setting. The perspective grid is
developed from an off-center view
rather than on the center line.
(a) The floor plan with grid. (b) The
perspective grid. (c) The final
sketch.

Three-dimensional Perspective

The use on the stage of three-dimensional forms, both architectural and abstract, is the sculptural use of space. It is the use of actual space and not the illusion of space. This is best dealt with in three dimensions by the use of models or real forms.

Sometimes, however, the scene designer has to produce the illusion of more space with three-dimensional forms, or combine two-dimensional with three-dimensional forms to create an illusion of space on a shallow stage. With careful study, the same techniques of space perception applicable to two-dimensional forms can be adapted to three-dimensional forms. Figure 5–32 illustrates a method of foreshortening a three-dimensional form. In this example a structure representing a garden shelter has been foreshortened in perspective into a much smaller space than it actually appears to occupy.

The technique of foreshortening a three-dimensional object is dependent upon two views, the plan and side elevation. View (1) in Figure 5–32 is the plan or view looking down on the structure. The dotted lines designated a, b, c, d represent the actual size of the plan while a', b', c', d' represent its foreshortened size. Each foreshortened point is located on a sightline drawn from the observation point to its original position on the actual plan. The position of the foreshortened points a', b', c', d' is arbitrary, depending upon how large or small a foreshortened plan is desired.

View (2) is a side view of the structure drawn next to and in alignment with view (1). The points a, b, c, d are shown in side view as well as a dotted line drawing of the rest of the elevation. The side view also shows the height of OP through which is drawn the horizon line.

By projecting each point (a', b', c', d') of the foreshortened plan into the side view, being careful to relate each to its proper sightline, a foreshortened side view of the structure can be drawn. Because of the height of HL and the theatrical convention of stopping the perspective at the railing, most of the perspective appears at the top of the structure.

View (4) is a development of the four walls of the garden shelter based upon dimensions found in the two foreshortened views, plan and side elevation.

View (3) is a normal two-dimensional perspective drawing with OP and HL in the same positions as in (1) and (2). To a certain extent (3) represents how the foreshortened walls of view (4) will look when they are assembled.

A second method of solving foreshortening is to work directly from the three-dimensional sketch and related floor plan. Figure 5–33 presents the two views of a perspective street scene. The plan has been located in the sketch by the perspective grid technique (Figure 5–28). The base of each house has been produced to find its vanishing point on the horizon line. House (1), for example, has a base line vanishing point on HL at the point labeled B-VP(1). All horizontal lines above HL, however, vanish to a second temporary vanishing point T-VP(1). It is closer to the house to force the perspective and thereby foreshorten the house. To layout house (1) in elevation for a model or designer's elevations, T-VP(1) must be located in the plane of the element of scenery. This is accomplished by projecting T-VP(1) on HL directly upward until it intersects the produced base line of house (1) in plan.

The elevation of house (1) (Figure 5–34) can be drawn using T-VP(1) as a VP for all horizontal lines *above* HL. Note that the true distance of T-VP(1) in elevation is located in the plan view. The same procedure can be used to develop the elevation of all the foreshortened houses. Because the method is an approximation, it is subject to adjustment as the designer develops the sketch.

Figure 5-32
Three-dimensional Perspective

Illustrated are the steps necessary to foreshorten a scenic element (a gazebo or garden shelter) that in reality occupies in plan the space a, b, c, d to half the depth indicated a′, b′, c′, d′ in the drawing. (1) Using, jointly, the plan (1) and the side elevation (2) to work out the foreshortened heights of each corner, the four walls are redrawn into their new shapes (4). (3) A normal two-dimensional perspective drawing of the gazebo, which is the way it will appear if the foreshortened walls are carefully assembled on the foreshortened plan.

Figure 5-33
Foreshortened Scenery

A floor plan and sketch which has been drawn on a perspective grid. All horizontal lines *above* HL converge to a temporary vanishing point (T-VP) to heighten the normal perspective. House (1), for example, has a base line vanishing point on HL at point B-VP (1). All horizontal lines above HL, however, vanish to a second temporary vanishing point T-VP (1) to foreshorten the house.

Figure 5-34
Foreshortening in Elevation

To resolve the elevation of the foreshortened house (1) the distance of T-VP (1) from (1) is an important dimension. The true distance of T-VP (1) in elevation is found in the plan directly above T-VP (1) on HL. The degree of foreshortening in any of the houses is the decision of the designer. It is important to note in the elevations that there is no foreshortening or converging horizontal lines *below the horizon line.*

PART II

EXECUTING THE DESIGN

Scene Design and Technical Production

Before the ideas of the designer can reach the stage, the designs, in the form of working drawings, have to go through a preparation or construction period. The scaled model is transformed into full-scale elements of scenery, the graded wash in the sketch becomes a carefully painted backdrop, and the insignificant spot on the elevation is fashioned into a pointed bit of detail. Step by step all the scenery is fitted together on the stage under lights and in final form.

Although the study of technical production is placed here in the logical order of the development of a stage setting, it also, paradoxically, represents knowledge a scene designer should possess *before* beginning a design. For this reason a study of technical production is a necessary part of a scene designer's training and background. As the architect is familiar with building techniques and materials, so should the scene designer be acquainted with methods of constructing and handling scenery as well as the uses of theatrical materials and techniques. A logical place to begin is with a survey of the tools and materials that are used to make scenery and an examination of the working procedures of a scenery shop.

THE SCENERY SHOP

Scenery is frequently built and painted under the adverse condition of an inadequate shop. Designers soon learn that an ill-equipped shop with sparse working space places a limit on the kind and amount of scenery that can be built and painted. Occasionally they find themselves in the enviable position of being able to plan their own shop or at least asked to specify the space requirements of the ideal scenery shop. In preparation for such an occasion, the designer should have some knowledge of the space requirements and layout of a good scenery shop.

Space Requirements

The overall area of a scenery shop depends upon four things: the size of the stage the shop is to serve; the location of the shop in relation to the stage and storage areas; the number and kinds of productions to be produced in an average season; and the nature of the shop's working procedure and personnel.

The size of the stage, or, in some cases, several stages, which the shop is to serve, has a direct bearing on the size of the shop itself. A large stage requires large elements of scenery. A shop serving a large stage, of course, needs the space to execute the expansive proportions of such scenery. In a similar manner, the large amounts of scenery necessary to supply more than one stage would influence the size of the shop. The scale of the scenery may be smaller, but a shop serving several stages must be arranged to handle quantities of scenery.

The location of the scenery shop also affects its size. For example, a shop near the stage could utilize stage space for the construction of scenery and thereby supplement the shop area. On the other hand, a shop in a remote location needs additional space for the storage of scenery and properties as well as the necessary construction and painting areas. Although a distant shop has the disadvantage of causing the additional handling of scenery from the shop to the stage and back again, it does have the decided advantage of being able to operate free of preperformance uses of the stage. A shop adjacent to the stage is doomed to conflict with rehearsals and performances, which will render it inoperative a major portion of the time.

The number and kinds of productions also help determine the space requirements of a scenery shop. A repertory company, for example, would require enormous storage space to retain the scenery of numerous productions intact, while perhaps only building one or two new productions a year. An opera or musical-comedy production group would have a greater demand for scenery than would a company that mounts intimately scaled productions.

The final consideration that has some influence on the overall size of the shop is the shop procedure and personnel. The nature of the shop's personnel and working hours may vary from a staff of full-time professionals to scattered groups of part-time student apprentices or volunteers. A small highly skilled staff working steadily can use building space more efficiently than large sporadic groups requiring sufficient area to do many separate jobs at once. A further evaluation of the space requirements resulting from shop procedure includes an analysis of the areas of work, tools and equipment, and materials of the average scenery shop.

Work Areas

The shop is divided into areas related to the various steps in the process of building and painting. These areas are organized for: (1) storage of materials and tools; (2) the cutting and working of lumber (boring, cutting, and so on); (3) the framing and covering of basic units of scenery; (4) the trial assembly of basic units into portions or all of the complete setting; (5) a metal-working area; (6) a plastic-working area; (7) a property preparation area; (8) and finally an area for the painting of scenery.

Figure 6-1
Scenery Shop Layout

Represented is a schematic plan of a scenery shop and related areas for a modest producing theatre. The basic areas are:

1. Scenery shop including areas for the cutting and framing of scenic units as well as tool storage and technical director's office. The heavy tools are a pullover saw, table saw, band saw, drill press, sander and two movable templates.

2. Area for the construction and maintenance of set properties containing a spray-paint booth, wood lathe, work bench and low furniture work-table.

3. Metal working shop with forced ventilation. In the room are a welding table and electric welder, work bench with vise and emery wheel, an anvil, gas welding tanks, sheet metal brake and metal lathe.

4. Assembly and painting area which has enough space and height for a trial assembly of all or a portion of a set. There is enough floor space to stretch a drop as well as a vertical paint frame. Paint storage is in adjacent areas.

Overhead and off the balcony are:

5. Sewing room for draperies, drops and gauzes. On the balcony are stored draperies and drops.

6. Plastic working area which is well ventilated. Vacuum forming, blue printing and area for the construction of small properties are located here.

a

b

c

Figure 6-2
Template Bench

(a) The type shown is adaptable to a shop with limited working space where the same area may be needed for other operations. The template is a waist-high work bench with movable planks in the center (1) to provide support for framing the various widths of regular-shaped flats. The casters on one side (2) enable it to be tipped onto that side and pushed out of the way for storage. The casters on the base (3) provide easy movement when the bench is in working position. Although not equipped with built-in square corners and clinch plates, the template can also be used for such tasks as sabre-saw cutting and small assembly work. (b) Template bench with fixed working surface. (1) Storage space. (2) Casters for mobility. (c) Movable horse to support work longer than bench.

1. *Storage.* Within all shops it is necessary to provide space for the storage of materials and small tools. This means lumber racks, pipe and structural steel racks, paint bins, and hardware cabinets. Provisions should also be made for the storage of brushes near the painting area and for small tools near the woodworking area.

2. *The woodworking area.* This second area is related to the next step in building scenery. Here the lumber is worked (bored, planed, jig-sawed, and so on). Within the area there should be space for the large power tools such as table saws, band saws, drill presses, and the necessary work benches. A large shop would include an air compressor and storage tank for pneumatic tools. A heavy-duty compressor can also serve the painting area and property shop.

   Careful consideration should be given to the lighting of the woodworking area as well as the other work areas. The location of power outlets convenient to the working positions of power tools in all areas is essential.

3. *The framing area.* The framing and covering of scenery can take place in the center of the shop on template benches, but the joining or hinging of units of scenery together must take place in a larger area.

4. *The assembly area.* This fourth space ideally should be as large as the stage area and high enough to stand the scenery upright. Besides being a trial assembly area, its floor can serve as a space to layout or "loft" full-scale pattern of irregularly shaped scenery as well as flat painting on the floor.

5. *The metal-working area.* This area should ideally be near the assembly area since some metal work is used for the bracing of scenery or the support of weight-bearing forms. This is where metal will be cut, bent, and joined (bolted or welded). The welding area should be well ventilated and on a concrete floor.

6. *The plastic-working area.* The use of plastic in all forms (foam casting, thermoplastic, and the sculpturing of foam) needs a separate space to work. Because of the fumes and dust, ventilation is important. Occasionally plastic working can be done in a part of the property area.

7. *Property preparation area.* The most frequently neglected area in shop planning is a space to build properties. The altering, repairing, upholstering, and finishing of furniture is a specialized operation that requires different tools, materials, and paints from those found in the scenery shop. A property shop does not need a lot of space. It should, however, be an area near but separated from the dust and confusion of the scenery shop and the splatter of flying paint from the painting area.

8. *The painting area.* Another important space in the shop, the painting area should be convenient to a sink, gas or electric burners, and the paint bins. Vertical painting, which occupies the least amount of floor space, requires overhead clearance or sufficient height to stand the scenery upright. The simplest vertical-painting method is to mount the scenery on a fixed frame against a wall and paint from a rolling platform or boomerang. The most-con-

venient method is the use of a counter-weighted, vertical paint frame, which lowers into a well, or raises off the floor. The painting is done from different levels or decks (see "Painting Scenery," Chapter 9).

A more-precarious method is to raise and lower a painting scaffolding in front of a fixed frame. In addition to being laborious and dangerous, the scaffolding has the added inconvenience of usually being some distance from a sink, burner, and paint supplies.

With even the best equipment for vertical painting, it is sometimes necessary to paint horizontally on the floor. Certain painting techniques require horizontal painting. The floor of the assembly area, or stage floor, often serves this purpose if stage use can be worked into the production schedule.

SCENERY MATERIALS AND TOOLS

Although some materials will be mentioned in relation to the construction of certain types of scenery, it may be wise to consider briefly all the materials that are used for making scenery. To compile a comprehensive list is, of course, next to impossible, for designers and technicians are constantly bringing new materials into the theatre every day as well as discovering new uses for old materials.

Materials can be divided and classified into four groups of similar functions: (1) structural (lumber and metal); (2) cover stock (fabric and hard surfaces); (3) hardware (joining and stage hardware); (4) rigging (rope, cable, and chain); (5) paints and related supplies (Chapter 9).

Structural Materials: Wood

Lumber is the principal framing and structural material, supplemented and reinforced on occasion by structural steel, pipe, and aluminum. As supplies and prices change, aluminum may become the framing material and wood the supplementary or decorative material. Until this is an actuality, lumber remains the chief structural element.

Lumber • To fill the needs of scenic construction, lumber must be lightweight, strong, straight, and inexpensive. The best combination of weight and strength is found in white pine. Although woods such as redwood and spruce are lighter, they do not have the strength and tend to splinter and split. The hardwoods are stronger, of course, but weigh and cost too much.

Lumber is classified at the yard into quality groups. The straightness of grain and freedom from knots determine the quality. Hence, clear white pine is of the highest quality. It is further classified as to its expected use. A board that is to become trim or a finished surface is of a higher quality than a structural member hidden from view.

The finishing lumber or "select" grades are designated by the letters A, B, C, and D. Hence B-select or better is a high-grade pine. C-select is the usual quality of lumber used in professional scenery.

The common grades are numbered 1 to 5. They are not intended for a finished surface although many times 1- and 2-common are used as

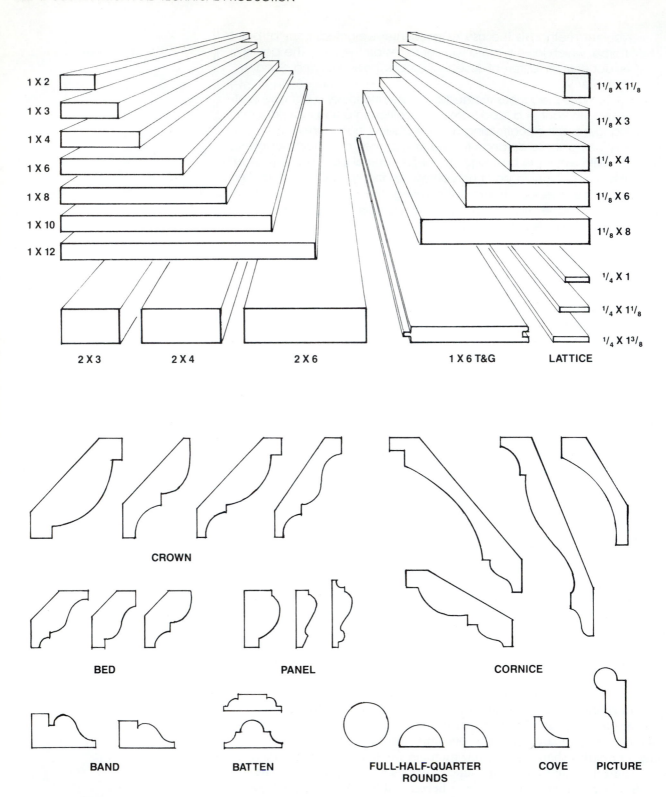

1 X 2
1 X 3
1 X 4
1 X 6
1 X 8
1 X 10
1 X 12

$1\frac{1}{8}$ X $1\frac{1}{8}$
$1\frac{1}{8}$ X 3
$1\frac{1}{8}$ X 4
$1\frac{1}{8}$ X 6
$1\frac{1}{8}$ X 8
$\frac{1}{4}$ X 1
$\frac{1}{4}$ X $1\frac{1}{8}$
$\frac{1}{4}$ X $1\frac{3}{8}$

2 X 3   2 X 4   2 X 6   1 X 6 T&G   LATTICE

CROWN

BED   PANEL   CORNICE

BAND   BATTEN   FULL-HALF-QUARTER ROUNDS   COVE   PICTURE

Figure 6-3
Stock Lumber Sizes and Molding Shapes

knotty-pine paneling. No. 2-common is the usual framing material for amateur scenery unless the theatre is in an area of the country where the better grades of pine are available at reasonable prices.

The stock sizes of lumber refer to the rough-cut size and not to the finished dimension after the wood has been dressed (planed or smooth on all sides). Thus 1 by 3 is really ¾-inch by 2½-inch. The longest stock length is 16 feet, although longer lengths can be obtained on special order.

Because lumber is cut in a variety of widths and thicknesses, it has a unit of measurement, the board-foot, common to all sizes. A board-foot is a 1-foot-square unit measuring 1 inch in thickness. A piece of lumber of any size can be reduced from its linear dimensions into board-feet. A 16-foot length of 1 by 3, for example, contains 4 board-feet. All lumber prices are based on the board-foot measurement.

Special shapes like "rounds" are stocked in diameter from ¾-inch to 1½-inch and sometimes as large as 3 inches in diameter. Dowel is available in ⅛- to 1-inch diameter and 3-foot lengths made of maple and birch.

Other special shapes are stock moldings which are made in a great variety of sizes and contours. A few of the most frequently used moldings are illustrated in Figure 6–3 along with the stock lumber sizes.

WOODWORKING TOOLS AND EQUIPMENT

The tools of a scenery shop are primarily for woodworking, with limited provisions for the working of metal. To build scenery it is necessary to cut, pare or shape, bore, and join the wood. The tools to work the wood are either hand tools for limited and special work or power tools for mass production and precision work. The working and joining of wood, however, is always preceded by careful measuring and marking.

Measuring and Marking Tools

Tools for measuring and marking are not only used with each technique of working wood but also in every step in the construction and assembly of the completed setting (Figure 6–4). Almost all mistakes in building are directly traceable to wrong measurements or a misinterpreted mark. The importance of accurate measurements cannot be overstressed.

Some of the tools are obviously for measuring only (6-foot rule and 50-foot tape) and others are made specifically for marking (tri-square, bevel gauge, scribe, spirit level, spline, and center square). A few tools are, however, designed for both measuring and marking.

The *protractor square* is able to measure an angle in degrees and provide a marking guide.

The *combination square,* with its adjustable sliding bar, is calibrated for measuring as well as establishing a marking guide for the 90-degree and 45-degree angles.

The *framing square* with calibrated edges is a useful tool in marking the angle cut of a stair carriage and for establishing a right angle for framing.

The *marking gauge* is calibrated to mark for a rip cut, an operation that can be duplicated by the combination square.

Within the group of marking tools, the *tri-square* is calibrated for limited measuring although its chief function is as a marking guide for

Figure 6-4
Woodworking Measuring Tools

a 90-degree angle cut. The *bar* or *beam* holding the trammel points is sometimes calibrated to measure the radius of the circle or arc it is to swing. The other tools in this group serve as marking guides only.

The *bevel gauge* is designed for transferring or saving a predetermined angle or bevel.

The *scribe* can follow an irregular surface with one point and scratch or mark the outline of the surface at a fixed distance with the other point.

The *spline* or *spring curve* is used to mark an irregular curve, or to plot a curved edge in full-scale lofting.

The *spirit level* establishes a true vertical or horizontal, and the *center square* locates the unmarked center of a circle or round stock.

The *chalk line* is for snapping an extremely long straight line that may be used as a framing guide, as a reference line for full-scale lofting, or as a guide for painting.

Wood-Cutting Tools

The chief cutting tool is the *saw*. Of the many saws in the scenery shop some are hand saws, others power saws that are hand-held, and the remaining are fixed power saws.

Hand Saws • The specific work a saw can do depends upon the shape of the tooth (pointed or chisel), the set of the tooth (flare of every other tooth in the opposite direction), and the tooth count (number of teeth per inch). Because wood has a grain, which is the alternating density of the fibers within its structure, it requires a different kind of saw to cut *across* the grain than to cut *with* the grain. The teeth of a *crosscut saw* are sharp and straight to cut through the wood fibers, while the teeth of the ripsaw are angled and flat-edged like a chisel to chip the wood with the grain. The *ripsaw* has the widest set and the lowest tooth count (6 to 8 teeth per inch). The crosscut saw has a tooth count of 8, 10, to as many as 12 teeth per inch.

The set of a saw is the degree of bend every other tooth has away from the norm of the saw blade. The set of the saw teeth keep the saw from binding because the width of the cut is wider than the blade. When a saw has lost its set it begins to bind in the cut (see inset of Figure 6-5).

An angled cut or miter can be cut freehand with a crosscut saw, or it can be accurately cut in a miter box with a *backsaw*. The *backsaw*, with a high tooth count (10 to 12 teeth per inch) is a stiff-bladed saw with a straight back which serves as a guide in the miter box. It is extremely useful in mitering moldings for a cornice, picture frame, or panel.

Irregular Cutting • Not all cutting in the making of scenery is straight-line cutting. As a matter of fact, a high percentage of the cutting is irregular or scroll work. Cutouts and profile edges require the greatest amount of scroll work.

A hand saw to cut on an irregular line must necessarily have a small blade to be able to turn and follow the irregular line. The *scroll saw* has a high tooth count of 12 per inch to produce a smoothly cut edge. It also has a removable blade for inside cuts. The deep throat of the frame that holds the blade allows the saw to reach well into the work.

The *keyhole saw* with a tooth count of 8 to 10 is made for heavy, coarse, and fast work. The small blade, although not as small as the scroll saw, allows irregular cutting beyond the limits a scroll saw can reach.

KEYHOLE SAW

RIP SAW

CHISEL
TEETH

SCROLL SAW

CROSSCUT SAW

KNIFE
TEETH

HAND SAWS

MITER BOX
AND
BACK SAW

PORTABLE CIRCULAR SAW

SABER SAW

CUT-ALL

HAND-HELD POWER SAWS

Figure 6-5
Wood Cutting Tools

IIII➤ *SAFETY PRACTICE*

When working with power tools such as circular saws, pull-over saws, drill presses and hand power tools:

1. Dress. Avoid loose clothing and long hair. Wear goggles.
2. Keep all blades and drills sharp. A dull blade can bind or skip and cause an accident.
3. Make sure the space under work is clear. Don't cut the saw horse in two.
4. If you use an unusual setting on the saw or drill press, return to normal set after work is finished.
5. Don't be afraid to ask for assistance to crosscut or rip a long board, for example.
6. When using a power tool, concentrate on what you are doing and know where your hands are.
7. After the work is finished, clean up and return tools.
8. Above all, listen to and follow the shop manager's work procedure.

Hand-Held Power Saws • The *portable circular saw* is designed to be brought to the work rather than for bringing the work to the saw. It can be used to advantage as a rip or crosscut saw on partially completed units of scenery. Because of its light weight and small blade it is limited as to depth of cut and accuracy. It is, however, a useful tool to have in a busy shop.

For irregular cutting, the *saber saw*, which is a portable jigsaw, does not limit the size of the work. It is a very versatile tool for scroll cutting at any stage of assembly.

The *cut-awl*, which is designed for light, detailed cutting, works best on profile and composition board. It also requires a padded bench or table for satisfactory results.

JIGSAW

TABLE SAW

BAND SAW

PULLOVER SAW

FIXED POWER SAWS

Fixed Power Saws • Power tools made for straight-line cutting are the table saw, pullover saw, and Skilsaw. Each may be fitted with a rip, crosscut, or combination blade for specific work.

A 10-inch, tilting-arbor, 1-horsepower *table saw* with miter gauge and rip fence is a basic piece of equipment. It is a heavy enough tool to do precision work in quantity. It miters and rips with ease and accuracy.

A 10- to 12-inch 1-horsepower *pullover saw* provides the necessary power for cutting heavy lumber. Its pullover action above the wood and long table make it an accurate crosscut and limited mitering tool. Because the guide fence becomes inaccurate from repeated crosscutting, it is not a very accurate ripping tool.

Power Tools for Irregular Cutting • Power tools that speed up the production of scroll work are the band saw and jigsaw. The *band saw* with its continuous blade is limited to outside cutting and to work as large as the depth of its throat. A band saw with a 20-inch throat will serve the average need of a scenery shop if it is supplemented with other equipment to do inside cutting.

The *jigsaw* with its removable straight blade and deep throat is made for both inside and outside scroll cutting.

Wood-Paring Tools

The simplest tool for freehand shaping of wood is the *chisel.* Although the hand chisel cannot compare in speed and accuracy to power tools, it can be used to do a limited amount of shaping and notching of wood. It is an excellent tool to clean up a power-cut dado, rabbet, mortise, or routed area. With skilled handling it can, if necessary, make any of these cuts itself. A set of chisels would include a variety of widths from ¼ inch to 1¼ inches.

The paring edge of the chisel is shown in the inset of Figure 6-6. The top bevel is forged, but the lower bevel is sharpened into a cutting edge. Note that the angle is about 45 degrees. When the edge becomes dull or nicked it can be resharpened by first reshaping the edge on the coarse emery wheel and then grind a new cutting surface at 45 degrees. The sharpening is finished on an oil stone.

The *drawknife* is not a precision tool. It is useful to pare away waste or roughly shape a surface before planing.

The *smoothing plane* can pare a surface to an accurate dimension. It is made to smooth with the grain of the wood while the small *block plane* is designed to work across the grain and to smooth or shape the end of a board.

The small *block plane* is designed to smooth cross-grain. It can be used to correct a bad saw cut or shorten a member to improve a delicate fit.

The *rasp* and *Surform,* a replaceable rasp blade in a holder, are also designed to work across the grain. They can do the same shaping faster than the block plane but leave a rougher finish.

Power Shapers and Sanders

Probably the most useful, small power tool for shaping is the *router*. In addition to routing to countersink hinges, it can cut tenons, dados, and

CHISEL BLADE

CHISEL

DRAWKNIFE

BLOCK PLANE

SMOOTHING PLANE

SURFORM

RASP

HAND PARING TOOLS

ROUTER

DISK SANDER

ORBITAL SANDER

HAND-HELD POWER SHAPING TOOLS

Figure 6-6
Wood Paring Tools

JOINER

POWER
SANDER

MORTISING
MACHINE

SHAPER

EMERY
WHEEL

LATHE

Figure 6-6, continued
Wood Paring Tools

rabbets. With special bits it can also do a limited amount of molding cutting.

Portable sanders are handy tools at the bench or when brought to the work. The *disk sander* is best to use when smoothing an end cut. With coarse sandpaper it can reshape or round a cut. It is less effective sanding a flat surface because it tends to leave sanding marks.

The *orbital sander* is excellent for smoothing a flat surface. It is light-weight and economical using a half sheet of regular 9″ by 11″ sandpaper.

Power tools designed to do various shaping and smoothing operations are limited mostly to special cuts. The *rotary planer* or *joiner,* for ex-ample, can smooth a board, size a board by changing the depth of cut, bevel the edge by angling the fence, as well as cutting a rabbet on one side of the board.

Likewise the *rotary shaper* is designed especially to cut moldings. It can cut a variety of molding by changing or combining different blades.

The *mortising machine,* or mortising attachment for a drill press, with its square chisel, is limited to cutting the deep square hole of a mortise. It is a time-saving tool in a professional scenery shop where there is a lot of mortise-and-tenon joining.

Although mortise-and-tenon joint for the framing of flats is not found in most shops, the *square chisel* is a useful tool. A well-built door, for example, has mortise-and-tenon joint and inset panels.

Some shaping operations can be performed on the table and pullover saw. The circular table saw can be equipped with a dado head, which is a set of special blades to cut a groove. Molding cutters can also be at-tached to the circular saw for simple molding cutting. The pullover saw can also be rigged to dado, shape, and rout. Any change-over, of course, takes time and ties up the saw for other uses.

For finished smoothing, a power *sander,* both belt and disk, quickly and accurately smooths the end, edge, or face of a board. In this same category, the *emery wheel* is used to smooth and shape metal as well as sharpen hand tools.

The *wood lathe* is a cylindrical shaping tool. A block of wood is rotated on its long axis and shaped with a chisel held on an adjustable rest that can be moved with the work. A baluster or spindle for furniture or stair railing can be turned on this tool.

The *joiner* is a power plane. Its rotating blades can smooth the edge or surface of a board. By setting the fence at an angle, the edge of the board can be planed with an angle.

Boring Tools

Tools with a cutting edge that revolves about a central axis to cut a circular hole are called boring tools (Figure 6–7). The tool consists of two basic parts: the bit, which is the cutting part of the tool, and the mech-anism to rotate the bit.

There is, of course, great variation in the types of bit, depending upon the size and depth of the hole, kind of hole (clean bore, taper, ream), and the nature of the material (hardness, thickness). Likewise the power-providing part of the tool will vary with type of bit used and the speed of rotation necessary to do the work. The types of bit and means of rotation found in the average scenery shop are:

BITS	ROTATING TOOLS
Auger bit (square shank)	Brace
Twist drill (round shank)	Hand drill
Twist drill (square shank)	Power hand drill
Twist drill (¼-inch round shank)	Drill press
Power bit (¼-inch round shank)	Cordless drill
Countersink, wood	
Countersink, metal	
Hole-cutter	
Expanding bit	
Extension shank	

The *auger bit* has a screw lead that, when rotated, pulls the cutting edges of the bit into contact with the wood. The auger bit does not need to rotate at a high speed. It is usually driven with the brace made to receive its square shank. The *brace* is a cranklike form designed to give the carpenter a mechanical advantage rather than to increase the speed of rotation. Augers are manufactured in size differences of $\frac{1}{16}$ inch. They are numbered by sixteenths; thus a ½-inch auger would be a No. 8 bit.

Twist drills have no screw lead and depend upon speed of rotation and pressure to advance into the material. The *hand drill* is designed to increase the speed of rotation as well as provide some mechanical advantage. The high-speed portable *power hand drill* is excellent for this type of work.

The *power bit* is a wood-cutting bit made for high-speed rotation with a small round shank (¼-inch) for the small power drill. The paddle end of the bit varies from ⅜ inch to 1¼ inch in width. The chisel-like edges do the cutting and depend on high speed for accuracy.

Also in the auger-bit class is the *expanding bit* which is adjustable and can bore a hole as large as 1¼ inches to 2½ inches in diameter.

The *countersink bit* is used on either wood or metal after the hole has been bored. It enlarges the top of the opening with a beveled cut of sufficient depth to set a flathead screw or bolt flush with the outer surface of the material.

The *hole-cutter* is used to cut oversized holes (1½ inches and up) at high speed. Although faster and cleaner than the expanding bit, it is limited in its depth of cut.

The hex *extension shank* can lengthen the depth-of-cut of a paddle drill by extending its shank. It is good for drilling the length of a block of wood, for example.

The *drill press*, which is a stationary power drill, has added advantages of such controls as depth of bore and speed variation for precision work. The drill press with a mortising attachment makes a very useful tool in the scenery shop.

The *cordless drill* with rechargeable batteries is useful away from the shop. It can do light work such as drilling to set a screw in a hinge.

AUGER BIT

**TWIST DRILL
W/REDUCED SHANK**

**COUNTER SINK
METAL**

HOLE CUTTER

TWIST DRILL

PADDLE DRILL

EXTENSION SHANK

**TWIST DRILL WITH
SQUARE SHANK**

**COUNTER SINK
WOOD**

EXPANSION BIT

BRACE

HAND DRILL

POWER DRILL

DRILL PRESS

**CORDLESS DRILL
W/BATTERY PACK
AND CHARGER**

Figure 6-7
Wood Boring Tools

Many shops have found the need of a heavy power drill to make larger holes or drill deeper. A power drill with speed control and a ½-inch chuck capacity is a valuable tool.

Wood-Joining Tools

The joining of wood is the last stage of carpentry. The tools are designed to drive or set the joining hardware (nails, screws, or staples) in such a manner as to hold the pieces of wood together (Figure 6–8).

Hammers • The *claw hammer* is used to drive a nail or set a screw. The rounded claw is used to correct mistakes by pulling a misdirected nail.

The *straight claw hammer* sometimes called the "ripper" provides a straight claw for prying apart joined members.

The *mallet* with a wooden or leatherbound head is not used for heavy driving. It can be used to tap a member into place without damaging the edge of the wood. The mallet is also used with the chisel.

The *magnetic tack hammer* is used primarily in upholstering to attach heavy material and padding to a wooden frame.

Screwdrivers • The *ratchet screwdriver* drives the screw by pushing down on the handgrip. It can be reversed to pull out the screw. The straight screwdriver comes with several types of heads to drive a screw with *slotted head, Phillips head,* or a hex head or *nut driver.*

Staplers • The *staple gun* drives the staple when the trigger is squeezed, while the *staple hammer* requires a hammering action.

Bolt Joining • When wood is joined together by bolting, a tool is needed to tighten the nut. Besides the nut driver already mentioned there are tools that grip the nut. The *plier* is a simple tool to grip the nut, however, too much stress will damage the sides of the nut. The *crescent wrench* has adjustable jaws to fit the sides of the nut, thereby applying even pressure.

The *socket wrench* with ratchet action and interchangeable wrench heads is a very efficient tool to tighten or loosen a nut. It also has an extension shaft to work in tight places.

A *bolt cutter* is often needed to trim or shorten a bolt. The ratio of the small jaw opening to the long handles gives it greater leverage.

To correct mistakes or take apart a joint the *crowbar* or *nail puller* is needed. Both are strong and, because of their long handles, have a very efficient leverage. Their leverage is based on the principle of the *lever.* A long bar placed over a fulcrum or point of pivot close to the work (a rock to be moved or a nail to be pulled) requires less energy at the long end of the bar (Figure 6-9).

In the process of framing scenery the corner and keystone blocks are attached to the back with nails that are bent or clinched on the face as they hit the *clinch plate.* The plate is usually a square foot of ⅛-inch steel. It is sometimes built into the template.

The final method of wood-joining is gluing. Since glue requires time to set, the clamp holds the members firmly in place. The *C clamp* holds boards face to face as does the *wood clamp* which, because it is made of

Figure 6-8
Wood Joining Tools

CLAW
HAMMER

STRAIGHT
CLAW
HAMMER

MALLET

TACK
HAMMER

CRESCENT
WRENCH

UTILITY
PLIERS

CROW-BAR

NAIL-PULLER

SCREWDRIVER

PHILLIPS SCREWDRIVER

NUT DRIVER

RATCHET SCREWDRIVER

SOCKET
WRENCH

STAPLE GUN

STAPLE HAMMER

BOLT-CUTTER

GROMMET-SETTING DIE

CLINCH PLATE

C-CLAMP

HAND
SCREW CLAMP

BAR CLAMP

Figure 6-9
The Lever

25 LB

100 LB

FULCRUM

FULCRUM

wood, does less damage to the surfaces. The *bar clamp* is designed to hold the boards edge to edge.

Pneumatic Tools

No well-equipped scenery shop should be without the speed and efficiency of the pneumatic hammer or staple gun (Figure 6–10).

Because these tools require about 90 pounds per square inch of air pressure to operate, the shop must have a heavy-duty compressor or compressed-air service at convenient positions in the shop. In addition to the air-hammer the shop should have a pneumatic reversible drill with socket wrench and screwdriver attachments.

The same supply system can provide compressed air to the painting and property areas to operate paint spray guns.

METAL AS SCENERY MATERIAL

Metal has been used in the theatre as a structural material for some time. In recent theatre there are many examples of metal being used as a design feature. For these reasons, it is important for the designer and technician to understand the many forms and techniques of using metal.

Iron and Steel • Iron is the basic metal. It is combined with carbon to make steel. A high proportion of carbon produces a harder steel. Steel can have other alloys such as chromium or nickel, however, the most useful combinations for the theatre are a low-carbon steel and malleable iron.

Figure 6-10
Pneumatic Tools

Two useful pneumatic tools, (a) a nailer. (b) A stapler for ⅜-inch to 2-inch staples. A 1–inch staple is suitable for attaching corner blocks to scenery framing.

a

b

Forming and Fabricating Metal • While the metal is still molten it can be *formed* in many ways: *rolling* to produce *plate* and *sheet* metal; *extruding* by squeezing the molten metal through a shaped aperture forming such shapes as rod, tubes, and so on; *casting* liquid metal into block forms; *drawing* the softened metal through a small aperture to make *wire*; and *forging* or stamping the metal into a prescribed shape.

Out of the forming we have the following familiar shapes: *plate,* rolled steel no thinner than ⅛ of an inch; *sheet,* rolled steel no thicker than ⅛ of an inch; *strip,* rolled steel narrower than plate; *strap,* narrow strip; *rod,* solid round and square; *structural* shapes such as channel, angle, and so on; *tube,* extruded round, square, and rectangular; *pipe,* round malleable iron; *wire,* drawn carbon steel that can be twisted into cable.

The *fabricating* of metal involves unique techniques and tools. The following terms are used in the fabrication of metal: *brake forming,* to bend plate or sheet metal; to *shear* is to cut sheet metal; *spinning,* sheet metal is placed into a lathe-like machine and spun (while spinning a blunt tool shapes the metal into bowl or bell shapes); *rolling,* the cold-rolling of sheet metal into curved or cylindrical shapes; *twisting,* a square bar can be twisted into a decorative shape or wire can be twisted into cable; *blanking,* the punching of holes or a pattern through plate or sheet metal; *wrought iron,* the twisting, bending, or rolling of soft iron into decorative shapes; *joining,* the bolting or riveting of structural steel or sheet metal together; *welding,* joining by fusing metals together at a high temperature; *soldering,* the joining of sheet metal or tin with solder.

Structural Steel Shapes • The numerous shapes of structural steel that will be shown and discussed represent typical cross sections (Figure 6–11). In all examples, the thickness of the metal and the length of a leg is manufactured in many combinations. The choice of the combination of size and thickness of the metal depends on the work the structural member is expected to do. In the beginning, it is wise for the designer and technician to become familiar with all the size and weight variations of any one shape.

Strap. If it is very thin it is called *band.* Its most frequent use is as a *silliron,* ¾ inch wide by ³⁄₁₆ inch thick.

Strip. It is a wide strap. A 2½ inch wide by ⅛ inch thick strip is sometimes cut and drilled for mending plates.

Angle. It is a good reinforcing shape to stiffen or brace scenery. It is a very useful cross section and comes in many sizes.

Channel. Its U-shaped cross section makes it stronger though not as adaptable as an angle.

Tee. The T shape is useful for stiffening. When it is used horizontally in a framework, it is stronger than an angle. The tee also serves as a guide for the arbor in a counterweight system.

I beam. As the name suggests, the I beam is best used as a beam where the major thrust or weight is on the top of the I.

Round tube. One of the many extruded forms. The larger tubes can become vertical support members while smaller diameter tubes can be bent into decorative shapes (see TWC, on p. 160).

Square tube. A popular shape that can be cut and welded into structural or decorative forms.

STRAP

STRIP

ANGLE

CHANNEL

TEE

I-BEAM

ROUND TUBE

SQUARE TUBE

RECTANGULAR TUBE

ROD

BAR

PIPE

STRUCTURAL STEEL SHAPES

SPECIAL SHAPES

UNISTRUT

TELSPAR

DEXION

Figure 6-11
Structural Steel Shapes

Rectangular tube. A good clean shape for design or structural uses.

Rod. A round solid, sometimes used as the internal member of a steel truss or easily bent into decorative shapes.

Bar. A square solid, sometimes used as a spindle in a metal railing or bent and twisted into ornamental shapes found in wrought-iron work.

Pipe. With heavier side walls than tube, malleable iron pipe can be threaded and joined with fittings (Figure 6–12). Although the inside dimension (ID) remains the same, pipe is available in three side-wall thicknesses: standard, extra strength, and double extra strength.

Figure 6-12
Various Uses of Iron Pipe

(a) Top batten for drop, cyclorama, or stage drapery. (b) Bottom batten for a drop-in pipe sleeve. (c) Curved bottom batten using tielines. (d) Free-standing platform legs. (e) Special bracing. (f) Lighting booms and battens. (g) Bent pipe and welded railing. (h) Cut pipe and fitted railing.

Special Shapes • *Uni-strut* with its fittings is a method of knockdown framing in special channel-shaped steel that is adaptable to platforming and trussing in the theatre. It eliminates the necessity of welding and cutting and is available in different forms.

Thin-wall galvanized-steel *conduit* (TWC) pipe has become a very popular structural and decorative material in the theatre. With walls too thin to thread and therefore easy to bend, it has many uses in scenery construction (Figure 6–25). It comes in three diameters, ½-inch, ¾-inch, 1¼-inch, in 10-foot lengths. It is lightweight, inexpensive, and easy to gas-weld with fluxcoated brazing rod.

The types of *Telspar*, a telescoping square tube, are: (1) solid sides; (2) punched with round holes; and (3) punched with square holes.

Dexion, a slotted angle iron designed to bolt together in a variety of shapes, is also made in strap and channel shapes.

Flat Steel • Steel plate and sheet metal have been mentioned as forms of flat steel.

Plate is ridged and comes as thin as ⅛ inch. It can be cut-to-order to sizes for various needs such as a clinch plate or pipe stand base to add weight to the bottom.

Expanded metal plate is steel plate that is punched with a pattern of slits and then stretched from opposite edges to expand the plate into a grille surface. Expanded metal is weight bearing and has been used as platform flooring thereby allowing light through in interesting patterns. Lightweight expanded metal has been used as a screen surface for light projections.

Sheet metal is rolled steel under ⅛ inch thickness. The various thicknesses are indicated in *gauges*. They decrease in steps of 1.5 hundredth of an inch, hence, the larger the gauge, the thinner the sheet.

Galvanized steel, aluminum sheet, tin (tinned steel), zinc, and copper have been used as scenic materials as has highly polished stainless steel. Light pans, shadow boxes, and special effects are a few of the uses of sheet metal in scenery construction.

The *metal screening* such as hardware cloth (¼-inch mesh), galvanized screen (¹⁄₁₆-inch mesh), and chicken wire (1-inch mesh) are primarily used as structural materials. Occasionally, galvanized screening is used to simulate window glass.

METALWORKING TOOLS AND EQUIPMENT

The use of metal in the theatre requires special tools to cut, shape, and join the many forms of metal as well as ways of coping with the various methods of fabrication. Although some woodworking tools can be used on metal, most metalworking tools have special functions. The following *hand tools* are used for the measuring, marking, shaping, and cutting of metal.

Measuring and Marking • Most marking on metal is done with a *scriber.* Its sharp point scratches a line on the surface of the metal. Pencil and chalk lines smudge and are not feasible. A measuring tape is usable for

Figure 6-13
Metal Working Tools

VERNIER CALIPER   SCRIBE   COMPASS   INSIDE CALIPER   FRAMING SQUARE   CENTERING PUNCH   METAL STRAIGHT EDGE   MEASURING AND MARKING

ANVIL   MACHINIST'S VISE   MACHINIST BALL PEEN HAMMERS   FILES

FORMING ROLL   LIGHTWEIGHT BREAK   SHAPING TOOLS

long dimensions; however, a *flat steel rule* not only gives measurements, but also serves as a straight edge for marking. The large *framing square* is also useful for layouts.

The *compass scriber* will mark a circle or arc as well as scribe an irregular shape or pattern.

The *center punch*, as its name implies, marks the center of a circle or provides a start hole for drilling in metal.

Shaping Tools • The *anvil* is the original tool for the shaping and bending of steel and malleable iron. The metal is shaped, hot or cold, by hammering on the flat or rounded surfaces of the anvil. The heavy *blacksmith hammer* and the *ball peen* hammer do the shaping.

Strap iron can be bent in a *machinist's vise* with its steel jaws and small anvil. The vise can hold metal for shaping with a file. The *metal files*, flat and triangular, can smooth a rough cut or round an edge.

Pipe and tube also can be shaped. The *conduit bender* is a hand tool for bending thin-wall conduit (TWC). Besides bending, pipe can be shaped by cutting and threaded to be joined in numerous ways (Figure 6–12).

To cut and fit pipe several hand tools are needed. The pipe is held in a *pipe vise* and cut with a *pipe cutter*. The pipe cutter, technically a cutting tool, rotates around the pipe to make a clean cut. The *pipe*

Figure 6-14
Decorative and Structural Uses of
Rod and Strap Iron

LEAF FORMS

CHANDELIER

BRACKET

SPECIAL
JACK

WAGON GUIDE

SILL IRON

SADDLE-SHAPED
SILL IRON

threader with several *die heads* to fit the various pipe sizes, cuts threads on the end of the pipe. The numerous fittings are shown in Figure 6–16.

Some shaping tools, although operated by hand, are too large to be hand-held tools. The *sheet-metal roll*, for example, is hand operated. Sheet metal is fed between three rollers, two fixed and one adjustable. The position of the adjustable roller will increase or decrease the degree of curl in the shaped sheet metal.

The *brake form* is hand or foot operated to cleanly bend sheet metal to a prescribed angle. The *Hossfeld metal bender,* with a variety of attachments, can bend metal into intricate shapes.

Cutting Tools • The hand *hack saw* with a fine toothed blade is normally used to cut metal bar or bolts. The *pipe cutter* has been mentioned as a necessary tool for cutting and threading pipe. The hand tools to cut sheet metal are the *tin shears,* for cutting a straight line; *nippers,* for end cutting, and *side cutting pliers.*

Metalworking Power Tools • To cut sheet metal or aluminum, both of thicker gauges, a *saber saw* with a metal cutting blade is a noisy but effective method. Two tools designed to cut sheet metal are the *power shear,* which is hand-held and will cut straight or curved, and the *power nibbler* for inside cutting. It requires an .87-inch starting hole.

The major tools to crosscut pipe, tube, or any structural steel forms are the *powered hack saw,* and *band saw,* and the *abrasive wheel cutoff saw.*

HAND HACKSAW

**RECIPROCATING SAW
WITH HACKSAW BLADE**

POWER HACKSAW

POWER BANDSAW

**ABRASIVE WHEEL
CUTOFF SAW**

TIN SHEARS

**END CUTTING
NIPPERS**

SIDE CUTTERS

**METAL CUTTING BLADE
IN SCROLLSAW**

POWER SHEAR

**POWER
NIBBLER**

Figure 6-15
Metal Cutting Tools

Figure 6-16
Pipe Cutting, Threading and Bending Tools

Hand tools used for cutting, threading and bending pipe include: (a) pipe cutter, (b) pipe threader with ¾-inch, 1-inch, and 1½-inch die heads, (c) pipe vise, (d) portable vise stand, (e) Stillson wrench, and (f) pipe bender.

The *power hand drill* with ½-inch chuck capacity is a heavier tool than the wood drill. The *drill press* is a fixed tool for precision work. A *drill press vise* is used to hold the work in position. Another fixed power tool is the *bench grinder.* With one coarse and one fine emery wheel the bench grinder can sharpen tools or grind down a metal edge.

Metal-Joining Tools and Materials

The various forms of metal can be joined with bolts, screws (sheet metal), rivets, solder, or by fusing the metals together with a weld. Pipe joining, besides the many fittings, can be accomplished on the outside. The *saddle tee* is strapped on the surface of the pipe providing a right-angle coupling. The *rota-lock* clamps the adjoining pipe also at a 90-degree angle (Figure 6–17). The *Stillson wrench* with jaws to grip and long arm is used to tighten the pipe into a fitting. The *vise-grip wrench*, along with other uses, can be used to tighten smaller diameter pipe.

The wrenches and screwdrivers from woodworking that can be used to join metal are the *socket wrench*, *nut driver*, and *cresent wrench*. The Phillips screwdriver can be used to set *sheet metal screws*. With a small starter hole, the self-threading sheet-metal screw easily joins two or more pieces.

Sheet metal can be firmly joined with rivets. A hole is drilled through overlapping sheets; the rivet is inserted through the hole from the back;

1 COUPLING
2 NIPPLE
3 REDUCING COUPLING
4 TEE
5 CROSS
6 7 UNION RING & SCREW END
8 CAP

9 90 DEGREE ELBOW
10 45 DEGREE ELBOW
11 STREET ELBOW
12 FLOOR FLANGE
13 ADJUSTABLE ELBOW (RAILING)
14 PIPE STRAP

15 16 17 18
BATTEN SLEEVE SPLICE   SADDLE TEE   ROTOLOCK   PIPEHANGER

Figure 6-17
Pipe Joining

Some of the screw fittings used to join sections of pipe: (1) coupling, (2) nipple, (3) reducing coupling, (4) tee, (5) cross, (6) union, ring end, (7) union, screw end, (8) cap, (9) 90-degree elbow, (10) 45-degree elbow, (11) street ells, (12) floor flange, (13) adjustable elbow (railing fitting), (14) pipe strap, (15) batten inside sleeve splice, (16) saddle tee, double strap, (17) rotolock, (18) pipe hanger.

RIVET

METAL SCREW

POP RIVETER

SOLDERING IRON

SOLDERING GUN

PROPANE TORCH

Figure 6-18
Metal Joining Tools

a washer is placed over the shaft of the rivet; and, to finish the joining, the shaft is *peened* or flattened with a ball peen hammer. When the back is inaccessible a *pop rivet* can be used. The *pop riveter* compresses the rivet in place with a squeeze or two of the handles.

Soldering

As a method of joining metal, solder functions as a *bond.* The strength of the bond depends upon the preparation of the surfaces to be joined and an even application of solder.

The surfaces should be cleansed of oil, paint, or oxidation (rust). A flux, borax, or rosin is applied to further clean the metal and prevent oxidation.

An electric *soldering iron* or *soldering gun* supplies sufficient heat at the tip to melt the solder along the joint.

The soldering of pipe to a fitting requires a torch. The *propane torch* supplies heat to a large area of the fitting so that when the solder is applied it is sucked into the joint. The joint surfaces are cleaned and polished with emery cloth and coated with flux, before applying the heat and solder.

For the soldering of electrical connections, a rosin flux is used to prevent corrosion.

Welding

Welding is the fusing of metal. It provides a more permanent joint than soldering. It is a faster method of joining but requires specialized equipment. The two most useful welding processes adaptable to the construction and designing of scenery are *gas-welding* and *arc-welding.*

Gas-Welding Equipment

Oxy-acetylene welding (OAW) ignites an oxygen and acetylene mixture to produce one of the hottest flames known. Welding is possible with or without a filler metal. Gas-welding can perform a wide range of work. In addition to joining or fusing the metals together it can be used for low-temperature welding or *brazing,* to cut metal with a cutting attachment, and to preheat metal for reshaping on the anvil. The chief disadvantage to gas-welding is heat warpage.

Unless handled very carefully, gas-welding can cause warping of the metal near the welded point. The choice of a welding rod that will melt at the same temperature as (or slightly lower than) the melting point of the steel will minimize the amount of distortion.

The relative harmlessness of the flame is another advantage of gas-welding when used in the scenery shop or on the stage. The only exception is when the cutting tip is being used. To cut metal with a torch, a tiny jet of oxygen is directed onto the white-hot metal, producing a rather spectacular shower of sparks.

The most cumbersome parts of a gas-welding outfit are the heavy tanks containing the two welding gases, oxygen and acetylene. A tank truck is essential to make their movement easier. The methods of acquiring oxygen and acetylene vary with the suppliers. Some gas suppliers charge a fixed deposit on the tank which is refunded when the empty tank is returned, while others rent the container on a per diem basis. If

> ||||⮞ *SAFETY PRACTICE*
>
> Gas welding operators should wear goggles and gloves, more for protection from flying sparks than from the intensity of the flame itself. Because there are no ultraviolet rays generated in the flame by gas-welding, it does not have to be isolated or shielded from other shop activity. Precautions should be taken, however, to guard flammable materials from the sparks by using sheetrock pads under and around the work.

a supplier insists on the tank-rental arrangement, it pays in the long run to purchase a set of empty tanks to exchange for each tank of gas and thereby eliminate the per diem rental charge which, though small, can mount up during idle times between productions.

A listing of the parts and attachments of a gas-welding outfit including the gas tanks is found in (Figure 6–19).

Arc-Welding Equipment

The heat of arc-welding comes, as the name implies, from the arc of a high-amperage short circuit between the metal and the rod or electrode. The work has to be grounded to complete the circuit from the rod to the holder through the electrode cable to the transformer. *Shielded metal arc-welding* (SMAW) is the most-adaptable, arc-welding technique for the theatre workshop. Upon striking, the arc is enveloped in a shield of inert gas as the coating of the rod burns. This shield of inert gas keeps the oxygen in the air out of the critical metallurgical change of the welding process.

Of the two welding methods, arc-welding requires more skill. It takes practice to develop a steady hand to strike an arc and draw a good bead. Arc-welding's chief advantage is in the speed of the welding operation. Because a welding temperature is reached almost instantaneously and in such a small area, the amount of heat warpage is negligible. This is important in the welding of a preassembled part when its fit is critical to the final shape of the completed structure.

Gas-Metal Arc-Welding

A third welding process, which is rapidly becoming adaptable to theatre shop use, is the gas-metal arc-welding method commonly referred to as *metal inert gas* or MIG. MIG uses a wire-fed electrode through a gas hose and gun nozzle to the work. The arc is surrounded with an inert gas shield and is automatically fed with a wire electrode in the center of the nozzle. MIG welding is a simple one-handed operation that is easy to learn. The heat of the arc and gauge of the wire can be altered to weld various metals including aluminum. A special spot-welding fitting can be attached to the end of the nozzle for temporarily tacking or permanently joining adjacent surfaces. Some MIG units can also switch to stick-welding (regular arc-welding with rod) without the use of gas.

As welding equipment MIG is more expensive than arc or gas but is easier to operate and provides a variety of uses. Its chief disadvantages

Figure 6-19
Gas-Welding Equipment

(a) Oxygen tank. (b) Acetylene tank.
(c) Tank truck. (d) Gauges: oxygen
regulator and acetylene regulator.
(e) 25-foot twin $\frac{3}{16}$-inch hose with
connectors. (f) Welding butt.
(g) Cutting attachment. (h) Welding
nozzles, sizes 00, 1, 3, and 5. (j) Tip
cleaner set. (k) Flint lighter.
(l) Welding gloves. (m) Goggles.
(n) Rods: $\frac{1}{16}$-inch fluxcoated brazing
rod (for thin-walled conduit), $\frac{1}{8}$-inch
mild steel rod (for structural steel).
(o) Flux. (p) Wrench.

are its weight and bulk. It is not very mobile for other than metal-shop use.

Because an arc is involved in gas-metal arc-welding it is subject to all the safety precautions of arc-welding mentioned earlier. The components of MIG equipment are found in Figure 6–20.

Figure 6-20
Gas-Metal Arc-Welding Equipment

(a) Power unit MIG—160 amperes DC at 22 volts (60% duty cycle). (b) Gas cylinder—mixture of argon and CO_2 or helium. (c) Gauges—tank pressure, work pressure. (d) Gas hose-cable. (e) Automatic wire-feeder, built-in wire-feeder is a feature of this particular unit (AIRCO, DIP/STICK 160). (f) Gun and nozzle. (g) Ground cable. (h) Electrode cable for stick-welding. (i) Spot-welding attachment. (j) Helmet, fiberglass with ray-absorbing viewing window. (k) Gloves. (l) Apron or smock. (m) Rods for stick-welding. (n) Folding screen. (o) Angled grinder to smooth-weld.

Figure 6-21
Gas-Metal Arc-Welding
Note the expanded-metal welding table top.

Figure 6-22
Metal Scenery
(Below left) Sheet metal (16 to 18 gauge) over square tube structural framing. (Right) Rear view of welded frame. The Tyrone Guthrie Theatre production of *Oedipus the King* by Sophocles. Designer— Desmond Heeley. *Photo courtesy Kewley*

Figure 6-23
Steel Staircase
Spiral staircase for a production of Molière's *Tartuffe* framed with 1-inch square steel tube. (Bottom left) Full assembly. (Top) Framing of tread supports. (Bottom right) Bending the sweep of the helix. Designer—Douglas Maddox. Construction—Eric Harriz and Roger Segalla. *Photo courtesy Mark Baird*

Figure 6-24
Decorative Use of Thin-Wall Conduit

Forest scene from Shakespeare's *As You Like It*. Designer—John Kavelin. Carnegie-Mellon University. *Photo courtesy Nelson*

Figure 6-25
Pipe-Scaffold Design

A scaffolding of black iron pipe held with rota locks and plank platforming make-up the setting for a production of *'Tis a Pity She's a Whore*. Stainless steel sheet metal covers the central floor in an interesting use of metal as scenery. *Photo courtesy Nelson*

Cover Stock

The material used to cover the structural frame of scenery, thereby providing a surface for painting, is known as *cover stock.* The frame can be covered with a fabric or hard surface depending upon the use and handling of the particular piece of scenery. A translucent backing, for example, is framed and covered differently from a section of wall that must support the weight of an actor.

Covering Fabrics • The usual covering fabrics for framed scenery are 8-ounce canvas duck and 5- to 6-ounce unbleached muslin. Muslin is more frequently used as a drop material than as cover stock for framed scenery. However, almost any fabric can become a covering material to serve as a special effect or as an unusual painting surface. Burlap, velour, scrim, terry cloth, and even string rugs have been used as covering fabrics. The thin, translucent materials are backed with canvas, of course, if the surface is supposed to be opaque.

Hard Surfaces • If the surface has to withstand active handling during the action of a play, the frame is covered with a harder surface than canvas. The most frequently used hard-surface material is ⅛-inch plywood board called EZ curve or profile board. It is lightweight but still strong enough to supply a hard surface with a minimum of framing. Tek board, ⅛-inch laminated wood and paper, is a close substitute for profile board although not quite as strong.

Other hard-surface materials include ⅛-inch and ³⁄₁₆-inch Upson board, an inexpensive but weaker substitute for profile board made of laminated paper; ¼-inch fir three ply, a very sturdy but heavy board (also used for keystone and corner blocks); ½-inch Homosote, a paper-pulp board with very little strength but thick enough to be carved or textured; and ³⁄₁₆-inch Masonite, a very heavy, hard surface of compressed wood pulp. The tempered Masonite is an extremely hard surface that is occasionally used as a floor covering. Double-faced corrugated cardboard is an inexpensive hard surface for limited profiling and covering providing the scenery is not subjected to excessive handling. Some shops also include ¾-inch and 1-inch five ply as cover stock, although its chief use is for platform tops.

Most of the cover-stock materials are available at the local lumber yard in stock 4-by-8-foot sheets. Occasionally, oversized sheets, such as 5 feet by 9 feet, 4 feet by 10 feet, and 4 feet by 12 feet are stocked.

Plastic Surfaces. Because the use of modern plastic as a scenery surface is usually related to a textured or relief-sculptured surface, it is reserved for discussion in Chapter 7, where the techniques of working plastics such as Styrofoam, urethane foam, and thermoplastics are treated.

HARDWARE

In the scenery shop, hardware is divided into two categories: joining hardware and stage hardware. The latter is further broken down under the categories of stiffening hardware, bracing hardware, joining hardware, and rigging hardware.

Joining Hardware • This is an important part of normal scenery construction. It includes all the necessary nails, screws, and bolts for joining wood or metal. Stage hardware is a part of knockdown construction methods, stage assembly, and handling techniques peculiar to scenery.

A list of joining hardware most frequently used in the construction of scenery would include:

Nails	Common—8d, 10d
	Box—3d, 6d
	Finish—4d, 6d, 8d
	Clout—1¼-inch (or 3d box nail)
Screws	Flat-head bright steel:
	No. 8—¾-inch, ⅞-inch, 1¼-inch
	No.10—2-inch, 3-inch
Tacks and Staples	Carpet—No. 6, No. 10
	Gimp—½-inch
	Staples—⅜-inch, ½-inch
Bolts	³⁄₁₆-inch stove—2-inch, 3-inch
	⅜-inch carriage—3-inch, 4-inch, 6-inch
Washers	¼-inch ID (inside diameter)
	⁷⁄₁₆-inch ID

Supplementary to this list are many special items that might or might not be stocked, depending upon the personal style of the shop carpenter's construction techniques. Such items as lag screws and machine bolts are sometimes used under special conditions. Corrugated fasteners, wire brads and nails, screw eyes, eye bolts, and decorative-headed tacks are often needed.

Stage Hardware • The necessary portability of scenery leads to the use of many pieces of hardware made especially for the stage. Most of it is designed to brace, stiffen, and temporarily join units of scenery as well as provide rigging hardware for the flying of scenery (Figure 6–26).

Stage hardware has been broken down into categories that relate to their function:

Stiffening hardware. The *loose-pin back-flap hinge* is used to attach a horizontal stiffening member to the back of two or more units of scenery. A *keeper hook* over the toggle rails of two or more units can receive a horizontal stiffener.

Bracing hardware. An adjustable stage-brace hooks into a *brace cleat* to function as a vertical brace. A *strap hinge* is used to brace and hold a door frame in position. A *hinged foot iron* and a *bent foot iron* with a stage peg secures the bottom of a unit of scenery for better bracing. There are two types of *stage screws.* The first has bolt threading to screw into a pre-set plug. The second is the traditional *stage screw* or peg as it is sometimes referred to. A *straight foot iron* is sometimes found on the

Figure 6-26
Stage Hardware

LOOSE PIN
BACK-FLAP HINGE

BATTEN
HOOK

BRACE CLEAT

STRAP HINGE

HINGED FOOT IRON   BENT FOOT IRON

STRAIGHT FOOT IRON

STAGE SCREW
AND PLUG

STAGE SCREW

FLOOR STAY

LASH
CLEAT

STOP
CLEAT

PICTURE
HANGER

HOOK AND EYE

LASH
EYE

TURN BUTTON

LASH
HOOK

TURN BUCKLE

CYC KNUCKLE

CABLE
CLAMP

STRAIGHT HANGER IRON

SQUARE PLATE&RING

HOOKED HANGER IRON

PLATE AND D RING

SHACKLE BOLT

SWIVEL EYE
SNAP HOOK

CEILING PLATE

bottom of a jack, which is a hinged brace. A *floor stay* is designed to hook over the bottom batten of a drop.

Joining hardware. To lash two flats together is one method of joining. Shown are a *lash cleat* and a *lash eye.* Both are attached to a style of a flat. The lash line is fastened to the eye and hooks around alternating lash cleats. The *stop cleat* holds flats together in a corner lash. A *lash hook* is used when there is not enough space for a lash cleat. The *picture hanger* and *socket* is used for fastening a picture to a toggle rail or picture batten. The *hook and eye,* although not strong, is a quick way to make a joint as is the *turn button.*

Rigging hardware. As the name suggests this hardware is used in the flying of framed or soft scenery. A *straight hanger iron* is used at the top of a framed unit of scenery while a *hooked hanger iron* is used on the bottom. Attached to the bottom hanger iron is a *turn buckle* to adjust the trim of the hanging piece.

The following are various types of plates and rings for hanging scenery flat such as a ceiling: A *square plate and ring;* an *oblong plate and D-ring;* a *ceiling plate;* and a *cable clamp,* used to fasten cable after passing through a hanger ring. A *shackle bolt* is designed to grip and bolt through a horizontal member. A *cyc knuckle* slips along a pipe batten to support an arm of a cloth cyclorama. A *swivel-eye snap hook* provides a quick means of attaching and detaching a light load.

Rope, Cable, and Chains

A number of specific types of rope, chain, and cable are important in the rigging and joining of scenery. A listing of their specification and uses on the stage follows. Rope used in the theatre is of two general types: cotton braid and stranded manila. The cotton braided rope is softer, easier to handle, more flexible, but of course not as strong as the stranded manila rope.

COTTON BRAID ROPE
No. 8 sash cord—used as *lash line, lightweight rigging,* and as an occasional *draw line* on a lightweight traveler.
No. 10 braided rope—*draw line* for heavy traveler track.
1/8-inch awning cord—lightweight *curtain rigging* and *trick line* to trigger a mechanical effect from an offstage position.

MANILA ROPE
3/4-inch three-strand manilas—*purchase line* of counterweight system (see Chapter 7) and heavy rigging line.
1/2-inch, 3/8-inch manila—lightweight *rigging, breasting,* and *bridling.*

Wire rope or cable is used to hang scenery when the supporting wires will be in view. The wire rope is very strong for its small diameter and can inconspicuously support a fairly large unit of scenery. The types of wire rope used most frequently in the theatre are aircraft cable, tiller rope, and hoisting rope.

AIRCRAFT CABLE
1/32-, 1/16-, 1/8-inch—nearly invisible at a distance, very strong for size, flexible but expensive.

TILLER ROPE (6 BY 42)
1/8-inch (smallest diameter)—strong, flexible, and less expensive.

HOISTING ROPE (6 BY 19)
1/4-inch (smallest diameter)—extremely strong, less flexible, and not too expensive for its weight.

Chain, outside of instances of special rigging, is used primarily as *weight for stage draperies.*

JACK CHAIN
1/2-, 3/4-inch (single or double)—*curtain weight.*

Constructing Scenery

Scene designers and technicians are interested in the construction of scenery not only to become familiar with building techniques but also to become aware of the uses and limitations of various materials. The more they know about present-day theatrical materials and techniques the better they are able to introduce new materials and original methods into designs as well as to develop a knowledgeable use of contemporary types of scenery.

TYPES OF SCENERY

Scenery construction may seem at first glance to be unduly flimsy and unnecessarily complicated. This is due, chiefly, to the unique demands placed upon scenery by the theatre. First, it must be portable and lightweight in structure so as to move easily on the stage and from theatre to theatre. Second, scenery has to be able to assume large-scale proportions for either decorative or masking reasons. Therefore, large areas of scenery must be furnished with the minimum of structure and the maximum of portability. And last, because scenery is here today and gone tomorrow, its construction must be economical. To be economical does not necessarily mean to buy the cheapest materials. It means to balance costs against the weight and structural demands of a material. It also implies the economical use of scenery. Higher material costs can be afforded if a scenic element has more than one use or can be reused at a later date.

For the purpose of discussing construction techniques, the various types of scenery are divided into groups that are similar in construction and alike in function as well as related in handling methods. Scenery is broadly divided first into two general classifications: two-dimensional and three-dimensional.

Two-dimensional scenery, under this broad division, is meant to include all flat scenery with reference to its basic shape rather than to the way it is used on the stage. Although units of flat scenery, for example, may be assembled together to make a three-dimensional form on the stage, the individual pieces are still classified as two-dimensional scenery.

Two-dimensional scenery is further subdivided into two groups: framed and unframed, or soft, scenery. Within these two groupings falls the bulk of the scenery that is used on the stage either in the form of stage draperies and drops or wings and flats.

Three-dimensional scenery obviously refers to the pieces that are built in three dimensions to be handled and used as solid forms. Some three-dimensional units, particularly platforms, knock down into smaller, nearly flat, pieces for ease of handling, but, because of their weight and use, they are still classified as three-dimensional scenery.

Three-dimensional scenery is also separated into two basic groups: weight-bearing solids, meaning the weight of the actor, and nonweight-bearing forms. Steps and platforms are examples of weight-bearing scenery as compared to such nonweight-bearing examples as tree trunks, logs, and the like.

SOFT-SCENERY CONSTRUCTION

Such large unframed pieces as stage draperies, the drop, and the cyclorama, or "cyc," are counted as soft scenery. They all have the same function, to provide a large area of scenery with a minimum of construction and a maximum of portability. Being soft, they are dependent upon hanging from a batten or pipe for support. As a result they can be easily folded or rolled for transportation or storage.

Stage Draperies

The large panels of stage draperies are made by sewing small widths of materials together with vertical seams. There are three sound reasons for using vertical seams. First, because the direction of the weave or decoration is with the length of the fabric, it hangs and looks better in a vertical position. Second, a vertical seam is less conspicuous because it is lost in the folds of the drapery. Third, there is less strain on a vertical than on a horizontal seam, which carries the cumulative weight of each width of material from the bottom seam to the top.

The seams are face to face to present a smooth front surface. The top is reinforced with a 3- to 4-inch webbing through which are set the grommet rings at 1-foot intervals for the tielines. The bottom has a generous hem containing a chain that functions as a weight for the curtain. Occasionally, the chain is encased in a separate sound-deadening pocket that is sewn on the backside of the drapery instead of being enclosed directly in the hem.

Drapery fabrics may be sewn on the top webbing or may be gathered or pleated onto the webbing to give a fixed fullness to the curtain. Fixed fullness is an advantage for a front curtain or traveler curtain. However, it is not as flexible as a flat curtain panel, because the latter can be hung either flat or with varying degrees of fullness in a greater variety of uses (Figure 7–1).

a   b   c

BORDER

LEG   PANEL

Figure 7-1
Stage Draperies

(a) Flat drapery construction. Webbing with grommets and tie-lines at top; hem enclosing chain weight at bottom. (b) Gathered drapery. Fullness gathered on top webbing; chain pocket attached above hem at the bottom. (c) Types of stage draperies: border, leg, panel.

Drapery Materials • Stage draperies can be made of a variety of fabrics, depending upon the specific use they are to serve and the limitations of the budget. Are the draperies to be opaque, translucent, or transparent? Are they to be pictorial, decorative, or just masking? Are they to be stock draperies or a one-shot special effect? Answering such questions helps decide the kind of material to choose and its relationship to cost and use.

Velour, although expensive, is the favored drapery material. Its pile weave has a rich texture under the stage lights that cannot be duplicated with cheaper substitutes. It hangs and drapes beautifully and is also easy to maintain, handle, and store. Among the more-economical velour substitutes which bear mentioning are duvetyn and flannel.

Duvetyn is almost as opaque as velour but drapes poorly and lacks as rich a surface quality. Flannel drapes a little better than duvetyn, and it has almost the same opacity. Its woolly nap surface has a fair texture under stage lights.

Stage draperies are made of other materials not with the intention of imitating velour but to create their own effect. Cotton rep and monk's cloth have enough texture to make an interesting inexpensive curtain when hung in fullness. Wide-ribbed corduroy is another drapery texture, which though semi-opaque, drapes and hangs well.

Sometimes draperies are expected to be translucent or, on occasion, transparent. Dyed muslin is the least-expensive translucent fabric. It has a further advantage of coming in wider widths than such materials as satin or nylon crepe in the translucent class.

Gauze, the general term applied to all transparent materials, is available in a variety of fabrics such as cotton or nylon net, chiffon, and organdy, to name a few familiar commercial textiles. Although these fabrics are available at the local dry-goods store, their chief disadvantage

NET

BOBINETTE

SHARK'S-TOOTH SCRIM

Figure 7-2
Gauzes

The three basic gauze materials: net, bobinette, and scrim are illustrated to show their difference in weave. Net, square weave. A larger mesh (1 inch) is knotted like a fish net. Loose, tabby-weave materials are sometimes called gauze. The fabric, which looks like surgical gauze, has very little strength. Bobinette, hexagonal weave. Very transparent and strong, but stretches out of shape easily. Shark's-tooth scrim, ladder weave. Strong, not as sheer as bobinette; best for dye painting

is their narrow width, which increases the number of seams in a curtain. The seams become visible when the transparent curtain is back-lighted. There are gauzes, as well as muslins, that are woven on wide looms especially for theatre use. Bobbinet and shark's-tooth scrim, two transparent materials, are made in 30-foot widths. Bobbinet is a hexagonal net that is more sheer but weaker than shark's-tooth scrim, which has a rectangular or ladder pattern. The shark's-tooth, in addition to draping well, is dense enough to provide a dye-painting surface and still become transparent when back-lighted.

Drops

Another large-area piece of scenery is the drop, taking its name from the fact that it hangs on a batten and is dropped in, as opposed to the older method of the shutter that slid on stage from opposite sides. The drop is made with horizontal face-to-face seams to create a smooth surface. The horizontal seams, when the drop is hanging, are under enough tension from the weight of the material and bottom batten to stretch into a smooth surface. A drop can be made to fold or roll depending upon whether it is to be translucent or opaque.

A translucent drop is dye-painted and can be equipped with tielines at the top and tielines or a pipe pocket at the bottom. The position of the seams of a translucent drop are important, because if they are not carefully hidden in the design they produce a distracting shadow line. For this reason, translucent drops are sometimes made with vertical seams and with irregular spacing, or, if the budget permits, they are made seamless by using 30-foot-width muslin.

Since opaque scene paint is used on a regular opaque drop or a drop with opaque areas, it cannot be folded and therefore is rolled on the bottom batten. The opaque drop has a top and a bottom batten. Its construction and shape variations are shown in Figure 7–3.

Drops are commonly made of muslin because it is available in wide widths and is an excellent inexpensive translucent material. Drops are

a

DOUBLE TOP BATTEN

FACE TO FACE SEAM

DOUBLE BOTTOM BATTEN

b

WEBBING WITH GROMMETS & TIE LINES

NET

PIPE IN PIPE SLEEVE

PIPE BATTEN

Figure 7-3
Drop Construction

(a) Rear view of a roll drop. (1) Top batten, double 1 x 4. (2) Face-to-face horizontal seam. (3) Bottom batten, doubles 2 inches half round. (b) Rear view of a folding drop. (1) Top webbing with grommets and tie-lines. (2) Netting glued over openings or cut edges to support loose ends. (3) Drop bottom with pipe sleeve for the removal of bottom batten. (4) Drop bottom made with grommets and tie-lines. (c) Types of drops: (1) Plain back drop. (2) Cut border. (3) Cut drop, netted. (4) Leg drop. (5) Also referred to as leg drop or leg.

c

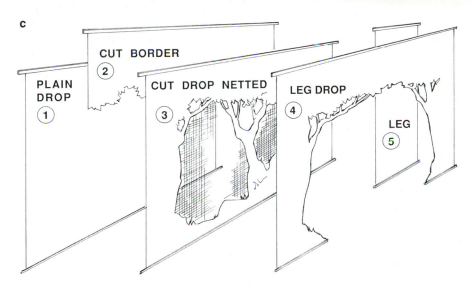

CUT BORDER
(2)

PLAIN DROP
(1)

CUT DROP NETTED
(3)

LEG DROP
(4)

LEG
(5)

sometimes made of other materials, frequently for an unusual textural quality, such as burlap, velour, and terry cloth. And, of course, drops can be made of the gauze materials. Shark's-tooth and bobbinet are used more often than other sheer fabrics because they come in wider widths.

The cut-drop in Figure 7–3c is often backed with bobbinet or scrim more for a lighting effect than for strength. The cut edges of a drop or border are better supported with a special lightweight net that has a 1-inch-square mesh. When the net is dyed to match the background it becomes nearly invisible.

The Cyclorama

The largest single piece of scenery in the theatre is the cyclorama or "cyc." As the name implies, it encircles or partially encloses the scene to form the background. The cyclorama's most familiar use is as a sky or void backing a setting or elements of scenery placed in the foreground. Because the flat center of the cyclorama blends into the sides in a gentle arc, it cannot be made on rigid battens like the drop can. It is kept soft by using dyed material that is fastened by the tielines to a curved top-and-bottom batten of pipe.

A cyclorama is not always a sky or void. Occasionally it is painted with a decorative or pictorial scene to fit a specific show. Sometimes, stage draperies are hung in the same position to form a drapery cyclorama.

The sky cyclorama presents the greatest problem in its necessity to create a large, uninterrupted, smooth surface. Because the "cyc" material, dyed or dye-painted canvas, is hung flat without fullness from a curved batten, the direction of the seams becomes important. If the seams are horizontal the tension on the seams draws the surface smooth, but the resulting strain distorts the shape of the curve as the seams turn the corner.

Vertical seams round the corners better than the horizontal seams, but they do not present as smooth a finished surface. In both cases the seams are sure to show under a high level of illumination. This can be corrected by hanging a large flat panel of dyed (very light blue) shark's-tooth scrim directly in front of the canvas cyclorama, using the same batten. Because it is a wide material the number of vertical seams can be reduced to two on the normal cyclorama. The scrim becomes the reflecting surface and the canvas acts as a backing (Figure 7–4).

FRAMED SCENERY

The structure of framed scenery is planned to support itself in a standing position. Although a framed piece may be aided by hanging support, or may be flown altogether, the basic framing principle remains the same. Framed scenery, as a construction technique, does not lend itself easily to the framing of a large area. It is possible to develop the framing for a large area, but to do this, it has to be hinged to fold into a smaller size or be dismantled into smaller parts to move in and out of the theatre. Most framing, then, deals with relatively small modules when compared to the large sizes of unframed scenery.

Wood Joints

Scenery construction, although special in its framing techniques, employs the normal methods of joining wood. The various wood joints are derived from the many ways of combining lumber surfaces. The surfaces of lumber are described as its face (flat surface), edge, and end. The surface-joining combinations are classified as end to end, face to face, end to face, edge to end, edge to face, and edge to edge.

The making of a joint has two steps: first, the cutting and fitting of the joint; and second, the securing of the joint with hardware or glue. In scenery construction the joint is not always fixed but is many times

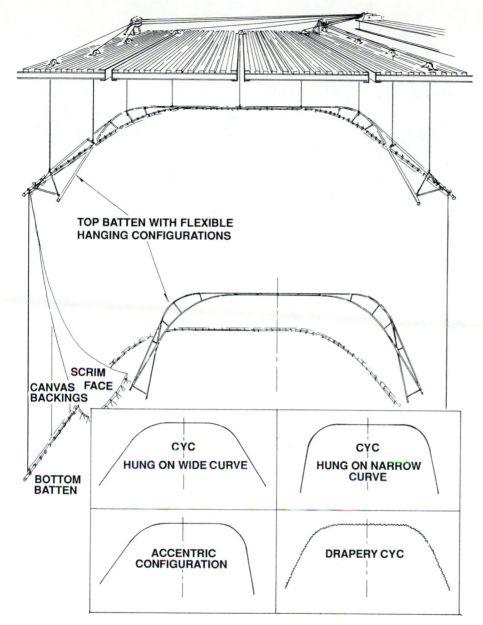

Figure 7-4
The Cyclorama
Rigging, construction and hanging
patterns.

TOP BATTEN WITH FLEXIBLE
HANGING CONFIGURATIONS

SCRIM
CANVAS FACE
BACKINGS

BOTTOM
BATTEN

CYC
HUNG ON WIDE CURVE

CYC
HUNG ON NARROW
CURVE

ACCENTRIC
CONFIGURATION

DRAPERY CYC

temporarily secured or hinged. The fixed or permanent joint is used on
standard-sized units of scenery, or smaller. The knockdown or temporary
joints are used on oversized pieces that must be dismantled to get in and
out of the theatre.

Figure 7–5 illustrates the numerous joints used in scenery construction classified in groups that combine the same surfaces. Fixed joints are
secured with nails, clout nails (soft nails that clinch on the opposite side
of the joint), screws, and glue. Knockdown or temporary joints are held
with bolts, loose-pin hinges, keeper hooks, pegs, and turn buttons.

SURFACE JOINING COMBINATIONS

Figure 7-5
Typical Wood Joints Used in Scenery Construction

BUTT JOINTS

CORNER BLOCK

KEYSTONE BLOCK

SHOE

NOTCHED

D

EDGE TO END

BLOCKED   **MORTIS & TENON**   **MITERED**

BUTT JOINTS

E

EDGE TO FACE

BLOCKED REVEAL   **LOOSE-PIN STIFFENER**   **DADO**   **DADO**   **NOTCHED**

PLANKING

F

EDGE TO EDGE

BUTT   **TONGUE & GROOVE**   **SHIPLAP**   **NOTCHED**

Figure 7-6
Framed Scenery

The framing of a simple flat illustrates the basic technique that is applied to any size or irregular shape (Figure 7–6). The area is enclosed with a lightweight frame of 1-by-3 white-pine lumber. The face of the lumber is kept flat in one plane, causing end-to-edge butt joints at the corners. In this way, the wide surfaces of the framing boards are in position to support the canvas which is tacked to the inside edge of the outer frame and then pasted down. The end-to-edge joint is strengthened by one of two methods, or both. The joint can be mortised and tenoned with glue or a simple butt joint reinforced with a ¼-inch three-ply plate or corner block. The mortise and tenon, although a stronger joint, takes longer to cut because it requires special power machinery or special attachments. It also reduces the amount of lumber that can be salvaged if the scenery undergoes remodeling. Unless the scenery is going to be subjected to excessive handling, the butt-joint keystone and corner-block method provides a simple, sturdy joint.

Toggle rails and diagonal braces are the internal members that function to strengthen and hold square the rectangular shape. A rectangle is basically a weak structure and can be very easily racked out of shape. The triangle, on the other hand, is very rigid and resists a change of shape. Hence, two diagonal braces off one side of the rectangle will resist a change of shape. Bracing on opposite corners, however, is not as strong and can be racked out of shape (Figure 7–6).

Toggle rails should be spaced at about 5-foot 6-inch intervals unless a *shoe* is being used which allows a greater distance between toggles.

Framing Curved Scenery

The framing of a curved surface requires a different technique. All framing members are on edge rather than flat. The toggles are *sweeps* cut to the curve of the surface. The surface covering must be firm yet be able to bend such as luan board (⅛-inch ply) or easy curve. Scenery canvas is glued to the finished form to provide a matching surface to the rest of the scenery (Figure 7–7).

The Framed Drop

As mentioned earlier, it is possible to frame a large area of scenery. The framed drop and ceiling piece are examples of this technique. They use a droplike construction except that the battens are single instead of double and therefore are made of heavier lumber stock (1-by-4 or 1⅛-by-4). The top and bottom battens are held apart by stretcher bars at about 6- to 8-foot intervals. They are bolted by means of ceiling plates to the battens. The loose ends of the drop are laced around the two end stretchers (Figure 7–9). A ceiling piece is made in the same manner, but will of course hang flat instead of vertically like the drop. Both the drop and ceiling fold and roll on their battens when the stretchers are removed.

Doors

Doors and windows are those important details that are often neglected in the haste of preparing a set. A door, in a sense, is a moving piece of scenery that is used by the actor. In a split second, its malfunction cannot only give away the scenic illusion but can also break up the carefully built-up mood of a scene.

The building and hanging of a door is a skilled and time-consuming job. For these reasons, the average amateur group is better off to make or have made a set of good stock door casings that can be used in a variety of ways.

In the making of a door the normal scenery-framing techniques are often too lightweight. There was a time when the audience would accept a canvas door painted to look like oak planking but sounding and handling like a screen door. The modern audience, schooled by years of

REAR VIEW

SWEEP-TOGGLE

Figure 7-7
Framing Curved Scenery
The styles are 1x3 lumber on edge separated by curved toggle rails or *sweeps*, also on edge. The curved surface, inside or out, is of ⅛-inch plywood covered with scenery canvas to provide a matching paint surface.

Figure 7-8
Types of Framed Scenery

(a) The framing of a set-piece with profile edges of three ply. (b) Detail of sill iron used across the bottom of a door opening in a flat. (c) Detail of canvas-covering technique. Note that tacks or staples are set on the inside edge of the external framework. The loose outside edge of canvas is then pasted to the flat surface of the frame. (d) Flat with profile edges, of three ply. (e) Door flat. (f) Window flat. (g) Two-fold flat with double-door opening. Note hinged sill iron.

movie and television realism, is jarred by this obvious theatricality. There is a limit, however, to the weight of a door that can be supported in framed scenery that does not have the solidity of the stud framing or masonry it is simulating. Hence it is necessary to reach a compromise in a construction technique that will keep the door portable and light-weight enough to shift while at the same time achieving a degree of solidity and sturdiness for the action.

A door unit is made up of three basic parts: (1) the actual door, some-times called "shutter"; (2) the reveal, comprised of the jambs (vertical members), header (top), and sill (bottom); (3) the trim, which forms the decorative frame around the door opening. The door is always hinged to

Figure 7-9
The Framed Drop and Roll Ceiling
(a) Rear view of a framed drop. Notice how the canvas is laced around the ends and through the openings. The canvas is permanently attached to the top and bottom battens. The vertical stretchers and braces are removable. (b) Rear view of a roll ceiling which is very similar to the framed drop in construction. (1) Detail of ceiling plate on the end of the stretcher. The stretcher is bolted to the two battens. (2) Same technique used on the diagonal brace. (3) Detail of lacing. (4) To roll, stretchers are removed and battens are brought together, face to face. (5) Ceiling rolled on battens.

the reveal. The trim, however, is constructed in one of two ways: it may be attached to the reveal, or it may be kept as a separate member and applied to the face of the flat. The first method, called a "cased door," is a complete unit. With the trim permanently attached to the reveal, the reveal of the cased door assembly slides through a prepared opening in the flat which is considerably larger than the size of the door itself (Figure 7–10a).

In the second method, referred to as a "scene door," the trim is not attached to the reveal, which is built to the exact size of the flat opening. The reveal, containing the shutter, "butt fits" to the opening from behind (Figure 7–10b). The scene door provides a great deal more flexibility in the ways the trim can be handled. It can, for example, be completely painted or attached and set away from the opening to increase the apparent size of the doorway (Figure 7–11a).

The action of a door affects its construction. For example, a door that swings onstage requires double facing; a double-action door (kitchen door) takes special hinging as does a Dutch door; sliding doors involve tracking; and additional rigging becomes necessary for the trick door that, as if by magic, opens and closes by itself.

Windows

Similar to the door, a window has a reveal and trim, but the window sash takes the place of the door. The arrangements of panes within the sash varies with the style of the window. Because the window sash is

Figure 7-10
Stock Door Construction

(a) Cased-door unit. (1) Door reveal and trim built as one unit. (2) Flat with a standard door opening. (3) Detail of door construction. (4) Angled strap hinge on jamb to hold door unit in the opening. (5) Blocks to hold trim in place. (6) Cross section of door unit through the header. (7) Plan of the cased-door unit showing the hinging. (8) Butt hinge on door. (b) Scene-door unit. (1) Separate trim. (2) Flat with a standard door opening. (3) Door and reveal. (4) Corner blocks to hold reveal frame square. (5) Rim lock. Attached on back side of door. (6) Tubular latch. Sets into edge of door.

more open than a door, it is difficult to build. The pattern of the thin mullions often becomes too fragile for normal stage framing unless the window is far enough upstage to fake them in profile board. Delicate tracery is frequently reinforced by a backing of galvanized screening that passes for glass and strengthens the mullions at the same time. To simulate glass, panes are sometimes left clear or backed with netting. The net, although nearly invisible, has enough density to give the feeling of glass. It is more apparent by contrast if the window is opened during the action of the play. Real glass or plexiglass is difficult to use on the stage because of the reflection of the many stage lights.

Figure 7-11
Variations in Door Trim and Paneling

(a) Various methods of handling the trim around the same-size door opening, possible with a scene-door unit. (1) Wide-set trim. (2) Close-set and high trim with transom. (3) Painted trim. (b) Door paneling. The paneling for (2), (3), and (4) are all constructed within the basic paneling of a stock door (1). (5) The flush side of a stock door painted and cleated to look like a planked door.

Figure 7-12
Window Construction

(a) Double-hung window. Trim is attached to reveal in the same manner as the cased door.
(b) Casement window. The reveal is constructed in the same way as the scene door with hinged sashes.
(1) A bent T-strap hinge in place of the butt hinge. (2) Notched mullions.
(3) Galvanized screening to strengthen the sash and simulate glass.

a

b

Figure 7-13
Cornice Construction

A cornice is a lightly framed three-dimensional element of trim designed to attach along the length of a wall. The perspective view shows the block-framing technique and a method of attaching the cornice to the scenery.

CORNICE
PROFILE

CROWN

BLOCK

FACE

BASE
SUPPORT

BED
MOULDING

BOLT

STIFFENER

SET
WALL

Window action, like that of the door, involves sliding or swinging on hinges. A window may have the vertical sliding action of a double-hung window, or slide horizontally. It may have the vertical hinging of a casement window or the horizontal hinging of the awning-type window.

It is a little more difficult to plan a set of stock windows than doors because of the greater variation in sash styles. Certain often-used, conventionally styled windows can be standardized and put into stock. Also the casing (reveal and trim) may be kept in stock to be used with interchangeable or new sashes for each show (Figure 7–12).

Trim

Decorative trim appears in a set in places other than around door and window openings. Some additional areas of trim, painted or practical, are baseboards, chair rails, wainscoting, cornices, and overmantel decoration. Trim that is attached in these areas must be removable so the flat scenery will fold easily.

The attached trim requires additional framing within the flat for support. Chair rails and baseboards are easy to attach but the construction and hanging of a cornice is more complicated. Although trim details are slightly oversized for the stage, the average cornice can be made up of stock moldings. To keep the framing lightweight, the molding is nailed to blocks set at about 2-foot intervals and backed with 3-ply or longitudinal framing strips. The whole assembly is attached to the wall flats with bolts or turnbuttons (Figure 7–13).

THREE-DIMENSIONAL SCENERY

Weight-Bearing Structures

Certain elements of scenery cannot be reduced to flat planes. Others, because they are so small, are more practically built as three-dimensional forms. This is especially important if the form is to bear the weight of a sitting or standing actor. Weight-bearing structures are present in such architectural forms as steps, ramps, and raised levels; in the irregular forms of rocks; and in the free form of an abstract design. The raising of a large portion of the stage floor and the use of steps and ramps brings excitement to the design composition, variation to the staging, and headaches to the stage technician. In the absence of any mechanical means of raising sections of the stage floor, the problem becomes one of creating a second floor at a specific distance above the stage floor. The level must be structurally sound enough to support actors and furniture with a minimum of deflection and, at the same time, be portable and economical. A large expanse of platforming is subdivided into smaller units for ease of handling. A single unit is made to knock down into even smaller parts.

The Parallel • The familiar way of providing a raised level for the stage is the parallel method. The parallel is a hinged trestle structure that opens to support a top and folds into a flat pack when not in use (Figure 7–14).

As a stock platforming method, the parallel has the advantage of being lightweight, easy to assemble and transport, and fairly sturdy. It also can

Figure 7-14
The Parallel Platform

(a) Basic parallel construction with open-corner hinging. (1) Top ¾-inch 5-ply with cleats. Typical trestle framing includes (2) top rail bearing on (3) the post, tied by (4) the bottom rail, and strengthened by (5) the diagonal brace. The framing may be joined either by (6) corner blocks or (7) by mortise-and-tenon joints. (b) The parallel technique used on a slanted platform or ramp.

be adapted to irregular shapes as well as to the conventional rectangle. Its chief disadvantage is a storage problem. To maintain any variation in levels, duplicate sets of parallels of different heights have to be kept in storage.

A convenient stock size for regular-shaped parallels depends first upon general handling and storage conditions; second, the construction of the top; and last, the riser heights of stock steps that work with the platforms.

If the top is to be made of ¾-inch 5 ply, a 4-by-8-foot top is the most economical size. Planked tops, however, can be made smaller or larger without material waste if space permits the storage of larger parallels.

PLATFORM PIN

(4)

PIN TO HINGE
(5)

CORNER
(6)

(7)

CORNER

FOOT
(8)

SPACER
(2)

(1)

(4)

(3) FOOT

(9)

EXTENDED FOOT

(5)

(3)

(1)
TOP
d

c

b

a

Figure 7-15
Other Platforming Techniques
(a) Post-and-rail method which knocks down into individual 2 x 3 units. (b) Detail of post-and-rail corner bolting. (c) Scaffold method. (1) Tubular steel or aluminum scaffold unit. (2) Spacer to interlock units. (3) Foot. (4) Cross braces to space and stabilize scaffold units. (5) The stacking of one scaffold unit upon another to gain height. (d) Steel parallel method. A smaller moduled tubular steel and angle iron-framed parallel. (1) Top overhangs unit to allow for facing flat. (2) Spacer to interlock and stack units. (3) Corners become hinges. (4) Pin attached to top to lock it in place. (5) Internal pin of hinge corner made up of (6) opened-end trestle and (7) closed-end trestle. (8) Foot. (9) Extended foot.

    Stock parallel heights, obviously, should be at intervals related to riser heights of the steps, 6- or 7-inch intervals being normal. Parallel heights usually vary at double-riser intervals such as 12-, 24-, and 36-inch, or 14-, 28-, and 42-inch intervals.

    There have been various attempts to standardize platforming construction with the aim to cut down the size of stored parts, to reduce the amount of internal framing (by using material other than wood), and at the same time to provide a sound structure. The post-and-rail and scaffolding methods (Figure 7–15) are ventures in this direction. Both succeed in reducing the storage space of spare parts and each provides a very sturdy platform with a minimum of framing. The techniques, although very practicable for regular shapes, do not lend themselves readily to irregular shapes. The limits placed upon design, however, are minor when compared to the stage-space and sightline limitations imposed by some theatre buildings.

Steel pipe and aluminum tubing have been used as platforming materials in two different methods. The first method involves the adaptation of construction scaffolding for stage uses. Each scaffold unit is made out of aluminum tubing and at heights of 1 to 3 feet at 1-foot intervals. Figure 7–15c illustrates how the various heights of scaffolds interlock, or stack, one on top of the other. Each set has its own system of cross bracing.

A more recent use of pipe for platforming is in the parallel method (Figure 7–15d). The unique feature of the design is the making of the corner into its own hinge. The unit takes a 4-foot-square top that is overhung 1 inch for a facing flat.

Other examples of steel in platform framing involves the use of manufactured shapes of structural steel. The shapes are designed to interlock and bolt together. Figure 7–16 illustrates the use of the Unistrut channel, and the Telspar and Dexion slotted angles as platform. Dexion, with its slotted flat angles, offers ample surfaces for combining wood with steel in platform construction.

Regardless of whichever type of platforming is favored, the parallel method is, like the framing of a plane flat, an example of basic structural framing. With this basic knowledge the carpenter can modify or embellish the technique to fit all special needs.

Platform Construction • Any platforming technique can be resolved into the three structural members that are always present in some form or other: they are the top, rail, and post. The top, which is the actual bearing surface, is directly supported by the rails. Crossrails run parallel to the shortest dimension of the level. Their interval is linked to the material and thickness of the top. The average top, made of 1-by-6 tongue-and-groove planking or ¾-inch 5-ply board, should be supported at 30-inch intervals. The span, however, can be increased by use of cleats or stiffeners on the underside and thereby, in effect, increase the thickness of the top material.

The rail is, in turn, supported by the post. The interval of posting is dependent upon the size of the rail. A 1-by-3 rail (on edge) should be posted at not more than 3-foot intervals and at 4-foot intervals for a 1-by-4 rail.

The framing of a single trestle or "gate" of a parallel employs the post-and-rail technique. In Figure 7–14a note that the top rail is borne by the two vertical members, or posts, which carry through to the floor. The bottom rail is merely a tie-rail that completes the rectangle. The diagonals are necessary to hold the gate square and eliminate side sway or "rack" in the finished platform. The single gate, though lightweight, gathers strength when it is hinged to the other members of the parallel. The parallel to fold flat must hinge as shown.

Any irregular shape that can be reduced to flat planes may be constructed by the parallel method. The gates can be loose-pin-hinged together rather than folding, for many times the pattern of the supports is so irregular the parallel cannot fold flat (Figure 7–17).

Figure 7-16
Platforming Techniques Using Preformed Steel

(a) Commercial preformed steel shapes. (1) Unistrut channel. (2) Three types of Telspar, a telescoping square pipe shape manufactured by Unistrut Corporation. (3) Dexion, a slotted angle iron also made in bar and channel shapes. (b) A corner view of a platforming technique using Unistrut channel as the basic corner post. Longer extensions of optional lengths are attached with stock Unistrut fittings and cross bracing. (c) Slotted angle framing with a basic post of slotted channel. Iron pipe is used as the extension. (d) Slotted angle framing with a slotted channel or Telspar basic post. The extension is Telspar. *Drawing after designs by Philip Eck and Ned Bowman*

Truss Construction • A truss is a lightweight framing system which is designed to counter the same stress-forces as those of a beam. Truss framing involves two long horizontal members, top and bottom, and a series of vertical posts spotted at intervals to hold the members apart. The framing is completed by inserting a diagonal at each interval.

The stress-forces on a beam or beam-type structures can be illustrated with an exaggerated stress condition by placing the beam in an unstable condition. As the beam sags the top face is under compression while the bottom face is in tension.

The stress-forces within a truss are similar. When the top member is compressed in a horizontal direction, the bottom member is in tension. The vertical members are compressed and the diagonals are also in tension (Figure 7–18).

Figure 7-17
The Irregular-shaped Platform

(a) The hinging and assembly of an irregular-shaped platform are solved individually. (b) To fold: (1) Loose-pin-hinged internal trestle is detached after top (2) has been removed. (3) By unpinning the hinges of one corner, the parallel will fold into a flat pack. (c) The use of a "spanner" allows the removal of internal trestles in cases where it is necessary to keep the area under the top clear. (1) Spanner is of heavy enough stock, usually 2 x 4 or 2 x 6, to make strong span. (2) Detail of keeper-hook on end of spanner.

Figure 7-18
Truss Construction
A lightweight framing designed to
function as a beam or joist. (a) A
beam in unstable condition to
illustrate the direction of stress-
forces. (b) Simple truss showing
direction of stress-forces. (c) Truss
technique for steel joist. (d) Bridge
truss hidden in the railing of a
scenic bridge.

A long single truss has a tendency to torque or twist. As a result, a long span has to be stiffened with a second truss, forming a box truss. Repeated trusses, when used as a joist, are bridged or cross braced.

Free Forms • The irregular surfaces that cannot be reduced to a series of flat planes have to be constructed as a three-dimensional unit. Rock pieces and abstract forms that have to bear weight are examples of this type of irregular surface.

The framing of an irregular surface is, of course, more or less extemporaneous and dependent upon some final sculptural touches by the designer to complete the form. For this reason the design drawings of a free

Figure 7-19
Construction of Rock Forms
(Right) (1) Shape of form on floor.
Conventional framing. (2) Contour
pieces. (3) Cross bracing. (4) Wire
screening. (5) Burlap. (Photo, left)
Three-dimensional shape before
covering with burlap. (Right) Same
shape covered.

form should be accompanied by a scaled model. The form usually suggests the manner of construction; nevertheless there is a basic method that can be adapted to most irregular shapes.

The method of construction of a rock piece demonstrated in Figure 7–19 goes through the following steps: (1) The exact shape of the base of the rock is framed in the conventional flat-scenery technique. (2) Across the shortest dimension of the base is set a series of contour pieces that follow the contour of a section taken at that point (see "Sections," Chapter 5). (3) The contour pieces are stiffened with cross bracing and all bearing surfaces are reinforced. (4) Over the contour pieces is placed 1-inch chicken wire or ½-inch screen wire, which is pinched or stretched in the desired shape. (5) The final surface is applied to the screen wire. The kind of covering material depends upon the nature of the texture that is desired. The best results are usually obtained with burlap. It is applied by first dipping it into a mixture of strong glue size and base color. The burlap is then draped over and tacked to the framework and allowed to harden. A form made in this manner is lightweight, inexpensive, and surprisingly sturdy.

Ramps • The parallel as a platforming technique can also be adapted to a ramped surface (Figure 7–14b). The side trestles are built to the angle of the incline. Gates of varying heights connect the outside trestles and are hinged to fold like a regular parallel.

Steps • Whereas the ramp is a gradual change of level, the step is more direct, dividing the change into a series of intermediate levels. A flight of steps is made up of risers and treads. The tread is the bearing surface and the riser is the interval of change in level. The rule of thumb guiding the size relationship of the tread to the riser is based upon the ease of movement up and down the steps. The sum of the riser and tread in a continuous flight of steps is kept about 18 inches. Hence a 6-inch riser would require a 12-inch tread; an 8-inch riser a 10-inch tread, and so forth. Obviously the low-riser and wide-tread combination is more desirable for the onstage steps, permitting the actor to move easily and gracefully up and down.

A flight of steps can be built for the stage in one of two ways. One method is a modified platform trestle construction with each tread supported by a complicated post-and-rail framework (Figure 7–15a). This way the steps are a part of a bulky three-dimensional platform that is difficult to store and move.

Steps can be made to knock down into more easily handled parts by the use of the cut-carriage method of construction (Figure 7–20b). The pattern of the riser and tread is cut from a wide board running parallel to a line drawn through the nosing of each step. The nosing is at the intersection of the top of the riser and the outside edge of the tread.

A carriage is cut from a wide enough board to retain at least 3 inches of uncut board along the bottom edge. The thickness of a carriage depends somewhat on its unsupported length. Frequently 1⅛-inch pine stock is used, chiefly for its lightness as well as strength. Sometimes 1-inch pine stock is substituted for lightweight construction while 2-inch stock is used for a heavier structure.

Figure 7-20
Stair Construction Techniques

(a) Trestle method. (1) Trestle with the top edge framed to riser-tread pattern. (2) Three ply used as riser stock. (b) Cut-carriage method. (1) Carriage cut to riser tread pattern. Step unit leans on platform for support. (c) Closed-carriage method. (1) Closed carriage can only be used on the outside of stair unit, hence this type of construction limits the width of the stairs. (2) Cleat to hold tread. Note that no riser is used. (d) Cut-carriage method used on an irregular-shaped flight of steps. (1) Carriages with same riser height but varying tread dimensions. (e) Stair facing, framed out of 1⅛-inch baluster stock (1) which is pin-hinged to steps (2). If both faces are covered with 3 ply (3), the facing unit becomes reversible with minimum alterations.

The choice of carriage stock is also affected by the nature of the riser material. Is the riser made of 1-inch pine or ¼-inch 3-ply or is it left open? As the riser material becomes lighter, the carriage stock should increase in thickness.

A flight of steps would have, of course, two carriages. Additional carriages would depend upon the thickness of the tread and the width of the steps. For example, a ¾-inch-thick tread would need a carriage every 30 inches of width.

The lower step of the carriage sits on the floor and the top step rests on a prepared cleat fastened on the front of a platform, thus eliminating the need of a post underneath. The steps, or carriage unit, can be lifted off the cleat to be handled and stored separately.

The facing of stairs (also levels) is a separate piece of scenery attached to the downstage edge of the step or platform. The facing of a stair is a more complicated unit because it includes the stair rail, balusters, stringer, and newel post (Figure 7–20e). The stringer, which parallels the carriage, supports the bottom ends of the balusters. It can be an "open stringer," revealing the tread and risers, or it may be a "closed stringer," masking the ends of the steps with an uncut surface.

The railing completes the stair facing. It spaces the top ends of the balusters while being supported by them. The whole assembly of the stair-facing flat and steps must be kept to a practical size or it can become too large to handle.

Stress-skin Panels • The stress-skin technique sandwiches a paper honeycomb core between two plywood sheets. A wooden outside edge completes the panel. A hollow-core flush door is a stress-skin panel.

To adapt the technique to theatre use, the plywood skin is increased to ½ inch and is glued to a 4-inch paper honeycomb. The outside edge is increased to a 2-by-4 inch thickness (Figure 7-21).

Stress-skin panels are used commercially as roofing material thereby allowing rafter spacing to increase to 4 feet.

1/2" 5 PLY TOP & BOTTOM

1 1/2" STOCK SIDES

PAPER HONEYCOMB INTERIOR

Figure 7-21
Stress Skin Panel

Nonweight-Bearing Structures

Columns, tree trunks, and any other objects that have to have dimension but do not bear weight form the last type of scenery. Since these kinds of structures need only be strong enough to hold their shape, framing is lightweight in comparison to weight-bearing structures.

An irregular shape is built in three dimensions by the use of two structural elements: the basic silhouette of the object and numerous contour pieces. In a tree trunk, for example, the basic silhouette is the vertical outline of the trunk and branches. The contour pieces are spaced at intervals perpendicular to the silhouette frame. After sufficient bracing and stiffening, the form of the trunk is rounded into shape by attaching chicken wire or wire screening over the contour pieces (Figure 7–22a). The chicken wire is covered with burlap or canvas for the finished surface.

In a rock, the basic silhouette is horizontal and the contour pieces are vertical, which, as has been mentioned, can become structural if the rock has to bear weight.

Figure 7-22
Construction of Columns and Tree Trunks

Columns have regular shapes and lend themselves to a slightly different construction method. It is not necessary to use a silhouette piece. The circular or semicircular contour pieces can be attached to a central core or be held at intervals by slats on the outer surface (Figure 7–22b).

The exterior surface of the column can be handled in two different ways. The surface can be made up of thin vertical slats (best for a column with a taper or entasis) that are covered with canvas after all of the slats have been rounded with a plane or rasp.

The column can also be covered with a flexible paperlike ⅛-inch EZ curve, or for a temporary column, heavy building paper can be used. When a light exterior covering is used, the amount of bracing between contour pieces has to be increased to stiffen the column.

TEXTURED AND SCULPTURED SURFACES

Designers are always fascinated by a deeply textured surface. It reacts well under stage lights and gives the scenery a feeling of authenticity and stability. A deeply textured surface like the stone wall in Figure 7–23 is usually accomplished by using the laborious technique of applied papier-mâché. New plastic foams and forming techniques have made it easier to texture a surface or to create sculptural relief, architectural details, and many three-dimensional forms.

Rigid Foams

The demand for greater perfection in the design and construction of decorative details on both properties and small elements of scenery, which grew out of the intimacy of the thrust and arena theatres, has led to easier methods of simulating a sculpture form. The closeness to the audience, the increased amount of handling, and the change of design focus from scenic background to set properties are the basic influences on new theatre forms.

Styrofoam, the trade name of Dow Chemical's low-density rigid polystyrene foam (RPF), has been used successfully as a lightweight material that is easy to carve into three-dimensional details or textured surfaces. Blocks of Styrofoam can be glued together or to a scenery surface for convenient carving.

Regular Styrofoam is low-density and therefore very porous. This limits detailed carving and reduces its strength. *Urethane* is a high-density, rigid foam (RUF) that, because of its high density, is easier to carve in detail or turn on a lathe. It also has greater strength than a low-density foam.

Sections of rigid or flexible foams can be glued to reinforcing wood or adjacent surfaces with Illbruck Adhesive PA–02. Hyde glue is a good second choice.

Sculpture surfaces can be primed with casein paint or flexible glue and then finished with scenery paint. For an extremely hard finish the surface can be coated with a mixture of fiberglass resin and hardener in about five-to-one proportions. Further uses and techniques can be seen in Chapter 11.

Both foams, of course, are very lightweight and many times have to be counterweighted or attached to heavier units of scenery to maintain

Figure 7-23
Three-dimensional Surface

Shown are the steps in the construction of a highly textured surface such as a stone wall. (1) Hard undersurface, either ⅛ plywood, upson board, or double-faced corrugated cardboard, shellacked to reduce warpage. (2) Surface is diagramed into areas representing the shape of each stone. Cutout appliqués of corrugated board are helpful in reaching a desirable composition. (3) Each stone surface is built up with glue-soaked newspaper or rough-hewn Styrofoam. (4) Individual stone is covered with a square of cheesecloth to give it its final form. (5) After the covering has dried, the entire surface is covered with a thick coat of texture paint and then painted.

Figure 7-24
Carved and Turned Rigid Foam
(Far left) Turned rigid urethane foam: left, baluster with wooden core: right, turned finial. (Left) Relief carving, Styrofoam, sealed with flexible glue, finished with casein paint. (Below) Sculptured Styrofoam and mulched wood embedded in polyurethane foam with welded iron cyclone fencing. *Oedipus Rex* by Stravinsky/Cocteau. Final ritual masks were each 9 to 12 feet high. The set measured 54 feet at the highest point. Designer—John Ezell.

the proper esthetics. Nothing is more disconcerting than to see a supposedly quarter-ton Greek statue bounce like a ping-pong ball if accidentally knocked over.

Ethafoam rod is a commercial insulation material. It is a flexible, closed-cell foam-extruded rod in various diameters of ½ inch to 2 inches. It can be easily cut with a knife or saw into half-round and glued to a surface as a decorative relief or curved molding. It covers best with a vinyl or acrylic paint.

Foam Casting

If a sculptural element or decorative detail recurs several times on a set it is often better to prepare a mold and cast the detail to ensure a matching likeness. The mixing and casting of a polyether or urethane foam into a negative mold is the easiest method. It brings together two chemicals that produce a rigid foam of considerable strength and stability.

The chemicals are described by the supplier, IASCO (Industrial Arts Supply Co.), as, first, a Prepolymer A and, second, a Resin-Catalyst B. When mixed in equal parts they provide a rigid polyether foam.

Flexible Foam • The application of relief detail on a curved or flexible surface requires a flexible foam. IASCO's Isofoam F is a flexible urethane foam that serves this function. There is, however, a new flexible foam known as *Hydrofoam,* which is a hydrophilic polyurethane prepolymer that has the unique property of being formed with the addition of *water.* Different densities of foam are obtained by varying the amount of water.

All foams should be mixed in a disposable container such as a No. 10 can, beaten with a high-speed mixer for about thirty seconds. The creamy mixture is then poured into a hollow mold, the surface of which has been sealed with shellac and coated with paraffin or a prepared parting agent. If it is necessary to delay the action, Acetone is a solvent before the foam sets-up. The foam can be demolded in about thirty minutes (Figure 7–25).

|||▶ *SAFETY PRACTICE*

Because the chemical action in all foam systems is highly toxic, precaution should be taken to ensure proper ventilation and protection of the hands. The use of a respirator mask and disposable surgical gloves is strongly recommended. Any contact of the foam chemicals with skin should be washed with soap and water immediately.

Foam Texture

Polyurethane foam applied under pressure hardens into an interesting deep-textured surface. Two chemicals are brought together under pressure inside a spray gun and mixed in the air as they are shot onto a surface, where the mixture foams into a bubbly texture in a matter of seconds. To control the chemical proportions that establish the density of the foam requires a high-compression tank, specific spray gun and nozzles (two hoses), and the necessary valves and gauges to vary the

B
RESIN-CATALYST

A
PREPOLYMER

MIXING

POUR MIXTURE INTO MOLD

① ② ④ ⑤

SAFETY EQUIPMENT

CAST FORMS

POUR MIXTURE INTO MOLD

③ ⑤

CAST FORM

Figure 7-25
Foam Casting

Demonstrating one of the many forms plastic foam casting can take. Drawings show the steps taken to duplicate various forms of bakery goods. (1) Mixing IASCO's Prepolymer (A) with a Resin-Catalyst (B) in equal parts. (2) Mixture is stirred vigorously for about 30 seconds. (3) Mixture poured into hollow mold prepared with parting agent. (4) Mixing tool and a visual reminder of mixing precautions, disposable surgical gloves and respirator mask. (5) After liquid foam expands into the mold (about 20 minutes) the casting is removed from the mold. With the excess foam cut away, the foam is ready for painting. Photo: bakery shop full of foam cast bakery goods, *Cyrano de Bergerac*, Guthrie Theatre. Designer—John Jensen. *Photo courtesy Kewley*

quantity of chemical from each tank. If all of the above equipment is not available, it is easier to use *Insta-Foam,* a trade name for aerosol urethane foam in a disposable kit form.

Although developed for the building trades, Insta-Foam is adaptable for stage use. Insta-Foam, manufactured by Insta-Foam Products, Inc., is sold in a variety of mixtures for specific commercial uses and construction techniques. The Insta-Foam *Froth-Pak* in the Standard Foam mixture is ideal for the textured surface just described. The kit consists of two aerosol tanks of chemicals, two hoses to a mixing spray gun, and a variety of nozzles. The several nozzles not only give a selection of distribution (fan to round), but are also expendable. The nozzles clog with hardened foam very quickly if work is stopped for any length of time and have to be replaced. The chemical content of the two tanks is Polymeric Isocyanates in the first and Polyops with Amines and Fluorocarbons in the second.

||||⮕ *SAFETY PRACTICE*

Insta-Foam is toxic and thus the mixing process should be performed only in a well-ventilated room. Prolonged breathing of the vapors or spray mist should be avoided. The empty tanks should be vented, the valves removed with caution, and the chemicals drained. An unvented aerosol tank can be dangerous if handled carelessly or if stored near heat (over 120° F). Safe storage for full tanks is 60° to 80° F.

Figure 7-26
Foam Texture

(a) Froth-Pak mixing nozzles and foam spray in action. (b) Detail of texture finished and ready to paint. (c) Foam texture and welded metal sculpture for *The Song of the Lusitanian Bogey*, by Peter Weiss. Designer—Dessis McCarthy.

a

b

c

Insta-Foam will adhere firmly to any surface except polyethylene (a transparent filmlike plastic called Vis-queen, which, incidentally, can be used as a parting agent or separator between units of scenery). After it has hardened, the foam can be painted with dye or scene paint. For added texture, materials or objects can be imbedded and held by the foam. The hardened foam is quite durable and compares in density and hardness to high-density rigid urethane foam. It will withstand normal handling on the stage but would have to be handled with care were it to go on tour.

Thermoplastics

Another method for the shaping of three-dimensional details such as arabesques, props, masks, armorplate, or the duplication of real objects is the vacuum forming of sheet plastic. Formerly a manufacturing technique that was out of reach of the average scenery shop, it is fast becoming an important construction method for those hard-to-execute details. Thanks to detailed research by Nicholas L. Bryson on thermoplastic scenery (see "Additional Reading on Technical Production" in the Appendix) the trial-and-error approach has been taken out of the process.

The chemical structure of a thermoplastic is such that when heated it loses its rigid state and becomes ductile. While it is in this pliant condition it can be reshaped or stretched over a positive (or negative) mold, then allowed to cool and return to a hardened state. The fact that

Figure 7-27
Thermoplastics
The cut-away drawing of a vacuum-forming machine suitable for a scenery shop. (1) The oven has slanted metal sides with asbestos lining. The floor of the oven is covered with a pattern of coiled resistor wire forming a heating element. (2) Plastic sheet in angle-iron frame. (3) Frame is hinged to swing off of the oven and onto the mold and forming table when the plastic sheet is ductile. (4) Forming table. Floor is pierced with ⅛-inch holes spaced at 1-inch intervals to vent the vacuum chamber underneath. (5) Mold. (6) Vacuum chamber. (7) Bleed valve; can be rigged for pedal action. (8) Gauge reading inches of mercury. (9) Air hose or pipe to reservoir tank. (10) Vacuum pump. (11) Reservoir tank. The photograph is of a vacuum-forming machine suitable for piecework and original designing but not mass production. Note that the reservoir tank is made of wood. It is reinforced internally to resist pressure or sealed on the outside with canvas, flexible glue, polyethylene, mastic, and enamel paint. *Constructed after designs by N. L. Bryson, by Les Zellan*

a true thermoplastic can be reheated and reshaped without a discernible change in its physical properties makes it economically feasible for theatre use.

Of the many thermoplastics available there are three that seem best suited for use in the theatre. They must be opaque, translucent, or transparent, have a selection of color or take paint and dyes, be noncombustible, and be strong enough to withstand normal handling onstage and the mechanics of fastening (nailing, stapling, and so on). The three thermoplastics meeting these requirements are high-impact polystyrene, low-density polyethylene, and cellulose acetate. The working thickness need not be greater than .0040″ (40 thousandths of an inch); it depends on how rigid or flexible the final form is meant to be.

High-impact polystyrene, as the name implies, has a high impact strength, great flexibility for intricate forming, a wide range of colors, and is obtainable in opaque or translucent sheets.

Low-density polyethylene is also tough and flexible. It is normally milky white (no colors) and opaque, but turns translucent when heated and formed.

Cellulose acetate is a well-known plastic with excellent forming characteristics. It is also very sturdy with the distinct difference of being completely transparent.

Vacuum Forming

The heated thermoplastic sheet, in order to take an accurate impression copy of the mold, must be tightly drawn or sucked by a vacuum around the form. The process is called vacuum forming. The basic steps of vacuum forming are: (1) Heat the plastic sheet uniformly to the temperature that renders it flexible (750–1000° F). (2) Transfer it quickly to a forming table where it is stretched over the mold and its edges clamped to the table in an airtight seal. (3) The air is removed through the forming table by a vacuum tank and pump, thereby sucking the heated plastic sheet over the mold. (4) Allow the plastic to cool and harden into its new shape. (5) Break seal and remove the plastic form for trimming, painting, and attaching to scenery, costume, or any other formed unit.

The use of a reservoir tank permits a rather rapid vacuuming action that is necessary or the plastic will cool and return to a rigid state. The pump then recovers the vacuum in the tank while the next sheet of plastic is being heated. Figure 7–28 illustrates the various components that make up a vacuum-forming machine.

Heat Gun • There are some additional tools that are useful accessories to the thermoplastic-forming process. The heat gun, which is capable of delivering a blast of hot air (750–1000° F) from an enclosed heating element and turbo fan, is used at close range to soften portions of the plastic sheet that may not have taken to the mold accurately.

|||➡ *SAFETY PRACTICE*

When cutting ridged urethane or Styrofoam, certain precautions should be followed. Because the heat of *hot wire cutting* releases toxic gases, prolonged cutting should be well ventilated with the operator wearing a respirator mask.

Shaping rigid foam with sandpaper creates an irritating dust. A nose mask is excellent protection.

Figure 7-28
Thermoplastic Forms

A few of the many architectural and decorative details that can be vacuum formed for use on the stage setting. (Above left) A cornice section. In this category, column capitals and bases, pilasters and panel molding can be included. (Above right) Open grill work, split baluster, and decorative details. (Right) Low relief panel decoration. Additional thermoplastic forms can be seen in Figure 11-10.

Figure 7-29
Fabrication of Rigid Foam

Armor has fiberglass under form. A
one-to-one mix of 16-pound density
IASCO rigid foam to build pea-pod
form, caskets, gauntlets, and details.
Latex and graphite surface with
paper-doily appliqué as decorative
detail. *Armor and photo courtesy
Jim Bakkom*

Figure 7-30
Cast Plastics

This altar for *Oedipus the King* was
designed to look like an oversized,
polished half of a geode. The top
surface is made of layers of tinted
Clear-cast, a clear polyester
available at local craft shops,
supported on a hollow frame of
wooden ribs with a Celastic
covering. The crusty edge is
modeled fiberglass resin and
Cab-o-sil (formed silica), an inert
powder that gives the mixture body
for modeling. *Photo courtesy
Bakkom*

Welding Gun • Similar to the heat gun, the hot-air welding gun produces a fine jet of hot air (400–700° F) that, when directed at a seam or thermoplastic welding rod, can weld plastic sheets or plastic forms together. Because the welding gun needs a jet flow of air it has to operate from an air compressor.

Hot-Wire Cutter • Although not used in the thermoplastic process, the hot-wire cutter is a handy tool for cutting and shaping rigid foam. Both the table hot-wire cutter and the hand cutter using the flexible wire loop (Figure 7–31) are useful to cut large blocks and to carve small forms. The wire loop is made of a high-resistance wire conductor (Chromel or Nichrome resistor wire). The wire's resistance generates enough heat to melt the rigid foam, thus enabling it to cut the block cleanly and quickly.

Figure 7-31
Hot Wire Cutters

Table and hand hot wire cutters for sculpting rigid foams. (1) Nichrome resistance wire. (2) Low-voltage, high-amperage transformer (about 16 amperes). (3) Adjustable arm to facilitate the cutting of large blocks of foam. (Left drawing) Table hot wire cutter rigged to shape molding. (4) Nichrome wire bent into the shape of the molding. (5) Strip of styrene foam or rigid urethane foam. (6) Fence guide clamped to table top. Photo: hand hot wire cutter.

Figure 7-32
Commercial Vacuum Forming of Stage Products
Shown are process pictures of the more sophisticated vacuum-forming equipment developed in the Tobins Lake Studios for the mass production of stage properties, armor, and architectural elements. Although this special equipment is capable of producing more than the average scenery shop, the studio's output is still far short of commercial manufacturing production. (a) View of forming table. Note overhead oven. (b) Plastic sheet in place over molds. (c) After the "pull" with the oven raised. (d) The making of a permanent mold to withstand the heat and pressure of numerous pulls. A fresh pull from the prototype is used as a negative mold. It is backed with sand for stability. (e) The negative mold is filled with epoxy resin sometimes loaded with aluminum to save weight. The final mold is drilled with a pattern of small holes to improve the suction of the pull. (f) Storage shelves of permanent molds.

Other three-dimensional forming techniques such as fiberglass, Celastic, and the like are discussed in Chapter 11, because they relate to properties, furniture, and costume accessories.

MIRROR SURFACES

Highly reflective surfaces and optical mirror surfaces have always fascinated the scene designer as a theatrical effect. Until the mylar surface entered the theatre, large mirrors were heavy and awkward to handle. A mylar mirror surface, when rigidly mounted or tightly stretched, provides the reflection optics of a real mirror that is lightweight and easy to handle.

Silver Shrink Mirror

This technique utilizes a vinyl-backed reflective surface designed to be tacked to a frame and then shrunk with heat to a smooth mirrorlike surface. The heat source can be a normal portable electric heater or a heat gun. The 54-inch width of the material, however, limits the size of the individual frame. A full stage mirror, for example, would have to be made of several frames. However, if the planes of the frames are parallel, the divisions are not noticeable.

Scrim-Backed Mirror

This form of stage mirror is backed with a scrim instead of vinyl and thus has the added advantage of being transparent when lighted from behind. When stretched and heat-shrunk, it serves as a mirror surface, transparent scrim, or a rear projection screen.

Both mirror surfaces in silver or gold are available at Rosco Laboratories.

Color in the Theatre

8

The final step in the execution of the design, the painting of scenery, is yet to be discussed, but it is imperative to examine first the use of color in the theatre as it relates to painting, lighting, and the designing of scenery and costumes. This might be begun by asking the question "What is color?"

"Color is *light*," says the physicist when referring to the small visible portion of the electromagnetic spectrum. "Color is *paint*," replies the artist, "light merely reveals it." "Color is in the *eye*," says the physiologist, "for no two people see color in the same way and some are color-blind." "Color is in the *mind*," the psychologist insists, to explain why some experience color with their eyes closed or in their dreams. All these attributes, of course, are present in any color experience. To these the artist in the theatre might add, as a part of its creative use, critical analysis and emotional response—the *philosophy* of color.

Although scenery, costume, and lighting designers desire knowledge of color to the same degree, they have slightly divergent interests in its use. The lighting designer, for example, is more involved with the physics of color, while the scene and costume designers are interested in the painting and dyeing of color as well as the manipulation of colored materials. Whatever the final use of color may be, each designer has need of the same knowledge of color, for eventually all areas of design must come together onstage to form the total visual effect. The beginning designer in the theatre must be aware of the separate uses of color and seek a color explanation that satisfies both the use of color as light and as paint.

It can be seen that any explanation of color in the theatre must, therefore, involve not only the separate study of color in light and color in pigment but also the integration of the two in an inclusive definition.

It is important that all workers in the theatre understand at least the basic terminology of color to be able to communicate in the language of color.

THE LANGUAGE OF COLOR

It is always difficult to talk or write about color, for words trigger individual images and do not convey accurate information. There are, however, a few terms that are so much a part of the description of a color that it is impractical to converse without knowing their meanings.

The three variants of color, *hue, value,* and *chroma,* are the most familiar terms used to describe a specific color. All will be discussed and illustrated in detail later, but briefly one can describe a color by hue identification (red, yellow, and so on); value level, or the black-to-white relationship of a color; and the degree of chroma or freedom from neutralization by mixture with another hue.

Within the framework of these variants an elusive color can be described in simple semiscientific terms by referring to its hue, degree of chroma, and value level. In normal communication their use brings to mind a more consistent image of a specific color than would the use of such emotionally charged labels as "blushing pink" or "passionate purple." Because descriptive labels are so firmly a part of the advertising and merchandising of color in fabric, paint, and the light-color medium, a designer soon learns to translate them into more communicative terms. A "chocolate" shade, for example, might be described more precisely as a spectrum orange neutralized to one-half chroma but retaining its normal low-light value position.

COLOR IN LIGHT

A basic knowledge of color begins with its presence in light. Without light there would be no color. Everyone has seen in some form or other the breaking up or refraction of sunlight into a spectrum of color. The refraction of sunlight through a bevel-edged window or in a rainbow are simple examples. The physicist with more precise laboratory prisms can produce an accurate spectrum with wavelength values for each hue and can explain the existence of these hues, from infrared to ultra-violet, as a visible part of the electromagnetic spectrum. This is the beginning of *hue,* the first variant of color (Plate 8–1).

Hue

The position of a color in the spectrum determines its hue. The number of hues that can be separated or identified as principal hues in the spectrum is arbitrary. Six easily identified hues are: *red* (R), *orange* (O), *yellow* (Y), *green* (G), *blue* (B), and *violet* (V). The expanding of the number of discernible hues depends upon their ultimate use or application in a color theory or system of color notation. The use of color by the artist, for example, is linked to a medium such as paint or dye. Light, on the other hand, is colored by passing it through stained glass or colored plastic. Because of the purity of the color mediums in light, it is possible to establish *light* primary hues.

A primary is a basic hue that is suitably located in the spectrum to mix secondary colors (see "Additive Mixing"). Red, green, and blue are light primary hues. The intermediate hues, or secondaries, are produced by mixing any pair of primary hues.

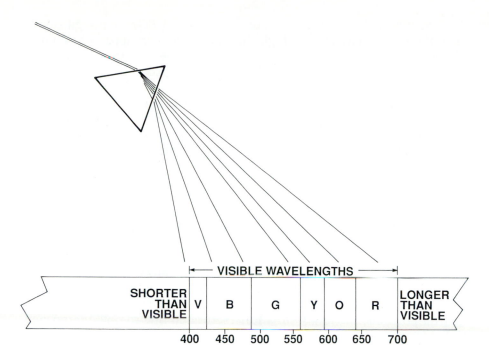

Figure 8-1
Spectrum and Six Basic Hues

It is important to mention at this point that mixing of paint as a color medium is not as accurate as the mixing of colors in light. It involves a different physical process, hence the painter requires a finer separation of spectrum hues to creatively mix and use color (see "Color in Paint").

Value

The light-to-dark relationship of a hue or mixed color is its value. The lighter values, nearer white, are known as *tints* and the darker values, approaching black, are referred to as *shades*. Both represent a variation from the true hue.

The use of value as a color variant or control is more the tool of the painter than of the lighting designer because of the necessarily greater range in pigment mixing. Subtle value differences are easier to accomplish in paint, particularly in the darker ranges, because in the use of colored light there is no black.

The number of steps in a value scale is arbitrary. The limiting factor is usually the ability of the eye to distinguish the difference between adjacent steps. Seven steps between black and white seem to be a comfortable number (Figure 8–2).

The value in the center of the scale is referred to as *medium* (*M*). The steps above *M* towards white are *low light* (*LL*), *light* (*L*), and *high light* (*HL*). Below *M* towards black is *high dark* (*HD*), *dark* (*D*), and *low dark* (*LD*). Within this range the artist can create form without the use of color.

Some hues come from the spectrum with a natural value difference. The light-to-dark difference of yellow and violet is the most extreme example. Other hues have less value difference and some, of course, are about equal (Plate 8–2). Hues that have little value difference, such as *RO* and *BG*, contrast each other with another force. They are *hue op-*

Figure 8-2
Value Steps

WHITE

HIGH LIGHT HL

LIGHT L

LOW LIGHT LL

MEDIUM M

HIGH DARK HD

DARK D

LOW DARK LD

BLACK SOLID

posites. When certain hue opposites like *RO* and *BG*, are placed side by side, the color contrast is so high that it produces an apparent vibration in the eye. This phenomenon involves both the physics and optics of color and will be discussed later, after all the aspects of color have been examined.

Hue opposites, however, do perform another function. When mixed in equal parts they tend to neutralize or offset each other. Hue opposites in light produce white, while their mixture in paint results in neutral tones. This change in the purity of a hue is the third variant of color, *chroma.*

Chroma

The instant the purity of a principal hue is modified, the change is referred to as a change of its chroma. The degree of pureness, or freedom from neutrality, like the value scale, can be measured in steps. The number of steps from pure hue to complete gray varies according to color theories. A very precise measuring and mixing method can produce a great number of steps. The artist, however, can see and work easily in quarter portions, moving from a fully saturated hue to one-quarter neutral through one half, then three-quarters to full neutrality. This serves merely as an explanation of chroma, and the artist is free to use more steps for a more subtle change.

It is interesting to note in Plate 8–3, which shows the value and chroma changes produced by the mixing of orange and blue hues, that when the value of either orange or blue is raised or lowered its chroma is also changed as the tint or shade becomes more neutral. On the other hand, the quarter steps on the direct horizontal line to the value scale represent a chroma change without a value drop. This is accomplished on the orange side by the proportional mixing of blue (the hue opposite or complement of orange) after it has been raised to the matching value of orange. In other words, it is possible to change the chroma of a hue without affecting its value, but it is impossible to change the value of a hue without modifying its chroma.

All neutralization can be accomplished, theoretically, by the use of black or white paint. It is possible under scientifically controlled conditions of paint manufacturing, but the scenic artist knows that certain opaque colors do not respond to mixing with black. The use of a complementary color to neutralize a hue gives the painter a chromatic neutral that has a little more life under the stage lights. The neutralization of a pigment hue or its modification by another color is due to the particular method of mixing colors in paint. When painters mix colors on the palette or in the bucket they are using *subtractive mixing.*

Color Mixing

Although hue, value, and chroma are theoretical variables of color, a designer must understand them also as a means to describe a color and use them to create new shades and match old ones. Color is varied by mixing. The two methods are *additive mixing* and *subtractive mixing.* While both methods effect hue changes, additive mixing also noticeably alters value, and subtractive mixing modifies chroma.

Additive Mixing • The blending of colored *light* from two or more sources is additive mixing. It is best demonstrated by the three overlapping fields of the light primary hues in Plate 8–2a. The additive mixing of the light primaries red, green, and blue produces, first, the secondaries. Green and blue cross to make a turquoise (*BG*); red and blue produce the light secondary magenta (*RV*), and red and green make an amber (*YO*). The white in the center is the additive mixing of all three primaries. Note that the additive mixing of two hues raises the value of the mixed color.

Figure 8–3 diagrams the physics of additive mixing of red (*R*) and blue (*B*). A single red color filter, for example, absorbs all other hues from the spectrum and transmits only red. When red rays overlap with light from a blue filter (see diagram) the colors are "added," resulting in a red-violet or magenta hue. The most spectacular example of additive mixing is the combination of two contrasting colors, for example, red and green. Their mixing produces a yellow or amber. (Note that the yellow and orange hues fall between red and green in the color spectrum.) The additive mixing of a secondary and primary hue, or of all three primary hues, results in a synthetic white. Remember that all colors resolve into white before being refracted into the color spectrum.

Primary and secondary hues are frequently used to light the actor. The favorite combination of Lavender and Bastard Amber, for example, are tints of primary blue and secondary amber. Medium Straw and Steel Blue, for example, are tints of complementary hues, blue and orange. The additive mixing of the two colors models the actor's face in a flattering white light than can be warmed (more red) or cooled (more blue) by changing the intensity of one of the spotlights (Plate 8–4b).

Subtractive Mixing • The opposite of additive mixing is subtractive mixing—the crossing or combining of color mediums in front of a single source of light. Plate 8–5 illustrates the effect of combining two color

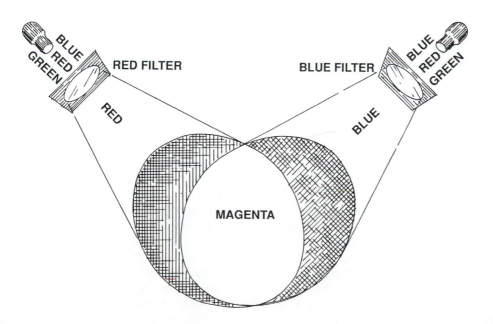

Figure 8-3
Additive Mixing

Light represented in its primaries—red, green and blue—is passed through a blue filter. Red and green are filtered out, resulting in a blue-colored light. Red filter absorbs green and blue, passing red. The fields of red and blue light overlap and additively mix a third, magenta. Magenta is red-violet raised in value because additive mixing raises the value of the mixed color.

Figure 8-4
Subtractive Mixing
The basic hues of light are passed through two successive color mediums, first red, then blue. All hues are absorbed and no color is transmitted.

mediums, blue-green and yellow, in front of a light source containing all the spectrum hues. The green color that is transmitted is the only hue not subtracted or filtered out of the light by the combined color mediums. It is not as visually apparent, but the same subtractive results are present when the artist mixes blue-green and yellow in paint.

Subtractive mixing in paint and light is characterized by a move toward neutrality and darker shades. This is particularly evident when the hues are complementary colors. It is understandable that the closer the color mediums are to hue opposites the less light can be transmitted until a block or point of negative transmission is reached. The mixing of complementary colors in paint results in a nearly black neutral for the same reason. Because painters use subtractive mixing most of the time, they have a slightly different attitude toward color than the lighting designer.

COLOR IN PAINT

Color in paint, of course, depends upon light to realize its physical properties. The color of a surface reaches the eye by the reflection of the light that is illuminating it. Just as a light color medium transmits a color by absorbing some spectrum hues and letting through others, so a colored surface reflects only the colors of the paint (Plate 8–6). These are the physical properties of a paint surface that begins with its coloring agent, pigment.

Pigment

The term *pigment* is an inclusive term that refers to the coloring agent in paints, dyes, and nature. It can be best explained as the chemical properties of color that create hue. At first, pigments came from natural sources; the indigo and madder plants are familiar examples. Minerals and semiprecious stones were also pulverized and made into pigments. The crude chemistry of the past established many of the traditional names of colors still used today, such as madder lake and indigo blue.

Colors, other than those found directly in nature, were often made synthetically from known minerals and their compounds. In the mid-nineteenth century, organic colors made their first appearance as organic dyes. Most present-day colors are a product of organic chemistry, which essentially deals with the carbon compounds. The names of organic colors often signify their chemical origin, such as chrome green, alizarin crimson, and calcium red.

Modern chemistry has given artists many new colors, which have allowed them to increase their palette. Because of the subtractive result of most paint mixing the painter cannot begin with a palette of primary hues to develop a full range of colors. The intermediate colors of combined primaries are not pure and do not relate to the spectrum hues. Hence, the painter prefers to begin with a larger palette that might include all the principal hues of the spectrum. While a small palette made up of the six principal colors already mentioned is usable, the scenic artist favors a palette of twelve principal colors for reasons of flexibility and economy.

Twelve Principal Hues • Beginning with the six original hues (red, orange, yellow, green, blue, and violet) six additional hues may be created through intermediate steps. The new hue thus formed takes its name from the two original hues on either side. The hue between yellow and orange, for example, would be *yellow-orange* and so on around the color wheel (Figure 8–5).

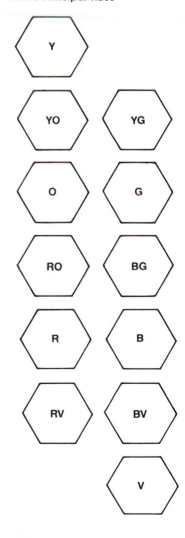

Figure 8-5
Twelve Principal Hues

The new intermediate color is not thought of as a paint mixture of the two adjacent colors but as a full chroma hue from the spectrum. The result is a working palette of twelve full-intensity hues that will reduce the degree of neutralization from subtractive mixing that might have occurred with a smaller palette. Some scenic artists even prefer a palette with more than twelve hues. Also, in certain situations, such as the commercial or industrial use of color, the number of principal colors may be expanded to 24 or more. In any event, the expansion is based on the twelve principal hues that become a basis of reference for individual use.

The Color Wheel

To better show the physical relationship of spectrum hues most color notation systems use a color wheel. The circular arrangement of colors brings into view the diametric and adjacent correlation of the twelve spectral hues and thus provides designers a schematic view of primary and secondary hue relationships as well as pairs of complementary colors that appear diametrically opposite each other around the wheel. A knowledge of complementary hues is not only necessary for mixing both light and pigment, but it also is important in composition. This is apparent in the choice of tints and shades in a production color scheme. Because color in light and pigment are constantly brought together in the theatre, they must be aligned in a compatible arrangement so that both have the same complementary colors (Figure 8–6).

Integrating Light and Pigment • The attempt to bring color in light and pigment into one system of notation is best illustrated in the color wheel. The steps taken toward the merger are shown in Figure 8–7. The light primaries and secondaries are represented in diagram *a* and the pigment primaries in *b*. Note that the complementary colors within each circle

Figure 8-6
Color Wheel

Twelve principal hues arranged in a circle or wheel. Diagonals are hue opposites or complementary colors.

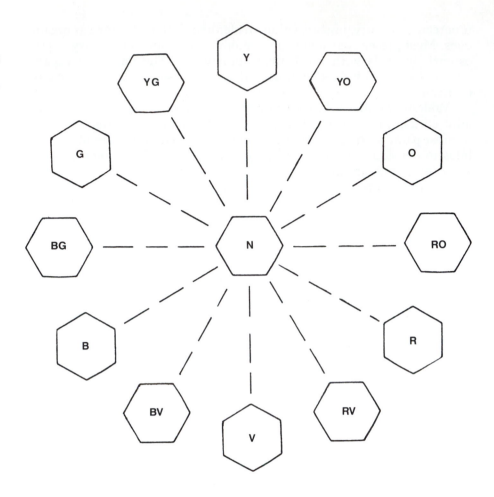

are different. The complement of blue in light, for example, is yellow, while its opposite in pigments is orange. To integrate light and pigment into one wheel, *c*, the light primaries have been moved slightly to fit into the pigment wheel. Light primary red becomes red-orange (*RO*), green a yellow-green (*YG*), and blue a blue-violet (*BV*). The maneuver also more accurately represents the light primary hues.

The Pigment Color Wheel • In addition to showing a contiguous relationship of the twelve principal colors, the pigment color wheel (Plate 8–7) also emphasizes hue opposites of complementary colors. The hues are full chroma and represent the basic pigment colors of the painter's palette.

Because most pigment mixing is subtractive, the gray tone in the center indicates the neutralizing effect of any pair of complementary colors. The many tints and shades resulting from the mixing of one pair of complementary hues, orange and blue, has been shown in Plate 8–3, where the flexible relationship between *chroma* and *value* was demonstrated. The subtlety of neutral shades and almost unlimited combinations of hues is the major advantage of subtractive mixing in pigments.

The Light Color Wheel • Although the conception is different, the arrangement of the twelve principal colors in the light wheel is the same as the pigment wheel. The primary, secondary, and intermediate colors are developed from the additive mixing of the light primaries. As the additive mixing of colored light tends to move toward white, the secondary and intermediate colors are therefore lighter in value than their companion colors in the pigment wheel.

The light color wheel in Plate 8–8 represents the interrelation of the colors in light with the twelve principal hues more than it indicates a complete range of colors in light. A full range of saturated color mediums of all spectrum hues is available for selective use.

Figure 8-7
Integrating Light and Pigment Colors

(a) Pigment primaries and complementary hues. (b) Light primaries and complementary hues. (c) Because true light primaries are described as red-orange, blue-violet and yellow-green they can be integrated into a single color wheel with both light and pigment now having the same complementary colors.

COLOR VISION

The source of color can be scientifically explained; the mixture of color can be diagrammed; and all the variants of color can be arranged in a system of notation. However, what the eye sees and the brain interprets is an individual color experience. Although the eye functions very much like a camera, it is not a scientific instrument. It receives light through its lens, which focuses the image or impression onto the layers of the retina in the inner eye. The innumerable nerve endings (rods and cones) of the retina culminate in the optic nerve, which carries the impression signal to the brain for interpretation. The impression is registered in terms of color and intensity (brightness); which, in a sense, is another way of saying hue and value. The eye sees value differences because of the variation of reflected intensities. Lighter pigment tints, for example, reflect more light (intensity) than do lower value shades. A few people can only distinguish value differences and not variations of hue. Because the greatest difference in hue falls in the middle of the value scale, most color-blind individuals cannot see the difference between red and green.

The eye's sensitivity to high and low levels of light affects the color we see. Since the rods of the retina, for example, produce most of the low level or night vision, their sensitivity to green-blue would tend to add a greenish-blue cast to all hues seen under a low level of light. Moonlight, for example, though it is the reflection of the sun greatly reduced in intensity, appears to have a blue tint. However, blue tint, as far as the brain is concerned, is a *color impression.* All this a designer has to consider within a stage composition. The high-intensity vision of the cones in the retina are more sensitive to yellow; the sun at noon, although a brilliant white, appears to have a yellowish tint. In a stage composition, however, there is a less-apparent shift in color under high intensities.

Intensity and Color Overload

The retina of the eye assimilates light energy. When it is saturated (isomerized), it is said to be *bleached.* Hence after any sudden change of intensity or color, the retina has to regenerate itself. This process takes place over a noticeable period of time. Since the rods are sensitive to *intensity* and the cones are sensitive to *color*, there is a difference in the time it takes the eye to readjust from a sudden intensity change than to a color change. It takes the eye about one to one and a half minutes to adjust in a blackout, for example (rod regeneration); while a color change (cone regeneration) may take as long as five minutes.

The time lag the eye experiences after a sudden change of color explains *after image,* a phenomenon of color vision. Until the eye has recovered, it retains an image of the object and a color impression long after the object has been removed or changed. The after image, however, is in the *complementary hue* of the original image color.

An ingenious demonstration of after image was immortalized in Diaghilev's Ballet Russe production of *Le Coq d'Or* with decor by Natalya Concharova. The first scene, a garden, was dominated by a brilliant red-orange tree. During twenty minutes of dancing the eye was saturated with an unbalanced color scheme; upon changing to the next scene the audience was reportedly plagued by a blue-green after image of the first-scene tree floating ethereally about the stage. The impression, of course, was in the eye of the beholder.

The phenomenon of after-image, or the color-balancing tendency of the eye, is present in another form. It was first referred to in 1886 as the *simultaneous contrast of color* by M.E. Chevreul, an early color theorist. In 1960, Joseph Albers called the same effect *interaction of color.*

The Interaction of Color • How a color reacts to an adjacent hue or to its background is known as the interaction of color. Certain reactions are painfully obvious while others are extremely subtle. The degree of color interplay is a critical element in the use of color by all stage designers. Aside from the mixing and creating of colors itself, the designer's choice and arrangement of colors become one of the most forceful elements in stimulating an emotional or intellectual response on the part of the audience.

The interaction of colors affects all variants of color. The *value* of a color can seem to change by juxtaposition; a neutral can be influenced by a surrounding color and appear to take on a *hue*; and the *chroma* of a color can be sharpened or deadened by its background. Plates 8–9, 10, and 11 are a few classic examples of obvious color interactions that have an influence on the designer's use of color or choice of a color scheme.

COLOR SENSATION

The experience of color includes elements of sensation or emotion as well. Designers in the theatre must be aware of the scope of this emotional response on the part of the audience (which is often subconscious) when they choose colors to establish a mood or specific atmosphere on the stage. The psychological effect of color, however, is difficult to measure. To some extent the designer must depend on a measurable individual response and hope it will multiply.

Most emotional response to color is conditioned by a lifetime of reaction to colors in nature and under natural light. We are repulsed, for example, by strong colors in light that produce unnatural flesh tones or discolor our food. We are also influenced by centuries of social and religious conventions that are buried deeply in the subconscious. Finally, we react to symbolism in color, some primal and others more contemporary (such as traffic lights and color-coded road signs).

The psychological description of a hue is, at best, very general. The emotional response to a color can be countered or modified by adjacent colors, as well as the color of the background. The intercolor experience, which involves both the psychological response and the physiological limitation of the eye, can also be tricked by an optical illusion. This phenomenon of fooling both the eye and the mind is dependable enough to be considered an important part of the impact of color on a theatre audience.

COLOR MANIPULATION

Some designers have an intuitive sense of color. The colors they put together seem right for the specific dramatic moment or atmospheric scene. A designer in the theatre, however, frequently has to suppress personal preferences to bring a color scheme into harmony or contrast with the colors in the show. To ensure the chances of a unified color solution, all designers—scenery, costume, and lighting—rely on advance color schemes to coordinate the final color impression.

With these psychological influences in mind—the natural, traditional, and symbolic sensations of color—we will attempt to describe the general emotional connotations attached to the six basic spectrum hues.

Yellow	Radiant, light-giving, golden, saintly; in light values near white, virginal.
Orange	Festive, earthy, peasant colors, neutral shades, nature in the fall.
Red	Active, passionate, full of inner warmth, fiery, strong, forceful.
Violet	Royal, piety, deeper shades, shadows, terror, chaos, a reddening color.
Blue	Passive, receding, deep, cool, purity, icy tints.
Green	Tranquility, compassion, nature in the spring and summer.

The Color Scheme

The development of a production color scheme may be as simple as deciding on the overall tonality of a single hue, or it may involve selecting a number of related or contrasting colors. The *harmony* or *contrast* of hues becomes the basic control of a production color scheme. The mood of the production is often expressed in the interrelationship of the colors in the scheme. Although the basic control is established in full chroma on the color wheel, all the variants of color (hue, value, and chroma) are called upon to provide interest and flexibility to the final colors in the composition. Aside from the obvious harmony of a *mono-chromatic* color scheme, which relies on the manipulation of the value and chroma of a single hue, various schemes can be created in terms of *chords* on the color wheel.

The Geometry of a Color Scheme

One way to develop a color scheme is to draw chords from color to color on the circumference of the wheel. A short chord system, of course, furnishes a closer interval between hues than a scheme of longer chords. As the interval grows longer hue contrasts will increase until hue opposites or a complementary scheme is reached.

To show a few of the unlimited color combinations enclosed in the geometry of the chords, Figure 8–8 demonstrates all of the possibilities on a single axis (yellow and violet). They vary from the close *harmony* of one hue to the vibrant *contrast* of a pair of complementary colors.

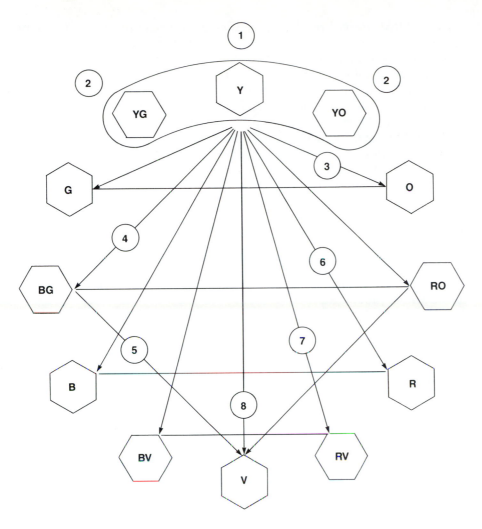

Figure 8-8
Color Chords
Various color schemes related to color wheel. Shown is one of the six complementary areas, yellow to violet. The various schemes are: (1) monochromatic; (2) analogous or neighboring colors; (3) third interval triad; (4) fourth interval triad; one pair of complementaries; (5) fourth interval quadrate; two pairs of complementaries; (6) fifth interval triad, primaries or secondaries; (7) split-complement triad; and (8) complementary. Although this chord is on the yellow-violet axis, it can be rotated to any of twelve other possibilities.

1. A *monochromatic* scheme. The natural high value of yellow limits its range. It can be neutralized into ochres, warmed with orange, and cooled with green to add variety to a one-color control.

2. An *analogous* scheme combines neighboring hues with the shortest chord into a harmonious scheme. The three hues in this example are yellow-orange, yellow, and yellow-green.

3. A *third interval* triad of hues derives from a triangle including yellow, orange, and green. The chord has lengthened, thereby increasing the interval between colors and providing slightly more contrast to the scheme (Plate 8–12).

4. The *fourth interval* scheme is first illustrated as a three-color combination—yellow, red-orange, and blue-green. A fourth interval chord always involves one pair of complementary colors, which increases the contrast of the scheme.

5. A *fourth interval* scheme is shown involving four colors. The quadrate of chords includes two pairs of complements when violet is added to the triad of yellow, red-orange, and blue-green. The designer can soften the contrast of the scheme by varying the value and chroma of one or all of the hues.

6. A *fifth interval* triad. The equilateral triangle of chords takes in the pigment primaries red, yellow, and blue as a scheme. The fifth interval scheme is not as obvious when the axis is between intermediate colors such as yellow-orange, red-violet, and blue-green.

7. *Split-complement* is a rather arbitrary selection of chords. It is usually used to soften the high contrast of a complementary scheme. In this example, yellow is in combination with red-violet and blue-violet, which flank the complementary hue, violet.

8. *Complementary* hues offer the highest contrast as a color scheme. The two-color scheme, yellow and violet, also have a high value contrast. The most vibrant pair of complementaries is red-orange and blue-green.

The Color Plot

The control of color within a composition is only a portion of the color planning that occurs in designing for the theatre. The color scheme for each setting of a multiscene play must also be considered in the content of the *whole* production.

Most scene designers use some form of a *color plot* to make preliminary studies of the entire production. Although it is a view of the show the audience will never see, it does serve as a color guide for the lighting and costume designers. Through the color plot the overall development of color can be studied. The functional relationship of connecting colors and hue accents is clearly visible. The progressive unfolding of color change within a scene or throughout a production, as well as moments of high contrast or subdued uniformity, can be demonstrated in the color plot.

The color plot is very important to the costume designer. It shows the overall relationship of all costumes in the production and enables the costume designer to plot small scenes and families of color that may help to visually define sympathetic characters and rival groups or individuals. The focus or center of attention in a large group scene can be planned as well as the control of the overall emotional impact or mood within the scene. The color plot also establishes the progression of colors from scene to scene and act to act.

A character's age and position in society (deacon, servant, master, and so on) can enter the color plot in the broad, symbolic statement of a single color note. The costume designer, however, frequently uses more than one color to note a single costume as a means of studying color accents and harmonies between characters. The costume color plot in Plate 8–13 illustrates in particolor swatches the color interaction and character relationship within Molière's *The Misanthrope*.

Color Modification

We have seen how color can be changed by mixing, influenced by interaction with other colors, and created by optical illusion. Surface color can also be modified by colored light. The constant use of colored light on a colored surface is unique to the theatre. Designers in the theatre not only have to consider the colors of a painted background, costumes, and other materials of a set, but also the colors of the lights that will reveal them. This is especially true if the lighting for the scene is unusual, such as a romantic moonlit scene or the flooding of the stage with red or green hues to provide an unnatural effect.

Fortunately, color modification is not quite as complicated as it seems. The effect of colored light on a colored surface is a result of subtractive mixing. In other words, if a red light is thrown on a yellow surface, the yellow is modified into orange tones.

The modification of a color in a costume or on scenery by colored light is a theatrical example of the joining of two color media, pigment and light. Designers in the theatre are constantly aware of how colored light and pigment influence each other. They are always prepared to compensate in either medium to create a natural effect or to deliberately cause dramatic reversals of color.

Color modification charts can be prepared for the reference of all designers in the theatre by systematically matching the shade of the modified color chit on the white-light side of the dividing shield of a testing apparatus similar to the setup indicated in Plate 8–14. If each of the twelve principal colors is subjected to the influence of at least the light primaries, a rather informative set of color notes is collected. It will be noted that when like hues are brought together, blue light on blue pigment, for example, the modified pigment hue is raised in value. This slight alteration of value is true of all alike color combinations. The degree of value change in a given situation depends upon the relative value of the background surrounding the color chit and the comparative intensity of the two light sources.

The chart will indicate the many possibilities under light primaries; however, unusual color combinations should be checked under the exact lighting conditions. Some designers prefer to use a miniature duplication of the planned stage lighting setup to check their color schemes and plan color effects. The consideration of the color of the stage lights is, of course, most important to the scene designer when preparing to paint the scenery.

Painting Scenery

Scenery painting is a highly skilled and specialized portion of creating a setting. It is also a very interesting and fascinating part of scene design and technical production. Most of the methods and techniques of handling scene paint are familiar to anyone with visual-arts training. The main difference between scenery painting and easel painting is one of scale. Instead of painting at a small drawing board, the scenic artist paints at life-size or larger.

Because the scale of scene painting is so large, the scenic artist uses a broad technique, sometimes so broad that what appears to be slaps and dashes up close does not take form until viewed from a distance. Learning to paint on a large scale and in broad technique is an easy adjustment for the visual artist. The uninitiated, however, should first become accomplished in handling watercolors in sketch form before attempting large-scale painting. Sketching and painting from still life or landscape not only improve student designers' drawing and painting ability but also increase their perception of light and color in nature. These processes also serve to underscore the significance of color as an element of design.

PAINT AND COLOR

The design of a setting can succeed or fail on the strength of the painting. Hence, the designer should carefully plan how the scenery is to be painted. The most important consideration is the use of color. A scene designer must be familiar not only with the mixing and use of pigments but also with the use of colored lights.

The prominence and forcefulness of color as an element of design was mentioned in Chapter 3. The attributes of the color experience and the philosophy of the use of color in the theatre were discussed in Chapter 8. The scenic artist or scene designer employs the same philosophy, terminology, and mixing procedures in the use of color for scenery as would any other visual artist.

Scene-Painting Palette

The scenic artist's first act is to create a working palette of scene paint that will relate to the twelve principal hues of the spectrum. The size of the palette will vary from at least twelve to many additional pigments depending on the individual artist's tastes and working methods; on pureness of hue and mixing behavior of the available pigments; and finally, on the relative cost of individual colors.

When designers choose their paint they must judge how the pigment color compares to the corresponding spectrum hue. If the paint sample does not match favorably in hue, value, and chroma, they may have to

---

Yellow

Light Chrome Yellow   A straight yellow, close to a primary hue. It is important to have a yellow with a sharp cut-off (minimum green or orange content).

Yellow Orange

Medium Chrome Yellow   Excellent yellow-orange hue. Not necessary to stock with light chrome yellow. Some painters, however, prefer stocking two yellows, warm (slight red content), and cool (slight blue content).

Orange

French Orange Mineral   Excellent spectrum hue. Heavy, therefore a little expensive.

Red Orange

American Vermilion   Brilliant red orange.
Bright Red   Also a brilliant red orange.

Red

Turkey Red Lake   Good red, slight yellow content.
Red   Close to spectrum red.
Dark Red   Deep red with blue content.

Red Violet

Magenta Lake   A brilliant bluish red, makes rich violets with blue. Expensive but goes a long way.

Violet and Blue Violet

Purple Lake   A rich, brilliant violet. Very expensive. Special, not necessary to stock with magenta lake at hand.

Blue

Cobalt Blue   A pure primary blue although a little high in value.

Ultramarine Blue	A rich blue with a touch of red content. Mixes well to make purples, but poorly for greens.

Blue Green

Italian Blue	A brilliant turquoise, although not a true blue green (high in value), it is a very useful color. Mixed with primrose yellow, it makes vibrant yellow greens and greens.
Celestial Blue	Dark turquoise.
Prussian Blue	Dark, rich blue green. Difficult mixer, good for near-black tones.

Green

Emerald Green	Intense green, slight yellow content.
Medium Chrome Green	A straight green but a little low in value.

Yellow Green

Primrose Yellow	A cold yellow. Not necessary to stock with light chrome yellow, except as a special color.
Primrose Yellow and Emerald Green	A cold yellow mixed with an intense green, makes an excellent yellow green.

Earth Colors*

French Yellow Ochre	Rich ochre or neutral yellow shade, extends into good cream shades.
Raw Italian Sienna	Warmer and richer than ochre.
Burnt Italian Sienna	Terra cotta and brick color
Raw Turkey	A cold brown, has greenish cast. Not too useful by itself. It is used to neutralize other colors.
Burnt Turkey Umber	Rich brown, good wood-graining color.
Van Dyke Brown	Very rich brown, but hard mixer. Excellent wood color.
Ivory Drop Black	A bone black. (Avoid using lampblack, which is commonly mistaken for bone black. Lampblack is greasy and therefore a hard mixer).
Zinc White	A white pigment, not whiting. Sometimes called permanent white.
Danish Whiting	Pure whiting, does not settle out. Excellent filler.

*The earth colors are inexpensive neutral shades that can be used in place of the expensive method of neutralizing the more intense colors.

compensate by choosing colors on either side of the spectrum hue and stock two pigments instead of one. The pigment yellow is a good example. Because a true spectrum yellow may not be obtainable, two yellows are usually stocked, one that will mix with blue or green and the other with orange.

There are two types of scene paint: the unmixed dry pigments and ready-mixed paints. Mixture in this case refers to the presence of all or part of the properties of paint as a medium, which will be discussed separately under mixing procedures. The choice of a palette in either type of paint is related to the mixing of colors or of one pigment with another.

Dry Pigment Palette • Dry pigments are ground for theatrical use and, therefore, the spectral hues at least are available only at supply houses specializing in scenic paints and supplies. Earth colors (ochre, sienna, umber, and the like) can be found in local paint shops, although many times they are of inferior quality for painting scenery.

In preparing a list of stock scenic colors it is natural to compare the quality of the pigment's hue to the twelve principal colors of the color wheel. A good scene-painting palette would include them as well as some special colors and the earth colors.

The following hues have been selected from Gothic Scenic Paints (Gothic Color Company, Inc.) and Iddings Dry Pigments (Rosco Products).

Ready-Mixed Paints

The color range of ready-mixed paints is not as extensive as that of dry pigments. Although their colors are brilliant there are not as many intermediate tones. The following paint colors are from three major sources, Gothic Fresco Paints, Iddings Deep Colors, and Roscopaint. They are fairly representative of the range of colors found in all premixed paints.

MIXING PROCEDURES

Components of Scene Paint

The three basic components of scene paint are *pigment* (color), *binder*, and *vehicle*. The pigment and binder are suspended in a liquid that allows the paint to be brushed or sprayed onto a surface. The vehicle then evaporates and the binder holds the pigment to the surface.

The dry colors used for scene paint are the pigments suspended in a water vehicle with a water-soluble glue as a binder. A filler is frequently added to scene paint: whiting, which is an inexpensive chalk and not a pigment, is often added to the mixture to give the paint body and opacity. Because whiting affects the intensity of the color, it is not used in pure or full-intensity colors.

The mixing of scene paint begins with the preparation of the binder and vehicle which the scenic artist calls "size." The mixing proportions of a working size depend upon the kind of glue that is being used. Ordinary flake or ground glues are strong and usually have to be cut about 16 to 1 to make a size. Rubber and gelatine glues, although more flexible and easier to handle (they dry slower), make into about a 10-to-1 size. Both types require advance preparation. They have to be soaked and cooked in a double boiler to soften them into a liquid state. Once the glue has been made into size, it stays in a liquid state. The size will deteriorate, however, if it is allowed to stand for too long a period. A small quantity of carbolic acid or Lysol added to the size acts as a preservative.

Yellow
Lemon Yellow — A good straight yellow close to spectrum hue.

Yellow-Orange
Golden Yellow — Not quite a full yellow-orange in hue. Closer to an orange-yellow.

Orange
Orange — Has more red than a spectrum orange.

Red-Orange
Bright Red — Excellent spectrum hue.

Red
Red — Good spectrum hue. Just a shade off in chroma.
Dark Red — A step lower in value than red and has a little blue content.

Red-Violet
Magenta — The hue is right but it is about three steps too high in value.

Violet and Blue-Violet
Purple — Excellent spectrum hue. When mixed with ultramarine blue it produces fine blue-violet.

Blue
Ultramarine Blue — A blue with a red content. Too deep in value to be a true spectrum blue.

Blue-Green
Turquoise Blue — Excellent spectrum hue.
Cerulean Blue — A brilliant blue-green but high in value. Makes vibrant yellow-greens when mixed with lemon yellow.

Green
Emerald Green — Excellent spectrum hue.

Yellow-Green
Cerulean Blue and Lemon Yellow — No prepared yellow-green available.

Earth colors
Yellow Ochre — Rich neutral yellow.
Raw Sienna — Neutral yellow. Warmer and richer than ochre.
Burnt Sienna — Darker and less red than traditional burnt sienna.
Raw Umber — Cold brown. More blue than green, the cast of traditional raw umber.
Burnt Umber — Good rich brown.
Black — Deep flat black. Covers and mixes well.
White — Opaque. Good tinting white.

Because scene paint dries about two to three values lighter than it appears when wet, it is easier to mix the dry colors together first to acquire the desired tone. The size is then added to the premixed pigment, thereby saving repeated testings and sometimes the mixing of twice as much paint as is needed in the attempt to match an elusive shade. The size is added slowly, first making a pulp or paste. If the paste is vigorously stirred to make sure all the dry color is thoroughly moistened before thinning it to painting consistency, there is no need to break up the unmixed lumps by hand. If the dry paint refuses to go into suspension (some colors such as Van Dyke brown and Prussian blue are poor mixers), a little alcohol added to the paste helps to wet the troublesome color.

Ready-Mixed Paints

The pigment color, binder, and vehicle are premixed in proper proportions into a creamy paste. Since most scenery paints are suspended in water, ready-mixed paints are identified by their binder. Casein, acrylic, and latex-based paints are those most often used in the theatre. Although casein, a milk derivative, has given way to other protein binders such as soybean, the term is still used to identify this type of ready-mixed paint. Gothic Casein Fresco Paints and Iddings Deep Colors are two brands of protein-based premixed paints that have already been mentioned.

Roscopaint, a product of Rosco Laboratories, is an acrylic-based paint. Although most premixed paints are somewhat concentrated, Roscopaint is supersaturated and is made to extend to a dye consistency without losing brilliance. For easier mixing with other colors, the basic paste can be thinned with equal parts of water. It can then be further extended with up to three parts of water, depending upon the degree of opacity that is desired. The acrylic binder is compatible with any water-extended paint.

Latex-based paints are also adaptable to scenic painting. Vivid-Deep Color (Long Island Paint & Chemical Co.) produces a complete range of colors. Although most Vivid colors are in full chroma and concentrated, they are liquid in consistency and therefore do not go as far as a pulp mixture. Because latex and casein paints are compatible, the painter is free to select favored hues from each system as stock colors.

PAINTER'S ELEVATIONS

Designers must prepare for scene painting even if they do their own painting. Painting ideas are expressed in painter's elevations, which, unlike sketches, remove all the atmosphere of stage lighting to show true colors and exact form. The painter's elevation is a scaled drawing showing in detail the cartooning, or line drawing, a notation of actual color, and a clear indication of the painting technique. The scale of the drawing varies with the designer. The larger the scale, however, the more accurately it can be interpreted. The painter's elevations for most settings can be done at ½-inch scale, with details shown at a larger scale.

If a designer is doing the painting, the preparation of painter's elevations is the point at which to think through the appropriate painting technique and procedure. If lights are to play an important part of the design, the designer can check the painter's elevations under colored lights to foresee the effect of the stage lights on the setting colors.

Working from the painter's elevation, the scene painter can proportionally enlarge the drawing to full scale. A grid of horizontal and vertical lines is placed over the drawing, spaced, in the scale of the drawing, at 2-foot intervals. A similar grid, at full scale, is drawn on the priming coat of the surface to be painted.

Ways of numbering or lettering the grid vary. In Europe, for example, the artists prefer to number the spaces (Figure 9–1), while in the United States the numbering of the lines is favored. Proceeding square by square, the painter transposes the small-scale elevation into a full-scale layout of the design.

PAINTING PROCEDURE

The three steps toward preparing a surface for decorative painting are the size, prime, and base coats of paint. Their individual use or omission varies in accordance with the complexity of the design, the nature of the surface, and the painting technique.

Size Coats

The first step toward preparing new canvas or muslin is the size coat, which shrinks the canvas and glazes the surface without filling it. There are several uses and ways to mix size coats that bear mentioning. The *starch size* is used to prepare canvas or muslin for dye painting or very thin opaque paints. It can also serve as a surface for opaque paints, especially if the opaque coat is not completely covering the surface but is applied to leave large areas of unpainted background. A starch size is made by adding a cup of cooked Argo glossy starch to a 16-quart bucket of hot working size of about 20-to-1 proportion. A touch of dye or scenic color is added to make it more visible for brushing on the canvas. The resulting coat is a taut, slightly glazed surface that is excellent for dye painting.

The *alum size* is used over old painted canvas to stop an old coat of paint from picking up or bleeding through succeeding coats. A small quantity of powdered alum (½ cup to a 16-quart bucket) is mixed into working size of about 10- or 16-to-1 proportion.

A third use of a size coat is as a *glaze.* A glaze is a thin, transparent coat that is more of a painting technique than a preparation step. It gives the surface a slight gloss without covering up the undercoat. A glaze mix is prepared by weakening or strengthening the working size, depending upon the degree of gloss that is desired. The stronger the size, the higher the gloss. The technique can vary from a filmy, transparent wash to a fairly glossy finish. A glaze technique is tricky and difficult for a beginner. It has to be applied quickly and lightly to avoid moving the painted detail underneath.

Prime Coat

The second step in preparing new canvas is the prime coat, which has the function of filling the canvas. When painting on new canvas it is necessary to have it filled or the colors will "strike in" and lose brilliance. This phenomenon is very noticeable when old canvas is used beside new canvas on a flat.

Figure 9-1
Methods of Proportional Enlarging
(a) The designer's elevation with a grid of two- or three-foot squares. Spaces are numbered from right to left and lettered from bottom to top. (b) Full-scale layout of the drawing with the same labeling method. (c) Full-scale grid with the lines numbered from the center line in opposite directions and from the bottom to top. The base line and center line are established first.
(1) A perpendicular center line is constructed off the base line through the intersection of two arcs swung from centers equidistant from the center point.

A prime coat is made of working size and whiting with a touch of color to facilitate the application. It is kept thin in order not to overload the canvas. Because the prime coat fills the canvas, it tends to be an opaque coat and therefore cannot be used over areas of canvas that are to be translucent or dye-painted. If there are no translucent areas on the flats, the size and prime coats are sometimes combined into one operation, shrinking and filling the canvas at the same time.

All cartooning or layout drawing is done in charcoal on the prime coat. After the drawing is completed, key points or portions of the cartoons are "inked" in a fine line of dye or indelible pencil. The rest of the charcoal is "flogged" or dusted off the surface in preparation for the base coat. The inked-in portions of the design will bleed through the base coat and serve as a guide for later detailed painting.

a

Figure 9-2
Scenery Painting Procedure: Painter's elevations to finish scenery

(a) Painter's elevation of an oleo drop prepared by the designer. The drawing has been gridded with 2-foot squares in preparation for enlarging. (b) Proportional enlarging. The muslin has been sized and the drop has been gridded with charcoal and snap line to full-scale dimensions. The design is sketched in with charcoal so that mistakes and construction lines can easily be "flogged" or dusted off. (c) Inking the cartoon. The charcoal drawing or cartoon of the design is fixed to the muslin with a thin dye outline. (d) Painting into the cartoon. Wash backgrounds and detail painting can proceed without fear of losing the cartoon since the dye will bleed through the paint and be visible as guide lines. (e) Finished drop. An oleo drop for *Under the Gas Lights* by Augustin Daly. Designer—Glenn Gauer. *Photo courtesy Nelson*

b

c

d

e

Base Coat

The base coat is the under-painting for the final decorative painting and texturing. The application and color of the base coat depends on what is to follow. For example, a base coat may be one tone as a basis for a slick, modern paneled wall; it may be a scumbling of two or three tones in preparation for an antiqued, weather-beaten surface, or it may become a graded wash under a stenciled wallpaper design.

As a mixture, the base coat is kept thin in order not to overload the canvas. Because it is more intense in color than the prime coat, it will have less whiting and more pigment.

Detail and Decorative Painting

The final step in scene painting is the definition of form or the illusion of form through the various painting techniques of lining, texturing, and stenciling. We will also discuss the designing and painting of trees and the technique of pouncing.

Lining • The technique of lining, with straight edge or free hand, is to represent in two dimensions the complicated surfaces of the moldings in a cornice, chair rail, panel, or door trim.

Careful lining, in addition to local color, is done with a minimum of three tones: high light, shade, and shadow. Sometimes in showing a large cast shadow, two shadow tones are used consisting of a light and dark shadow. The high light is cooler and, of course, lighter in value than the local color, while the shade and shadow are in warmer and darker tones.

The order of lining for a panel or cornice is determined after first studying a cross section of the molding and the direction of the light that would reveal the molding if it were real. The position of a window or artificial-light sources are clues for fixing the general direction of light for each wall in the set. If the paneling is for a stock set that will be used in many positions, the light source is standardized as if it were coming from above and left of the surface (Figure 9–3).

Texturing • To avoid the starkness of a single tone and to bring more depth to a flat surface, the painter uses various texturing techniques. Because stage lighting is from many sources most natural shadows and reflected-light tonalities are eliminated. Much of this natural variation of tonality has to be painted into the set through the use of texturing techniques.

One of the simplest texturing techniques is to wet-blend or scumble three or more tones of a color on a surface. Using three brushes, one in each bucket, the three tones are brushed or blended together on the canvas while the paints are still wet. The result is an impression of one color with more depth and quality than is found in a single flat tone. This technique is usually handled on a broad scale with subtlety or obviousness depending upon the contrast or harmony of the tones.

A scumbling technique can also be done over a dry surface by blending the tones together with a dry-brushing or feathering. Dry-brushing, as the name implies, is done with the tip of a relatively dry brush in order to cover the under surface only partially and thus let it show through. Feathering refers to the direction of the brush stroke. The brush is drawn from the wet surface toward the dry so that the stroke ends in a feath-erlike pattern.

Other texturing techniques on a smaller scale include sponging, stippling, spattering, combing, use of a paint roller, and spraying. Each technique creates an individual feeling of texture as well as blending the tones into a vibrant surface (Figure 9–4).

All these techniques can be used to simulate the textural qualities of a specific material such as stone, plaster, wallpaper, and the like. Some materials, however, require texturing techniques that border on decorative painting; wood and wood graining are a prime example (Figure 9–5).

The painting of wood graining employs the same movement of color found in the other techniques. The grain pattern, of course, will vary with the type and use of the make-believe wood. Is it to be matched-grain walnut veneer on a late Empire breakfront secretary, or knotty-pine vertical paneling? Any attempt at realistic representation of wood graining on the stage should be preceded by a careful study of the real wood's color and grain characteristic.

If the wood is a door or door trim and should appear as a varnished finish, the graining can be glazed. Glazing, however, not only reduces the contrast between colors but also lowers their value. This must be taken into consideration in the preparation of the grain colors.

Figure 9-3
Lining Techniques

(a) Profile of cornice to be painted. (b) Lining of cornice. (c) Lining of a raised panel molding. (1) Assumed direction of light. (2) Local color. (3) Highlight. (4) Shadow, darkest tone. (5) Shade.

Plate 8-1
Spectrum Hues
The breakdown of sunlight through prism refraction into first six, then twelve, spectrum hues.

Plate 8-2
Hue-Value Relationship
The twelve principal spectrum hues are
arranged next to the value scale in their
natural light-to-dark relationship. The middle
value of the seven steps between black and
white is referred to as *medium* value while
the three steps above are known as
lowlight, light, and *highlight.* The lower
value steps are called *highdark, dark,* and
lowdark.

The following labels appear on the figure:

HL

L

1/4   1/2   3/4

ORANGE

LL

M

HD

ORANGE
DROPPED TO
HIGH DARK VALUE

D

LD

BLUE
RAISED TO
LOW LIGHT VALUE

BLUE

Plate 8-3
Value and Chroma

The complementary hues, blue and orange, are subjected to value and chroma changes first by alternately mixing each color with white and black in the outside ring to effect a value change. Chroma changes at a fixed value are accomplished horizontally by mixing the color with its complementary hue after it has been raised or lowered to the same value (arrow). Note that to change the value of a hue automatically alters its chroma without necessarily affecting value.

It is possible, of course, to alter chroma at each value step and completely fill the circle with a variety of tints and shades. This mixing procedure (although impossible to reproduce accurately), applied to any set of complementaries, is important to the stage designer as a method of creating new and unusual colors as well as matching existing shades.

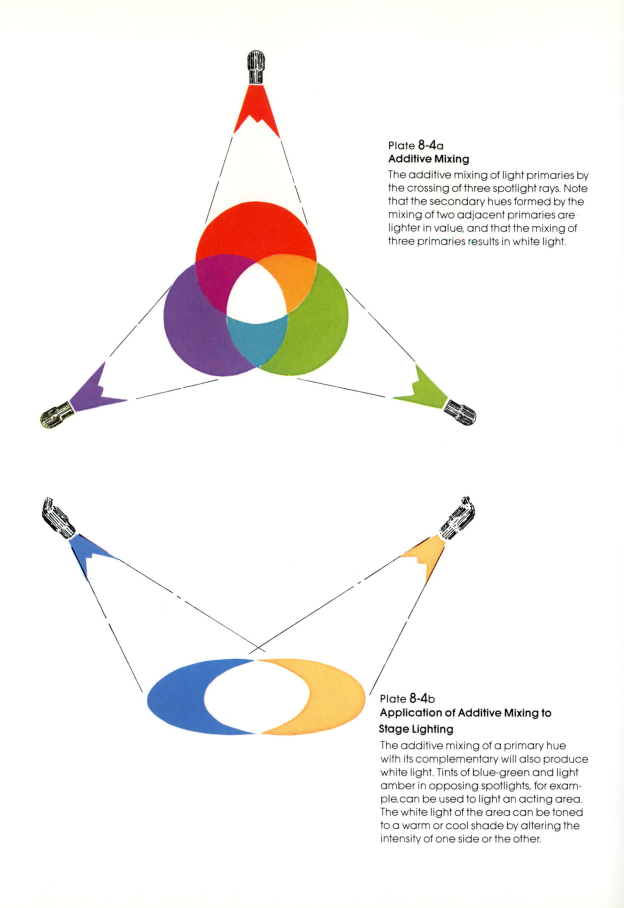

Plate 8-4a
Additive Mixing

The additive mixing of light primaries by the crossing of three spotlight rays. Note that the secondary hues formed by the mixing of two adjacent primaries are lighter in value, and that the mixing of three primaries results in white light.

Plate 8-4b
Application of Additive Mixing to Stage Lighting

The additive mixing of a primary hue with its complementary will also produce white light. Tints of blue-green and light amber in opposing spotlights, for example, can be used to light an acting area. The white light of the area can be toned to a warm or cool shade by altering the intensity of one side or the other.

Plate 8-5
Subtractive Mixing

(a) Six basic hues of the spectrum are shown passing through two color mediums, first yellow and then blue-green. All hues except green are absorbed or subtracted by the two filters. (b) Subtractive mixing in paint. The result is the same when blue-green and yellow paint are mixed.

Plate 8-6
Color Reflection

The horizontal orange strip represents an orange-colored surface. It appears orange under sun light because only red, yellow, and orange hues of the spectrum have been reflected. The other hues have been absorbed.

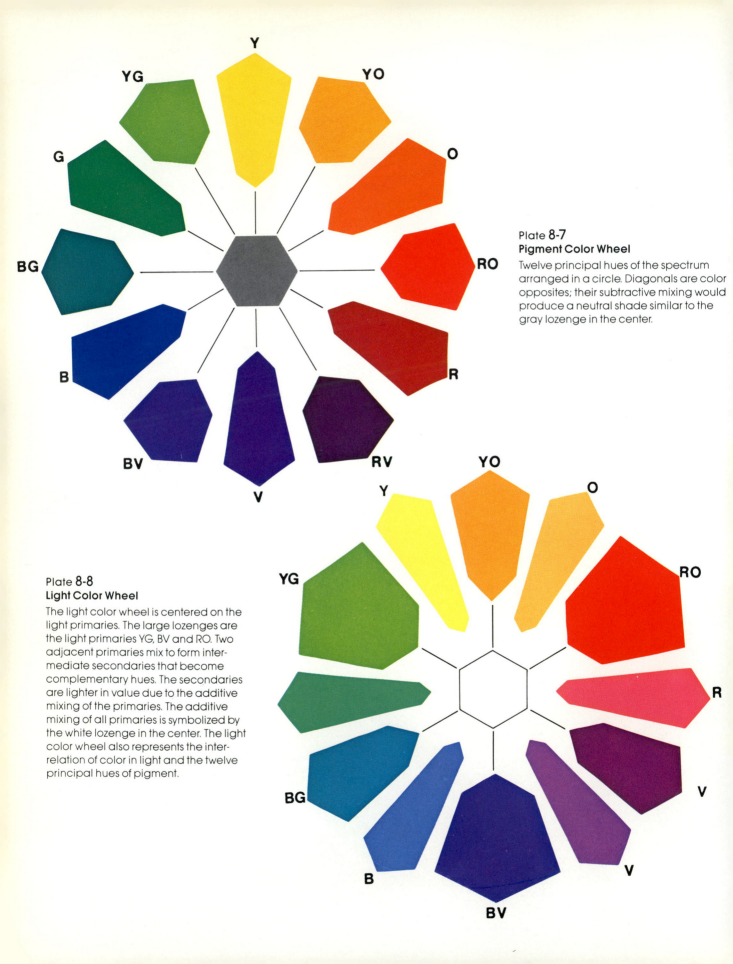

Plate 8-7
Pigment Color Wheel
Twelve principal hues of the spectrum arranged in a circle. Diagonals are color opposites; their subtractive mixing would produce a neutral shade similar to the gray lozenge in the center.

Plate 8-8
Light Color Wheel
The light color wheel is centered on the light primaries. The large lozenges are the light primaries YG, BV and RO. Two adjacent primaries mix to form inter-mediate secondaries that become complementary hues. The secondaries are lighter in value due to the additive mixing of the primaries. The additive mixing of all primaries is symbolized by the white lozenge in the center. The light color wheel also represents the inter-relation of color in light and the twelve principal hues of pigment.

Plate 8-9
Interaction of Color Hue Reaction Influencing a Neutral

A small neutral figure is influenced by the color of the ground surrounding it. The neutral in each of the six basic spectrum hues appears to be tinted with the complementary color of the background. The influence can be noted in each case when compared with the same gray tone to the right of each hue.

Plate 8-10
Interaction of Color Chroma Reaction
The chroma of the six basic spectrum hues appear to take on more brilliance as the background is darkened.

Plate 8-11
Interaction of Color Value Reaction
The value of the center of each area of color is the same. It appears to be lighter or darker as it is influenced by the surrounding color.

Plate 8-12
Third Interval Triad Color Scheme

This vibrant designer's sketch by Jo Mielziner for the dance hall scene in *Can Can* is a third interval triad: green, yellow, and orange. *Courtesy Jo Mielziner estate*

Plate **8-13**a
Color in Light
Projected blue light forms the monochromatic graveyard scene from Elmer Rice's *Adding Machine*.

Plate **8-13**b
Color in Light
Color and form in this projected scene is from one of the many scenes in Eugene O'Neill's *Emperor Jones*. Designer—June DeCamp.

Plate **8-14**a
Chroma Interaction

The intensity of the red hue is increased by the surrounding black in this sketch for *Carmen*,
Act III, San Francisco Opera. Designer—Howard Bay.

Plate **8-14**b
Chroma Interaction

The yellow becomes vibrant because of the encircling black detail in a scene for *Dido and Aeneas.* Designer—Donald Oenslager.

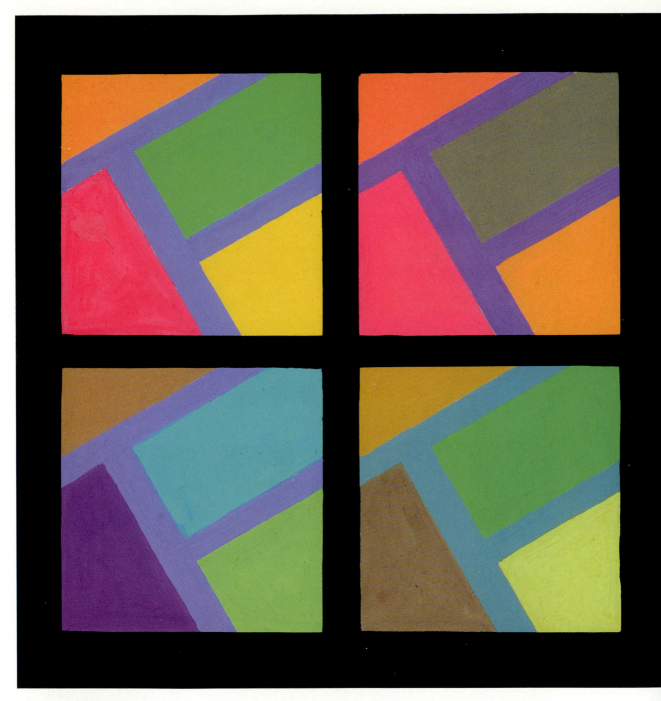

Plate **8-15**
Color Modification

A multi-colored design is seen under three different colors of light. The color of light on the two upper squares (left) clear, (right) medium-red. On the lower squares (left) sky-blue, (right) moss green.

Plate **8-16**
Costume Sketch
Two costumes for Brecht's *Three Penny Opera*. Designer—Susan Tsu.

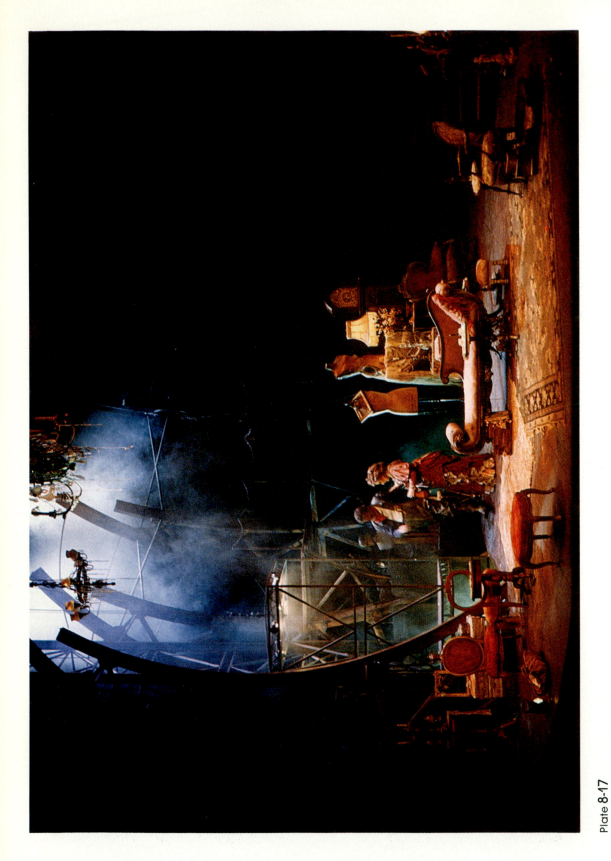

Plate 8-17
Scene Design and Lighting

The Madwoman of Chaillot by Jean Giraudoux. Set design—Cameron Porteous. Lighting design—Sholem Dolgoy. Courtesy Shaw Festival Theatre, Canada

Plate 8-18
Monochrome Color Scheme
Sketch for a velour dye-painted traveler curtain in shades and tints of one color, blue.

Plate **8-19**
Complementary Color Scheme
Sketch for a setting using orange and blue as a color control.

The glazing of grain that has a varnished finish can be accomplished in two different ways. The first method is to grain the surface first, then apply a glue, shellac, clear latex, or flat-varnish glaze. Of the three glazes, clear latex is the easiest to handle and gives the best results. The results, however, are hard to predict especially if there is a change of surface materials, as from wood to canvas or vice versa.

If it is dry color, a safer and easier approach is to put something with the paint that will give a gloss and eliminate the necessity of glazing the surface at all. Scene paint can be mixed directly with a flat varnish, which serves as a binder as well as giving the paint a slight sheen. Liquid wax mixed with scene paint produces the same effect as does clear acrylic. Both are easier to mix than varnish or shellac. Either method can be brought into a higher luster by polishing with paste wax later. Glazed surfaces must be handled with caution, however, for there is always the danger of creating a surface that is too reflective; it then becomes annoying to actors and audience.

Foliage • The designing and painting of trees and foliage requires practice and a study of natural forms. The designer should first study trees in their natural state, perhaps painting them in watercolors. A designer will soon learn to see the overall mass of foliage, then the subdivisions of smaller units relating to the branches of the tree's structure, and finally, the detail of a single leaf. It is interesting to see how light reveals the forms, passing through translucent areas. Some branches catch light while others are silhouetted.

The conceptual treatment of a tree on stage can assume many forms. Stage foliage can be translucent, opaque, or textured. The tree style may be real or stylized, or it may even be suggested with light patterns. Foliage can be carefully painted leaf by leaf or boldly painted in block areas loosely suggesting the organic form.

A landscape artist often starts with the darkest tones. Leaf masses in the shadow or silhouette are blocked in first. The lighter shades and highlights are painted last in opaque paint. If the foliage of the tree is to be translucent and painted with dyes, the technique is reversed: the lighter tones are painted first and the darker shades last.

Stenciling • The chief use of stenciling is for a painted wallpaper (or something similar) in which a design motif is repeated in an interlocking overall pattern. The cutting and printing of a stenciled design is the fastest and most effective method of repeating a small motif. After the means of interlocking the motif has been carefully figured out in relation to the size of the wall area, the motif is traced upon a sheet of stencil paper. Stencil paper is a tough, oil-impregnated paper especially for stencils. It is readily available in art shops or paint and wallpaper stores or can be made by applying a half-and-half mixture of linseed oil and turpentine to a heavy wrapping paper.

A well-planned stencil has at least one full motif with portions of adjacent motifs to key the stencil into an interlocking scheme. The size of the motif and the amount needed for interlocking the design more or less determines the size of the stencil sheet. Care should be taken not to create too large a stencil that might become awkward to handle. The

Figure 9-4
Texture Painting Techniques
(1) Wet blending or scumble. (2) Dry scumble. (3) Spattering.
(4) Combing or dry brushing.
(5) Rag rolling. (6) Spraying.
(7) Feather duster. (8) Paint roller.
(9) Taped paint roller to add a pattern to texture.

motif is cut out of the paper with a sharp knife, razor blade, or Exacto knife. Be sure to leave some tabs within the open parts to support the loose ends and strengthen the stencil as a whole. Two or more stencils can be cut at one time, for it is wise to have more than one stencil, especially if there is a large area to cover. They can be alternated in use so as to minimize the tendency of a stencil to become damp and misshapen from hard use.

After the stencil is cut, it is framed at the outside edges with 1 by 2 on edge to further strengthen it and at the same time provide a shield to the spray if the paint is being applied with a spray gun. The stencil is coated with clear shellac or any water-repellent plastic spray as an additional protection from the water-soaking effect of scene paint.

The stencil print can be made by three different methods: by spray gun, by brush, or by sponge. The spray gun is fast but sometimes messy. Stenciling with a brush is slower. The brush should be kept fairly dry

7

8   9

a   b   c

Figure 9-5
Wood-grain and Marble Texturing

(a) Pine grain. (b) Oak grain.
(c) Marble.

and stroked toward the center of the openings to avoid dribbles. The use of a sponge or soft cloth to apply the paint works best on an open stencil, for the print is purposely textured and not clean cut (Figure 9–6).

Pouncing • Pouncing is another method of transferring and repeating a design motif. It is generally used when the motif is either too large for a stencil, does not repeat enough times for one to bother cutting a stencil, or is repeated in reverse. Pouncing differs from stenciling in that only the outline or cartoon of the motif instead of a painted print is transferred.

The pounce pattern is made by first drawing the design on a piece of wrapping paper and then perforating the outline with a pounce wheel. The best type of pounce wheel (Figure 9–6c) has a small swivel-mounted perforating wheel. It works better on a padded surface, such as a blanket or fold of canvas, than on a hard table top or floor.

After the design is perforated and the back-side rough edges are lightly sanded, the paper is laid on the canvas in the desired position. The pattern is rubbed with a pounce bag made of a thin material such as cheesecloth filled with a dry color or charcoal dust. The outline is strengthened after the pouncing with charcoal, paint, or dye, depending upon the painting technique to follow.

TEXTURED SURFACES

Although their value on the stage is debatable, textured surfaces are sometimes desirable. Important points to consider before texturing a surface are: (1) a textured surface cannot be reclaimed for a different use without re-covering the piece of scenery; (2) deeply textured surfaces will not stand excessive handling or wear; (3) unless the texturing is in a position on the stage to get the proper lighting (preferably side lighting), it may as well be painted.

Texture Compounds

Spackle • The use of a prepared mixture of plaster and whiting called *Spackle* is the most familiar method of texturing. Because of the tendency of any texture coat to crack and flake off, Spackle is applied on a base of the same color unless, as an aging technique, some areas are purposely knocked off to reveal an undercoat of a contrasting color. The Spackle, which can be obtained at local paint shops, is mixed in cold water, colored with dye, and applied in about ¼-inch layers. While it is damp it may be roughed, combed, or grained for more texture. Sawdust, cork, or wood chips may be added to the mixture for extra texture. After the Spackle coat dries (about 24 hours), it can be shellacked and detail painted.

Sawdust Coat • Sawdust or wood chips can be mixed directly with scenic paint and applied as a texture coat. The size should be stiffened a little to bind the sawdust firmly. A sawdust coat requires less preparation and dries more quickly than Spackle but does not have as deep a texture.

Water Putty • Durham's Water Putty, a commercial surface repair mixture in powder form, can be used as a texture coat. It works best on a hard surface (3-ply or wood) and can be combed or stippled into a deep texture. Although it dries off-white it can be colored either with dye during the mixing or with paint after it has dried. When hardened it is tougher than Spackle but still subject to chipping.

Joint Cement • A compound developed commercially to cement tape over dry-wall joints in house construction, joint cement will hold a deep texture if a little white glue is added to the compound before application.

Texture Paints

J.C. Penney Texture Paint • J.C. Penney makes a prepared texture paint that is easy to apply. It holds a deep texture on a hard surface and is flexible enough to hold a medium texture on canvas.

Marble Coat • A texture paint made of marble dust sets up extremely hard. This marble coat takes a deep texture, can be colored when mixing, and when hardened it can be handled with the minimum of chipping. It is the hardest of the prepared texture coats.

SURFACE MATERIALS

Surface materials used mainly for textural purposes exist in a variety of forms. Each has its special handling and individual effect.

Irish linen has, of course, long since disappeared from the U.S. theatre as the standard covering for framed scenery. Its durability and excellent texture have not quite been replaced by the scene canvas in common use.

Figure 9-6
Stenciling Techniques
(a) Unframed stencil for dry-brush application. (b) Framed stencil for spray-gun application. Note how the stencil is keyed at the top and bottom. Because this stencil follows a vertical line it is not necessary to key it horizontally. (c) Pouncing: (1) Pounce, or perforated design. (2) Pounce wheel. (3) Pounce bag. (4) The pounced design transferred onto the canvas. (d) Border stencil. (e) Brick stencil. (f) Lining and spattering the stencil pattern. (g) Finished brick pattern.

Canvas, which is 8-ounce cotton duck, has been discussed (see "Size Coats") as a painting surface. It is the standard and most frequently used painting surface for all types of scenery. All other surfaces are limited in use to a special effect.

Muslin (unbleached) is the next most frequently used covering material. Although it lacks the texture and durability of canvas, its light-weight weave is useful for other purposes. As was mentioned, muslin is an excellent dye-painting surface for translucencies.

Scrim can be used as a painting surface in addition to its general use as a dye-painted transparency. It can also be used as a covering material if backed by canvas or some other opaque fabric.

Unbacked scrim can also be painted (dry brushed) with thin scenic colors. They are not as good as dyes, for they tend to stiffen the scrim, which is a disadvantage if it has to fold or roll. If large areas of scrim must be painted, it is best to use a spray gun to avoid stretching the scrim out of shape.

Filling Scrim. The open mesh of a scrim can be filled to create opaque areas. One means of doing so is to squeeze pure undiluted clear latex mixed with a casein color in a paste consistency onto the scrim to fill a   b

Figure 9-7
Textured Surfaces

Above. (a) Preparation for textured surface. Burlap, muslin, and random shapes of upson board glued to the surface of scenery units.
(b) Appliquéd surface is covered with a mixture of joint cement and sawdust. After it is dry, the surface is painted in dark tones and then higher surfaces are dry brushed with lighter tones. For a deeper textured surface see Figure 7-23.

Figure 9-8
Wallpapering

Occasionally the scenic artist is expected to hang wallpaper. The surface, if canvas, should be sized and based with casein or latex paint. If the wall surface is hard a size coat is sufficient. (a) Wallpaper strips of approximate length face down on pasting board. Wheat paste is used for regular wallpaper, or vinyl paste on vinyl wallpaper.
(b) Paste-covered strip is folded one third as shown. (c) Exposed portion of pasted strip is smoothed onto wall, being careful to match the pattern. Bubbles are smoothed out with wallpaper brush. (d) Strip is unfolded and brushed flat.
(e) Cutting wheel and roller. Edges are trimmed and, if paper is being applied to a hard surface, the edges are rolled. (f) Wallpapered unit of scenery. (g) Wallpapered panels.

a

b

c

Figure 9-9
Textured Details

Decorative details such as this rinceau pattern are often in slight relief. (a) A cut-out of the border pattern is prepared in upson board. Thick texture paint (J. C. Penney) is applied with a cake decorator to the cutout, which is then glued to the architrave position of the entablature. (b) When dry, all recessed surfaces are stained dark and later brushed with metallic gold paint. (c) Final assembly.

the mesh. A table-mustard squeeze bottle is a good applicator. If the scrim is to be filled while it is on the floor in a horizontal position, steps should be taken to prevent the latex from sticking to the floor. Vis-Queen, a clear transparent plastic, is a good separator. More expensive premixed fillers are also available (for example, Roscofiller).

Burlap is frequently used as a covering material chiefly for its texture. Burlap should be backed or fastened to a firm surface, for it is made of jute and may stretch or sag under a heavy coat of paint. Sometimes it helps to paint and dry burlap horizontally.

Burlap needs to be heavily sized to keep the color from "striking in." However, this may be a desirable effect if it is to be an old tapestry or wall hanging.

METHODS OF PAINTING

Scenery is painted in two different positions, horizontally and vertically. The various methods of painting are devised to facilitate either way of painting.

Figure 9-10
Painting on the Floor

Extensive floor painting is made easier with the use of proper tools and the right type of brushes.
(a) Individual paint-bucket carrier.
(b) Long handles for the brushes.
(c) Paint cart with palette area for mixing paint. (d) Straight edge with handle.

Horizontal Painting

Painting on the floor is the oldest and simplest method and requires the least mechanical assistance. Long handles on the brushes, charcoal holders, and straight edges help to take the backache out of horizontal painting. The most essential requirement is lots of smooth floor space (preferably wood) and good overhead illumination (Figure 9–10).

Although some painting techniques are best employed horizontally, others are accomplished more easily in a vertical position.

Stationary Frame and Boomerang

It is easy to fasten scenery against a wall or on a stationary frame along a wall, but it is not so easy to paint all areas without using a ladder. A rolling platform, or *boomerang*, as it is called, provides the painter with two or three painting levels (Figure 9–11).

Moving Frame

The moving paint frame that raises or lowers past the working level brings the greatest flexibility to vertical painting (Figure 9–11). The frame lowers into a well or to a second painting level. Some unusually high frames many times have two or three decks so that the painters can work at different levels at the same time.

TOOLS AND EQUIPMENT

The painter's most important tool is, of course, the *brush*. A good brush should have long bristles and a full shape. (Avoid hollow centers.) Pure bristles are so expensive, especially in the larger sizes, that many painters have turned to nylon brushes. A nylon brush with sandblasted tips is about half the price of the pure-bristle brush of the same size. The difference in price is offset by the slight disadvantage of nylon, for watercolor tends to run off nylon, causing it to hold less paint than a pure-bristle brush.

Because scene-painting brushes are used predominately in watercolors, the bristles should be rubber set. Some brushes set in glue are suitable for oil paint but will break down with the continued use in watercolor.

Types of Brushes

The types of brushes for scene painting are classified by the work they do, such as priming, base-coating or "lay-in," decorating, and lining (Figure 9–12).

The *priming brush* is the widest brush (6 to 8 inches). It holds a large quantity of paint, which makes it good for spreading size and prime coats quickly and efficiently.

The *lay-in brush*, about 4 inches wide, is used for the more careful painting of a base coat, blending, spattering, and similar techniques.

A *decorating brush* is from 1½ to 3 inches wide with a long handle. Sometimes called a *foliage brush*, it is used for most decorative painting, including tree leaves. The foliage brush is a pure-bristle brush made especially for scene-painting and is quite expensive. A *sash tool*, which is a long-handled brush for painting window sashes, is an inexpensive decorating brush.

Liners are also long-handled brushes varying in width from ¼ to 1 inch. Liners should have long pure bristles to perform well. A 1-inch sash tool can do limited lining, but there is no substitute for the smaller brushes.

Cleaning Brushes • Water-based paints "set up" quicker than most oil-based paints. This is an advantage while painting, but a disadvantage when cleaning brushes. Also, latex and acrylic paints are water-repellent when they are dry. To keep brushes from building up paint in the heel, an unclean brush should not be allowed to dry. An uncleaned brush not in use at the moment is usually kept in a pail of clean water.

Figure 9-11
Vertical Painting Methods

(a) The moving paint frame raises and lowers into a well extending below the the main working-deck level. Scenery is attached to the frame and is painted in a vertical position by raising and lowering the frame. (b) The boomerang, a stepped-level platform on casters, provides a variety of working levels for the painter.

When brushes are cleaned at the end of a work day, attention is focused on getting all paint out of the heel of the brush. A wire brush is useful to comb out stubborn paint. After washing, the bristles of the brush should be shaped while damp and left to dry.

If the brush has been in dye, it may need to be soaked overnight in a mixture of whiting and water to draw out all the dye.

PAINTING TOOLS

In addition to brushes and paints, the painter uses other implements to prepare, lay out, and paint scenery. Other necessary painting tools are:

1. Beveled straight edge (6 feet)
2. Rule or steel tape
3. Snap line (50 feet)
4. Charcoal stick and holder
5. Large compass (36 inches)
6. Tank sprays
7. Spray gun and compressor
8. Pounce wheel
9. Plumb bob
   Buckets (14 and 16 quarts)
   Small pots or cans (No. 10 cans)
10. Bow snap line (6 to 8 feet)
11. Burner and double boiler for glue
12. Flogger
13. Paint roller

RELATED MATERIALS

Aniline Dyes

Aniline dyes are available in almost all the standard colors. They are used for inking in outlines, thin wash glazes, translucencies, and for dip-dyeing fabrics.

Dyeing or painting with dyes is a different process than painting with scene paints. Scene paint changes the color of a surface by covering it with a pigment that is held in place by a binder. Dyeing, on the other hand, is a chemical process. The dye color becomes a part of the material it is dyeing. It is important that the dye and material have an affinity for each other, or a complete chemical action will not take place.

To dye cotton duck or muslin it is sometimes necessary to add a small amount of acetic acid or vinegar to the dye solution. The acetic acid increases the affinity of the cotton for the dye, causing the fabric to absorb more color from the dye bath. The addition of a small quantity of salt also helps to increase the amount of absorption. Salt counteracts the tendency of dyestuffs to go into solution, making it easier for the dye color to be absorbed by the material.

However, the presence of too much salt in the mixture, possibly from salted dyes or flameproofing compounds frequently mixed with the dye bath, can keep the dye from going into solution. All crystals must dissolve, or streaks of concentrated color will appear on the surface of the canvas. If the dye separates, the addition of some alcohol will ensure a complete solution. Normally, the crystals go into solution in hot water without any trouble.

For extensive *dye-painting*—when painting a translucent drop, for example—the muslin is prepared with a starch size (see "Size Coats"). If

Figure 9-12
Brushes and Tools

Scene-painting brushes: (a) Lining brushes, flat and oval. (b) Decorating brushes. (c) Lay-in brushes. (d) Priming brush. Painting tools and accessories: (1) Beveled straight edge. (2) Yard stick. (3) Snap line. (4) Charcoal and holder. (5) Large compass. (6) Tank spray. (7) Spray gun and compressor. (8) Pounce wheel. (9) Plumb bob. (10) Bow snap line. (11) Burner and double boiler for glue. (12) Flogger. (13) Paint roller.

the painting is being done on a fabric that cannot be starch-sized, such as velour or silk, a small amount of starch can be added to the dye mixture to keep it from spreading on the fabric.

Dip-dyeing is used mostly on small pieces of fabric, such as window drapes or tablecloths. Occasionally, large gauze pieces are dipped with excellent results.

The preparation of the dye for dip-dyeing is the same as for dye-painting except, of course, larger in quantity. It is important to be sure that enough dye has been mixed, for to run out of dye mix in the middle of a dipping is disastrous. The color of the mix should be checked by dipping a sample of the fabric before preparing it for dipping.

In preparation for dip-dyeing, the fabric is first dipped in water. If it is new material, it should be washed to remove the size. After wringing, the still-damp fabric is dipped into the dye mix. If it is a stage gauze, after squeezing or wringing out the excess dye, it should be stretched to dry, or hung in place and stretched back into shape as it dries.

An important thing to remember is that dip-dyeing will take out any flameproofing that might have been in the material. It has to be reflameproofed later, or better still, flameproofed directly by a mixture added to the dye. The regular sal ammoniac and borax mixture can be cut to half strength by adding water and still give a satisfactory result. It is best, however, to run some test experiments under dipping conditions before taking a chance with a large piece.

ADDITIONAL SUPPLIES

There are some additional supplies that supplement dry colors, glue, and dyes that are directly associated with scene painting. Some have already been mentioned in relation to a particular painting technique. These supplies and their uses are:

White shellac	For glazes, water-repellent finishes, binder and hardener.
Alcohol	Solvent for shellac and speeds the dissolving of colors that are poor mixers.
Flat varnish	Glaze finish and paint binder.
Turpentine	Solvent for varnish and oil paints.
Liquid wax	Glaze finish and paint binder.
Metallic paints	Powder mixed with strong size or clear acrylic for metallic surfaces. All right for scenery, but not for props. Spray cans (Krylon) have harder finish, good for props, more expensive.
Glycerin	Added to paints for slow drying.
Lysol	Preservative.
Alum	For alum-size preparation.
Sal ammoniac	Flameproofing chemical.
Borax	Formula—l lb borax, l lb sal ammoniac to 3 qts of water.

Flameproofing

Canvas and muslin can be purchased already flameproofed, but if the scenery has been washed for reuse the canvas will have to be flameproofed again. A mixture of one pound of sal ammoniac, one pound of borax, and three quarts of water is an inexpensive flameproofing formula. It is brushed or sprayed onto previously dampened material for the best results. Sheer materials, such as scrim or bobbinet, should be dipped to ensure successful flameproofing.

Because the flameproofing mixture is highly corrosive to metals, brushes and spray cans should, after use, be washed thoroughly in cold water. A small amount of acetic acid in the water helps to counteract the corrosive action.

Testing Flameproofing • The term "flameproofing" does not mean that a treated fabric will stop a flame, but that it will *not support* a flame. Hence when an obscure section of a drop or flat is *tested*—by bringing a lighted match to the surface—it will burn a hole; but it will stop burning when the flame is removed signifying that the fabric is flameproof.

Testing and other fire regulations vary over the country. It is wise for the designer and technician to become familiar with local regulations before beginning production.

||||➡ *SAFETY PRACTICE*

Most of the paints and solvents that have been mentioned are relatively safe. However, there are precautions that should be taken for prolonged use.

Paint is most hazardous during the mixing and application stage.

Dry pigments have a dust hazard. Inhalation can be avoided by wearing a nose mask until paint is wet.

Acrylic paints release a small amount of ammonia and formaldehyde during mixing and while the paint is drying. Forced ventilation not only speeds drying but also dissipates the fumes.

Alcohol is very volatile. Avoid inhaling. Use in a well-ventilated room.

Krylon Sprays should be well ventilated or used in spray booth. Use a respirator mask for prolonged spraying.

Metallic colors are safest when mixed with clear acrylic.

Alum may be allergic to some.

Turpentine is marginal. Some may have skin allergies.

Gloves of the EPT Neoprene type are the best for all purposes.

Goggles should be used for overhead spray painting.

FIRE HAZARDS

Solvents, such as alcohol and turpentine, oil-based paints, and Krylon spray cans should be stored in a separate fireproof chamber. Care should be taken in their use to ensure proper ventilation. There should be no smoking, open flame, or sparks in the area.

Handling Scenery

10

Confronted with a multiscene play, a designer has to consider, early in the planning, a method of handling the settings. A production scheme is developed from the numerous ways of moving scenery, and this scheme frequently influences the design concept. Consequently, the more designers know of the mechanics of the modern stage and of theatrical techniques for moving scenery, the closer they can come to fully realizing their design concept. This is especially true of some theatre outside New York, where the designer has to be clever to overcome limited funds and poorly equipped stages. Thus, technical knowledge can help a designer solve scenery-shifting problems with an ingenuity that often becomes inventively original.

METHODS OF HANDLING SCENERY

The four basic methods of handling scenery, in the order of their increasing complexity and additional construction are: (1) the moving or running of scenery on the floor; (2) the flying of scenery; (3) the moving of scenery on casters, including such large units as wagons and revolving stages; and (4) the handling of scenery through the stage floor by elevators.

How scenery is to be handled is influenced by four major factors: the play, the theatre and its stage, the design of the production, and the budget.

Play Structure

The form of the play and its plot structure are the primary influences on the handling of scenery. A play, for instance, may have many unrelated episodic scenes, a flash-back technique, several simultaneous scenes with continuous action, or the conventional three-act form. The structure of the play, in addition to determining the number of scenes or locale changes in their order of appearance or reappearance, also establishes the *kind* of change.

The most common interval for a change of scene is between acts. The act change, which can be as short as three minutes or longer than fifteen minutes, presents no great problem under optimum conditions, assuming the stage has adequate flying and offstage space. Even under limited stage conditions, an act change usually allows enough time to maneuver the scenery, although it may require more ingenuity and hard work.

A change within the act, or a scene change, can be as short as thirty seconds to as long as a minute and a half. A scene change, by necessity a fast change, can be handled in several different ways. It may be a hidden change, taking place behind a curtain, or without a curtain but hidden by a blackout. It may be a *visible* change (avista) made in full view of the audience with a display of theatrical magic, or by actor-stagehands openly moving elements of scenery as a part of the action.

In contrast to the other kinds of changes, the avista becomes a part of the play by calling attention to the movement of scenery. As a theatrical technique, it obviously fits only certain types of plays and production schemes.

Theatre and Stage

The shape of the theatre and the size of the stage, of course, have an important influence on the movement of scenery. The amount of flying space and equipment, the extent of offstage and wing space, the size of the proscenium opening, and sightline conditions obviously help determine the way scenery can be handled.

Some stages have more elaborate mechanical aids or stage machinery for shifting scenery, such as a built-in revolving stage, tracking and offstage space for full-stage wagons, or elevator stages. The existence of one or more of these mechanical aids in a theatre cannot help but influence scenery-handling techniques.

Traveling productions have other scenery-shifting considerations. Instead of one theatre and stage the designer has to consider the size and sightline conditions of many stages and auditoriums as well as the physical limitations and extreme portability expected of scenery for a road show.

Elaborate scenery-moving devices such as turntables and treadmills are sometimes duplicated in order to reduce the setup time in each theatre. Two crews are used. The first specializes in assembling shifting machinery, for example a turntable. They work in advance of the second crew, who run the show. When the run is finished, the second crew moves the show from theatre *A* to theatre *B* and onto preassembled turntable No. 2, leaving behind turntable No. 1. The first crew then returns to theatre *A* and moves turntable No. 1 in leap-frog fashion to theatre *C*, and so on.

Design and Scheme of Production

The scene designer reconciles the needs of the play and the stage and adds a third control, the scheme of production. The designer's production scheme stems from the kind of scene or locale change inherent in the play, the physical limitations of the stage, and a concept of the play's setting (Chapter 4). A designer cannot design a large production without thinking through, at least in basic terms, a method or scheme for handling the changes.

Budget

The influence of budget on the handling of scenery is felt directly through the control of the scale of the set designs and general size of the productions. Although the operational budget has little direct effect on the form of the physical stage, it does influence its operation through the provision of funds for an adequate production staff. A large stage with a small technical staff, for example, would limit the amount of scenery that could be efficiently handled.

An operational budget also is tied in with the estimated length of a run. A Broadway show with a prolonged run, for example, can reduce its operational costs by spending more money on costly mechanical aids to shift the scenery, thereby cutting down the number of stagehands on the weekly payroll.

The operational budget of a university or community theatre influences scenery handling in a slightly different way. The decision to use an extensive mechanical aid is based upon its reuse value for other productions. Cost is thus spread throughout the season's operational budget.

BACKSTAGE ORGANIZATION

Anyone who has seen a fast change from a backstage vantage point has been amazed by the teamwork and precision with which the large pieces of scenery, properties, lights, and actors seem to move. This is due, to some extent, to careful rehearsing, but largely it is the result of normal backstage organization and its division of responsibility. Under the coordinating management of the stage manager, a production has two major divisions: acting and technical. The technical responsibilities are divided between the scenery, electrical, property, and costume departments.

Stage Manager

Although the primary responsibility of the stage manager is to the director and the actors, he or she is also of great assistance to the designer and the production side of the show. The stage manager officiates at the first technical rehearsal, without actors, to allow all hands to become familiar with the timing of shifts, light and sound cues, and the placement of properties.

Once the production is on the stage, the stage manager becomes its field commander, fully responsible for the performance. The stage manager starts each performance, gives all cues, calls the actors, posts all daily calls, and is charged with maintaining both the production standards set by the director and company discipline onstage.

Stage Carpenter

Although taking cues from the stage manager, the master carpenter is in charge of the shifts, the rigging, and the general condition of the scenery. The crew, which is made up of assistant carpenters, grips (stagehands), and flymen, report to the master carpenter.

Master Electrician

The responsibilities of the master electrician include the hanging and focusing of lighting instruments, the maintenance of all electrical equipment, and operation of the switchboard for the lighting cues. Any movement of lighting equipment during a shift comes under the supervision of the stage carpenter but may be done by grips assigned to the electrical department.

Property Master

The property person's duties include the care and maintenance of the set and hand props, rugs, ground cloth, mechanical sound effects, and any trick device handled by the actors that is too small to be classified as scenery. The property master supervises handling of props during a shift, helped by grips assigned to the property department.

Sometimes electrified props cause what may seem to be double handling. A living room lamp, for example, is placed on the set by a member of the prop crew, but it is connected and lighted by the light crew. The offstage storage and visual appearance of the lamp is the responsibility of property people, while all electrical maintenance is done by the electrician. The division of responsibility is clearly and logically defined.

Sound Technician

Although traditionally a member of the electrical department, the sound technician is established in many theatre organizations as a separate function. The increasing use of high-fidelity recording for a major portion of sound effects and incidental music warrants, in many cases, the creation of a sound department.

The sound technician is responsible for the recording and editing of each show tape as well as the operation of sound equipment for sound cues. He or she supervises the placement and installation of speakers and microphones, maintains all sound equipment, the stage manager's inner-communication, and, for a permanent producing group, might organize and service a sound-recording library. More on *sound* can be found in Chapter 12.

Wardrober

The care and maintenance of all costumes is the responsibility of the wardrobe supervisor (and, during a fast costume change, of the actors as well). The backstage organization of community and university theatres often places the supervision of makeup in the costume department.

RUNNING SCENERY ON THE FLOOR

Running or "gripping" of scenery is the simplest handling method and requires the least additional construction. If the units are strong enough to support themselves, usually the only additional support that is needed is horizontal stiffening, the vertical bracing of the piece in an upright position, and a quick and easy method of joining together the various parts of the set. Occasionally the extreme height of scenery combined with its traditional thinness makes it difficult to move for anyone not experienced in handling scenery.

Some of the many ways of handling single flats, twofolds, and partially assembled units of scenery on the floor are illustrated in Figure 10–1. Since the stagehands are called *grips*, "gripping scenery" refers to the handling of scenery by stagehands.

a   b   c   d

e   f   g

The drawing (*a*) illustrates how a large unit of scenery is raised off the floor. The grips on the backside are *footing* or holding the bottom edge with their feet while the other two grips walk-up the piece by pushing on solid surfaces, such as the stiles.

To "edge-up" a single flat is a similar maneuver (*b*). With the flat on edge, one grip is holding the point down while the second is walking-up the unit by pushing along the edge.

To run or "grip" a single flat (*c*), the grip has one hand low and other high for balance. By lifting the lead corner slightly off the floor, he or she handles the flat in perfect balance.

To make a lash (*d*) is a part of handling scenery. It takes a little skill to swing the lash line so as to catch each lash cleat and make fast with a tie-off knot (Figure 10–7k).

Running a twofold (*e*) is similar to running a single flat. The lead grip guides the move while the second balances the unit by keeping the fold slightly open.

Running a top-heavy piece (*f*) often requires a third grip to balance the awkward unit of scenery.

To float down a single flat (*g*) is a simple move. Because the construction of a flat is similar to a heavy kite, the grip, by putting a foot on the flat's bottom to control its descent, can let go and the flat will float gently to the floor.

Figure 10-1
Running Scenery

The running or "gripping" of scenery is the simplest handling method although, occasionally, the awkward shape or extreme size of a piece may require experience to handle it successfully. (a) "Walking-up" a stiffened two-fold.
(b) "Edging-up" a single flat.
(c) Running or "gripping" a single flat. (d) Making a lash. (e) Running a two-fold. (f) Three men running a top-heavy piece. (g) "Floating" down a single flat.

Stiffening, Bracing, and Joining

Because scenery has to travel in units of relatively small, lightweight sizes to get in and out of theatres, the joining or unfolding of these smaller units into larger shapes is crucial. The new larger shape requires stiffening to be safely handled in a shift.

A stiffener is usually a horizontal stiffening member (1-by-3 or 1-by-4 on edge) that is loose-pin-hinged into place as the set is assembled. A vertical stiffener is often called a "brace," especially if it is in the form of a "jack." A "brace jack," often shortened to just "jack," is a triangular form with a small base providing maximum bracing. A jack can be loose- or tight-pin hinged to the scenery it is bracing. Bracing and stiffening can take a variety of forms depending upon the shape and size of the scenery they are reinforcing (Figure 10–2).

Figure 10-2
Bracing and Stiffening

(a) Stiffening a flat wall: (1) Vertical stiffener. (2) Horizontal stiffener. (3) Bracing or "jack." (b) Stiffening a jogged wall: (4) A framed stiffener which conforms to the shape of the wall. (c) Other bracing and stiffening techniques: (5) A swivel keeper bar and keeper hooks. (6) Bent footiron and stage screw. (7) Adjustable stage brace. (8) L-jack and sandbag (no stage screw). (9) Hinged jack. (10) Folding jack.

The three different categories of joining are related to the portable nature of scenery and the degree of permanence of the joint. Elements of scenery may be joined together by fixed or permanent joining, by assembly joining, or by temporary joining. The kind of joint and its location are often important to the design, for the designer will seek ways to avoid a crack or open joint in a conspicuous area of the setting.

Fixed joining occurs as the scenery is being built (with use of nails, screws, and so on). A fixed hinged joint is made with tight-pin hinges so that larger units composed of several small pieces may unfold into larger sizes. The smaller pieces remain fixed together and travel or move folded from shop to stage, to be unfolded and stiffened into their final shape in the theatre (Figure 10–3a-d).

Figure 10-3
The Joining of Scenery

Fixed joining: (a) Tight-pin hinge and dutchman. (b) Two-fold, two flats tight pin-hinged together. (c) Three-fold, two jogs, and a flat hinged together. (d) Three-fold and "tumbler" to hinge three full-width flats together. Assembly joining: (e) Loose-pin hinge. (f) Bolting. (g) Picture hanger. (h) S-batten hook. (i) Keeper hook on end of a spanner. Temporary joining: (j) Lashing, flush and around corner. Note stop cleat. (k) Hook and eye. (l) Tongue and socket. (m) Turn buttons.

On the other hand, large areas of scenery may be made in separate small pieces to be assembled in the theatre. Loose-pin hinges, bolts and wing nuts, and turn buttons are some of the most frequently used methods of assembly joining pieces of scenery together into a larger unit. After a larger unit is stiffened and braced, it can be handled in its assembled form until time to leave the theatre (Figure 10–3e,f,m).

The temporary joining of scenery occurs at the time of the striking and making of a set during an act or scene change. The lashed joint is the most common means of temporarily joining units of scenery. Loose-pin hinges, turn buttons, and hooks and eyes are some additional ways scenery may be temporarily joined (Figure 10–3e,j,k).

A lip is often used to cover a flush temporary joint between two flats. The lip, which is made of a 4-inch strip of ¼-inch plywood with both edges beveled, is secured to an edge on the face of one of the joining flats. It is attached under the canvas with about an inch overhang.

FLYING SCENERY

The designer is always interested in the size of the stage house and type of flying system, if any, over the stage. A good stage house that is designed to handle scenery in the air will have an adequate flying system and a generous amount of hanging space, which means a high and wide loft. The two common methods of flying scenery are the pin-and-rail and counterweight systems. Both are based on the presence of a gridiron over the stage to support the sheaves or pulley blocks and the extended control of the line-sets to one of the side walls. They differ in the complexity of the rigging, cost of installation, and the flexibility of use.

Gridiron

As the name implies, the gridiron is a grid or open floor of iron high over the stage. The average gridiron has at least three and sometimes four or five channels that run up and down stage and are spaced at approximately 10-foot intervals across the stage. Across each channel opening, which is about 6 to 8 inches wide, sit the sheaves that make up the line-sets. Each line, as it runs over the sheave, drops through the channel to the stage floor.

The space between the channels is floored with strips of 3-inch channel iron running parallel to the main channels. The channel-iron strips are set far enough apart to allow the spotting of additional sheaves for special spotlines (Figure 10–4c[1 and 2]).

Recent gridiron designs employ the use of many more channels at about 4-foot intervals. Swivel loft blocks are suspended above the gridiron floor from beams over each channel. The multichanneled gridiron is discussed in more detail later in this chapter and is illustrated in Figure 10–5.

Line-Sets

A line-set refers to the grouping of three or more lines into a set to be handled as one line. The sheaves of a line-set are usually placed over each channel opening and are all at the same distance from the proscenium, thus forming a line parallel to the footlights.

Figure 10-4
Flying Systems

(a) Pin-and-rail or "hemp" system:
(1) Short line. (2) Center line. (3) Long line. (4) Tandem head block.
(5) Double pinrail on fly door.
(6) Sandbag counterweight.
(7) Clew or "sunday" on a line-set.
(b) Counterweight system: (1) Pipe batten, a fixed line set. (2) Hoisting cable for liftlines. (3) Head block, multi-grooved. (4) Trim chains at top of arbor. (5) "T" track. (6) Purchase line. (7) Lock and safety line on lock rail which may be on a fly floor or the stage deck. (8) Idler pulley.
(c) A demonstration of the flexibility of the pin-and-rail system: (1) Spot sheaves used to fly a drop at an askew angle. The spotlines use the same or adjacent head blocks.
(2) The separation of a single line from a line-set to use in a spot-sheave.

The number of lines in a line-set depends upon the number of channels in the individual gridiron. A stage with a wide proscenium opening might have as many as five lines in a set, while a small stage usually has only three lines to a set.

The lines are named by their length and position on the stage. The line nearest the control side (pinrail or lock rail) of the stage is called the short line and the line to the far side of the stage is the long line. The line in between is, of course, the center line. A four-line set would have two center lines, a long center, a short center, and so on.

Pin-and-Rail

The pin-and-rail system is the older though more flexible of the two flying systems. It is a less costly installation but does require more skill and more people to operate. The hemp system, as it is sometimes called,

Figure 10-5
Motor-driven Spotline System

(a) A pictorial drawing of the rigging for one line-set: (1) Driver motor, a ¾ horsepower, variable speed D-C motor. (2) Sprocket and roller chain drive. (3) Movable bull-winch to retrieve empty arbor for loading. (4) Arbor. (5) Grooved pulleys to return the four liftlines to (6) grooved muling pulley, the normal dead-tie position on the regular double-purchase counter-weight system. (7) Trimming winches to adjust the length of each liftline. (8) Swivel head blocks in tandem mount. (9) Swivel loft blocks. (10) Channel openings at about 4-foot intervals. (11) Underslung channel supporting loft blocks for rigid line sets. (12) Head block for rigid line-set. (13) Pipe batten. (b) Schematic diagram of the motor-driven spotline system.

uses ¾-inch manila rope for liftlines. As illustrated in Figure 10–4a, the individual line in a line-set (1), (2), (3) comes up from the stage, passes through the loft block, and travels horizontally to one pulley in the head block (4) located on the left or right stage wall. From the head block, in which the pulleys are mounted in tandem, the lines are brought together as a set and tied off at the pinrail (5). The lower rail of the pinrail is usually the trim tie for the drop in its "in" or working position, and the top rail receives the tie for the "out" or stored position. A line-set can be "clewed," or bound together (7), and sandbagged (6) to counterweight a heavy piece for easy handling.

As can be seen, the pin-and-rail system has great flexibility in its ability to use only part of a line-set, add a spotline to a line-set, or, in some instances, cross line-sets. The adding of a spotline employs a single rope and loft sheave occasionally placed in a remote position on the gridiron to fly a raked, or angled, piece of scenery (Figure 10–4c[1]).

The chief disadvantage of a "hemp house" is in the number of hands required to run a show, as well as in the professional skill necessary to rig and safely counterweight heavy pieces of scenery. To the designer, this disadvantage is far outweighed by the greater design possibilities inherent in the flexibility of the pin-and-rail system.

The Counterweight System

Unlike the pin-and-rail system, which can separate lines or add a single line to the line-sets, the counterweight system uses fixed line-sets. Although the counterweight system was born in an era of box settings and raked scenery as theatrical styles, it is, paradoxically, rigidly based upon wing-and-backdrop staging. It keeps the lines in sets fixed to a pipe batten parallel to the footlights.

The system, as illustrated in Figure 10–4b, begins at the pipe batten (1) and the permanently attached wire-cable liftlines (2). Lifting the batten, the lines pass through the individual loft blocks at each channel, over a multigrooved, single-pulley headblock (3) and attach to the top of the counterweight arbor (4). The arbor is guided by a "T" track (5), or guy wire, and controlled by a separate purchase line. The purchase line (6) is also attached to the top of the counterweight arbor and passes through the large groove in the head block. It then turns toward the floor and after going through the lock (7) on the lock rail and around the idler pulley (8) fastens to the bottom of the arbor.

Pulling down on the outside purchase line lifts the arbor and lowers the scenery hanging on the batten. A corresponding amount of weight placed on the arbor balances the weight of the scenery. Although the counterweight system is easy to run with parallel scenery, it is less flexible because of the fixed line-sets. Most of the rigging time used to hang an angled or raked piece is spent in overcoming rather than using the system.

Winch Systems

There have been attempts in the past to electrify a flying system, for example, by using a single, electric motor-driven winch to lift a battened line-set. In this system, all the lines in the set are wound upon a single drum that turns in only one direction to lift the batten. A mechanical clutching and braking device disengages the drum from the motor, allowing the weight of the attached scenery to bring the batten back down to the stage floor. Its only advantage over the counterweight system is that it requires only one person to run the remote-control operation. The slow fixed speed and insensitivity of the system combined with the rather hazardous braking operation has caused the "electric batten," as it was once called, to fall into disuse.

A new but short-lived method of flying scenery was the synchronous-winch system designed by George Izenour. It was based on a radically different approach to the control and placement of the winches and on a unique gridiron concept. Although the synchronous-winch system promised to give the theatre both the flexibility of the pin-and-rail and the weight-lifting capacity of the counterweight system (plus the added feature of a centralized electronic control), it failed in its initial obligation — synchronization. Repeated attempts to improve the design only proved that the system could never provide a dependable trim over a group of winches. While the synchronous winch has fallen short of being the ultimate method for flying scenery, it proved moderately successful in installations where it was combined with both the pin-and-rail and counterweight systems. It functions best when limited to scenery loads involving a scattered pattern of liftlines and conditions where accurate trim is not critical.

Perhaps the most important by-product of the synchronous-winch venture is the new look of the gridiron. The two features that have improved the gridiron for any flying system are, first, the increased number of channel openings positioned to extend from wall to wall of the stage, and second, the use of swivel loft blocks suspended at head height over each channel.

More channel openings at closer spacing (about 4- to 5-foot intervals) make it easier to spot lines away from the playing area to positions offstage. This gridiron can provide a spotline in any area of the stage without involving a major rigging problem to overcome rather than extend a flying system.

The overhead swivel loft block allows a cleaner gridiron floor, which is normally filled with sheaves and fixed line sets. A single bolt or pin holds the swivel block in the overhead channel beam, making it a simple operation to loosen and slide up or down stage or move to another channel. An additional feature contributing to an uncluttered gridiron floor is the mounting of all fixed line-sets under the gridiron floor in a lower set of channels at the conventional spacing of a counterweight system.

An equally important outgrowth which, perhaps, made the new gridiron possible was the increasingly widespread use of ⅛-inch aircraft cable as liftlines in place of hoisting cable or hemp rope. The use of the smaller, more flexible steel cable resulted in smaller sheaves and working parts.

Motor-Driven Spotline System • In an attempt to bring to the counterweight system the flexibility of the pin-and-rail, Izenour and associates developed the motor-driven spotline system (Figure 10–5). It is apparent from the drawing that the basic concept of the system is to use an individual driver motor on a specially designed double-purchase counterweight line-set. The theory is that after the weight of the scenery on the individual arbor has been counterweighted, the work load on each motor would be more or less the same, thus keeping the horsepower of the drive small and eliminating the need for line-to-line synchronization within the working set. The electronic read-out of the exact position of the arbor has been retained from the synchronous-winch system, but the operational accuracy is greatly improved.

The driver, which is a variable-speed ¾-horsepower DC electric motor, is placed either under the stage floor or behind the stage wall to minimize noise. It is attached to the lower portion of the purchase line by a sprocket and roller chain drive and utilizes both dynamic and electromechanical braking.

The top of the arbor is not connected to the conventional fixed line-set arrangement but utilizes new spotline and trim adjustment features. The head block, although in tandem-mounted position, is made up of individual caster-mounted swivel pulleys, which increase the "fleet angle" or spread of the lines in the set. The swivel head block, while allowing a wide spread to the pattern of the loft blocks in the line-set, is dependent upon the adjustable length of each line in the set to be completely flexible. The length adjustment of an individual line is accomplished by taking up each line on a trimming winch at the trimming gallery position. This small hand winch is located at what would normally be the end or "dead tie" of a single liftline in a double-purchase system.

To base the motor-driven arbor on a double-purchase counterweight system, however, gives the flyman cause for concern because of the tremendous demand for counterweights. The nature of the rigging produces a mechanical disadvantage of two to one, thereby creating a counterweight load twice the weight of the scenery it is lifting. The storing of counterweights and the endless job of loading and unloading an arbor are tasks that are not eliminated but are *doubled* when the double-purchase system is employed.

The advantages of the new motor-driven spotline system over the synchronous-winch are threefold. First, the number of lines to each motor is quadrupled; second, the synchronizing problem within a line-set is eliminated and improved between line-sets; and last, by using the double-purchase rigging, the top speed is doubled from 2 feet per second to 4 feet per second.

The motor-driven spotline system in its present form is not intended to be the sole method of flying scenery. An installation including 12 to 24 motor-driven arbors interspersed with several counterweighted rigid line-sets, as well as the always flexible pin-and-rail line-sets, would be considered ideal.

Hydraulic Flying System • The general principal of the hydraulic system is to use the power generated by an hydraulic cylinder and ram to provide the lift. The *piston* in the hydraulic cylinder, which is mounted vertically on a side wall of the stage, is double-faced and can be driven by fluid pressure from either side. Because of the short stroke of the ram in the cylinder, the system relies on a complicated rigging to reduce the ratio of the travel of the batten to the length of the ram stroke.

The 3/16-inch plastic-coated lift cables run horizontally over each loft block to a pair of head blocks that reverse the direction to meet a running pulley block or double-purchase rig. This maneuver not only shortens the distance of the lift cables by half but also provides a mechanical advantage of 2:1. The pulley block is moved by a single 5/16-inch flexible lead cable to a second moving pulley block. The second moving block, which is attached to the top of the ram, however, is doubled. The double moving block reduces the run of the lead cable by a 4:1 ratio.

The combination of the two double-purchase rigs, the first 2:1 and the second 4:1, reduces the ratio of the ram stroke to the batten travel to a 8:1 ratio. Figure 10–6 diagrams the rigging of a four-line batten system. A single cylinder can be isolated for a single spot-line rig.

Rigging

Whether a stage is equipped with a pin-and-rail, counterweight, or synchronous-winch system, there are several flying and rigging techniques common to all systems. While many of the routine problems

Figure 10-6
Hydraulic Flying System

inherent in the older systems are eliminated in a winch system, certain specific problems pertaining to the movement of scenery in relationship to its hanging position and loft height will be forever present.

Stage rigging begins with the relatively simple process of hanging scenery and includes the more complicated maneuvers of breasting and tripping scenery elements. The handling of stage curtains (such as the traveler, tableau, and contour curtains) and the unframed drop are also a part of stage rigging.

Hanging Scenery • An early step in rigging is the preparation of scenery to hang by providing hardware or some other means of attaching the liftlines. Hanger irons or D-rings, which are used on framed scenery, should be bolted to a vertical member of the framing for greater strength. On extremely tall or heavy pieces two rings are used, the one at the top serving as a guide for the liftline that is attached to the bottom. To lift the load from the bottom is not only a safer procedure, but it also provides a convenient position to trim each line (Figure 10–7a,b). The use of the turnbuckle or trimming hitch as illustrated is, of course, not necessary on the pin-and-rail system, for each line can be brought into trim from the flyfloor. The same is true of the winch system, which can "inch" an individual line into exact trim.

Cable Clamps • Occasionally framed scenery is hung a distance below the batten on a thin cable. These extensions are called "legs" and have to be fastened to the batten and to the scenery with a special technique. Although the cable may be very flexible, it is important not to allow a kink to form in the method of attaching, or the cable will lose its strength.

a

TOP HANGER IRON

(1)

CEILING
PLATE
(2) & RING

(3) BOTTOM HANGER
IRON

b

(1)
TRIMMING HITCH

(2)
SNATCH HOOK

(3)
TURN
BUCKLE

c

(1)　(2)　(3)

(4)　(5)　(6)

d

CABLE CLAMP　SLEEVE　NICRO PRESS　THIMBLE

Figure 10-7
The Hanging of Scenery

(a) Hanging hardware: (1) Top hanger iron, straight. (2) Ceiling plate and ring. (3) Bottom hanger iron, hooked. (b) Trim adjustments: (1) Trimming hitch using hemp rope or sash cord. (2) A snatch line. The snap hook on the end of the liftline makes it possible to unhook a flown piece of scenery. (3) Turnbuckle on wire cable, another way to adjust the trim of a flown piece of scenery. (c) Various methods of hanging a drop: (1) Tie around top batten. (2) Tie through batten. (3) Drop holder. (4) Tie-lines to pipe batten. (5 and 6) Floor stays. (d) Cable Clamps.

Figure 10–7d illustrates cable clamps and thimbles that secure the cable to the batten and the scenery.

The cable clamp is not very effective on very fine cable. The *Nicopress* clamp is a very secure, though permanent, fastener. The soft-metal tubes are designed to slide over the cables and are crimped into place with a Nicopress tool (Figure 10–7e).

Unframed pieces of scenery, such as drops and borders, are hung from their top battens and can be fastened to a pipe batten or can be picked up by a set of lines in many ways (Figure 10–7c). The long thin batten requires numerous pickup points, about every 6 feet (see ''Bridling''), to keep it from sagging and thereby spoiling the trim of the drop.

Figure 10-8
Knots Used in Stage Rigging

(a) Half hitch or overhand knot.
(b) Figure eight, used to put a knot in the end of a line to keep it from running through a pulley or eye.
(c) Square knot, for joining ropes of the same size. (d) Sheetbend, for joining ropes of different sizes.
(e) Bowline. A fixed loop used on end of liftline through ring. (f) Clove hitch on a batten, finished with a half hitch. It grips firmly under tension, but is easy to adjust or untie. (g) Fisherman's bend. Excellent for a tie onto a batten. Not as easy to adjust as the clove hitch. (h) Half hitch over a belaying pin. Used as tie-off on pinrail.
(i) Stopper hitch, made with a smaller line in the middle of a larger rope. The safety line on the counterweight lock rail uses a stopper hitch on the purchase line. (j) Sunday: (1) A method of joining the ends of a small loop of wire cable without putting a sharp kink in the cable. (2) The loop is then used to clew a set of rope lines together so as to counterweight them with a sandbag. (k) Lashline tie-off. (l) Trimming hitch, to adjust the trim of a hanging piece of scenery.

Knots • Safe stage rigging requires the use of many familiar knots. The stage technician and the designer who has to supervise rigging should both be skilled in the use of at least a few of the knots and hitches that appear in stage rigging. Some of the most frequently used knots are illustrated in Figure 10–8 along with notations of their uses for stage rigging. A more detailed and comprehensive manual of knots and splices can be found in the catalogues of cordage companies (see bibliography at the back of the book).

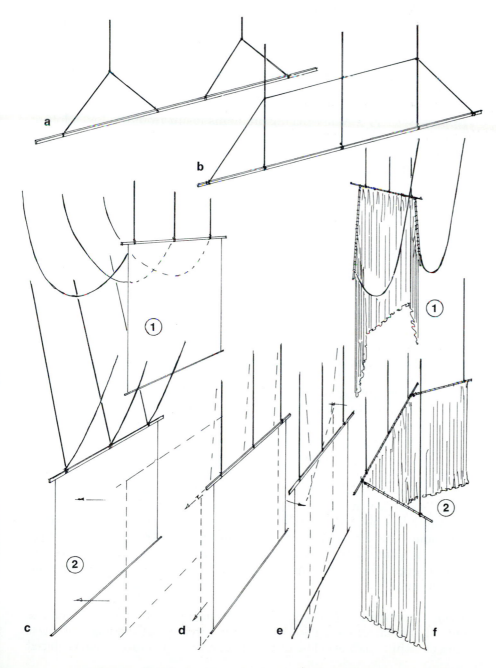

Figure 10-9
Bridling and Breasting Techniques
(a) A simple bridle. (b) A bridle of a set of lines to suport the overhang of an extra-long batten.
(c) Breasting a drop up- and downstage: (1) Stored position. (2) Working position. (d) Breasting across stage. (e) Twisting a batten into an angled position. (f) Breast lines on the side-tab arms of a drape cyc.: (1) Stored position, arms hanging down. (2) Working position, arms pulled by breast lines into spread position.

Breasting Scenery • Regardless of which flying system is being used, two pieces of scenery cannot occupy the same space at the same time, although the designer may wish they could. Consequently, it sometimes becomes necessary to hang a unit away from its working position and rely on breasting lines to bring it to its proper location. A breasting line (sometimes called a *checkline* or restraining line) is usually dead-tied at one end to the gridiron or side-stage position and fastened to the scenery at the opposite end. When the piece is in its flown position the breasting line is slack, but as the piece comes into its working position the breasting line becomes taut and breasts the unit off dead-center hanging. (Several breasting maneuvers are illustrated in Figure 10–9c-f).

Bridling • The bridle is a simple rigging used to spread the load picked up on one line (Figure 10–9a,b). The number of lines in a set can be reduced, or the number of pickup points increased by the bridling technique.

Tripping Scenery • Many rigging problems result from too low a loft or the complete absence of one. Tripping, which can only be used on soft or semisoft scenery, is one way of flying scenery in a limited space (Figure 10–10d-f). By picking up the bottom of a drop as well as the top, it can be flown in half the height necessary to clear a full drop. The height can be further reduced by picking up the drop a third of the height off the floor and thereby tripping it in thirds.

An extreme variation of tripping is to roll a drop on its bottom batten or drum at the bottom edge (Figure 10–10a-c). The old opera house "oleo" drop was rigged in this manner, and it still is a good way of flying a drop on a stage with reduced flying space.

Levitation • The flying of objects or persons, as if in defiance of gravity, requires special rigging. To create a workable setting for flying actors or objects, a designer should be familiar with the special rigging that is required for a flying effect. The right kind of background, properly planned exits and entrances, and atmospheric lighting can serve to mask or camouflage any exposed support wires and highlight the illusion.

To create the illusion of floating in space, an object must be supported on as fine a wire as possible so that the support will disappear from view at a distance. Lightweight objects, such as a bat or bird, can be supported on fishing line (20-pound test), which becomes invisible at a very short distance. The size and strength of the support wire to fly an actor, however, is more critical. The kind of wire used depends upon whether or not it has to go over a pulley. Wire rope, such as airplane strand, is extremely flexible and strong for its size — $\frac{1}{16}$-inch aircraft cable tests at 500 pounds and has a recommended safe load of 100 pounds; 20-gauge (.045-inch) piano wire has great tensile strength (500 pounds) for its size but is a single strand and cannot be run through a pulley. Any sharp bend or kink quickly weakens piano wire to the point of breaking.

Flying Apparatus • A flying apparatus begins with a harness for the actor. It is made of strong webbing and is fitted about the legs and chest like a parachute harness. The ring, to which the wire is attached, is placed approximately in the middle of the back, a little above the actor's center of gravity. The harness, of course, is worn under the costume with only the ring protruding.

Variable Load · Of the many rigging problems experienced with conventional flying systems, the most annoying is the variable load or unbalanced condition resulting from the removal of part or all of the scenery load from a set of lines. The *deus ex machina,* descending with a live cargo of gods or goddesses and then ascending to the heavens empty, is an example of a variable load.

Figure 10-10
Tripping Techniques

(a) The "oleo" drop, which rolls on the bottom batten or drum. Note: the rigging of the rope gives operator a mechanical advantage of two. Drop is made with horizontal seams to make roll flat. (b) An alternate rigging. Liftline has equal turns on the end of drum, in reverse direction of drop. When liftline is pulled, it unwinds as the drop winds onto the drum and thus rises.
(c) Detail of drum construction:
(1) Contour pieces. (2) Linear stiffeners. (3) Lattice slats.
(4) Padding and final cover.
(d) Tripping a drop; back set of lines is attached to bottom batten:
(1) Working position. (2) Stored or tripped position. (e) Tripping in thirds. Upstage batten is attached at one-third height of the drop off the floor: (1) Working position.
(2) Tripped position. (f) Tripping a drop which has the lower portion framed: (1) Working position.
(2) Tripped position. (g) Book ceiling rigging: (1) Working position.
(2) Booked position. (h) Carpet hoist, handling a variable load: (1) Free arbor (no batten attached) carrying counterweights. (2) Working arbor with batten that handles the variable load. (3) Free arbor is locked off at top position allowing working arbor to run free of counterweight after load has been removed from batten (rigging is only usable on light loads of 100–150 pounds).

If the weight variation is not too great (100–150 pounds), the carpet hoist is one way of compensating. The counterbalancing weight to the variable load is not directly attached to the load-bearing batten but is handled on a separate purchase line. Figure 10–10h shows a carpet hoist rigging on a counterweight system. The counterbalancing weight is on the first arbor (1), which is a "free arbor," meaning that it is not attached to a batten or line-set.

The second arbor (2), which carries only enough weight to bring the arbor down, is attached to the batten handling the variable load. The

Figure 10-11
Levitation

Types of rigging for flying objects or persons: (a) Pendulum and breast line: (1) Pendulum line, placed off center, has long arc when it is swinging free of breast line. (2) Breast line shortens arc and lifts object up and out of sight. (b) Pendulum and double breast line: (1) Pendulum line. (2) First breast line. (3) Second breast line. (c) Harness for actor. (d) Schematic diagram of Joseph Kerby's flying rig for *Peter Pan*: (1) Piano wire lead. (2) ⅛-inch wire cable feeds through swivel sheave at gridiron to a drum off stage. (3) Operating line turns large drum, thereby achieving a mechanical advantage and avoiding the use of counterweights. (e) Double-line counterweighted rigging provides a very flexible lateral movement although the actor has to remain attached to rig.

extending hooks on the bottom of this arbor pass under and engage the first arbor to utilize its weights. Note that when the first arbor is locked or tied off in an up position at the moment the variable load is being removed, the second arbor is free to disengage and return to a down position. The counterbalancing weight can be returned to the second arbor by reversing the procedure and unlocking the first arbor.

Any larger weight variation has to be handled by an electric floor winch or a hand winch which provides a mechanical advantage to offset the unbalanced load condition. The synchronous-winch system, of course, eliminates any variable load problem because it is based upon a direct, not a counterbalance lift.

The type of rigging for levitation depends upon the movement of the actor both in the air and on the floor. For instance, the Rhine Maidens in Wagner's *Das Rheingold* keep flying in a lateral pattern back and forth across the stage. On the other hand, Peter Pan, in addition to flying in all directions, also lands and walks about on the floor.

Most flying apparatus is based on a pendulum action whether the pattern of movement is lateral or in all directions. The pendulum is usually placed off center for a lateral movement and center stage for a free-movement pattern. Figure 10–11 illustrates, schematically, the various pendulum riggings as well as other methods of flying actors, some of which require two wires and more complicated apparatus.

Curtain Rigging

The actions or movements of a stage curtain, other than raising or lowering on a batten, are classified into three groups. A curtain can be drawn horizontally from the sides, tripped diagonally into a tableau shape, or tripped vertically into the varied patterns of a contour curtain.

Traveler or Draw Curtain • The conventional action of a traveler curtain is the drawing together of two curtain halves on two overlapping sections of track. The track guides the carriers, which are attached to the top edge of the curtain at about 1-foot intervals. The draw line is fastened to the first or lead carrier, which pushes or pulls the rest of the carriers to open or close the curtain. The many track and carrier designs and the rigging of the drawline are illustrated in Figure 10–12.

Sometimes a one-way traveler is needed, which means that instead of coming from opposite sides of the stage, the curtain is drawn on stage from one side on a single long track (Figure 10–12b). Also illustrated is a rear-fold device that causes all carriers to move at once rather than being pushed or pulled by the lead carrier (Figure 10–12c).

Tableau Curtain • Like the traveler, the tableau curtain is made up of two curtain panels hung, with a center overlap, from a single batten. Each panel is lifted or tripped by a diagonal drawline attached to the central edge, about a third of its height off the floor, that runs through rings on the back of the curtain to a pulley on the batten (Figure 10–13a). The tableau has a quicker action than a traveler, but does not lift completely out of sight unless the batten is also raised at the final moment. Because of its picturesque quality, the tableau curtain drape is frequently left in view as a decorative frame for the scene.

Figure 10-12
Traveler Curtains and Tracks
(a) Rigging of a draw curtain or two-way traveler: (1) Draw line. (2) Head block. (3) Lead carrier on downstage curtain, fastened to drawline. (4) Change-of-direction pulley. (5) Lead carrier on upstage curtain also fastened to drawline. (6) Floor block. (b) One-way traveler curtain. (c) Detail of rear-fold attachment. All carriers move at once with drawline and curtain folds offstage rather than bunching onstage. (1) Lead carrier. (2) Drawline. (3) Rear-fold attachment grips drawline until it is straightened up by bumping into the next carrier. (4) Drawline now passes through the rear-fold attachment. Various Types of Traveler Tracks and Carriers: (d) wooden track with ball carriers, (e) square steel track with double-wheel carrier, (f) round steel track with ball carriers, (g) triangular steel track with side opening and single-wheel carriers, (h) I-beam track.

Figure 10-13
Front Curtain Riggings

(a) Tableau curtain. (b) Contour curtain. The lift lines are numbered 1–6. The lines are paired 1–6, 3–4, and 2–5. (c) Brail curtain.

Contour Curtain • The contour curtain is made in a single panel with great fullness, usually about 200 percent of the curtain width. The curtain, which is made of thin or soft material to drape well, is tripped by a series of vertical drawlines attached to the bottom edge of the curtain and running through rings on the back to pulleys attached to the batten. By varying the lift on certain lines the bottom edge of the curtain takes on many different contours (Figure 10–13b).

Brail Curtain • The front curtain in a no-loft stage is sometimes rigged as a Brail curtain to achieve a faster and more-desirable lifting action than the slower side motion of a traveler curtain. In this case the amount of lift on each drawline is equal, eliminating the need for the abnormal fullness of a regular contour curtain. To add a decorative quality the curtain may have the horizontal fullness that is obtained by gathering material on the vertical seams, thereby producing a series of soft swags (Figure 10–13c).

SCENERY ON CASTERS

Moving a three-dimensional piece of scenery on the floor is made easier and faster if it is mounted on casters. Such mounting can vary from a single caster on the edge of a hinged wing to the large castered platform or wagon to move an entire set. In between are such techniques as castered tip and lift jacks and outrigger wagons for rolling.

Casters

The stage places special demands on casters. A good stage caster should first of all run quietly, which requires a rubber wheel or a rubber-tired wheel. The rubber-tired wheel is a better long-time investment because the tires can be replaced as they wear.

Secondly, the caster wheel should have as large a diameter as possible (3½ to 4 inches). A wagon on 4-inch diameter caster wheels rolls with little effort and is not as easily stopped by small obstructions such as rugs, padding, ground cloth, or lighting cables.

Casters are of two general types: those made to move freely in any direction and those made to move in a fixed direction. The *swivel caster* has a free action that allows it to move in any direction, while the *fixed caster* is limited to one direction in a guided or tracked movement. It is more economical to invest in swivel casters which, when necessary, can be blocked into a fixed position for a tracked movement (Figure 10–14). An alternate method is to purchase swivel casters and a matching set of fixed forks without the wheels. The wheels of the swivel casters may be removed and inserted into the forks to create a fixed caster that is easier to mount.

Lift and Tip Jacks

Mounting scenery on casters in order to make it move easily creates a paradoxical problem of anchoring, preventing the unit from moving at an undesirable moment. Lift and tip jacks are methods of lifting or tipping a piece of scenery from a standing position onto casters to move (Figures 10–14d; 15e,f). The scenery, however, sits firmly on the floor when it is in its working position.

Figure 10-14
Castering Techniques

(a) Single caster mounted on rear of flat. (b) Single caster mounted in corner. (c) Outrigger wagon. (d) Tip jack: (1) Scenery tipped back to rest on casters. (2) Scenery upright, blocked-off caster in working position. (e) Castered jack: (1) Side view showing how scenery is held clear of floor. (2) Caster jack on a hinged or "wild" piece of scenery. (f) Flat-top swivel caster. (g) Flat-top fixed caster. (h) Stem-type swivel caster for furniture. (i) Small stem-type ball caster for furniture. (j) Large stem-type swivel caster. Mounts into bottom of scaffolding pipe.

Another way to anchor a castered platform or a bulky three-dimensional piece of scenery is to attach it to units that are sitting on the floor or by tipping the piece onto casters mounted on its offstage or upstage edge (Figure 10–15d).

Outrigger Wagons

An outrigger wagon is essentially a pattern of castered jacks or braces around the outside of a set or portion of a set. The scenery remains on casters. It is a skeleton wagon intended to brace and caster the scenery. The action of the scene is played not on a wagon but on the stage floor (Figure 10–14c).

Figure 10-15
Methods of Stabilizing Castered Units

(a) Barrel bolt fits into hole in stage floor. (b) Hinged footiron and stage screw. (c) Portion of platform not on casters: (1) Steps hinged to castered platform folds on top for easy movement. (2) Unfolded and resting on the stage floor, the steps stabilize the platform unit.
(d) Casters on offstage edge of platform: (1) Platform in working position, casters on back edge.
(2) Platform is tipped onto casters to move. (e) Lift jack: (1) Pictorial view of lift jack. (2) Side view showing jack lifting scenery. (3) Jack released, scenery rests on floor.
(f) Lift jack under a platform: (1) Jack released. (2) Jack depressed to lift platform on casters. (3) Sectional view. (4) Note eccentric hinging.

Wagons

The low-level platform (6 to 8 inches) on casters or wagons can carry a large portion of a setting including the set props. Large wagons often carry an entire setting, which can swiftly and easily move into place for a scene change. Although requiring ample floor space, the wagon is a flexible and efficient method of handling scenery.

Wagon Construction

Wagon construction is basically the same as platform construction. The caster in a sense becomes the post of the platform. If the casters are mounted on caster planks (2-by-6 feet or 1⅛-by-6 feet) the minimum span between supports can be increased. The caster plank, in addition to providing a sturdy mount for the caster, serves as a cleat for the top to increase the overall strength of the wagon. Normally, unless the wagon is to carry an extremely heavy load, such as a piano, the spacing of casters at 3-foot intervals is sufficient to remove any noticeable deflection.

Stock wagon units made in a convenient size (3-by-6-foot or 4-by-8-foot modules) for handling are pin-hinged together to make larger units (Figure 10–17). Although stock wagons use more casters than are necessary for the total area, the flexibility of arrangements and handling and ease of storage justify the module system.

Figure 10-16
The Air Bearing Caster

Basic air bearing unit. Cross section of the unit showing the flow of the compressed air into the flexible inner tube and out through the vent holes, thereby lifting the object on a film of air for a frictionless movement. *Photos courtesy of Rolair System, Inc., Santa Barbara, Calif.*

The Casket Lock • Wagon modules can be fastened together to make up a larger wagon unit with loose-pin hinges on the top. If the decoration or action on the top of the wagon prohibits the use of loose-pin hinges, a hidden fastener, the casket lock, can be used. The two halves of the lock are mounted opposite each other in countersunk slots. Through an access hole in the top, the two halves of the fastener are locked together with an Allen wrench-type key (Figure 10–17e).

Wagon Movements

Aside from the free movement of a wagon carrying a full or partial set, there are several controlled or tracked movements that can become a scheme of production for handling scenery entirely on casters. The scheme may be based upon a pair of alternating wagons that allow the scenery and props to be changed on the offstage wagon while the alternate

Figure 10-17
The Wagon Unit

(a) Construction of a stock wagon: (1) 4-inch swivel casters. (2) 2 × 6 caster planks. (3) 2 × 3 frame. (4) 4 × 8-foot, ¾-inch 5-ply top. (b) Cross section. (c) Large wagon made up of stock units: (1) Stock unit. (2) Units pin-hinged together. (3) Facing boards. (d) A different shape made of three stock wagons and two special corner pieces. (e) Casket Lock. A unit to lock together wagons.

wagon is in the playing position. The transverse, jackknife, and split-wagon movements operate on this principle (Figures 10–18; 10–20).

When there are small sets in a production it is sometimes desirable to keep each set intact on separate wagons. The stage then becomes packed with wagon sets and the shifting is accomplished by shuttling each wagon into position. The pattern of movement varies with the size and shape of the sets and their order of appearance in the play.

Figure 10-18
Tracked Wagon Movement

(a) Tracks on top of the stage floor. (1) Steel angle irons. (2) Beveled wood which though subject to wear is quieter than steel on steel. (b) Section detail. (c) Section showing track cut into the stage floor. In an elaborate tracked-wagon scheme such as those diagramed in d, e, and f, a temporary stage floor is installed with space beneath the track groove for cables to drive the wagon unit by hand winch from an offstage position. Types of Tracked Wagon Movements: (d) Transverse movement. (e) Split transverse wagons and a large single wagon moving up- and downstage. (f) Multimovements: transverse, diagonal, as well as up- and downstage.

The Revolving Stage

Another controlled movement is that of a castered unit around a fixed center: a revolving stage. Such a stage that is not permanently built into the stage floor is similar to the wagon in structure. To remain portable, a turntable is made in small pie-shaped sections that are bolted or pin-hinged together (Figure 10–21). The casters are mounted in a pattern to properly support each unit and are fixed in a position perpendicular to a radius line drawn through the point of attachment. If the casters are carefully mounted, the turntable will revolve about its pivot point with very little effort.

Another method of assembling a portable turntable is to reverse the normal position of the casters under the table and place them upside down on the stage floor (Figure 10–21c). The casters are placed in concentric circles as bearing points on a prepared rolling surface on the under side of the table. Each caster is shimmed to the same height to ensure a level turntable floor. Although the assembly time is longer and the table is a little higher off the stage floor, the result is a smooth-running, quiet turntable. Figure 10–22 illustrates the assembly steps as well as the cable-drive and motor method of powering a revolving stage.

Single Turntable • The revolving stage as a basic device can have a variety of sizes and uses. The most familiar is the large single turntable. Unless the stage is especially designed for a large turntable, its diameter is limited by the depth of the stage. If the stage happens to be shallow in proportion to the proscenium opening, a single turntable will leave an awkward corner in the downstage right and left positions. Attempts to fill the area with a show portal or with hinged pieces on the turntable that unfold and mask the corner more or less negate the basic function of the single revolving stage (Figure 10–24a).

Two Turntables • A shallow stage is adaptable to the use of two turntables that either touch in the center or are held slightly apart. This method removes the awkward corners of the single turntable, but it creates a design problem—that of joining all the sets in the center (Figure 10–24b).

Three Turntables • Occasionally, a large turntable is combined with two small disks in the downstage right and left positions. The small disks either carry scenery related to the large set in the center or are small independent sets. The production scheme for *I Remember Mama* designed by George Jenkins used this technique (Figure 10–24e).

Ring and Turntable • A great deal more variety of movement is achieved by using a ring and turntable combination. The ring and turntable are individually powered so that they can turn in the same direction at identical or different speeds, or they may revolve in opposite directions. The possible combinations of fixed units on the ring and turntable are almost endless. If the changes are made avista it becomes a delightful scheme of production. The settings for *Protective Custody* designed by Peter Larkin were handled in this manner (Figure 10–24f).

CABLES

PLATFORM

STAGE PLATFORM

GUIDE TRACK

GUIDE   GUIDE

Figure 10-19
Cable Drive for a Moving Wagon
A schematic drawing showing the drive cable, hidden from view under a raised stage floor, and attached to wagon guides, right and left. The cable turns on the drum of the winch to pull the wagon to the right or left.

a

① ②

③

Figure 10-20
Pivoted Wagon Movement
(a) Pivot mounted on the corner of the wagon: (1) Pivot detail. (2) Socket fastened to the floor at the pivot point. Although the pivot and socket positions are often reversed in a turntable installation, it is best under the illustrated conditions to place the socket on the floor. A corner pivot, besides being an awkward mounting position, may also have to bear weight because the nearest caster is usually about four feet away. (3) Fixed caster set perpendicular to radius. (b) Jackknife wagons. (c) Type of jackknife in combination with split wagons. (d) Pivoting a segment of a circle, semi-revolving.

b

2   1

P   P

c

2R   1R   1L   2L

P

d

2   1

P

Figure 10-21
The Revolving Stage

A portable revolving stage or
turntable can be built many ways.
Shown here are two methods.
(a) Turntable made up of stock
wagon units with special-shaped
wagons to form the curve of the
outside edge: (1) Stock wagon.
(2) Special wagon to complete
circle. (3) Casters blocked perpendicular to radius. (4) Section.
(b) Turntable made of wedge-
shaped units around central core.
Fewer casters are used, creating
less noise: (1) Basic wedge-shaped
unit. (2) Top removed showing the
position of casters. (3) Central core.
(4) Section. (c) Turntable
construction, reverse castering.
(1) Basic wedge-shaped unit.
(2) Central core, ball-bearing pivot.
(3) Single unit viewed from
underneath to show framing.
(4) Bearing surface in path of
casters, ¾-inch 5-ply or particle
board. (5) Casters mounted on the
stage floor in patterns that are the
same circumference as the caster-
bearing surface on the underside of
the turntable (6) Spirit level and
rotating bar to check the level of
each caster mount to ensure a
steady, level rotation. Although the
reverse caster turntable takes
longer to assemble, it is quieter and
easier to turn than the
conventionally castered unit.

a

b

c

Figure 10-22
Motorized Cable Drive for
a Single Turntable
(a) Sketch shows: (1) Tension idler.
(2) Mule pulley to change direction
of the cable. (3) Centering pulley, it
keeps cable from creeping and
binding as it winds and unwinds on
the edge of the turntable. (4) Winch
to control the tension on the cable.
(b) Motor and reduction pulley
system. The drive is a 2.5
horsepower, variable speed,
reversible, 230-volt DC motor.
Instead of a drum, a system of
pulleys is used to keep the cable
from binding and still provide
enough friction to move the
turntable. (c) A diagram of the
threading of the cable, which is
one-quarter inch of flexible steel
long-spliced into a continuous loop.
Photo courtesy Tom Eaton

a

c

b

Two Rings and Two Turntables • Although less adaptable to revolving fixed units than the single ring and turntable, two rings around two turntables are a very flexible method of changing elements of scenery and properties. This was demonstrated in the production of *Lady in the Dark* designed by Harry Horner. With the help of flown pieces of scenery, the settings were able to blend from one scene to the next in full view of the audience (Figure 10–24c).

Semi-revolves and Combinations • The remaining variations of the revolving technique are the semi-revolving stage and combination of a turntable and a wagon.

The semi-revolving stage is a portion of a ring or turntable tracked to swing in half an arc and then return to its original position (Figure 10–24g). The semi-revolving stage may be large or small, used singly or in pairs, or, in some cases, combined with a turntable.

Figure 10-23
Methods of Powering a Single Turntable

(a) Cable and winch: (1) A spliced cable with one turn around the outside edge of the turntable is held taut by (2) a tension idler and powered by (3) a hand winch. (b) Motor-driven turntable: A reversible and variable-speed electric motor underneath a highly mounted turntable. (1) Motor. (2) Reduction gear box. (3) Spring loaded friction drive wheels, or bevel gears. (4) Drive ring for friction drive, or gear ring for bevel gear drive. (5) Raised, fiber-padded track for fixed casters. (6) Steel channel-beam framework. (7) Roller-bearing pivot. It should be noted that both a and b turntables are usually surrounded by a raised temporary stage floor flush with the top of the turntable. (c) Drive wheel power unit. An example of a turntable on top of the stage floor with an eccentric pivot position making the use of the ring drive or cable drive impracticable: (1) Basic platform structure on fixed casters perpendicular to radius. (2) Pivot located off the center of the platform. (3) Wheel drive power unit hidden by (4) superstructure of the setting. (5) The path of rotation. (6) Components of the power unit: 5-horsepower, reversible DC motor linked to (7) gear reduction box. (8) Drive wheel which turns the platform by friction drive off of the stage floor. It is connected to the gear box by a sprocket and roller-chain drive. (9) Ball-bearing socket fixed to the platform. (10) Turn indicator. A self-synchronizing motor (SELSYN) mounted on the wagon with its shaft fixed to the pivot and wired to a companion motor mounted offstage. An arrow attached to the shaft of the second "selsyn" becomes a pointer to indicate the exact position of the turntable. (11) Dial face of the turn indicator. (Original installation designed and constructed by George B. Honcher and Pat Mitchell.)

b

c

Figure 10-24
Turntable and Ring Combinations
(a) Single large turntable. (b) Two small turntables. (c) Two small turntables with rings.
(d) Single turntable in a transverse wagon. (e) Large turntable with two small disks. (f) Large
turntable with ring. (g) Semi-revolving ring-segment and small turntable. (h) A pair of rings.

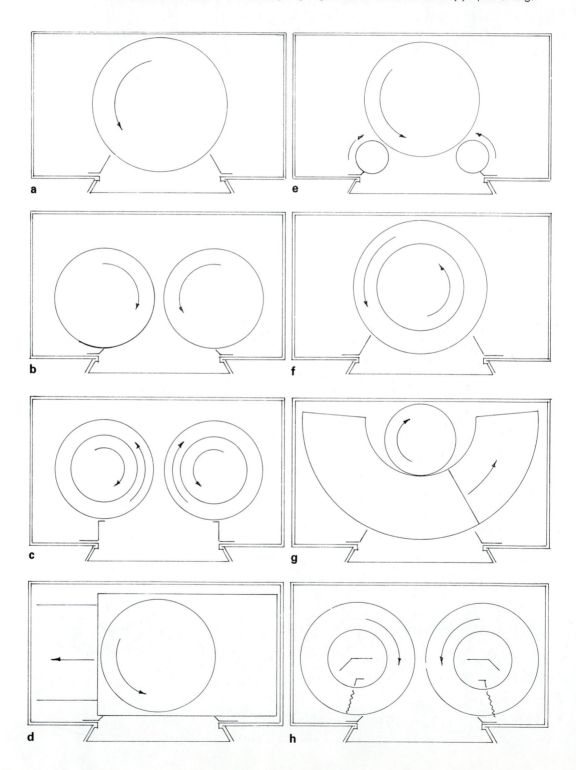

A combination of revolving and lateral movements can be accomplished by building a turntable into a full-stage transverse wagon (Figure 10–24d). This combination works best when a portion of one set is reused many times during the show. The lobby of *Grand Hotel,* for example, was saved in this manner. Most of the lobby settings remained on the left side of the wagon while a portion moved on the turntable. The smaller rooms and other scenes in the hotel occupied the remainder of the turntable and were moved into better sightlines by sliding the wagon to the left.

The scheme can be varied by setting the turntable into the center of the wagon and having elements of scenery on both sides instead of one side.

ELEVATOR STAGES

As a means of moving scenery, the elevator stage requires the maximum amount of stage machinery. Unless the theatre is in the position to make constant use of the equipment, or the elevators have a second function such as a scenery and property lift to remote storage areas, the installation is extravagant. With few exceptions (The Metropolitan Opera, Radio City Music Hall, and similar presentation houses), the normal legitimate theatre in the United States has little use for the elevator stage as a method of changing scenery (Figure 10–25).

Figure 10-25
Elevator Stage

A backstage view of the elaborate elevator installation at the Metropolitan Opera House, New York.

Figure 10-26
Beneath the Stage

(a) Counterbalanced disappearance elevator. (b) A highly specialized example of rigging through the stage floor to raise a curtain batten up from the floor.

a

b

The financial organization and scale of production of numerous state theatres in Europe make the elaborate elevator stage a more feasible method of handling scenery than could be supported by the unsubsidized theatres of the United States.

Small Elevators and Traps

Although the average stage may not have an elevator system, it usually has a portion of the floor area made in sections or "traps" that may be used to raise small elements of scenery through the stage floor. The traps can be removed to give access through the stage floor into the trap room below. Entrances by stairs or ladder can be made from below through such an opening. Trap openings are made between transverse beams that run parallel to the footlights. As a result, the designer has great freedom in planning the size and position of an opening running across stage. Openings running up and downstage, however, are limited by the transverse beams.

The construction of a temporary lift that can be used for scenery or actors is shown in Figure 10–26a. Although the elevator platform can be as large as a single trap opening, the example illustrated is smaller. A larger elevator would require more guides and liftlines. Figure 10–26b is an example of an elevatorlike mechanism under the stage floor designed to raise a small curved batten supporting a curtain. The technique is probably very similar to the methods used to raise a curtain out of the front pit of the Roman theatre.

The Elevator Floor

The elevators designed to move scenery should not be confused with the short-run elevators used to shape the stage floor in some of the more recent theatres. In this instance, sections of the stage floor can be raised or lowered by elevators to make levels or pits but are not used to move scenery. They can, however, be considered as a means of changing the appearance or form of the stage floor, thus creating a new scene without moving scenery.

Stage Properties and Effects

I n addition to large scenic background elements of the stage setting, the designer is responsible for the design and selection of stage properties and smaller bits of scenery used by the actors. This may vary from finding a marble-topped Louis XV console table to making an exotic sofa for a Turkish cosy corner, or from borrowing a Victorian tea set to fashioning tree leaves. Whether borrowed or constructed, each property must be carefully coordinated into the design composition and adjusted to the production scheme and must also be checked for size and ease of use by the actors.

Stage properties are in essence the design details of the overall visual composition. Although the visual significance of properties applies more specifically to a realistic interior setting than to an exterior or abstract scene, their contribution cannot be overemphasized. Stage properties are, many times, the accent or artistic touch that makes or breaks the effectiveness of a stage setting.

Perhaps a more significant use of properties occurs on the thrust and arena stages, both of which are almost entirely dependent on properties to set the scene visually. Because of the close audience-stage relationship in both cases, the finished detail and quality of all properties are subject to closer inspection than they are on the proscenium stage.

Another important visual consideration of a stage property is its "rightness" for the play. The designer has to continually ask such questions as: Is this chair in the right historical period and nationality? Is the sideboard the kind Mama would choose? And so on. The selection and designing of furniture and properties is done in close collaboration with the director in order to ensure their appropriateness for the play and to check how they fit into the staging of the action. For example, large furniture may hinder movement, or a high-backed chair may block off a view of upstage action.

Real furniture is, of course, used in the modern theatre, although it is often altered to become stageworthy. Scale and color are sometimes changed to improve its relationship to the stage composition. Because of these alterations even real furniture may take on a theatrical look. It becomes a stage property suggesting, sometimes faintly, sometimes openly, that it is no longer real. The name, property or "prop," is often synonymous with the unreal or theatrical.

Properties of a setting should be planned and built simultaneously with the rest of the scenic elements. Their importance to the design and production scheme is sometimes overlooked in the planning period. The construction of built properties is often started too late, or too many decisions in the selection of furniture or decorative features are postponed until the final hectic rehearsals. This often occurs when the designer, overworked and pressed for time, places the responsibility of organizing the properties on the shoulders of a willing but not-too-able apprentice.

To make better use of their time, designers should have a competent background in historical furniture styles and period decorations and should be thoroughly acquainted with the traditional uses of properties in the theatre. They must also be able to evaluate a property in terms of its importance to the action of the play and its sheer decorative qualities.

PROPERTIES VERSUS SCENERY

What is a prop? When does a small piece of scenery become a property or a large property become scenery?

Stage properties are traditionally defined as: (1) all objects carried or handled by the actor; (2) separate portions of the set on which the actor may stand or sit, such as rocks, stumps, or logs; (3) decorative features not permanently built or painted on the scenery (pictures, draperies, and so on); (4) the ground cloth and rugs; and (5) all sound and visual effects that are not electrically powered such as a gun shot or door slam.

In the average show, the categorical division of properties is based for the most part upon these traditional definitions of a property. An occasional exception or collaboration is made with the agreement of all concerned. Hence, a tree trunk may be scenery and foliage a property; a pair of glasses discovered on the stage is a property while those brought on stage by the actors are considered costumes. Heavy properties often become scenery because of their size or necessity to be fastened to the scenery for movement.

Properties may also be classified according to their size and use. Properties can be designated as either hand, set, or dress properties, or as visual or sound-effect properties.

Hand Properties

The small objects handled by the actor on the stage are hand props. They include such items as teacups, books, fans, letters, and many more similar articles.

Set Properties

As the name implies, set properties are the larger elements more closely related to the scenery but still used by the actor. This group includes furniture, stoves, sinks, rugs, ground cloth, and any domestic object. Exterior set props consist of small rocks, stumps, bushes, foliage, real dirt (*Tobacco Road*), grass mats, and so on.

Set properties are in the care of the property person, who supervises the placing of the set prop on the stage and its removal to a stored position offstage.

Dress Properties

Dress properties are more closely related to the setting. Their chief function is decorative. Dress properties consist of all the elements not specifically used by the actor that serve to fill in and complete or dress the set. Window curtains, pictures, wall hangings, flower groupings are a few typical dress properties.

As a class, dress properties are not necessarily superficial. They can become a strong decorative feature in a setting. Because they are not used by the actor they can often be faked in order to be handled more easily or in a different way from the normal set property. Bookcases, for example, may have faked books and be attached to the scenery. A saloon back bar is often dressed with fake plastic or papier-mâché bottles to cut down the weight. A period piano or spinet, which is hard to find and harder to borrow, can be easily built and faked as a dress prop (Figure 11–1). These are, of course, just a few of the many, many types of faked dress properties.

SELECTING SET AND DRESS PROPERTIES

The designer is responsible for the compositional unity, period continuity, and color relationships of the set and dress properties. Their first notation appears in the designer's sketch, which may or may not be clear as to the indication of the real form. Once the general idea of the design has been accepted the designer can turn to a more careful study of period line and availability of each piece.

Figure 11-1
Dress Properties

(a) Fake spinet piano. (b) Dummy books in book case. (c) Papier-mâché bar bottles.

a   b   c

The final decision on each piece of furniture is made by the designer with the director's approval. To help reach this decision at an early stage in the planning, the designer uses individual sketches or illustrational clippings. The selection of set properties can be further facilitated by the use of a furniture plot and compositional elevations as suggested in Chapter 5, which give exact references to the size of an individual piece in relation to its surroundings.

Period Styles and Ornamentation

Needless to say, scene designers must be well grounded not only in furniture styles but also in period interior decoration and architecture. The more familiar designers are with the historical background of a period style, the easier it will be to design, select, and make up set and dress properties that bring a feeling of authenticity to the setting.

Throughout the period of selecting or designing the properties and setting designers draw heavily on a knowledge of period style. They cannot hope to recall at an instant the details of a certain period, but they should have a general sense of period style at the tip of their pencils. For detail and enrichment of the general form designers must depend on research. Research does not always mean leafing through reference books or old periodicals. It frequently involves study of the real thing in a museum or in actual surroundings. Designers frequently resort to sketches or photographs to collect this information. Although these are not presentation drawings they can become important to the designer as personal reference material.

Designers soon learn to conserve energy and legwork when doing research by avoiding duplication. Generally much more material is gathered than is finally used. If all the research examples are filed and catalogued, they may come in handy at a later date on another show. Designers in this way soon find themselves in possession of an efficient reference library. They should also have several inexpensive illustrated books (such as those listed in the bibliography) containing collections of furniture styles and ornamentation. More extensive research, of course, may be needed to back any one style, depending upon the needs of the play.

Draperies

Of all the dress properties used onstage, draperies are the decorative detail that brings character to an interior setting. Their elegance or cheapness, style or lack of style or even their complete absence contributes immeasurably to the visual expression of the kind of place and people in the play.

From historical references, the designer can plan to use draperies which, depending upon the period, may include window, door, fireplace mantel, picture, and mirror draperies. The designing of draperies is based upon a knowledge of the way the material drapes or hangs and the methods of cutting and assembling the material into the desired effect.

A New York designer needs only to prepare a carefully scaled or dimensioned drawing of the assembled drapery, specifying the material and the action, if any. Window curtains, for example, may have to be drawn for a tableau during the action of the play.

For university and community theatre production, the designer is expected to guide the execution of the draperies and therefore needs to know something about drapery patterns and assembly techniques.

Window Drapery • Although draperies may occur in many positions other than at the windows of a setting, the fundamental parts making up the decorative portion are the same. The basic parts of the window drapery, which may or may not be used all at the same time, are: glass curtains, shade, overdrapery, and valance. The overdrapery and the valance are the frame, so to speak, while the glass curtains and shade diffuse the light or cut off the view into the room from the outside. Each is made of a different type of material.

Figure 11-2
Types of Draperies and Valances

(a) Festoon valance and pattern.
(b) Eccentrically draped festoon valance. (c) Crossed festoons as valance. (d) Valance of swag and wing pieces. (e) Festoon valance and side draperies showing pattern for side drapery. (f) Swag pattern.
(g) Draping swag. (h) Pattern of wing piece or tail. (i) Draping or folding a wing piece. (j) A double or central tail. (k) Pattern of a central tail.

Drapery Materials • The materials for window draperies are divided into three groups: the transparent or sheer fabrics for glass curtains and some types of draped shades; the translucent materials for the shade, unless it is opaque; and the opaque materials of the overdrapery and valance. The sheer materials may be chiffon, organdy, net, or theatrical gauze, to name a few. Muslin, silk, and handkerchief linen are samples of translucent fabrics. Though the opaque materials for overdraperies are numerous, they usually are made of a fabric that will drape well such as velour, velveteen, corduroy, or monk's cloth.

Types of Draperies • Because most of the decorative emphasis of a drapery is in the valance, it requires the greatest variety of draping techniques. A valance may be made up of plaits, swags, tails, or wing pieces, or even festoons. The festoon, which is one continuous piece of material, is the basis for the more exaggerated shape found in the swag and tails. Although the swags and tails are cut separately, they are frequently sewn together to look like a continuous piece of drapery. Examples of the types of draperies and their patterns are shown in Figure 11–2.

The side draperies, which are vertical members of the overdraperies, are usually a simple rectangular piece of material hung in fullness and drawn into a gentle or deep swag with a "tie-back" or decorative loop. Side draperies are sometimes shaped by cutting the bottoms on the diagonal similar to the festoon pattern (Figure 11–2e). Side draperies, although frequently draped symmetrically, can take on an eccentric draping depending upon the design and period style.

Shades

A shade normally is not included in a stage window unless there is action in raising or lowering it. Roll shades are fairly easy to make and install. A dye-painted shade of muslin or handkerchief linen can be attached to a commercial spring-loaded roller that has been cut to fit any special size of window.

A more special type of shade for a very grand window is the festoon-draped shade, sometimes called a French drape or Brail curtain. It is pulled up from the bottom by a series of vertical liftlines, which have been threaded through rings on the back of the curtain like the rigging of a contour curtain (Figure 11–3). The bottom of the festoon-draped shade is shaped so that its top position becomes part of the valance design. The shade may work in front of or behind the side draperies.

Borrowing or Renting Properties

Nonprofessional producing groups must rely on renting and borrowing furniture or maintain in storage a collection of stock period furniture for continuous use. Storing select period pieces is by far the most satisfactory method of securing properties for a repertory or stock company. Stock furniture can be varied with new upholstering and painted for reuse in future productions.

A producing group that depends upon borrowing furniture and other articles must make an effort to maintain good will with the community. It pays to be businesslike when borrowing properties. Unfortunately, many a property room has been furnished with unreturned props, which

Figure 11-3
Shades and Valances

(a) Café-curtain valance. (b) Boxed-festoon drapery valance.
(c) Festoon drapery shade.

a

b

c

is obviously not the way to build good will. A few simple rules for borrowing will help create a friendly, businesslike way of handling a loan.

1. Make a list of each borrowed article that includes the name and address of the owner, date borrowed and date to be returned, estimated value, description noting condition (scratches, cracks, or parts missing), remuneration (cash, complimentary tickets, or program credit), and request a signed receipt from the owner upon return of the article.
2. Centralize all borrowing in one person rather than in different people for each production.
3. Never borrow priceless heirlooms or irreplaceable antiques.
4. Take special care of all borrowed properties on the stage, using dust covers and padding to prevent damage from movement of the scenery.
5. Return borrowed pieces promptly on the date promised and in the borrowed condition.
6. Secure and file a receipt. Records become an excellent source for quickly locating and reborrowing for another production.

FLOOR COVERING

Traditionally, all floor covering (such as rugs and ground cloth) was handled by the property department. In present-day theatre, however, with its greater emphasis on floor design, floor covering has become more and more a part of scenery. Many modern proscenium theatres have an increased seating gradient that allows the audience to see more of the floor; on the thrust and arena stage, the floor is an important part of the overall design. As a result, the modern designer must be conscious of the floor covering as a means of unifying the stage composition.

A floor-cover design might involve painting the ground cloth to simulate wood or mosaic or creating a related hue to help anchor the design to the floor. Any stage setting on an unrelated or contrasting floor seems to float in space. If it does, it should be an intentional effect and not an accident of design.

A built-up or sloped stage floor will often be made of real materials, such as a planked floor that has the look and sound of wood. Such a floor can also be marbleized by using paint on a tempered masonite or particle board to create the highly polished surface of marble.

Latex and acrylic-based paints are durable enough to use on rigid surfaces, especially when they are later glazed with clear latex or acrylic. Such a surface can be damp-mopped and polished to perfection for each performance.

There are many examples of unusual floor coverings that go beyond conventional ground cloth or painted floor: the real dirt in *Tobacco Road*, for example, and the artificial snow in *Ethan Frome*. An unusual Spanish production of Aristophanes' *Lysistrata* comes to mind. The entire stage floor and scenery were covered with free-form overstuffed canvas, which obviously encouraged very unconventional movement.

Functional Floor Covering

A stage floor may have to be covered for purely technical reasons. An entire stage, for example, may be built up to surround a turntable or to provide slots to guide wagon movements. Stage floors are also notorious for their poor condition, a situation that bothers dancers the most. To correct this, most ballet companies and dance groups prefer to cover an imperfect floor with a vinyl covering. Some dance companies even carry their own portable floor. D'Anser, the trademark name of a portable modular floor, is transported in 4-by-8-foot units. This floor is 3 inches thick with offset wooden supports and gives the "bounce" dancers want. The units connect with interlocking hardware and can cover the entire stage area. D'Anser was designed by Ronald Bates and Perry Silvey of the New York City Ballet.

MAKING AND REMAKING FURNITURE

Cabinetmaker styles of furniture are often too difficult to produce in the average scenery shop, which is not equipped to finish or work hard woods. There are, however, several carpenter styles and rustic pieces of furniture that may be easier to make than to find or borrow. Some of the unupholstered, carpenter-style pieces shown in Figure 11–4 can be made without too much trouble.

Furniture can also be altered easily, especially if the alteration involves reducing rather than adding to the original structure. The practiced eye of the designer will be able to see in an otherwise hideous late Victorian "masterpiece," after a little painting, reupholstering, and trimming away excess parts, a Louis XIV side chair that would fool Molière. Armed with knowledge of period style, a designer can turn a second-hand furniture store into a treasure house of antiques (Figure 11–5).

Upholstering

When sundry set properties are brought together on the stage for the first time, some or all may have to be upholstered for either color or compositional reasons. Extensive reupholstering is not recommended on borrowed pieces, although it is possible to cover the existing surface with a new material by catching it lightly with a needle and thread. This should not be attempted on antiques, however, which might have weak upholstering. Bright colors or shiny materials on a borrowed piece can be dulled by covering them with a black net.

Figure 11-4
**Examples of Carpenter-style
Furniture That Are Easy to Make**

To reupholster furniture that belongs to the theatre, it is best to follow the same method of covering used originally. If the old covering is removed carefully, the pieces can serve as a pattern for cutting the new material. While the upholstering is off, repairs can be made to the springs, webbing, and padding (Figure 11–5b). If the furniture is going to be kept in stock, the padding can be covered first with muslin, which serves as a base for any future changes in upholstering.

Expert upholstering will hide or cover the tacking. This may be accomplished in many ways. The material can be tacked on a hidden edge in back or underneath or tacked to a surface that is later hidden by a covered panel. Exposed tacks can be covered with a decorative gimp braid or fringe. Sometimes tacks may be studded and left exposed as a decorative feature in themselves (Figure 11–7).

FABRICATING AND CASTING TECHNIQUES

Properties often require decorative details or bold relief at an exaggerated scale beyond that of conventional furniture. These and other forms (such as architectural details, costume armor plate, small properties, and various free forms) are often made in the shop to obtain the exact shape and dimension the designer seeks. The forms may be fabricated or cast from a real object or the prepared mold of a three-dimensional shape.

Mâché Work

The term *mâché work* has grown to include all techniques and materials used to mold or fake carved relief detail on furniture or scenery. The original papier-mâché technique used paper or paper pulp, which was either modeled directly on the surface, or, in order to duplicate a large number, was fashioned from a plaster mold.

a

b

c

d

Figure 11-5
Remaking Furniture
Remodeling a sofa: (a) The original sofa before alterations. (b) Back removed, reupholstered, and freshly painted. Reupholstering, tufting: (c) Tufting a sofa. (d) Rear view of ties used to form tufts. *Photos courtesy Gene Diskey*

a

Figure 11-6
Making New Furniture

(a) A hard-to-find tête-à-tête is
constructed in the property shop.
Frame and webbing ready for
padding and upholstering.
(b) Finished settee. (c) Plexiglass seat
and back give a side chair a new
look. On the left, rigid urethane
foam with wooden core carved
into legs for a console table. In the
right background, turned rigid foam
baluster.

b

c

Figure 11-7
Upholstering Techniques

(a) Tacking: (1) Hidden tacking. (2) Tacking covered by a panel. (3) Tacking kept on an unexposed surface. (4) Decorative tacking. (5) Tacking covered with gimp braid. (6) Tacking covered with fringe. (7) Upholstering tacks, 4, 6, 12, and gimp tacks, 3, 4. (b) Fringes and braid: (1) and (2) Ball fringes. (3) and (4) Tassel fringes. (5) Bullion fringe. (6) Braid. (7) Gimp braid. (8) Ruffle. (c) Plaits: (1) Pinch plait. (2) Box plait. (3) Accordion plaits. (4) Gathering.

Papier-Mâché • When modeling directly with papier-mâché, a porous paper is used, such as tissue, paper toweling, or newsprint. The paper, after being torn into convenient strips and dampened in water, is dipped into binder consisting of wheat paste and strong glue size. Any excessive binder is lightly squeezed out of the now near-pulp mass, and then is applied to the furniture surface to be modeled into the desired shape. If the relief is high, some preliminary modeling can be done with wire screening, to which the mâché is applied as the final surface. The technique is very similar to that described in Chapter 5 for construction of irregular shapes.

To duplicate identical forms, the same process can be applied to a greased positive or negative mold. In molding mâché there is a noticeable amount of shrinkage in the size of the final shape that has to be taken into consideration.

Celastic

Because papier-mâché is fragile, a sturdier substance may often be needed. Although more expensive, Celastic, or Sculpt-o-fab, can be used for small relief details and irregular forms that need to be resistant to the effects of excessive handling.

Celastic is a cheesecloth impregnated with cellulose nitrate and a fire retardant. This rather stiff fabric, when softened in a special solvent, becomes pliable and can be shaped or molded in a negative or positive mold. As the very volatile solvent evaporates, the cellulose nitrate hardens into the new shape. The Celastic form will separate easily from a mold that has been covered first with aluminum foil. There is very little shrinkage and the resulting shape is extremely sturdy (Figure 11–8).

A word of caution: Because of the volatile nature of the solvent, the softening and shaping process should be done in a well-ventilated area.

Styrofoam • Architectural details, sculptural pieces, and out-of-the-way dress props may often be fashioned out of Styrofoam. However, unprotected Styrofoam is fragile and its surface has to be hardened. For an extremely hard finish, the foam surface must first be sealed with flexible vinyl glue. It is then coated with a mixture of catalyzed fiberglass resin and Cab-o-sil, a silica glass filler. (The use of Styrofoam and other foams adaptable to scenic use is discussed in Chapter 7.)

Fiberglass • Fiberglass is easily adaptable to three-dimensional details on scenery or properties. The technique, like the papier-mâché and Celastic procedures, shapes a fiberglass cloth over a positive form or into a negative mold after first coating the mold with a releasing agent. The pieces of fiberglass cloth are saturated and cemented together with a solution composed of a fabricating resin and a hardener. Because the hardener is the catalytic agent of the mixture, the amount present controls the degree of hardness of the final form. The proportion of resin to hardener is usually about five to one, but, because the strength of these plastics may vary from dealer to dealer, any mixture should be tested for its finished hardness before beginning extensive fabrication. Acetone, which is the solvent for the plastics, is used to clean brushes and hands.

Figure 11-8
Celastic

(a) Fabric is softened in special solvent. (b) Softened fabric is draped over prepared understructure. (c) Final form after Celastic has hardened. (d) Celastic used in negative mold. (e) Over a positive mold. (f) Greek statuary. Celastic No. 411 (lightweight) over an armature, spray-enameled white, then antiqued. *Statue and photo courtesy Jim Bakkom*

There are many types and weights of fiberglass cloth. Woven glass cloth is available in light, medium, and heavy weights. The woven glass cloth is not suitable for making objects with opaque surfaces that are to be painted. The medium and heavyweight cloth works very well for making costume armor plate and helmets. The matted glass cloth is generally lightweight and quite translucent and is often used for fabricating shapes like lamp globes or similar translucent forms.

An easy way to experiment with the technique is to purchase a fiberglass boat-repair kit and follow the directions in the manual. Although the kit may not supply a releasing agent, that may be purchased separately.

Body Armor and Mask Making • Some of the mâché techniques can be applied to the making of full or partial masks, or, in some cases, to appear as decorative details on scenery. Figure 11–9 illustrates the designing and making of masks in the three basic forming techniques: papier-mâché, Celastic, and rubber latex. Fiber glass and thermal plastics lend themselves to the forming of body armor, such as breast plates and helmets (Figure 11–10).

Laminated Felt • Another method for constructing small set or dress properties is the laminated-felt technique. It is a process that works best for hollow forms, such as vases, goblets, and body armor. It can also be used to make open filigree or oversized costume jewelry.

Working over a position form covered with aluminum foil to ensure its "parting," the shape is built up with laminated strips of felt coated with Elmer's or poly-vinyl glue. Decorative detail is appliquéd in the same manner. Once the shape is hardened, it is painted with a glaze made up of shellac cut one half with thinner. The glaze is applied in successive coats to build up a hard surface. Aniline dye may be added to the glaze to serve as an undercolor or as an antique effect if it is the final coat.

Figure 11-9
Mask-making Techniques
(a) An example of a full face mask and its negative mold. Ritual or larger decorative masks can be reproduced in number by using the vacuum forming technique if water clay is used in place of plasticine to make the mold. Designer—Pat Moser. (Below) Positive mold technique using Celastic.
(b) Plasticine clay original. (c) Foil covering the clay mold as a parting agent. (d) Softened Celastic strips applied to the mold. The hardened form is then cut off the mold and sealed together to complete the raw mask. (e) Finished mask with a velour covering and applied hair. Designer—Louise Krozek.

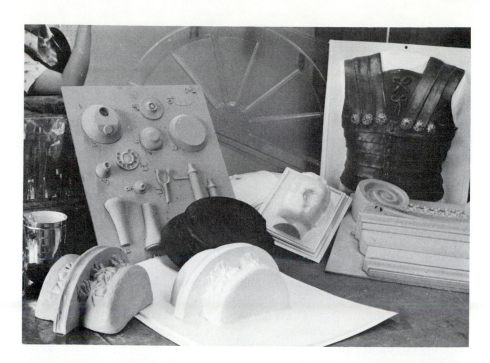

Figure 11-10
Properties and Armor
A few of the innumerable vacuum-formed articles for theatre use from Tobin Lake Studios. (Left) Prop telephone, architectural details, armor breastplate, and other articles are shown in various stages of assembly and surface finish. (Below) Full armor and shields vacuum-formed from vinyl plastic sheets. The swords in the display are made of tempered steel.

If the surface is metallic (to simulate silver, gold, or bronze) the dry metallic powder is brushed into one of the glaze coats as highlights. A metallic surface developed in this manner has a very authentic look on the stage.

Felt can be kept flexible by using a flexible glue rather than Elmer's. A flexible glue made by Swift and Company, Adhesive Division, is a transparent poly-vinyl that can, with dye staining, make felt look and feel like leather. The same flexible glue is also an excellent sealer for Styrofoam and Artfoam prior to painting.

EFFECT PROPERTIES

There was a time in theatre history when visual and sound effects were the major concern of the property department. Before the advent of high-fidelity recording many sound effects were created mechanically by the property person. Most of these old machines are now gathering dust in the property room. An adequate sound system can bring any effect to the audience with a truer quality and a more sensitive control than any mechanical sound effect. There is one possible exception: the effect of offstage gunfire. The recordings of distant battle scenes are fairly convincing, but close rifle or revolver shots are better when a gun with blank cartridges is fired backstage.

More as historical record than as modern practice, Figure 11–11 shows some of the mechanical sound effects that are a part of the property department. Directors, on occasion, have requested old mechanical sound effects for their theatrical quality rather than having the movielike realism of electronic sound.

Although some visual effects have become electrified, most are still produced mechanically. Smoke, fire, and flash explosions are usually electrically controlled; however, smoke also can be made nonelectrically by combining solid carbon dioxide (dry ice) and water.

Some familiar visual effects that are mechanical are the snow cradle and rain pipes, which are shown in Figure 11–12, along with other special effects that call upon the ingenuity of the stage technician and property person to rig and trigger on cue.

Breakaways

Many times pieces of furniture, dishes, or other objects have to break on stage. The chairs that collapse and the flagpole that falls down in *Cockadoodle Dandy,* or a railing that breaks during a fight scene are a few examples of properties or scenery breaking on cue and in a predetermined manner.

In Figure 11–13, a railing breakaway is prebroken and lightly glued together. Thin strips of orange crate are tacked to the back of the repair to give a convincing splintering sound as the railing breaks again. The pattern of the break is carefully planned in order to control the fall of the pieces in the same manner for each performance.

Breakaway Windowpanes and Mirrors • Breaking real glass on stage is somewhat dangerous. Flying glass and broken glass left on the floor can be a hazard. If an actor must be close to breaking glass it is sometimes desirable to use other materials. One familiar substitute used often in the motion picture industry is candy glass. Candy glass, or hardened sugar and water, is prepared like old-fashioned rock candy. After a su-persaturated solution of sugar and water is brought to about 260 degrees Fahrenheit it is poured on a smooth surface into a thin sheet. The sheet hardens into a clear, transparent solid. Candy glass, however, has a low melting point and may soften under stage lights or excessive handling.

Figure 11-11
Mechanical Sound Effects

(a) Wind machine. (b) Rain, shot in rotating drum. (c) Rain, shot in tray with wire-screen bottom. (d) Thunder sheet. (e) Rumble cart. (f) Falling rubble after an explosion. (g) Wood crash. (h) Gun shots. (i) Slap stick. (j) Horses' hoofs.

a

b

d

c

e

f

g

h

i

j

Figure 11-12
Visual Effects

(a) Snow cradle. (b) Rain pipe.
(c) Water reflection.

Figure 11-13
Breakaway Railing

(a) Railing prepared for breaking:
(1) Prebroken spots, lightly glued.
(2) Loose spindles, lightly glued.
(b) Railing after breaking:
(1) Prepared hinge points.

Pottery Breakaways • Opaque shapes, such as teacups, dishes, or small objects of art are much easier to make into breakaways. Because they are not transparent, inexpensive pottery or china pieces may be prebroken and lightly glued together again to ensure their breaking on stage. As the second breaking usually shatters the piece beyond reclaiming, a breakaway should be prepared for each preformance.

Special opaque breakaway shapes can be prepared by casting a mixture of plaster and Styrofoam into a mold of the shape. To keep the casting hollow for easy breaking requires a core mold, which makes the whole casting process very complicated and time-consuming.

If the authenticity, both in sound and looks, of the breakaway object is extremely important to the play a replica can be made in clay bisque. A clay slip or solution of powdered water clay and water is poured into a mold of the object and after setting a few minutes is poured out. A thin shell of clay adheres to the mold, making a hollow casting of the object. After drying thoroughly (48 hours) the raw-clay casting is fired in a ceramic kiln to bisque hardness. A great number can be prepared this way.

Foliage

Artificial flowers and the foliage of hedges, bush pieces, and small trees are considered properties, as are live flowers, potted plants, and sprays of real leaves used to dress the setting. The expression "prop bush" means that the bush is not real but also implies that it is shaped in three dimensions, as opposed to a flat, painted set piece.

Lifelike artificial flowers can be obtained easily from display houses, local variety stores, or the home-decoration section of a department store. (Although they are more expensive than real flowers, with proper care they can be used over again.)

Stylized or caricatured blossoms have to be specially made. Their scale and design determine the material used. Exotic tropical flowers in a musical comedy, for example, have been made of velveteen or satin with leaves made of wire loops covered with sheer chiffon.

Banks of blossoms and box hedges can be made of shaped 1-inch mesh chicken wire with ruffle-edged colored crepe paper or silk pushed into the openings. A more realistic box hedge can be made of chicken wire holding sprays of artificial boxwood or ilex leaves (Figure 11–14). Large-mesh chicken wire can be used to support clumps of leaves on a tree branch, or as a hanging border related to a tree trunk. The leaf material, which can be either paper or fabric, should have sufficient stiffness to hold a leaflike shape, or it will have to be stiffened with wire. Window-shade stock, which comes in several shades of green, makes a good leaf fabric to staple onto a branch or chicken-wire frame.

Figure 11-14
Foliage

(a) Artificial leaves wired or taped to real tree branches or section.
(b) Trimmed boxwood hedge made of frame covered with inch-mesh chicken wire. Crepe-paper or fabric squares are pushed into openings (color is more convincing if two or three shades of green are used).
(c) Untrimmed box or ilex bush; chicken wire shaped over basic frame and filled with sprays of artificial boxwood or ilex.

a   b   c

PART III

STAGE LIGHTING
& SOUND

12

Designing the Sound

While a number of theatre organizations remain rooted in the past, there is no doubt that the design of sound and music for stage production has finally achieved "status" in the theatre. Not so many years ago, theatre sound was primarily comprised of mechanical effects supervised by the properties department; while anything, like bells and buzzers, requiring electricity was relegated to the electrics department. With the advent of high-fidelity recording and playback equipment, sound reproduction has become a practical theatre tool. More recently, the synthesizer, digital recording, compact discs, and sophisticated, even computerized, electronics has allowed sound the freedom to reach a new level of artistry in the theatre. It is an exciting time for sound designers for stage production; and the theatre world greatly anticipates collaborating with yet another powerful design element—not visual this time, but auditory.

FUNDAMENTALS OF SOUND

Whether it be familiar music and talk from a radio station; records, tapes, or discs of a recording artist; or even background chatter from an unwatched television, we are surrounded by sound. Our brain has the capability of focusing in on a particular sound or rejecting all sound in order to concentrate on something else. Music affects us emotionally, heightening or relieving tension; and it has the power to alter our perception of time.

The Phenomenon of Sound

We are most familiar with sound as air waves or vibrations existing within a certain range of wavelengths of the electromagnetic spectrum (Figure 12–1). However, nearly all of us have experienced hearing under

322

water, an occurrence that illustrates the fact that sound moves more or less easily through nearly all materials. In fact, sound moves very slowly through air compared to most other mediums—only about 1,130 feet per second under usual conditions of altitude, humidity, and temperature (approximately 1 foot per millisecond). Sound cannot travel through a vacuum due to the fact that nothing exists from which waves can be created.

Sound can be thought of as pressure waves moving in all directions from the source. As the sound waves move, they diminish in height (loudness or *amplitude*), but the wavelength itself (*frequency*) does not change (Figure 12–2). Sound bounces off some hard surfaces with little absorption; and, if this reflection happens several times before being absorbed, *reverberation* occurs. Finally, the sound may reach a receptor, like our ears.

The Ear • The ear (Figure 12–3) is made up of several parts: the *pinna*, or outer ear, acts like an antenna to collect sound waves and direct them into the *ear canal* (the pinna also is instrumental in the location of sound direction); the ear canal terminates at the *tympanum*, or ear drum, which is caused to vibrate by the sound waves; the middle ear contains three tiny bones that take up and intensify the vibrations; the fluid-containing *cochlea*, or inner ear, houses the many nerve endings that receive the vibrations, transferring them into an electrochemical signal that is sent to the brain for analysis. Our ears "hear" everything within a certain range of frequencies; it is the brain that has the power of selectivity and analysis.

Measuring Sound

In order to describe a certain sound we must have a technical vocabulary that defines the components specifically enough to be meaningful. While very few sounds are made up of a single frequency, they all can be broken down into their various component frequencies and amplitudes.

Frequency • The length of the sound wave is referred to as frequency or pitch. It is measured in *Hertz* (Hz) or cycles per second. Frequency is the prime way by which we discern one sound from another. The normal human ear can hear frequencies from 20 Hz to 20,000 Hz (these frequencies represent wavelengths from approximately 75 feet to 1 inch long!). Figure 12–4 shows some common frequency ranges.

Amplitude • The height of the sound wave is called its amplitude, which is synonymous with the volume or intensity of sound. The *decibel* (dB) is the measure of amplitude, with 1 dB being the smallest difference that can be heard by the normal human ear. The decibel measurement is not on a linear scale, however; it is technically a ratio of two intensities. Decibel levels will be explained in greater detail in our discussion of equipment.

The following are important terms and concepts concerning the volume of sound: *sound pressure level* (SPL) is a common measurement of loudness that uses decibel values (Figure 12–5); *threshold of hearing* refers to the quietest sound we can hear, or 0 dB on a frequently used scale

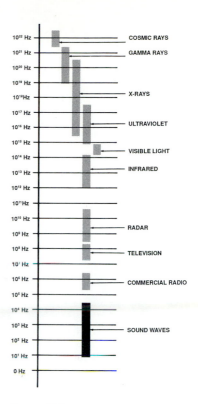

Figure 12-1
The Electromagnetic Spectrum

The normal range of human hearing is generally considered to be between 20 and 20,000 hertz (cycles per second).

called *dBA*. Finally, it is important to remember that sound intensity drops off by the square of the distance from the source (*inverse square law*).

Timbre • Very few sounds are pure (containing a single frequency and amplitude). Most sound is made up of a variety of frequencies and amplitudes, or *timbre*. Timbre allows us to distinguish between two different musical instruments even when playing an identical note at the same volume. A determining factor in timbre is *harmonics*, a musical term that refers to the specific quality of sound from a given source.

Figure 12-2
Various Sound Waves

These four photographs are from an oscilloscope display of various sound waves. (a) A simple sine wave. (b) A sine wave illustrating higher frequency with equal amplitude. (c) Wave form generated by a single note from a flute. (d) Complex wave form generated by orchestral music. *Photos courtesy Bill Isenberg*

Figure 12-3
The Human Ear

Sound is gathered by the outer ear or pinna and directed down the ear canal to the ear drum or tympanum. Vibrations of the ear drum are conveyed through the hammer, anvil, and stirrup (the ossicles) of the middle ear to the fluid filled inner ear or cochlea. Here tiny hair cells stimulated by traveling waves send nerve impulses to the brain via the auditory nerve.

Figure 12-4
Frequency Ranges

A comparison of some common sounds and their frequency ranges.

Figure 12-5
Sound Pressure Levels (Loudness)

A sound pressure level (SPL) chart illustrating various common sounds and their loudness in decibels.

Acoustics

Simply stated, the acoustics of a theatre refer to how a specific auditorium responds to sound. While the study of acoustics is a subject of its own, there are several factors that are of such significance to the sound technician and designer that they need to be discussed here.

Reverberation • The reflection of sound waves creating the prolongational effect of a sound is called *reverberation*. A major element in acoustical study, reverberation must be controlled in order for sound to be heard well. Too little reverberation makes a room sound "dead," lacking in richness and fullness; too much causes complete lack of intelligibility. Naturally the key to good sound parallels the reflective qualities of a room; however, the matter is complicated by the fact that ideal reverberation time for speech is not the same as that for music. To be heard well, the speaking voice prefers .8 to 1.4 seconds of reverberation time; while musical instruments require more time in order for the sounds to blend well—from 4 to 5 seconds.

Reflective Surfaces • Because sound emanates in all directions from a source, it is reflected by a number of different surfaces in the typical theatre. Scenery on stage, as well as the walls, floor and ceiling of the auditorium, all reflect sound. It has been found that parallel side walls of an auditorium tend to bounce sound back and forth between them, often creating reverberation that may destroy intelligibility. A hard flat ceiling can act as a valuable sound reflector, but a convex ceiling serves better because it disperses the sound more evenly (Figure 12–6).

In order to control reverberation, acousticians treat walls and ceilings with absorptive materials; carefully design the shape and interrelationship of walls and ceiling; and pay close attention to the rake (slope) of audience seating, seats themselves, as well as floor treatment. While still in the experimental stages, several new auditoriums have been built with adjustable ceilings and side walls that either increase or decrease reverberation time in order to accommodate both speech and musical instruments.

Figure 12-6
Sound Distribution

These drawings illustrate how building architecture can affect the distribution of sound. Not only does this apply to ceilings, but to side and back walls as well as the floor. As indicated, concave reflectors focus the sound and can cause echo.

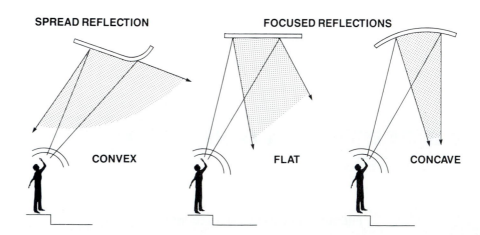

SOUND IN THE THEATRE

In addition to the performer's natural voice, sound in the theatre can be broken into four functional categories: reinforcement; live music; communications; production design.

Reinforcement

Perhaps the most difficult of sound tasks, reinforcement is the process of amplification and/or processing of any live sound—most often, but not restricted to, a performer's voice or a musical instrument. What makes this endeavor difficult is the usual desire to maintain as natural a quality as possible. Reinforcement is typically necessitated by either poor acoustics or the desire to balance two or more sounds (an orchestra and the singing voice, for instance, which is common in the musical theatre).

Amplification • Our hearing determines the source direction of a sound by distinguishing either the loudest of several sounds or the earliest perceived sound. Reinforcement requires the use of microphones and speakers; this introduces the rather complex problem of timing when the sound will reach an audience member. If the live sound slightly precedes the reproduced sound, the audience will recognize the live sound as the source. However, sound sent electronically to a speaker moves a great deal faster than live sound through the air and therefore must be delayed. Recent technology in the form of digital delay equipment has allowed acoustical engineers to design reinforcement systems that maintain the apparent source on the stage.

In addition to the need for delay of amplified sound, the requirements of a reinforcement system for the musical theatre will most likely change for each and every production. The design of such systems involves speaker selection and placement; microphone selection and placement; as well as a sophisticated, mixing control console that must be located in the auditorium so that the operator can hear what the audience hears.

A final reinforcement concern is that of amplification not *of* the performer, but *for* the performer. Such an arrangement is called a *foldback* system and allows the performers to better hear recorded or live music and even themselves. Speakers with individual control, called either foldback or monitor speakers, are located backstage so as to direct their sound to the performers.

Sound Processing • Treating sound with electronic equipment in order to change its quality is considered sound processing. Extremely valuable in the design of sound and used to a lesser degree in reinforcement, processing involves routing the sound through equipment such as an *equalizer* (Figure 12–7a). Although certainly a matter of opinion, both the female and male voice, as well as most musical instruments, can benefit from proper and judicial equalization—a process of electronically boosting or cutting selected frequencies. An equalizer will often be found as an integral part of a reinforcement system.

Live Music

While live music in the theatre is certainly not limited to the musical theatre orchestra, electronic sound requirements tend to be most elabo-

Figure 12-7
Processing Equipment

(a) Shown is a ⅓ octave equalizer. The upper unit provides both cut and boost while the lower is cut only. *Photo courtesy JBL Professional.* (b) A digital reverberator used to create effects such as reverb., echo, pitch-shifting, flanging, and so on. *Photo courtesy Yamaha*

a

b

rate when contending with a full orchestra. The live orchestra is an integral part of the magic and attraction of musical theatre, an art form having its roots in the theatre in the United States. There are occasions when the live musical requires no electronic treatment of sound at all, but these tend to be the exception rather than the rule.

The Orchestra • Traditionally found in a pit located at the front of the stage, the musical theatre orchestra of today may just as likely be found backstage behind a scrim, or on a side stage, or even on the stage itself. Such changes have been brought about by the healthy desire to break with the traditional structure of the American musical, as well as an increased interest in stages other than the proscenium. However, moving the orchestra is often fraught with numerous problems including sound. Individual musical instruments, instrumental sections, or even the entire orchestra may need to be covered by microphones in order to provide sound that is properly balanced with that of the performers. Even a small orchestra requires a great deal of physical space that must include room for music stands and lights, details that might fall under the auspices of the sound department.

The Conductor • An orchestra's conductor usually has no special sound requirements with the possible exception of necessary communications (discussed below). However, the conductor must be able to see the stage and the orchestra; and the performers must be able to see the conductor. These seemingly obvious details can require extensive treatment, often demanding closed-circuit television. A single camera set up to cover the stage can be sufficient for the conductor equipped with a small video monitor. Another camera on the conductor along with several large monitors situated about the stage may be necessary to enable the performers to see the baton. If this is the case, sufficient light must be provided on the conductor to accommodate the television signal.

Audio Communications

The necessity for a number of people scattered all over a theatre to be in constant touch with the stage manager and each other during a performance requires a flexible and reliable system of audio communication. Usually such a system is built into the theatre; if not, a portable system

---

HEADSET SUGGESTIONS

1. A system with more than one channel is often very useful, sometimes imperative.
2. Use headsets with one earphone rather than two so that live sound can be heard also (an exception might be high-volume sound situations such as rock concerts).
3. Always have working spare headsets and the belt packs that power them available and readily accessible.
4. Treat headsets with the care and respect they deserve—they are fragile instruments.
5. Know what to do if headsets fail—have a back-up system.

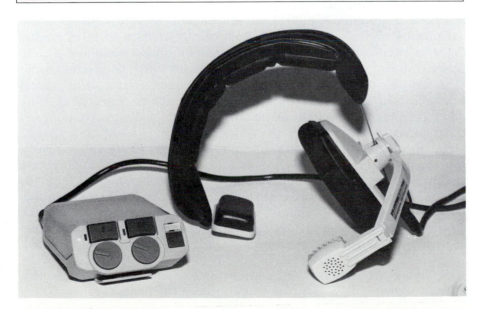

Figure 12-8
Headset and Belt Pack

A modern two-channel headset and belt pack manufactured by RTS. *Photo courtesy Doug Leighton, RTS Systems* is necessary, and the sound technician may have to attend to such details. Headsets are the most common and useful system, and several companies manufacture a sturdy and reliable product (Figure 12–8).

There are certain locations in the theatre that are best served by speaker stations rather than headsets. These include the fly rail and loading dock where stagehands cannot wear headsets, as well as soundproof booths such as the lighting control booth.

Production Sound Design

The design of music and audio effects for theatrical production is certainly the most creative and perhaps the most important function of sound in the theatre. Such design requires that a person have a strong background in general theatrical production; a good knowledge of sound equipment; more than a passing interest in and familiarity with music and sound; as well as that ineffable sense of design, which is so very difficult to define. The manner in which sound design may contribute to theatrical production can be broken down into three categories:

> *Evoking* a specific atmosphere or mood
> *Reinforcing* the action of the play
> *Commenting* upon the action of the play

Evoking Atmosphere or Mood • The most-familiar way sound can evoke a specific atmosphere or mood is by using environmental sounds in a realistic manner. Examples are abundant: the bright chirping of birds for a cheerful morning scene; the ominous rolls of thunder preceding a storm; or the sad notes of waltz music coming from a nearby dance hall. While it must be handled with some degree of caution, realistically motivated sound is one of the easiest to use due to an audience's inclination to accept such sound.

Nonrealistic or unmotivated (lacking in any apparent source) sound created by the designer for a specific effect can also be used to evoke a feeling of atmosphere or mood upon the audience. *Musical underscoring,* the process of playing music or sound effects under a performer's dialogue, is a good example. Such usage is more difficult for an audience to accept, but can be extremely effective. A subtle touch is recommended.

A designer must never forget the power of silence! The artful process of establishing an atmospheric sound, such as crickets chirping, and suddenly cutting off the sound can be more dynamic and effective than any other device.

Further examples of the use of atmospheric sound are pre- and postshow incidental music, as well as musical "punctuations." Punctuation effects are most often used for entrances or exits of characters or at the end of scenes. They may be realistic, such as a clap of thunder; or stylistic, such as musical fanfares; or frankly presentational such as the abstract grinding of stones together upon each entrance of a particular character as a leitmotif. Once again, subtlety should be the watchword.

Reinforcing the Action • Normally using sound in a realistic manner, reinforcing the action of a play helps to keep the audience informed of current or upcoming events. Sound coming from a television just switched on is an example, as is the ringing of the telephone or the sound of an approaching delivery truck. These sounds usually fall into the category of effects. In addition, offstage voices or "voice-over" effects might be used to reinforce a central action.

Commenting upon the Action • The designer can comment upon an action by using sound in a symbolic manner. Such usage may or may not be motivated; and a wide variety of approaches might be taken. For example, a tympani roll on the entrance of a character might be either comic or sinister depending on its treatment; and comic music playing under a very straight and serious scene will certainly affect the audience's reaction to the scene.

ELEMENTS OF DESIGN

The tools with which the designer works are the building blocks of any sound design. Choices are made based upon the script and the production concept as arrived at by the design team. At the designer's command are music (live or recorded); sound effects (live or recorded); synthetic or processed sound; and speaker placement.

Music

Most production designs will use either live or recorded music to some degree. Pre-show music may be playing when the audience enters the theatre. Selection of this *incidental* music is never left to chance, for the designer would be wasting a great opportunity to put the audience in the proper frame of mind for the upcoming performance. In addition, a special type of sound (electronic music, for instance) specifically selected by the designer for the production can be introduced at this time in order to acclimate the audience to the sound.

In making selections from existing music, the designer must proceed with great caution. Music carries with it associative memories that stick with people for a very long time; in fact, if it is a strong enough association, all their lives. The *William Tell Overture* (used as theme of "The Lone Ranger"); *Also Sprach Zarathustra* (used in *2001*); and the much-played *1812* Overture are just a few examples of music selections that obviously would have to be used with great care. Most designers like to work with original music in order to avoid the possibility of such associations. Employing a composer is highly recommended in situations where music is intended to play a major emotive role in the production.

Music accompanying a well-choreographed scene change can make pleasurable a potentially painful experience. Yet, music used solely for covering changes and nowhere else in the production may appear obvious and out of place. Of course, so-called change music must be as carefully selected as any other, always allowing for greatly variable playing lengths.

As mentioned earlier, *underscoring* involves playing music during a character's dialogue. Perhaps the trickiest of ways to use music in a production, the danger lies in competing with the spoken word to the extent of distraction (an effect called *masking*). In addition, the technique itself, which is used more favorably in television and film production, can become obvious and ridiculous: The camera focuses the attention of an audience to a much greater degree than in the theatre where the normal field of focus is considerably less specific. Therefore, underscoring, while not to be avoided, must be approached with great care and consideration by the designer. Many stage directors may at first find underscoring distracting to the point of being unacceptable. Introduce the technique slowly and at very low levels and use limited dynamic range.

Finally, when music is necessitated as an *effect* (motivated by a phonograph playing, a radio, a piano in the sitting room, an orchestra, or a jazz combo across the street), selections require not only a good design sense but a thorough knowledge of music of all periods.

Sound Effects

While it is possible that any use of sound in a stage production could be labeled an effect, it is convenient to consider most music and processed sound as separate from effects. Sound effects may be found prerecorded, they can be self-recorded, or they may be created; sources of sound effects are only as limited as the designer's imagination.

Pre-Recorded Sound • Pre-recorded sound can be found on records, tapes, or compact discs. Sound-effect libraries vary in quality, but several of the better collections available for purchase are the BBC Sound Effects Library (currently three volumes of 50 records covering a wide variety of well-recorded effects); Major Sound Effect Records (24 volumes with a good selection but recording quality varies); Sound Ideas Company (with sound effects as well as music on compact disc); and Elektra Authentic Sound Effects (a large, uneven, collection including a section on the "sounds of Europe"). While the purchase of an effects library is a significant investment, the ready availability of effects is absolutely necessary for even the modest production studio. Records are still less expensive than tape or compact discs, but clearly the compact disc is the best choice if affordable.

Other sources of pre-recorded effects might be local radio stations or a professional recording studio, where both the quality and cost will be high. Become familiar with the studio nearest you, their personnel are usually audio experts and can be of great assistance.

Self-Recorded Sound • Recording sound yourself, from either environmental sources, musical instruments, or the human voice itself, constitutes the second category of sound effects. Recording on location can be fraught with problems that range from special equipment demands to the need for sound isolation. While not to be totally avoided, this technique of sound gathering should never be left to the last moment and a back-up plan is advisable. Studio work is much safer and a huge variety of recording can be accomplished in the well-equipped studio space.

Created Effects • Created effects are by far the most interesting and offer the most potential for exciting design results. Found objects such as pieces of metal, noise-making machines, and everyday things such as squeaky screen door hinges all have possibilities for interesting effects.

Investigate objects made up of as many different materials as possible (tin interacting with fiberglass, metal tubes striking glass, for example) and imagine how each sound might be used—record your findings if necessary.

Processed Sound

Some of the most-exciting created effects fall under the category of processed sound. One of the primary reasons sound processing is so full of potential in the creation of effects is the *synthesizer* (Figure 12–9). Synthesizers come in a variety of types and price ranges, one type being primarily intended for performance and another for production. Due to the fact that a basic synthesizer will be made up of a number of components such as sound oscillators, amplifiers, and filters, they are easily custom designed for special applications. Digital synthesizers, currently the most sophisticated and versatile units available, can be made to produce almost any sound. In addition, a process called *sampling* uses the synthesizer like a digital recorder to record and reproduce any sound.

Figure 12-9
Synthesizers

Shown are two types of synthesizers: the popular Yamaha DX7 (a) and a more complex computer-assisted model (b). *Photos courtesy Charles Weeks*

There are also a number of other ways to alter sound in order to create a particular effect. One of the most popular and reliable is *speed distortion:* the process of speeding up or slowing down a recorded sound in order to change its quality. As a sound is slowed its pitch is lowered resulting in a "bigger" sound; for instance, a small engine can be made to sound like a huge turbine by slowing the playback speed. This is the primary reason for a variable-speed tape machine in the sound studio. Other valuable techniques are mixing *sound on sound;* playing back in the *reverse direction; filtering* using an equalizer; adding *echo* or *reverberation;* and *pitch shifting* (altering frequency). Sound-on-sound mixing can be very subtle by just adding a "richness" to the sound; or its effect can be quite abstract and bold. Use of the equalizer to filter sound can add as well as subtract hiss and noise to a tape by boosting the high and low frequencies. The last three techniques (echo, reverberation, and pitch shifting) can all be achieved either with a synthesizer or the use of specialized equipment such as a digital reverb unit (Figure 12–7b).

The final tool available to the sound designer has to do with the critical choice of how the sound will reach the audience.

Speaker Placement

While the selection of speaker type will have a significant effect upon the quality of sound, the placement of speakers is of primary concern to the sound design. It is important to realize that the location of our ears

SOUND SCORE : HYPOTHETICAL PRODUCTION							
	CUE DESCRIPTION			REASON	ORIGIN	SOURCE DIRECTION	TREATMENT
SCRIPT PAGE	NAME	TYPE	APPROX. LENGTH				
6	ALARM CLOCK RING	REALISTIC EFFECT	45 SEC.	REALISM	EFFECT LIBRARY	CLOCK ITSELF	NONE
12	BETH'S MUSIC	UNDERSCORING	2½ MIN.	ESTABLISH BETH'S CHARACTER	FOUND MUSIC	GENERAL NON-DIRECTIONAL	NONE
21	HEART-BEAT	UNDERSCORING	6 MIN.	INCREASE TENSION	EFFECT LIBRARY	GENERAL NON-DIRECTIONAL	SPEED UP 2X
26	PHONE RING	LIVE	3 RINGS	REALISM	PHONE ITSELF	PHONE ITSELF	AMPLIFY IF NECESSARY
28	WIND AND STORM	UNDERSCORING	10 MIN.	REALISM AND ATMOSPHERE	EFFECT LIBRARY	EXTERIOR	NONE
41	INTERMISSION MUSIC	INCIDENTAL	15 MIN.	ATMOSPHERE	FOUND MUSIC	GENERAL LOBBY SPEAKERS	NONE

Figure 12-10
The Sound Score

Shown is an example of what form the sound score might take. It is intended to aid the designer in formulating and presenting early sound ideas to the director and fellow designers.

gives us a greater horizontal than vertical sensitivity to sound direction. Therefore, principles of sound *reinforcement* state that speakers should be located above the performers in order to minimize an audience's directional acuity. This is a good rule to remember but may not always apply to performance music and sound effects.

For effects that have a distinct source (for example, a gutted radio prop located on stage), the speaker should be located as close as possible to the object. Speakers come in a variety of sizes and good sound is being reproduced from some very small speakers these days, so do not hesitate to locate the speaker right on stage if possible. Distant effects can often be achieved by speakers aimed in some direction other than at the audience. The theatre's grid and auditorium ceiling are also valuable speaker positions.

Many sound designers like to hang their speakers above the stage. This is desirable for a variety of reasons, including clearing valuable deck space, keeping sound cable in the air (off the floor), and source direction. However, if planning to hang speakers, be very sure that the scenic and lighting departments are advised well in advance. They also need that air space and, if consulted, will be less likely to place a black border immediately downstage of your hanging position.

Finally, it must be realized that flexibility of speaker placement is absolutely necessary to good production sound. While not true for reinforcement, playback requires that the designer have the ability to place speakers in any position.

DESIGNING SOUND FOR THE THEATRE

The Sound Designer

Several earlier references have been made to qualities that a designer of sound for the theatre should possess: a working knowledge of theatre production in general and sound production specifically; a passion for music with interest in all types and periods; a technical knowledge that provides understanding of the equipment involved in sound production; and a keen environmental awareness that will facilitate design creativity. In addition, a trait that is essential for every designer in the theatre is the ability and desire to share in the design process—to be a member of a design *team*. Being a collaborative art is the most significant aspect of theatrical design, making it unique from the rest of the arts. Relating to other designers and their ideas in a positive manner is not only exciting but is the very basis of collaboration.

Design Steps and Considerations

The sound designer is involved with the production and production team from its inception. A production *concept* is the result of script analysis and design meetings with all the designers, the director, and, perhaps, the playwright. This concept will be the product of much thinking and input, and must suggest in what direction the production will go—including, but not necessarily limited to: the period, thematic elements of the script being emphasized, and the production style. From this information will grow design ideas that will be unified by the fact that each stemmed from a single concept. Only then will the sound designer be ready to begin the exciting process of making specific choices.

Design Stage • Design for the theatre always begins with the script, for it embodies the playwright's ideas upon which all other production choices will be based. Several thorough readings of the script will eventually lead to a *sound score.*

The early sound score (Figure 12–10) is a visual representation of what the sound might be like. It embodies a preliminary presentation of ideas of style and period which may or may not include specific cues. This valuable paperwork can aid in the presentation of a sound designer's ideas to the rest of the production team and will act as an initial outline of the final sound design. While there are no set rules concerning what information the score should contain, some suggestions are:

1. A description of the cue (not a cue number at this point, might include cue type and an approximation of length)
2. The reason for the cue (could be as simple as the telephone rings, or as complex as underscoring intended to affect the audience psychologically)
3. The origin of the sound (what will the designer record to make the cue — this has to do with many decisions including style, period, and quality)
4. Treatment (equalization, distortion, speed change, and so forth)
5. The source direction of the actual cue (where the speakers will be)

A great deal of thought goes into the creation of the sound score with all decisions being based upon the production concept. The period decided upon will undoubtedly affect the ultimate style and quality of the sound. Period research, an essential step towards any good sound design, must take place as soon as possible; for a sound score cannot be developed without proper research. Of course, films and actual period music are good research sources; but do not ignore reading about the period, reading books from the period, looking at art of the period, and looking at photographs from the period. Photographic records of architecture, clothing, and interiors will be a tremendous aid in discovering the feel of the times.

Pre-Production • Once the sound score is complete, the designer may begin to collect the required music and effects as well as start the recording process. As sounds are found, they should be recorded onto a *master* tape which will later be used to produce the show tape(s). This master needs to be of the highest quality possible. Recording tape is available in different thicknesses directly related to playing time (more thin tape fits on a reel). Since thinner tapes tend to stretch, the master must be 1 or 1½ mil thick and recording speed should not be any slower than 7½ inches per second (i.p.s.) because the higher the recording speed, the better the reproduction quality. Each copy of a master is called a *generation,* so a copy of the first copy would be labeled "third generation" (the master itself being "first generation"). Since the quality of analog sound production decreases with each generation, it is wise to plan carefully to need as few generations as possible. One final piece of advice is to always record the master tape with more than enough of a sound required for the production and be sure to keep careful track of what and where each effect is on the tape.

A director may need a rehearsal tape well in advance of the actual show tape. Such a tape should be recorded from the master onto a cassette for ease of playback and should contain sound that is as close to the final product as possible. Use of a rehearsal tape can prove to be of great advantage to the sound designer, allowing for immediate feedback from the director.

Sound processing such as equalization or digital reverberation treatment should happen next. Always process a second-generation tape, keeping the original sound on the master for possible use later.

The next step is that of editing and building the show tape, but this must be preceded by the creation of a *sound plot.* Another planning tool for the designer like the sound score, the plot is similar but much more detailed and technical (Figure 12–11). The components and format vary with requirements, but important information includes: sound cue number; script page number; cue description and length; deck, track, and speakers in use. This is the time when the designer plans exactly how the production sound will be run: how many decks are necessary; exact speaker requirements and control; how long cuts should be on the show tape; and how many cues there will be. Often the stage manager can be of help and should at least be consulted for last-minute changes. The formulation of the sound plot will give the designer enough information to intelligently proceed with the making of the show tape, but a tape must never be attempted without this paperwork. In addition, if sound requirements are complex with many overlapping cues, it is advisable to do additional charts (sometimes referred to as *work sheets*) detailing in time line form each track of each tape.

Production • The production period is usually thought of as beginning with technical rehearsals, but the sound designer needs to have several details taken care of before this. Cues should be written into the stage manager's script several days before the technical rehearsal. The director may wish to be present at this session, so schedule it well in advance. Running cue sheets must be written for the operator(s). The sound plot will serve as their basis, making them very easy to write. Cue sheets should be arranged with columns headed: cue number; action ("fade up," for example); fade time; cue length; deck in use; track(s) in use; volume (usually mixer level); speaker selection and comments or notes ("visual cue," for example).

It is very wise to take a quiet moment in the theatre before the first technical rehearsal and set preliminary sound levels for each cue, checking speaker function at the same time. This is also a good time to brief and check out your operator(s) on the equipment; be sure to allow plenty of time for problem solving. If the headset communication system is the responsibility of the sound department, find out what is required from your stage manager and prepare and check out the equipment. Leaving these details for the day of the technical rehearsal is a serious mistake and will waste much time. Good preparation and planning is never more evident than at the technical rehearsal and every effort should be taken to make this experience a painless one.

REVISED SUNDAY FEB-19

SOUND PLOT

RAT   *TAITE*

PAGE: <u>one</u> of ____

production <u>Saratoga</u>   Issue # <u>two</u>   Director: <u>O'Brien/ James</u>   Feb. 19, 1989

PAGE	TENT. CUE #	TIME	SPEAKER		"A"	"B"	"C"
B I-1	1	27 sec. from the entrance on. What ever at the top.		OVERTURE	X		
		[5:06					
B I-1	2	a full song		Underscoring Salon Music from off stage	X		
B I-42	3	a full song		Underscoring Salon Music from off stage	X		
B I-52	4	15-20 Secs		Button/Music tag end of I	X		
7 GUCKSTERS ORGAN WALTZ							
B II-1	5	33 sec. or 9 sets of 8 plus something at the top		OVERTURE Act II	X		
5.2	*6 MIN EXT.*	VOICES		*SL*			X
| II-1-2	5.3	3 or 4 sentences		small children's voices *SL*		X	
| II-1-6	5.7	10 min	*U.S.*	summer sounds, cicadas (this cue will fade in and out)		X	
B II-1-56	6		*S.R.*	~~Bugle reveille~~ *DINNER BELL*		X	
B II-1-56	7			Button/Music tag end of II-1		X	

Figure 12-11
The Sound Plot
Shown is a sound plot for a production of *Up In Saratoga* at San Diego's Old Globe Theatre with sound designed by Tony Tait. The sound plot aids the designer in making and communicating operational decisions.

Arrive a bit early for the technical rehearsal and be sure that you, your operator, and your equipment are ready to begin on time. Every sound cue should be run under performance conditions so that length and level can be properly judged. Make sure that the stage manager calling the cues and your operator take careful notes of all changes—nothing is more frustrating than mistakes being repeated because changes were not properly noted. Remember to give yourself and your crew proper breaks. Be aware that an audience absorbs roughly 3 dB of sound.

Often the designer will need to make adjustments after the technical rehearsal and before the dress rehearsals begin. These changes will usually be minor if everything has gone well, but may require a great deal of studio time if there are problems. It is imperative that the corrected tape be ready for the first dress, so plan ahead. Once the dress process has begun, sound problems must be dealt with while the run goes on—you may not stop a dress for a problem unless it is an emergency. Make sure that you touch base with your director, stage manager, and operator after every rehearsal. Be sure that a back-up recording of the final tape is readily available in case of emergency.

THE SOUND SYSTEM

Sound plays several different roles in the theatre, and the requirements of a sound system vary slightly with each.

The *reinforcement system* is comprised of microphones, a mixer, amplifiers, and speakers; with most systems also having an in-line equalizer located between the mixer and the amplifier. The *playback system* used for music and effects during a production requires the addition of tape decks and possibly additional processing equipment. This system will probably need speakers and microphones of a different type than those best suited to reinforcement. The *recording system* adds input sources such as a turntable, compact disc player, and synthesizer. In addition, specialized remote recording equipment may be necessary. Microphone requirements may again vary from those of the other systems, and the recording system has very limited need for amplifiers and speakers. It is possible that this system may be located in a studio rather than the production sound booth; but such an arrangement, while more desirable, is also more expensive due to the need for duplicate equipment.

Figure 12–12 illustrates a *combination system* typical of most theatre facilities. It introduces the patch panel in order to allow for flexibility in connecting one piece of equipment to another. Our discussion of individual components carries this system in mind.

Input Sources

Anything that sends a sound signal to the system is considered an *input* source. Two basic methods of transmitting a source's signal are in use today: *digital* and *analog.* It must be understood that the distinction between these two lies in the method of sending the signal, not the source itself. For instance, while normally analog, a microphone's signal could be converted to digital if so desired.

Analog signals have been with us for a long time. They are signals of varying electrical voltage transmitted to a receiver/transducer (such as a

Figure 12-12
Block Diagram of a Combination Sound System

A system such as the one shown is typical of most theatre sound systems in that it combines reinforcement, playback, and recording possibilities.

tape head) that interprets the variation and translates it. Digital technology is a fairly recent development that seems likely to replace analog in many applications. The digital process sends a more exact signal than analog because rather than a varying voltage it sends a rapid series of on-or-off (binary) pulses to its receiver. These pulses can be read and recorded with great precision, resulting in a more accurate reproduction of the source.

Major input sources are microphones, tape, records, compact discs, and the synthesizer.

Microphones • A microphone converts sound into electrical energy for transmission to another location. The microphone shown in Figure 12–13a is a good choice for multipurpose use, but most tasks are performed best with specialized types. Reinforcement uses floor microphones enclosed in foam covers called "mice" (Figure 12–13b) or a special microphone manufactured by Crown International called a pressure zone microphone (PZM) (Figure 12–13c). In order to capture sound from upstage and other remote locations, a long-range microphone called a *shotgun* may be put to use (Figure 12–13d). Shotguns work fairly well for groups, but off-axis sounds tend to be muddy. Another alternative is a *personal microphone:* either hand held or miniature, with or without cable attached. The popularity of wireless miniature microphones has grown as they have become more dependable. If used properly the modern wireless mike works very well for many stage applications.

Tape • Recording tape is film coated with ferrous oxide particles that can be magnetized, allowing it to store sound sent to it in the form of an electrical signal. A tape deck receives the signal and transfers it to the

Figure 12-13
Microphones

Four commonly used types of microphones: (a) A cardioid vocal mike. *Photo courtesy Shure Brothers.* (b) Top and bottom views of a stage microphone "mouse". *Photo courtesy Electro-Voice.* (c) A Crown PZM (Pressure Zone Microphone) often placed on the stage apron. *Photo courtesy Crown International.* (d) A hyper-cardioid "shotgun" microphone used for long-range pick-up. *Photo courtesy Shure Brothers* tape by means of small magnetic "heads." While most tape decks in use today require an analog-type signal, new digital recording techniques are replacing them. The two are not compatible without a converter. The standard tape used in theatrical recording is ¼-inch wide with speeds of 3¾ i.p.s., 7½ i.p.s., and 15 i.p.s. Faster analog-recording speeds provide higher quality playback because the magnetic information is spread over more tape.

The tape-deck record head forms magnetic paths along the length of the tape called *tracks*. The most-useful tracking configuration for nearly all theatrical application is two tracks running in the same direction capable of reproducing stereo sound. While there are a multitude of track formats and widths, the 2-track stereo arrangement is by far the most common.

Be aware that quality of tape varies to the degree that poor recording tape can stretch in playback and/or "print through" when stored. Print through is a transfer of magnetism from one part of the tape to another and will render a production tape useless. Being magnetic, recording tape is sensitive to all magnetic fields and should be stored "tail out" (end of tape first) in a cool, dry location out of direct sunlight. An entire reel of tape may be erased by using a tool called a bulk eraser which is essentially an electromagnet. Your tape machine should be protected from dust and dirt with a proper dust cover.

Records and Compact Discs • The compact disc will replace standard records. In the meantime, the recording studio must have both a turntable and a disc player for sound input to a tape recorder. Seldom will either kind of disc be used in live playback, rather its contents will be put on tape and then edited for playback as necessary. Sound-effect libraries are expensive and should be handled with care. Like tape, discs should be stored properly, out of sunlight; it is often a good idea to provide a special lock-up for effect libraries.

Synthesizer • The synthesizer as an input source is a fairly new concept, but one that is becoming more and more accepted. Like that on a compact disc, synthesized sound will not ordinarily be used live in a production, but will be recorded onto tape.

Sampling refers to the synthesizer's ability to receive an analog sound signal, convert it to digital, store it on computer disk, and reproduce it at will. One can easily process the sampled sound for a wide range of effects.

Perhaps the most versatile of input sources, the synthesizer is expensive and takes time to learn. It should not be made available for general use by the novice and must be taken care of like any fine musical instrument.

Signal Processing

Various pieces of equipment are used to take the sound from an input source and get it ready to move on to the amplifiers and speakers; this is called *signal processing*. The most simple system might be comprised of a microphone, an amplifier, and a speaker; however theatre sound must be as flexible as possible.

The Patch • The patch or interconnect panel (Figure 12–14) is an often confusing-looking collection of jacks that allow the operator the freedom of connecting any input source into any signal-processing unit. For example, a tape deck's output could be patched into the equalizer or into the mixer or into another tape deck depending upon the needs of the job at hand. The patch bay is made up of single ⅛- or ¼-inch phono jacks that are labeled by function; for instance, "MIX 3 IN" translates to Mixer channel number-3 input. Once the purpose of a patch panel is understood and the various pieces of equipment in the system are known, using the patch becomes a fairly easy task.

The Mixer • The primary function of a mixer (Figure 12–15) is to combine several different input signals into one or more output channels while providing volume and tone controls for both the input signals as well as the mixed output. A mixer is useful in reinforcement, recording, and playback situations. In reinforcement when various performers are using microphones, the mixer and its operator are located in the house and will "ride" the sound levels. That is to say, the operator will bring up a mike when needed, take it out when not required, and balance the sounds from more than one microphone. Since the power of a signal from a microphone (called *low-level*) is relatively slight, the mixer contains preamplifiers that take low-level signals and boost them up to a power level normal for processing equipment (called *line-level*). In recording and playback the mixer will be used to accept several sources, balance them, mix them into one or more channels, and send them on to the next piece of equipment which may very well be an equalizer.

Figure 12-14
The Patch Panel
A patch panel such as the one shown allows interconnection of one component of the sound system with another. *Photo courtesy Charles Weeks*

Figure 12-15
Mixers

(a) A compact 8-channel in, and 2-channel out, audio mixer. *Photo courtesy Sonosax SA.* (b) A larger audio mixer which allows 32 channels in, and is commonly used for musical theatre reinforcement. *Photo courtesy Yamaha*

The Equalizer • While a mixer provides some degree of equalization through its tone controls, an equalizer offers a great deal more potential for altering specific frequencies. Two types exist: *graphic* and *parametric* equalizers. The graphic type will have sliding faders permanently assigned to frequency bands that are at least one octave in width. The parametric type shown in Figure 12–7a allows the operator to select specific frequencies for control. Like the mixer, the equalizer is a valuable component of reinforcement, recording, and playback systems.

Specialized Equipment • While a great variety of very specialized sound-processing equipment is available, two units that are particularly useful for theatrical sound are the synthesizer and the digital reverberation/echo unit. While the synthesizer's value as an input source was discussed above, it can have equal or even greater import as a piece of processing equipment. Synthesizers contain processing components that could replace everything but a mixer and certainly would make a reverberation/echo unit unnecessary. However, for those many facilities not yet with synthesizer capability, the digital reverberation/echo unit is a valuable piece of equipment. It can alter a sound in varying degrees: from simply making it richer by adding a slight amount of reverberation to the creation of echo (repetition of a whole sound). In addition it will provide pitch shifting, flanging, auto-pan, and so on.

Output Sources

The amplifier and the speaker constitute the only output source used in theatrical production other than live sound.

Amplifiers • Line-level voltage is not enough to make a big loudspeaker work properly (in technical jargon, to "drive" the speaker). Therefore, an amplifier matched to the loudspeaker's power rating is assigned to each speaker. The amp rack should be remotely located somewhere between sound control and the location of most of the speakers, and then left alone.

Loudspeakers • Like microphones, loudspeakers are rather specialized and come in a wide range of sizes, types, and prices. They receive the sound signal from the amplifier and change it into pressure waves that we can hear. The more accurately a speaker performs this task, the better it is for theatrical use; but quality varies greatly.

THE EQUIPMENT

The sound designer or technician must have enough knowledge of how and why a piece of equipment works in order to make intelligent choices when using or specifying the equipment. The following section describes the functional aspects of input, processing, and output equipment.

Microphones

Most microphones are categorized in two ways: by how they perform the task of changing sound into electrical energy, and by the various pick-up patterns available. While there are a number of different types, we are only concerned with three: the *dynamic, condenser,* and *ribbon* microphones.

Ribbon Microphones • As the name implies, these microphones operate by virtue of a velocity-sensitive metal ribbon located within the housing. They have best sound pick-up at the front and back, are relatively delicate, and will primarily be found in the sound studio rather than live performance.

Dynamic Microphones • Rather than a ribbon this microphone uses a diaphragm to pick up sound waves; the name is short for dynamic moving coil, referring to the metal coil that is affected by the diaphragm movement. Probably the most common microphone, the dynamic can be designed with any sound pick-up pattern, is the least fragile of types, and can be of excellent quality depending upon manufacturer.

Condenser Microphones • Also using a diaphragm to initially receive the sound, the way the condenser works requires a DC power source which may be in the form of a small battery; or, more likely, an electrical supply called "phantom." While being of the highest quality available, this microphone is also more delicate than the dynamic and on the expensive side. It is most common to find a condenser microphone used for the more demanding or critical sound tasks.

Microphone Pick-up Patterns • The reason for various sound pick-up patterns is that a microphone will receive all sound, not just the desired sound. For instance, a microphone located on the floor will receive direct sound from a performer's voice, bounced sound from the floor, as well as the sound of footsteps. Restricted pick-up patterns can help the microphone be more selective. Figure 12–16 illustrates four general pick-up patterns: *omnidirectional, bidirectional, cardioid directional,* and *hypercardioid directional.*

An omnidirectional pattern receives sound from all directions and is used for body mikes and in situations where all sound is required, such as monitor mikes or group recording. *Feedback* (sound from a speaker picked up by a microphone and continuously reamplified) can be a particular problem with this pattern.

A bidirectional pattern, which looks like the figure eight, works well in recording two-person interviews or in any other situation where the desired sound comes primarily from two opposite directions.

Figure 12-16
Microphone Pick-up Patterns

OMNIDIRECTIONAL

HYPERCARDIOID

BI-DIRECTIONAL

CARDIOID

Figure 12-17
Wireless Microphones

(a) A body pack wireless microphone transmitter with lavalier mike and diversity receiver. (b) A hand-held transmitter with a cardioid-type microphone and compact receiver. *Photos courtesy HM Electronics, Inc.*

The cardioid pattern is the most useful for general theatrical applications. Sound rejection increases as one moves around the microphone and is nearly total at the rear, reducing the possibility of feedback.

For long range and very directional pick up, the hypercardioid pattern is chosen. This pattern is typical of "shotgun" microphones.

Wireless Microphones • A body microphone without the nuisance of a cable attached to it is a very desirable thing, particularly for vocal reinforcement. The wireless microphone shown in Figure 12–17 is actually a miniature FM radio station. The mike is wired to a low-power transmitter worn on the performer's body which sends a radio signal via a short antenna to a receiver located offstage. The receiver then sends the signal to the sound system for amplification. The transmitter and receivers can be made to operate on a variety of frequencies in order to isolate one microphone from another. Care must be taken in selecting these frequencies to avoid interference from other broadcasting; using vacant television channel frequencies (7 through 13 in the United States) is often a good solution. The batteries that power the transmitter must be checked before every performance and often require changing on a daily basis. The system is fairly delicate and the good ones are expensive, but the negative aspects of the system are more than outweighed by the convenience and quality of sound reproduction. The latest trend is to wear the tiny microphone on one's forehead at the hair line with the wire running through the hair.

MICROPHONE CARE

Microphones are pieces of equipment that need to be cared for in order to perform well over their life span:

1. Never blow into a microphone to test it.
2. Store microphones in a cool, dry cabinet on a padded shelf or in their cases.
3. Don't thump or bang microphones on a hard surface.

Tape Machines

The distinction between a tape recorder and a tape deck is that the former refers to a machine primarily intended for home use that contains an amplifier and possibly speakers. A tape deck is a professional machine, more durable and capable of reproducing sound of a higher quality than that of the home tape recorder.

The Basic Tape Deck • The tape deck (Figure 12–18) is a very important piece of equipment in theatrical performance, for unless the music or sound effect is intended to be live from the stage, it will be recorded and then played back on the tape deck. A sound-studio tape deck has three magnetic heads that perform the functions of *erasing* or demagnetizing, *recording* or magnetizing, and *playback* or reading the encoded tape (Figure 12–19).

Located first in line as the tape runs (tapes run from left to right), the erase head is active when recording, providing a clean tape for the record

Figure 12-18
The Tape Deck

Shown is a professional 2-track stereo tape deck. *Photo courtesy Studer Revox America, Inc.*

Figure 12-19
Tape Deck Heads

This illustration shows how recording tape passes by the three heads of the tape deck.

SUPPLY REEL   TAKE-UP REEL

CAPSTAN

HEAD UNIT   TAPE GUIDE

TAPE GUIDE   PRESSURE ROLLER

ERASE HEAD   PLAYBACK HEAD

RECORD HEAD

head to magnetize. During recording the playback head, which is third and last in line, is also active, making it possible for the operator to monitor what was just recorded on the tape. In playback mode, both the erase and record heads are automatically shut off.

A desirable feature for a deck used in the preparation of tapes is an edit mode. This will allow the operator to precisely locate a sound by rolling the tape by hand past the playback head while monitoring the signal. Better decks will have a three-motor transport: one for each tape reel and one for the *capstan*, which has the important responsibility of precisely controlling the tape speed as it travels past the heads. One final feature, very valuable to sound processing, is continuously variable speed.

The Electronics • While features will vary from machine to machine, some general comments are in order:

Function control switches (play, fast-forward, and the like) should be electrical or solenoid-operated. This will provide for better start-ups, protect the machine from an inexperienced operator, and assure compatibility with remote control devices including computer control.

Most machines provide a *monitor select switch* which gives the operator the option of monitoring either the actual input signal or the recorded signal from the playback head and, more importantly, allows for comparison of the two.

Volume controls will be found for both input and playback channels. Two important volume-monitoring features found on most machines are the *VU meter* and a *peak reading* LED or meter (Figure 12–20).

The VU (volume unit) meter measures volume in decibels, but on a scale (called dBM) different from the dBA scale with which we are most familiar. The basic difference is that 0 dBA is equated with the threshold of hearing while 0 dBM is considerably louder (electrical value of .775 volt into 600 ohms). Little else matters as long as the operator understands that both negative and positive dB readings are routine on the dBM scale. The VU meter indicates sound levels from −20 dB to +3 dB

Figure 12-20
Volume Monitoring
An illustration of a VU meter used to indicate volume.

for each channel or track (a quadraphonic machine will have four VU meters). In most situations no distortion will occur if the sound peak levels are kept at or below +3 dB. Most sounds and music will benefit from being recorded at maximum level. Because a VU meter is rather slow in reacting, many machines will be provided with peak indicator LEDs. These register when a volume peaks over +3 dB.

Some tape decks will be provided with a noise reduction system brand-named *Dolby.* This system works well in reducing or eliminating unwanted noise (tape hiss) introduced during the recording process. Dolby electronics boost certain low-level frequencies before recording and return them to their original value during playback. The only problem this presents for the sound designer is if the Dolby tape is played back on a non-Dolby system.

Finally, clean the tape heads on a regular basis (see "How To . . ." section at the end of this chapter).

Turntables and Compact Disc Players

A good turntable cartridge is a must; and the stylus should be cleaned and checked frequently. The proper way to clean a stylus is with a fine brush and alcohol; moving the brush over the stylus from back to front only.

The compact disc player is one of the newest additions to the studio's input source equipment. The players themselves are easy to use, many being available with remote control. It is fairly common knowledge that sound quality from a compact disc is superior in dynamic range and frequency response to that from a standard record; and a disc will maintain that quality indefinitely.

The Mixer

Mixers (Figure 12–15) are available in a wide variety of styles dependent upon function. As mentioned earlier, theatrical mixers may need to serve several purposes to the extent of being portable for inhouse reinforcement mixing as well as studio recording. Mixer capacity is specified in terms of input and output channels; six to eight channels in and two channels out is a minimum requirement.

Figure 12-21
The Mixer Sound Path

(a) Photograph of the Yamaha Model M508 audio mixer. It features 8 channels in with 2 main outputs, 2 auxillary outputs, and 3-band equalization. *Photo by Charles Weeks.*
(b) Block diagram illustrating the signal path of the M508 mixer. *Diagram courtesy Yamaha International Corporation*

Sound Path • The mixer is a complex piece of equipment; necessarily so in order to perform its function of controlling a large number of inputs and directing them to various output channels. Each input channel will have a line-level as well as a low- or microphone-level input; the low-level being wired directly to a preamplifier located within the mixer (Figure 12–21). The sound signal then travels to an input attenuator or trim pot, which is just a volume control, and on to tone controls, which can be rather sophisticated in a large system. Next is another fader called a "pan pot" and switches that determine how much volume will be routed to each output channel. Yet another fader will master the level of the selected output channel. Finally, the VU meter, bridged across the outputs, registers the sound on its way to another piece of equipment.

An operator can monitor the sound at one of two locations: either completely mixed just before the VU meter, or unadulterated just before the input fader. (This is referred to as PFL or pre-fade listen.)

Auxilliary feeds for processing equipment can be found as part of many mixers. A mixer, like a synthesizer, can be custom designed for particular use.

The Equalizer

The equalizer serves two basic functions for theatrical sound: this piece of processing equipment can adjust certain frequencies of an output signal in accordance with room acoustics; or it can alter voice, music, or sound frequencies in order to improve tone quality. Because of this dual function, the location of equalization in the sound's path from input source to output source should be made variable through the patch panel. An equalizer used only to adjust room acoustics should be of the cut-only graphic type, and can be left alone to do its job. However, equalizers used to control tone quality will need adjustment with each task. In this case, an easily accessible parametric equalizer might be preferable.

The Synthesizer

The sound-processing power of a synthesizer has already been elaborated upon. It remains only to say that the potential offered by good and creative use of a digital synthesizer has not yet been investigated by most theatrical sound designers. It takes time to learn a synthesizer; but, like a computer, it will ultimately make a world of difference in one's ability to produce superior sound.

Figure 12-22
The Amplifier
Shown is a 2-channel professional power amplifier. *Photo courtesy Altec Lansing Corporation*

Amplifiers

Power amplifiers such as the one shown in Figure 12–22 have come a long way since the days of a metal box filled with glowing tubes. However, something that has not changed is the important fact that amplifiers and speakers must be compatible. Proper matching involves *impedance* (similar to resistance in an AC circuit, measured in ohms) as well as *RMS power rating.* RMS (root mean square) is a way of describing power or wattage capacities of amplifiers and speakers. An amplifier's RMS power rating which will be measured in wattage must never exceed that of the speaker. While loudspeakers can have impedances varying from 2 to 30 ohms (most common are 8 and 16 ohms) and amplifiers usually are designed for 4, 8, or 16 ohm loads, they must be matched for proper sound reproduction. It is highly recommended that a theatrical sound system have amplifiers permanently assigned to speakers.

a

b

Figure 12-23
Sectional Drawings of Two Speaker Types
(a) Cone-type driver. (b) Compression driver without horn. *Drawings courtesy JBL Inc.*

Loudspeakers

Two general speaker types exist: the *cone speaker* (Figure 12–23a) and the *compression driver speaker* (Figure 12–23b). In both cases a moving diaphragm generates pressure waves, but the diaphragm in the compression driver is made of a stiff material such as aluminum which has the advantage of being able to produce louder sounds in the higher frequencies than the cone speaker with its paper or plastic diaphragm. A horn is usually coupled to a compression driver to control the sound dispersion.

Most speakers will be enclosed in a cabinet that plays a significant acoustic role in the sound production. Sometimes housed in or attached to the cabinet will be a crossover network. This clever electronic device receives the sound signal from the amplifier and separates the frequencies into ranges that are more acceptable to the individual speakers. The low frequencies are handled by the *woofer*, a large cone whose size is determined by the sound volume it is required to generate: the more volume, the larger the cone diameter. The middle frequencies are processed by *mid-range* speakers, and the highest frequencies are handled by the *tweeters*. The horn-type speakers seen either attached to or independent of a cabinet are either mid-range or tweeters. The woofer only takes the form of familiar cone-type speakers (Figure 12–24).

Power Ratings • As noted above, speakers have an RMS power rating that serves as a guide to their performance in terms of volume. However, it must be realized that some speakers are more efficient than others. Do not rely on RMS figures alone, but compare them with the sound pressure levels published by the manufacturer (SPL at 1 meter with 1 watt input).

Phasing • Proper electrical phasing is important in hooking up speakers. What this simply means is that one must always pay attention to the positive and negative connections from amplifier to speaker and never cross them. Doing so will cause the diaphragm of one speaker to move in while that of another moves out, resulting in a cancellation of sound.

Selection • Of course speaker selection depends completely upon application. Theatre speakers should be able to produce 115 dB of sound pressure level without distortion; they should have as wide a frequency response as possible; and they should be kept to a minimum physical size. All this translates into money: be prepared to pay top dollar for your speakers. They are the weakest link in the reproduction system and must be of the highest quality to make up for this fact.

Wiring and Connectors

Sound signals vary in voltage from low-level microphone signals of less than 1 volt to high-voltage speaker lines carrying 70 volts. There are two types of wiring used to connect one piece of audio equipment to another;

Figure 12-24
Speaker System

A horn-loaded compression driver mounted on a cabinet containing two cone-type woofers. *Photo courtesy Electro-Voice* they are referred to as *balanced* and *unbalanced* lines. In addition, connections from amplifiers to speakers deserve special attention because of the relatively high voltages used.

General Audio • An unbalanced line is a power cable made up of a single conductor with a shield of metal wrapping around it (Figure 12–25a). The single conductor is the positive wire while the shield acts as both the negative and ground. A balanced line has two conductors with a shield (Figure 12–25b). The two conductors carry the signal while the shield simply acts as a ground.

Unbalanced lines are less expensive but are subject to electrical interference. They tend to be used from one piece of equipment to another. Balanced lines are used for microphone lines and other long runs of cable. It is most desirable to have the entire system balanced.

Even with a completely balanced system, it is best to keep audio cable away from higher voltage electrical cables which tend to produce a significant magnetic field resulting in interference.

Speaker Lines • If the distance from amplifier to speaker is short, there are no special power cable concerns. However, if the run is long, a voltage increase may be necessary to ensure that the speaker receives adequate power. Many amplifiers will have connections that allow for 4-, 8-, or 16-ohm normal voltage or an increase to either 25 or 70 volts. In the case of higher voltage use, a small transformer must be located at the speaker in order to step-down the voltage from the amplifier to a normal speaker level.

Computerized Sound Control • The idea of using the power of a computer to expand the potential for complex, theatrical sound design and operation has been resisted just as it was in the field of theatrical lighting. It is high time to reverse such thinking. Equipment such as that shown in Figure 12–26 is being installed in major theatrical sound facilities throughout the country.

Computerized control allows for memory storage and playback of highly complex sound cues with the press of a single ''GO'' button by the operator. Interface with existing equipment is routine, operation is as simple as a lighting control system, programming is by keyboard or a standard mouse, and cost is not prohibitive. Just as the lighting computer has freed the designer from hardware restrictions, so will the sound computer allow theatrical sound the opportunity to reach its full potential.

Figure 12-25
Balanced and Unbalanced Lines

(a) An unbalanced line with a matching jack plug. (b) A balanced line with matching jack plug.

a

b

```
          Richmond Sound Design Command/Cue(TM)   Sound Cues

                          Up in Saratoga

1.                   Pre-Show Music           A Dk   x000   PRESS F10   Y
1.1.                 Overture Act I           A Dk   x000   PRESS F10   Y
1.2.                 Overture Fade to Stage          x000   PRESS F10   N
2.                   Underscore               A dk   x000   PRESS F10   Y
2.2.                 Underscore DOWN                 x000   00:00:12.0  Y
3.                   Underscore               A dk   x000   PRESS F10   Y
3.2.                 Underscore DOWN                 x000   00:00:12.0  Y
4.                   Button to I              A Dk   x000   PRESS F10   Y
4.2.                 Button to I Fade UP             x000   00:00:02.5  Y
4.5.                 Intermission 1 music     A Dk   x000   PRESS F10   Y
5.                   Overture Act II          A Dk   x000   PRESS F10   Y
5.2.                 Kids under               C Dk   x000   PRESS F10   Y
5.3.                 Childs Voice             B Dk   x000   PRESS F10   Y
5.7.                 crickets\Cicadas         B Dk   x000   PRESS F10   Y
5.7.5.               crickets\Cicadas    OUT         x000   00:09:45.0  Y
6.                   Dinner Bell VARY SPEED!! B Dk   x000   PRESS F10   Y
7.                   Button to II-1           B Dk   x000   PRESS F10   Y
7.3.                 Beautiful Dreamer        A Dk   x000   PRESS F10   Y
7.3.5.               Beautiful Dreamer Fade to Stg   x000   00:00:17.9  Y
7.4.                 Soft Gunshot             B Dk   x000   PRESS F10   Y
7.5.                 Soft Gunshot             B Dk   x000   PRESS F10   Y
7.6.                 Soft Gunshot             B Dk   x000   PRESS F10   Y
7.9.                 crickets\Cicadas         C Dk   x000   PRESS F10   Y
7.9.2.               crickets\Cicadas    OUT         x000   PRESS F10   N
7.9.3.               crickets\Cicadas    restore     x000   PRESS F10   N
7.9.5.               crickets\Cicadas    OUT         x000   00:07:00.0  Y
8.                   Chase to Act II          A Dk   x000   PRESS F10   Y
```

Figure 12-26
Computerized Control

(a) Shown is the Richmond "Command/Cue" computerized control system. *Photo courtesy Richmond Sound Design Ltd.*
(b) A cue sheet printed by the Command/Cue for a production of *Up In Saratoga* at the Old Globe Theatre; Tony Tait, sound designer.

HOW TO . . .

The following sections give practical information on how to make a tape, including recording and editing; hints for placing speakers; how to select and place microphones; and how to clean and demagnetize the heads of a tape deck.

HOW TO MAKE A PRODUCTION TAPE

Once the sound designer has located the necessary music and sounds for a production, the next step is recording and then editing the tape for playback during the performance.

Dubbing. The simplest of recording processes, dubbing refers to tape recording of prerecorded sound from a record, compact disc, or another tape. Follow these steps:

1. Place a reel of blank tape on the left spindle of the tape deck and thread it past the heads onto a take-up reel.
2. Prepare the deck by making sure that the power is on, the speed correct, the monitor switched to "source," the counter at zero, and the "record" volume up.
3. Check to make sure the source machine's playback volume settings are up.
4. Play the source sound and adjust the deck's record volume as necessary according to VU meters (see "Record Levels" below).
5. When satisfied with levels; begin recording deck, wait a few seconds to allow tape to roll and reach speed, and then begin source sound. Switch the monitor to playback and listen off the playback head.
6. When source sound is ended, allow the tape to run a few seconds before stopping.

Handle the recording tape as little as possible. Keep good records: what was recorded, where, and how long.

One final thing to remember is always to record more music or effect than you think you will need. It is easy to edit sound out, but much more difficult to add in.

Record Levels • While a general rule for recording is to keep the volume as high as possible without distortion, a few suggestions for specific situations follow. Normal speech should be recorded between −5 and 0 dB. Music with a wide dynamic range such as classical must be carefully monitored so that the peaks hit, but do not exceed, +3 dB.

Live Recording • Live recording of a synthesizer is simply a matter of patching its output into the recording deck, but recording sounds with a microphone is another matter entirely. The mike input will want to go through a mixer and then into the recording deck, allowing the operator volume and mixing control. In most instances, it is safest to record "flat" (without equalization) and make adjustments later. The recording studio normally should be quite "dead" with walls and floors covered with absorbent material (carpeting works fine); and ambient sound must be eliminated.

Allow ample time, especially if you are a novice recording artist. Before your "talent" arrives, make sure all equipment is in good working order and make a recording of the room to see what you hear. Do not be afraid to experiment; mistakes often reveal the best of techniques. Try a variety of different microphones as well as placements. Remember that microphones (especially omnidirectional microphones) pick up *everything*, including the sound of your tape machine (which should be in another room).

Selecting and Placing Microphones • If recording the speaking voice, either a directional or an omnidirectional microphone may be used. The directional mike will eliminate more ambient sound, but the omnidirectional will have more "presence" and is less likely to "pop." Place the microphone so that it is from 6 to 12 inches away from the speaker and run a series of tests with the speaker talking into the mike. A distant effect is best achieved with the speaker off-axis or to one side of a directional mike; or, it can be added later with reverberation.

Group recording can be done with a single omnidirectional mike; or, if stereo is necessary, try a stereo microphone or two directional mikes crossed as in Figure 12–27. More microphones may be used as fill, and large groups may require several more.

Moving sound is best accomplished by doing just that: moving the sound, not the microphone. Better yet, try panning in post-production.

How to Edit Tape

Editing a tape for production playback is as important as any other step in the design process. Editing should only be attempted after the sound plot is complete so that the designer knows precisely how the operator will perform the various functions of running the show.

Determining the Sound Plot • Working closely with the script, the director, and the stage manager and attending rehearsals, the sound designer will determine exactly how each production sound tape will be compiled. Perhaps this will be as simple as determining the order of effects and music on one reel of tape. But, more likely, it will involve figuring out the use of each track on several tapes playing simultaneously.

Building a Show Tape • A standard show tape will have a 5-foot piece of leader tape at the beginning or "head" and the same at the end or "tail" with recording tape in between. The head and tail are carefully marked as such, and the show name and deck number should be included. Between each cut, more leader tape (approximately 2 feet long) will be inserted with the cue number clearly marked on the tape just preceding that cut.

Never force a sound operator to return to a cue by rewinding. If a sound is repeated, a second cut should be made and placed in order within the show tape.

Figure 12-27
Stereo Microphone Arrangement
Illustration showing crossed
microphones to achieve stereo
pick-up.

Every sound studio will have one tape deck that is used whenever editing a show tape. This deck should be mounted flat with a splicing block such as the one illustrated in Figure 12–28 permanently fixed to the table top in front of the deck.

Making a Tape Loop • Sound continuing for long periods of time, such as a fog horn or the chirping of crickets, is easiest to record if you use a tape loop of the sound. An endless loop cassette is a good solution, or you may build your own loop. The length of the loop depends on the effect, but tension must be maintained on the loop at all times while dubbing. Running the tape around a homemade jig of noncoated nails works well, but the loop's splice must be absolutely silent. Also, be careful that no moment on the loop is terribly discernible unless repetition is desired, as in the fog horn example. Never attempt to use a tape loop for live playback.

How to Place Speakers

Elementary speaker placement for reinforcement and general sound was discussed earlier: it is best to place loudspeakers above and just in front of the performer. However, other locations may be desirable or necessary due to source direction or physical limitations.

If stereo sound is required, two sources separated by some distance will be necessary. This can be achieved by placing speakers above and to each side of the performer perhaps with a fill-in center speaker. Be aware that this arrangement may be fine for sound effects and music, but will cause the spoken word to be less intelligible.

Column speakers located at each side of the proscenium arch are very good for voice reinforcement. Their pattern tends to spread the sound horizontally, which is ideal. They should be directed straight out at the audience, tilted down only slightly or not at all.

Speakers for the arena should be located as closely as possible to center above the performance space pointing out toward the audience. If such an arrangement causes microphone feedback, the speakers will have to move towards the audience until the problem is alleviated. Cabinet-type speakers may work well for the small arena.

It is good to remember that the higher frequency sounds are most directional. It may be possible to locate just the tweeter in a desirable position for source direction while placing the mid-range and woofer in a more-convenient location.

How to Select and Place Performance Microphones

We will discuss two categories of microphone use: vocal reinforcement and musical pick-up.

Vocal • Other than body mikes, the best solution for vocal microphone selection and placement in the reinforcement system is a floor mike mounted in a mouse or a PZM (see Figure 12–13) and placed in the footlight position. Microphones mounted on stands do not work as well due to the disparity between direct and reflected sound. The only advantage of a mouse compared to the PZM is that the mouse arrangement can employ hand-held microphones commonly found in a sound studio's inventory. The PZM generally will deliver superior sound quality.

Position several directional microphones pointing upstage with their angles of coverage sufficiently overlapped. While the number needed will depend on the width of the proscenium opening and the microphone pick-up pattern, an odd number with a center mike is most useful. Be aware that floor mikes will not be effective much more than about 15 feet upstage. A hypercardioid "shotgun" can be useful in an upstage position. Hang the shotgun at an angle pointing down about 60 degrees below horizontal.

Keeping the total microphones in use to an absolute minimum is an important rule to follow. As the number of live microphones increases, the possible volume before feedback decreases significantly. A good operator will never have a microphone pot open if it is not needed.

Musical • Any electronic musical instrument should be fed directly into the mixer (except for electric guitars, which use a device called a "direct box"). Most other instruments can best be miked by placing a directional microphone as close to the sound source as possible. In addition, special microphones are manufactured specifically for musical instrument pick-up: some are standard microphones and others, called *contact microphones,* react to sound vibrations. A PZM mounted on a closed piano lid produces good sound. Manufacturer's catalogues will provide additional information on the various microphones made for musical pick-up.

How to Clean and Demagnetize Tape Heads

Oxide from magnetic recording tape builds up on the heads, capstan, and tape guides of the tape machine. This residue will reduce recording fidelity and eventually may result in tape spillage. Cleaning is a simple process that should be done periodically and after every heavy use of the machine.

Figure 12-28
Four Steps of Splicing
Recording Tape

(a) Placing the tape in the splicing
block. (b) Placing leader tape in
the block. (c) Cutting the tape.
(d) Placing splicing tape over
the cut.

Use denatured alcohol and a clean cotton cloth or cotton swab. Rub the damp swab over contact surfaces and allow to dry.

The heads should be demagnetized with the inexpensive machine made for just this purpose every 25 to 30 hours of use. Be sure not to leave recording tape in the vicinity of the demagnetizer.

HOW TO SPLICE

A splice is necessary in attaching leader tape to recording tape. The equipment necessary for splicing are a metal splicing block (EdiTall), splicing tape, a single-edge razor blade, a china marker or grease pencil, and leader tape. Read carefully the instructions that come with the EdiTall splicing block.

1. Locate the sound to be spliced by rolling the tape at normal speed. Once found, engage the deck's editing mode and roll the tape by hand until the sound is exactly located. Mark the location of the sound with your grease pencil. Do not mark directly on the playback head; devise a system of marking a set distance from the head and measuring that distance.
2. Transfer the tape from the deck to the splicing block. Handle the recording tape by its edges and place the tape in the block with the nonmagnetic back side up.
3. Assuming that you are attaching leader tape to the beginning of a sound cue, place your sound location mark ½-inch to the left side of the splicing block's 45-degree cutting groove (Figure 12–28a). Lay the leader tape in the splicing block directly on top of the recording tape with its end just overlapping your sound location mark (Figure 12–28b).
4. Draw the *demagnetized* razor blade along the 45-degree cutting groove, cutting through both recording and leader tape (Figure 12–28c). Remove the excess leader tape to the left of your cut and pull out the unwanted recording tape from the right of the cut.
5. Slide the splice to one side of the cutting groove and carefully butt the two ends together. They must not overlap, but meet perfectly.
6. Apply a ¾-inch length of splicing tape across the splice, pressing it down to eliminate any air bubbles (Figure 12–28d). It is best to use tape that is $7/32$-inch rather than ¼-inch wide, for the splicing tape must never overlap the edges of the recording tape. Many designers prefer "Editabs," a brand of pre-cut splicing tape.
7. *Do not pull the tape straight out of the block!* Remove the tape by holding it by the edges and turning it out of the block's groove.
8. Check your splice by running it by the heads at proper speed and with proper tension.

13

Introduction to Stage-Lighting Design

While each one of us reacts to our environment in a unique manner, it is generally true that we take light and lighting for granted. Like a veterinarian who will be aware of things in an animal that even its owner does not notice, the lighting designer is acutely aware of the presence of light: its quality, color, shadow and direction, warmth or coolness, texture, and movement. The first thing a student of lighting must develop is such an awareness; not for theatrical lighting, for that will come later, but for the light that surrounds us each and every day.

The design of lighting begins with an *idea.* In the theatre this idea is rooted in the ensuing interpretation of a script by a director and production design team (lighting, scenic, costume, and sound designers). In dance, the idea comes from the choreographer and the movement and the music. In concert lighting, it begins with the music; and in advertising, it is inspired by a product. It matters not whether the lighting designer is found working in a theatre or a museum or a restaurant or a film studio or an exhibition hall, the design will be based upon a collection of feelings, an idea. Our discussion will primarily be concerned with stage-lighting design; for the theatre has historically been the source of lighting design and continues to be the prime training ground for today's lighting designer.

STAGE LIGHTING

What is the magic of stage lighting? The demands on it are many. The costume designer, while considering period, silhouette, color, and character in choosing the fabric for a costume, also wonders how it will look *under the lights.* The scene designer, in selecting the colors of draperies and upholstery or deciding the scale of detail on the scenery, hopes they will show *under the lights.* The actor in the dressing room ponders if makeup will look right *under the lights.*

Good lighting—and there is much that is not good—should tie together visual aspects of the stage. The primary concern of stage lighting is, and will always remain, *visibility* (a rule that the designer must never forget). Yet, we will see that visibility is much more than simple intensity or brightness of light. The lighting designer must also be concerned with revelation of form, with the mood of the scene, and with the overall composition of the stage picture.

Scripts often call for startling effects such as an explosion, a fog, a flashing sign, lightning, or a hearth fire. Effects usually occur either to advance the plot or establish the mood for a scene and are most often the responsibility of the lighting designer.

The Scenic Designer

Scene design, unlike the other visual arts, is deeply dependent on the use of light as a part of the final composition: the dramatic picture. Stage lighting holds such importance in contributing to the total visual effect that every designer should be familiar with its techniques.

The design of lighting often begins with the scene designer's sketch which presents a suggestion of the light that will illuminate the scene. It may appear to be coming from such natural sources as the sun, the moon, or a fire, or from artificial sources such as table lamps or ceiling fixtures. In contrast, the sources may be frankly arbitrary and depend on the position and color of the instruments used to build the composition. The sketch or rendering, as opposed to a model, is the scene designer's only means of conveying a sense of mood; and, if carefully done, the direction and color of the light will be apparent. If necessary, the designer will have prepared several sketches to show major changes in composition or color (Figure 13–1).

Such sketches, however, are only a start in the planning of stage lighting. Although a sketch represents an artistic concept, it must be technically sound to be properly realized. The floor plan and section that accompany the sketch give the first clues as to the credibility of the designer's lighting ideas. Many a beautiful sketch has been based on a floor plan that revealed, on closer study, impossible lighting angles and insufficient space for the lighting instruments.

Ideally, a single person should design the entire production—scenery, costumes, and lighting—thus assuring a unified concept. But more often today we see a production design team made up of several designers and the director. Diverse ideas and views must be brought together into a single outlook or concept by active and open communication among all designers as well as strong leadership from the director.

The Lighting Designer

In contemporary theatre, the lighting designer is the newest member to join the visual design team. Except for a few scene designers who enjoyed lighting their own scenery, the lighting of most Broadway productions in the first half of this century was neglected and became, by default,

Figure 13-1
Scene Designer Sketches
The planning of stage lighting may begin with the scene designer's sketches where the kind of illumination, its distribution, color and general atmosphere are indicated. These two sketches were done for a production of *Follies* designed by Beeb Salzer. See color plate 23-1 for a production photograph.

one of the innumerable duties of the stage manager or stage electrician. It was inevitable that lighting specialists would eventually move into this neglected field and demonstrate with startling results what could be done if one person devoted his or her sole attention to the planning of lighting. This trend continued as lighting designers, inspired by the work of people like Jean Rosenthal, Stanley McCandless, and Abe Feder developed their art and craft.

Contemporary theatre training and awareness of total theatre on the part of the lighting designer have brought greater unity to the visual side of today's theatre. The lighting designer must have compassion for and understanding of the total design effort since he or she is the only design member who does not make an advance statement in visual terms of what is intended. The costume and scene designers submit a multitude of sketches, material samples, and models as visual examples of their intent. The lighting designer, on the other hand, may submit sketches in light in the form of a *storyboard* or possibly a lighting *score*; but most often simply submits a light plot and a verbal description. Fortunately, the lighting designer will commonly have the advantage of seeing and discussing the work of the other designers and the director before the final plot is completed.

Training • Of course, there is no formula that outlines exactly what makes a good lighting designer—or, for that matter, a good lighting design. It is clear though that the student of lighting must seek, before all else, a well-rounded background in the art of the theatre. Ideally, he or she should know what it is like to be on stage before an audience, understand how a flat is constructed and why it is done that way, be aware of the choices the costume designer goes through in creating a design and in choosing fabric; and understand why an audience enjoys Shaw, how to feel the poetry of Shakespeare, and why O'Neill captivates an audience with hours of dialogue. The lighting designer should know what it is to back-paint a flat every bit as well as how to wire a pin connector. Only then can the young lighting person begin to learn what it is to design lights.

On the surface, the mechanics of lighting design are fairly simple. The script is read (many times), conferences are attended, rehearsals are viewed, a light plot is drafted, instruments are hung and focused, levels are set and cues adjusted, and another production opens. While a more detailed examination of process will be found in later chapters, it must be understood at this point that the first thing the young lighting designer must concentrate on is learning to *see*. There is not a practicing lighting designer worth his or her salt who does not possess a strong visual memory. In order to develop a mental file of visual experiences, one must first learn to notice, to observe, and to analyze light and shadow. Light is a constant part of our lives. The lighting designer must enjoy neon for its uniqueness, realize the effect of mercury vapor, feel the qualities of fluorescence, and see the color of the noonday sun. Learning to see is an ongoing process, not one to be learned in a month or even several years. We are constantly seeing anew.

STAGE LIGHTING AND THEATRICAL FORM

Several factors have a great effect upon the development of a lighting idea and the subsequent plot. The *production concept* and resulting scene and costume design will influence color palette as well as style. *Scenery* will affect specific placement of lighting instruments. The *style* of the production as well as the *script itself* guides the lighting designer toward an approach. Finally, *budget* and the *physical form of the theatre* will have significant impact upon the lighting design.

Production and Lighting Style

While the term *style* is subject to overuse and misunderstanding (see Chapter 3), we use it here in its broadest sense. At the most basic level, there are two styles of lighting: motivational and nonmotivational. Motivational lighting will attempt to reinforce a specific source or sources (the sun, a candle, a window, and so on) as well as be concerned with actual environmental conditions such as time of day, weather, time of year, and locale (Figure 13–2). Nonmotivational lighting will ignore the above rationale as a basis for color selection, instrument choice, and lighting angle. Instead, the lighting designer will make these choices as a result of the desired mood, compositional requirements, or simple "feeling" about a scene.

The young lighting designer should begin by concentrating on motivational lighting but must realize that a nonmotivational approach can be quite as valid and sometimes more expressive and exciting. The production style will help the designer select an approach that will employ one or perhaps both of these two basic lighting styles (Figure 13–3).

Figure 13-2
Motivational Lighting
The documentary style of Brecht's *The Measures Taken* illustrates a highly motivational approach to the lighting. Designer—Frederic Youens. *Photo by Nelson*

Figure 13-3
Lighting Style

(a) Highly stylized motivational lighting is shown here from a production of *You Can't Take It With You.* Set Design by Craig Wolf, Lighting Design by Doug Grekin. *Photo by Mountain Mist.* (b) Abstract non-motivational lighting is appropriate for this production of *A Midsummer Night's Dream* with scenery by Michael Yeargan and lighting by Pat Collins. The Hartford Stage Company, copyright 1989. *Photo courtesy T. Charles Erickson*

Physical Plant

The shape of modern theatre has had an influence on the development of stage lighting. Beginning with the *proscenium theatre* and its traditional audience and stage arrangement, lighting, for the most part, is essentially shadowbox illumination catering to theatrical realism or the illusory theatre. Lighting instruments are traditionally concealed behind masking on stage and in "ports" or "beams" front-of-house. In many older theatres, front-of-house positions are often limited, possibly to only a balcony rail. Worth noting is the fact that, scenery permitting, the proscenium stage is the most versatile form for side lighting possibilities.

The *thrust stage,* with its audience on three sides, minimizes the use of scenery and makes illusion a greater responsibility of the lighting designer. This new-old form of theatricality (popular in the sixteenth century) relies chiefly on lighting, costumes, and properties for its visual

Figure 13-4
Distribution

Both specific and general distribution are illustrated from four different theatrical light sources.

composition. Thrust staging requires full coverage (360 degrees) lighting and is an exciting and challenging theatre form. The modern thrust theatre provides great flexibility in lighting positions both front-of-house as well as overstage.

Arena staging surrounds the stage area with audience. The arena-theatre form increases the demands on stage lighting and virtually eliminates scenery. Like thrust, the arena requires 360-degree coverage but is often a bit more restrictive in terms of lighting possibilities. A good arena theatre will be equipped with a lighting grid that covers the entire space and allows total flexibility in hanging position.

Theatre of total environment, the most recent form, not only brings back scenery elements but also expands the use of lighting to even greater dimensions by surrounding or immersing the audience in the atmosphere or environment of the play. The circle has been completed by returning to a proscenium form. The production, however, is not contained behind the frame, but is allowed to spill out and surround the audience.

Flexible or *black box staging* should not be neglected, for it is capable of achieving, on a small scale, any of the aforementioned audience-stage arrangements and even more. It is, by its sheer flexibility, a frankly impromptu form with its exposed lighting instruments and temporary seating arrangement.

It can be seen by now that, between the rapid expansion of imaginative theatrical forms and the numerous physical forms in the explosion of new theatres, lighting designers are facing demands on their skills that are totally different in taste and technical capabilities of only a generation or so ago. And this is only the beginning, for the demand for designed lighting is becoming greater and greater; not only in the entertainment industry, but in advertising and architecture as well. The opportunities are challenging.

Setting aside the technical aspects of electricity, instrument and control design, and the nitty-gritty of plotting, scheduling, and handling of equipment, the lighting designer is concerned first with the esthetics of light. To develop a sense of composition and taste in color, a lighting designer must start with qualities and limitations of the medium, light, itself.

QUALITIES OF LIGHT

Once light is created, whether it be from the sun or an artificial source, it has certain inherent qualities that become characteristic of the light medium. Just as paint has traits particular to its medium, so light conforms to its own set of attributes. The physical characteristics of light as a design potential are discussed in Chapter 3, where light is presented as a very important element of design in context with the development of scene design as a visual art. The separate study of light in its application to stage lighting involves these same qualities: intensity, distribution, and color—with the addition of movement.

Intensity

The first and most obvious quality of light is its intensity or brightness, which may be actual or comparative brightness. The actual brightness of the sun, for example, can be contrasted to the comparative brightness of automobile headlights at night. Spotlights in a darkened theatre offer the designer the same comparative brightness under more controlled conditions.

Varying intensity of a light source is achieved by means of a dimmer. Groups of dimmers working together can direct audience focus as well as alter the stage composition.

Distribution

By far the most common way we see light is through its reflection off various surfaces. The manner in which it is distributed upon these surfaces is dependent upon the source *direction* and *quality*. The designer is in complete control of the source and, therefore, its direction and quality (Figure 13–4).

Direction • A change in lighting direction can radically alter the perception of size and/or shape of any form. Highlight and especially shadow are our best indicators of direction. A theatre audience feels most at ease with light coming from a "natural" direction.

Quality • The concept of "quality" is very closely related to texture and is dependent upon a source's intensity and diffusion. A highly diffuse light tends to have divergent rays while a less diffuse light has coherent and parallel rays. Diffuse light is perceived as soft and lacking in intensity. More coherent light is harsher, more intense, and has harder edges.

The considered use of the direction and texture of light can introduce highlight, shade, and shadow into the composition.

LIGHT QUALITIES

Intensity
Distribution
Color
Movement

Color

The third property of light is its ability to transmit and reveal color. Color, in addition to being a forceful element of design in all phases of the visual side of the theatre, is often considered the most effective and dramatic quality of light. Setting aside the physics of color and its origin in the electromagnetic spectrum (see Chapters 8 and 14) and turning to the design aspect of color in light, we find that its chief contribution is the transmitting of color or colored light. The modification of the local color of a scenic form or costume by colored light is a design technique unique to the theatre. Color modification and the additive mixing of colored light are two rather basic concepts of color as a quality of light that has to be understood by all designers in the theatre.

Movement

While not an intrinsic quality of light, movement is an extremely important characteristic of stage lighting. It implies a change in intensity, distribution, or color that might be as subtle as a slow color shift from pre-dawn to daybreak or as blatant as a blackout. Movement will take and control focus. Movement alters composition. A lighting cue is movement.

STAGE LIGHTING AND THE FUNDAMENTALS OF DESIGN

The principles of composition are the same for the lighting designer as they are for the scene designer or any graphic or visual artist. Composition is the organizing of the visual elements of design into a unified form or arrangement of forms. Lighting is the final unifying force of the stage composition.

The Elements of Design

The role of the lighting designer as a member of a design team demands that he or she be acutely aware of the elements of design that affect the creative process of the scenery and costume designers. The elemental factors that make up any visual form or arrangement of forms can be listed in the order of their importance to the creative process. They are: line, dimension, movement, light, color, and texture.

Line as an element of design defines form. Its force is present in a composition in many ways. Line can enclose spaces as outline creating shape (two-dimensional form), or as contour-line suggesting three-dimensional form. Strong backlighting, for example, would emphasize the silhouette or outline of a form while directional side lighting reveals its contour. Light has the power to deny, alter, or accentuate line (Figure 13–5).

Line can appear in a composition as real line in many different modes (straight, curved, spiral, and so on) or as suggested line simulated by the eye as it follows a sequence of related shapes.

Line as a path of action frequently assumes direction. A strong beam of light cannot help but establish direction. The linear shape of the beam coupled with a concentration of brightness creates a strong focus in the composition.

Figure 13-5
Textured and Low-relief Surfaces
Demonstrating the affects of angle and distribution of light on a highly textured surface or low-relief carving. (left) A low-relief sculptural form lighted with a single source from the front. (right) The same form lighted with two side-angle sources of different intensity or color.

Dimension is the size of form. As an element of design, it is not only concerned with the *size* of a shape or mass, but also with the relationship of the size of one shape to another—large to small, large to large, and so on. Hence the size of the interval has a definite effect on the apparent size or mass of a form and to its proportional relationship to other forms in the composition.

Control of light on either the form or the interval influences the dimension of one or the other. Light can reverse the feeling of dimension by making a two-dimensional shape look three-dimensional and vice versa.

Movement is the action of form. It is the kinetic energy of composition. Motion can exist in a stage design as real movement and as the movement of the eye or optical motion within a static composition.

The real movement of lights, of the actor, and on occasion, animated elements of scenery, are all very much part of a theatrical production.

Optical motion is the movement of the eye over a composition. When a form or arrangement of forms is static, optical motion is dependent on the sequential arrangement of forms or elements of design. The movement of the eye can easily be altered through a shift in light intensity or composition. Strong directional light rays or the sequential arrangement of light sources are examples of the use of light as optical motion.

Light reveals form. The dominant presence of light in all areas of stage design makes it imperative that light be considered as a basic influence in the beginning of the creative process and not something to be studied later. The early awareness of light as a design element is as important to the scenery and costume designer as the appreciation of all the elements of design is to the lighting expert to whom this section of the book is devoted.

Color modifies form. As an element of design it is a powerful stimulus within the composition. It can change the dimension of form, reverse the direction of line, alter the interval between forms, and generate optical motion. Color in the theatre comes from two basic sources: pigment or dye colors present on the surface of the form, or colored light that modifies the color of the form.

Texture is the tactile aspect of form. It is the treatment of surfaces that is of interest to the lighting designer. Surfaces may be highly polished, rough-hewn, or rusticated, to name a few that may reflect light or cast interesting shadows. Real texture is best revealed by directional side light (distribution), while painted or simulated texture appears more real under a wash of light without a strong sense of direction (Figure 13–5).

In its simplest form, the texture of light is the product of a specific type of lighting instrument (Figure 13–4). Certainly one of the considerations in choosing the type of instrument to use involves the textural quality of its light. In addition, the designer can alter texture in light by adjusting focus or breaking up the light with specially designed patterns or frost media.

THE FUNCTIONS OF STAGE LIGHTING

The basic obligation of stage design is to give the actor or performer *meaning* in his or her surroundings while providing an atmosphere in which the role may be logically interpreted. Through the manipulation of light in all its aspects—intensity, color, distribution, and movement—the lighting designer assists in creating an environment for the play by achieving *selective visibility*, appropriate *composition*, and *revelation of form*; and by *establishing mood* and *reinforcing* the theme.

Selective Visibility

It is important to understand that the actor must be seen in order to be heard. We cannot define visibility as a fixed degree of brightness or an established angle of distribution. It is the amount of light needed for a moment of recognition deemed appropriate for that point in the action of the play. "To see what should be seen" may mean the revealing of only the silhouette of a three-dimensional form, the solidity of its mass, or the full detail of all surfaces with decoration and texture.

Figure 13-6
Compositional Lighting

These photographs from a production of *A Christmas Carol* at San Diego Repertory Theatre illustrate the use of compositional lighting to enhance both mood and locale. Designers: Lighting by Peter Maradudin, Scenery by Kent Dorsey, Costumes by Nancy Jo Smith.

Composition

Unlike a painting, a stage composition is not static but is an ever-changing arrangement of forms with a moving center of interest. More than any other design element, light is able to direct the audience's eye and control what is and is not seen. Since light possesses the additional quality of incredible fluidity, stage composition can be altered with relative ease. Although light can have composition of its own (projected patterns, for example) its chief function is to reveal stage forms in the proper relationship to other forms and to the background. And here the complexity of compositional lighting begins.

```
┌─────────────────────────────┐
│  ┌───────────────────────┐  │
│  │   LIGHT FUNCTIONS     │  │
│  │                       │  │
│  │   Selective Visibility│  │
│  │      Composition      │  │
│  │   Revelation of Form  │  │
│  │   Establishing Mood   │  │
│  │     Reinforcement     │  │
│  └───────────────────────┘  │
└─────────────────────────────┘
```

Compositional lighting means lighting one form and not another; lighting two-dimensional forms to make them look three-dimensional; keeping shadows off the background; lighting three-dimensional forms to make them look three-dimensional (not as easy as it seems); and many other similar problems, the most important of which is the compositional lighting of the actor (Figure 13–6).

Revelation of Form

Figure 13–7 illustrates that a form can be revealed in a variety of ways. The three-dimensional form of the actor must be shown in a consistent and predictable manner while moving through space—something best not left to chance. Control of form is one of light's greatest powers.

Establishing the Mood

The lighting designer begins with a feeling for the overall mood of the play or scene. A color impression comes from the mood as well as a suggestion of the intensity and distribution of light. The word *mood* tends to suggest dark and gloomy surroundings, but bright comedy or nonsensical farce also indicates a type of mood.

Occasionally a lighting designer will allow concern for mood or atmosphere to override all else: sacrificing other functions, including visibility. Unfortunately, this has happened frequently enough for directors to have become wary of "mood lighting" and shy away from any such discussion. Two things must be understood:

1. Mood and atmosphere are *unavoidable* features of light and to ignore that fact is as dangerous as overstating the mood.
2. Mood is only one of five equally important light functions; to slight any one for another *must* be a conscious decision made by the entire design team and director.

Although an abstract or dramatic mood is more impressive and eye-catching than the realistic visibility of a conventional interior setting, it is also far easier to accomplish with light.

Reinforcing the Theme

The key word here is *reinforcing.* Because the visual expression of theme depends on the scene designer's interpretation of the playwright's message, the lighting designer is concerned with compositional revelation of the thematic forms of the setting. The theme-dominated play (Tennessee Williams' *A Streetcar Named Desire,* for example) asks the lighting designer to reveal the fragmented setting first as a structure having solid walls, then as a transparent, see-through skeleton; finally the designer is

Figure 13-7
Visibility

Illustrating the effect of four different kinds of visibility. (a) An object visible in silhouette only. (b) With front light added, the object is visible as a three-dimensional form. (c) With the addition of another angle of light, the object's detail becomes visible. (d) An example of detail and form becoming less visible as a result of too much light.

Figure 13-8
Theme
Tennessee Williams' *A Streetcar Named Desire* is an example of a theme-dominated play. The lighting designer is asked to support the theme with a distribution of light which follows the action in all areas within the apartment as well as revealing the outside through transparent walls. Design by Edward Pisoni. *Photos by Nelson*

asked to illuminate the constantly moving center of attention from room to room, interior to exterior (Figure 13–8).

In the more extreme theme-oriented or documentary plays of Bertolt Brecht, the theme is often stressed by eliminating the theatricality of stage lighting and playing the show under a clear, uncolored wash of light. Lighting, however, is used to reinforce the theme visually through the use of projections. These take the form of propaganda pictures or subtitles and are used in place of scenic background.

THE ROLE OF THE LIGHTING DESIGNER

Each designer in the production team functions differently according to the demands of the separate areas. The scenic and costume designers must begin their work well in advance of the production in order to allow sufficient time for purchase of materials and construction. The lighting and sound designers have the pleasure of more time to assimilate and observe the production process unfold, but must accept the added responsibilities that are implicit in that knowledge.

Design Stage

It has been made clear that *all* designers are involved in the creative development of a production concept. Once a concept is in place, the lighting and scenic designers will work closely together in order to anticipate any lighting requirements that may affect scenery. Adding an onstage follow-spot position after the scenery drawings have gone into the shops will be terribly expensive if not impossible. Consultation with the costume department is usually not necessary or even desirable until designs are more solidified.

Preparation • The designer must really know the script before anything happens. The number of readings will depend upon the individual designer as well as the script, but we reiterate: at the very least three readings are necessary. The first is to simply enjoy the play as a piece of literature; the second identifies technical concerns such as time of day, effects, and specific lighting action; and the third develops thematic elements of the script. The well-prepared designer will be familiar with the playwright and the period as well.

Before attending rehearsals, it is a good idea to meet with the director on an individual basis if only to explain why you will be there.

Figure 13-9
The Lighting Laboratory
Shown is a human-scale lighting lab where students are able to experiment with various instrumentation, color, and angles of light.

Rehearsals • The reason for attending rehearsals may seem obvious, but one discovers that many directors believe that blocking is the lighting designer's sole interest. While blocking and spatial concerns are important, other benefits include an increased awareness of the director's intent, deeper understanding of how the director works, and a feeling for both mood and pace. Planning for compositional lighting is very difficult without prior knowledge of blocking, however every rehearsal need not be a run-through to satisfy other equally important lighting needs.

Pre-Production • The light plot which has been developing in the designer's head for awhile is usually put on paper during the week before lighting move-in day. While every designer has an individual way of working, most who draft their own plots create at the same time. After initial technical drawing of the theatre and scenery, lighting areas are determined. Next will come choice of specific instrumentation and distribution. Finally, the designer makes color and control choices.

Good and thorough pre-planning is of the utmost importance. Lighting cues are written and conveyed to the stage manager who will call them during performance. The designer is present to answer questions during the put-in, but crews are supervised by a master electrician who is well acquainted with the theatre facilities and equipment.

Production • Dimmer readings for each lighting cue are written by the designer before lighting rehearsals begin. The paper information is given to the light board operator and adjusted visually during an acting rehearsal just previous to technical rehearsal. This procedure allows the technical rehearsal to be just that—a *technical* rehearsal rather than a lighting rehearsal. If the production is complex enough to require a separate lighting rehearsal, it should be scheduled. During subsequent dress rehearsals the lighting designer watches from the auditorium and makes level and timing changes, a procedure which may continue through previews in some cases.

THE LIGHTING LABORATORY

More and more institutions that are genuinely committed to training lighting designers are seeking and finding the space and equipment for lighting labs. The light lab comes in many sizes and forms; most exist in found spaces that have been equipped by students and faculty with a limited budget. The available equipment is often ancient and may be less than useful in an actual production. However, the lab is also the place

Figure 13-10
Using the Lighting Lab
In lieu of the training advantages of actual production lighting, a well-equipped lighting lab offers a simulated but parallel experience. The student lighting designer can reconstruct lighting angles and position for any stage form—proscenium, arena, or thrust—and discover, in a hands-on manner, some of the compositional properties of light. In this exercise the scenic form purposely contains a variety of surfaces. Sweeping curves, sharp corners, openings, and texture lend interest. The photographs show some of the effects.

for experimentation with state-of-the-art instrumentation; many facilities select for purchase one or two new pieces of equipment each year to be used in the lab.

Ideally the light lab will be on a human scale, with a grid somewhere between 12 and 15 feet high. It should have its own control system and circuitry, although neither need be elaborate. The lab shown in Figure 13–9 is a converted, high-school auditorium stage. Another intelligent arrangement is to combine the lighting lab with a makeup classroom, for makeup instruction often requires stage lighting. Lab exercises vary from reproduction of light in a painting to demonstrations of angle and quality of light.

An excellent example of the use of a large-scale model in the lighting lab is seen in Figure 13–10. Note the various uses of light angle for texture and composition.

DEVELOPMENT OF A LIGHTING DESIGNER

Designing for the theatre requires a great deal from an individual. Not only must one have artistic talent and technical knowhow, but the designer must also be able to communicate. The next few chapters will instruct the young designer in the nuts and bolts of lighting, but it must never be forgotten along the way that a *designer* is being nurtured. The importance of "learning to see"—of establishing visual memory—must always be in the forethought of the reader. Experimentation is essential: lighting instruments should be examined, dimmer systems operated, and colors mixed. The lighting designer can learn only so much from theory and example; he or she must have opportunities to put theory into practice. Since production space is always in great demand, a lighting laboratory becomes a tremendous aid to practical training.

But always remember, while wandering through the maze of technical information, pause now and then—and *look*.

Color and Light

Color is a dominant force in a stage composition. It can be subtle or dramatic, decorative or atmospheric and, by its very absence, call attention to itself. Color in light animates the scene. The energy of light reveals, brightens, and adds color to inert forms thereby increasing their vitality.

There are, however, many definitions of color. The chemistry and physics of color are the most familiar because they directly influence the use of color in the theatre. But we must not overlook the fact that the eye sees color and the brain interprets the color experience. Also, within the physiology of the eye are phenomena of color vision that should be considered by all designers in the theatre.

The design element of color often seems most complex to the lighting designer. It is for this reason that it was first introduced in Chapter 8 and again here, early in our study of stage lighting. No pressure must be felt to "master" the subject of color usage, for it will take time and experience. The beginning lighting designer must attend to color in dye and pigment as well as in light, for most often they interrelate.

COLOR AND LIGHT

Color would not exist without light. The breaking up of white light into spectral hues by means of a prism is a common sight that illustrates the fact that such light is actually made up of a variety of colors. If we perceive a light as white, the receptors in our eyes are actually receiving a mixture of colors that our brain calls "white." It is believed that the color receptors in our eyes (*cones*) are most sensitive to three color wavelengths; however, the physicist with more precise laboratory prisms can produce an accurate spectrum with wavelength values for each hue (Plate 14–1a).

The Visible Spectrum

Color and light are the visible wavelengths of the electromagnetic spectrum (Figure 14–1). The visible portion of the spectrum measured in

Figure 14-1
The Electromagnetic Spectrum

nanometers (one-billionth of a meter) is a minute section falling in the vicinity of 400 to 700 nanometers in length. The shortest, 390 to 430 nanometers, produces what we call violet light. The next length is blue followed by green, yellow, orange, and finally (between 630 and 700 nanometers), red light. The wavelengths shorter than 390 nanometers are called ultraviolet (beyond violet) and those longer than 700 nanometers are infrared (below red).

THE LANGUAGE OF COLOR

In describing a color it is important to use a common language that will be understood by other designers and co-workers. The three variants of color in pigments and dyes (discussed in Chapter 8's scene-design section on color) are hue, value, and chroma. The lighting designer uses these variants as a basis of color terminology. A color can be described in simple terms by referring to its hue (blue, yellow, and so on); value (lightness or brightness); and chroma or saturation.

Hue

The position of a color in the spectrum determines its *hue.* Hue is the quality that allows us to differentiate one color from another or from a gray of the same value (brightness). Six easily identified hues are red, orange, yellow, green, blue, and violet. As mentioned earlier, the color receptors in our eyes respond most strongly to the three hues of red, green, and blue; and, as a result, the lighting designer often finds it useful to think of hue in terms of a mixture of these three primary colors in light. The primary hues are suitably located in the spectrum to mix to what we perceive as *white light* (Plate 14–1b).

Value or Brightness

In paint or dye the term *value* refers to the amount of white or black added to the color hue. In light, value is closer to intensity or brightness of a color. A tint refers to a color filter that transmits a brighter light, higher in value. The pale colors often used to light an actor from the front are tints of high value.

Chroma or Saturation

Lighting terminology prefers the term *saturation* to that of *chroma*. Saturation refers to the amount of pure spectral hue present in a color. A primary blue for example is considered a highly saturated color. The instant the purity of a spectrum hue is modified by mixing, the change is referred to as a difference in saturation.

Kelvin Temperature

The lighting designer has yet another concern: the color of the source of light itself. We tend to think of the light emitted from almost any lamp as white, but in reality the actual colors of light given off by various sources can be quite different. The method we have of identifying the color make-up of any light source is called *color temperature* and its measurement is in degrees Kelvin (after the British physicist, William Lord Kelvin).

Unlike literal temperature, the higher the Kelvin temperature the cooler or more towards the blue end of the spectrum is the source. For instance, candlelight which tends to be very reddish is rated at 1,800 degrees Kelvin (K); the standard incandescent household lamp will be somewhere around 3,000° K; and sunlight is suprisingly blue at a cool 6,000° K. More detailed information about Kelvin temperature will be found in Chapter 22, but the concept of a scale of measuring the color of light is important to understand at this point.

COLOR FILTERING

Most stage-lighting instruments deliver a light that we consider "white" rated at approximately 3,200° K. Currently, the only practical means of significantly altering this color is by interrupting the beam of light with a filter. Clear glass vessels containing red wine and other colored liquids were once employed as filters, but we have advanced into the age of modern technology and now use colored plastic.

Color filtering of stage lights is considered subtractive mixing (discussed below) because, as its name implies, selected colors are filtered or blocked from passing through the plastic. This is an important concept to understand. In theory, if a pure blue light is shone through a pure red filter, no light at all will be allowed to pass (Figure 14–2).

COLOR MIXING

Color in light and pigment is varied by mixing. The two methods of mixing are *additive mixing* and *subtractive mixing*. While both methods affect hue changes, additive mixing also noticeably alters value, and subtractive mixing modifies chroma.

Additive Mixing

The mixing of colored light from two or more sources is additive mixing. It can be demonstrated by the overlapping of sharply defined fields of two or more spotlights each with a separate color filter (Plates 14–2a and b). A single filter such as red, for example, absorbs all other hues from the spectrum and transmits only red. When the red rays overlap or are

Figure 14-2
Subtractive Mixing (Filtering)
(top) White light, when filtered through two secondaries, produces a tint of the latters' common primary. (bottom) Light, when filtered by two primaries, is completely absorbed so that no light whatever emerges.

added to the light from the blue filter the result is a red-violet or magenta color. A hue produced by additive mixing is always higher in value.

The most spectacular example of additive mixing is the combination of two contrasting colors, red and green. Their mixing produces a yellow, which is not too surprising when it is noted that yellow and yellow-orange hues fall between red and green in the color spectrum.

Mixing Primaries • The additive mixing of the three primaries in light produces a synthetic white light. When the field of each primary color is partially overlapped it is possible to see the forming of secondary colors. The secondaries are hue-opposites to the primaries, which are referred to as complementary colors. Blue and amber, for example, are complementary colors. Their mixing produces white light (Plate 14–2a).

Primary and secondary hues in lighter values (tints) are frequently used to light the actor. Tints of the complementary hues, yellow and blue, for example, may be used from opposite sides of the stage or in pairs from a single direction. The additive mixing of the two colors model the actor in flattering white light that can be warmed or cooled by changing the intensity of one of the spotlights (Plate 14–2).

Subtractive Mixing

The opposite of additive mixing is subtractive mixing. In light it is the crossing or combination of color filters in front of a single light source. Figure 14–2 illustrates the merging of a magenta and amber filter (secondaries) to produce red light. The magenta absorbed or subtracted all spectral hues but red as does the amber filter. If two primaries are crossed, such as red and blue, all hues are subtracted and no light is passed. It should be noted, however, that the lighting designer seldom finds it necessary to use more than a single filter in front of a light source due to the very large range of colors available.

Color Reflection

Just as light allows us to see an object, it also allows us to perceive the color of an object. Unfiltered light is a result of mixing together the various colors of the spectrum to create a color that we call "white." The eye sees the color of a surface by *reflection*. A colored surface lit with white light will selectively reflect certain light colors while absorbing others. So a colored surface acts somewhat like a color filter except that it selectively reflects color rather than allowing it to pass through. An orange surface, for example, absorbs all spectrum hues except yellow, orange, and red to reflect the orange color we see (Figure 14–3). In theory, a pure red object lit by a pure blue light will reflect no light and therefore be invisible.

The Color Wheel

Sir Isaac Newton, who first observed the phenomenon of refraction and the spectrum, was also the first to bring the ends of the spectrum together into a continuous circle or *wheel*. The circular arrangement of hues brings into view the diametric and adjacent correlation of the twelve spectrum hues and thus provides designers a schematic view of primary and secondary hue relationship in both pigment and light (Plate 14–1b).

In the light color wheel the additive mixing of diametrically opposite hues produces the white in the center.

The location of the light primaries in the light wheel represents more accurately their spectral hue. Red, for example, is red-orange (*RO*); blue, blue-violet (*BV*); and green, yellow-green (*YG*).

With some latitude light primaries can be described in terms of Roscolux color mediums (Rosco Laboratories, Inc.) as (1) a red with some orange content (Roscolux No. 26, light red) designated as *Ro* (small orange). (2) A blue containing some red (*Rv*) Roscolux No. 47, light rose purple plus No. 65, daylight blue, is very close to primary blue. (3) The remaining primary, green, is obtainable by combining No. 89, moss green, and No. 12, straw. These primary hues are close enough to be thought of as red-orange (*RO*), blue-violet (*BV*), and yellow-green (*YG*) as they appear in the pigment color wheel.

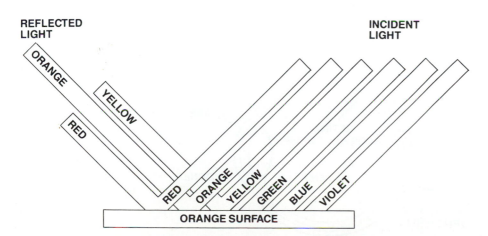

REFLECTED LIGHT

INCIDENT LIGHT

ORANGE
YELLOW
RED

RED ORANGE YELLOW GREEN BLUE VIOLET

ORANGE SURFACE

Figure 14-3

Selective Color Reflection

The horizontal orange strip represents an orange-colored surface (a costume, for instance). It appears orange under white light because only the red, yellow, and orange hues of the spectrum have been reflected. The other hues have been absorbed.

The light secondaries are the result of the additive mixing of the primaries. They are complementary colors and are located directly opposite each primary in the pigment color wheel. Yellow-orange (*YO*) is opposite light-primary blue-violet (*BV*) and can be produced in light by doubling Roscolux No. 03, dark amber. Blue-green (*BG*), across from primary (*RO*), is near Roscolux No. 71, sea blue; and red-violet (*RV*), the complement of primary (*YG*), is almost the same as Roscolux No. 48, rose purple. Note that the light secondaries are lighter in value than their corresponding pigment hues because of the additive mixing that formulated them.

COLOR VISION

The source of color can be scientifically explained; the mixture of color can be diagrammed; and all the variants of color can be arranged in a system of notation. However, what the eye sees and the brain interprets is an individual and personal color experience. Although the eye functions very much like a camera, it is not a scientific instrument. It receives light through its lens, which focuses the image of impression onto the layers of the retina in the inner eye. The innumerable nerve endings (rods and cones) of the retina culminate in the optic nerve, which carries the impression signal to the brain for interpretation. The impression is registered in terms of color and intensity (brightness), which in a sense is another way of saying hue and value.

Color Physiology

The lens of the eye can focus objects from a distance of approximately eight inches to infinity by changing the curvature of its surface — in effect, changing its own focal length. The iris contains the pupil, located just in front of the lens, that opens or closes to allow more or less light into the eye (Figure 14–4). It closes quite a bit faster than it opens. Two types of nerve endings located in the retina area of the eye detect light intensity and color: the rods and the cones. Rods are sensitive to intensity or brightness only. The color-sensitive cones are of three types: one most sensitive to colored light in the red range, the second most sensitive to blue, and the third to green light. Rods and cones send an electrical signal to the brain that varies in frequency with the intensity of the light. It is important to realize that the brain then *interprets* the signal. This interpretation is affected by many factors including viewer expectation and need.

Figure 14-4
The Eye

COLOR PERCEPTION

Knowledge of *how* we see color is perhaps of greater interest to the lighting designer than to other designers in the theatre. An understanding of the physiology of the eye as it relates to color vision gives the designer some indication of how the audience reacts to both intensity and color.

Intensity and Color

The eye's sensitivity to high or low levels of light affects the color we see. Since the rods of the retina, for example, produce most of the low-level or night vision, their sensitivity to green-blue would tend to add a greenish-blue cast to all hues seen under a low level of light. Moonlight, for example, though it is the reflection of the sun greatly reduced in intensity, appears to have a blue tint. However, blue tint, as far as the brain is concerned, is a *color impression* a designer has to consider within a stage composition. The high-intensity vision of the cones in the retina are more sensitive to yellow; the sun at noon, although a brilliant white, appears to have a yellowish tint. In a stage composition, however, there is a less apparent shift of color under high intensities.

Intensity and Color Fatigue

The retina of the eye assimilates light energy. When it is saturated it is said to be *bleached.* Hence after any sudden change of intensity or color, the retina has to regenerate itself. This process takes place over a noticeable period of time. Since the rods are sensitive to intensity, and the cones are sensitive to both intensity and color, there is a difference in the times it takes the eye to readjust to a sudden intensity change and to a color change. It takes the eye about one to one-and-a-half minutes to adjust in a blackout, for example (rod regeneration), while a color change (cone regeneration) may take as long as five minutes.

Our eyes tire of a constant color, especially if it is at all saturated and tending toward one of the primaries (blue is a good example). A stage picture washed only in blue light will soon lose its color quality because of this fatigue effect. Color contrast or variation will counter fatigue and maintain the intended look.

After-image

The time lag of the eye experienced after a sudden change of color explains *after-image,* a phenomenon of color vision. Until the eye has recovered, it retains an image of the object and a color impression long after the object has been removed or changed. The after-image is in the *complementary hue* of the original image color—a result of color fatigue.

The Color of Cast Shadows

The phenomenon of after-image or the color-balancing tendency of the eye is present in other forms. The shadow cast from a colored light source, for example, appears to the observer to be in a complementary color. Plate 14–3a illustrates the pale red-orange shadow cast from a blue-green light which is not there in reality but is an optical illusion or color impression within the eye. It should be mentioned that the shadow has to be faintly illuminated with a colorless light to accomplish the demonstration accurately.

The Interaction of Color

How a color reacts to an adjacent hue or to its background is known as the interaction of color. Certain reactions are painfully obvious while others are extremely subtle. The juxtaposition of hue opposites such as colors blue-green and red-orange seem to vibrate in violent interaction. To experience the same interaction in light it is necessary to compare surfaces that are independently colored by two or more light sources. It is a condition where colored light is not mixed but is viewed side by side. An example of the interaction of color in light is illustrated in Plate 14–3b. The angled position of the surfaces separate the contrasting colors from the two right and left sources. The third softer tint in the center seems bluish as it interacts with the blue-green on the left and has a reddish cast when influenced by the red-violet on the right.

Another phenomenon of color interaction and perception has to do with colors that appear to recede or move away from the viewer and those that seem to accede or move toward the viewer. The cool colors (blues and greens) fit into the former category of those that recede, while the warmer colors (reds and ambers) tend to accede. This phenomenon may be put to use by the lighting designer only in specific instances but is one that should always be kept in mind.

DESIGNING WITH COLOR

We all make numerous color choices in the course of our everyday lives, but the average person will make many or most of them on a subconscious level. The interior designer, fashion designer, and theatre designer must force such choices to the conscious level and begin to analyze how and why specific color determinations are made.

Before examining color usage in greater detail, several other important points should be made. First of all, the term "white light" is heard a great deal in the theatre when talk turns to color. The fact is that so-called white light is relative, and our eye will accept an astonishing range of colored light as "white," depending on the circumstances. For this reason, the term "no color" (abbreviated N/C) is preferable to "white" when one discusses color and filtering. The concept of color temperature discussed earlier (measured in degrees Kelvin, or K) is also valuable to a discussion of color.

Finally, the lighting designer must always keep in mind the effect of *dimming* on the color of a light source. In almost every case we will control the intensity of a theatrical lighting instrument by means of a dimmer. Dimming lowers the voltage or current sent to the instrument's lamp; and, as a result, the lamp's filament burns less brightly. As it is dimmed it also gives off a significantly warmer color of light. A blue filter in front of an instrument burning at 100-percent intensity emits a very different color than that of the same filter in front of an instrument burning at 70-percent intensity.

Mixing on a Surface

Mixing occurs anytime two colors of light are used on the same area. The resultant color depends on colors and angles of the two light sources as well as the surface on which they fall. If two light sources strike a surface from different angles, and if the surface is three-dimensional and sculpted (an actor's face, for example), many interesting things happen. First of all, one source will cast shadows that will be filled or partially filled by the other source's light and color. Second, an overall even color mix will not be achieved because the sources are coming from different directions. What will be seen, instead, is a heavy coloration from one source that merges gradually to an even mix with the second color and finally moves into the color of the second source. Such coloration adds to the three-dimensionality of a figure on stage and can help establish a direction of light (Figure 14–5).

Mixing in the Air

Another form of color mixing involves the placement of two or more light sources very close to one another so that they effectively act as a single source. The most common example of such mixing in the theatre is the use of striplights on a cyclorama or backdrop. But this technique is also employed for area lighting using spotlights placed very close to one another. The point of this is to give the designer a large range of color options through mixing while only using two lighting instruments. Of course, this type of mixing depends on dimming, and therefore each instrument must have separate control.

Choosing Color

The designer chooses colored light for one of four reasons:

1. The light is motivated by a specific source (the sun, a lamp, the fireplace), and colored light will help convey that motivation.
2. The mood of a scene is reinforced by the light, and color will heighten the effect.
3. A visual contrast between light sources is desirable, and color will increase that contrast.
4. Change or dramatic effect for its own sake is desired.

Figure 14-5
Color Mixing

Two complementary colors striking a three-dimensional object, such as an actor's face, from different angles will gradually mix toward white.

The dilemma most often is not whether to use color, but which color to choose. The lighting designer's job in this respect is often made easier by the fact that most design teams will decide upon a production's *color scheme* early in the design process. The scenic and costume designers will have made their color choices based upon these earlier discussions, and the lighting designer will follow suit.

A METHOD OF USING COLOR

As indicated earlier, successful designing with color depends on taste, knowledge, and experience. Let us begin with a technique developed by Stanley McCandless, a man who more than any other might be considered the founder of lighting design in the United States. McCandless suggested that one way to achieve the most *natural* look when lighting the actor on stage is to position lighting instruments to each side of the actor at an angle of approximately 45 degrees, and 45 degrees up from the horizontal (Figure 14–6). Two complementary colors will then be placed in the instruments—say a light blue in one and a warm amber in the other. The amber will act as a "key" or primary source light while the blue will read as a "fill" or reflected light. The colors mix with each other on the actor's face and body front to a shade that will be read as white. This technique has formed a basis for color use in modern lighting design.

Warm and Cool Colors

In general, most people will consider the color red as bloodlike, typifying anger and war. Amber is likely to be perceived as sunlight, warm and comfortable. Blue will typify restraint and coolness, while green may be seen as restful. These and similar identifications must always be taken into consideration when a designer selects stage colors. But there is little advantage in going too deeply into the psychology of color, about which there are many (often contradictory) theories.

Figure 14-6
45-degree—45-degree Mixing
A stage-left blue and a stage-right amber will mix toward white light at the center of the actor's body (See Plate 14-2).

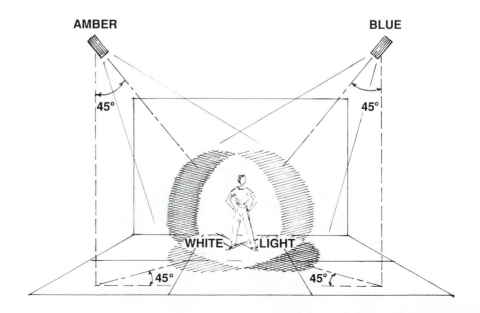

There is one psychological aspect, however, that cannot well be ignored: the matter of the relative warmth and coolness of colors. Few people would deny that a bright red-orange suggests warmth; most would agree that a brittle blue-white gives an impression of coolness.

Given samples of twenty different tints and shades, rarely will two people list them in exactly the same order from most warm to most cool. But in general we can say that the reds, oranges, and ambers are considered in the warm group, while the blues, violets, and greens fall within the cool range. Some mixtures of hues from the opposing groups seem on the border line, and the particular effect they give at any moment is in contrast to whatever other color is seen in relation to them (Interaction of Color).

As a matter of fact, the precise feeling given by most tints is purely a matter of contrast. A pale blue that seems positively icy in contrast to a strong amber will appear quite warm when placed next to a stronger shade of blue. Pink and lavender are frequently used on the stage as freewheeling tints whose effects we can reverse merely by changing the hues used in association with them.

Unfiltered light may also seem to have warm or cool characteristics. Opposite a cool color, such as the palest of blues or greens, uncolored light will appear quite warm. But when it is opposite a pink or pale amber, white light will definitely be on the cool side in contrast.

Remember that as dimmer readings are changed the color of light produced by a source changes. A low dimmer level will generate a very warm light compared to a reading at full intensity.

Color Modification

Designers in the theatre not only have to consider the colors of a painted background, costumes, and other materials of a set, but also the colors of the lights that will reveal them. This is especially true if the lighting for the scene is unusual, such as a romantic moonlit scene or the flooding of the stage with red or green hues to provide an unnatural effect.

Fortunately, color modification is not quite as complicated as it seems. The effect of colored light on a colored surface is a result of subtractive mixing. In other words, if a red light is thrown on a yellow surface, the yellow is modified into orange tones.

The modification of a color in a costume or on scenery by colored light is a theatrical example of the joining of two color media, pigment and light. Designers in the theatre are constantly aware of how colored light and pigment influence each other. They are always prepared to compensate in either medium to create a natural effect or to deliberately cause dramatic reversals of color.

Colored Light and the Actor

In a later chapter, we will suggest specific colors to use in different situations, but here we will consider general effects desired in various portions of the stage picture. For acting area front light, for example, it is best to stay clear of saturated and unnatural shades that will adversely affect the faces and costumes of the actors.

Preserving color integrity of costumes can be a difficult task. Often the acting areas are lighted with tints of pinks and ambers, flattering enough to the human face, but deadly to green materials. Because the scene may definitely call for such colors in the light, the lighting designer must at all times keep abreast with the costume designer's color palette.

Knowing what will happen to a given costume under colored light is simplified by breaking down the colors into primaries. For example, let us assume a yellow dress will be lit by a cool blue light from one angle and a straw or cool amber from another. The cool blue contains some mix of green and blue, the cool amber is made up of both red and green, and the yellow dress is going to reflect red and green. The conclusion, reached by simply noting the preponderance of green, is that we are probably going to be in trouble. A warmer blue or a lavender and a warmer amber light might be a better choice.

Beware of Green! • Green light has limited use on the acting areas of the stage. Green on the human face is extremely unbecoming, muddying the natural healthy colors of cheeks and lips, deadening blonde and reddish hair, and exaggerating to the point of grotesqueness the slightest blemish in the complexion.

This does not mean that green should never be used. It is an extremely useful color, especially for the enrichment of costumes and scenery. But it should be handled with considerable care, unless, of course, a distorted effect is actually desired.

Colored Light and the Scenery

Always operate on the assumption that the scene designer has painted the settings the way they should appear. Thus, for a lighting designer to attempt to improve on the scene designer's artistry would be impertinent. Enhance it, yes, but strictly in accordance with the scene designer's wishes. Close collaboration between scene and lighting designers is crucial. The result will usually be that nearby scenery, such as the walls of an interior setting, will, like the acting areas, receive tints of light only. Strong colors, as we have made clear, will tire the audience and will alter the appearance of the painting. Furthermore, being so close to the acting areas, it is almost impossible to separate light on such scenery from other portions of the stage.

A good rule of thumb for a lighting designer to begin with is "If you are debating whether or not to light the scenery—don't." Generally, light on scenery such as flats and drops will cast unwanted shadows and possibly create a situation where the walls and the actors are competing for focus. On the other hand, color washing the scenery can help to create some very nice and useful effects (Plates 14–4a and b). Nearly any scenic or costume color can be made to appear warmer or cooler—more or less inviting—through the use of colored light. A scene designer may, in addition, actually paint the set in several different colors that can be selectively accentuated or deemphasized by colored light.

Color on the Sky

At some point a lighting designer will be called on to use color on a sky drop or cyclorama. Specific lighting techniques are discussed later, but the use of color deserves some comment here. Careful consideration and experimentation must be given before choosing a color to light a backdrop. The color of the drop itself will affect the lighting choice, for sky drops can vary from numerous shades of white to blue.

Is it better to select a single color medium that gives the exact hue desired or is a blending of several colors preferable? Of course, if there is to be a color change during the scene, then more than one color must be provided. More delicate and precise shadings can also be achieved if several different colors are blended into one.

Mixing of the three primaries is a traditional method of achieving variable color on a sky drop, and striplights will commonly be supplied with glass color filters (roundels) in the three primary colors. Remember, however, that light transmission from primary colors is extremely low, and pale tints usually are too pale for a sky drop. Therefore, colors closer to the secondaries are often the best solution.

Selecting Color

Experimenting with color mixing is especially important for the young lighting designer. Colors projected by stage-lighting instruments can be seen in the theatre or in a lighting laboratory — in fact any place that has

Figure 14-7
The Color Mix-Box
Three Fresnels on dimmers allow the designer freedom to mix colors in a space other than the theatre.

dimmers. However, a useful tool for experimentation outside the theatre is the color mix-box (Figure 14-7). Three-inch Fresnels and three common household dimmers are used in the mix-box shown. The box is portable and can be plugged into any household circuit. With the mix-box, the task of color selection is made easier and more convenient.

COLOR MEDIA

In order to use a mix-box, a lighting designer must have available a file box of color media that contains a frame-size cut of every color the designer may need. There are three kinds of color media in use today: acetate, Mylar, and glass.

Gelatin

It is common to refer to any color filter as a "gel," being short for "gelatin"; the first material to be manufactured as a color media. However, except for very special applications, gelatin is no longer in use.

Plastic Media

Two types of plastic color media are available: acetate and Mylar. While acetate is less expensive than Mylar, it will fade and even change color over a period of time. Both plastics are waterproof and considerably more durable than gelatin was.

Acetate • Only one acetate color gel is in common use in the United States: "Roscolene" manufactured by Rosco Laboratories. Roscolene is available in a wide range of colors numbered in the 800 series.

Mylar • Mylar filters were developed a number of years ago for use with the hotter, quartz stage-lighting instruments. Like acetate, Mylar is available in sheets (20" by 24"), but also comes in rolls (24" by 50'). It is quite durable and may be reused. Three companies supply Mylar filters in the United States: Great American ("GamColors"), Lee ("Lee Filters"), and Rosco ("Roscolux").

GamColor is numbered in the 100s through 900s; Lee Filters are numbered in the 100 series and spill over into the 200s; and Roscolux begins its numbering at 001 and goes into the 100s. So as to avoid the confusion this may cause, use an "R" prefix before Roscolux numbers, an "L" prefix before Lee Filter numbers, and a "G" prefix for GamColor.

Most often the choice between acetate and Mylar is simply a matter of durability. Mylar is now available in a wider range of colors than acetate, but its higher cost can be prohibitive. However, the use of Mylar is recommended in the following situations:

1. In sky drop or cyclorama lighting, particularly if the lighting instruments are placed on the floor shooting up.
2. When using high-intensity lighting instruments with lamp ratings of over 1,000 watts.
3. In scenic projection or follow spotting.

Handling Plastic Media • A new piece of plastic may, when placed in the heat of a light beam, give off considerable steam for a period. This effect, which appears to be smoke, can be quite distracting, if not alarming, to the audience. It is wise, therefore, to test new plastic well before curtain time and, if it smokes, leave the instrument switched on to dry it out before the show starts.

To allow the heat of an instrument to escape when acetate is used as its color medium, it is a good idea to perforate it with numerous small holes. These will not affect the performance of the plastic in any way, except to prolong its life, nor will the holes appear in the beam pattern. An ice pick, nail, or awl may be used for this purpose, but the neatest and easiest method is to run a pounce wheel several times over the full sheet before cutting it to size.

Colored Glass

The most expensive medium of all is glass. While gelatin and plastic may be cut to any size or shape desired, glass must be ordered for exactly the purpose required. It comes in few colors, is heavy and bulky to store, and although it never fades, is rarely affected by heat, and stands up well under ordinary usage, it can be smashed. Glass has two great advantages: it is heat resistant, and it can be molded into markings and prismatic lines that will spread light.

Roundels can be obtained with the following features:

Plain	For color filtering only
Stippled	For color and also to diffuse the beam
Spread	For color and also to spread the beam laterally, so that the various colors will blend more readily
Stripped	Very thin glass in narrow strips to color the light from extremely hot-beamed instruments

Diffusion Material

Diffusion material, often called "frost," diffuses light from an instrument and softens or even eliminates a shutter cut or beam edge. Although not a color medium, it is manufactured by the companies that produce color media, is listed in their "swatch" or sample books, and is commercially available in sheets. Several years ago Rosco expanded their line of frosts from several to nearly 20 varieties that range from a very light frost, which just barely takes the edge off a sharply-focused instrument; to a heavy frost, which makes a beam edge all but disappear; to a "silk," which will actually spread the beam of light in two directions (Figure 14-8).

A lighting designer who chooses to ignore the nearly endless possibilities of the various frost media available is overlooking an important tool of the trade.

Figure 14-8
Diffusion Material
The effect of three different diffusion materials: (top) A light frost such as Rosco's "Hamburg Frost" #R114. (middle) A heavy frost which keeps a hot center similar to Rosco's "Tough Frost" #R103. (bottom) A spread frost such as Rosco's "Tough Silk" #R104.

Color Manufacturers

It is good practice to replace swatch books every two or three years to avoid faded color samples and keep aware of newly added colors. For a variety of reasons, a manufacturer may not be able to match exactly the color of a filter from one batch to another. Rosco has taken to adding a letter suffix to the number of a color filter that was not able to be adequately matched (R35A).

Finally, never trust the color names that the various manufacturers assign to each color. Names are assigned to aid in communication and to make a particular color easier to remember, but one need only compare GamColor's "Light Steel Blue" (G720) with Roscolux's color of the same name (R64A) to fully understand why such labels are meaningless.

To obtain color swatch books contact your local color media supplier or write the following manufacturers:

GamColor: The Great American Market
826 N. Cole Avenue
Hollywood, CA 90038

Rosco: Rosco Laboratories, Inc.
36 Bush Avenue
Port Chester, NY 10573

Lee: LeeColortran Inc.
1015 Chestnut Street
Burbank, CA 91506

15

Stage-Lighting Practice: Distribution

The beginning lighting designer should first study motivational lighting. Accordingly, the early part of this chapter will involve a discussion of the types of light from those sources with which we are all familiar: daylight, night light, and light from artificial sources.

As in any creative process, the means and methods toward accomplishing a finished design will vary a great deal. As you read remember that only one of many solutions is being discussed and, while it most certainly will be a proven technique, it may not be the best in every instance. There are very few firm rules in lighting design.

LIGHTING THE ACTOR

Actors must be seen in proper relationship to their backgrounds. This relationship, of course, is different for each play or dramatic situation. In general, the designer must vary the intensity, distribution, and color of light to solve the problem. Distribution is of primary importance because it involves the angle and direction of light that reveals the actors, especially their faces, in natural form.

Angles of Light

The expression ''in natural form'' is the clue. It means the actor's face should be seen as it appears under natural lighting. Our eyes have been schooled by a lifetime of seeing one another under sunlight or interior lighting coming from above. We are so accustomed to seeing the features of a face disclosed by light from an overhead direction that to light it from below, for example, produces for us an unnatural look (Figure 15–1).

Figure 15-1
Lighting the Actor
Upward angle from the footlights or apron. An unnatural, though dramatic, angle.

The primary way we determine the direction of a light source is by the *highlight* and *shadow* created. It is the shadow in Figure 15–1 that makes it seem unnatural. Highlight and shadow, which give dimension to a form, are controlled by source angle. Figure 15–2 further illustrates the relationship of highlight and shadow to perception. Shadowless illumination is uninteresting and reduces visibility.

Anyone who has done outdoor photography knows how to maneuver a subject into a position where the sun will reveal the face most favorably. Overly bright sunlight from a single direction will cast such deep shadows that visibility of the face will be reduced. In the diffused light of shade or of an overcast sky the face appears in full visibility, although it is missing the dramatic accent of the brilliant sunlight.

The proscenium theatre offers numerous possibilities for varying the angle and direction of a light source. Figure 15–3 shows the various standard positions available in a simple proscenium house. Those positions on the audience side of the proscenium arch (referred to as "front-of-house" [FOH]) present the designer with a good variety of angles from the front. In terms of extreme angles, the backstage positions are even more varied including lights from side, top, and back as well as front.

Through the elaborate control of intensity and distribution possible in stage lighting, the face of the actor can be lighted to appear the way it does in nature.

Front Lighting • It has long been a practice of artists and architects to render their drawings as though light were falling on the subject from over the artist's shoulder at an angle of about 45 degrees. Lighting designer Stanley McCandless adopted the same concept. Using spotlights, the beams may be directed on the actor at a 45-degree angle above and at 45 degrees from the right and left. To give the face an accent of brightness or color difference on one side, the intensity or color of the right or left spotlight may be varied, as discussed in Chapter 14. The face is then disclosed by a *fill-light* on one side and an accent or *key-light* on the opposite side. This slight difference in color and intensity not only improves the visibility of the face but also adds interest to the composition (Figure 15–4).

This is not to say that the McCandless 45°/45° system is the *only* way to achieve natural lighting, but it is a good way. Another method, which originated on Broadway, is often referred to as "jewel lighting." This

LIGHT FROM BELOW

LIGHT FROM ABOVE

Figure 15-2
Depth Perception As Influenced by Lighting Angle

An illustration of how we assume the direction of light to be from above is shown in Figures (a) and (b), identical rectangles each containing five convex domes. With lighting from below as in Figure (a), the domes appear to be concave; while lighting from above as in Figure (b), they appear convex.

Figure 15-3
Lighting Positions in the Proscenium Theatre

(1) Ceiling beams or ports. (2) Box booms or coves. (3) Balcony front or balcony rail. (4) Apron or footlights. (5) First electric or bridge. (6) Boom. (7) Second electric (midstage backlight position). (8) Ladder. (9) Third electric (backdrop or cyclorama lighting). (10) Cyclorama base or horizon lights. (11) Translucent drop backlight. (12) Followspot.

approach, probably developed because of a lack of front-lighting positions, depends on low-angle, balcony rail lights to fill from the front while side and back light create accent. The inhouse-box boom positions, another Broadway innovation, act more as side light on the apron than front light. This system particularly makes sense knowing that more often than not frontal follow spotting is used on main characters, supplementing other front lighting.

In conceptualizing lighting, however, the wise designer begins not with hanging position restrictions, but determines ideal angles based upon desired effect. It has been stated that 45 degrees to the actor is a fairly natural angle. As a light moves higher in angle toward top light, shadows become steeper and the light appears harsher. Moving a light downward from 45 degrees progressively causes shadows to disappear, a condition called "flat" lighting (Figure 15–5).

Back Lighting • A third angle also can be employed to further define the actor: lighting from overhead and behind (Figure 15–6). Back lighting is a stratagem borrowed from movie and television lighting. Because of the need to separate an actor from the background, back light is necessary in television lighting. (The tendency of the television camera is to flatten or shorten distances appearing on the reception screen.) The use of back lighting on the stage to separate an actor from the background adds another dimension to the stage composition. It allows the lighting designer to put a brighter light on the background than would otherwise be possible, and it permits the scene designer to use colors without fear of failure to bring the actor's face into relief. Back lighting produces highlights on the head and shoulders of the actor that give a halo effect if the light is too intense. When it is kept in proper balance with the front lights the actor is etched clearly against the background.

Because back light tends to "edge" an actor, stronger colors than those used in front lighting may be employed. Such creative use of color can help to establish an overhead motivational source or simply color and texture the stage floor for a specific mood or effect. Back light will normally require a more intense source than front light. Care must be taken to keep back light from shining into the first row of audience seating. This often presents a problem, and the lighting designer may be tempted to compromise the back angle, making it more of a top or down light. Top light is not at all the same as back light, for it tends to "squash" rather than edge an actor (Figure 15–7).

Figure 15-4
Lighting the Actor
(a) Front light from stage-left, 45-degree angle. Lack of visibility on the dark side of the face.
(b) Front light from the left and right, 45-degree angle. The stage-right side of the face has a higher-intensity light suggesting the direction of the motivating or "key" light.

Figure 15-5
Lighting the Actor
Low angle full-front light. Note lack of definition.

15-4a

15-4b

15-5

15-6

15-7a

15-7b

Figure 15-6
Lighting the Actor
Three angles: right and left front light at 45-degrees and back light.

Figure 15-7
Lighting the Actor
(a) Backlight providing a halo or "rim" effect. Note shadows. (b) Downlight or toplight, 90-degree angle. Normally not a complementary angle.

Figure 15-8
Lighting the Actor
(a) Side light from the right, 45-degree angle. (b) Side light from the right, 30-degree angle.

15-8a

15-8b

Side Lighting • Side lighting gives the designer additional flexibility. Both color and angle add variety as side lighting is used in combination with frontal sources. Side lighting comes from the wings or tormentor positions and is best when directed parallel to the apron. A great variety of vertical angles, however, are available to the designer—from the low, straight-side angle of dance lighting to a high side that edges an actor from the side (Figure 15–8).

Because side lights hit the actor from the extreme right and left, their color need not be as unsaturated as the front lights. They may be used with more chromatic colors to accent costumes or to add colored highlights to white or neutral costumes. Strong side lighting is frequently used for musical production as a part of this more-presentational style of theatre.

Like back light, side light also can be used to establish a motivational source through color, angle, and intensity. In addition, such light is more apparent to the audience simply because more surface area is exposed to light than with back light. Thus, dramatic lighting effects can be established through the creative use of strong side light.

LIGHTING THE ACTING AREA

Lighting an actor from various positions and angles is, of course, easy if the subject is posed or remains in a fixed position on stage. The actor, however, usually moves. Therefore, to produce the same uniformity of coverage as on a stationary figure, the lighting designer must constantly duplicate the focus of spotlights on many similar areas over the entire playing area.

By dividing the playing portion of the setting into convenient areas and then lighting each area with the same number of spotlights, the acting area is covered with a balanced illumination. The area method of lighting the actor, first developed by Stanley McCandless in the 1930s, has proved a very efficient and systematic technique. As scenery style has changed and lighting instrument design has improved, the method has been modified and expanded. The original concept of providing a smooth coverage through the use of a minimum of instruments has given way to double and triple hanging in the name of greater flexibility in color control and distribution. The resulting number of lighting instru-

Figure 15-9
Beam Alignment

For smooth and even coverage of the acting area, light beams must be overlapped as shown.

NANOMETERS

| 400 | 450 | 500 | 550 | 600 | 650 | 700 |

V   B   G   Y   O   R

Plate 14-1a
The Spectrum
Shown are the spectral hues and their respective wave lengths measured in nanometers.

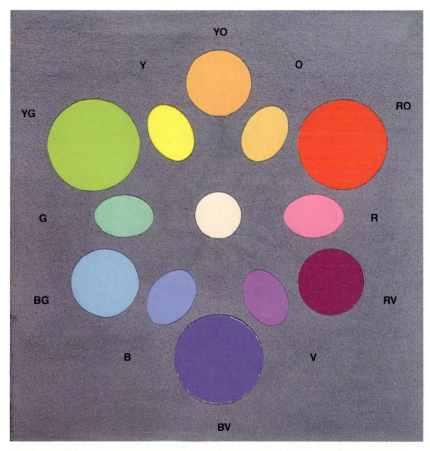

Plate 14-1b
Light Color Wheel
While we consider the primary colors in light to be red, blue, and green, the color wheel is best illustrated using primaries of red with a bit of orange, blue with a bit of violet, and green with a bit of yellow (indicated by the large circles). Mixing complementary colors across the color wheel produces white light. Mixing adjacent primaries (red-orange and blue-violet, for example) produces a secondary color (red-violet).

Plate **14-2a**
Additive Mixing of Primary Colors

When the three primary colors of light are mixed, white light is the result. Any two primaries will mix to form secondary colors.

Plate **14-2b**
Additive Mixing in Stage Lighting

The mixing of complementary tints will produce white light. The "white" light can be warmed or cooled in color by dimming one of the instruments. The different colors on each side of an actor's face adds a sense of direction and source to the light while still mixing to a natural white in the middle.

Plate 14-3a
The Color of Cast Shadows
A cast shadow will appear to be a color that is complementary to the hue of the light source. This illustration shows the primary light source to be blue-green in color. The shadow appears a red-orange tint, the hue opposite of blue-green.

Plate 14-3b
Interaction of Color in Light
Here are two pylons and three colors of light, yet the center tint seems to be two tones of lavender. The left is bluish, the right reddish. This illustrates the interaction of the brilliant blue-green and red-violet washes from the right and left that is sometimes referred to as the push-pull effect.

Plate 14-4
Color on a Scene
Two photographs from a production of *As You Like It* illustrate the strong effect color has on a scene.

ments used in some shows is staggering. Although the area method was first developed for the proscenium theatre it has been readily adapted to other theatre forms such as thrust and arena (see Chapter 23).

Area Alignment

In using the area system, one of the things a designer learns is that areas must overlap considerably or the actor will pass through dark spots ("dips") in lighting when moving from one area to another. A properly focused stage-lighting instrument shines a light that has maximum intensity along the center line of its beam and falls off in brightness towards the edge. If light beams are overlapped so that the fall-off of one beam is compensated by that of an adjacent light, a smooth and even coverage is achieved (Figure 15–9).

Television and film designers will often check intensity variation by using a light-sensitive meter. If the meter readings indicate that intensity levels are uneven, the designer will either add instruments to fill in the gap or adjust focus. The acceptable degree of variation is determined by camera sensitivity or film stock and design considerations. Live-audience designers (theatre, concerts, industrials, and the like) will visually check instrument focus for good alignment, relying on experience and their own perception of design requirements. While being less precise than studio focus, this method promotes a higher level of intuitive design during the focus process.

In either case, focus techniques and procedures are passed along from designer to designer; the apprentice or assistant system is very much alive and well in the relatively small world of lighting design. A beginning designer is wise to observe focus sessions of as many experienced designers as possible, for each will exhibit individual ways of working.

Area Placement

The placement and choice of the number of areas are the lighting designer's decision and, of course, vary with the size and shape of the setting (Figure 15–10). However, in general, areas will vary from 6 to 10 feet in diameter, with 8-foot areas being a good average.

While Chapter 18 supplies more detailed information on beam and field spreads, for now suffice it to say that a lighting instrument produces a pre-determined size beam of light. Being cone-shaped, this beam may be measured either in degrees or diameter of its circle of light. As is apparent in examining Figure 15–11, the diameter of a light beam when it strikes a surface will be determined by throw distance as well as beam angle or spread.

Normally using front light as a basis, the designer determines lighting area size by specifying instruments with certain beam spreads. The smaller the area, the better the control, provided enough dimmers are available (see Chapter 16 on control).

The action of the play or the staging of the production also helps to determine the number of areas and the distribution of the coverage. Attending rehearsals and paying particular attention to blocking will immensely benefit the designer when the time comes for assigning areas. In a multiscene production some of the areas can be planned for use in more than one set, providing the floor plans are close to the same configuration.

Figure 15-10
Lighting Areas

(a) A conventional box setting. Note the numbering of the areas from down-stage left to up-stage right. The total number of areas will vary with the shape and number of settings in the production as well as the desired tightness of control.
(b) An irregularly shaped interior setting. Some designers prefer to designate the areas with Roman numerals to avoid confusion. (c) A complicated set. Various levels often require the use of more lighting areas.

Figure 15-11
Light Beam

One bit of advice: Most directors and actors have a tendency to love center stage (actors have been known to be attracted to center stage much like moths to a flame), so the prudent lighting designer will be sure to have a controllable center area.

Instrument Placement • Using as illustration a simple, two front-light area system, the designer places one instrument up and to the right front of the area as indicated in area number 2 (Figure 15–12). The second instrument is located opposite at approximately the same angle. This procedure is repeated for each lighting area until all are covered in a similar manner.

Ideal lighting angles often must be compromised. An example particular to lighting the proscenium stage is illustrated by the placement of instruments 1-L and 3-R in Figure 15–12. Since the desired 45-degree angle is impossible to maintain because of the proscenium arch, these instruments must be shifted toward center until they adequately cover the area.

Figure 15-12
Lighting the Acting Areas:
Front Light

Illustrations show the area system with a minimum of front lighting. The beam or ceiling positions (1) cover the downstage areas while the first electric position (2) lights the upstage areas.

Back and side angles are normally determined and instruments plotted based upon front-light areas. However, coverage from side light will not duplicate that of front light (Figure 15–13); and, while often not a problem, it could be troublesome if the side light is being used as a key source. In such instances, it will be wise to develop a second area layout exclusively for side-lighting angles.

Area Flexibility

The demand for greater and greater flexibility in area lighting stems from the trend toward increasingly complex staging, more frequent repertory organizations (where several shows are kept in rotation), and high labor costs that force the elimination of unnecessary handling or manual operation of equipment. It is cheaper, for example, to hang a few extra instruments than to pay an electrician to be present at each performance to change a color medium.

Double Hanging • To improve the limited flexibility of simple cross lighting the designer can hang more instruments, right and left, as additional lights for each area (Figure 15–14a). By duplicating the area coverage on each side, several possibilities for color control are created. The designer can (1) change the warm-cool accent from left to right; (2) change the area color by independently mixing the colors from either the right or left; or (3) flood the stage with only one of the two area colors. If the setting is open enough to permit it, the back lights can also be double hung, providing even further flexibility.

Triple Hanging • A third spotlight may be added to each position lighting an area (Figure 15–14b). The extra light can give further dimension to color control, increase the intensity of the area, and provide greater flexibility of distribution for the area. An area, for example, can have

Figure 15-13
Lighting the Acting Areas: Side Light
Illustration shows three side lights from both right and left lighting across the stage in a "zone." Side light areas will not correspond in shape to those of front light due to the elongation of the light beams.

both tight and wide coverage. To achieve tight coverage, the two extra spots are focused onto a smaller portion of the stage so that the focus on the scene is more concentrated.

Distribution Flexibility • Double and triple hanging offer the designer excellent color control, but an additional degree of flexibility can be achieved by varying the angle and direction of light. If side lighting (either from the wings or from a more-frontal side position such as the traditional box booms) is added to area lights, the designer can then alter color as well as direction. For example, front-of-house right instruments can work with the stage-right side lights.

High side lights can be hung in addition to low side ones to create a different quality and color tonality for a given scene. Low-angle front-of-

a

b

Figure 15-14
Double and Triple Hanging

(a) Double hanging on the stage-left side. Only the downstage areas 1, 2, and 3 are shown. The stage-right lights are colored with a neutral filter while the stage-left lights are both warm and cool to allow color mixing in the acting area. (b) Triple hanging on area 2 with double hanging on areas 1 and 3. The center area has tight and more open focus while all areas provide a selection of color and direction of key and fill sources.

house sources called "washes" are often hung on a balcony rail and can be subtly used to change color tonality as well as the texture of a scene. However, care must be taken in using this rather flat angle in order not to lose dimensionality and lighting quality.

Remote Control • The newest means of providing the designer with distribution and color flexibility is achieved by remote control. Color changers, which fit onto any standard instrument, offer a wide range of choices at the push of a button. The only drawback for theatre production has been operational noise, but much is being done to overcome this problem.

In addition to remote color control, the remotely controlled instrument is now a standard feature of more-elaborate, concert lighting plots. Automated fixtures change color and focus (both direction and beam) on cue from nearly any computerized control system. Lighting with such equipment will change the very nature of how a designer thinks. Automated fixtures are ideal for studio lighting where hanging positions are infrequently changed: units are simply refocused for new requirements. The theatre might accept this technology slowly with typical caution, but accept it *it will*.

The possibilities are endless, and the more a lighting designer experiments with area flexibility, the more diverse and exciting the product can be.

Area Specials and Special Visibility

Area specials are a variation of regular area lighting that uses instruments to specifically define or emphasize a part of the setting or draw attention to an actor at a given moment and in a certain position on the stage. Examples include a door special, an extra light carefully framed to catch an actor in the doorway; a couch special, extra punch on the couch or settee where an important scene takes place; or a pin spot, a narrow beam of light on an actor's face that is held a moment longer than the rest of the stage lights on a final dim-out. Area specials influence composition by pulling the eye to the center of the action.

Special visibility deals with the moving actor under more arbitrary or abstract conditions. The movement of light can be achieved in one of two ways. The actor can be covered by a series of carefully focused spotlights on the path of movement that dim up and down at the proper moments. The more traditional method is to use a follow spot.

Follow Spots • The movement of the actor is followed by a single, freely mounted spotlight. The follow spot has long been in use in musical comedies, revues, and other presentational productions, where realism is of minor importance. It usually appears as a sharply defined, brilliant circle of light outshining all the stage lights.

Another form of follow spotting, often referred to as "European follow spotting" after the practice of placing follow spots and operators on a first light bridge, has become fairly popular for more dramatic productions. Unlike Broadway-musical follow spotting, the goal of European follow spotting is subtlety. A soft-edged incandescent follow spot is used to highlight the action unobtrusively. A vertical angle closer to 60 degrees than 45 degrees is preferable in order to minimize shadows around the actor. With good operation European follow spotting can be an extremely effective lighting technique.

LIGHTING THE BACKGROUND

The mood of the environment surrounding the action of the scene is often so fully expressed in the intensity, color, and distribution of the area lighting that, except for special occasions, the area lights provide the major portion of the illumination of the setting.

In the case of a conventional interior or box setting, the area light will usually suffice to light the walls of the set. However, several precautions are necessary to make such wall illumination successful. Too often we see a box set with the stage-right wall a totally different color from that of the stage-left wall. This appallingly common mistake, a result of poor color mixing from the frontal-area instruments, can be corrected by making sure that all frontal colors hit the walls with relatively equal intensity. Instruments lighting the walls of a box set should be softly focused in order to blend well and reduce shadow.

Shadows from actors or furniture are a problem that may be difficult to solve. The best solution is to change the angle of light causing the shadow, but at times this may not be possible. A wall wash comprised of lights specifically hung, focused, and colored for this purpose may help.

Background areas and backings, however, are a different matter. Many times the lighting problem may be small, for example the backing behind a doorway, rarely seen for more than a moment at a time, and then not directly by most of the audience. Not very elaborate equipment is needed to give these backings enough illumination so that an actor, when leaving the stage, does not seem to be retiring into a dark closet. However, such attention to detail can make the difference between an adequate and a good design.

Backdrops

Backings can assume greater proportions, for example a section of exterior seen through a large window which might contain groundrows of distant hills or hedges and a section of sky. Rooftops or the exterior walls of an adjoining building may also be seen in a more-detailed backing. Such backings usually demand greater attention to distribution and color control (to perhaps simulate different times of day) than would the simple doorway backing.

For the most-complicated backgrounds, such as vast areas of sky sometimes with a painted scenic vista, large backdrops or cycloramas are usually used. These require rows of high-wattage instruments, both from above and below, in order to give the proper amount of light as well as even distribution and blending of color over the entire surface (Figure 15–15). Greater control of color is required if the mood of the background is expected to change with the time of day. Changes in distribution can also occur, especially if the backdrop is partly translucent, allowing a cross-fading from front lighting to back lighting furnished by an additional bank of lights behind the drop.

Figure 15-15
Lighting the Background

A painted backdrop or sky drop lit from above and below (a) and lit only from above (b). When lighting from below, a masking "ground row" is necessary. Lighting only from above often requires two sets of lights, one aiming high and the other low.

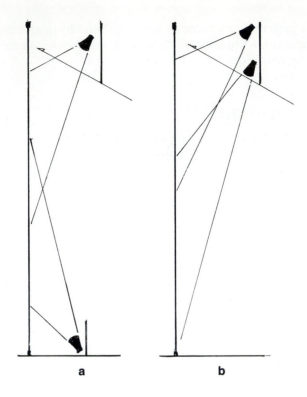

a   b

Figure 15-16
Lighting the Background

(c) A translucent drop (1) illuminated by backlight reflected off a reflecting drop (2) lit from above and below. In addition, the translucency is lit from the front with a set of lights from above. (d) A translucent drop (3) positioned upstage of a scrim (4). The drop has both front and back lighting to change effect and the scrim is also lit from the front to add depth and atmosphere.

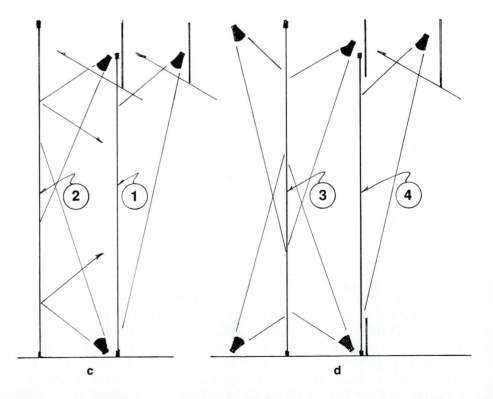

c   d

Scrim is a particularly useful material because of its capability to appear either opaque or transparent. Scrim in front of a backdrop or cyclorama will add the somewhat hazy quality of distance to the backing. The scrim itself can be lit, or, better yet, the drop behind the scrim may be illuminated (Figure 15–16). Scrim may also be used alone as a drop, in which case the designer will most certainly need to pay close attention to the light that falls directly on as well as behind the scrim. A high-angle top light is the best means to create an opaque scrim. To make a scrim transparent, keep as much light as possible off the scrim itself while illuminating objects behind it.

Successful background lighting depends on the close cooperation of the lighting and scene designers. All too often the scene designer does not leave enough space between groundrows and the backdrop or between borders and the cyclorama to allow sufficient distance for proper distribution of the lighting instruments. Backgrounds representing distant fields are sometimes so close to a window or door that it is impossible to keep the area lights from casting shadows on the background, thereby destroying any illusion of distance.

16

Intensity Control

Intensity is the controllable property of light that refers to the brightness of a source. Intensity is controlled by the use of dimmers. To dim a lighting instrument, the electrical voltage to the lamp is reduced resulting in the metal of the filament glowing less brightly as well as giving off a warmer light. The minimum requirement of any dimming apparatus is the capability of dimming a lamp completely to black in a smooth and even manner. When this is possible, dimmers can be used to alter the composition of the stage picture by dimming (up or down) one or a whole series of lighting instruments. Such movement of light can suggest time change, alter the mood or feeling of a scene, or shift emphasis from one area of the stage to another.

Huge advances in lighting control have taken place over the past ten years thanks to the electronic revolution and to the theatre's insatiable need for better equipment. New control systems have been springing up so quickly that it is difficult to keep track of them all. Computer memory-storage systems have replaced preset systems in all but the smallest applications, and dimmer-per-circuit has become "state of the art."

ARCHAIC FORMS OF DIMMING

The history of the use of dimming is a long one. On seventeenth-century stages, cans on cords were lowered over the candles to vary the light; and in the eighteenth century, candles in the wings were frequently mounted on vertical boards that could be revolved to turn the light away from the stage or back toward it. In the nineteenth century the gas table—a complex of pipes, rubber tubes, and valves—adjusted the flow of gas to the various jets about the stage and provided quite a complete control over intensities, as well as an increase in theatre fires.

With the advent of the incandescent lamp, crude forms of dimming control were introduced almost from the start. These all utilized the principle of placing in line with the lamp some sort of electrical resistance that could be varied at will. The carbonpile and salt-water dimmers were among these. But the most popular of all, and one that only recently has been retired, is the resistance dimmer, often called a *rheostat*.

Resistance Dimmers

Most commonly found in the form of a large disk, the resistance plate consisted of lengths of wire used to create electrical resistance. When properly loaded, these dimmers could fade a light source or sources in an even and smooth manner. "Road boards" consisting of several plates mounted in close proximity to one another (Figure 16–1) would be arranged backstage amidst an incredible array of stage cable and connectors. From here as many as six or eight electricians would operate the dimmer handles and switches on cue from the production's stage manager. To be replaced only by the electronic dimmer, resistance road boards remained a part of rental house stocks well into the 1970s.

Disadvantages • Because the resistance dimmer consumes full current as soon as it is switched on—whether the lamp burns full up or otherwise—it is extremely wasteful of electric power. And the heat generated by the coils can be quite overwhelming unless adequate ventilation is provided. But these are less important from the artistic point of view than is the problem of fixed capacity. The length of wire in each dimmer is determined by the exact wattage of the lamp it is expected to control. If a lamp of a smaller wattage is used instead, the dimmer will not put it out completely, and what dimming it does accomplish will be at a different rate from those lamps of proper size on adjacent dimmers. This must be corrected by the expedient of connecting, in parallel with the stage light, a second lamp or "ghost load" hidden offstage and of sufficient wattage to make the total load on the dimmer approximate what it was designed to control.

Figure 16-1
A Resistance Board

Example of an early switchboard, built into a box for travel. At the right end of the row of dimmer handles is the long interlock handle and beyond it the master switch.
Photo courtesy Strand Lighting

Autotransformer Dimmers

Many complaints about resistance control were solved by the autotransformer dimmer. This device consists of lots of copper wire wound around an iron core. The wire is wound in such a manner that the magnetic fields created anytime electricity flows through a conductor are made to work against each other, causing a phenomenon called back-electromotive force (back-EMF) or back-voltage. If the wire is arranged properly, a variable voltage will be available along the coil.

By means of a sliding contact shoe called the "brush" moving over the bared turns of the coil, the exact voltage required is drawn off. Because this tapped-off voltage does not depend on a resistance relationship between the coil and the lamp, it will be the same regardless of what load is placed on it. Thus any lamp from the smallest to the highest allowable can be dimmed smoothly and effectively between full out and full up.

Because the only current drawn is that actually used by the load, the autotransformer is not wasteful of power nor does it create any appreciable amount of heat.

Package Boards • The most-common configuration for the autotransformer, the *package board* is a bulky unit by today's standards, containing several dimmers, circuit breakers, and often a plugging panel. Although heavy, these boards were transportable and a popular means of control for a number of years. Figure 16–2 shows two styles of the package board, both manufactured by Superior Electric and called Luxtrol control boards. In the early 1980s, the final Luxtrol package board rolled (or lumbered) its way off Superior Electric's assembly line — the electronic dimmer had finally and rightfully taken over the entire market of intensity control.

ELEMENTS OF ELECTRONIC CONTROL

Under older methods of control, a simple shift of emphasis in the stage lights required the designer to instruct (either directly or through a boss electrician) several operators, who probably could not even see the results, in what they were expected to do and coach them repeatedly and carefully on timing. If what was desired was executed correctly once out of five times, the designer would probably be considered fortunate.

With the low-voltage, miniaturized control systems provided by electronics, all facets of stage lighting, or any portion of it (submastering or group mastering), can be mastered. Readings for future changes can be stored and brought into effect on cue and at whatever rate of speed is desired. The dimming devices are multicapacity: each dimmer will successfully control any lamp load from the top capacity of the dimmer down to the smallest load desired. And because the electrical current is low and the controls are miniature, the control panel is compact and may be located anywhere in the theatre that is practical rather than being pushed into a corner backstage. This allows the operator to follow the action on stage with ease and to make changes with accuracy.

The basic thing to understand about electronic control systems is that the operational or control part of the system can be (and in larger systems almost always is) separate from the actual dimmers. The way this works is quite simple: a low-voltage current (somewhere between 11 and 20 volts, depending on the system) is sent to the remotely located dimmers telling them what to do. This signal is either generated by a small fader called a *controller* or *potentiometer* in the "preset" system, or by a computer-stored intensity level in the memory system. Of course, the actual electronic dimmer handles full-voltage current (120 volts) and alters the flow of this current to the lighting instrument per instructions from the low-voltage control signal.

Silicon Controlled Rectifiers

Usually referred to as the *SCR dimmer,* its name meaning "a silicon rectifier under control," this little marvel performs its dimming task by switching on and off at a very high speed. The rapid switching effectively alters voltage to a light source without using the principles of resistance.

Figure 16-2
Autotransformer Package Boards

(a) A package containing six 1,300-watt autotransformer dimmers and one of 6,000-watt capacity. By means of the white switches one or more of the small dimmers may be put under control of the large one, thus providing proportional dimming for up to a total of 6,000 watts. (b) A package with six 2,500-watt autotransformer dimmers and an interlock handle to which several or all of the other dimmer handles could be connected. *Photos courtesy Superior Electric*

a

b

Recent miniaturization has allowed the creation of high-density dimmer racks containing hundreds of dimmers in a very small space (Figure 16–3).

Two SCRs are required for a single dimmer, but the actual SCR is only the diameter of a nickel and is ¾-inch thick. These little "buttons" are mounted in metal finlike devices called "heat sinks" which dissipate the heat generated by the rapid switching. An entire SCR dimmer (never larger than a shoe box) will also include a circuit breaker and a printed circuit card that contains the other necessary electronic components (Figure 16–4). The dimmer module can normally be slid out of its rack for servicing, making electrical connection by virtue of plugs located at the rear. Always remember to turn off the circuit breaker(s) in the front panel of the module before removing or replacing the dimmer.

In the days when electronic dimmers were quite expensive, a flexible system was necessary to allow the connection of any stage circuit to any dimmer. The major component of this system is called the *patch panel*.

Figure 16-3
High-Density Dimmer Racks
(a) The rack shown will hold either 288 1.2 K or 144 2.4 K dimmer modules. (b) A 48-channel touring rack complete with amperage and volt meters. *Photos courtesy Teatronics Incorporated*

The Interconnect System

Figure 16–5 illustrates the flow of power from the service entrance of a theatre to a lighting instrument in a typical electronic system using an interconnect or patch panel. In all but the smallest theatres it was normal to have many more stage circuits than dimmers. In order to make possible the connection of any circuit to any dimmer, or indeed to place several lights under the control of a single dimmer of suitable capacity, flexible systems, variously referred to as interconnecting, cross-connecting, or patching, have been devised.

Possibly the simplest and most common form of cross-connecting panel is the type that has all the stage circuits terminating in plugs at

Figure 16-5
Typical Theatrical Power Flow

A block diagram illustrates the flow of power from the service entrance through control and to a lighting instrument.

the end of retractable cables, much like the old-fashioned telephone switchboards (Figure 16–6). The dimmer circuits end in jacks mounted in the panel. Any plug may be pushed into any jack; therefore any instrument may be under the control of any dimmer. Usually there are several jacks for each dimmer circuit, thus providing a simple way to gang several instruments on the same control if desired.

The "slider" patch is a full-voltage, sliding contact system arranged on a grid. Stage circuits are normally represented by vertically sliding clips while each dimmer is assigned a horizontal buss bar. One need only align the slider (circuit) with the dimmer in order to complete the patch. This system eliminates the "spaghetti" of cable too often found in the telephone-type patch board, but several problems have surfaced with the slider patch:

1. The circuit-to-dimmer connection is not a sure one, and it is easy to make a poor contact.
2. Often the sliders are not built to take the rugged treatment and frequent use given nearly every patch panel.
3. It is quite simple to overload a dimmer by placing too many circuits on it.

Figure 16-6
Telephone-type Interconnect or Patch Panel

Single plugs representing each circuit in the theatre are plugged into one of several receptacles assigned to each dimmer. Circuit breakers for each individual circuit are located on the face of the panel. Repatching during a show is often accomplished by throwing the proper circuit breakers.

A welcome result of the SCR's gain in popularity was the steady decrease in cost to the point where today we are experiencing patch or interconnect panels being replaced by dimmer-per-circuit systems.

The Dimmer-per-Circuit System

Although patch systems are still very common, new installations and renovations are most often opting for the dimmer-per-circuit system. The dimmer-per-circuit concept has been with us for many years, but only recently with the introduction of high-density dimmers, computer control, and lower dimmer cost has this system been considered a truly competitive alternative to the interconnect system. Dimmer-per-circuit is exactly what its name implies: a system with an individual 2,000- or 2,400-watt dimmer assigned to every circuit in the house. Patching still exists, but it is of a different kind. Instead of patching a circuit into a dimmer, circuit and dimmer (being one) are patched electronically to a control channel at the console. This patch is totally flexible, allowing as many circuits and dimmers to be controlled by an individual channel as is desired. Note that a slight change in commonly used terminology is necessary with this system: no longer is the control channel referred to as a dimmer, for the relationship between the two is not constant.

Figure 16–7 shows the electronic patch display of Strand Lighting's "Light Palette" control console. Selecting a new patch configuration is simply a matter of several key strokes.

This system is an exciting one for the lighting designer because of its great flexibility—provided, however, that the number of stage circuits has not been compromised in the initial installation. Where this has occurred the theatre would be better off with an interconnect system.

Figure 16-7
Electronic Patch
Shown is the dimmer-to-channel arrangement of Strand's "Light Palette" electronic patch display.

DIM	001	002	003	004	005	006	007	008	009	010
CHN	58	70	30	61	62	1	2	18	3	64
DIM	011	012	013	014	015	016	017	018	019	020
CHN	63	4	16	17	5	6	67	31	32	33
DIM	021	022	023	024	025	026	027	028	029	030
CHN	34	66	22	53	41	21	56	69	54	46
DIM	031	032	033	034	035	036	037	038	039	040
CHN	11	37	38	36	19	20	43	51	51	59
DIM	041	042	043	044	045	046	047	048	049	050
CHN	60	42	43	44	45	46	47	48	54	51

PATCH : DIMMERS

TYPES OF ELECTRONIC CONTROL

For all practical purposes, only two types of electronic control exist: the manual system and the memory system. The manual system always consists of at least one controller or potentiometer per dimmer as well as a master controller. It may be quite sophisticated, with a great number of possible presets, masters, submasters, and group masters.

Manual and Preset Systems

The simplest and least expensive of the manual electronic-control systems provides one controller per dimmer and might very well be contained in a single housing (Figure 16–8). Although these systems are inexpensive and quite portable, they are also inflexible and can be poorly built. When considering purchasing such a control system, pay close attention to the following considerations:

1. Are the dimmers themselves easily accessible for repair?
2. Have the dimmers been properly protected from power surges?
3. Is proper dimmer ventilation provided?
4. Are chokes installed to prevent excessive lamp-filament vibration?
5. Is a master controller provided?
6. Do the controllers work smoothly and seem sturdy?
7. Finally, can the system be expanded?

The only advantage these systems provide over the older autotransformer package boards are in compactness, lightness of weight, and electronic mastering.

Of value to the very small facility is the system shown in Figure 16–9. This "Dove" control system provides six dimming channels, an optional two-scene preset (shown), and plugs into two normal, household, electrical outlets. Care must be taken in using this system not to exceed circuit capacity.

Presetting • The first truly electronic dimming system was put into operation by George Izenour in 1947 at Yale University. The two-scene preset console shown in Figure 16–10, built by Izenour in 1955, served as a model for preset systems for the next two decades.

In addition to the direct, manual control of each dimmer from the console, preset systems provide one or more additional sets of controllers. When only one duplication of controls is provided, it is usually identical to the manual control and located in the same panel. This is referred to as a two-scene preset board. The set of controllers energized at a given moment also acts as the manual control, while the readings on the other set of controllers are being adjusted as a preset that will shortly be used.

When there are several duplicate controls, usually five or ten, they are placed in a panel adjacent to the console, and an assistant sets the readings on them. Multi-preset systems will still be found in some facilities, but for the most part have been replaced by computer memory control.

The presetting approach does create certain problems, however. A completely new preset is required for most lighting changes. It is sometimes possible to make a minor change in the preset panel itself, but this is frequently awkward and, in some models, impossible.

Figure 16-8
Portable Control

Shown is a six-dimmer controller with master and circuit breakers. Each dimmer has a capacity of 2,400 watts. Circuit plug-ins are located on the rear panel. Also shown is a remote control unit. *Photo courtesy Electronics Diversified, Inc.*

Figure 16-9
Small Capacity Dimming

Shown is a portable two-scene, six channel control system unique in its ability to be powered by two normal household circuits. *Photo courtesy Dove Systems*

Figure 16-10
An Early Two-Scene Preset Console

The transparent disks with the white handles are the controllers for the 30 dimmers, one apiece for each preset. Below is a row of on/off switches for each circuit. At the right end of the white plate is the cross-fade handle. *Photo courtesy George Izenour*

Figure 16-11
Concert Lighting Control

Shown is Celco's "Gold" control board: 90 channels, 450 possible presets, and 24 sequence patterns for chases. *Photo courtesy Celco, Ltd.*

Group Mastering • Another method of designing a control board does not depend exclusively on separate preset panels but divides the manual board into various groups and subgroups, each with its own master control. This system is known as *group mastering*. The groups may be used as presets independent of each other, operated together, or used to "pile on" (add new readings on top of the old ones).

While a favorite of concert lighting designers, the operation of such a console can unfortunately become extremely complex if a great many changes are needed in rapid succession. There are just too many things for an operator to keep track of in a swiftly moving play. But for fewer cues and with a tempo that permits careful checking and preparation for the next change, this type of system has much to offer.

A product of the group-mastering control board, the modern Celco "Gold" control system remains a favorite for concert lighting where the operator/designer will often "play" the board during performances (Figure 16–11).

Combination Systems • The most-desirable manual system obviously will combine the virtues of presetting with those of group mastering and sub-mastering. An incredible variety of such control systems exist today, each with its own idiosyncrasies. Although computerized memory systems have almost eliminated large preset systems from the market, smaller systems such as Strand Lighting's Mantrix and Colortran's Patchman have a great deal to offer (Figure 16–12). These manual control systems are equipped with a two- or four-scene preset, sub- and group mastering, matrix patching, and timed split cross-faders. They are economical, portable, and offer a good alternative to small, computer memory control.

Computerized Memory Systems

The combination of the SCR dimmer, low-voltage control circuits, and miniaturized parts has led inevitably to computerized control of lighting. The ability of the computer to store information enables it to hold preset or cue information in whatever quantities a production situation might

Figure 16-12
Two-Scene Preset Control
The "Mantrix" control system shown has 24 channels, 8 submasters, split cross-faders, and a grand master. Also included is an electronic dimmer to channel soft patch (left side of board). *Photo courtesy Strand Lighting*

desire. A computer can be programmed with the digital information of a cue that is randomly recalled with push-button speed. The only limit to capacity is the size or number of storage elements in the memory bank.

Early Memory Control • Compared to those being manufactured today, early memory systems were generally large and bulky. They would often have a single set of controllers or potentiometers as well as a keyboard, and cue information could be placed in memory by either means. A split-fader, often a timed-fader, and possible group and/or sub-masters were also standard equipment. The main memory storage was either disc or core, and only later was disc or magnetic tape "library storage" added as a standard feature. Q-File, developed by Thorne Electric of Great Britain and by Kliegl Brothers, was one of the first systems to eliminate a full set of controllers and add library storage (Figure 16–13). Autocue, manufactured by the now-defunct Skirpan Lighting Control Corporation, introduced the video monitor (a standard television screen) to their control system. Although more complex than necessary, Autocue led the way to the development of current state-of-the-art equipment.

Kliegl took Q-File off the market and replaced it with their more sophisticated and less complex Performance system. Colortran introduced Channel Track, a rather bulky system which has since been replaced with their very fine Prestige series; and Strand Lighting developed Multi-Q and Micro-Q, the forerunners of "Light Palette."

State-of-the-Art Control • While the design of early memory systems varies a great deal from manufacturer to manufacturer, the current trend is toward more standardization. Trial and error has proven what features and functions designers and operators prefer in a control system, and most manufacturers have listened. Today we find three categories of theatrical control systems: the nondedicated computer system; the small-capacity dedicated system; and larger-capacity dedicated systems.

WestStar Corporation captured the *nondedicated control* market with systems designed to work with an IBM personal computer as well as the Apple computer. One need purchase only the software from WestStar,

Figure 16-13
An Early Memory System

Shown is "Q-File," the first successful preset memory system. Originally developed for television, it was designed and manufactured by Thorn Electrical Industries, Ltd.

Figure 16-14
Non-Dedicated Control
Shown is the "ProStar" system which can be expanded to control up to 192 channels. *Photo courtesy WestStar Corporation*

Figure 16-15
Computer Display Cue Sheet
Shown is the cue sheet from the "ProStar" system illustrated in Figure 16-14. Channel levels are shown for the currently active cue (#10 in this case).

although optional control features such as manual cross-fader and mouse controller are available. Figure 16–14 shows the complete "ProStar" system used with an IBM computer. The operator is able to select onscreen displays of patch information, channel levels, or a cue sheet used during playback.

Figure 16–15 is a close-up of the "ProStar" cue sheet. The main body of the screen is dedicated to a sequential list of cues, fade times, and information. To the right of the cues is a listing of operational functions from which the operator can choose.

The advantages of the nondedicated system are low cost and the fact that the computer can be put to uses other than stage lighting. Bookkeeping, box office, and a host of other software programs can all be run

Figure 16-16
Small Capacity Control Systems

(a) Kliegl's "Performer II." *Photo courtesy Kliegl Bros.* (b) The 48-channel "Access." *Photo courtesy The Great American Market.* (c) The 100-channel "Vision." *Photo courtesy Electronic Theatre Controls, Inc.* (d) Strand's new 96-channel "Lightboard M." *Photo courtesy Strand Lighting*

a

b

on this single computer. The disadvantages of the system are lack of functions, limited channel capacity, and relatively difficult operation.

The systems illustrated in Figure 16–16 are typical of *small-capacity dedicated systems.* The modern smaller system will offer all the common operational features as well as some specialized ones according to the whim of the manufacturer. However, they will be limited in channel and cue storage capacity. A good example is "Vision" (Figure 16–16) the fine and inexpensive system from Electronic Theatre Controls (ETC). This console will operate 100 control channels, has a memory capacity of 200 cues, a battery back-up, and proportional patching (discussed later in this chapter). Usually the smaller systems will have one video monitor that will display various information according to operational needs. Features necessary in a quality system are a reliable battery back-up, and easy-to-use entry keyboard, and a video monitor. Important functions include the ability to insert additional cues into an existing cue list; electronic patching (called *softpatch*); the ability to link one cue to the next; split time fades (time of the incoming cue differs from that of the outgoing cue); and a help display for the operator.

Several *large-capacity dedicated systems* are shown in Figure 16–17. As a means of comparison with the smaller systems, ETC's "Concept" control system is included. This console has a capacity of 400 cues per show and can handle 500 control channels. In addition, this larger system offers sub-masters and groups as well as a number of more-sophisticated functions. Nearly all of the larger systems have two monitors with selectable onscreen displays. Normal operation will have the cue sheet displayed on the primary screen with channel levels or other information as needed on the second screen.

The displays shown in Figure 16–18 are from a Strand "Light Palette" control system. The cue sheet display includes cue number, time, and other playback information such as cue parts, delays, and effects. The channel display lists each control channel along with its assigned level in the designated cue (in this case, the live cue on stage).

One of the major functional advantages of the larger and more-sophisticated control systems is programmable effects. Several systems offer "effect packages" that allow a limited number of effects such as a forward chase or a random flicker useful for fire effects; but only a few allow for operator-designed effects. To be most useful, such a program must be easy to write and operate as well as flexible enough to accommodate any kind of effect desired.

a

Figure 16-17
Larger Capacity Control Systems
(a) Strand's "Light Palette." *Photo courtesy Strand Lighting.* (b) ETC's "Concept" will control up to 500 channels. *Photo courtesy Electronic Theatre Controls, Inc.* (c) The Avab "Viking" will control 1000 channels. *Photo courtesy AVAB America, Inc.*

Figure 16-18
"Light Palette" Displays

(a) The set-up sheet. (b) The cue
sheet. (c) The channel/level display.

```
 1  LIGHT PALETTE V6B        15  CHANNELS      100
 2  MEMORY AVBL   89.        16  DIMMERS       100
 3                           17  MULTIPLEX DIMMERS
 4  LOAD MEMORY              18
 5  LOAD BACKUP   ON         19  PRINT CUE SHEET
 6  RECORD DISK              20  PRINT CUES
 7                           21  PRINT GROUPS
 8  SUBMASTERS   INHIBITIVE  22  PRINT EFFECTS
 9  CHANNEL FORMAT           23  PRINT PATCH,PROFILE,SUBS
10  REMOTE CONSOLE           24  HALT PRINTER
11  REMOTE CONTROL           25
12  COLOR MONITORS           26
13                           27  RUN DIAGNOSTICS
14  CLEAR MEMORY             28  INITIALIZE DISK

SETUP :
```

a

```
 Q   10        TIME    20                          R
 Q   10.5      TIME     3                           A
 Q   11        TIME     3                           T
 Q   12        TIME     3                           E
>Q   13        TIME    20
 Q   13.3      TIME    20
 Q   13.6      TIME     1                           1
 Q   14        TIME    20                           0
 Q   15        TIME     7                           0
 Q   16        TIME    10                           %


     20
 Q   13.3
```

b

```
001 02 03 04 05 06 07 08 09 10 11 12 13 14 15 16 17 18 19 020
                                                                

021 22 23 24 25 26 27 28 29 30 31 32 33 34 35 36 37 38 39 040
                                                                

041 42 43 44 45 46 47 48 49 50 51 52 53 54 55 56 57 58 59 060
                              30 30 20 25

061 62 63 64 65 66 67 68 69 70 71 72 73 74 75 76 77 78 79 080
```

c

```
081 82 83 84 85 86 87 88 89 90 91 92 93 94 95 96 97 98 99 100

STAGE
```

DESIGNING WITH ELECTRONIC CONTROL

When Tharon Musser, one of our most-outstanding lighting designers, insisted on a "Light Palette" control system for her Broadway production of *A Chorus Line,* it became obvious that even New York was going to have to accept memory lighting control. There is no doubt that lighting designers can achieve a higher level of artistry with the help of the computer. Cue writing is simplified, the potential for more complex and sophisticated cues is greatly expanded, and changes are made quickly and accurately—every time. The systems offer the designer a choice of manual or automatic operation with manual override (the operator simply presses a "go" button), simultaneous fades, channel tracking, electronic patching, and a variety of more-specialized functions. In effect, these memory systems have passed the artistic "buck" back to the designer. No longer does a control system place severe limitations on what can be achieved. New levels of creative lighting design are being reached every day with the help of computerized control.

Area Control

Well before considerations of a specific control system, the designer must think about *control.* Unless fortunate enough to be working in a situation offering unlimited dimmer control (such as that provided by dimmer-per-circuit installations), the designer must soon face the task of assigning instruments to dimmers. Color control is normally a high priority; seldom will it be desirable to have two sets of instruments of differing colors on the same dimmer. Area control is the next priority: which stage areas should be controlled individually and which "ganged" or grouped together? The latter is a critical decision, for the designer must work with the chosen control flexibility throughout the production. Before a choice is made, the designer should view rehearsals and discuss questions of control with the director.

Although there will never be absolute rules of control priorities, the following is suggested as a beginning:

1. Control of the front-of-house "visibility" area lighting is most important.
2. Area control of side-lighting sources, although of secondary importance, is still important.
3. Area control of back or top light is of least importance unless the stage floor and its composition are visible to the majority of the audience.

Of course, most specials require their own control channel but can be repatched at an intermission in many instances. Do not forget to assign control for practicals, house lights if necessary, and curtain warmers or stage toners. Also, it is always good practice to save a couple of dimmers as spares in case of dimmer failure or additional control requirements are made during final rehearsals.

Patching

Before the days of electronic controls, dimmer board layout was a critical operational concern, for the designer had to anticipate the best way to help the various operators perform their sometimes octopus-like maneuvers. Today these concerns are less critical, but dimmer layout is still important to the designer for two reasons. The first is operational: it being much faster and easier for an operator to keystroke channels 23 through 31 than a random series of nine channel numbers. Channels that are frequently controlled together should be grouped together.

The second reason is for the designer's convenience in remembering channel assignments. If, for instance, front-of-house lights are always assigned lower channel numbers, the designer will be able to identify them more quickly. Board layout is then transferred to an easily read designer's "cheat sheet" for quick reference (Figure 16–19).

If a patch panel exists, most of the desired, dimmer channel-to-circuit assignments can be made there. However, in the frequently encountered case of some dimmers having limited capacities, a softpatch comes in handy to assign those dimmers to a different control channel.

Softpatch • The electronic patch or softpatch is of primary value with a dimmer-per-circuit system, for it alone allows the designer flexibility in dimmer layout. In addition, many of today's memory control systems contain a useful feature called *proportional patching*. This simply means that if two dimmers/circuits/instruments are assigned to a single control channel, one can be given a proportional intensity level. For instance, if lighting instrument *A* is assigned a proportional level of 90 percent while instrument *B* is assigned nothing (default being a level of 100 percent), the intensity readings of *A* will always be 90 percent of those of *B*.

Part of the set-up procedure in preparing to store a production's lighting levels and cue information into memory is the creation of patch assignments. If the system's patch is left unassigned, dimmer to channel will assume a one-to-one relationship. Patch assignments never need to be touched during playback, a good reason for using the "record lock" key switch found on many control consoles.

Figure 16-19
Designer's "Cheat Sheet"

This is the form of cheat sheet generated by Rosco's micro-computer lighting program, Assistant Lighting Designer (ALD). Other styles of cheat sheets will be found in Chapter 20.

```
===========
CHEAT SHEET
===========

SHERLOCK HOLMES LAST CASE                                                Page   1
JERRY ROBERTS
MAYFAIR THEATRE, SANTA MONICA, CA                                        01-29-1985
Design by DAVID C. PALMER & R. CRAIG WOLF
=================================================================================

DIMMER INFORMATION:
    Dimmers 1 through 36 are 2.4 kw

DIMMERS

     1     AREA I WARM
     2     AREA II WARM
     3     AREA III WARM
     4     AREA IV WARM
     5     AREA V WARM
     6     AREA I COOL
     7     AREA II COOL
     8     AREA III COOL
     9     AREA IV COOL
    10     AREA V COOL
    11     R60 AREA LIGHT
    12     R60 WALL WASH
    13     DS HI-SIDE
    14     US HI-SIDE
    15     R04 AREA LIGHT
    16     161 AREA LIGHT
    17     WINDOW
    18     BRICKWALL
    19     US DOOR BACKING
```

System Features

As noted earlier, available functions vary from one system to another. However, the designer can normally depend upon a number of fairly common operational features. Among these are split time fades, a cue copy function, and the ability to insert and/or link cues. Other features which may or may not exist but deserve comment are groups, channel tracking, follow cues, a level/rate wheel, simultaneous cue playback, and direct dimmer access.

Common Features • Movement of light is greatly enhanced by *split time fades* because the designer has the option of leading with a new look or area as opposed to the execution of a simple linear cross-fade.

Probably the single most time-saving feature in writing cues live on the board is *cue copy*. This allows the operator to take an existing look in the form of a cue and assign it to another cue number, thereby exactly reproducing levels so that they can be built upon.

When making corrections and additions, *cue insertion* is a must. *Linking* one cue to another is also handy and can be used in some cases to form effect "loops" (link cue 6 to cue 10; then cue 10 back to cue 6).

Specialized Features • The concept of *groups* originated with preset-type control systems and, therefore, is not a new one. Any number of selected channels can be labeled a group and accessed as such with a single command. This is valuable for the rapid building of various stage looks.

The operational concept of *channel tracking* is a holdover from the days of resistance dimmers when a dimmer lever was up until the operator was told to take it down. In a tracking system such as the "Light Palette," a channel assigned a level in a cue will retain that level in all subsequent cues until told otherwise. While making perfect sense, tracking can sometimes be confusing with channels apparently popping up out of nowhere. Some new systems provide the designer with the useful option of working in a tracking or nontracking mode.

The action of one cue automatically following another is normally not desirable in live production; for timing on stage may change, but the light cues will not. However, *follow cues* can be valuable for a sequence effect or for timing to something other than live action. While the operational term "delay" has different meanings depending upon system manufacturer, a *delay button* will most often allow for a preset time delay between the execution of a cue and that of a following cue.

With proper use the *level/rate wheel* can be of great assistance both in writing cues as well as playback. Anything from a single channel to a group to an entire preset can be assigned to this wheel. If a group of dimmers is "put on the wheel" and the wheel is rolled down, the intensity levels of all channels in the group will be lowered. If an active fade is suddenly assigned to the wheel, the speed of the fade in progress can be altered. In other words, the operator is able to seize control of any fade speed by using the rate wheel. An experienced console operator will perform a great number of operations with the aid of this wheel.

Simultaneous playback of several cues is a valuable feature which most control systems provide. The slow sunset can now continue undisturbed while any number of other lighting movements take place.

Finally, *direct dimmer access* is a feature that is not used very often, but is extremely helpful when needed. In the event of several dimmers being softpatched into a single control channel, this option allows the operator access to any one of the individual dimmers.

Every control system comes with an operation manual which, despite the fact that some are very poorly written, should be read by both the designer and operator. Systems vary enough that the designer will discover new and exciting possibilities by reviewing the manuals of unfamiliar boards.

Paperwork

Too many designers do not realize how very important proper planning and the resulting paperwork is to a successful design. The best lighting designers are individuals who are both creative as well as methodical—character traits not very often found together. Paperwork relating to lighting control includes hookup schedules that record patching, cue sheets, dimmer level or preset sheets, and designer "cheat sheets" (see Figure 16–19).

Paperwork Software • As would be expected, the widespread use of computers has fostered software programs that are designed to create the necessary lighting paperwork for a production. Several such programs exist and, depending on the circumstances of a production, can save the designer or assistant designer a great deal of time. Once the entry of lighting data has been made, changes and/or additions in order to keep the paperwork up to date are extremely fast and simple. This is of particular advantage to productions that will tour or be revived. A hookup produced by Rosco's ALD (Assistant Lighting Designer) microcomputer program is shown in Figure 16–20.

Figure 16-20
Hook-Up

This hook-up sheet was generated by Rosco's microcomputer lighting program, Assistant Lighting Designer (ALD).

```
======
HOOKUP
======

SHERLOCK HOLMES LAST CASE                                      Page   2
JERRY ROBERTS
MAYFAIR THEATRE, SANTA MONICA, CA                              01-29-1985
Design by DAVID C. PALMER & R. CRAIG WOLF
=======================================================================

Dim#   Position    Unit Cir   Watts Type      Color         Purpose/Focus
-----------------------------------------------------------------------
  13   OVER          5        750 6X12        LEE 205        DS HI-SIDE
       STAGE PIPE
       OVER          6        750 6X12        LEE 205        DS HI-SIDE
       STAGE PIPE
       OVER         10        750 6X12        LEE 205        DS HI-SIDE
       STAGE PIPE
-----------------------------------------------------------------------
  14   OVER          4        750 6X12        LEE 205        US HI-SIDE
       STAGE PIPE
       OVER          7        750 6X12        LEE 205        US HI-SIDE
       STAGE PIPE
-----------------------------------------------------------------------
  15   HL BALCONY     2       750 6X12        R04            R04 AREA
                                                             LIGHT
       HL BALCONY     4       750 6X16        R04            R04 AREA
                                                             LIGHT
       HL BOX         2       750 6X12        R04            R04 AREA
       BOOM                                                  LIGHT
-----------------------------------------------------------------------
  16   HL BALCONY     1       750 6X12        LEE 161        161 AREA
                                                             LIGHT
       HL BALCONY     3       750 6X16        LEE 161        161 AREA
                                                             LIGHT
       HL BOX         1
```

Preset Sheets • For many years it was accepted practice for an electrician and the director and stage manager to sit in the darkened theatre for hours on end in what was euphemistically called a "lighting rehearsal." Actually it was the time set aside for the director to create lighting looks for a production. Today this work is done by the lighting designer and most often presented to the director at the technical rehearsal. In preparation for this all-important presentation the designer has written dimmer levels for each cue on preset sheets (the name being a hold-over from the days of writing cues for preset systems) that are then given to the board operator to be placed in memory (Figure 16–21). Some designers prefer to then use the sheets as "cheat sheets" as well as "hard copy" of the dimmer levels.

Hard Copy • Despite the fact that computers and computerized control have become much more reliable in the past few years, it remains extremely important that an accurate written record of cues and presets be maintained. Any number of things can happen to a control system necessitating the re-entry of cue and dimmer level information into memory. Such an occasion is only a nuisance rather than a tragedy if good *hard copy* has been kept.

LIGHTING PRESET SHEET: RICHMOND BALLET — CARPENTER CTR - 1984 //R.C.W.

CUE # | COUNT: 1

Channel #	1	2	3	4	5	6	7	8	9	10
Use	H.R. D.S.C.	R05 D.S.L+R	MID-SC.	MID-S.LR	U.S.C.	U.S.L+R	CTR R59	H.R. Box Boom Blue	H.L. Box Boom Pink	H.L. Box Boom Red
Level										

Channel #	11	12	13	14	15	16	17	18	19	20
Use	H.L. D.S.C.	R61 D.S.L+R	MID-SC	MID-S.LR	U.S.C.	U.S.L+R	S.R. SIDE – AMB. ZONE 1	ZONE 2	ZONE 3	ZONE 4
Level										

Channel #	21	22	23	24	25	26	27	28	29	30
Use	SIDE ZONE 1	S.L. ZONE 2	ZONE 3	ZONE 4		SHIN ZONE 1	S.L. ZONE 2	ZONE 3	ZONE 4	
Level										

Channel #	31	32	33	34	35	36	37	38	39	40
Use	SIDE ZONE 1	S.R. ZONE 2	ZONE 3	ZONE 4		SHIN ZONE 1	S.R. ZONE 2	ZONE 3	ZONE 4	
Level										

Channel #	41	42	43	44	45	46	47	48	49	50
Use	BACK							PAR HOT CTR.		SM. B-U GOBOS
Level										

Channel #	51	52	53	54	55	56	57	58	59	60
Use	SOLDIER'S TALE FRONT DIAG.	BACK DIAG.	WAR/DEATH SP.	D.S.L. SP.	C.S. SP.	D.S.C. SP.	GLORIA U.S.L. SP.	C.S. DOWN FRES.	C.S. BACK FRES.	C.S. 6x12 FRONT
Level										

Figure 16-21
Designer's "Preset Sheet"

Levels for each lighting look or "preset" are pre-written on these sheets and then recorded into the control system's memory. Sheets are up-dated as changes are made and serve as "hard copy."

Of course, a back-up copy of the disc is always necessary, but this alone will not suffice. Many larger systems will have a printer available to make copies of the stored material. Otherwise, the designer must record and constantly update dimmer levels on paperwork such as preset sheets.

THE OPERATOR AND REMOTE CONTROL

As we have pointed out, the low amperage and low voltage used by the control system permit the operator to be placed at any distance from the stage and in any location that seems appropriate. Of the practical places, the rear of the main floor of the auditorium is unquestionably the best. It is a good place from which to run the show—the view of the stage is satisfactory, and the operator and light designer are, during rehearsals, in easy and direct communication with director, scene designer, and others. It is inexcusable to place the control panels backstage, although the cross-connecting system should be there, while the actual dimming apparatus can be tucked away in the basement or other convenient location. This applies equally to a permanent installation consisting of console and preset panels and to the controller units of a portable board.

It would not be wise to leave the subject of electronic dimming without speaking of the person who will operate the controls. This is a very different task from that presented to an electrician standing backstage and manipulating several large handles, heavy with friction, under the direct supervision of a stage manager or a chief electrician.

A console operator is usually in a booth out in the house. Cues may be taken from the stage manager, but if the show is being called from backstage, the operator should take sight and sound cues from the stage action itself. Often the control apparatus is delicate and complex, not at all like a bank of simple and rugged resistance or autotransformer dimmers. An error could very well result in every light on the stage assuming the wrong reading. Nothing is more agonizing than watching an operator fade to a blank or totally incorrect preset in the middle of a subtle stage moment. While a good memory-control system will lessen the chances of operational error, a highly competent operator is still essential.

A good operator will have confidence, a cool head, and enough understanding of the control system to rectify an error before it gets out of hand. In addition, the operator must know the show and fully understand the lighting designer's intentions. He or she *must watch the stage.*

Perhaps, most of all, the operator requires a sensitivity and sense of timing akin to that of an actor's. In a very real sense, the operator is also an actor. An operator does not merely snap lights on, but dims in gently, with feeling, perhaps at a varying pace to suit best the action on the stage. If the actors are fast in their pace one night, an adjustment must be made to the new tempo. Many highly competent electricians cannot adjust to this sensitivity. They may understand, but the delicacy of feeling is not there: their lights are always a trifle off cue, a bit jerky on the fade-up, a little slow on the dim, a trifle rushed on the cross-fade sequence. A lot of sensitivity and a little know-how is a good formula for a successful operator of today's control systems.

Distribution Control: Lenses and Reflectors

Distribution of light is a complex subject because it not only involves direction, as discussed in Chapter 15, but it also very much concerns itself with lighting *quality*. Quality, which may be thought of as texture or physical attributes, can be affected by the light source itself; but most often it is a result of the manipulation of light after it leaves its source.

When a beam of light passing through air encounters anything in its path, three things can happen. The light may be absorbed (for example, by a sheet of black material); it may be bent or refracted (through a lens); or it may be reflected (by any opaque substance it strikes). Actually, none of these things will happen completely: a mirror or a lens will absorb a small portion of light and the blackest of materials will still reflect some light. All stage-lighting instruments use reflectors to increase the efficiency of a light source, and many use lenses to gather and redirect light from the source. By understanding the laws by which reflection and refraction operate, we can better understand how stage-lighting instruments work and why light behaves as it does when it strikes the stage and actors.

REFLECTION OF LIGHT

The law of *specular reflection* explains what happens to a light beam when it strikes a smooth, shiny surface, such as a mirror. It is reflected

Figure 17-1
Specular Reflection
i = incident light. r = reflected
light. N = the Normal (a
perpendicular drawn to the
surface).

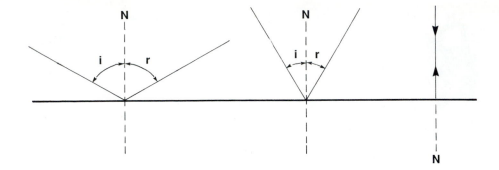

at an angle equal to the angle at which it struck, but in the opposite direction. (The angle of incidence is equal to the angle of reflection.) If the beam strikes the surface head on, it will reflect directly back over the same path (Figure 17–1).

If the beam strikes a surface with slight irregularities, for example etched aluminum or foil paper that has been crumpled and smoothed out again, the same law applies. However, because there are now innumerable small surfaces rather than a single, perfectly flat one, the reflected rays will tend to be scattered but will not diverge too greatly from one basic direction. This phenomenon is known as *spread reflection.*

A piece of blotting paper or soft cotton cloth will produce a *diffuse reflection* because of the vast number and varied angles of the surface. In the case of these surfaces, there will be no single direction to the reflected light. Rather the whole surface will appear much the same from whatever angle it is viewed.

A combination of specular and diffuse reflection is known as *mixed reflection.* A piece of crockery with a high glaze will produce this: the rough surface of the ceramic will create diffusion, while the shiny glaze will act like a mirrored surface to give specular reflection. (Figure 17–2).

REFLECTORS

Early stage-lighting instruments used reflectors that were molded glass mirrors, but modern reflectors are constructed of a lightweight spun metal. After fabrication, this metal shell is given a highly reflective and durable surface treatment named Alzak processing. The Alzak reflector has become an industry standard.

Figure 17-2
Types of Reflection

SPREAD REFLECTION   DIFFUSE REFLECTION   MIXED REFLECTION

Stage-lighting instruments use one or possibly a combination of three reflector types or shapes:

1. *spherical:* found in the Fresnel-type spotlight.
2. *parabolic:* found in beam projectors and PAR-, MR-, and R-type lamps.
3. *ellipsoidal:* found in ellipsoidal reflector spotlights (ERS).

By redirecting the light that leaves the back of a lamp toward the front, a reflector increases the amount of light available from any source. As one would expect, the shape of the reflector determines in what manner it will redirect the light. Each of the above three reflector shapes has a specific point where the light source must be placed in order to achieve the desired reflective pattern; this point is called the reflector's *focal point.*

Spherical Reflectors

If polished metal is made into a reflector in the form of a part of a sphere, and a source of light is placed at the center of the curvature of this form (the focal point), each ray of light that strikes the reflecting surface will do so squarely. It will be returned through the source, thereby increasing the amount of light emanating from the source in the opposite direction (Figure 17–3).

Figure 17-3
The Spherical Reflector

These drawings illustrate light reflection from the spherical reflector under different conditions.

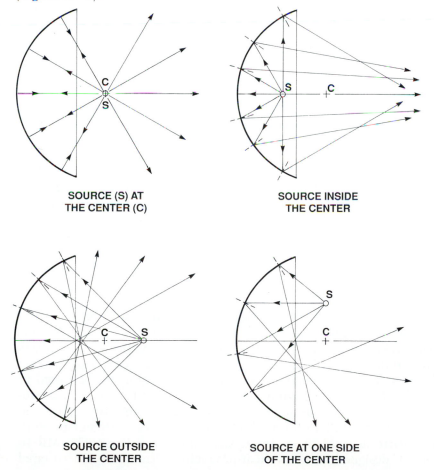

SOURCE (S) AT
THE CENTER (C)

SOURCE INSIDE
THE CENTER

SOURCE OUTSIDE
THE CENTER

SOURCE AT ONE SIDE
OF THE CENTER

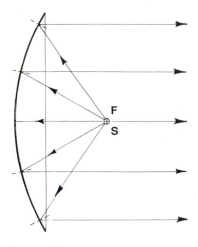

Figure 17-4
The Parabolic Reflector

This drawing illustrates light reflection from a parabolic reflector with the source (s) at the focal point (f).

Naturally, it is necessary for the source, say the filament of a lamp, to be located precisely in relation to the reflector, or its rays will not strike the reflector straight on but at various angles. Although not doubled, the efficiency of a light source in combination with a spherical reflector is increased significantly.

Fresnel spotlights use a spherical reflector in combination with the special Fresnel lens to create a light that, while still concentrated in a tight beam, exhibits qualities of softness and diffusion.

Parabolic Reflectors

The nature of a parabolic reflector is such that if a light source is placed at its focal center, or focal point, all rays that strike the reflective surface will emerge parallel to one another (Figure 17–4). This will naturally give a great concentration of light in a tight beam, rather than the spread effusion from a spherical reflector.

Moving the source from the focal point toward the reflector will spread the light, while moving it away from the reflector causes light rays to converge.

The harshest quality of light achievable is that from the parabolic reflector; for parallel rays produce the extremely sharp-etched shadows most commonly associated with sunlight.

The only problem with the parabolic reflector in stage-lighting instruments is that in addition to the valuable parallel rays being reflected, the lamp or light source itself also emits nonparallel rays out the front of the instrument. When we study the beam projector we will look at attempted solutions to this problem (Chapter 18).

Ellipsoidal Reflectors

The ellipsoidal reflector is more efficient than either the spherical or parabolic reflectors. By mathematical definition an ellipsoid has two focal points. When a reflector is constructed in the form of half of an ellipsoid and a source is placed at the focal point at that end, all rays of light that strike the reflector will be diverted through the second or conjugate focal point (Figure 17–5). The result is that an enormous percentage of the light from the source is directed in a manner that makes it easily usable, as we shall examine in the next chapter.

The quality of light produced by the elliposidal reflector spotlight is harsh, falling somewhere in between that of the more-diffuse Fresnel instrument and the sharpness typical of the parabolic reflector.

Dichroism

A technology fairly new to the stage, *dichroic filtration* refers to the ability of a material to pass certain wavelengths of light through its surface while rejecting others. This principle has been applied to color filters as well as reflectors, but is primarily practiced in reflector treatment.

The most common example of a dichroic reflector can be found in the lamp and reflector assembly used in the Kodak Carousel slide projector. Developed for slide projection in particular, this tiny lamp and reflector called an MR-16 (miniature reflector) was rapidly put to work in the theatre because of its small size and low voltage. The MR-16 reflector is designed to allow heat-producing ultraviolet and infrared

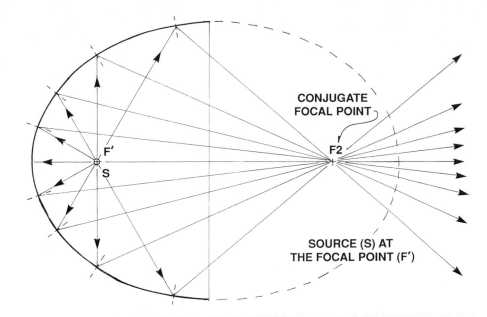

CONJUGATE
FOCAL POINT

F2

F'
S

SOURCE (S) AT
THE FOCAL POINT (F')

Figure 17-5
The Ellipsoidal Reflector
This drawing illustrates light
reflection from an ellipsoidal
reflector with the source at the
primary focal point.

wavelengths to pass through the reflector while reflecting all visible
light. It is available in several "beam spreads" which are determined by
the shape of the reflector itself. More details on the MR-16 will be found
in Chapter 23.

REFRACTION OF LIGHT

Refraction is a phenomenon observed by anyone who looks into a pool
of water and notices how a straight stick will seem to bend sharply as it
passes beneath the surface. The law of refraction states that when a ray
of light passes into a denser medium (for example from air into water),
it is bent toward a perpendicular drawn to the surface at the point of
entry (the normal); when it reemerges into the less dense medium, it is
bent away from the perpendicular drawn at that point.

Plano-Convex Lens

If the two surfaces of a sheet of glass are parallel, the path of an emerging
ray will be parallel to its entering path but slightly offset (Figure 17–6).
But if the two surfaces are not parallel, then the emerging ray will take
a different course depending on the angle at which it strikes each surface.
This is the principle of all lenses, of which there are many forms, but
the plano-convex lens, with one flat side and one curved surface (or modifications of this) is the only one of importance to us. It is the simplest
and least expensive lens for concentrating spreading rays into a compact
beam of great brightness.

Focal Point and Focal Length • Every lens has a focal point. If parallel
light rays (such as those from the sun) strike a lens, they will converge
at the focal point. Conversely, if a source of light is placed at the focal
point of a lens, all the rays of light that emerge from the lens will be
parallel one to another (Figure 17–7a).

Figure 17-6
Refraction of Light
(left) Refraction of rays of light passing through a sheet of glass. (right) Refraction of rays of light passing through a plano-convex lens.

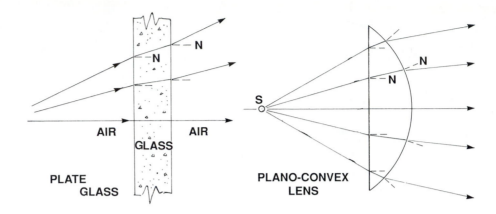

Lenses are traditionally identified by two numbers. The first gives the diameter in inches, while the second gives the focal length (the distance from the focal point to the approximate center of the lens). Thus, a 6-by-9-inch lens (6 × 9) will have a diameter of 6 inches and a focal length of 9 inches. The greater the curve of the convex face, the greater the refracting power of a lens. Therefore, a thick lens will have a shorter focal length than a thin one.

It is usually desirable to know the focal length of a lens. However, because this information is rarely marked on lenses, a quick method of determining focal length is valuable. If the sun is shining, the lens may be carried outdoors and held, plano side down, so that the sun's rays are concentrated on the ground. Then, using a ruler, measure the distance from the ground to the focal plane. For lenses used in stage-lighting equipment the focal lengths are measured in even inches.

Field Spread • A second and probably more useful way of identifying lenses used in stage-lighting instruments is by degrees. A single, or pair of, plano-convex lens is assigned an angle in degrees determined by the field spread of light produced by the particular lens. Beam and field spread is discussed in Chapter 18, but for our purposes field spread can simply be defined as the size of the beam of usable light. For instance, the 6 by 9 lenses mentioned above would have a field spread of approximately 40 degrees and would be identified as 40-degree lenses.

Figure 17–7 illustrates how emerging rays diverge if a source of light is placed between the focal point and the lens. If the source is placed farther from the lens than the focal point, the rays will converge and eventually cross one another. Since the light from a stage-lighting instrument should spread in the shape of a cone, the lenses of some ellipsoidal reflector spotlights will cause the light to converge and cross beyond the lens barrel (Figure 17–7c).

Fresnel and Step Lenses

The thick glass of a lens with a short focal length has a tendency to crack because of excessive heat from the source. Ellipsoidal reflector spotlights often compensate for this deficiency by using a combination of two lenses rather than one. In this way, each lens is thinner and therefore less likely to crack from heat build-up.

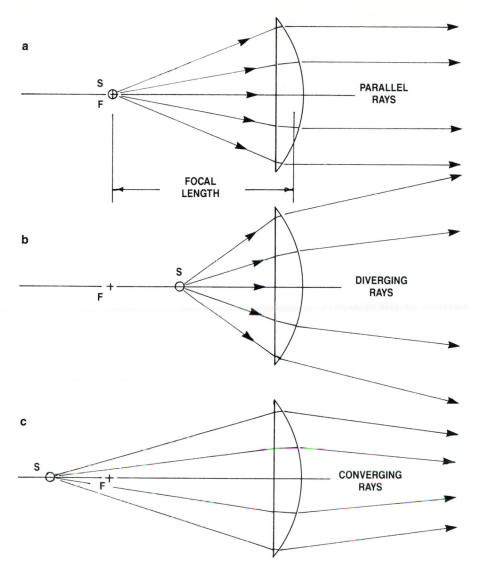

a

S
F

FOCAL
LENGTH

PARALLEL
RAYS

b

F

S

DIVERGING
RAYS

c

S

F

CONVERGING
RAYS

Figure 17-7
Refraction

These drawings show the refraction
of light passing through a plano-
convex lens under different
conditions. (a) Source (s) at the focal
point (f). Note the focal length.
(b) Source inside the focal point.
(c) Source behind the focal point.

Two other solutions have been developed, both using the technique
of cutting away part of the thick glass yet retaining the basic relationships between the curved and the plano surfaces. The first of these is the
Fresnel (pronounced Fre'nel) lens, in which the plano face is retained,
but the curved face is cut back in steps. More recent is the step lens, in
which the convex side retains its shape while the plano face is cut back
(Figure 17–8).

The Fresnel spotlight derives its name from its lens. The plano surface
of the lens is broken up by either a light frosting technique or by a series
of dimples molded into the glass. This breaking up of the light results in
the very smooth and soft illumination distinctive of the Fresnel spotlight.

The step lens was put to use in ellipsoidal reflector spotlights and
became fairly popular because of its low cost and light weight. Yet, the
light from a step lens simply is not of the same quality as that from a
plano-convex lens. Disturbing ring patterns from the step risers are commonly projected by a step-lens instrument, and the light is never as clean

Figure 17-8
Fresnel and Step Lenses

These simplified diagrams show
how the Fresnel and step lenses are
derived from the plano-convex lens.

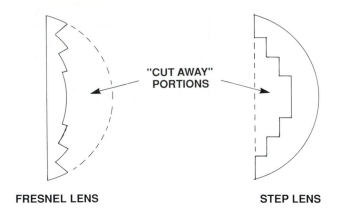

FRESNEL LENS   STEP LENS

or crisp in quality. As a result, instrument manufacturers have returned to the plano-convex lenses, using them in adjustable relationships to allow variable beam spreads.

Lenses in the Theatre

An ellipsoidal reflector spotlight will be designated either by its lens diameter and focal length (6 × 12, for instance) or by the spread of its light beam in degrees. Both designations are accurate, but the labeling by degrees is probably the more helpful. A general rule to follow is that the shorter the focal length, the wider the beam spread (given identical lens diameters).

The following table illustrates some standard instrument designations and their approximate field spreads in degrees:

INSTRUMENT	FIELD SPREAD
4½ × 6½ ERS	50°
6 × 9 ERS	40°
6 × 12 ERS	30°
6 × 16 ERS	20°
6 × 22 ERS	15°
8 × 9 ERS	15°
10 × 12 ERS	10°

Always consult the specifications published by instrument manufacturers to determine the exact light-beam spread for a specific instrument.

Care and Treatment • The quality of light from a stage-lighting instrument greatly depends on its optical system. This not only involves the type of reflector and lens but also their condition. Mistreated or dirty lenses and reflectors can turn a very fine spotlight into little more than a lamp in a can. Keep lenses and reflectors clean; replace cracked or chipped lenses; and treat your spotlights with the care they deserve. You will have a happier bunch of luminaries, and your work as a designer will be much more gratifying.

18

Distribution Control: Lighting Instruments

Recall that the term *distribution* refers not only to direction or angle of illumination but also to quality of light. Will the light be soft or harsh; will it be textured and broken up or coherent and smooth; will it have sharp, linear edges or a soft, rounded shape? The lighting designer must always go through a specific (although often subconscious) process of matching known instrument capabilities with specific requirements of a production. Assuming the designer has an image of the quality of light desired, the next step is to determine what lighting instrument will be most capable of delivering that specific feeling. Several factors will affect this determination:

1. Instrumentation available
2. Physical (theatre) restrictions
3. Quality of light
4. Beam shaping and control

INSTRUMENT DETERMINATION

Instrumentation Available

Choices of lighting instruments would be unlimited with a large budget; but the lighting designer is seldom in such an enviable position. Most often, the designer will be working with a limited and specific equipment list and with a restricted budget. It is always wise to confirm the accuracy of an equipment list before completing the design work.

Physical Restrictions

Physical restrictions invariably affect lighting possibilities. They include the throw distance (distance from lighting instrument to target); the amount (if any) of offstage space for side-lighting positions; the adequacy of hanging positions both front-of-house as well as overstage; and space restrictions limiting the physical size of the instrument.

Quality of Light

The designer must now consider the quality of light possible. Perhaps an 8-inch Fresnel would be a better choice than a 6-by-12 ERS because of the softer quality of its beam. Perhaps an ERS is the only answer because we want to break up the light with a template. Perhaps a PAR will best deliver the strong yet soft-edged illumination sought by the designer.

Beam Shaping and Control

The final consideration is a simple one: will the chosen instrument provide the desired beam shaping and control? Some types of stage-lighting instruments come equipped with devices intended to shape the beam of light; others require that additional equipment be added to the instrument; while still others do not allow any type of beam shaping at all.

The following information on stage-lighting instruments will give the reader a basis for making intelligent decisions. Because stage workers have a habit of referring to whole classes of instruments by trade names or other slang terminology, there seems to be a bewildering complexity of such instruments. Actually, there are just a few basic types.

Figure 18-1
Parts Common To All Lighting Instruments

C-CLAMP FOR ATTACHING TO 1 1/4" OR 1 1/2" PIPE

C-CLAMP BOLT FOR SWIVEL ADJUSTMENT

YOKE

HOUSING

SIDE HANDLE FOR TILT ADJUSTMENT

CONNECTOR

COLOR FRAME HOLDER

SPOTLIGHTS

The spotlight is by far the most-important lighting instrument on the modern stage. Broadly defined, the spotlight is a metal hood containing a high-powered source of light which is made more effective by use of a lens and usually a reflector as well (Figure 18–1). The resulting beam of high-intensity light can be altered and shaped by various means to the designer's specifications. There are two basic types of spotlights in common use today: the Fresnel and the ellipsoidal reflector spotlight.

Fresnel Spotlight

The Fresnel gets its name from the inventor of its unique lens, Augustin-Jean Fresnel (1788–1827). In a simple housing a spotlight lamp is mounted on a sliding carriage to which is attached a spherical reflector that rides behind the lamp and is always in correct relationship to it (Figure 18–2). Such a reflector sends all rays that strike it back through the original source, thus increasing output (Chapter 17).

In front of the lamp is the Fresnel lens which gathers the light and redirects it into the cone-shaped beam typical of spotlights. When the lamp is moved all the way forward toward the lens, the light beam is at its largest size and the instrument is referred to as being in *flood* focus.

Figure 18-2
Fresnel Components

(a) A cut-away view of a typical Fresnel showing: (1) Three prong twist-lock connector. (2) Rubber coated lead wires. (3) Spherical reflector. (4) Ventilation holes. (5) Yoke. (6) T-shaped lamp, base down (incandescent shown). (7) Fresnel lens. (8) Color frame holder. (9) Hinged lens front for interior access. (10) Worm-screw drive for movable lamp socket and reflector. (11) Movable lamp socket. (b) An 8-inch Fresnel that uses a tungsten-halogen lamp. *Photo courtesy Kliegl Bros.*

Figure 18-3
A Fresnel with Barn Doors
The 4-way barn doors at the front of the instrument allow beam shaping. This unit, designed especially for film and television applications, allows remote spot and flood focus by turning the knob at the side. *Photo courtesy Lee Colortran*

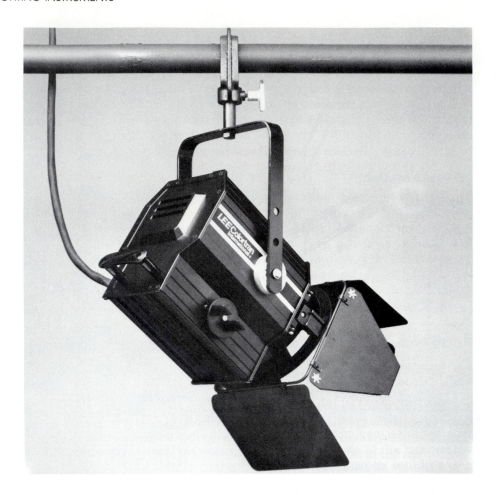

As the lamp is slid back away from the lens, the light beam becomes narrower until it reaches its smallest dimension which is called *spot* focus. Movement of the lamp and reflector assembly is accomplished by means of a worm screw or a simple thumbscrew extending from the bottom of the instrument.

Beam Shaping • While internal beam shaping is not possible, accessories called "barn doors" can be placed in the color frame holder to effectively shape the beam by cutting it in a linear manner from either of four sides (Figure 18–3). The well-equipped theatre will have barn doors for every Fresnel in its inventory. It is wise to "safety" a barn door to the pipe or yoke of the instrument by means of a small chain or wire rope. This is particularly important for the larger Fresnels, whose barn doors tend to be heavy and are easily dislodged by scenery flying on an adjacent batten.

Another spotlight accessory which is particularly useful with a Fresnel is the "top hat" or "snoot." A top hat is nothing more than a tin can open on both ends, attached to a rectangular metal frame that fits into the color holder and is painted flat black inside and out. The top hat controls lens flare by absorbing stray light refracted by the risers of the Fresnel lens. If the lens is in audience sight, lens flare can be quite distracting.

Fresnel Sizes • Fresnel spotlights come in a number of sizes, the smallest of which has a 3-inch lens and burns a 150-watt lamp. Fondly called an "inky," this little instrument, although not possessing much punch, is very handy for tucking into small corners.

The most common Fresnel is the 6-inch, burning 500- and 750-watt lamps. This spotlight is a true workhorse, being invaluable for the up-stage acting areas, where its soft-edged beam fades away on the scenery without leaving obvious and distracting lines and patterns. It throws a good punch with a typically smooth beam pattern. For the larger stage the 8-inch Fresnel can be almost as valuable and with its 1,000- to 2,000-watt lamps has a powerful beam that can be put to many uses.

The Fresnel spotlight is also sold with lenses from 10 to 20 inches in diameter. These have little importance for the conventional stage, being primarily designed for television and motion-picture studios. They might be useful in outdoor productions, where exceptionally long throws are often the rule. Another feature that has been introduced for television purposes is the Fresnel lens that throws an oval beam. This can be very useful on the stage as well, to spread the light laterally, making cross-stage blending easier.

Fresnel Beam Characteristics • The beam of light from a Fresnel is soft in quality, with a smooth, even field. The light will appear to "wrap around" a figure and shadows will be soft edged and not very harsh. Being a spotlight, the light from a Fresnel exhibits a good sense of direction, but it can also be used for wall washes or blending. In a proscenium theatre the Fresnel is limited, however, to use overstage because of its scattered beam characteristics. Also, throw distance of even the 8-inch Fresnel is restricted for the same reason.

The following table lists beam spreads for typical 6- and 8-inch Fresnels at both flood and spot focus:

	SPOT FIELD ANGLE	FLOOD FIELD ANGLE
6-inch Fresnel	16°	60°
8-inch Fresnel	14°	50°

While the Fresnel is an ideal instrument for some spaces and certainly a practical instrument for almost all spaces, the ellipsoidal reflector spotlight is a more-versatile lighting instrument.

The Ellipsoidal Reflector Spotlight (ERS)

In Chapter 17 we saw that if a source of light is placed at one of the focal points of a reflector built in the shape of half an ellipsoid, all the light rays that strike this reflector are diverted through the conjugate focal point. By placing a lens or lenses beyond this secondary focal point a spotlight of great efficiency and power can be constructed (Figure 18–4). Such an instrument, properly called an ellipsoidal reflector spotlight (ERS) is, unquestionably, the most important, useful, and common stage-

Figure 18-4
The Ellipsoidal Reflector Spotlight

(1) Pin connector. (2) The lamp's filament, with its center located at the focal point of the reflector, "f." (3) Ellipsoidal-shaped reflector. (4) Bottom shutter which shapes the top of the beam. (5) Color frame holder. (6) Medium prefocus base socket. (7) Standard incandescent lamp designed to burn base-up. (8) Top shutter which shapes the bottom of the beam. (9) The aperture or "gate" with typical reflected rays crossing at the conjugate focal point, "f'." (10) Two plano-convex lenses. (11) Spring ring holding lenses (older models). (12) Alternate position of lens system.

lighting instrument today. It is commonly referred to as a Leko or a Klieglight, the trade names of Strand Lighting and Kliegl Brothers, respectively.

ERS Beam Shaping • Just before the conjugate focal point, where the various rays are still converging, is a metal baffle known as the "gate." This cuts off stray rays of light that are not useful in forming a well-controlled beam. It is an image of the opening in this gate, called the aperture, which appears as a round and reasonably smooth pattern when the ellipsoidal spotlight is focused on a plain surface. Various other features to shape the beam may be placed at the gate, a standard device being four *shutters* which, by proper manipulation, can change the beam pattern into almost any simple linear shape. An iris is sometimes inserted here, allowing the circular form of the beam to be made smaller or larger at will, though this is most significant when the instrument is to be used as a follow spot.

A well-equipped ERS will also have a pattern or template holder located just in front of the four shutters. A template, commonly called a "gobo," is a metal plate with a pattern cut in it. When equipped with a gobo an ERS can serve as a shadow projector. Light can simply be textured, or specific patterns can be projected on scenery, actors, or the stage floor. Stainless steel templates available in a large variety of patterns can be purchased, or homemade gobos can be cut out of pie tins or aluminum lithoplates. (You can probably get lithoplates free from a local printer.) In using a gobo, remember that the pattern image will be inverted because of the crossing of the light rays. Consequently, the gobo should be placed in its holder in an upside-down position.

ERS Beam Characteristics • The ellipsoidal reflector spotlight throws an extremely powerful beam of light capable of creating harsh and sharp shadows. An "edging" of light can best be achieved with an ERS, whose light is much more controllable than that of other theatrical lighting

Figure 18-5
Axial Ellipsoidal Reflector Spotlight

(1) Three-wire pin connector. (2) Lamp filament (coiled-coil). (3) Ellipsoidal reflector. (4) Bottom shutter which shapes the top of the beam. (5) Color frame holder. (6) Axially mounted socket. (7) Tungsten-halogen lamp. (8) The aperture or "gate" with typical reflected rays crossing at the conjugate focal point. (9) Top shutter. (10) Double plano-convex lenses. (11) The lens barrel in alternate positions.

Figure 18-6
Beam and Field Angles

In a typical ellipsoidal reflector spotlight, 100 percent intensity is found at beam center. The beam and field angles are designated in degrees.

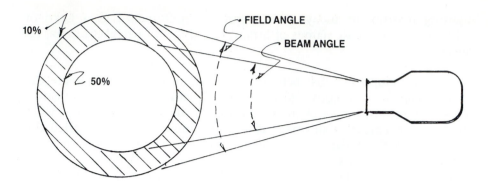

instruments. Because the lamp, reflector, and lens are in static relationship, there is no flood and spot focus as in Fresnel spotlights. But the lenses may be moved a few inches, allowing the beam pattern to be thrown out of focus and thus softening the hard, sharp edge of the field.

Because of the delicate relationship between filament and reflector, it is easy for the instrument to get out of adjustment, particularly if an inexperienced electrician tampers with the adjusting devices on the socket cap of older ellipsoidals. Sometimes the lamp base has not been properly seated in the socket. At other times it is necessary to focus the spotlight on a plain surface and manipulate the adjusting devices until a firm, circular field is found again. The better of the new axial-mount ellipsoidals will have the lamp socket mounted on a ball-and-socket type joint and attached to a "joy stick" handle or knob (Figure 18–5). This arrangement allows for rapid and simple lamp alignment.

ERS Sizes • The ellipsoidal reflector spotlight comes in several sizes, from one with a 3½-inch lens that burns 400- and 650-watt lamps suit-

If the intensity of light from an ellipsoidal is considered in terms of percentages, and the beam center line illumination is 100 percent, the beam and field angles are defined as follows:

Beam angle is the point where the illumination falls off to 50 percent.

Field angle is the point where illumination falls off to 10 percent.

ERS TYPE	BEAM ANGLE	FIELD ANGLE
3½ × 6	25°	32°
3½ × 8	18°	24°
3½ × 10	16°	20°
4½ × 6½	33°	50°
6 × 9	24°	40°
6 × 12	16°	28°
6 × 16	15°	20°
6 × 22	8°	15°
8 × 9	7°	15°
10 × 12	7°	10°

able for small stages and auxiliary use on large stages, up to a 12-inch model that uses a 2,000-watt lamp for a very narrow and extremely powerful beam intended for long throws.

The workhorse of the ellipsoidal line is the 6-inch, which is available in a variety of focal lengths (see table on page 454). Older 6-inch units will accept either a 500- or 750-watt lamp, while the newer quartz-light units can be lamped to 1,000 watts. The 8-inch and 10-inch ERS will provide a narrower beam as well as allow for higher wattage lamps, usually up to 2,000 watts.

Beam and Field Angle • The table on page 454 lists typical beam and field angles for various sizes of ellipsoidal reflector spotlights. Note that these figures are approximate and may not correspond exactly to the performance of any specific unit. Consult manufacturer specifications before using.

When an ERS is properly aligned, its cone-shaped beam of light will be most intense along the center line of the cone and drop off evenly toward the edge of the beam (Figure 18–6).

It is important to note, however, that many of the newer axial-mount ellipsoidals allow an additional adjustment of the lamp in respect to the focal point of the reflector. By moving the entire lamp housing either in or out, an electrician is able to change the field of light from an extremely "hot center" to a "flat" field. The hot center concentrates a greater percentage of the light into a small beam, while the flat field evens out the intensity through the beam. This adjustment does not alter the effective field angle but obviously changes beam angle considerably. Because of this new design feature, manufacturers have begun exclusively to use field angle-degree designations for their ERS instruments.

New Silhouettes • The development several years ago of the smaller and more-efficient tungsten-halogen lamp (also called "quartz" lamp) triggered new instrument design, particularly in the ellipsoidal reflector spotlight (Figure 18–7). The near point source, reduced size, and greater intensity of the lamp has increased the efficiency of the reflector and changed the hood design. The forerunners in new instrument design were Electro Controls with its Parellipsphere and Colortran; with Strand, Kliegl, and Altman rapidly following suit.

In addition to an improved hood design, the new ellipsoidals provided a means of changing the instrument's beam spread by adjusting the relationship of the now common, double plano-convex lenses. The Colortran 6-inch ellipsoidal is adjustable from 20 degrees, to 30 degrees, to 40 degrees by opening the lens barrel and either moving the two 6-inch lenses or adding a smaller 4½-inch lens. While something of a bother, this feature greatly increased the flexibility of a single ellipsoidal instrument.

Likewise, the introduction of Colortran's Mini-ellipse made a significant contribution to the line of short-throw ellipsoidals. Like its bigger 6-inch counterpart, the mini has a three-position lens adjustment allowing field spreads of 30 degrees, 40 degrees, and 50 degrees. Its 500-watt, compact quartz lamp delivers a gret deal of intensity and is relatively inexpensive (Figure 18–8).

Figure 18-7
The Modern 6-inch E.R.S.
Shown is a 6 × 12 axial "leko."
Photo courtesy Strand Lighting

Figure 18-8
The "Mini-ellipse"
An efficient short-throw 4-inch ellipsoidal developed by Colortran.
Photo courtesy Lee Colortran

Figure 18-9
The Parellipsphere

Although basically an ellipsoidal reflector spotlight, the Parellipsphere has a more sophisticated reflector design and beam spread flexibility like a zoom ellipsoidal. *Photo courtesy Electro Controls, Inc.* (1) Three-wire twist-lock connector. (2) Parellipse part of the reflector—apex is parabolic in action. (3) Kickback reflector with slight spherical configuration. (4) Bottom shutter. (5) Baffles. (6) Nonsymmetric bi-convex lens. (7) Plano-convex lens. (8) Color frame holder. (9) Prefocus medium base socket axially mounted. (10) Quartz lamp. (11) Top shutter. (12) Lens adjustment knob to change focal length of objective system. (13) Lens adjustment knob to change beam spread.

But even before Colortran marketed the adjustable lens ellipsoidal, Electro Controls had introduced the variable focal-length Parellipsphere—forerunner of the modern zoom ellipsoidal.

Zoom Ellipsoidals • The adjustable beam Parellipsphere derives its name from a new reflector design involving three surfaces. The basic shape of the reflector is ellipsoidal with a parabolic apex at the lamp position and an off-axis spherical reflector in front facing the lamp to redirect outside rays back into the ellipsoidal portion of the reflector (Figure 18–9). Another unique feature was the ability to slide both lenses backwards and forwards resulting in a continuously variable beam spread.

The modern, 6-inch zoom ellipsoidal (Figure 18–10) costs a bit more than the standard fixed-lens instrument, but offers this same beam-spread variability. Normally the range will be between 20 and 40 degrees with some units offering an even narrower spread. While the instrument itself is larger and heavier than a non-zoom, its advantages outweigh disadvantages in many stage and studio applications.

Of course, the logical evolution of the zoom ellipsoidal is the automated fixture that provides remote control of beam spread, among other things. This instrument is discussed later in the chapter.

The Plano-Convex Spotlight

The first incandescent spotlight, and for many years the only kind, was the plano-convex spot. In the United States this old workhorse has long since been replaced by the ellipsoidal reflector spotlight; but in many European countries the P-C, as the plano-convex spot is frequently called, remains the standard stage-lighting instrument.

Built and operated much like a Fresnel spotlight, the modern P-C gives off a high-quality sharp beam of light that is adjustable in size similar to our zoom ellipsoidals. A disadvantage of the P-C, as compared to the ERS, is that beam shaping is more difficult and the use of gobo patterns is restricted. Typical sizes are 6 and 8 inch with lamps of 1,000 or 2,000 watts.

Figure 18-10
The Zoom Ellipsoidal
The 4½-inch instrument shown has a variable focus which allows field spreads from 25 to 50 degrees. *Photo courtesy Strand Lighting*

BEAM PROJECTOR

Despite its narrow beam and intense output, the beam projector is not a true spotlight. It has no lens, and, more important, its beam pattern cannot be greatly altered from the small and very bright circle that is its characteristic. The lamp can be moved slightly in relation to the reflector, which results in a somewhat larger pattern but one which has a "hole" or dark spot in its center. In no case is the beam projector's pattern very smooth, and masking (with barn doors, for instance) will not alter the shape in any way but instead dims it in an erratic fashion.

This instrument makes use of a parabolic reflector that sends all the rays that strike it forward and parallel one to the other. In order to eliminate diverging rays of light that would not contribute to the tight beam pattern, but would prove undesirable and distracting, a spherical reflector is often placed in front of the lamp to redirect such rays back to the parabolic reflector, from which they may augment the other parallel rays (Figure 18–11). In some styles of beam projector baffles or louvers serve to intercept and absorb such diverging rays. The beam projector is basically a searchlight adapted to the theatre. Its stage uses are largely limited to strong shafts of light of great intensity but confined to small areas, for example sunlight through a window. For musical comedy and the like, great banks of beam projectors may be employed, but for the modest stage this instrument has limited uses.

The beam projector comes in various sizes, from 10 to 30 inches in diameter. The 10-inch style takes either a 750- or 1,000-watt lamp, while the larger types use 1,000- to 2,000-watt lamps. Anything larger than 16 inches would scarcely be required for even a sizable stage. The beam projector continues to be used because of its uniquely harsh light quality, but many of its previous applications are being assumed by the popular PAR instrument.

PAR CAN

The heart of the PAR can lighting instrument is the parabolic aluminized reflector (hence, PAR) lamp; for this lamp, invented by Clarence Birdseye, the pioneer of frozen foods, is itself a self-contained instrument, lacking only a housing and conventional plug. The extruded-metal, PAR-can housing simply secures its PAR-64 lamp in place by means of a large

Figure 18-11
The Beam Projector
Pictured is the 11-inch "Kliegsun" beam projector. *Photo courtesy Kliegl Bros.* (1) G-shaped lamp (older models). (2) Parabolic reflector. (3) Concentrated filament. (4) Adjustable lamp base. (5) Connector and lead wires. (6) Spherical reflector (baffles or lenses also found here). (7) Color frame holder.,

spring ring and absorbs immediate flare created by the built-in lens of the lamp (Figure 18–12). The butt of the housing hinges opens to allow access to the lamp and socket, and color frame holders are fixed to the front of the unit.

The PAR-64 lamp is rated at 1,000 watts and is available in the following beam spreads:

	ANSI CODE	BEAM ANGLE	FIELD ANGLE
Very Narrow	FFN	6° × 12°	10° × 24°
Narrow	FFP	7° × 14°	14° × 26°
Medium	FFR	12° × 28°	21° × 44°
Wide	FFS	24° × 48°	45° × 71°

The oval-shaped beam of light cannot be effectively altered or adequately controlled, however the direction of the oval can be changed by simply rotating the lamp within its housing. Because of its parabolic reflector, the quality of light is very harsh; but, the beam edge remains quite diffuse due to the lens. Relative to other stage instruments, the PAR can is nearly indestructible, and the lamp life is long. Although not an ideal stage-lighting unit because of its lack of beam-shaping capabilities, the PAR can is economical and may be perfect in certain applications.

Figure 18-12
The PAR-64

(1) Color frame holder. (2) Light baffle. (3) PAR-64 lamp, 1,000 watts. (4) Three-wire cord and pin connector. (5) Yoke. (6) Lamp socket. (7) Rear hinge allowing access to lamp.

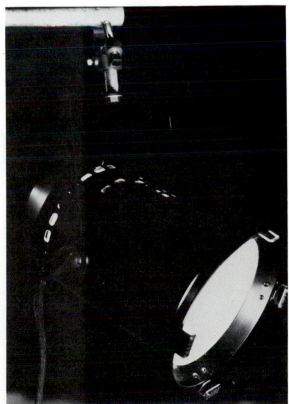

Figure 18-13
Floodlights

(a) Ellipsoidal Reflector Floodlight, often called ERF's or "scoops" can be lamped up to 2,000 watts.
(b) "Soft lite" used for even more of a reflected light quality are most often found in television or film studios. *Photos courtesy Kliegl Bros.*

FLOODLIGHT

A floodlight is, as its name suggests, a device for throwing a broad wash of light over a wide area. For many years the so-called Olivette was the standard instrument for such a purpose. Large and unwieldy, burning a 1,000-watt lamp, the Olivette reflected a smooth wash of light from its boxlike hood and white-painted interior.

The most common floodlight today is the ellipsoidal reflector flood-light (ERF), or "scoop" (Figure 18–13). It has a matte finish that distributes the light smoothly and without a sharp edge to the beam. A single such instrument can be valuable for lighting a fair-sized window backing, while a bank of them may be used to illuminate a drop. They are especially useful for washing any curved surface, such as a cyclorama.

Most of these floodlights are about 15 or 16 inches in diameter and burn lamps of up to 2,000 watts. There is also a small 10-inch model that uses 250- and 400-watt lamps, or, occasionally, gives good service with a 100-watt lamp when only a very low illumination is required.

STRIPLIGHT

One form of stage-lighting instrument that predates electricity is the striplight, which produces the effect of a line of light by means of a number of sources—formerly candle or gas, but now electric—adjacent to each other. In its crudest form, the striplight can be found as footlights, a row of bare bulbs, sometimes as far apart as 12 inches, extending the entire width of the proscenium opening.

In today's theatre, permanently installed footlights are rare; the more-accepted approach being portable striplights manufactured in 6-foot sections. These sections may then be placed about the stage, including the usual footlight position on the apron's edge or hung from overhead. This system allows far greater flexibility in the use of equipment than do permanently installed striplights.

Certain basic principles in striplight design must be understood. The lamps should be wired in several color circuits, three or four being the most common. Then, by using different colors in each circuit and properly controlling their respective intensities, practically any color or tint of light may be attained. Obviously, the lamps should be closely spaced, so that their various beams will blend together more readily.

Types of Striplight

Since the days of Birdseye, the most common style of striplight has been the 6-foot section containing twelve PAR-36 or R-40 type lamps (Figure 18–14). With their common screw bases and built-in reflectors, these lamps adequately serve the purpose of producing a broad and smooth sheet of light. The 150-watt R-type floodlight is most popular for short throws, though occasionally the 300- or 500-watt R floods may be needed for extra punch in lighting a large cyclorama. The spot type of either R or PAR lamps can be used in lighting the lower part of a backdrop from above (see "Lighting the Background" in Chapter 15).

The color frames of most striplights will accept either plastic (Mylar) color media or glass roundels. While either may be used when the striplight is in a hanging position, it is recommended that only glass be used if the striplight is placed on the floor shooting up with lamps of the 300- or 500-watt variety. Since heat rises into the filter, glass holds up much better than plastic.

The Quartz Strip • With the advent of the quartz lamp came a new design in striplights. Although each manufacturer uses a different trade name for its particular unit, they all use 1,000- to 2,000-watt quartz lamps and are available with one to four lamp compartments per section. As can be seen in Figure 18–15, the reflector is curved in order that more light be projected to the bottom of a backdrop or cyclorama. Also due to reflector design, each color compartment can be spaced as far as 8 feet apart and still maintain a smooth wash of light on a cyclorama or a drop. Quality of light as well as output is far superior to the older R and PAR strips for general wash applications. Roundels (glass color filters) are generally not made for the newer quartz strips, but the use of Mylar color media is perfectly satisfactory.

FOLLOW SPOTS

The traditional follow spot is a specialty instrument intended to produce a very bright and small beam of light over a long throw distance (Figure 18–16). A necessary element of a certain style of Broadway musical, these instruments and their operators are most often situated at the very rear of the auditorium in the uppermost balcony.

A spherical reflector is used to help direct the light to an aperture similar to that of the ERS. Mounted at the aperture will be an iris, a mechanism called a "damper" or curtain shutters that chops the beam of light horizontally, and possibly a mechanical dimmer called a "douser." Mounted in a long barrel in front of the aperture will be a lens

Figure 18-14
The Striplight
Shown is a strip unit with PAR-type lamps (spot) for a long throw.

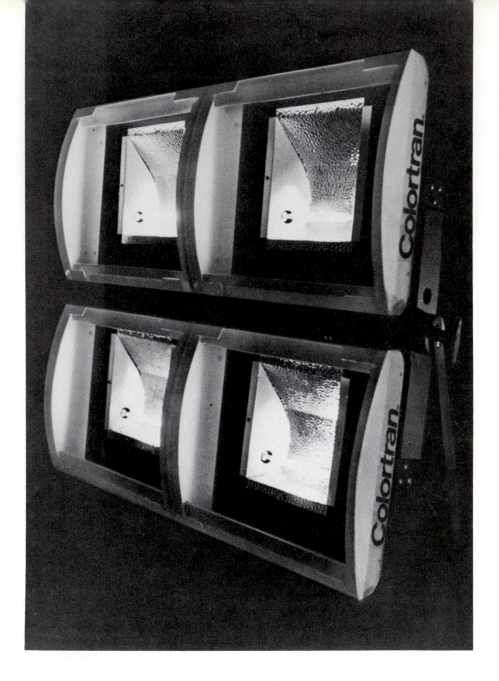

or lenses that can be moved to adjust beam size and sharpness as well as a color boomerang that allows for rapid color changes.

In the carbon-arc follow spot, adjustments for the reflector and the arc source itself are found at the rear of the instrument. These adjustments move the carbon rods forward or back in relationship to the fixed reflector for better source alignment. They also tilt the reflector itself for more accurate focus. An arc source is desirable for throw distances of 75 feet or more, while one of the various quartz-lamp follow spots is sufficient for shorter throws.

The newer xenon and HMI sources (see Chapter 22) have stimulated change in the design of follow spots. More compact units which are generally easier to operate are currently available (Figure 18–17).

Figure 18-16
The Carbon Arc Follow Spot
(1) Arc and reflector adjustment assembly. (2) Spherical reflector. (3) Arc light source. (4) Cooling and exhaust vent (carbon monoxide gas). (5) Mechanical dimming control (Douser). (6) Horizontal shutter control (Damper). (7) Iris control. (8) Lens system. (9) Zoom track. (10) Rear pan/tilt handle. (11) Compact solid state switching regulator. (12) Pan lock. (13) Tilt lock. (14) Lock-down stabilizer. (15) Front pan/tilt handle. (16) Six-color filter boomerang. *Photo courtesy Lee Colortran*

Figure 18-17
High Intensity Arc Lamp
Followspots

(a) The Strong Xenon Super Trouper uses a xenon arc lamp for high intensity over long throws. *Photo courtesy Strong Electric.* (b) The Long Throw Ultra Arc Followspot uses a G.E. Marc 350 projector lamp for high intensity and is one of the lightest followspots available. *Photo courtesy Phoebus Mfg.* (c) The "Unispot," made in West Germany, is available with a range of lamps from 1,000-watt quartz to 1,200-watt HMI. *Photo courtesy AVAB America, Inc.*

AUTOMATED FIXTURES

Recent technology, good research and design, and the lighting industry's demand for more flexible equipment has introduced us to what may become the lighting instrument of the future: the automated fixture. Two remote-control servomotors tilt and pan a lighting instrument to any position with accurate repeatability and variable speed. A third small motor may change instrument focus (lens adjustment) while yet another drives a color changer equipped with either dichroic or standard filters (Figure 18–18).

Control of automated fixture can be from a conveniently located station or built into the user's dimming system. Typically, various focus and color settings are stored into the memory of a control system as cues and then played back just as any other lighting cue would be. Currently the prime market for units like Strand's ParScan is not the theatre. One will be more likely to find them on tour with industrial shows or "rock" concerts or in television and film studios where one automated fixture might replace a dozen standard instruments — thereby saving time, space,

Figure 18-18
The Automated Fixture

(a) Strand Lighting's "Parscan" automated fixture. *Photo courtesy of Strand Lighting.* (b) The "LightWiz," a remote control yoke which will hold a variety of different kinds of lighting instruments. *Photo courtesy of The Great American Market.* (c) The AVAB/Niethammer "Varimot" remotely focusable profile spotlight is similar to an ellipsoidal reflector spotlight. *Photo courtesy AVAB America, Inc.*

and ultimately money. However, theatrical application is growing and as the automated fixture becomes quieter, less expensive, and more reliable it will find its way onto the stage.

LOW VOLTAGE

As stage lighting becomes more sophisticated, the use of light sources that require a lower-than-normal electrical voltage is becoming more common. As will be discussed further in Chapter 22 on light sources, a low voltage lamp offers certain advantages over traditional voltage sources. Simply stated, it is possible to more exactly control by means of a reflector the light from a low-voltage source.

Until recently, the user of low-voltage lamps such as ACLs (aircraft landing lamps) and MR-16s (the Kodak Carousel lamp discussed in Chapter 17) had to self-manufacture a housing, for none were available from the standard sources. Today, however, manufacturers are paying more attention to the needs and desires of the industry and are building instruments that feature low-voltage sources. This trend will continue.

CARE AND HANDLING

While standard practices will naturally vary from one situation to another as well as from one locality to another, there are good practices that should be observed everywhere. By far the most important concern should be with maintenance of equipment. Instrument hanging, circuiting, and focusing are made simpler if the equipment is in good condition.

⫸ SAFETY PRACTICE

The best way to prevent accidents from happening is to keep equipment in good operating order.

Sticking shutters, bent bolts, and missing knobs or handles all frustrate an electrician and encourage mistreatment. A conservative estimate would be that 25 percent of all lamp "burnouts" are caused by an angered electrician attempting to free a stuck part by giving it a tap with the old wrench.

Some houses require that lighting equipment mounted overhead be secured to the pipe with a safety chain or wire in addition to the C-clamp. While the likelihood of an instrument falling during a performance is slim, nothing could be more unnerving for a theatre patron than to have a 10-inch Leko fall from 30 feet and land nearby. To prevent accidents, the safety cable should ideally be attached to the instrument itself (as opposed to the yolk) and then around the pipe. A second cable clipped to the color frame will ensure that it stays with the instrument. Other theatres may require that a wire mesh separate all instrumentation from the auditorium.

When working overhead, remember to carry a minimum of tools and always tie off your wrench. Take special precautions to avoid falling gel frames, pens and pencils, and gobo holders.

The Hang

A definite schedule must be published at least a week before the actual "put in" of equipment. This is to ensure adequate participation by crew members and minimize any space conflicts. Equipment must be ready and waiting to be hung. There are certain tasks that are best accomplished by a large crew and others that are more suited to one or two people. Preparing equipment (lamps, lens adjustment, color, gobos, cable, and so on) is best done by the head electrician and perhaps one assistant, while the actual hang requires a larger group of four to eight individuals. Therefore, the master electrician (M.E.) must have all equipment needed for the hang in good ready condition before the larger crew is called. This simple policy allows the M.E. a fighting chance of doing a good job as crew head.

Just as the goal of the preparation period should be to make the hang go smoothly, the goal of the hanging session should be to make the focus uneventful. It is most efficient to split the crew into groups of two or three people with a group leader reporting to the head electrician. In this way, one group can begin working on the booms (which always take a good deal of time), another on the first electric pipe, while a third starts hanging front-of-house. The M.E. coordinates all, checking from time to time on a crew's progress and seeing that everything is being done properly. A given hanging position should be completely hung before cabling is begun, C-clamps should all face the same way (bolts either up or down stage) so that the focusing electrician knows where they are. If the designer indicates focus on the light plot, instruments should be roughly aimed in that general direction—this also saves valuable focus time. Instrument adjustments for pan and tilt should be snug but not so tight that a wrench is required before setting focus.

Cabling • Depending on the circuit layout of the house, cabling may be the most time-consuming part of the hang. It is often better for the designer not to specify circuits, thereby allowing the electricians freedom to cable to best locations. If this is the case, a single person (designer's assistant perhaps) should be assigned the task of recording circuits onto the hook-up or instrument schedule. The only disadvantage of this system is that patching cannot be completed until circuiting is done and recorded. Begin circuiting as soon as each position is hung, with one or at most two electricians assigned to the task. It is best to allow one electrician to cable a hanging position alone due to the complexity of the work, unless the position is very large. Cable should be attached to the pipe with tie line (cotton sash cord works well) using bow ties. Adequate slack must be left in the instrument leads, never cabling so taut as to prohibit free instrument focus. If a connection is loose, it should be taped or repaired at the time rather than later during focus. A quality electrician will constantly be anticipating the needs of the upcoming focus.

The Focus

A focus crew normally consists of the designer, two focusing electricians, the board operator, and one or two additional electricians. The production's master electrician has done a full checkout and completed all necessary repairs well before the focus crew arrives. With communications set up, general focus philosophy discussed, and coffee drunk, the focus begins. The designer will often focus two electricians simultaneously in the front-of-house position, and have the two focusing electricians take turns on the ladder overstage.

A good focus team in action is wonderful and awe-inspiring to watch. Talk is kept to a bare minimum as the electricians keep ahead of the designer, anticipating his or her next move. The team works like a well-oiled piece of machinery and soon a pace is established and the job is done before anyone realizes that they are hungry or tired. On the other hand, an unprepared and/or unskilled focus team is dreadful to observe and even more painful to be a part of. Headsets do not work, lamps are burned-out, one instrument is discovered without a lamp in it at all, shutters stick, cables short out, barrels do not move, and three instruments are hung upside-down. By lunch time, 18 instruments have been focused with 108 left to do, and everyone is tired and feeling mean. The reality of the situation is that the good team is prepared and their equipment is well maintained while the poor team is sorry.

The Equipment

When not in use, cable should be neatly coiled in large coils (diameter approximately 2 feet), tied with tie line, and hung up for storage. It is a good idea to permanently attach a length of black tie line next to the female connector on all pieces of cable. Cable length marking codes should be maintained and connectors checked for strain relief periodically.

Older instruments can be valuable if they are used properly and taken care of. Do not attempt to increase light output of an older instrument by exceeding recommended limits with newer quartz lamps. These older instruments simply do not dissipate heat as well as newer equipment and they were made for lower wattage lamps—use them that way.

The single most-important factor in instrument maintenance is keeping everything clean. Lenses can be washed in mild soap and water or with a good glass cleaner. Reflectors should be wiped with a soft cloth or washed with vinegar and water. Keep body parts as free of dust as possible. A clean spotlight will dissipate heat better, thereby increasing lamp life and decreasing warpage, and will also deliver more light. Commonly needed spare parts such as shutters, knobs, and lenses should be kept on hand so that repair is not delayed by waiting for a parts order. Be advised that most instrument manufacturers require a fairly large minimum charge for parts orders and, adding insult to injury, take forever to fill the order.

19

Projection, Practicals, and Effects

T his chapter covers several diverse subjects important to lighting and the lighting designer, the most significant of which is the use of light as a scenic element. Light is commonly part of scenery as a practical property, such as a lantern; it can be used in the form of projected backgrounds; and, it can even be used as a basic scheme of production.

LIGHT AS SCENERY

Light begins to be a scenic element the moment an open source is present on the stage. Such motivating lights as realistic chandeliers and sconces generally bring elegance and high style to the scene. On the other hand, gaudy carousel lights or burlesque runway lights are frankly decorative and theatrical in their impact. Although motivating lights can make a strong visual contribution to the total design, they are a supporting element and normally not the basic scheme of production.

Designer/directors like Robert Edmond Jones (1887–1954), Edward Gorden Craig (1872–1966), and Adolphe Appia (1862–1928) envisioned using light as a central production scheme in their work, but technology of the time could not support their imagination. It took the genius of the Czechoslovakian scenographer Josef Svoboda to show the theatre world what could be accomplished with light. An example of his work is illustrated in Figure 19–1, a photograph of the scenery for Wagner's *Tristan und Isolde*. Svoboda has experimented extensively with low-voltage light sources, electrostatically charging particles in the air to act as reflectors of light. In addition, his use of projected images has pioneered new ways of thinking about scenic projection.

Figure 19-1
Light as Scenery

A curtain of light. The shape of visible light rays turns light into substance and becomes the design form in this early use of high-intensity, low-voltage light sources by Josef Svoboda, the Czechoslovak scenographer. Light rays are caught in a special aerosol spray of minute, electrostatically charged oil-emulsion droplets capable of staying suspended in the air for a prolonged time. The light column is the central portion of the design by Svoboda for Wagner's *Tristan und Isolde. Photo reprinted from* The Sceneography by Josef Svoboda *by permission of Wesleyan University Press. Copyright 1971 by Jarka Burian.*

Light being used as a scheme of production has become most common in the more-abstract presentation of modern dance and performance art. Not only do we see light being projected on actors and dancers, but moving light is used as a character itself. The modern-dance/performance-art piece illustrated in Figure 19–2, called *First Light*, was choreographed only after a lighting "score" was developed. The air is filled with fog (see "Special Effects" at the end of this chapter) to accentuate the continuously moving intense beams of side lighting, while the dancers act with and react to the light. Costumes and support lighting were designed after the piece was conceived.

Another quite different but equally effective use of light and projection is shown in Figure 19–3. These illustrations and photographs are from the English National Opera's 1979 production of Britten's *The Turn of the Screw.*

The expanded metal screens shown in Figure 19–3a were reception surfaces for both front and rear projection. Kodak Carousel projectors and Pani 5,000-watt projectors as well as Strand's Patt 752 projectors were all employed from front-of-house, stage-left and stage-right wings, and backstage. Note the extremely effective use of texture on the stage floor in Figure 19–3c.

Projected Scenery

The most familiar and accepted application of light as scenery is through the use of projections. Projections and projected scenery (usually backgrounds) are not new to the theatre. They are as old as the "magic lantern," which entered the theatre in the 1860s, before the incandescent lamp. The early experiments with the projection of moving images, first as crude animations and then later as motion pictures, are well-known events in theatre history. The resurgence of projections in modern theatre is the result not only of improved equipment design but also of a change in attitude toward their use.

Figure 19-2
Light as a Scheme of Production
These photographs of a production of *First Light* performed by Nancy Karp + Dancers, a San Francisco based modern dance company, illustrate the use of light as a scheme of production. Choreography by Nancy Karp, visual design by Wolfram Erber, costumes by Sandra Woodall, and lighting by Craig Wolf.

Figure 19-3
Projection as a Scheme of Production

Bly, a gloomy Victorian country house, is the locale for the English National Opera's production of *The Turn of the Screw* by Benjamin Britten. The eerie mood of the opera lends itself to the extremely effective use of projected scenery as the action moves rapidly through fifteen variations. (a) Line drawing shows the arrangement of screens that form the basic setting. A third screen, upstage, occasionally adds greater depth to the composition. The surface of the basic set is an expanded metal screen allowing projections from the front and rear as well as a clear view of the upstage screen when necessary. (b) Floor plan shows relationship of screens and location of projectors.

a

b

Figure 19-3 cont.

(c) Photographs of two of the many variations. Scene design and projections by Patrick Robertson; lighting design by David Hersey. *Photos courtesy Noel Staunton, Technical Director, English National Opera, London Coliseum*

c

Paint versus Light • It is most important to realize that a projection is *light* and not *paint* and that there is a world of difference between the two media. Because color in light is more brilliant than in paint, and has a limited value scale by comparison, its use in a projection is more dramatic and eye-catching. For these reasons, when projections are used as background to substitute for painted scenery, the actor may have to fight for attention. This is not to say that projections do not work as background, for they can, either at controlled levels of intensity or in a highly dramatic situation. The director and designers soon learn that the most successful use of a projection is not as a substitute realistic background, but as a medium of its own, where it expresses itself best in abstract or thematic terms and almost becomes an additional actor (Figure 19–4).

The inexperienced designer may be tempted to consider projection as a means of saving either time or money. This reasoning is totally fallacious. Good projections require a great deal of effort and often more lead-time than standard theatrical scenery; they must never be considered a last-minute production detail. In addition, projection equipment is very expensive to buy and often difficult to rent.

Both paint and light, as individual mediums of expression, have their advantages and disadvantages. Thus, it is important to realize that one is *not* the substitute for the other. This is one of the places where everyone concerned, the director and the scene and lighting designers, must be in full agreement and completely knowledgeable, or misconceptions will develop that will adversely affect the end result.

The Projection Surface

Aside from the increased efficiency of projection equipment, the innovative exploitation of the screen or projection surface is perhaps the greatest contribution to the imaginative use of light as scenery. Projected scenery has graduated in a very short time from the large single-screen background to multiscreen compositions and to an infinite variety of sizes, shapes, and three-dimensional forms.

As soon as the use of projections has been confirmed as the desired technique for a given production, the scenic designer turns to consideration of surfaces. Any material capable of reflecting light may be used as a projection surface; anything from smoke in the air to the auditorium walls is fair game. Of course, some materials reflect more light than others, and the brightness of a projection is almost always of primary concern for the designer.

Figure 19-4
Projected Scenery

A simple, direct use of projected images as a design form in a show curtain for *Anastasia* by Guy Bolton. Shown is a dye-painted, translucent muslin curtain with projected photographs from the balcony front. Designer—John Ezell.

Figure 19–5 illustrates a few of the many screen arrangements and projector positions. They range from a single rear-projection screen, a mixture of both rear- and front-projection screens, multishapes and sizes to three-dimensional front-projection surfaces.

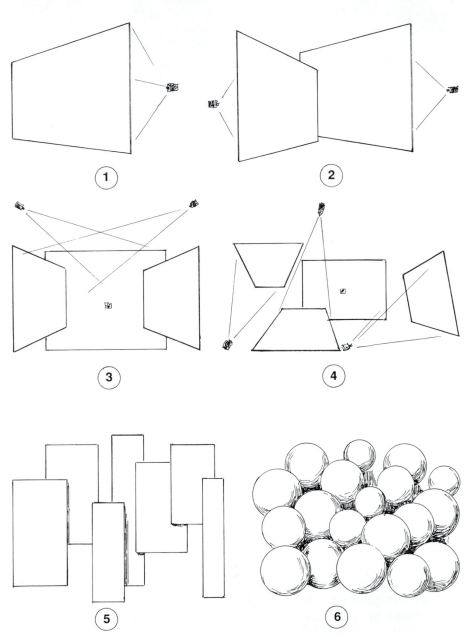

Figure 19-5
Projection Screen Arrangements

(1) Single screen rear projection. (2) Double screen rear projection. (3) Front projection screens right and left with rear projection center. (4) Multiscreen arrangement. (5) Three-dimensional surface made up of flat planes designed for a single projection. (6) A projection surface made up of spheres. (7) Sculptural surface planned for many angles of projection. (8) Slanted surfaces. The downstage screen is scrim, providing the possibility of front, rear, and see-through projections.

Rear Projection • The single screen, rear-projection technique has been used as background for dramatic productions for some time. The original location of the projector and screen was governed by the need of having an operator, as well as the reluctance to stop thinking of the screen as a painted drop. A rear-projection screen is translucent enough to diffuse the bright spot of the projector's source, yet transparent enough to transmit the image. A professionally made rear-projection screen is constructed with the greatest density in the center to offset the hotspot of the projector source and is polarized to allow for equal distribution of the light. Because of the general high density of a rear-projection screen a lot of light is stopped; consequently a rear projection requires a higher intensity to equal a similar projection from the front.

The advantage of rear projection is that the projectors themselves need not be hidden from audience sight as in front projection. Image distortion created by the obtuse angles of projection necessary to hide equipment is not a concern. However, any type of projection requires that the projectors be a considerable distance from the screen. A rule of thumb is that a projector must be at least 1 foot away from its screen for every foot of image size desired. Thus, for a 10-foot image, the rear projection must have at least 10 feet clear upstage of its screen. Some theatres have been designed with extra depth or rear projection booths, but many stages in the United States are simply too shallow to accommodate rear projection on any large scale.

Before concluding that rear-screen projection is a possible technique for your production, make sure that screen purchase or rental cost has been considered. Be aware that projecting on surfaces other than a good rear-screen material will produce an inferior image. Rear-screen material is available in many sizes and colors from several theatrical suppliers, including Rosco.

Front Projection • Front projections have become more popular and practical for two reasons: the first, which has been mentioned frequently, is the change in attitude from thinking of projections as a substitute for painted scenery; and second, the great improvement in the efficiency and reliability of remote-control projection equipment.

7

8

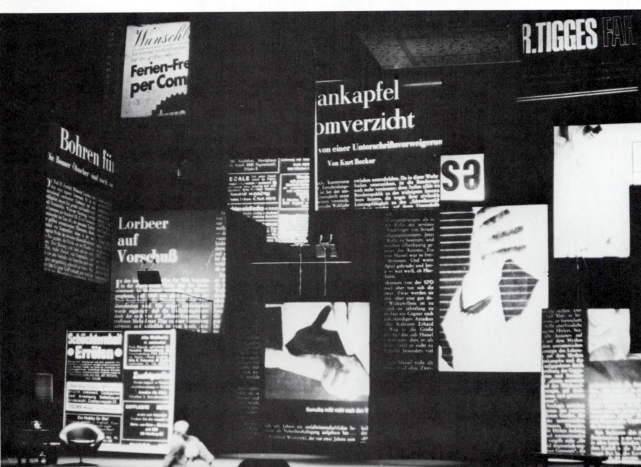

Front projection does have the disadvantage of having to throw from a more extreme angle or a greater distance than does a rear projection. The extreme angle of a front projection also causes distortion problems. They are not insurmountable but do necessitate extra drawing for the scene designer. If the slide is to be a photographed transparency, the designer has to make two designs. The first is the projection as it is to appear free of distortion, and the second shows the built-in counter-distortion that is to be photographed and processed into a color transparency for the slide. If the slide is not too small or too detailed it can be painted directly on the slide glass using the same counter-distortion control.

Not all distortions need to be corrected. There are times when the distortions of an angled projection are accepted as part of the design, especially if the slide is abstract or nonobjective in style.

A distinct advantage of front projection is that it allows greater creativity in the design of the screen. It may be three-dimensional or it may be pieced, to permit action behind or through the screen. Multiscreen techniques such as those illustrated in Figure 19–6 are best accomplished using front projection.

A technique for determining exact shape and size of images to be projected upon screens of complex shape has been developed by Svoboda: Once the screen and projector are in position, it is simply a matter of placing a piece of unexposed photographic film in the projector where the slide would normally go. Shining a light on the screen will expose the film, producing an exact image of the screen shape and size for the slide.

Lighting the Actor

The lighting of the actor in relation to a projected background is quite tricky and varies with the direction of the projection, front or rear. Any projection suffers from reflected light on the front of the screen, which tends to wash out the intensity of colors and design in the image. Care must be taken to choose angles to light the actor that will not reflect off the floor onto the screen (Figure 19–7).

In addition to the control of distribution, bounce light can be minimized in other ways: (1) The reflective quality of the floor can be deadened with a cover of black or dark gray felt or carpeting; or (2) reflected light can be kept off the rear projected screen by hanging a seamless black scrim about a foot in front. It serves to absorb the reflected light but does not affect the quality of the image.

The reflected light problem can also be helped by the design and position of the screen or the image on the screen. If, for example, the screen or the image on the screen begins about 4 feet or more above the floor, it is less likely to suffer from bounce light. This elevation coupled with the directing technique of keeping actors away from the screen by

Figure 19-6
Multiscreen Technique

The use of many screens is well illustrated by the work of its originator, Josef Svoboda. While this production of *The Journey* repeats the rectangular screen, the technique can involve screens of various shapes and sizes, each with its individual slide projector. *Photos reprinted from* The Scenography of Josef Svoboda *by permission of Wesleyan University Press. Copyright 1971 by Jarka Burian.*

Figure 19-7
Projections and the Actor

The effective use of large-scale projections as a background requires special lighting techniques. To avoid undue spill of reflected light onto the screen, the acting area lights are kept at a steep angle along with use of back and cross lighting to throw the actors' shadows away from the screen. (1) Rear-projector. (2) Rear-projection screen. (3) Black scrim hung in front of screen to absorb reflected light from the front. (4) Ground row. (5) Unit area, called neutral zone, about 3 or 4 feet in front of screen. (6) Back light on actor to help definition. Note top hat to prevent flare onto the screen. (7) Sharply angled upstage area spotlights to keep light and shadows off the screen. (8) Front-area ceiling spotlight. The normal angle is usually acceptable. (9) Center of the first electric or bridge position for front projection. The drawing on the right illustrates a front-projection setup. The lighting of the actor remains the same. The black scrim is removed to allow projections from the front. Note that the angle is planned to miss actors at the edge of the neutral zone.

maintaining a so-called neutral zone of about 4 feet makes it easier to light the actor and not lose the intensity of the projection.

Back lighting and side lighting are especially helpful in separating the actor from a projected background. Otherwise, it is difficult compositionally to balance the intensity of the background and the area lights without one or the other becoming dull.

Projection on the Actor • Modern dance and performance art have found that projections can also frankly involve the actor as a projection surface or use the shadow that he or she casts as a part of the image. The imaginative mixture of light, projections, and performers is so successfully executed by Alwin T. Nikolais and his dancers that their performances are both a stimulating experience in the theatrical form of sight and sound and epitomize light as scenery (Figure 19–8).

PROJECTION TECHNIQUES AND EQUIPMENT

Reduced to its simplest elements, the projection process requires a light source, the object or slide, and the projection surface most commonly known as the *screen*, although it is possible to project the image onto almost any type of surface.

The projection apparatus may be placed in front (downstage) of an opaque screen for a front projection, or at the rear (upstage) of a translucent screen for a rear projection. For a front projection the source is normally hidden from view of the audience. It must also be placed so that it has a clear throw onto the screen. In a rear-projection arrangement the problem of hiding the source is solved, although backstage space still has to be kept clear of the throw to the screen.

The image may be projected by one of two different methods: shadow projection or lens projection.

The Shadow Projector

Of the two methods of projection, shadow projection is the easier to achieve. Because the process depends upon direct emanation from the light source, without lens, the image is not as sharp or intense as a comparable lens projection.

The Linnebach Projector • The basic instrument for straightline, shadow projection is the familiar device known as the Linnebach projector (Figure 19–9). It is a large, plain hood with a source of light at the center of a system of diverging sides. The outer edge of the hood has a slot for holding the slide.

Being such a simple device, the Linnebach projector is often home-made, thereby reducing the cost of this type of projection. The most important part of the projector is the lamp, whose socket should be mounted in a manner so as to allow adjustment towards and away from the slide. The lamp itself must be high intensity with the filament remaining as small as possible. This indicates a low-voltage source such as General Electric's 24-volt FCS quartz lamp. The smaller filament will project a clearer image—although a transformer is necessary to reduce the voltage.

Figure 19-8
Projections on the Performer

The abstract form of the dance adapts easily to the unconventional use of projections on the actor or performer, thereby heightening theatricality and visual impact. Shown is *Scenario*, a production of the Nikolais Dance Theatre. *Photo by Oleaga.*

Figure 19-9
The Linnebach Projector

(a) This instrument's key components are: (1) Slide holder.
(2) Concentrated-filament lamp.
(b) A low-voltage, high-intensity Linnebach. A small, specially built shadow projector using a small source for a sharp projection.

The slide of the Linnebach projector or any variation of shadow projector can be a simple cardboard cutout, clear plastic such as acetate or Mylar, or painted glass. If the slide is kept parallel to the screen there is no distortion of the image on the screen. It is not always possible to place the instrument and the slide in this ideal relationship, hence the designer must be able to cope with distortion. Once the position of the instrument has been determined image distortion can be corrected by building in a counter-distortion in the slide. Distortion on one plane is, of course, easier to correct than on two planes.

The Cinebach Projector • Another variation of the Linnebach is the Cinebach projector, a homemade device that has proved extremely satisfactory for lighting the curved plaster cyclorama of a small stage. In its simplest form it is two D-shaped plywood panels, each about 20 inches wide, fastened about 24 inches apart to a plywood back piece. A sheet of acetate or of plastic color medium, clear or tinted, is tacked around the edges. On the bottom panel is a socket with a large-wattage lamp. Ventilation holes are drilled through both bottom and top panels, and frequently light baffles are built to shield these (Figure 19–10).

Any sort of design may be painted on the plastic, just as on a conventional Linnebach slide. If the Cinebach is to be placed at the bottom of the curved cyclorama, the top panel may be built smaller than the bottom one to permit the light to spread upward more smoothly.

The Lens Projector

The second and more complex type of instrument for projecting an image is the lens projector. The light source in a lens projector is concentrated on the slide surface by a condensing lens system. The image of the illuminated slide is then transmitted through another set of lenses called the *objective-lens system* (Figure 19–11).

Normally the body of the projector will include the lamp, condensing lens(es), slide holder, and perhaps a fan or fans to cool the lamp and slide. In order to provide a choice of image sizes, the objective lens assembly is a separate attachment, usually in the form of a tube that fits onto the front of the projector body. Image size is determined by throw distance as well as the focal length of the objective lens assembly (see "The Mathematics of Lens Projection," page 488). A designer will usually determine the desired image size first, the necessary throw distance next, and the proper focal length for the lens last.

Excluding effects projectors, the designer's choice of projectors is limited to a very few and is further restricted by application. The size of the slide a projector uses varies from the convenient 35mm (1.346 by 0.902 inches) to the large continental size of 9 by 9 inches. However, a specific projector will accept only one size. There are several guidelines to follow:

1. The longer the throw or the larger the image, the brighter the light source should be.
2. A large slide size will produce a clearer image than a small slide.
3. The larger the slide format, the more expensive and bulky the equipment.

The small 35mm slide is by far the easiest to produce and project, but its image size and intensity has limits. The designer may be forced to use larger format projection systems if large and bright images are required and/or if the throw distance is great.

The Kodak Carousel Projector • Very few people in this country are unfamiliar with the Carousel projector. While the theatre has used this projector for years, it has only recently become the best choice of 35mm projectors because of its improved lamp.

Figure 19-10
The Cinebach Projector

(a) A pictorial representation.
(b) Section View. (1) High wattage lamp. (2) Socket for lamp. (3) Ventilation holes. (4) Curved sheet of clear or colored plastic.

a   b

Figure 19-11
The Lens Projector

Shown is a drawing of the optical train of a typical lens projector.

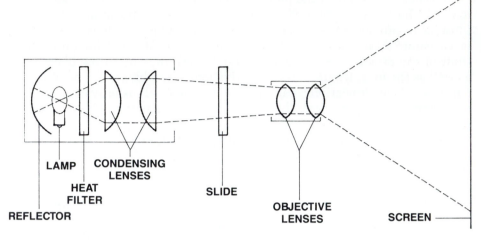

LAMP | CONDENSING LENSES
HEAT FILTER | SLIDE
REFLECTOR | OBJECTIVE LENSES | SCREEN

Kodak sells 25-foot extension cables for the projector's remote controller, allowing control over projectors hung overstage or placed in the auditorium. However, only three or four extension cables can be used together. One final thing to remember is that the Carousel operates on a gravity-feed principle for changing slides. This means that the projector cannot be tilted too much in any direction without danger of slides jamming.

Keep in mind the following valuable bits of information about the Kodak Carousel slide projector:

1. The standard lamp recommended by Kodak is the ELH (300 watt, 30-hour life). An acceptable substitute is the ENG (300 watt, 4-hour life). While the life of the ENG is only a fraction of that of the ELH, its light output is greatly increased. It is the ENG that enables the Carousel to be a viable scenic projection unit.

2. The Carousel as wired cannot be dimmed because of its fan and slide-changer motor, although Kodak manufactures a dissolve unit that will cross-fade two projectors. However, it is possible to add an external dimmer in-line with the projector's lamp without any sort of rewiring. A two-pin male plug (Radio Shack Cat. No. 274–342) fits into a pair of holes in the rear of the projector and interrupts power to the lamp. Power need only be directed through any remote dimmer of 300-watt or greater capacity. *Caution*: Power is supplied from the projector, through the dimmer, to the lamp—one may not connect the projector to a conventional stage circuit and dimmer without causing a short circuit.

3. While Kodak sells a large range of its own lenses, Buhl Optical Co. manufactures an even larger range of superior lenses. Focal lengths of Buhl lenses made to fit the Carousel projector begin at a very wide angle 1 inch and go to a narrow 9.5 inches. These lenses are available in varying speeds, with the faster lenses being best for scenic projection.

Slide Production • Anyone with access to a 35mm camera can produce slides that will project very well in a Kodak Carousel projector. If copying other photographs or designs, a copy stand will come in handy. Using plastic or glass mounts is preferable to the commercial cardboard mounts because they tend to warp over time and with heat. Do not attempt to use the Carousel trays which hold more than 80 slides—they will jam.

Experience has proven that it is best to shoot many more slides than considered necessary in order to have choices without further slide production.

Slides for larger format projectors are much more expensive than 35mm, the glass alone costing several times that of a 35mm slide. Common sizes are 4 by 5 inches; 13 by 13cm (approximately 5″ × 5″); 18 by 18cm (7″ × 7″); and 24 by 24cm (9½″ × 9½″). Photographic production houses will be able to make either black and white or color transparencies from any original material in any size desired. Such slides will be expensive and take time to produce—allow for both. Of course, it is possible to transfer design work directly onto the clear glass slides of larger format slide projectors.

Large-Format Slide Projectors • Three companies manufacture large-format slide projectors commonly used in the United States: Ryudensha Company of Japan; Ludwig Pani of Austria; and Reiche and Vogel of Germany.

Ryudensha Company's "Scene Machine," distributed in the United States by The Great American Market, uses the 4-by-5 slide and is available with 600-, 1,000-, and 2,000-watt lamps in addition to a new 2,500-watt, high-intensity HMI lamp. Lenses come in a range of focal lengths between 4 inches (23cm, 50-degree beam spread) and 16 inches (59cm, 12-degree beam spread). A manual as well as a remote-control slide changer with a five-slide capacity can be purchased. Optional effect equipment includes a film loop machine, a spiral machine, and a disc machine. The Scene Machine has proven to be a good reliable projector.

The projectors from Ludwig Pani are distributed in this country by Production Arts Lighting. Projectors with 2,000- and 5,000-watt quartz lamps as well as 1,000-, 2,000-, and 4,000-watt HMI lamps will take an 18-by-18cm slide. A larger 6,000-watt HMI unit takes a slide size of 24-by-24cm. Remote-control slide changers holding 15 slides, film loop machines, effects attachments, and a rather-impressive lightning generator are optional equipment. Lenses are available with focal lengths from 60cm (8-degree beam spread) to 13.5cm (60-degree beam spread).

The German Reiche and Vogel projector was for a long time the only, very high-powered scenic projector available in this country. The 2,000- and 5,000-watt projectors take a 13-by-13cm slide, while the larger unit accepts an 18-by-18cm slide. The usual lenses and optional equipment are available.

Other Projectors

Several other types of projectors are available, which can be extremely useful for special applications. They include the overhead, opaque, and video projectors.

Figure 19-12
The Kodak Carousel Slide Projector
The Buhl Optical Company modified the Kodak Carousel Projector by increasing the wattage of the lamp and adding a better cooling system. The "Hi-Lite" projector shown is also available with a higher intensity arc lamp.

a

b

c

Figure 19-13
Larger Format Slide Projectors

(a) This Pani projector has a 4,000-watt HMI lamp and takes a slide size of 18 × 18 cm (approximately 7 inches). (b) The Pani BP 1.2 takes a 1,200-watt HMI lamp with 18 × 18 cm slides. *Photos courtesy Production Arts Lighting, Inc.* (c) Shown is a 2,000-watt "Scene Machine" projector which takes a 4 × 5 inch slide. *Photo courtesy The Great American Market*

The Overhead Projector • The most unusual instrument in the lens-projector category is the overhead projector. Its large slide deck (about 12″ × 12″) is a translucent, horizontal surface with the light source underneath. The slide image, after passing through a vertically mounted objective-lens systems, is redirected by a mirror onto the screen (Figure 19–14).

The advantages of the overhead projector, which was originally designed to animate or illustrate the classroom lecture, are twofold: (1) The large area of the slide permits handpainted slides, allowing the photographic process to be omitted, thereby saving time and money; and (2) the horizontal position of the slide deck provides the opportunity to bring movement to the image. On-the-spot animation is possible by such actions as moving transparent film across the slide deck, agitating with an air jet a shallow transparent dish of colored dyes in oil or water, or blowing smoke across the deck. The movement of smoke across the deck can appear on the screen as a descending fog, rising smoke from a fire, or the engulfing black cloud of an approaching storm.

The overhead projector is not as efficient as a regular lens-projector, but because of its wide-angle objective system it can work close to the screen. It functions best with short-throw, small-image projections.

The overhead projector obviously requires an operator and therefore cannot be used in a remote position. It is best for rear projections, although it has been used for front projections from an extreme offstage side position.

The Opaque Projector • There is another lens projector that has not been mentioned: the opaque projector. The slide, which is opaque, is reflected by mirrors into the objective-lens system and projected onto the screen. Because the slide is not transparent the image is not as bright; thus, the inefficiency of the instrument renders it impractical for stage use. Its chief use in the theatre is to facilitate the cartooning and painting of scenery. If a drawing bearing a grid of scaled squares is projected to match over a corresponding full-scale grid of a scenic element or drop, it can serve as a quick guide for drawing an enlargement of the original painting.

The Television Projector • The television or video projector is a complex and highly specialized piece of equipment that is capable of projecting a live televised image. It has been used as a dramatic extension of action on stage or of a scene occurring just offstage. Intimate business or emotions expressed by live actors can be supported by simultaneously enlarged television projection elsewhere on the stage.

Gobo Projection

One form of lens projection that does not require any special apparatus other than a common ellipsoidal reflector spotlight is the gobo, also known as a *cookie.* The gobo is a sheet of highly heat-resistant material from which some shape, pattern, or design has been cut. When placed at the gate of an ellipsoidal spot, this pattern is projected by the lens (or lenses) onto any appropriate surface (Figure 19–15 and Color Plate 24–2).

Commercial equipment houses sell gobos in a variety of designs; some are fairly realistic, but most are simply pleasant patterns. These are frequently used in television, where the background is rarely in sharp focus, to give interest to an otherwise plain drop or wall.

Patterns may be home-designed and cut from heavy aluminum foil or the bottom of a cheap tin pie plate. Two especially useful effects are clouds, cut from foil, which may be wrinkled slightly to give out-of-focus soft edges, and stars, made by pricking tiny holes through a piece of tin kept carefully flat to make all edges sharp. Both are projected in a white light against a blue drop or cyclorama.

Regrettably, neither color nor fine detail can be used at the present because the only transparent material that will withstand the terrific heat at the gate of an ellipsoidal spot is a very expensive clear ceramic requiring special paints and a carefully controlled fixing process not available to the public.

Figure 19-14
The Overhead Projector

Shown is a wide-angle overhead projector with a 10 × 10 inch transparent slide deck. *Photo courtesy of Buhl Optical*

a

b

Figure 19-15
Gobo Projection

(a) Shown are several of the many gobo patterns available from Great American. *Photo courtesy The Great American Market.* (b) This is a photograph of Rosco's "Realistic Leaves" gobo template and the image it projects. *Photo courtesy Rosco Laboratories, Inc.* Also see Color Plate 24-2a and 24-2b.

THE MATHEMATICS OF LENS PROJECTION

To eliminate trial-and-error methods of selecting lenses and placing projectors, use the following simple formulas:

F = Focal length of lens

D = Projection throw distance

S = Slide size

I = Image size

$$F = \frac{D \times S}{I}$$

$$D = \frac{F \times I}{S}$$

$$I = \frac{D \times S}{F}$$

Remember that all these distances must be expressed in the same units, usually inches. If the horizontal dimension of the slide is used, the horizontal dimension of the image will be obtained; if the vertical measurement of the image is needed, one must use the vertical measurement of the slide.

PRACTICALS

Practicals refer to onstage, working light sources such as lanterns, lamps, fireplaces, or candles. The wiring and maintenance of such units are the responsibility of the electrical department, and their use is sure to be a concern of the lighting designer. Playwrights or directors will call for practicals for any of several reasons:

1. The particular light given off by a practical will enhance the desired mood of a scene.
2. The use of a practical will indicate time of day, season, or even period.
3. Practicals help reinforce the reality of a scene or location.

One rule to remember in dealing with practicals is that whenever possible they should be controlled by dimmers. Never allow an actor to switch on a major motivating practical and then expect your light-board operator to support it on cue—it simply does not work.

Fire Effects

Often prohibited by fire codes, open fires on the stage are rarely convincing. Yet play after play calls for them. If it is possible to design the setting so that the hearth is located in a side wall, reasonably good results can be attained by simply letting a flickering light move over the far corner of the fireplace. Even this must be kept at low intensity so as not to take attention from the actors.

All too often the demands of the script force the designer to put a fire in full view of the audience. If no flames are required, then a mere glow, through crumpled gel (orange and red), broken glass splashed with translucent orange paint, or the like, will suffice. If flames must be shown, then a glow on some form of rising smoke, or on thin streamers of chiffon or China silk, blown upward by a small fan, can be used. Another method of simulating fire from a fireplace is to use a slowly rotating drum covered with crumpled foil and painted in various fire colors. Lights mounted above the drum in the hearth and out of audience sight are then trained upon the turning cylinder.

Several electronic options are available, including: a color organ, flicker generator, or a random chase effect programmed into the control system. Any of these can control several low-wattage, R-type lamps colored in various fire colors and directed out from the hearth. In a pinch, one can use the inexpensive flash buttons (available from electronic stores) that insert into a medium screw-base socket, flashing the lamp. The problem with this solution is that the flash is slow, and the button capacity is only 60 watts.

In every case, however, the designer is placed on the horns of this dilemma: whether to make the fire effects so realistic as to grab the attention of the audience or so phony as to arouse their ridicule. It must be stated emphatically that, on the whole, the less fire effect you can get away with, the more fortunate you and your production will be.

Flames • Torches are particularly difficult to simulate. Perhaps a flashlight hidden in the handle and focused on streamers of very light silk is as good a solution as any, but it is not very convincing, even when the torch is stationary and the silk can be blown upward by a hidden fan. Perhaps a smoke device can be incorporated and the flashlight trained on its fumes. If real flame is necessary and legal, a can of Sterno is securely mounted in the top of the torch. Liquid fuel is never used.

Oil-burning lanterns should never be used on the stage. To begin with, their use is strictly against all fire rules and insurance regulations. A real hazard is presented by their use, for in case of accident the stage will become flooded with blazing oil. Fortunately, oil lanterns conventionally have glass chimneys which can be realistically smoke-stained to hide a small lamp bulb placed inside (Figure 19–16).

If the lantern is never moved during the action, it can be connected to the regular stage wiring and dimmed up and down from the control board. Of course, actors, when pretending to adjust the wick, or touch a match to it, or whatever, must always be careful to mask this fakery by placing their bodies between the lantern and the audience until the process of dimming has been completed. If a lantern is to be carried about the stage a battery must be hidden within it and a silent switch provided for the actor to control.

Small flashlight lamps can be colored using the commercial transparent dye called *lamp dip*, available from Rosco. Always test the color first. Amber works well, but you may want to experiment with mixing various colors.

Figure 19-16
Practicals

An actress uses a practical oil-type lantern which is illuminated by battery and a small flashlight lamp.

Candles • Unlike oil lanterns, candles, which usually extinguish themselves when dropped, are permissible on most stages if properly handled. In some locations they must be encased in transparent mica shields. If you have any doubts about the legality of using candles on stage, consult the local authorities. In no case should candles be placed near draperies or other easily flammable materials, including human hair and frilly costumes.

Even if candles are allowed, however, they probably should be avoided, for their bright light and particularly their flickering at the smallest breath of air can be most distracting for the audience. Very effective faking of candles can be done by means of a small battery or pencil flashlight hidden in a white paper tube. A tiny lamp on the top, colored with lamp dip, gives a steady and quite convincing glow.

||||▶ *SAFETY PRACTICE*

It is best not to use open flame on stage at all; but if absolutely necessary, take these precautions:

1. Have a crew member with a fire extinguisher stationed on both sides of the stage ready to react to any emergency.
2. If entrances and exits are made with open flame, establish the policy that anytime the flame is offstage it is handled by crew only.
3. *Never* use a filled oil lantern on stage.

Lighting Fixtures

Chandeliers, wall sconces, table lamps, and similar household lighting fixtures generally offer no vast problems except for the wattage of the lamps actually used in them. Such fixtures should never be counted on to produce all the light that seems to emanate from them. Frequently they are in quite the wrong locations to light the faces of the actors playing near them, so additional illumination must be provided by spotlights especially mounted for the purpose, or the acting area lights may be varied to give the effects desired.

This is particularly true when the fixtures have bulbs visible to the audience, for these, if at all bright, will throw a most annoying (even blinding) glare. Such bare bulbs must always be of extremely low wattage, and even then may have to be dimmed still further. Obviously little light will emanate from such fixtures, so the extra instruments become doubly important.

But if the bulbs are shielded by shades, then the glare is hidden and extra large-wattage lamps may be used to give a more realistic effect on an already bright stage. Such shades must be quite opaque, of course, or brown paper linings can be put inside them. Often an additional baffle must be placed over the bulb to prevent an unsightly hot spot on the walls and ceiling of the setting.

SPECIAL EFFECTS

All uses of light that are not directly involved in lighting the actor or illuminating the scene may be grouped in the category of special effects. Examples include explosions, fires, ghosts, or psychedelic lighting. Working out special effects is almost always enjoyable but can take a great deal of time. It should not be left to the end as an afterthought.

Moon and Stars

Some day a playwright undoubtedly will call for a realistic sun on the stage! Until then we have quite enough trouble with the moon and stars that are so often required. If the background is in the form of a cloth drop or cyclorama, quite a realistic moon can be devised by cutting the desired shape—fully round or crescent—into a large sheet of thin material such as cardboard or plywood, which is pressed firmly against the back of the drop. A small spotlight is then focused on the cutout from the rear. If the background is not a cloth, then a projection from an effects machine or an ellipsoidal reflector spotlight with an iris or a gobo may be used from the front.

Stars can be quite effective, but are tricky to handle. The tiniest bulbs obtainable look like great blobs of light against a darkened sky. It is advisable to tape these over; a mere pin-prick will pass enough light. If a dark-blue or black scrim is hung a few feet in front of the sky drop, it will help cut down excessive brightness and also will hide the wiring to the star bulbs.

Lightning

Lightning is a device in many plays. Fortunately, it is usually not necessary to show forks of light springing from the sky, but only the sudden, rapid, and irregular bursts of high illumination as seen through windows or coming from the wings. By striking and breaking the contacts rapidly, a carbon arc can be used to give excellent results for this purpose. In fact a so-called arc striker that makes this even easier to handle is available commercially. *Caution:* The light from a carbon arc is bright enough to blind—shield the source!

Another method is to switch rapidly on and off a number of intense sources. A momentary contact switch which acts like a "bump button" is the kind of switch to use. Many lamps can work well, but remember that smaller filaments react quicker and can produce a more-convincing burst of light. Therefore, low-voltage sources may be the answer.

Large photoflash bulbs, although fairly expensive, create a wonderfully bright burst of light. They can be mounted in an old plano-convex housing (with or without lens) or a simple tin can to avoid unwanted spill. Photoflood lamps such as the R-32 photoflood have a quick response time and also deliver a good deal of intensity.

If the lightning flash has to be seen against the sky, a projection must be used. Because of the slow response of the high-wattage lamp, it is well to have the instrument already turned on and an operator stationed at it to reveal and conceal the beam of light by means of a cap or other masking device. And several different slides should be provided, rather than show the same shaped flash again and again. Scratches on black-painted slides can be drawn quite realistically for these or lighting gobos for use in an ellipsoidal reflector spotlight are available.

Explosions and Flashes

To produce explosive flashes offstage, in the wings, the same general techniques can be applied as were suggested for lightning, with the addition of mechanically produced noises when required. But for the same effects on the stage, in view of the audience, a *flash pot* is necessary.

A flash pot is a device that will ignite a highly explosive powder called "flash powder." Still available from theatrical supply houses, flash powder was used as a light source for still photography. The safest flash pots are those available from reputable manufacturers such as the "Pyropak" system (Figure 19–17). However, an old theatre practice was to use homemade flash pots with exposed electrical wires—and sometimes even filled with black gunpowder. Use of such devices is extremely dangerous and should be discouraged.

Figure 19-17
Flash Pot System
Shown are photographs of the Pyropak concussion mortar and a 2 channel, 6 circuit controller. While the concussion mortar is designed for maximum report volume, Luna Tech manufactures several devices for various effects. *Photo courtesy Luna Tech, Inc.*

Figure 19-18
Fog Machine (Dry Ice)
(a) Assembled fog machine. (b) Top removed showing dry ice basket on end of the plunger.
(c) View into the tank revealing electric heating element to heat water. (d) Loading basket
with crushed dry ice. (e) The plunging of the ice into hot water produces a blanket of fog.
Photos courtesy Richard Thompson

Smoke and Fog Effects

Two acceptable methods of producing smoke on stage are dry ice and fog machines. While both are equally easy to use and cost roughly the same, each has unique properties.

Dry Ice Fog • As the name implies, dry ice acts more like fog than smoke in that it will tend to cling to the floor and creep along at a low level. Machines to produce dry ice fog are easily and cheaply built or can be purchased from various theatrical suppliers (Figure 19–18). Solid carbon dioxide (dry ice) changes from a solid state to a vapor without becoming a liquid. The rapidity of the change is increased if the dry ice is exposed to hot water.

A 55-gallon drum, an electric immersion heater like those used in home hot-water heaters, and a wire basket to suspend the dry ice is all that is needed to make the dry-ice fog machine. When the water is hot, dry ice is dropped in producing a good deal of fog. This fog can be directed over a short distance by using flexible dryer hose connected to a vent in the lid of the 55-gallon drum. Such fog gives a splendid effect, but dissipates rather rapidly. Note that the dry ice tends to bubble rather loudly. Avoid dry ice burns by wearing gloves.

Figure 19-19
Portable Fog Machine (Smoke)
Shown is Rosco's model 1500 fog machine which is designed to carry a bottle of "fog juice" with it. *Photo courtesy Rosco Laboratories, Inc.*

Smoke/Fog Machines • Several manufacturers make very fine portable machines that produce a smoke by heating up a special liquid called "fog juice." This mist tends to rise, but a cage is provided that may be filled with dry ice and fastened over the nozzle of the container. When this is done, the fumes hug the floor. Plastic hose hidden about the stage has proved an easy way to make this mist appear wherever wanted. A second fluid may be used to help disperse the smoke, and several essences are available to scent it pleasantly. Their value is strictly a matter of individual taste. Actually, the fumes are not dreadfully unpleasant (Figure 19–19).

Controlling Smoke • Anyone using smoke of any nature on the stage is frequently faced with the problem of preventing it from flowing or blowing to where it is not wanted. Heavy fog that tends to hug the stage floor may easily spill over the footlights into the auditorium—a touch that is seldom appreciated by the audience.

The lighter-than-air smoke that rises is subject to the slightest breeze or draft. A ventilator at the top of the stage house may draw it swiftly upward, a cross-draft may set up eddies and swirls, while an exhaust fan that evacuates stale air from the auditorium can bring the smoke billowing into the house.

Each theatre and auditorium will affect smoke and fog in a different manner. The only way to discover how best to use these effects in a given space is to experiment in that facility under conditions that are as close to performance as possible.

Electrically Triggered Effects

It is often necessary to create the illusion on stage that an occurrence has been affected by something other than what it appears to be: a trick. For instance, a bottle shattering as if hit by an onstage bullet requires either an actor who is a sharpshooter or a stage effect. Breakaway properties, pictures falling off the wall, or any number of magical occurrences can be achieved with the help of the electric department and a device called an *electrical solenoid.*

The magnetic power of the solenoid coil can be used to withdraw the support of a picture on the wall or as a trigger for any other breakaway (Figure 19–20). When a current is passed through the coil of the solenoid it becomes an electromagnet which draws the spring-loaded center pin into the coil. Upon breaking the circuit the pin is released with considerable force. Either action can be used to trigger a breakaway.

Ultraviolet Effects

One field in which it is impossible to surpass the carbon-arc follow spot is in the use of ultraviolet effects. Because the output from this instrument is rich in these very short waves, a black-light filter that removes practically all the visible waves will still permit the ultraviolet ones to pass through in good quantity. Objects painted with a medium susceptible to such waves will glow under this stimulus and, if all other light is removed from the stage, weird and unworldly effects can be achieved.

Figure 19-20
Electrically Triggered Effects
(1) Falling picture. (2) Solenoid coil mounted on rear of picture batten. (3) Picture batten. In its off position the spring-loaded pin is extended through the batten to hold the picture frame in place. When current is sent into the coil the pin withdraws and the picture falls.

Stage-Lighting Practice: The Light Plot and Production

We now come to a discussion of the lighting designer's basic communication tool: the light plot. The creation of a light plot signifies the end of pre-production and signals the exciting beginning of actual production. A great deal of time, preparation, and thought goes into this plot which presents the lighting designer's "working drawings."

DESIGN DECISIONS

The designer is constantly making decisions concerning type and position of instruments, color filtering, and dimmer readings. Before going into the specifics of plotting the lights, let us review these all-important design decisions: instrumentation, angle, color, and finally, control.

Choice of Instrument

As previously noted, a particular stage-lighting instrument will be chosen because it comes closest to satisfying requirements of intensity, coverage, and quality of light. Adjustability of beam spread and field quality of most of the new *ellipsoidal reflector spotlights* (ERS) along with increased light output certainly make this instrument the most valuable for the lighting designer (Figure 20–2). While the ERS is the logical choice for front-of-house, this workhorse of a unit also serves well backstage and should be considered along with the Fresnel, beam projector, and PAR can.

The *Fresnel* delivers a soft light whose beam blends very easily and therefore is ideal for upstage areas of a box set (Figure 20–3). Fresnels, having a tremendously variable beam spread, can be used over a wide range of throw distances: the 6-inch Fresnel lamped at 500 or 750 watts is effective to somewhat more than 20 feet, and the 8-inch Fresnel with lamps up to 2,000 watts can be useful up to 40 feet. The soft light of a candle, the quality of dusk or an overcast sky, or the scattered, almost shadowless light from fluorescent tubes will all be most closely reproduced by using the Fresnel.

The light from a *beam projector* cannot be shaped, but its near-parallel rays come closest to those of the sun (Figure 20–4). This quality can serve as a motivational source, whereas Fresnel and even ERS light will act as fill or bounce. Banks of beam projectors have been employed as "walls" of light shooting from an overstage batten.

The *PAR can*, like the beam projector, has a parabolic reflector, but the lens of its lamp breaks up the light enough to cause a softer-edged beam than that of a beam projector. Yet, the PAR still delivers a sharp and intense light, harsh in quality. Remember, its beam is oval and cannot be shaped. PAR cans make good back lights and deliver a nice quality of light for dance.

Choice of Angle

Angle and color are probably the two most-difficult choices for the beginning designer to make.

Figure 20-1
Design Decisions

Choice of Instrument—Does it support an incandescent or fluorescent source, a practical, daylight, sunlight, moonlight, and so on? *Choice of Angle*—What is the best position for the actor, director, costume, or set designer? View from the balcony? *Choice of Control*—Intensity, movement, focus, quality, nonverbal communication. *Choice of Color*—Motivation: nature or optional. Brilliance, atmosphere, style and texture.

Figure 20-2
Ellipsoidal Reflector Spotlight

Figure 20-3
Fresnel Spotlight

Figure 20-4
Beam Projector

The purpose of two *front lights* at angles of 45 degrees each, rather than a single unit straightaway, is to add dimension to the actor's body and face. As the angle of front light is lowered, it tends to flatten features more and more. As the angle is raised, features become sharper and sharper, with deeper and deeper shadows. Remember that front light is what the audience will "read" more than any other angle of light.

Whether it be a bit frontal or straight out of the wings, *side light* is an exciting angle for both variety and revelation of form. A low-angle side, such as that commonly used in dance lighting, will light the entire height of the body fairly evenly. The problem is that it is quite difficult to control. Therefore, a slightly higher-angle side (from 30 degrees to 60 degrees) is often used in the theatre. Here is where the designer can begin to use richer and more expressive colors in order to establish a motivational source or simply set the mood for a scene.

Back light is primarily used in order to create three-dimensionality, separating actor from background. However, colored light from the back is extremely useful in toning the stage floor; and back light textured by means of gobos can be of great help in establishing mood. Rear gobos are not nearly as noticeable on the actors as is a more-frontal distribution; yet, they texture the stage floor well, creating a broken light through which the actors move.

Choice of Color

Color selection requires experience—experience in observing traditional theatrical usage (blue = night); experience in color mixing; as well as experience in knowing how a given color will act on stage. The lighting laboratory and color mix-box will help, but the lighting designer ultimately has to do some experimenting with the real thing. A masterful use of color can be one of the most-exciting elements of stage lighting, but it takes time and taste.

Careful consideration must first be given to scenic and costume color. Unless intended, colored light must not significantly alter the true colors of an actor's skin, clothing, or environment. The varying colors of an incandescent lamp under different dimmer settings must be considered along with color filters.

Try to analyze color by feeling as well as seeing—how does sunlight feel? Then translate the feeling into color. This is why a visual memory is so important, for we tend to store feelings more than angstrom units. Why does the warmth of sunlight *feel* different than the warmth of a fireplace fire? It has something to do with color.

Throw distance tends to affect the intensity or saturation of a color— colors appear more saturated over shorter throw distances.

Choice of Control

At the mention of "control" one normally thinks of dimmer levels, however this design consideration additionally includes how instruments and dimmers are assigned to channels. If made arbitrarily, such assignments will cause the process of cue writing and level setting to be more difficult. The designer must be able to anticipate necessary control assignments based upon the viewing of rehearsals, discussions with the director, and anticipated design needs.

Setting dimmer levels for the first time will probably be a painful and time-consuming experience, but be assured that it gets easier. Force yourself to write your dimmer levels "blind" several days before actually seeing them on stage. Take the time to think through each preset or stage picture: Which sets of instruments should be reading highest and which control areas should take focus? Write the levels on your "cheat sheets" (more information to come) and have your board operator transfer them to standard preset sheets or directly into the memory of a computer system. You will find that this process of writing blind takes a good deal of time, but it ultimately results in a better-looking product and can cut hours off a technical rehearsal.

In general, it is best to write and design for the highest dimmer levels to be between 80 and 90 percent. Then, if more light is required, you have room to maneuver. Depending on the curve of your dimmers, a reading of 10 percent will barely warm the filament, and a reading of 20 percent will just begin to deliver light. Keep in mind the saturation of color filters, for the more-saturated filters will cut down light transmission significantly. Finally, always remember that the perceived intensity of light is relative.

THE COLLABORATIVE PROCESS

An attempt has been made throughout this book to emphasize the great importance of working together for all members of a production team. The lighting designer, in particular, must be an excellent collaborator because it is often expected that the lighting will, in the end, unite all the production elements. Compounding the importance of good collaboration skills on the part of the lighting designer is the fact that visual as well as verbal presentation of lighting ideas is difficult at best.

Production Collaboration

The very first contact between a director and designers sets the stage for the collaborative process that follows. The success or failure of this all-important exchange of ideas is determined first and foremost by *attitude*. If the atmosphere surrounding a production team's collaboration is one of acceptance and openness, the process has a good chance of being a positive experience. If such an environment exists and the members of the team become excited by the prospect of shared creation, the experience can be positively exhilarating.

While no formula for success exists, good preparation coupled with a positive attitude will go a long way. The preparation of lighting storyboard and score, two techniques for communicating ideas between lighting designer and production team, were briefly mentioned in Chapter 13.

The Storyboard

A lighting storyboard consists of a series of sketches illustrating important aspects of a production's intended lighting. A complete storyboard will consist of as many sketches as there are major lighting changes in the production; the drawings will often be value sketches, sometimes referred to as "thumbnail" sketches; and they will almost always concentrate on the lighting mood or atmosphere of a given scene. Figure 20–5 is an example of a pair of storyboard-type sketches for a production of *Tosca*. Obviously, a lighting designer's storyboard presentation would take place well after production concept meetings, for a completed scenic

Figure 20-5
Storyboard Sketches
Shown are two examples of
storyboard sketches from the opera
Tosca by designer Susan Gratch.

Tosca   ACT I   7/25/85 S.GRATCH

Tosca   ACT II   7/25/85 S.GRATCH

design is fairly necessary. On the other hand, the lighting score is a tool
that can be useful at the very early design meetings.

The Lighting Score

A lighting score is less intimidating than the storyboard for a designer
who is insecure with rendering and drawing skills and, at the same time,
is capable of presenting more information. As can be seen by the example
in Figure 20–6, the score consists of a horizontal axis time-line breakdown of the script along with a vertical axis composed of various design

EMPEROR JONES *by Eugene O'Neill* A LIGHTING SCORE

	SCENE 1: THE PALACE	SCENE 2: FOREST'S EDGE	SCENE 3: THE FOREST	SCENE 4: THE FOREST
TIME OF DAY	AFTERNOON	DUSK	NIGHT	NIGHT
MOTIVATIONAL SOURCE	BRIGHT SUNLIGHT	SKY LIGHT	MOON LIGHT	DIRECT MOON
OVERALL BRIGHTNESS				
MOOD	"OPPRESSIVE HEAT"	GLOOMY	EERIE	GHASTLY AND UNREAL
FOCUS	BROAD AND GENERAL	GENERAL	TRIANGULAR CLEARING	DIAGONAL ROAD
KEY		NONE		
CONTRAST				

	SCENE 5: THE FOREST	SCENE 6: THE FOREST	SCENE 7: THE FOREST	SCENE 8: FOREST'S EDGE
TIME OF DAY	NIGHT	NIGHT	NIGHT	DAWN
MOTIVATIONAL SOURCE	DIRECT MOON	MOON LIGHT	DIRECT MOON	SKY LIGHT
OVERALL BRIGHTNESS				
MOOD	FRIGHTENING	DESPERATE	RESIGNED	RELIEF
FOCUS	CIRCULAR CLEARING	SOFT CAVE-LIKE	HARSH CLEARING	GENERAL
KEY		NONE		
CONTRAST				

concerns and considerations. The *time-line* can be constructed in a variety of ways, with commonly used divisions being acts or scenes for simple lighting requirements, and French scenes for productions that demand more lighting movement. A complex production may require that the designer use lighting "pictures" as time-line categories, relating each to an action in the script.

The list of design considerations in the vertical axis will also vary from production to production, but almost always will include categories of mood, focus, motivational source, and time of day. Rising and falling action, sense of conflict, brightness level, contrast, color, temperature, and atmospheric conditions are other possibilities. It is recommended that the lighting designer keep the score pictorial (as opposed to verbal); using graphs and color whenever possible and pictographs instead of words. In this way, the director, as well as the rest of the production team, can "see" the lighting images along with the lighting designer well before the actual plot needs to be considered.

THE LIGHT PLOT

The light plot and its accompanying paperwork (the instrument schedule, hookup, and section) forms the link between the designer's ideas and the reality of theatrical production. The importance of this piece of paper cannot be overstated. It must be 100-percent accurate and complete so that the "put-in" (hang, circuit, focus) can proceed in an orderly and rapid fashion. The simple process of executing a plot enables the designer to discover and eliminate many artistic as well as technical problems well before ever setting foot in the theatre.

Drafting the Plot

The lighting designer must learn mechanical drawing in order to read and understand scenic draftings as well as execute a lighting plot and section. (If review of the tools and techniques of drafting for the stage is necessary, the reader is referred to Chapter 5, "Drafting the Design.")

The light plot is drafted in the conventional sense in order to allow reproduction through a process known as *blue printing*. The advantages of "blue line" reproduction (a variation of blue printing) are cost and availability. The disadvantage is that color cannot be reproduced; for it would be handy to be able to use color coding in place of some of our current drafting conventions.

Theatre Plan • The theatre plan should show all rigging for the production, including masking, flying scenery and drops, as well as electric pipes. Critical audience sight points must be included. It is permissible to show distance to front-of-house lighting positions in a smaller scale, but this deviation should be noted. A lighting position is indicated by a single, solid line of medium weight. All positions must be clearly labeled.

Figure 20-6
The Lighting Score
Shown is an example of a lighting score for a production of *Emperor Jones* by Eugene O'Neill.

Working on the premise that some standardization is desirable for any communicative tool, the light plot should include the following:

1. A plan of the theatre drawn to scale (preferably ½ inch—*never* ⅛ inch) showing and labeling all lighting positions.
2. A plan of the stage setting drawn to scale in lightweight lines.
3. The lighting areas indicated by Roman numerals in heavyweight lines beginning downstage left, working stage right and then upstage.
4. Exact instrument placement, type and size, color and number.
5. Title block in lower right-hand corner, instrument key, instrument annotation key, and color key (if needed).

Some designers prefer to include a plaster line scale and sometimes an up- to downstage scale in order to facilitate hanging and placement of instruments. Refer to Figure 20–7 for examples.

A blue-line plan and center-line section will be available from the technical director, electrician, or production manager of the theatre. These prints should include all the information needed to draw the theatre plan; however, they may not show circuits and/or all of the possible lighting hanging positions. If this is the case, ask the appropriate producing agent to provide a circuit chart and/or a lighting hanging plan. In addition, the house should be able to provide the designer with an up-to-date instrument inventory as well as control specifications.

It is advisable to draft the basic lighting plan (without instruments) as early as possible in the design process. Several weeks before the plot deadline is not too early. This will allow you time to digest the theatre and scenic information as well as save you valuable drafting time later.

The Stage Setting • The lighting designer's set plan need not be as complete as the scene designer's floor plan, but it should include elements important to lighting such as walls, doors, major levels, large pieces of furniture, and so forth. Plaster line and center line should be included. If the production requires several sets, the lighting designer may use transparent overlays of each set.

Instrument Annotation • One of the several available lighting instrument templates should be used to trace outlines of the various instruments (Figure 20–8). Templates can be ordered in either ¼- or ½-inch scale as well as in plan or sectional view. These outlines must be bold enough to stand out from all the other information on the plot. While the lighting instrument should intersect the lighting pipe, the pipe

Figure 20-7
The Light Plot

A lighting plot for a production of Ibsen's *A Doll House*. The theatre is a fairly typical proscenium with limited front-of-house lighting positions. A ½-inch scale hanging plot was developed in addition to the ¼-inch scale plot shown in order to clarify circuiting and distribution.

Figure 20-8
Lighting Templates

Shown is a ½-inch scale section template (above) and a ½-inch scale plan template (below).

should never be drawn through the instrument. In most situations, instruments are numbered by position beginning house right at the rear and working onstage. Numbering by position means that all instruments in each position are numbered consecutively beginning with 1 (Figure 20–7). Some situations, however, may make numbering by position rather confusing (for example, a flexible theatre with a full, overhead lighting grid). In such cases, *all* instruments should be numbered consecutively.

The instrument annotation illustrated in Figure 20–9 is recommended: Instrument number is centered in the rear body of the instrument; instrument type is indicated by either a symbol or beam spread in degrees (see also Figure 20–10) and located at the barrel position; focus area (if used) goes behind the instrument; and the color number is located in front of the lens of the instrument. In addition, the dimmer or channel number is placed within a hexagon and the circuit number is circled with both connecting to the rear of the instrument as shown.

Explanation of symbols indicating type of instrument are found in the instrument key.

Figure 20-9
Instrument Annotation

Some designers prefer to place the focus area in front of the instrument with the color number.

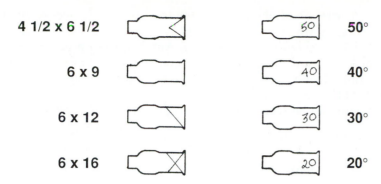

4 1/2 x 6 1/2	50	50°
6 x 9	40	40°
6 x 12	30	30°
6 x 16	20	20°

Figure 20-10
Instrument Types

Instrument and Color Keys • The instrument key indicates exactly which symbol the designer is using for a specific instrument. This key, which should include the wattage as well as the focal length or beam spread of the instrument, is normally located in the lower left corner of the plate.

The color key explains what numbering and lettering system the designer is using for each brand and type of color medium. For example:

"R" series = Roscolux
800 series = Roscolene
100 and 200 series = Lee
"G" series = Gam Color

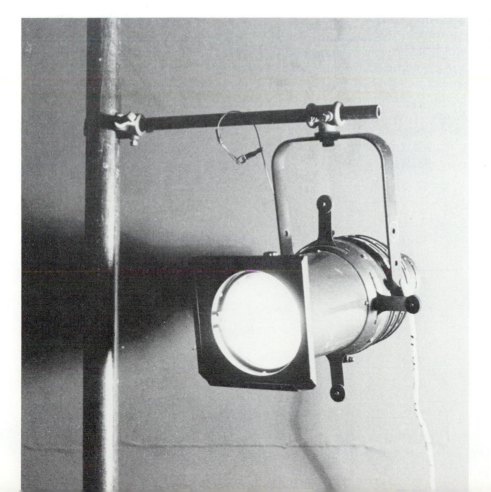

Figure 20-11
Lighting Instrument with Side-Arm Mounted on a Boom

Booms • A brief word about floor stands or booms is necessary at this point. A boom normally consists of a heavy metal base into which screws a length of 1¼- or 1½-inch black pipe. Any length of pipe may be used, but booms of any great height must be tied off above for safety. A lighting instrument is then hung off the boom by using a cross-pipe or "side-arm" (Figure 20–11).

The boom can be represented on a light plot in one of two manners:

1. Drawing the pipe at scaled length and at an angle of 45 to 60 degrees directly out of its base. The various instruments are then shown in relationship to their boom pipe (Figure 20–12a). This is similar to an isometric view.
2. Showing the boom base and pipe in plan view, but without instrument specifications, with an additional elevation of the boom placed on the side of the drafting plate. The elevation will specify instrumentation (Figure 20–12b).

If the second method is used, instruments shown in plan view should be cross-hatched to indicate that another view of them appears elsewhere in the plot.

In both methods of plotting boom positions, instrument height must be indicated (Figure 21–12b).

Similar drafting conventions should be used for ladder, box boom, and cove positions where a number of instruments are stacked above each other.

Lighting Areas • As discussed earlier in Chapter 15, lighting areas are determined by the lighting designer based upon several factors: shape and size of the setting, tightness of control desired, blocking of the actors, and equipment available. Of course, area size is determined by beam spread along with throw distance of a given lighting instrument. The beginning designer should consider making up a beam-and-field spread template for each of the instruments in common use. Such a template, drawn to scale on drafting or tracing paper, can be used as an overlay on a sectional view of the theatre and will quickly show approximate area coverage (Figure 20–13).

Figure 20-12
Representing a Boom on the Light Plot

(a) The isometric method shows the boom base in its actual position on stage. (b) The plan and elevation method is often desirable when space on the plan is tight.

a

b

S.R. BOOM # 2

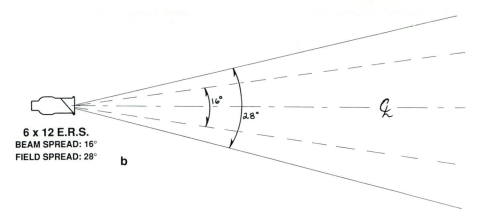

6 x 12 E.R.S.
BEAM SPREAD: 16°
FIELD SPREAD: 28°

b

a

Figure 20-13
Beam Spread Templates
(a) "Chart-A-Beam," plastic
templates available from Great
American, give spreads for 3½, 4½,
and 6-inch ellipsoidals, 6 and
8-inch Fresnels; and PAR-64s. *Photo
courtesy of The Great American
Market.* (b) The lighting designer
can make templates using a
protractor and drafting paper.

The heavyweight Roman numerals used as area indicators on the light plot should mark the center of the focus area. Roman numerals are suggested in order to distinguish area numbers from all the other numbers appearing on the plot.

THE INSTRUMENT SCHEDULE

The instrument schedule lists all instruments by location and instrument number and contains the following information in the following order:

1. Location and instrument number
2. Instrument type (specific)
3. Wattage/lamp designation
4. Color number
5. Use/focus area
6. Circuit
7. Dimmer/channel
8. Remarks

This schedule is simply a list of complete information about any given lighting instrument, some of which might not be included on the plot (Figure 20–14).

Designers today tend to include more information on the plot than in the past, thereby eliminating the need for an instrument schedule altogether. If this is the case, a simple hook-up (see "Additional Paperwork") will suffice.

The Lighting Section

The center-line section is important to the lighting designer as a tool to help ensure plot accuracy. An electrician need never see the section, but the designer will consult it for vertical sightlines, throw distances, acting levels above or below stage height, and accuracy of lighting angles (Figure 20–15).

Figure 20-14
The Instrument Schedule

The instrument schedule for *A Doll House* (Figure 20-7). Instruments are listed by position and number. Complete circuit information was added to the schedule during the put-in.

The sectional view is actually a side view with the picture plane being on center line. It is as if a large cut was taken through the theatre and auditorium along center line and we are looking into the cut surface. If the stage is drawn on the left-hand side of the drafting plate, we are looking stage left. If the stage is on the right hand side of the drafting plate, we are looking stage right. Only one sectional view is usually necessary.

It should be understood that the section is primarily a lighting designer's tool. If electric trims (height of pipes) are indicated on the plan, the electricians need never see the section.

The scene designer provides the lighting designer with a center-line sectional view of the stage that includes horizontal masking at trim height, critical audience sight points, as well as scenery placement. Occasionally various supplementary sectional views will be necessary; they can be easily and quickly drafted by the lighting designer.

Additional Paperwork

It should be fairly clear by now that the better prepared a lighting designer is before a production moves into the theatre, the easier the design will be realized. In fact, many professional designers would argue that preparation is as important as design or artistic work. As a result, a variety of additional types of paperwork have been developed by designers in order to simplify the put-in and the execution of the design.

Hook-ups • There are two types of hook-ups: one is arranged by dimmer number and intended for a traditional hard-patch system; while the other is arranged by channel number and used in the dimmer-per-circuit system.

Figure 20-15
The Section

The center-line section for *A Doll House*. Note that the only masking is on lines number 2 and 13, forcing the up-stage electric pipes quite high.

The computer-generated hook-up shown in Figure 16–20 (page 436) — with the first column heading being dimmer number — is set up for a standard hard-patch system. Note that it has a column for circuit numbers.

A hook-up designed for dimmer-per-circuit would be arranged as follows:

Column 1 — channel number
Column 2 — dimmer/circuit number
Column 3 — position and instrument number
Column 4 — wattage
Column 5 — instrument type
Column 6 — color
Column 7 — purpose/focus
Column 8 — remarks

However, as Tharon Musser's hook-up for *Teddy & Alice* illustrates (Figure 20–16), all the categories listed above may not be necessary. Originally the hook-up was intended as patching paperwork supplementary to

Figure 20-16
The Hook-up

Shown is one page from the hook-up for the musical *Teddy & Alice*, designed by Tharon Musser.

TEDDY & ALICE   87

PAGE 8 OF 9

HOOKUP PALETTE - 152 - 4K. DIMMERS

CHN	DIM	POSITION & UNIT NUMBER	TYPE	FOCUS	COLOR
114	132	NO. 6 ELEC. 3 - 20	6" x 16" 750W. L.	BED X-U.C.	02
115	133	NEAR COVE - 16	6" x 16" 1K L. I.	EAGLE	02
103	134	NO. 1 GROUND ROW - E	8'- 12 LT 500W. T-3	U.S. DROPS	79
104	135	NO. 1 GROUND ROW - E	"	"	67
105	136	NO. 1 GROUND ROW - E	"	"	58A
116	137	NO. 1 ELEC. 13	6" x 16" 750W. L.I	· PARTY · ALICE LEE	65
117	138	NO. 5 ELEC 12	6" x 12" 750 W. L.I	· WOODS · ALICE LEE	65
118	139	SCRIM - STARDROP	# 7153 - AS15 5VOLT - 115AMP. L4	STARS · A ·	
119	140	SCRIM - STARDROP	"	STARS · B ·	

the instrument schedule. With more information included on light plots, the hook-up may replace the instrument schedule.

Batten Tapes • To expedite hanging and circuiting the electric pipes, the designer may wish to prepare batten tapes for each hanging position. These consist of rolled strips of paper or cloth that have been premarked with center-line and specific instrument information. The tapes are simply attached to the batten, and electricians follow the instructions on the tape. Information may include instrument number, circuit number, instrument type, color, and even focus. Tapes eliminate any measuring and chalking of the battens and, in combination with hanging cardboards, could eliminate the necessity of an electrician ever having to consult the master light plot.

Hanging Cardboards • Hanging cardboards are pieces of stiff paper or cardboard onto which a single location and its respective instrumentation have been transferred from the master plot. A cardboard can be given to an electrician during the put-in, allowing him or her the freedom of hanging and circuiting the position without having to refer to the plot. Hanging cardboards may contain more detailed information than the plot and, like batten tapes, are especially useful for touring situations, where they can be reused a number of times.

a

LIGHTING PRESET SHEET: Rep. Christmas Carol '88 //R.C.W.

CUE #					PAGE # 2 OF 2				
CHANNEL #	81	82	83	84	85	86	87	88	89	90
USE	BELOW FRONT SL R53	FRONT SR R64	BACK	SCREEN S.L.	C.S.	S.R. →	MARLEY DOOR BACK	ALI BABA	UP THRU GRATE	
LEVEL										
CHANNEL #	91	92	93	94	95	96	97	98	99	100
USE	GOBO FUNERAL PIT	STAGE	GRAVE	COUNTRY PIT	C.S.	STAGE →	STREET H.R.	LOW L H.L.	STREET HIGH L	"RUDDY"
LEVEL										
CHANNEL #	101	102	103	104	105	106	107	108	109	110
USE	OFFICE SR SIDE R70	SCROOGE WALK HOME	PIT "FOOTS"	MARLEY DOOR FRONT	MARLEY GHOST TRAP LIGHTS	SCHOOL ROOM SP.	ROOM BACK	BOY SP.	GENIE	R. CRUSOE →
LEVEL										

b

CONAN DIMMER FOCUS/PURPOSE
JANUARY 1988

PAR FRONTS
1   UC, DC
(109) Rock
160   Off L, DL, DLC
161   L, UL, ULC
162   R, UR, URC
166   Off R, DR, DRC

PAR FRONTS DK BLUE
2   DC, UC
163   Off L, DL, DLC
157   DRC, DR, Off R

WARM FRONTS
12   DL, DLC
20   DR, DRC
22   DC

AREA WARM

PAR SIDE BK WARM
48   DC
58   DC
55   LC, DLC
53   RC, DRC
(49)   Rock

PAR SIDE BK COOL
51   DLC, DC
52   LC, UC
56   UC, RC
57   DC, DRC
(50)   Rock

GREEN SIDES
(3)   Stair L
(30)   Stair R
10   Off L
37   Off R

DRAGON PLATFORM
72   Sides
91   Down

COLUMN LEKOS
122   L   Neu. Density
129   R   Neu. Density
125   L   Lt. Neu. Den
126   R   Lt. Neu. Den
123   Aqua
124   Lt. Lav

COLUMN PARS
158   Blue L
164   Blue R
159   Aqua L
165   Aqua R

WALLS (COLM MT)

TREASURE LEFT
4   Lt. Lav
67   Warm
113   Cool

TREASURE RIGHT
27   Lt. Lav
94   Warm
114   Cool

STAIRS
82   L Cool Back
86   R Cool Back
(11)   R Area Warm
(24)   L Area Warm
(3)   L Green Side
(30)   R Green Side
(70)   L Fresnel Back
(92)   R Fresnel Back

c

TEDDY AND ALICE

FRONTS				PIPE AREAS				SIDES		
1	F. COVE A1 DDL	35A/62	26	1P	A-11	L	35A/02	54	1TL	68
2	F. COVE A2 DDLC	35A/62	27	3P	A-12	Lo/c	35A/02	55	1TL	34
3	F. COVE A3 DDC	35A/62	28	3P	A-13	C	35A/02	56	1TL DIAG	58a
4	F. COVE A4 DDRC	35A/62	29	3P	A-14	Ro/c	35A/02	57	WEDDING PATH	54
5	F. COVE A5 DDR	35A/62	30	1P	A-15	R	35A/02	58	2TL	68
6	N. COVE A-6 DL	35C/62	31	5P	A-16	L	35A/02	59	2TL	34
7	N. COVE A-7 DLC	35A/62	32	5P	A-17	C	35A/02	60	3TL	68
8	N. COVE A-8 DC	35A/62						61	3TL	34
9	N. COVE A-9 DRC	35A/62						62	4TL	68
10	N. COVE A-10 DR	35A/62			ENDS				63	4TL	34

Figure 20-17
The Cheat Sheet

Shown are examples of three different styles of designer's cheat sheets. (a) A cheat/preset sheet for a production of *A Christmas Carol,* designed by Craig Wolf for San Diego Rep. (b) A cheat sheet listing by function for the *Conan the Barbarian* show at Universal Studios in Hollywood, designed by Tom Ruzika. (c) Tharon Musser's cheat sheet for *Teddy & Alice,* listing by function/position.

The Cheat Sheet • The "cheat sheet," or "magic sheet" (names given to designer's paperwork that aid in setting and adjusting lighting levels) help the designer remember what is assigned to each control channel or group of channels. While each designer tends to customize his or her own sheets and nearly as many styles exist as do designers, Figure 20–17 illustrates several of the more common types.

Figure 20–17a is an example of a cheat sheet developed from earlier "preset sheets" used to record dimmer levels for a preset-type control system. The sheet lists all dimmers or channels, their function, and levels for any given preset or cue number. This information will allow the designer to quickly locate which dimmer controls a specific instrument or set of instruments as well as its intensity. Board operators can record prewritten dimmer readings from this style of cheat sheet into a computer memory with the written information then acting as "hard copy" in the event of memory loss or board malfunction. Obviously, these sheets must be kept up-to-date as levels are adjusted—a good task for an assistant.

Another very popular format for cheat sheets will list groups of channels by function. Figure 20–17b shows a sheet used by lighting designer Tom Ruzika to focus the *Conan the Barbarian* show at Universal Studios in Los Angeles. Likewise, Tharon Musser's cheat sheet for *Teddy & Alice* (Figure 20–17c) shows listing by function, including color numbers in an adjacent column.

Focus Charts and Shop Orders • Two paperwork items that are of primary importance in the commercial theatre are tour *focus charts* and *equipment shop orders*. Like cheat sheets, focus charts come in many styles and forms; but their function in providing a concise method of recording light focus is the same for all. A shop order is essentially a contract for the rental of lighting equipment and related hardware between an equipment rental house and a producer represented by the lighting designer. Both of these items are discussed further in the following section on the commercial theatre.

Computer-Generated Paperwork • A number of individuals and companies have developed software programs that are intended to ease the lighting designer's paperwork load. One such program, Rosco's ALD, will print information in the form of hook-ups, equipment lists, cheat sheets, instrument schedules, circuit schedules, and color lists (including purchase requirements). In addition, many programs will also check for paperwork errors such as dimmer or circuit overloads. The advantages of using these programs are accuracy, neatness, and ease; but time is not always saved. Specific show information must be entered in every case, usually taking two or three hours for an average-sized production. It would seem that use of computer-generated paperwork will remain subject to the preference of designers and electricians until the day comes when CADD light plots themselves are in common use.

Figure 20-18
The CADD Plot

Shown is a CADD (Computer Assisted Design and Drafting) light plot for a production of *Sgt. Musgrave's Dance*, designed by Bill Teague.

LEGEND

db – Drop Box
fp – Floor Pocket
wp – Wall Pocket

COLORTRAN 30 (1K)
6x9 LEKO (500)
8" CAP. ELLIPS. (1K)

6" FRESNEL (500)
8" FRESNEL (1K)
PAR 64–NSP (1K)

THE UNIVERSITY OF ALABAMA
MARIAN GALLAWAY THEATRE

SGT. MUSGRAVES DANCE
LIGHT PLOT

DIR: E. WILLIAMS	SET DES: E. WILLIAMS
LT DES: B. TEAGUE	DWN BY: WCT
DATE: 3-30-87	APRV BY: REV:
SHEET: 1 of	SCALE: 1/4"=1'-0"

CADD Lighting Plots • Computer-aided design and drafting programs such as the popular AutoCad, enable a designer to create a lighting plot using the computer. With access to proper equipment such as a plotter (a mechanical drawing machine capable of drafting a light plot from computer information), the designer need only input the desired lighting-instrument information and the system will generate a plot (Figure 20–18) as well as required paperwork.

REALIZING THE PLOT

The final step in lighting a production is, of course, realizing the plot. This process may be as short as two or three days or as long as two weeks and is always the most challenging time for the lighting designer. Let it be said once again that any preparation completed before move-in will pay off tenfold while in the theatre.

Final Preparations and Put-In

Cues • Writing lighting cues is one of the most simple tasks for the lighting designer, although at first this might not seem to be so. The *rhythm* of a production will tell an observant designer where most of the cues belong. (The designer must be sure to attend several rehearsals and to concentrate on things other than blocking.) It is a good idea to note cue placement in the script during one of the final run-throughs before move-in. Cues can then be numbered and presets written. Cues should be numbered sequentially, with inserted cues having a decimal point (Light Cue 12.1).

The cues and their placement, of course, must be given to the stage manager, who runs the show. This cue-writing session should take place at a sufficiently early date before the technical or first lighting rehearsal and ideally should include both the stage manager and the board operator. Set aside enough time for an uninterrupted discussion of the cues with both people so that they understand why a cue happens. Make sure that both know counts or cue times and, finally, make sure that your stage manager understands that the placement of some cues will most certainly change during the rehearsal process.

Cues should be called as follows:

"Warning Light Cue 12" (approximately 30 seconds before "go")
"Ready Light Cue 12" (approximately 15 seconds before "go")
"Light Cue 12 . . . Go"

The Put-In • The lighting designer or assistant must be present during the put-in, if for no other reason than to be available for questions. The lighting put-in should be carefully scheduled with the technical director in order to coordinate lighting and scenery, and step-by-step procedures should also be discussed with the master electrician.

While the responsibility for the put-in lies with the master electrician, the designer can do a great deal of good by being attentive and setting a positive tone. It is important that the master electrician and staff realize that the aim of their work should be toward a good and smooth focus session. If an electrician always keeps the focus in mind, quality of work will usually be excellent. The designer should not take a major role in physically hanging the show. This is the crew's job and a designer's energy is best spent elsewhere.

Focus • Lighting focus takes concentration. If at all possible, electricians should have the stage to themselves during focus hours. Be prepared for the focus: be alert, have a dimmer list or cheat sheet with you, and work in a logical order.

Never begin the focus before an accurate check-out has been completed. Interrupting focus for a lamp or a patch mistake or a bad circuit is a serious waste of time and, more importantly, concentration. Front-of-house is often focused first. Learn to focus two electricians at once. Learn to focus with your back to the light, looking at your shadow. Learn to focus fast. And do not forget to give your crew periodic breaks.

Technical and Dress Rehearsals

The first time a show's director sees the results of the lighting designer's work will probably be at the technical or lighting rehearsal. This should *not*, however, be the first time the lighting designer sees his or her work. The ideal situation is to look at presets during the final run-through before the technical rehearsal, explaining to the cast and director that you will be adjusting a few levels and will most probably not be in sequence with the action on stage. Simply remember to leave them enough light for rehearsal, never blacking out the stage. This gives the designer a good chance to see the lighting on actors without the added pressure of a technical rehearsal.

The technical and dress period is most crucial to the lighting designer, for this is when the majority of design decisions are made. This is the time when the lighting designer is working the hardest. Accordingly, the designer *must* be fresh and alert—one cannot see or think for very long with only four hours of sleep.

Technical Rehearsals • Infamous for being long and laborious affairs, technical rehearsals are disliked by technicians as well as actors. If proper and thorough preparation has been done and if someone keeps things moving, the rehearsal can be relatively painless. Good judgment must be used in determining when to stop and fix something and when to keep going. Tactless people must be banned from technical rehearsals.

It is a good idea for the stage manager to call this rehearsal from the house rather than an isolated booth somewhere. He or she will be in better contact with the director, the designers, the technical staff, as well as the actors. Always make sure that headsets have been carefully checked out well before the technical rehearsal begins. Nothing is more frustrating (and, unfortunately, more common) than communications problems during a technical rehearsal.

The purpose of a technical rehearsal is to solve technical problems— *not* constantly to adjust light levels, and *certainly not* to write lighting presets. If presets are not complete before the technical rehearsal, the rehearsal should go on without lights. Likewise, this is not the time for a director to adjust blocking, a temptation that sometimes is difficult to resist. If the director gives full attention to the process at hand, results will be better and a conclusion reached sooner.

Remember to take periodic breaks and that positive reinforcement is a good thing. Remain objective, observe time deadlines and, above all, be sure that your operators and stage manager understand and record changes as they are made.

Dress Rehearsals and Previews • A production will normally have two or three dress rehearsals, with the first primarily devoted to costumes. Level changes must be made during the dress rehearsal process, but the performance may not be stopped except for an exceptionally serious problem. Second and third dresses must never be stopped. The fewer changes made during dress rehearsals, the better your stage manager and operators will learn the show. Remember that the director's attention is divided among a great number of equally important things during this stage of a production. Never leave after a dress rehearsal without first talking to the director, the stage manager, and your operators.

Previews refer to performances with an audience that take place after the dress-rehearsal process but before official opening. The purpose is usually to expose the actors to audience reaction before the production is reviewed. The number of previews can vary from one or two to several weeks worth; and the role of the lighting designer often is dependent upon need. If the production's lighting is complete, there is no reason for the designer to attend all previews. However, if changes continue to be made during the preview process, the designer must be in attendance.

LIGHTING FOR THE COMMERCIAL THEATRE

In the not-so-distant past we saw an amazing rebirth throughout the country of professional theatre, too long confined to New York and a few other large centers. Now it is a rare city that does not have its own repertory or stock theatre, run by professional producers and directors and employing professional actors and designers.

Nearly all of these regional theatres (often called LORT houses after the type of union contract issued the actors) run apprentice programs which seldom pay much but which offer exceptional experience and valuable professional contacts. Theatre Communications Group (T.C.G.) publishes a complete list of theatres and programs which is available by writing to T.C.G. More and more college graduates, and even college students, are working in these theatres, on a full- or part-time basis. This section gives such people an overview of lighting practices in the commercial theatre.

Broadway Practices

New York's Broadway has always been, and still remains, the United States' premier theatrical-entertainment center. People come from all over the world to see Broadway hits. It is an extremely commercial theatre with tough competition and great reward for achievement. Many practices are identical to those of our regional theatres, however some are unique to Broadway alone.

Equipment in the Broadway Theatre • Most people would be surprised to learn that no commercial theatre on what is commonly referred to as Broadway has any lighting equipment of its own beyond the few items here listed: There will be a dimmer for the house lights; there will be a company switch furnishing considerable power, to which a show's dimmers may be connected; there will be current at appropriate locations for the use of follow spots; and, a fairly recent addition, there will be wiring in conduit to the front of the balcony and to the box booms, vertical pipes erected on either side of the auditorium in the upper boxes closest to the stage. Occasionally there will be conduit to a second balcony or other front-of-house lighting positions if any exist.

This means that everything else must come in with the show: all the instruments and their accessories, the dimmers and plugging boxes, cable sufficient to connect all instruments to the dimmers, booms for offstage instruments, work lights, all special rigging devices, everything!

The Broadway Lighting Designer • Before being permitted to light a show on Broadway or at a number of the larger commercial theatres across the country, the designer must become a member of the United Scenic Artists Union (U.S.A.). To be admitted to this organization, the applicant must pass a difficult two-day examination offered either once or twice a year in New York, Chicago, or Los Angeles only.

The lighting designer is hired, often at the suggestion of the director, by the producer of the play. Under the rules of U.S.A. he or she must receive a minimum fee, although established designers may ask for and get a great deal more than this minimum. It is not uncommon for a well-known designer to receive, in addition to a straight fee, a royalty based on a percentage of the gross receipts.

Renting Equipment • Because all expenses related to the play must be approved by the producer or business manager, the light designer must work within the figures that they have in mind. All the equipment is rented, the usual contract calling for a down payment of 10 percent of its price for the first three-week period, a lower charge for the next three weeks, and a reduced rental for the balance of the run of the play. Some producers make a practice of asking for competitive bids from the few companies that are engaged in the rental of lighting equipment for the stage; others always work with the same company. Some accept recommendations of the lighting designer to deal with a certain firm.

These bids are based on an equipment list called a shop order which must be drafted by the lighting designer or assistant well before the production moves into the theatre. For this reason, the Broadway lighting designer must complete the plot several weeks earlier than is required of a designer working primarily with in-house equipment. The shop order must carefully specify every piece of equipment to be rented or purchased.

Figure 20–19 shows part of the shop order for the production of *Teddy & Alice* with lighting designed by Tharon Musser. This show opened in Tampa, moved to Baltimore, and then played the Minskoff Theatre on Broadway. Note that the order includes instruments (complete with clamps and frames); cable and connectors; hardware such as side arms,

<u>TEDDY AND ALICE</u> - <u>Electrical Equipment List</u>

Load in: Performing Arts Center
Tampa, Florida
July 28, 1987

Producers:Shimberg and Gray
Ashley Tower
100 S. Ashley Drive
Tampa, Florida

Manager: Richard Seader
344 West 72nd St.
New York, N.Y. 10023

Designer: Tharon Musser
CH 3-9076

Electrician: Michael Scoville
586-0982

<u>BOOTH</u>

3 Colortran 2000 Follow Spots   *MINSKOFF THEATRE - XENON SUPER TROUPERS* ③

<u>FAR COVE</u>

32 6" x 22" 1000w. Lekos - Clamps and Frames   ① *IRIS*
Cable, Jumpers, Twofers

<u>NEAR COVE</u>

35 6" x 16" 1000w. Lekos - Clamps and Frames   ① *IRIS*
Cable, Jumpers, Twofers

<u>UPPER BOX BOOM LEFT</u>

8 6"x16" 1000w. Lekos - Double Side Arms, Clamps and Frames - Tophats
4 6"x16" 1000w. T. & S. Lekos - Double Side Arms, Clamps and Frames ② *# 294 LEAVES*
Cable, Jumpers, Twofers   ② *# 216 BRANCHES*

<u>UPPER BOX BOOM RIGHT</u>

Repeat Above

<u>LOWER BOX BOOM LEFT</u>

12 6"x12" 750w. Lekos - Double Side Arms, Clamps and Frames - Tophats
Cable, Jumpers, Twofers

<u>LOWER BOX BOOM RIGHT</u>

Repeat Above

<u>NOTE</u>

THE ABOVE F.O.H. LIST IS FOR BALTIMORE - LOAD IN
SEPT. 17, 1987. THE ONLY SHOP ORDER FOR TAMPA IS
<u>1 ZENON SUPER TROUPER.</u> * *TAMPA HAS SHORT THROW ARCS*

<u>FOOTS</u>

3 7½' 12 Compartment (Double) - 75w. R 30 FL. - Frames   *CUT* ② *SECTIONS!*
4 3'9" 6 Compartment (Double) - 75w. R 30 FL. - Frames
Hangers for hanging off front of Show Deck
Cable, Jumpers, Twofers

lamps, top hats, and barn doors; control system; color; and even tape and tie line. Equipment is listed by position so it can be properly packed and cable runs prepared.

Hiring Electricians • Even more significant than the equipment rental costs are the wages paid to the electricians who set-up and run the show. In New York and many commercial theatres elsewhere these people must be members of the International Alliance of Theatrical Stage Employees union, commonly called the I.A. Member electricians are paid a substantial hourly wage and prudent use of their time is imperative. Stringent regulations concerning working hours and conditions which may vary from one union local to another must be understood and adhered to by the designer.

It is most likely that the theatre itself will have an electrician as part of its regular staff. This person's title is *house electrician* and specific duties tend to be related to in-house equipment, including maintenance and repair. In addition, this individual will have a strong voice in determining put-in and running crew size as well as local interpretation of union rules and regulations.

The electrician who will work most closely with the designer is the *production electrician.* This person is hired by the show's producers and travels with the production. It is this electrician who works with the rental house and acts as a liaison between the production and the house staff. Obviously, the choice of who will serve as production electrician is an important one to the lighting designer.

Planning the Lighting • The biggest difference between designing for Broadway and elsewhere is time. The design period and time in the theatre is so compressed that only the best can survive. The rehearsal period is unusually short and the plot must be completed well in advance in order for the shop to have time to prepare the equipment. The old adage that "time is money" has never been truer than when one is in the theatre with an I.A. crew. Here is where superb preparation and an excellent production electrician really pay off.

Figure 20–20 shows the overstage plot for *Teddy & Alice.* Due to the large ½-inch scale required for commercial plots, two plates were necessary: overstage and front-of-house. Note that Tharon Musser only includes instrument numbers, but very carefully specifies spacing between instruments. Even more interesting is the fact that she does not distinguish between types of 6-inch ellipsoidals (6 × 16 and 6 × 12), but lists equipment by position at the stage-left end of each electric. Trim heights are given for each electric batten on the stage-right side of the plot. It is clear that this plot is intended to make the lighting hang go as quickly and trouble-free as possible. Refer to Figure 20–16 for the accompanying hook-up.

Figure 20-19
The Shop Order
Shown is page one from the equipment list for *Teddy & Alice,* designed by Tharon Musser.

Figure 20-20a
The over-stage Light Plot for *Teddy & Alice*, **designed by Tharon Musser.**

NOTE: CHECK LINE SETS FOR BOUNCE POSITION

NO. 2 GROUNDROW ⑤ 8'-12 LT. 500W. T-3 STRIPS
NO. 1 GROUNDROW ⑤ 8'-12 LT. 500W. T-3 STRIPS
NO. 10 ELEC. ⑤ 8'-12 LT 500W. T-3 STRIPS
NO. 9 ELEC. ⑤ 8'-12LT. 500W T-3 STRIPS

NO. 8 ELEC.
② 6"X16" 750W. LEKOS
① 1000W. WORK LITE
26'-0" L.o/L
NO. 4 TORM. L.

NO. 7 ELEC.
⑭ 6"X16" 750W. LEKOS

28'-0" L.o/L NO. 3 TORM. L.

NO. 6 ELEC.
22 6"X16" 750W. LEKOS

NO. 5 ELEC.
20 6"X12" 750W. LEKOS
① 1000W. WORKLITE
28'-0" L.o/L NO. 2 TORM. L.

NO. 4 ELEC.
② 3½"X12" 750W. LEKOS
② 3½" X 12" 750W. LEKOS
NO. 3 ELEC.
⑭ 3½" X 12" 750W. LEKOS
② 3½" X 12" 750W. T.#3 LEKOS
NO. 2 ELEC.
⑧ 6"X16" 750W. LEKOS
④ 6"X16" 750W. T.#3 LEKOS

NO. 1 ELEC.
⑨ 6"X16" 750W. LEKOS
28'-0" L.o/L NO. 1 TORM. L.

FOOTS
⑤ 7½-12 DBL. COMP. 75W. R-30 FL.
② 3:9"-6 DBL. COMP. 75W. R-30 FL.

+4"
C   B   A

1' 2' 3' 4' 5' 6' 7' 8' 9' 10' 11' 12' 13' 14' 15' 16' 17' 18' 19' 20' 21' 22' 23'

REV. 10-17 87 - DW'G. B.N.
REV. 9-2-'87 - DW'G. B.N.

"TEDDY AND ALICE"
FOR
TAMPA BAY PERFORMING ARTS CENTER
DESIGNER ROBIN WAGNER
LIGHTING DESIGNER THARON MUSSER
STAGE PIPES

| SCALE | DATE | ELECTRICIAN | DW'G |
| ½'=1'-0" | 7-7-'87 | M. SCOVILLE | 1E |

REPEAT S.R. SPACING
REPEAT S.R. SPACING
REPEAT S.R. SPACING
REPEAT S.R. SPACING
CONTINUE 1'-1" SPACING R.#L.
CONTINUE 1'-1" SPACING R.#L.
REPEAT SR SPACING

Figure 20-20b
Front-of-house and on-stage boom plot for *Teddy & Alice*, designed by Tharon Musser.

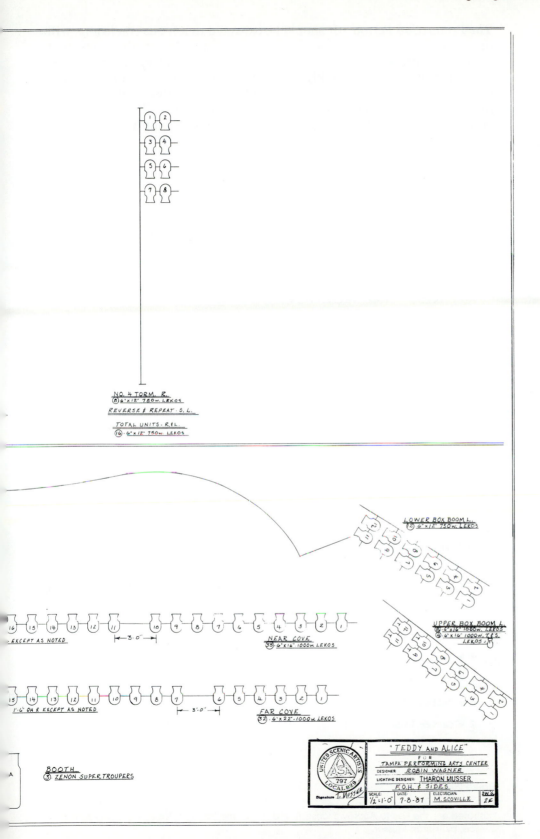

NO. 4 TORM. R.
⑧ 6"x 12" 750 W. LEKOS
REVERSE & REPEAT · S. L.

TOTAL UNITS · R & L.
⑯ · 6" x 12" 750 W. LEKOS

LOWER BOX BOOM L.
⑫ 6" x 12" 750 W. LEKOS

UPPER BOX BOOM L.
⑧ 6" x 16" 1000 W. LEKOS
④ 6" x 16" 1000 W. T. E. S.
LEKOS ·

· EXCEPT AS NOTED   ├ 3·0" ┤   NEAR COVE
                                              ㊳ 6" x 16" 1000 W. LEKOS

1'·6" ON R EXCEPT AS NOTED   ├ 3'·0" ┤   FAR COVE
                                              ㉜ · 6" x 22" · 1000 W. LEKOS

BOOTH
③ ZENON SUPER TROUPERS

UNITED SCENIC ARTISTS
ASA
LOCAL 829
797
Signature T. Musser

"TEDDY AND ALICE"
FOR
TAMPA PERFORMING ARTS CENTER
DESIGNER   ROBIN WAGNER
LIGHTING DESIGNER: THARON MUSSER
F. O. H. & SIDES
SCALE: ½"=1'·0" DATE: 7·8·'87 ELECTRICIAN: M. SCOVILLE DW'G. 2E

The Production Period • It should be expected that focus conditions will not be ideal. At best, a sound check will be going on simultaneously; at worst, carpenters will still be rigging scenery under a blaze of work lights. The job must be done quickly in order to avoid overtime wages for the electricians on the work call. It must also be done absolutely correctly, for a subsequent labor call in order to adjust focus will mean a ladder crew of four people hired at the union minimum of four hours.

a

FOCUS CHART FOR: ___TEDDY AND ALICE___

DATE ___87'___

KEY TO ABBREVIATIONS

O.O.H. = Out of House

O.O.P. = Off of Proscenium

Off Prosc. = . "

H.H. = Head High (To Fingers with Hand Held Above Head)

S.E. = Stage Edge

A.A. = As Above (Same cuts as previous lamp)

◁ = Angle Shutter

L = Stage Left

R = Stage Right

@ = At

F or FLD = Flood Focus for Fresnels

SP = Spot Focus for Fresnels

¼ SP = Lamp is ¼ way from Full Spot in a Fresnel

H = Hard Edge or Sharp in terms of focus of Lekos

S = Soft Edge or "Fuzzy"   "   "   "   "   "

M = Medium Edge

₵ = Center Line

O.F = OFF FOOTS

Figure 20-21
The Focus Chart

Illustrated are the Key to Abbreviations (a) and page one from the focus chart (b) for *Teddy & Alice*, by Tharon Musser.

b

FOCUS CHART FOR: __TEDDY & ALICE__
POSITION: __·UPPER BOX BOOM RIGHT.__

CH / UN	PLUGGED W/	FOCUS		F	TYPE	COLOR
11 / 1	0 -2- -U.B.L- 7-8	D.L. SL OFF PORTAL SR —	• +4 C 12L US H.H. DS O.F	S	6"x16" 1K LEKO	02
11 / 2	0 -1- U.B.L 7-8	D.L SL A.A. SR —	• +4 C 12L US H.H. DS O.F	S	"	35A
12 / 3	0 -4- U.B.L. 3-4	D.L O/C SL OFF. PORTAL SR —	• +4 C 4L US H.H. DS O.F.	S	"	02
12 / 4	0 -3- U.B.L 3-4	D.L O/C SL A.A. SR —	• +4 C 4L US H.H. DS O.F.	S	"	35A
13 / 5	-6- U.B.L 5-6	D. R O/L SL OFF COLUMN. SR —	• +4 C 4R US H.H DS O.F	S	"	02
13 / 6	0 -5- U.B.L 5-6	D. R O/L SL A.A. SR —	• +4 C 4R US H.H. DS O.F	S	"	35A
14 / 7	0 -8- U.B.L 1-2	D.R. SL — SR O.O.P.	• +4 @ 12R US H.H. DS O.F.	S	"	02
14 / 8	0 -7- U.B.L 1-2	D.R. SL — SR O.O.P.	• +4 @ 12R US H.H. DS O.F.	S	"	35A
78 / 9	10-11-12	(T) HOUSE FRONT SL O.O.P. SR —	• LEFT US OFF HEADER DS OFF FOOT	m s	" T & S	64A #216 BRANCHES
78 / 10	9-11-12	(T) HOUSE FRONT SL — SR —	• SL OF ¢ US CLIPS HEADER DS O.F.	m s	" T & S	"
7 / 11	9-10-12	(T) HOUSE FRONT SL O.O.P SR —	• LEFT US OFF HEADER DS O.F.	m s	" T & S	02 #294 LEAVES
79 / 12	9-10-11	(T) HOUSE FRONT SL — SR —	• SL OF ¢ US CLIPS. HEADER SLIGHTLY DS O.F.	m s	" T & S	"

POSITION & NO. __UPPER BOX BOOM RIGHT__

According to union regulations, under no condition whatever may the light designer or an assistant handle any lighting equipment, but must request one of the electricians to do so. This applies to even such innocent actions as handing a wrench to its owner, or steadying a ladder on which an electrician is working.

Moving the Show • The Broadway designer more than any other will find it necessary to design a production for more than one space. Perhaps, like *Teddy & Alice*, the production opens in one location and then moves to New York; or the show may premiere at one of the nation's regional theatres with the intent of then going to Broadway; or a production often will tour after it has had a Broadway run. In any event, the lighting designer needs to be proficient at designing for more than a single theatre.

A bus-and-truck road production will almost always carry less equipment than was on the Broadway plot. Various techniques have been developed to make setting up and focusing as easy as possible. Instrumentation might not only be reduced in numbers, but simplified in type. Lengths of pipe or track might be carried on the truck with instruments already attached. Focus charts such as the one for *Teddy & Alice* shown in Figure 20–21, as well as other time-saving devices, have been invented by those designers and electricians who frequent the road.

It is the designer's obligation to periodically drop in and check on a production during its run. If the lighting has slipped a bit from what was originally set, adjustments must be made.

The Regional Theatres

An enormous amount of exciting production is going on in our regional theatres, using both national and local designers. The chances of assisting a designer or working on the staff of these theatres are good for the talented and devoted theatre student. The first thing to do is send a resume to either the production manager or artistic director of the theatre. Then telephone and request an interview—it is that simple. Do not be discouraged if you are turned down or seemingly ignored, these people are extremely busy; but, you will get results if you are willing to be persistent.

Regional Production • Many of the professional practices that apply to lighting design on Broadway are also standard for the country's regional theatres. However, accepted practice in the regional theatres will vary a great deal from theatre to theatre. Production schemes, from repertory to stock, will influence how a lighting designer approaches his or her work. Local union rules and regulations will differ; inhouse equipment will probably exist, but will be radically different from house to house; and technical production practices will be unique to each situation.

Designing for Repertory • Traditional repertory production generally requires a daily changeover from show to show and may involve as few as two or as many as eight individual productions. The lighting designer will develop a repertory plot that acts as a basis for all shows and then add special instrumentation for each individual production. Repatching and sometimes color changes may take place during changeovers, but extensive refocusing should be avoided in repertory situations. As might be expected, a repertory design will require much more equipment than normal; and often the demands of an individual show must be compromised for the sake of the entire production scheme. Summer repertory—of Shakespeare or other classics, historical reenactments, and popular fare, especially musicals—has become a tradition in the United States. The repertory experience is an extremely valuable one in the developmental process of any lighting designer.

Designing for Stock • The vast majority of regional theatres will produce their shows in a stock arrangement, running each production continuously for a period of two to six weeks. (Summer stock productions may run only one week.) Such a scheme requires rapid changeovers from show to show and normally a new lighting design for each production. The stock designer must be able to work quickly and efficiently, remaining one step ahead of the production schedule at all times.

Those theatres that run a production for more than three weeks will most often job-in their lighting designers for each production, while those operations with shorter runs may very well employ a resident lighting designer. Either way, the lighting designer is always under a great deal of time pressure. Like repertory production, the stock experience is invaluable for the beginning lighting designer.

What To Expect • Some regional theatres will hire only designers who are United Scenic Artist members, while others pay no attention to requirements of union membership. Some will have a stagehand contract with the local I.A. union and just as many others will have no union labor affiliation. In essence, the regional designer should expect to find a new situation and new challenges in each place he or she designs.

Most cities have their own I.A. local. Rules and regulations will vary radically from local to local as will quality of workmanship. This fact is of particular concern to the regional designer, for he or she can only be sure of the quality of any local membership by previous experience or word-of-mouth. It is wise to carefully evaluate the potential work force in addition to local rule idiosyncrasies well before a production is mounted.

Stage-lighting rental houses have grown in numbers along with the spread of regional theatres across the country. Some of these local businesses will be surprisingly efficient and well-stocked, while others are woefully ill-equipped and lacking in knowledgeable personnel. The designer must anticipate the possibility of having to go to New York or some other major center for equipment needs, a situation which will surely affect budget and time considerations.

More important than commercial usage is the quite different matter of professional standards. No one should consider for a moment going into any level of commercial theatre unless he or she plans to devote total energy and ability to the routines and the problems that present themselves. It is no place for the casual enthusiast or the dilettante, nor for the easily discouraged, the supersensitive, or the noncooperative.

Stage Lighting and Electricity

An understanding of electricity may seem nothing more than a bother to the lighting designer/*artist*; but such information is essential for the lighting designer/*practitioner*. At the very least, we must understand electricity and basic electronics well enough to make intelligent choices concerning usage and safety. Unfortunately, too many people believe that electricity is solely an electrician's concern and, as a result, a curious mystique surrounds electrical practice and theory. The fact is that electrical theory and basic electrical practice are simple and quite unmysterious.

ATOMIC THEORY

According to presently accepted theories, all matter consists of molecules, which are made up of atoms. Each atom is composed of a postively charged center called the nucleus around which are distributed a number of negatively charged bodies called electrons. The nucleus of an atom consists of protons and neutrons. Neutrons have no electric charge, but each proton has a positive charge exactly equal to the negative charge of an electron.

Every normal atom has as many electrons surrounding the nucleus as it has protons within the nucleus, and thus has an equal quantity of positive and negative charges. Thus hydrogen has one proton in its nucleus and one electron outside it; helium has two protons and two electrons; lithium has three of each, carbon has six, copper has 29, and so on up to uranium, which has the most: 92 protons and 92 electrons. It is thought that the electrons are in constant motion, revolving around the nucleus in orbits much the same as the planets revolve around the sun. Figure 21–1 shows a few examples.

In the atom of lithium, the lightest of all metals, the three protons are balanced by two electrons in the inner orbit plus one in the outer orbit. Carbon also has two electrons in the inner orbit, plus four in the outer orbit, to balance the six protons. Copper requires four orbits to take care of its 29 electrons.

The various orbits are not all in the same flat plane, like a plate, but rather they are at angles to each other, somewhat like a number of rubber bands stretched haphazardly about a baseball.

The importance of all this is that the electron in the fourth and outer orbit of copper may be easily dislodged, providing a free electron, the basis of the flow of electrical current. The same is true of the outer electron in the lithium atom. In fact, all metals have electrons that can be readily dislodged and, therefore, are good electrical conductors.

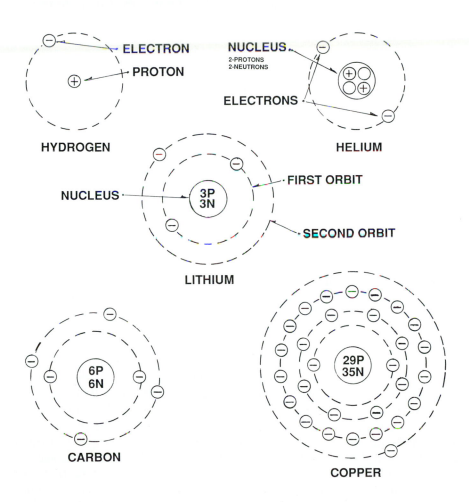

Figure 21-1
Schematic Diagram of the Structure of Certain Atoms

SOURCES OF ELECTRIC CURRENT

Just as you cannot get water to flow out of one end of a pipe unless there is water being poured into the other end, so free electrons will not move through a conductor unless there is a supply of free electrons being introduced into it. Such a supply of electrons is known as *voltage* or as an electromotive force (EMF). It can be established in a number of ways.

Battery

A common device for supplying an EMF is a battery, such as one consisting of a glass container filled with a dilute sulphuric acid solution into which are placed a strip of copper and a strip of zinc. If a meter is connected between these two strips, it will show a small electric current passing from one to the other through this connection (Figure 21–2). This is caused by the acid attacking the zinc, which dissolves into the solution and releases two electrons from each of its atoms. These electrons are left on the zinc strip, and because the acid will not permit them to return to their atoms, they flow through the wire to the copper strip.

Other Sources

An EMF may be built up in a number of ways other than the battery. *Electrostatics* produces electricity by rubbing two dissimilar substances together. *Photoelectricity* is the action of sunlight on certain photosensitive materials. *Thermoelectricity* is the application of heat to the junction of two dissimilar metals that have been welded together. *Piezoelectricity* is the mechanical compression of certain crystals. New techniques to produce electricity have been developed, but the method most important to the stage electrician is that of *electromagnetism*: the creation of an EMF through a generator, powered by water, steam, or atomic reaction.

Generator

The principle of the generator is the relative movement of a conductor within a magnetic field. The conductor may be moved while the field is stationary, or the field may be moved and the conductor remain stationary. The latter is usual in very large installations, but it is somewhat easier to comprehend the operation by considering a moving conductor in a stationary magnetic field.

The two diagrams in Figure 21–3 show a highly simplified AC generator, usually called an *alternator*. We see an armature in the shape of a single coil of wire being rotated through the magnetic field between the two poles of a magnet. This induces an EMF in the coil causing negative electrons to accumulate at slip ring 5 and flow off the slip ring through the brush and from there along the connecting wire and through a voltmeter to slip ring 4, from which they reenter the coil. In the second diagram the sides of the coil have reversed positions and directions, so now the electrons will accumulate at slip ring 4, pass through the connecting wire and meter and reenter the coil at slip ring 5. Each complete revolution of the coil is called a cycle, so for one half of each cycle the electrons move in one direction and for the other half in the opposite direction. Thus the current is said to be alternating (AC).

Figure 21-2
A Simple Copper-Zinc-Acid Battery

Figure 21-3
Diagram of an Alternator

(1) Side one of the coil. (2) Side two of the coil. (3) Direction of rotation of the coil. (4) Slip ring "A" and brush. (5) Slip ring "B" and brush. (6) Volt meter.

In Figure 21–4 we see the construction of the sine curve that represents the variation of the induced EMF for any portion of the complete cycle of the armature through the magnetic field. At the exact instant that the armature is passing the 0-degree point in its rotation it is moving parallel to the magnetic field, not through it, and hence is producing no EMF at all.

As it reaches the 30-degree mark it is cutting into the magnetic field somewhat and hence is generating a small EMF as depicted by extending a line from the 30-degree point to a somewhat later point than the 0-degree reading of 0. At the 60-degree position, an EMF of greater magnitude is produced and at 90 degrees the maximum EMF. After this the EMF drops back to 0; then in an AC generator it starts to build up in the opposite direction as depicted below the time line.

For the sake of economy it is practical to build not a single armature into a generator, but several of them. Because they must be at angles to each other, it is obvious that their respective EMFs will not reach any one point at the same instant, but rather they will produce sine curves as indicated in Figure 21–5. Here we see the very common arrangement of three armatures each producing its own curve. This is known as three-phase current and will be discussed later.

ELECTRIC UNITS OF MEASUREMENT

A *circuit* is an established path of electrical flow. Four basic measurements can be made in any electric circuit. Their definitions and relationships follow.

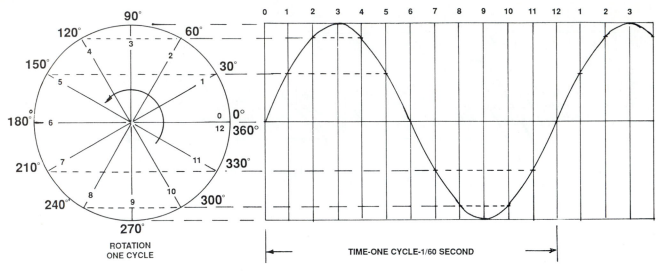

Figure 21-4
**The Construction of an AC
Sine Curve**

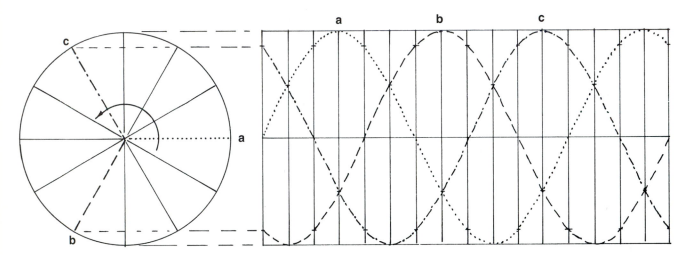

Figure 21-5
**Overlapping Sine Curves Produced
by an AC Generator with Three
Armatures at 120 Degrees to One
Another**

Volt

The volt is the difference in electrical potential between two points in a circuit. Another way of putting it is to ask how many more free electrons are there at point A than at point B, to which they will flow if a path is opened for them. Voltage is also called electromotive force (EMF), and its symbol is E.

Voltage can be thought of as the pressure behind electrical flow, although this definition is not completely accurate.

Ampere

The ampere is the rate of flow of current through a conductor: how many electrons pass a given point in one second? The symbol for the ampere in mathematics is I (for intensity of current flow). Amperage is used to describe a stage circuit's electrical capacity. For instance, most theatrical circuits will carry 20 amps.

Ohm

Every substance offers some resistance to the flow of current; some, such as copper, offer very little while others, such as rubber, offer a great deal. The ohm is the measurement of such resistance and its symbol is R.

Watt

The watt is the rate of doing work, whether it is turning an electric motor, heating an electric iron, or causing a lamp to glow. Its symbol is P, for power. Wattage can be thought of as "consumption" of electricity, although one must be aware that flowing electrons are never actually consumed.

The Power Formula

The power formula is important to remember because it expresses the relationship between wattage (P), amperage (I), and voltage (E). It states that the rate of doing work (wattage) is equal to the product of current flow (amperage) and potential (voltage):

$$P = I \cdot E \quad \text{(Called the "pie" formula)}$$

or

$$W = V \cdot A \quad \text{(Using first letters of unit names—called the "West Virginia" formula)}$$

An application of the power formula might be to determine how many 750-watt lamps one could plug into a single 20-amp circuit.

$$
\begin{array}{l}
W = 750 \text{ per lamp} \\
V = 120 \text{ (U.S. standard)} \\
A = 20 \text{ (given)}
\end{array}
$$

$$X \cdot 750 = 120 \cdot 20$$

$$X = \frac{2,400}{750}$$

$$X = 3.2$$

A 20-amp circuit thus will carry three 750-watt lamps.

Ohm's Law

Ohm's law introduces resistance (R) into a useful formula. It states that amperage (I) will equal voltage (E) divided by ohms:

$$I = \frac{E}{R}$$

DIRECT AND ALTERNATING CURRENT

Before the development of new techniques, direct current (DC) was not an efficient way to transport electricity over long distances. However, it was the only way known in the early days of electricity, and for that reason was installed in the downtown areas of many cities. Today, it has almost entirely been replaced by the more-versatile alternating current.

Alternating current has the great advantage of being easily changed from low voltage to high and from high voltage to low by means of transformers. A transformer consists of an iron core, frequently doughnut shape, about which is coiled two wires, the primary and the secondary. When an alternating current is sent through the primary coil, it sets up a magnetic flux in the iron core, and in turn this flux induces a new current in the secondary coil. It must be understood that there is no electrical connection whatever between the two coils, and that the voltage transformation is solely the result of fluctuating magnetic fields that surround any electrical conductor through which power is flowing.

If the primary has few turns about the core and the secondary has more, the voltage induced in the secondary will be higher than that in the primary, but if the primary has more turns than the secondary, then the induced voltage will be lower. These are known as "step-up" and "step-down" transformers, respectively.

Figure 21–6 depicts a portion of a typical arrangement for a modest alternating-current service. At the left side we see the AC generator station producing an EMF of 1,200 volts. This is fed to the substation where a transformer boosts it to 6,000 volts, because the higher the voltage the less loss there will be in transit (some high-power transit lines carry as much as 500,000 volts!). As the current nears the neighborhood in which it will be consumed, it passes through another substation where the EMF is reduced to 600 volts. This is sent out over a local wiring system until it reaches a house, where a small transformer on a pole by the highway reduces it still further to 120 volts for use in the home.

In this country the most common household service is 120 volts AC at 60 cycles. Many foreign countries use quite different voltages, ranging from 105 to as much as 240, and these are usually at 50 cycles or even fewer.

ELECTRIC SERVICES

It is essential for the stage electrician to know which of several possible wiring systems (referred to as "service power") is carrying electricity to the theatre. This is especially true when a touring company moves into an unfamiliar building and must connect up its portable control board and other equipment. Let us glance briefly at the three forms of service in common use (Figure 21–7).

The first is the two-wire system, in which one line is said to be "hot" and the other "neutral." The potential between them is 120 volts.

It should be noted at this point that 120-volt service is often, in fact, closer to 115 volts and may drop as low as 110 volts. But today's portable lighting equipment will operate well on any of these voltages.

The second form of service is the three-wire system, in which the two outside (hot) wires usually have a potential of 240 volts between

1200 VOLTS	6000 VOLTS	600 VOLTS	120 VOLTS
1-5	10-1	5-1	

Figure 21-6
Schematic of AC Transportation from the Generating Station to the Home

them. However, each hot wire has a potential of only 120 volts between it and the third wire, the common neutral. A familiar domestic application of this service is found in many homes, where the electric lights are on two or more circuits of 120 volts each, while the electric range operates on 240 volts.

The third type of service, and one that is popular because of its efficiency in distribution, is the AC 120–208-volt, four-wire system, also known as the three-phase system. The generation of these three phases is illustrated in Figure 21–5. The EMF produced by each phase is said to be at 120 degrees to the others. If the EMF in relation to a common neutral conductor is 120 volts, then any two phases will be 208 volts from each other, this being the product of 240 volts times the sine value

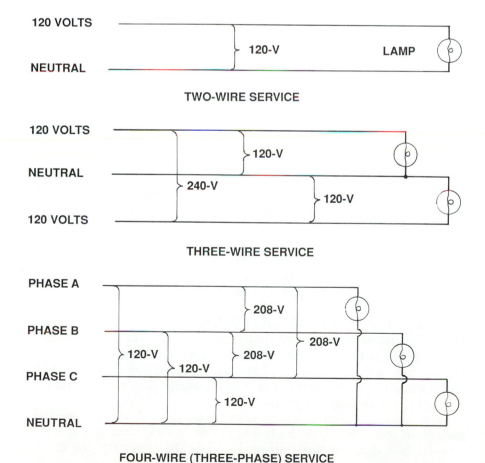

TWO-WIRE SERVICE

THREE-WIRE SERVICE

FOUR-WIRE (THREE-PHASE) SERVICE

Figure 21-7
The Three Kinds of Electrical Distribution Service

of angle 120 degrees, or .8660. Many motors are built to run on this 208 voltage, but this is of little concern to us, except that we must be sure never to connect standard-voltage equipment between two hot lines of a three-phase system. This type of service is quite commonly found in theatres.

||||➡ *SAFETY PRACTICE*

Great care must be taken with such a system to avoid connecting any apparatus designed for 120 volts across the two hot lines. The 240 volts will blow lamps at once, ruin other equipment promptly, and provide grave danger of fatal shock. The British, who use 240 volts for all their home lighting, must take precautions that would seem very irksome to us, who are used to our comparatively mild 120-volt service.

SERIES AND PARALLEL CIRCUITS

Once the current has been received from the supplying mains in any location, regardless of how it reaches the building (by two-, three-, or four-wire systems), it is distributed in two-wire systems, similar to the one diagrammed in Figure 21–7. The various elements that work in these circuits—lamps, switches, dimmers, fuses, and the like—may be connected in either of two ways.

One is the series circuit, in which the flow of current passes through the various elements successively. In the top diagram of Figure 21–8 we see that the current must pass through each of the four lamps, one after the other, before returning by the neutral wire. But in the center of the diagram the same four lamps are connected "in parallel," and it is apparent that a portion of the total current can flow simultaneously through each lamp.

Almost all practical lighting circuits are a combination of these two. The bottom diagram of Figure 21–8 shows a typical example. The switch and fuse are in series, and they are also in series with each of the lamps. But the four lamps are in parallel with one another. Let the switch be opened or the fuse blown and all the lamps will be extinguished. One of the lamps may be removed, however, and the remaining three will not be affected. In other words, the series portion is used to control the circuit as a whole, while the parallel portion is valuable as a distributor of the current.

In stage lighting we find that switches and fuses are most often replaced by circuit breakers and that these breakers and the dimmers are put in series with the stage lights for the sake of control. The circuit breaker can act as a switch, but its primary function is to protect the entire circuit against a short circuit or an overload that would result in a harmfully high flow of current.

The lights themselves are always in parallel, as several spotlights ganged on one dimmer or the lamps in one color circuit of a striplight. In each case they are simultaneously under the control of the dimmer

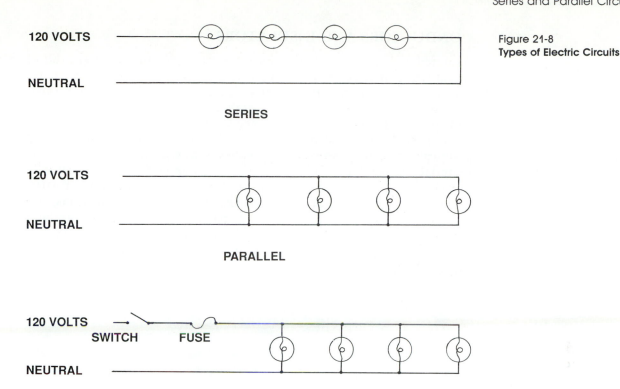

Figure 21-8
Types of Electric Circuits

and the circuit breaker, but each is independent of the other. If they were connected in series, none would burn at full brightness; and, like strands of old Christmas tree lights, if one lamp fails, no lamps can burn (the broken filament will act like a switch).

A calculation of the utmost importance in parallel circuitry is to ascertain quickly the ampere flow in a circuit. This is usually necessary when several stage instruments are ganged together or several striplights are fed through each other.

Suppose we have four spotlights ganged on one circuit, each one burning a 500-watt lamp. We may invert the power formula $(P = I \cdot E)$ to read $I = \dfrac{P}{E}$. Then:

$$I = \frac{4 \times 500}{120} = 16.67 \text{ amperes.}$$

If our circuit is fused at 20 amperes we are safe. But if we wish to change the lamps to the more powerful 750-watt variety, then:

$$I = \frac{4 \times 750}{120} = 25 \text{ amperes.}$$

This is too much for our 20-ampere circuit, so we must go back to the 500-watt lamps or put one or two of the spotlights on a different circuit.

CONDUCTORS AND INSULATORS

As noted earlier, materials that have few electrons in the outer orbit of the atoms that make them up tend to support the flow of electricity; they are called *conductors*. Actually all materials will offer some resistance to such movement, but all metals are relatively good conductors, and silver is the best of any substance known.

Because of cost, the use of silver for extensive wiring is not very practical, and some less-expensive material must be used. Copper is this material: its conductivity is almost as good as silver's, it is relatively inexpensive, and it is easy to work—to form into wires and other parts. Aluminum is coming more and more into use in some applications, and brass is valuable for large, permanent parts that need to be especially rugged. Other materials are also used for special purposes, but by and large when we think of electric wires, switch parts, and the like, we think of copper.

|||| ➡ *SAFETY PRACTICE*

An important rule to remember is that *electricity will always follow the path of least resistance.* Some sort of insulation is necessary to prevent the electrons that are flowing in a conductor from short-circuiting— that is, escaping into other channels. This "short" may result in severe shock to anyone chancing to come in contact with the new and unprotected channel of flow. And because it may offer little resistance, this new channel may allow a higher current than the legitimate circuit was designed to carry, thereby causing damage to it.

Just as there is no material that is 100-percent conductive, so there is nothing that has 100-percent insulative properties, but there are many materials that can serve various practical purposes. Glass and ceramics are excellent for small permanent parts such as sockets and switches; slate for larger switch and fuse panels; and asbestos where heat is involved. For wires and cables, rubber and fiber are used; while plastics are becoming increasingly common. The most-useful *insulator* of all is dry air. If this were not so, every open socket or wall outlet would drain off current!

Permanent wiring such as stage circuits, which should be laid by a licensed electrician only, may have a solid copper core through which the current flows, but the temporary wiring cable used on the stage always has a core made up of a number of small strands of wire. This is to provide proper flexibility in handling and laying. Standard stage cable consists of two or three such cores, each surrounded by a strong rubber insulation. For physical strength, tough fiber cords are laid alongside, and the whole surrounded by either a rubber and/or a fiber sheathing.

Grounding

National electrical codes now specify that all new electrical installations be grounded. Grounding requires that a circuit or cable have three rather than two wires. The third, the ground wire, is designed to offer an emergency path through which the current can flow in case of a short circuit. The wires of a stage cable or circuit are always covered with rubber insulation color coded as follows:

Black or red = "hot" line

White = "neutral" or "common" line

Green = ground

|||➡ *SAFETY PRACTICE*

Care must be taken in wiring plugs onto cable that the ground wire in particular is attached to the proper pin of the connector (see "Types of Connector").

Always remember that *Green is Ground.*

Stage Cable

Stage cable comes in different sizes, or gauges, each of which is designed to carry a specific maximum current or amperage. These limits should never be exceeded. The most-useful sizes are:

Size (gauge number):	18	16	14	12	10	8	6
Capacity (amperes):	3	6	15	20	25	35	50

The most-common (nearly standard) stage circuit will carry 20 amps. As a result, the most-common cable will be #12, Type SO (rubber coated). Occasionally, for a very small load and a very short run, ordinary lamp cord (or zip cord), which has an 18-gauge core, may be used, but this should be kept to a minimum and carefully guarded against abuse.

A final category of stage cable must be mentioned here because of its inevitable importance to a successful put-in. The first members of this category are cables that allow the electrician to plug several lighting instruments into a single circuit. These cables may be called "two-fers," "Y-connectors," "spiders," or "three-fers"; all of them allow the electrician to plug two or three instruments into one circuit. One must remember that 20 amps is circuit capacity. Adaptors are the other type of special category cable. Simple adaptors are seldom more than 2-feet long, with one of various connectors on each end. Applications are endless, but an example of the use of an adaptor would be plugging a backstage work light equipped with a pin connector into an "Edison" or parallel blade socket.

STAGE CONNECTORS

Types of Connector

Lights on stage are temporary. They are moved after each production and even between scenes of a play. Thus, it is not wise to make permanent

Figure 21-9
Connectors

(a) Female and male heavy duty parallel-blade plugs (ungrounded). (b) Female and male twist-lock connectors (ungrounded). (c) Female and male three-wire (grounded) twist-lock connectors. (d) Male and female pin connectors (ungrounded). (e) Male and female three-wire (grounded) pin connectors. (f) Full stage plug (no longer in common use).

connections of the cables to the various lighting instruments. Devices that can be easily connected and disconnected are needed. Ordinary household plugs with parallel blades are used on some small stages, but because they are easily disconnected in error and have limited capacities, they are not advisable. A departure from this style that is in popular use is the twist lock, roughly similar in appearance to a heavy-duty parallel blade plug but with a design that permits the male and female caps to be locked together quite easily yet firmly (see Figure 21–9).

Beware!

Unfortunately, the electrical industry has seen fit to manufacture an amazingly large number of twist-lock blade configurations. The most-common, stage twist lock is the 20-amp, three-prong variety, which, however, comes in several styles. The most significant difference among these styles is in the third or grounding blade, which will often have a part of the blade bent either toward the center of the plug or toward the outside. These two variations are commonly called "pin-in" or "pin-out," respectively, and cannot be used interchangeably.

When wiring a three-prong twist lock, always be sure that the grounding (green) wire is connected to the grounding prong (marked "G" or having a green screw head).

Pin connectors, heavy-duty fiber blocks with sturdy brass pins and sockets, are probably used as much as any other devices. They have the disadvantage of not always giving a firm electrical connection, and they can be easily pulled apart by mistake unless the two cables or connectors are tied together. Pin connectors have a "split" down the center of each brass male pin (hence the name split-pin connector). If a pin is not making a good connection, electrical arcing will occur and the connector will overheat. To avoid this, the individual pins can be "split" or slightly separated with a small knife blade.

Note that in pin connectors with three pins. the grounding pin is *always* the center pin.

As in the case with cables, all such connectors come in different sizes, each rated to carry specific maximum amperages. For the stage it is wise to settle on one size and one type of connector to avoid confusion and save time. The 15-ampere pin connector or the 20-ampere twist lock is the usual choice.

The connectors described above can all be used to join a lighting instrument to a cable, or two cables to each other, or a cable to a switch-board or cross-connect panel. There is also a nearly obsolete device, known as a stage plug, that is used solely to connect a cable to a switch-board or a plugging box designed to accept it. The stage plug is a block of hard wood with a strip of brass down each of its edges that fits into a porcelain receptacle of rectangular shape. The standard plug is about 1-inch thick and is rated to carry 50 amperes.

Wiring Connectors

Proper wiring of stage connectors is important to ensure against short circuiting or loose connections which can result in arcing within the plug. Stage cable and "leads" from lighting instruments will consist of small strands of copper wire. The easiest method of wiring a pin connector is to twist the small strands together (forming a more cohesive single strand) and then wrap the exposed wire around the screw terminal (Figure 21–10). Be sure to take the following precautions: (1) Expose only as much bare wire as is necessary. (2) Always wrap the wire in the direction the screw will turn when being tightened down (clockwise). (3) Be sure that the connector's strain relief is effective. The strain relief feature of a stage connector will ensure that any pulling tension is placed on the cable rather than on the connecting terminals.

Pin connectors are available for two different types of stage cable: rubber cable (Type SO) and individual fiber-covered leads from instruments. The rubber cable type will have a single hole in the back of the connector while the other type will have two or three smaller holes. These two connector types should not be used interchangeably.

A better and safer technique of wiring a connector involves "tinning" the exposed copper wire. The tinning process simply requires soldering all the small copper strands together to form one stiffer strand. This tinned lead will then be connected to the terminal as explained.

a   b   c

Figure 21-10
Steps in Wiring a Pin Connector

(a) Remove cover plate. (b) Wrap wire around screw terminal clockwise, making sure the green, or ground, wire is attached to the center screw terminal. (c) Tighten screws and replace cover plate, making sure the strain relief is effective.

A third technique involves the use of a small connecting device commonly called a "Sta-kon" (Figure 21–11). The "Sta-kon" is pinched onto the exposed wire with a crimping tool. The ring is then placed around the screw terminal of the connector. Make sure that the "Sta-kon" is the proper size for the wire and that the two or three "Sta-kons" cannot make contact with each other.

Perhaps it is obvious, but one should realize that a male connector must never be "hot" or "live." For example, leads from a lighting instrument will always terminate in a male connector so that the "live" shielded female connector will plug into it.

SWITCHES

A switch is a device put into a circuit to interrupt and restore the flow of current as desired, or, in more familiar terminology, to open and close the circuit. There are many types of mechanical switches, from the familiar domestic wall type to great knife-blade arrangements that handle many hundreds of amperes. Like everything else electrical, the type and size to use depends on the duty the switch is expected to perform and the load it is intended to carry.

The "disconnect" box is a heavy-duty switch housed in a metal box which may also contain fuses (Figure 21–12). A disconnect may be permanently mounted in the theatre to receive temporary lighting-control equipment, thus allowing quick and easy access to a power supply. In addition, a disconnect box, fused to the proper amperage for a traveling control system or other electrical apparatus, might also be carried by a touring production. In this case, the disconnect (fused at 100 amps, for example) would be connected to a larger amperage power supply (perhaps another disconnect) in order to protect the touring equipment from a power overload.

A contactor is an electrically operated device in which a small switch, located at some convenient place onstage, controls a magnet that operates a large-capacity switch in a remote spot. This has the double advantage of keeping the dangerously high current at a distance from the operator and allowing the heavy-duty portion, which is very noisy, to be placed where it cannot distract the audience.

CIRCUIT PROTECTION

No chain is stronger than its weakest link, and should an electric circuit suffer damage that causes a short circuit somewhere along the line, the ampere flow will increase to a point where *something* must burn out. The same thing will happen in the case of an overload—that is, if too

Figure 21-12
Disconnect Box

Shown is a 300-amp three-phase disconnect. Power in at the top goes through knife switches (shown in off position) and fuses to copper buss bars. Touring "road boards" and auxiliary equipment are connected to the buss bars by means of lugs or bolts.

a
250 AMP

b
150 AMP

c
100 AMP

d
60 AMP

e
30 AMP

f
5 AMP

h
30 AMP

i
3 AMP

j
25 AMP

k
10 AMP

g
20 AMP

Figure 21-13
Fuses and a Circuit Breaker

(a), (b), & (c) Knife-blade cartridge fuses, capacities as indicated. (d), (e), & (f) Ferrule-tipped cartridge fuses. (g) A typical circuit breaker. (h) & (i) Standard plug fuses. (j) & (k) Type-S fuses (note the difference in the threads as shown in the inserts).

many lamps are connected to the circuit. By using the power formula, we see that if six 500-watt lamps are connected to a 120-volt circuit, 25 amperes will flow through it. If 14-gauge wire, which has a capacity for only 15 amperes, is used in the circuit, its limit will be greatly exceeded and again something must burn out.

To protect against such occurrences, fuses of suitable capacities are inserted to form the weakest link in the electrical chain. Then, should the current flow increase to dangerous levels, it will be the fuse that gives way, thus breaking the circuit and preventing more serious damage. The fault is then located and corrected, and a new fuse is inserted with a minimum of trouble.

Figure 21–13 shows various forms of fuses in common use at the voltages usually encountered in stage-lighting circuitry. Everyone is familiar with the plug fuse which screws into a socket like a lamp. There is a special and very useful variation of the plug fuse known as nontamperable or "type S," which has one thickness of threading for ratings up to 15 amperes and a different threading for those rated 16 to 30 amperes. The socket is designed to take either one threading or the other but not both. When wiring up a switchboard, for example, the electrician will install a socket that takes only the proper-capacity fuse, depending on the other elements in that circuit. Thus no one can change to a higher-capacity fuse, and the circuit is always protected.

A different shaped fuse is the cartridge, which is available in contact types, sizes, and ratings as listed below.

CONTACTS	LENGTHS	CAPACITIES
Ferrule	2 inches	up to 30 amperes
	3 inches	31 to 60 amperes
Knifeblade	5⅞ inches	61 to 100 amperes
	7⅛ inches	101 to 200 amperes
	8⅝ inches	201 to 400 amperes
	10⅜ inches	401 to 600 amperes

If fuses continue to blow whenever replaced, it is a sign that there is either an overload or a short circuit, and immediate steps should be taken to eliminate the hazard. Overfusing, or bypassing a fuse, is a dangerous and foolish practice that can cause a fire.

Circuit Breakers

Today, in many installations, the fuse has been replaced by the circuit breaker. This, briefly, is a form of switch that automatically opens when

Figure 21-14
Neon Test Light

the current flow becomes higher than it should. For most installations the circuit breaker is a great convenience: it saves the trouble of keeping a supply of fuses on hand, it cannot be carelessly replaced by one of the wrong capacity, and it can also serve as a switch for the circuit.

TESTING EQUIPMENT

A stage electrician must have ready access to various testing tools in order to "troubleshoot" electrical problems which invariably arise precisely when time is most critical. These tools range from the simplest test lights to rather sophisticated meters. A test light such as the one shown in Figure 21–14 will indicate whether an electrical circuit is "live" simply by either lighting or refusing to light. Test lights should be inexpensive, easy to carry, and hard to break. The neon tester shown in the figure should prove most satisfactory.

A fairly recent addition to the line of stage testing equipment is the compact continuity tester (manufactured by Frontal Lobe, Ann Arbor,

Figure 21-15
Volt-Ohm Milliammeters
(a) V.O.M. with standard scale. (b) V.O.M. with digital read-out. *Photos courtesy Simpson Electric Company*

a

b

MI). This simple, female pin connector contains a small battery that passes a low-voltage electrical current through a connected circuit. If the circuit is complete (lamp good, connector good, cable good, and so forth), a small indicator lamp in the tester will light. This simple device eliminates the necessity of a circuit being live to test for a break. A continuity test, as its name indicates, will simply determine whether a circuit is complete.

More-sophisticated testing equipment in the form of meters can read voltage, amperage, and resistance (ohms) in a circuit. Most meters will combine functions (such as the V.O.M.—volt-ohm milliammeter), are fairly delicate, and are also fairly expensive (Figure 21–15).

|||▶ *SAFETY PRACTICE*

Electrical safety, like most everything else, is a matter of common sense. If you don't know what you're doing, don't do it! Attention to the following points will be helpful:

1. Always remember that electrical current will follow the path of least resistance and that your body could be that path.
2. Insulation is a good thing. Tools should be insulated with plastic or rubber handles. Soles of shoes should provide good insulation.
3. Electrical fires are most commonly caused by heat buildup caused by arcing or a short circuit.
4. Know the locations of electrical (red) fire extinguishers.
5. Fuses and circuit breakers protect equipment and ensure circuit safety. Never attempt to bypass them.
6. Never use a metal ladder for electrical work unless it is insulated with rubber foot pads on all legs. Wooden ladders are always safest.
7. Be particularly wary of damp or wet conditions. Water is a fairly good electrical conductor.
8. Strain relief in electrical connectors is important.
9. Green is ground.
10. Voltage kills.

Light Sources

The development of even an adequate lighting design depends on a strong working knowledge of light sources and instrumentation: quality of light, distribution of light, intensity of light, color of light, and shaping or control of light. Obviously, much of this has to do with the actual source of illumination. The theatre uses three basic types of light sources:

1. *Incandescence*—Light given off by a glowing metal filament.
2. *Arc light*—Electrical arc that gives off intense illumination.
3. *Gaseous discharge*—Light production that depends on reaction of gases within an enclosure, but also requires an electrical arc.

INCANDESCENT LAMP

The most common source of light used on the stage today is the incandescent filament lamp: a gas-filled glass bulb containing a tungsten filament that emits light when an electrical current is passed through it. Tungsten is a metal that is relatively resistant to electrical flow. As a result, it will heat up and glow when a current is passed through it. The three important parts (Figure 22–1) of an incandescent lamp are the bulb (the glass envelope that encloses the inert gas); the base (to hold the lamp in position and to make electrical contact); and the filament (to pass the current, yet offer enough resistance to effect the transfer of electrical energy into light energy).

There are two basic categories of incandescent lamps: the standard incandescent lamp and the tungsten-halogen lamp. Thomas Edison developed the standard incandescent lamp in 1879, and it really has not changed much over the years. The tungsten-halogen lamp (also called "quartz lamp," after the type of glass enclosure) was developed in the 1950s and has become a popular theatrical lamp for reasons that will be discussed throughout the chapter.

Lamp Filaments

A passing acquaintance with optics (not a bad thing for lighting designers) tells us that a reflector of light wants to see as tiny a source as possible.

Figure 22-1
Parts of a Standard
Incandescent Lamp

(1) Gas-filled G-shaped bulb.
(2) Barrel filament. (3) Filament
supports. (4) Lead-in wire. (5) Screw
base. (6) Bottom contact button.
(7) L.C.L. (light center length).

The smaller the source, the more efficiently the reflector will carry out
its job of gathering and precisely redirecting the light rays. Since almost
all stage-lighting equipment uses reflectors of various types, the ideal
lamp filament would be what we refer to as a "point source" (the size of
a pinhead would do nicely). We have a long way to go toward achieving
such a source, but attempts have been made to make tungsten filaments
as compact as possible. The tungsten wire is often coiled (designated "C")
and, in the case of tungsten-halogen lamp filaments, double-coiled (designated "CC" and called a coiled coil) in order to maintain as small a
size as possible (Figure 22–2e).

Among the standard incandescent filament forms used in stage-
lighting equipment are the barrel (C–5) and the corona (C–7). These are
designed to throw out their light equally in all directions. On the other
hand, the monoplane (C–13) and the biplane (C–13D) emit most of their
light in two opposite directions only, thereby permitting a larger proportion to be picked up and made useful by a reflector or a lens. The popular
tungsten-halogen lamp uses a filament that is double coiled and tends to
be a bit longer and narrower than the standard incandescent filament
(Figure 22–2).

The LCL (light-center length) of a lamp is the distance from the center
of the filament to some definite place in the base. With a screw-base
lamp, the measurement is to the contact button at the end of the base
(Figure 22–1). With a prefocus base it is to the fins, and with the bi-pin
to the shoulder of the pins. It is particularly important to know the LCL
when a lamp is to be used in conjunction with a reflector or a lens, for
the center of the filament must be exactly aligned with the focal points
of such optical devices.

One important characteristic of the incandescent filament is that
when voltage to a lamp is reduced by using a dimmer, the color of light
emitted is altered. This can be extremely important on the stage and also
in color television, for the appearance of colored materials such as costumes and scenery, and even the faces of the actors, may be changed.
This color shift will be discussed in greater detail later in this chapter.

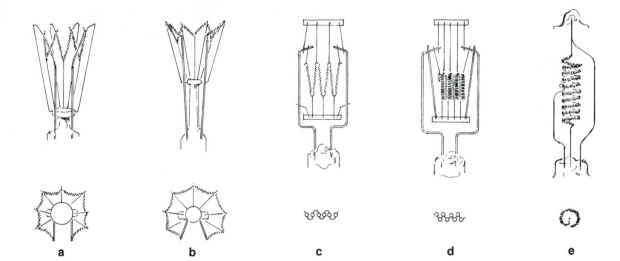

a   b   c   d   e

Lamp Bulbs

The bulbs of standard incandescent lamps are made of ordinary glass, while the bulbs of tungsten-halogen lamps are made of the more heat- and pressure-resistant quartz glass. As a result, the standard incandescent bulb needs to be larger in order to dissipate the heat given off by the filament. The smaller envelope of the tungsten-halogen lamp has an important advantage over the standard incandescent lamp, for the size of a stage-lighting instrument is often dictated by lamp size.

Bulbs come in a variety of shapes, sizes, and finishes. The shape of a bulb is designated by a letter. The A (for arbitrary) and PS (for pear-shape with straight sides) are common forms seen in the general line of household lamps (Figure 22–3). Lamps used in stage-lighting instruments may be globe-shaped (G) to permit the even dissipation of heat but are usually tubular (T) to allow the filament to be brought closer to some optical feature. There are a number of other shapes, some of which are purely decorative. The common and useful R and PAR reflector lamps will be discussed separately.

The size of a bulb is designated by a numbering system which may seem unnecessarily complex but which is, at least, standardized. The diameter of the bulb at its largest point is expressed in eighths of an inch, and this number is used to designate size. Therefore, a T–6 lamp (common in ellipsoidal reflector spotlights) means that the bulb is tubular in shape and $6/8$ of an inch (or $3/4$-inch) in diameter.

Bulb Finishes and Color • Lamps used on the stage usually are made of clear glass, which is essential for any source used in an instrument with reflector or lens. But the smaller wattage A and PS lamps are more readily obtained with an inner finish (called "frosting") that is intended to diffuse the light. If desired, these sizes can be ordered in the clear-glass style, but this is seldom necessary because they are rarely used in stage-lighting instruments of any precision. There are many kinds of finishes available, some purely decorative and others for some special application. The side-silvered showcase lamp that can be tucked away behind very little cover

Figure 22-2
Filaments Frequently Used in Stage-Lighting Instruments

The upper row shows a side view, the bottom row an end view of each. (a) The barrel. (b) The corona. (c) The monoplane. (d) The biplane. (e) The coiled coil.

Figure 22-3
Typical Bulb Shapes
(A) Arbitrary designation. (S) Straight
side. (PS) Pear shape. (T) Tubular.
(PAR) Parabolic aluminized reflector.
(G) Globular. (R) Reflector. (C) Cone
shape.

is often handy on the stage for throwing a little light in difficult corners.
Colored-glass lamps are obtainable in the smaller wattages only and are
not very useful on the stage except in the smallest installations.

Lamp Bases

The electrical contact part of the base of a lamp is generally made of
copper, though aluminum is now being used for many of the smaller
wattages. The base may be any of several sizes, but the medium size (as
in common household lamps) with a 1-inch diameter and the mogul with
1½-inch diameter are the ones most commonly used in standard incandescent theatre lamps. The tungsten-halogen lamp, because of its smaller
size, will almost always have a smaller base; bi-pin being the most popular type.

Bases also vary in type, with the common screw base (which comes
in all sizes) being the simplest (Figure 22–4). Occasionally this type is
sufficient, but it is often necessary to provide some sort of locking device
in the base so that the lamp and particularly its filament may be held in
a precise relationship with optical features of the instruments in which
it is designed to burn. This relationship is referred to as "lamp alignment." Standard incandescent lamps requiring specific alignment will
usually have medium or mogul prefocus bases. Smaller lamps such as
the 100–150-watt, 3-inch Fresnel lamp may use the bayonet base illustrated in Figure 22–4. The prefocus bases and the bayonet base slip into
the socket and require slight pressure downward and a turn before the
lamp "clicks" into alignment.

Tungsten-halogen lamps will normally have special bases, although
quartz lamps called "retrofits" are manufactured with standard incandescent bases so that the newer T-H lamps can be used in lighting instruments designed for standard incandescent lamps. Most T-H lamps
have one of two types of bases: the bi-pin base or the double-ended,
recessed single-contact base (Figure 22–5). The bi-pin lamp slides straight
into its socket and is held in place by a pressure plate. Excessive handling
or jarring may cause this lamp to dislodge from its base, so care must be
taken with instruments requiring the bi-pin lamp. The double-ended
lamp is held in place by two metal contacts mounted so that they pro-

Figure 22-4
Common base types

BAYONET   **MINI-CAN**   **BI-PIN**

SCREW   **PREFOCUS**

trude through the reflector of an instrument. Depending on the design of the lighting instrument, these lamps can be difficult to get properly seated. Care must therefore be taken not to damage either the contacts or the seal of the lamp base, which is most often porcelain or glass. A fairly recent addition to T-H lamp bases is the small-size screw base called a "mini-can" (short for miniature candelabra) base. This base is extremely easy to use and holds up quite well under the high heat conditions of the T-H lamp.

TUNGSTEN-HALOGEN LAMPS

The development of the tungsten-halogen lamp led to significant changes in the lighting industry. The most important, perhaps, was the creation of smaller and more-powerful lighting instruments designed specifically for these lamps, a development that freed the lighting designer from the restrictions of relatively archaic equipment. Not only are the T-H lamps much more compact than standard incandescent lamps (Figure 22–5), but they also have a much longer life and maintain initial intensity throughout their lifespan.

500W TO 1000W

1500W TO 2000W

500W TO 1000W

750W TO 1000W

BI-PIN   **DOUBLE ENDED**   **I**   **T-H**

Figure 22-5
Tungsten-Halogen Lamps

(Left) Two common types. (Right) Incandescent and tungsten-halogen lamp, both with medium prefocus bases.

The secret of this significant innovation is the halogen-family gas introduced into the bulb. As a tungsten filament burns, particles evaporate from the filament and deposit themselves on the cooler glass envelope. The result of this process is a gradual darkening of the bulb and, consequently, a lessening of light output from the lamp. In the T-H lamps, however, the halogen gas gobbles up the elusive tungsten particles and redeposits them at the hottest point within the bulb: the filament. (The lamp ultimately fails only because the halogen gas does not redeposit the particles evenly.) Because the desired reaction between the tungsten particles and halogen gas requires a great deal of heat, the glass envelope is made smaller and constructed out of strong quartz glass.

The tungsten-halogen lamp is more expensive than a standard incandescent lamp of comparable wattage; but its life is nearly two times longer and it is more efficient.

A disadvantage of the T-H lamp is that the quartz glass envelope cannot be touched by fingers. No matter how clean your hands happen to be, oil from your skin is deposited on the glass and will react with the quartz when it is heated. The result of this reaction not only weakens the envelope (possibly causing explosion) but also produces a frosted effect on the glass (if we had wanted frosted, we would have ordered frosted).

R AND PAR LAMPS

The R (reflector type) and PAR (parabolic aluminized reflector) lamps are discussed separately here because each is essentially a self-contained lighting instrument. Both the R- and PAR-type contain a parabolic-shaped reflector, either a standard incandescent filament or a small quartz lamp and a sort of lens. Because much of the light emitted by the filament is reflected out of the lamps in a useful direction, and because the reflector is sealed into the bulb itself, R and PAR lamps are extremely efficient.

PAR lamps are made out of molded, heat-resistant glass and can be used outdoors without danger of cracking if snow or rain strike them while they are hot. They are a good deal heavier and sturdier than the Rs, which are made of blown glass and are light in weight and more fragile.

A PAR lamp costs more than an equivalent wattage R-type, but it will deliver a more powerful beam of light. However, the R-type lamps have a smoother pattern of light. Both lamps are available in spot and flood beam spreads from 75 to 500 watts; higher wattage PAR lamps are available in wide flood and in medium, narrow, and very narrow beams. The lower wattage R-type and PAR lamps have medium screw bases (up to 500 watts); R-type lamps above 500 watts have mogul screw bases; and the larger (300–1,500 watt) PAR lamps have either side or end-prong bases (Figure 22–6).

Automobile headlights have used PAR lamps for years, but it took rock-concert lighting to introduce these high wattage lamps to the theatre (see "Instruments," Chapter 18). Quartz PAR-64 lamps are mounted in a very simple housing (aptly named PAR cans) and have the ability to throw a highly concentrated beam of light over a considerable distance. The light has a very distinctive quality because of its nearly parallel rays and its sheer intensity. The beam from quartz PAR lamps is more oval than round because of the filament shape and has a very soft and fuzzy edge, making it possible to blend one beam with another. The direction of the oval beam is altered simply by rotating the lamp within the PAR can housing. The PAR lamp has one distinct disadvantage over more conventional stage-lighting instruments: It is nearly impossible to control and shape the beam. Therefore, the application of PAR lamps to theatrical lighting, although significant, has been limited.

Because of the great breadth of beam typical of R and PAR lamps, they can be very useful in striplights, where it is necessary to blend the light from different color circuits smoothly and at close range. Since the reflectors are sealed into the bulbs, there is no worry about dirt or corrosion affecting their surfaces. If the same type and size of base is used, it is a simple matter to change from type to type depending on the precise effect desired. For example, PAR spots may be used for a long, very intense throw and R floods for a short throw where smoothness is more important than brightness. It should be emphasized that the beam pattern from the R-type lamp is quite superior to that of the PAR, and, as a result, the R-type is a better general purpose striplight lamp.

Small wattage (30–75 watts) R-20 and R-30 lamps, often used in showcase lighting applications, are frequently useful in lighting tight spaces where a standard stage-lighting instrument would be too large, heavy, or clumsy.

Figure 22-6
PAR-64 Lamp

Shown with extended mogul end prong base.

LAMP LIFE

The rated-average life for the common household lamp is usually 750 burning hours, but for many standard incandescent stage lamps it is only 200 hours. Rated-average life is determined by the manufacturer, who takes a number of lamps at random and leaves them burning under normal conditions until (1) they burn out completely or (2) their light output drops to 80 percent of what it was originally.

Rated-average life is presumed to apply under usual operating conditions. But a lamp's life may be shortened in a number of ways. It will give out more quickly if burned while enclosed in an excessively hot place such as one from which its own heat cannot escape (lighting instruments are specifically ventilated for this purpose). Rough handling may break some interior part, even though the outer appearance has not changed. *Never* jar an instrument with the lamp burning, for the supple tungsten filament will almost surely break. If connected to a higher voltage than it was designed for, a lamp will burn out rapidly, even abruptly. And in the case of many standard incandescent lamps used in stage instruments, burning in the wrong position results in rapid failure. The correct burning position, if important, will always be marked on the end of the bulb and should be consulted if any doubt exists.

Standard incandescent T-12 and T-14 lamps are particularly susceptible to failure if they are burned in the wrong position. A nonquartz T lamp designed to be used in an ellipsoidal spotlight should be burned base up, or nearly so, for the filament is close to the end of the bulb, which would be melted by the heat if it accumulated there. On the other

Figure 22-7
Dissipation of Heat from Incandescent Lamps
(a) A lamp designed to be burned base up. (b) Lamps designed to be burned base down.

hand, the T-20 lamp intended to be used in a Fresnel spotlight should be burned base down or no more than 90 degrees from the perpendicular, for the filament is close to the base and if the heat should concentrate there it would crack the cement seal between bulb and base (Figure 22–7). All T-H lamps (except retrofits) are designed to burn in any position.

If a lamp designed to be used on 120-volt service is fed with only 110 volts, the lamp will last almost four times as long as it would on 120 volts, but there will be only about 74 percent as much light.

On the other hand, if this same lamp is fed 130 volts, there will be 31 percent more light, but the lamp will last only a third as long.

This relationship of voltage, intensity, and life must be kept in mind, especially when bargains in "lamps that burn twice as long" or the like are offered. It also explains why stage lamps often last far longer than anticipated: they have been burned at low dimmer readings.

Wattage and Lumen Output

The general public has been taught by lamp manufacturers to equate the wattage of a lamp with its brightness. If our 75-watt reading lamp is too dim, we simply replace it with a 100-watt lamp. But, as we learned in Chapter 21, wattage is the rate of doing work and, therefore, is not necessarily an accurate measure of lamp intensity. Lamp manufacturers use a measure of intensity called the *lumen* to measure the light output of a lamp. Figure 22–8 shows how two lamps with identical physical specifications can be very different in brightness (compare DWT and FER). Note that as lumen output is increased, lamp life is significantly decreased.

Watts	GE Ordering Code	ANSI Code	National Stock No. 6240-00-	Std. Pkg. Qty.	Approx. Color Temp. °K	Approx. Hours Life	Approx. Initial Lumens	Lighted Length— Inches	Bulb Finish
1000	**Q1000T6/CL**	DWT	917-6915	6	3000	2,000	23,400	1	Clear
	FER-Q1000T6/4CL	FER	—	6	3200	500	27,500	3/4	Clear
1500	**DVV-Q1500T8/4CL**	DVV (11)	—	6	3200	500	42,700	1 1/4	Clear
2000	**FEY-Q2000T8/4CL**	FEY	231-0761	6	3200	300	59,000	1	Clear

COLOR TEMPERATURE

We tend to think of the light emitted from an ordinary lamp as being "white," but the fact is that so-called "white" light is relative, and the actual color of light given off by sources can vary greatly. The method we have to identify the color make-up of any light source is called *color temperature* and its measurement is in Kelvin (K) degrees. To standardize color notation, a light-emitting device called a "blackbody" was developed; when heated it emits light consisting of various color wavelengths. The blackbody responds to heat in much the same way that a tungsten filament does; it begins to glow a very warm red-yellow, moves toward "white" as more heat is applied, and will finally appear to approach blue when a great deal of heat is applied. The color wavelengths of light emitted by the blackbody are identified by a sophisticated meter called a "spectrophotometer." Any color can thus be equated with the temperature of heat being applied to the blackbody, resulting in a meaningful Kelvin figure.

This is fairly important for a lighting designer to understand because theatre sources will typically range from standard incandescence, which is around 3,000° K, to the much cooler arc lamps which can be as high as 6,000° K. Obviously, the same color filter placed in front of two such different sources will project very different colors. For all practical purposes, no one will notice a source color difference of less than 200° K; but any more of a difference will be noticeable. The color temperature of stage lamps is often printed on their containers and is always noted in catalogs. A general rule to go by is the higher the color temperature, the cooler the light. And always realize that dimming a source decreases color temperature significantly.

IDENTIFYING AND PURCHASING LAMPS

The American National Standards Institute (ANSI) has established a system for identifying lamps by a three-letter code called the "ANSI code." If one lamp differs in any way from another, it will be assigned a separate ANSI code (Figure 22–8). Although the three-letter codes are totally nondescriptive by themselves, they have greatly simplified the process of specifying lamps. One may now simply order a lamp by giving the supplier the ANSI code.

A lighting instrument is often designed with a certain lamp or lamps in mind. The instrument's ventilation, base type and size, and reflector specifications may all be determined by the choice of lamp. All stage-

Figure 22-8
Comparison of Wattage, Color Temperature, Life, and Lumen Output

Table courtesy General Electric Company. Publication SS-123: Stage Studio Lamps lighting manufacturers provide specific lamp recommendations for their instruments; usually allowing a choice of several different lamps depending upon the user's preference.

RECOMMENDED LAMPS

The table below is a sampling from the Colortran and Strand Lighting catalogs:

WATTS	ANSI CODE	COLOR TEMPERATURE	LIFE (HOURS)
Ellipsoidals			
1,000	FEL	3,200° K	300
750	EHF	3,200° K	500
750	EHG	3,000° K	2,000
6" Fresnel			
1,000	BTR	3,200° K	200
750	BTN	3,050° K	500
750	BTP	3,200° K	200
8" Fresnel			
2,000	BVW	3,200° K	250
1,500	CWZ	3,200° K	325
1,000	BVT	3,050° K	500
1,000	BVV	3,200° K	200

Note that several lamps of the same wattage are listed, but their color temperature and lamp life differ. If one investigates a bit further delving into a lamp catalog, it will be discovered that intensity (rated in initial lumens) also differs. For instance, initial lumen output of the 1,000-watt BVT is 24,500 lumens, while that of the 1,000-watt BVV is 28,500. The price paid is 300 fewer hours of life.

Of course, the wise electrician will be familiar with all possible variations in lamp manufacture and will have access to up-to-date lamp catalogs. Not only are these catalogs useful when ordering spare lamps, but they also offer quick access to special application lamps such as flashbulbs, low-voltage lamps, and photo-floods. The two major lamp manufacturers in the United States are willing to supply you with their current catalogs. Write to either their regional sales offices or to the following addresses:

SYLVANIA
GTE Products Corp.
Lighting Center
Danvers, MA 01923

GENERAL ELECTRIC
General Electric Company
Lighting Business Group
Nela Park
Cleveland, OH 44112

In addition to its lamp catalogs, Sylvania publishes a short and easy-to-use book called *Sylvania Lighting Handbook* (currently in its seventh edition), which will be sent to you upon request.

LOW-VOLTAGE LAMPS

Low-voltage light sources are lamps designed to operate with less than 120 applied volts. Sealed-beam automobile headlights operate to full potential with only 12 volts, while aircraft lamps operate with 24 volts. The advantage of low-voltage lamps for theatre application is in the intensity and quality of the light they emit. The lower the voltage applied to a lamp filament, the smaller the filament can be. Therefore, low-voltage sources have filaments that really do begin to approach the much-desired point source of light. The more closely we approximate a point source, the better we can control the light through the use of reflectors and lenses.

Low-voltage lamps such as aircraft landing lamps (ACLs) deliver an incredibly coherent light that is intense and harsh in quality. To use such lamps on the stage, however, a low-voltage power source is necessary. A variable voltage transformer is a good equipment investment for an active theatre, but it can be fairly expensive. Two substitutes come to mind. The first is the continuous-duty, car battery charger, which is actually a step-down transformer from 120 to 12 volts. The second is the auto transformer, which functions as a dimmer by reducing the voltage to a lamp (not true of the modern SCR and other electronic dimmers). One can put a meter on the output of an auto transformer dimmer and set the reading to any desired voltage.

When using low-voltage sources, care must be taken not to overload a circuit or the transformer. The power formula tells us that, given the same-wattage lamp, as the voltage is lowered, the amperage is subsequently raised.

The MR-16

Because of its unique dichroic reflector, the miniature reflector lamp (see Chapter 17) has become a popular theatrical source. Most MR-16s operate on 12 volts and are available in beam spreads from the very narrow 5 degrees to the wide 40 degrees. This lamp is used in a new striplight as well as a "bunch" light supplied by Great American (Figure 22–9); but its most interesting application is on its own as a tiny spotlight. Mounted in what appears to be an extremely small PAR can with a diameter of about 2 inches, this lamp can be tucked into the tightest of spaces. While it does require its own small transformer, recent development has led to a transformer that can be dimmed and located remotely. The light is of good quality with a harshness that is typical of low voltage, but unusual from such a small source.

ARC LIGHT

The first electric light source to be used in the theatre was an arc light in the form of limelight. Blocks of calcium oxide (lime) were used in place of the more-modern carbon rods in spotlights each requiring an

Figure 22-9
The MR-16 Lamp
Shown is a "cluster" of nine MR-16 lamps. Each of the three vertical rows can be aimed separately. Application is greater for television and film, but such a unit can be of great value for special theatre needs. *Photo courtesy The Great American Market*

operator. In fact, there are reports that the quality of limelight was so flattering that patrons bemoaned the installation of more-modern, incandescent light sources in many theatres. Arc light is impressive because of its brilliance—a streak of lightning during a thunderstorm is an example of arc light on a grand scale. The brief offstage striking of an arc is a theatrical technique used to simulate lightning on stage.

Carbon-Arc

The carbon-arc light source became popular in the theatre because of its intense and high-color temperature light. Popular taste in follow spotting, especially for Broadway-type musical productions, calls for a strong frontal source; and, because of physical restrictions on where one could place such a lighting instrument and operator in the typical Broadway house, an instrument with the potential of delivering a whole lot of light was developed. This instrument was the carbon-arc follow spot.

Two copper-coated carbon rods, about the size of pencils, are mounted within a housing along with a reflector and lenses. Electricity is conducted to the tips of the rods via the copper coating. The two rods are brought together to begin the flow of electricity (called "striking" the arc) and then backed off, forcing the electricity to jump the ¼ to ½ inch gap. This gap, which is air filled with a few flying carbon particles, offers a good deal of resistance to the electrical flow and, as a result, quite a bit of heat and light is generated. The arc is fairly small, so it works well with the instrument's optical system. As the carbons burn down (the life of a carbon should be at least 45 minutes), they are slowly fed toward each other, thereby maintaining a constant gap.

|||▶ *SAFETY PRACTICE*

Caution: A by-product of carbon-arc combustion is carbon monoxide gas, a lethal substance. Never operate a carbon-arc follow spot or projector without proper ventilation.

Caution: Unshielded arc light is extremely intense—bright enough to blind someone looking directly at the source.

The major manufacturer of carbon-arc follow spots in the United States is Strong Electric, a company well known for its Trouper and Super Trouper series of follow spots. While carbon-arc sources had a stronghold on follow spotting and projection for many years, recent developments in arc lamps will ultimately make carbon-arc as antique a light source as limelight.

Short-Arc Lamps

Two tungsten electrodes in a strong glass enclosure of gas under high pressure produce an intense light source when the current arcs between the electrodes. The result is a brilliant point source. Because the arc is shielded from the oxygen in the air, the tungsten electrodes do not burn up as do the carbons in the arc light.

Of the short-arc lamps currently available the *xenon lamp* is the old-est. The xenon lamp, which is filled with high-pressure xenon gas, burns with a brilliant, cool light. Its high efficiency and long life help to compensate for its high cost. Because of its efficiency and long life it has been standard installation in motion picture projectors and long-range follow spots.

The problem with the xenon lamp is that it has a tendency to explode because of the high pressure of the gas within the glass envelope. Several xenon lamp accidents (with small fragments of glass being propelled through the air at startling velocities) have prompted the enactment of safety regulations for the use of xenon sources. Among others, these include explosion-proof lamp housings that further increase the user's cost.

The more-recent *HMI lamp* is constructed like the xenon lamp but with the gas under a much lower pressure. It is a good projector lamp, although the light has such a high Kelvin temperature that it needs a warm filter to correctly project the colors of the film or slide (Figure 22–10). HMI follow spots are becoming more common, and this trend will probably continue unless an even more-acceptable, high-intensity source is developed.

A final note: The major disadvantage of any arc source for theatrical applications is that it cannot be electronically dimmed.

LASER LIGHT AND FIBER OPTICS

The world was introduced to laser light by inventor Theodore H. Maimann in the early 1960s. *Laser* is an acronym for Light Amplification by Stimulated Emission of Radiation—this title being descriptive of the inner workings of a laser. The light emitted from a laser is unique in that it is highly concentrated, made up of an extremely narrow wavelength band, and totally coherent in that all wavelengths are exactly in phase with each other. Due to the energy concentration and subsequent danger of laser light, its use is highly restricted, making it a very unlikely source of light in the theatre. While it is common knowledge that Peter Pan's Tinkerbell has been very well portrayed by a laser light, the cost of such a laser is prohibitive for most producing organizations.

Fiber optics refers to the transmission of light through certain kinds of transparent tubes, resulting in the tubes glowing either along their surface or at their end tips. A magical effect can be achieved in this way, but no great brilliance is possible. Unfortunately, both lasers and fiber optics have very limited use in the theatre.

Figure 22-10
Short-Arc Lamp
The HMI lamp, 2,500 watts.

GASEOUS DISCHARGE LAMPS

The most familiar form of gaseous discharge lamps is the fluorescent tube, which never achieved its promises of becoming a major light source in the theatre. Current passing through a pressurized mercury vapor causes a gaseous discharge, predominantly in the ultraviolet zone, which is absorbed by the phosphorous coating on the inside walls of the tube. The coating reemits the energy, becoming the light source itself.

Because the fluorescent tube is a line of light and not a point source, its uses in the theatre are limited to producing a wash of light on a cyclorama or backdrop. The shape of the lamp makes it difficult to achieve smooth color blending. The fluorescent hoods, however, can be installed with black-light fluorescent tubes to flood the stage with ultraviolet light for a black-light effect.

A black-light effect is the illuminating of a surface treated with fluorescent paint or dye with ultraviolet light (UV). The fluorescent surface becomes, in effect, the light source as it reemits the energy of the ultraviolet light.

The mercury vapor lamp with a UV filter is another effective instrument to produce black light. Both the black-light fluorescent tube and the mercury vapor lamp require a ballast and warmup time and can only be mechanically dimmed.

It should be also be mentioned that the arc-light follow spot can be equipped with a UV filter and be used for a black-light effect.

||||➤ *SAFETY PRACTICE*

A good electrician follows several simple rules when working with the various light sources found in the theatre:

1. Always unplug a lighting instrument before replacing a bad lamp.
2. Lamps are expensive, so be sure to treat them with care.
3. Keep fingers off quartz bulbs.
4. The envelope of a burning lamp gets too hot to handle even with the best of gloves.

Stage-Lighting Practice: Design

This chapter will investigate lighting layouts for different types of production in a variety of spaces. We will examine simplified designs for a realistic interior "box set" in the proscenium theatre; an "in-the-round" production in an arena theatre; and a drama designed for the thrust stage. In addition, we will look at two actual lighting plots: one for dance and a second for the opera, *Rape of Lucretia*.

The following examples have been greatly simplified for clarity and ease of presentation. The lighting layouts are deliberately designed to show the minimum number of instruments necessary to achieve acceptable lighting in each case.

THE PROSCENIUM THEATRE

Let us assume that the theatre we are using is of medium size. The stage will have a 30-foot proscenium opening. There will be ample provisions for hanging scenery and instruments above the stage. About 20 feet from the proscenium line will be a beam for mounting front spotlights.

The Realistic Interior

A realistic interior often calls for some variation of the conventional box setting, either with or without a ceiling piece. As one might expect, the existence of a ceiling will have a great effect on lighting possibilities. The primary interest is within the walls of this set, while the backgrounds seen through windows and doors are of less importance. The lighting is often motivated by apparent sources; in practically all cases it is realistically plausible.

Figure 23-1
Realistic Interior: Sketch

Figure 23–1 is a sketch of such a setting. In the upstage left wall, a door leads into the kitchen. Upstage center a flight of stairs comes down into the living room and to the right an exterior door leads out to the porch. In the stage-right wall is a four-window alcove which looks out on to the porch.

Two scenes are involved. Act I is an afternoon of a somewhat overcast day, and Act II is later that evening.

Sectional View • Figure 23–2 is a center-line section of the stage and auditorium showing lighting positions and angles. Especially useful is the elevation of the upstage landing and steps leading to it. The beam angles shown from several of the instruments indicate degree of coverage in a given area. The cross symbol located in the auditorium represents the first row of audience seating and is called a "sight point." Lines from this point past the masking borders indicate whether or not the lighting instruments are hidden from audience view.

Instrument Schedule and Layout • Figure 23–3a is the instrument schedule for the layout in Figure 23–3b. For sake of simplicity, the instruments are numbered consecutively throughout rather than consecutively by position. The two cross symbols on the plan indicate critical side sight points from the extreme seats house left and right in the first row. These sight points help to indicate what the audience can see through door openings, windows, and side masking.

Downstage Areas • In dividing the stage into lighting areas, we find that four across the front will be fine as long as a centerstage sofa special covers the overlap of areas #2 and #3. To cover these four areas we mount 1,000 watt 6-by-16 or 20-degree ellipsoidals in the ceiling position. We select the ERS over the Fresnel or PAR for sake of control. The beams from the Fresnel and PAR, although quite powerful, have such side spill that we would have light all over the proscenium wall. For a shorter throw than the one we have assumed for this theatre or for larger lighting areas, the 30-degree 6-by-12 ERS would be a good choice.

Plate 23-1

Follies

A photograph from the production of *Follies,* designed by Beeb Salzer, whose sketches are seen in Chapter 13, Figure 13-1. The projections were achieved by using multiple projectors, making sketches even more necessary in order to achieve the desired background look.

Plate 23-2a

Plate 23-2b
Gobos

(a) This dance production of *Gloria,* choreographed by Dennis Spaight and produced by The Richmond Ballet, used a number of gobo patterns front-projected on a scrim/ backdrop combination. These particular patterns depended upon a high angle source shooting across the scrim/backdrop with varigated color. The lighting was designed by Craig Wolf. (b) A more realistic use of gobos is shown here in a modern dress production of *Romeo and Juliet,* directed by Mack Owen.

Plate **23-3a**

Plate **23-3b**
La Sylphide

Two photographs from the ballet staged by Frederic Franklin and produced by
The Richmond Ballet, with lighting by Craig Wolf. (a) La Sylphide danced by Marianna
Tcherkassky with James danced by Fernando Bujones and (b) the Sylphides. A light plot
and section for the ballet will be found in Figures 23-14 through 23-16.

Plate **23-4**
Rape of Lucretia

Two photographs from the opera directed by John Eaton and produced by the Cincinnati Conservatory of Music with lighting by Cindy Limauro. (a) Act I, Scene 1, outside the Roman camp and (b) Act II, Scene 2, Lucretia's garden. The light plot, section, and hookup will be found in Figures 23-17 through 23-19. *Photos courtesy Sandy Underwood*

Figure 23-2
**Realistic Interior: Center Line
Section**

In choosing the mounting positions for these instruments, we have attempted to maintain the desired 45-degree angle, but note that we must mount instrument #2 somewhat in from the end of the beam in order to reach the extreme downstage-left corner of area #1 without being cut off by the proscenium arch. In addition, the color blend hitting the stage-left wall from the blue R60 instrument #6 and the warmer R02 in instrument #2 will be better with instrument #2 moved a bit towards center. In like manner, instrument #9 must move somewhat nearer the center.

Therefore, we have sacrificed to some extent the ideal angle, but this is a necessary compromise. The remaining area instruments can be placed just about where we prefer them. All instruments are carefully shuttered so as not to spill distracting light on the face of the stage apron and, in the case of #2 and #9, on the proscenium.

Back Light • Each of the four downstage areas is lit with two additional, 8-inch Fresnel back lights. A Fresnel is ideal for good blending from area to area; and the high wattage 8-inch instrument will punch through the area lights without any problem. Barn doors will mat the light beam from spilling too far downstage and, in the case of instrument #26, off the top of the scenery wall. The upstage areas could be back lit with another bank of Fresnels from a third electric pipe; but, for the sake of simplicity, we have chosen to exclude these instruments.

The back light helps to separate the actors from their backgrounds, giving them a pleasing sculptural look. In addition, its R09 color (pale amber gold) from the stage-left will reinforce the feeling of daylight in Act I and, when lowered on the dimmers, will be very nice for the glow of incandescent light in the night scene of Act II.

Upstage Areas • To cover the upstage areas #5, #6, #7, and #9, we will use 6-inch Fresnels mounted on the first electric pipe. Fresnels are picked for this location because the soft edge of their beams makes blending between the areas easy; and no sharp, distracting beam patterns will appear on the walls of the set. Numbers 13, 15, and 16 can be focused

INSTRUMENT NO. AND LOCATION	TYPE	USE	LAMP	COLOR	CHANNEL	REMARKS
1 – CEILING SLOT	6 x 16 ERS	AREA 2	1K	R02	2	
2 – " "	6 x 16 "	AREA 1	1K	R02	1	
3 – " "	6 x 16 "	AREA 3	1K	R02	3	
4 – " "	6 x 16 "	AREA 4	1K	R02	4	
5 – " "	6 x 16 "	SPECIAL	1K	R02	9	SOFA
6 – " "	6 x 16 "	AREA 1	1K	R60	11	
7 – " "	6 x 16 "	SPECIAL	1K	R60	19	SOFA
8 – " "	6 x 16 "	AREA 2	1K	R60	12	
9 – " "	6 x 16 "	AREA 4	1K	R60	14	
10 – " "	6 x 16 "	AREA 3	1K	R60	13	
11 – 1ST ELECTRIC	6 x 12 "	AREA 9	750	R02	27	
12 – " "	6" FRESNEL	AREA 5	750	R02	5	CIRCUIT w/ # 13
13 – " "	6" "	AREA 6	750	R02	5	CIRCUIT w/ # 12
14 – " "	6 x 9 ERS	SPECIAL	750	R02	26	STAIR + LANDING
15 – " "	6" FRESNEL	AREA 9	750	R02	8	
16 – " "	6" "	AREA 7	750	R02	6	
17 – " "	6" "	AREA 5	750	R60	15	
18 – " "	6 x 9 ERS	SPECIAL	750	R02	26	UPPER LANDING
19 – " "	6" FRESNEL	"	750	R02	28	WINDOW SEAT
20 – " "	3½" ERS	"	400	R60	37	FRAME ON TROPHY
21 – " "	6" FRESNEL	AREA 6	750	R60	15	
22 – " "	6 x 12 ERS	SPECIAL	750	R02	35	FRAME TO ARCH – AREA 9
23 – " "	6" FRESNEL	"	750	R02	28	WINDOW SEAT
24 – " "	6" "	AREA 7	750	R60	16	
25 – " "	6" "	AREA 9	750	R60	18	
26 – 2ND ELECTRIC	8" FRESNEL	AREA 1	1K	R09	21	BARNDOOR OFF SCENERY
27 – " "	6" "	STAIRS	750	R02	10	" " "
28 – " "	8" "	AREA 2	1K	R09	22	
29 – " "	6" "	AREA 1	1K	N/C	31	
30 – " "	6" "	AREA 8	750	R02	7	
31 – " "	8" "	AREA 3	1K	R09	23	
32 – " "	6" "	STAIRS	750	R60	20	
33 – " "	6" "	AREA 8	750	R60	17	
34 – " "	8" "	AREA 2	1K	N/C	32	
35 – " "	8" "	AREA 4	1K	R09	24	
36 – " "	3½" ERS	SPECIAL	400	N/C	37	FRAME ON TROPHY
37 – " "	8" FRESNEL	AREA 3	1K	N/C	33	
38 – " "	8" "	AREA 4	1K	N/C	34	
39 – BOOM # 1	6" "	KITCHEN	750	N/C	36	
40 – BOOM # 2	6" "	HALL	750	R02	25	CIRCUIT w/ # 41
41 – BOOM # 2	6" "	LANDING	750	R02	25	CIRCUIT w/ # 40
42 – SPOTLINE PIPE # 2	8" "	STREET LIGHTS	1K	R62	41	CIRCUIT w/ # 43
43 – " " # 2	8" "	" "	1K	R62	41	CIRCUIT w/ # 42
44 – " " # 2	8" "	" "	1K	R62	41	
45 – " " # 1	PORCH LIGHT	PRACTICAL	100	N/C	42	
46 – " " # 1	" "	"	100	N/C	42	FIXTURE IN VIEW
47 – " " # 1	14" ERF	WINDOW WASH	750	R02	29	
48 – HALL	9" ERF	WALL WASH	500	R02	30	
49 – "	CEILING FIXTURE	PRACTICAL	3 @ 40w	N/C	38	
50 – SR WALL	WALL SCONCE	"	2 @ 40w	N/C	39	
51 – STAIRS	" "	"	2 @ 40w	N/C	40	

a

Figure 23-3
The Realistic Interior

(a) Instrument schedule. (b) Lighting layout. Instruments have been numbered sequentially for ease of identification.

close to the 45-degree angle for their respective areas; but, #12 must move a bit center in order not to hit the wall just stage-right of the kitchen door. Likewise, #17, #21, and #24 are close to the desired angle, but instrument #25 into area #9 must slide onstage to avoid the stage-right set wall.

The special step area and landing area #8 are lit with 6-inch Fresnels from the second electric pipe. See the section (Figure 23–2) for an indication of vertical angle.

b

Color • All the area lights must be consistent in regard to colors. Because in both acts the light outside the window can be considered cool, the house-left instruments are colored in R60 (no color blue). The corresponding house-right front lights are colored a warmer R02 (bastard amber). This color choice is a useful one because the two colors mix toward white light and will look quite natural on the actors and scenery.

The Stairway • Of course, the stairway must not be overlooked. But rather than consider it another area, it is preferable to handle it as a special problem because of its different levels. To light it properly, yet avoid spilling, we use an ERS in soft focus from the first pipe, framing its beam to the stairs themselves and only high enough to cover the actor moving up and down. This would be instrument #14 (a 6 × 9 or 40 degree); and because a warm color is most appropriate, it will have an R02 filter. When the stairs bend stage-right toward the landing area #8, a pair of 6-inch Fresnels take over. These instruments (#27 and #32) are used to avoid, as much as possible, harsh shadows on the wall behind the staircase.

Practicals • There are five "practicals" on the set. Number 51 is a wall sconce at the first stair landing; #49 is a ceiling light located in the vestibule; #50 is another wall sconce on the upstage-right wall; and #45 and #46 are porch lamps. Each one should be on its own dimmer, and control of the fixtures should be in the hands of the light-board operator and stage manager, not the actors. The actors must be instructed to mime the switching on and off of the practicals while the light-board operator does the actual operation.

Backing and Support Lights • Beginning in the kitchen, we have hung a 6-inch Fresnel on a boom at a height of 14 feet to simulate a ceiling light. This light without a color filter will illuminate an actor moving through the kitchen door and shine an interesting light into the living room with the door open. A second boom holds two 6-inch Fresnels (#40 and #41) at 16 feet off the stage floor and focused down the "hallway" at the top of the stairs. These two instruments colored in R02 will light actors coming into view from behind the wall rather than forcing them to emerge from a black hole.

The upstage-right archway is an important area lit by a special ERS (#22) from the first electric. This instrument is placed in fairly soft focus and shuttered to the arch in order to light an actor entering from the porch door. In addition, the wall is washed with a small scoop (#48) colored in the warm R02 to dissipate shadows created by the frontal ERS.

Outside the stage-right window is another larger scoop (#47) that will be used as a window wash during the afternoon scene. In the night scene of Act II, instruments #42, #43, and #44 will shine in the bay windows imitating street lights, casting rather long and eerie shadows into the living room.

Specials • As mentioned earlier, the centerstage sofa specials (6-by-16 or 20-degree instruments #5 and #7) from the front-of-house ceiling beam will be important not only for accenting action on the sofa, but also because the sofa is located between two lighting areas. Several Fresnels act as specials into the window seat area from the first electric. These instruments (#19 and #23) will fill in where the light for areas #4 and #7 cannot cover adequately. Instrument #18 is a 6-by-12 ERS focused onto the stair landing for special accent on an actor playing there.

Control Even though we attempted to keep the number of instruments to a minimum, our schedule still lists a total of 51 units. While several instruments, such as the exterior street lights and the two hall-light Fresnels on boom #2 can be ganged, our layout will still require no fewer than 42 dimmers; and this figure means that we have to gang areas together.

Two areas to gang together would be #5 and #6. If we place the two R02 Fresnels (#12 and #13) into one dimmer, and the two R60 Fresnels (#17 and #21) into another dimmer, we save two dimmers. Other ganging choices must be determined by the blocking and desired movement of light.

ARENA PRODUCTION

The term *arena* is derived from the Roman amphitheatre where the audience surrounded the action on all sides and the lighting was nature's. Present-day arena theatres, such as the Arena Stage in Washington, D.C., are fine examples of modern technology working in combination with one of the oldest and most intimate of staging configurations: theatre in-the-round (Figure 23–4).

Special Considerations

Due to arena audience sight lines, scenery must be kept to a minimum so as not to block view. Lighting must be from all directions.

Functions of Arena Lighting • Visibility remains, of course, the primary function in arena production lighting, and this means that the actors must be effectively lighted for all members of the surrounding audience. Composition takes the form of holding the spectators' attention to the acting areas and thus the lighting must have definition and great precision of form. Tight and specific area control is often required in the arena, adding another compositional requirement to the designer's list. Mood must be accomplished by means of intensity and color toning but both within limited ranges. In addition, the color, texture, and compositional make-up of the stage floor takes on greater visual importance in arena production because of audience viewing angle.

Accuracy of Focus • With the spectators crowded closely—often too closely—about the playing areas, instruments that have hard-to-control beams are of little value. Floodlights are impossible. Striplights may be used discreetly and with side maskings to give an overall tonality of rather low intensity. Fresnel spots must be focused with particular accuracy and, in addition, a top hat or barn doors must be added to control the beam spill.

The smaller 3½- or 4-inch ellipsoidals are very useful in the arena space with a low grid. Adjustable field spread up to 50 degrees is a necessity, making a zoom ellipsoidal ideal.

Figure 23-4
Arena Stage Lighting Positions
(a) A perspective view of an arena stage showing the lighting grid.
(b) A sectional view of the same arena showing the various positions and angles of distributions. (1) A masking valance and the nearest frontal position behind it. (2) The extreme lighting position on the outer edge of the grid. (3) A central position over the acting area.
(4) Special boom position in the aisle for a very low angle.

Arena Lighting Areas • On the proscenium stage each area must be covered by a minimum of two spotlights, each ideally 45 degrees on the actor. In an arena, however, where the actor is seen from all sides, more instruments are necessary. There are two popular approaches to the solution. One is that three instruments per area be used, evenly spaced about the area and thus at 120 degrees from one another. The second approach is to use four spots on each area, putting them 90 degrees from each other and shooting along the diagonals of the space.

Color in the Arena • With either approach, the system of using one warm and one cool color on each area is no longer applicable. In the three-spotlight plan, the third instrument is assigned a neutral color, such as a light lavender which will appear cool opposite a warm filter and warm opposite a cool one. A light pink is also a possibility for scenes that are basically warm and romantic. No color also can be quite effective.

The four-instrument system suggests two color variations. In the first, a warm and a cool are used on opposite sides, while the two intermediate instruments have a neutral medium. An alternate approach is to use two warms, each opposite the other, and two cools, also opposite each other (Figure 23–5). The latter will most often prove more satisfactory.

A word of warning about the choice of colors in arena productions: because the directionality of the spotlights on each side of each area is so definite, colors show up much stronger on the actors than in a proscenium production, where there is far more mixing of different beams. Or perhaps this seems true to the audience because of its closeness to the action. In any event, use of the more-saturated colors is rarely advisable.

Unmasked Instruments • It would be fruitless in a temporary arena setup to attempt to hide the instruments from the audience. They can, of course, be hung and maintained in a neat manner, with wiring carefully tied off and the like. But a frank acceptance of the fact that the instruments are there for all to view is better than a lot of makeshift, dust-catching, and fire-prone draperies.

However, if a stage house has been designed especially for arena production, a false ceiling should be provided with openings through which the beams of light may be focused from instruments hung well above and out of sight. Catwalks must be installed so the electrician can reach all instruments with ease for maintenance, focusing, and color changes.

Better yet is the tension wire grid (Figure 23–11). Such a grid is suspended over the entire room, allowing great instrument-location flexibility as well as safe and simple hanging and focus. While the initial expense of such a system is greater than that of others, safety and lower long-term labor costs more than compensate.

Blinding the Spectators • A difficult problem in any form of arena production is to keep the beams of the area spotlights out of the eyes of spectators seated on the opposite side of the stage. As long as light persists in traveling in a straight line, and as long as directors wish to play their actors at the very edge of the arena stage, just so long will a compromise be necessary between a well-lighted actor and a half-blinded spectator.

To solve the problem, the angle of the instrument or instruments spilling into the audience can be raised, but this compromise only helps so much. If the first row of the audience can be raised higher than the stage level, or be set back from it, or both, the problem can be greatly eased. In any event, this is one of the greatest problems confronting the light designer in arena production.

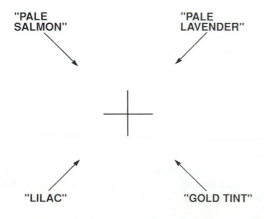

"PALE SALMON"   "PALE LAVENDER"

"LILAC"   "GOLD TINT"

Figure 23-5
Arena Color

Shown is a possible color key for the arena using four lights per area and a warm/cool approach.

Figure 23-6
Lighting an Arena Area

This drawing illustrates area #1 being lit from four angles. The numbers refer to instrument numbers found on the light plot, Figure 23-7.

Designing the Lighting for an Arena Production

Should the lighting designer attempt to create the same lighting picture for everyone in the arena audience? Experience has shown that such an approach is quite restrictive and leads to fairly bland lighting. Nonetheless, the designer should always be concerned about the quality of lighting from all viewing angles in an arena theatre.

Figure 23–6 illustrates our sample arena layout with properties in place on the stage floor. There are two boxes in which lighting instruments may be hung overhead. A layout and an instrument schedule for a suitable lighting design are also shown (Figure 23–7).

The designer has divided the stage into five areas, which have been numbered clockwise from one through four, with area five in the center. Dotted lines on the layout mark the approximate limits of these areas, although it is, of course, understood that actually they will overlap one another and their lights will blend smoothly. The instruments have been numbered systematically, from the top, clockwise around the stage, in the outer box first and then the inner.

From each corner of the outer box a pair of 6-by-12 ellipsoidal reflector spotlights is focused on the two closest areas, giving each of these two beams of light at approximately right angles to one another. From the inner box two 40° mini-ellipse spotlights are focused on each of the same areas. Looking at area #1 in Figure 23–7 for example, note that the ver-

Figure 23-7
An Arena Schedule and Plot

(a) Instrument schedule with instruments lighting area #1 indicated. (b) Layout of the lighting instruments. Note the various lighting angles to area #1. In the arena, lighting instruments will often be numbered sequentially.

a

1 - AREA 1

b

No.	INSTRUMENT	PURPOSE	LAMP	COLOR	REMARKS
1	6" ELLIPS'L-REF'L SPOTLIGHT	AREA 1	500T12	803	
2	" " "	" 2	"	803	
3	8" FRESNEL SPOTLIGHT	MOONLIGHT SPECIAL	1000G40	856	FOCUS CENTER
4	6" ELLIPS'L-REF'L SPOTLIGHT	AREA 2	500T12	848	
5	" " "	" 3	"	848	
6	" " "	DIVAN SPECIAL	750T12	826	FRAME TO DIVAN
7	" " "	AREA 3	500T12	805	
8	" " "	" 4	"	805	
9	" " "	" 4	"	842	
10	" " "	" 1	"	842	
11	40° MINI-ELLIPSE	" 4	500W Q	803	MAT TOP
12	6" FRESNEL SPOTLIGHT	" 5	500 Q	803	TOP HAT
13	40° MINI-ELLIPSE	" 3	500W Q	803	MAT TOP
14	" " "	" 1	"	848	" "
15	6" FRESNEL SPOTLIGHT	" 5	500T20	848	TOP HAT
16	40° MINI-ELLIPSE	" 4	500W Q	848	MAT TOP
17	" " "	" 2	"	805	" "
18	6" FRESNEL SPOTLIGHT	" 5	500T20	805	TOP-HAT
19	4½" ELLIPS'L-REF'L SPOTLIGHT	CENTER ACCENT	500T12	CLEAR	FOCUS CENTER
20	40° MINI-ELLIPSE	AREA 1	500W Q	805	MAT TOP
21	" " "	" 3	"	842	" "
22	" " "	DIVAN SPECIAL #2	"	802	MAT TO DIVAN
23	6" FRESNEL SPOTLIGHT	AREA 5	500T20	842	TOP HAT
24	40° MINI-ELLIPSE	" 2	500W Q	842	MAT TOP
25	FIXTURE	TABLE LAMP #1	40A	–	GANG WITH #26
26	"	" " #2	40A	–	" " #25

tical angle of the mini-ellipse spotlights is higher than that of the 6-by-12s. This is done to avoid distracting spill into the audience. In addition, the ERS is used here because the upper portion of its beam can be shuttered to prevent light from glaring into the eyes of the spectators.

Area 5, in the center, is hit from the four corners of the inner box by 6-inch Fresnel spotlights. Here the danger of spill light annoying the audience is less marked than in the outer areas, but top hats are used on the instruments just the same. The typical, soft-edged Fresnel-beam pattern is useful to blend this center light with the illumination on the adjacent areas.

Color • The color system in Roscolene plastic is that of opposite warms and cools. The warm light, working diagonally out of the upper-right corner of the layout, is from a Roscolene No. 803 (pale gold) filter. The identical color might have been employed also from the lower left, but the designer preferred to use a slightly different tint, Roscolene No. 805 (light straw). In like manner, the cools are not identical: from the lower right is a No. 848 (water blue), while opposite it is a No. 842 (special lavender). This is not an especially cool color, but it has been chosen here because we are assuming that this is a warm, pleasant type of play. Had it been a cold, stark drama, we might have selected a combination of No. 851 and No. 848 for the cools, while the versatile No. 842 might have been one of the warms, with perhaps no color at all in the opposite instruments.

Specials • A few specials have been provided. On the right side there is an 8-inch Fresnel with a No. 856 (light blue) gel to give the effect of moonbeams for a brief scene. Instrument #6 is focused carefully on the divan with a romantic No. 826 (flesh pink) for a tender moment. Toward the upper-left corner is another divan special with No. 802 (bastard am-

Figure 23-8
The Thrust Stage Lighting Positions

A perspective view of a thrust stage showing its various lighting positions. The stage division into areas would vary with each production. (1) Outer valance position. (2) Second valance and over-stage grid. (3) Wing ladder, side lighting. (4) Tormentor boom. (5) Vomitory rail. (6) Gutter. If a balcony exists, there will also be balcony rail positions.

ber) for a different scene. Also on the left, a wide-beamed ellipsoidal-reflector spotlight without color serves as an accent on the central area for some special action there. The two table lamps at either end of the divan are practical fixtures, meaning that they will be lit at some point in the production.

Control • Twenty-four dimmers would be necessary for this simple arena layout, assuming that we can repatch one of the specials. Arena and thrust lighting almost always require tighter and more individual control than proscenium production.

THRUST STAGE PRODUCTION

Thrust production shares many attributes with the arena. It is an intimate form, with the audience viewing the action from three sides. The stage floor almost always takes on a special importance due to steep audience rake. Concern must be taken for lighting angles that may cause light to spill into the audience; and, the performer must be lit from all sides.

The Theatre

Any theatre designed for a thrust stage should include provision for good mounting positions for the lighting instruments (Figure 23–8). The simplest manner of doing this is a grid of pipes or other mounting structure over the entire stage and extending over the audience as well in all directions as far from the edge of the stage as the height of the grid above the stage floor. There should be a great number of electrical outlets provided on this grid, unless it is the intention to string cables from the backstage to the specific instruments.

Boxes or valances to hide the instruments are often provided, but because of the necessity to be able to hang spotlights on any portion of the grid, especially over the stage itself, these devices are not wholly effective. Therefore instruments should be mounted and cabled neatly and securely so as to be neither a distraction nor a danger. Those spectators in the side seats particularly will find that the lenses of instruments focused in their general direction will be in full view. But as long as top hats are used, this should not prove too great a distraction. Care must be taken to mask or frame off the upper part of the beams from such instruments to be sure they do not glare directly into the eyes of those seated facing them. Ellipsoidal reflector spotlights can use their internal framing shutters to good advantage; Fresnels, if used, should be provided with barn doors. Once again, a tension wire grid rather than this awkward pipe grid would be a good choice.

Design Considerations

Often the arrangement of set pieces and properties will dictate how a thrust stage is best divided into acting areas, and each of these will require several instruments focused on it from several directions. Every actor on a thrust stage is seen from the three sides at the same time. Top or back lighting is also essential to set the actor off from the background. Blending and toning are best accomplished by use of softbeamed spotlights to throw color washes over large portions of the stage.

Figure 23-9
Thrust Stage Lighting

(a) Illustration of the lighting for area #4 from five angles. (b) The lighting layout with area #4 instruments indicated. (c) The instrument schedule.

a

b

No.	INSTRUMENT	LOCATION	PURPOSE	LAMP	COLOR	REMARKS
1	8" ELLIPS'L REF'R SPOTLIGHT	LEFT BOOM	AREA 1	1000 T12	144	L. BOOM TOP
2	6" " " "	" "	WASH - WARM	750 T12	134	" MIDDLE SOFT EDGE
3	6" " " "	" "	" - COOL	750 T12	119	" BOTTOM " "
4	6" " " "	2ND. VALANCE-L	AREA 3	1000 T12	141	
5	8" " " "	" " "	" 2	"	141	
6	6" " " "	" " "	" 5	750 T12	141	
7	6" " " "	" " "	" 3	"	144	
8	6" " " "	" " "	WINDOW SEAT	750 T12	144	
9	8" " " "	" " "	AREA 2	1000 T12	117	
10	6" " " "	" " "	LEFT TUNNEL	750 T12	115	FRAME TO TUNNEL
11	6" " " "	" " "	AREA 5	750 T12	117	
12	8" " " "	2ND VALANCE-C	" 3	1000 T12	117	FRAME OFF AUDIENCE
13	8" FRESNEL-LENS SPOTLIGHT	" " "	WASH - COOL	1500 G40	119	BARN DOOR- OFF "
14	8" " " "	" " "	" - WARM	"	134	" " " "
15	8" ELLIPS'L REF'R SPOTLIGHT	" " "	AREA 4	1000 T12	152	FRAME OFF "
16	6" " " "	2ND VALANCE-R	" 5	750 T12	152	
17	6" " " "	" " "	RIGHT TUNNEL	750 T12	115	FRAME TO TUNNEL
18	8" " " "	" " "	AREA 2	1000 12	152	
19	6" " " "	" " "	" 4	750 T12	151	
20	6" " " "	" " "	" 5	"	153(2)	
21	8" " " "	" " "	" 2	1000 T12	153(2)	
22	6" " " "	" " "	" 4	750 T12	153(2)	
23	8" " " "	RIGHT BOOM	" 1	1000 T12	151	R. BOOM - TOP
24	6" " " "	" "	WASH - WARM	750 T12	134	" MIDDLE-SOFT EDGE
25	6" " " "	" "	" - COOL	"	119	" BOTTOM- " "
26	8" " " "	LEFT LADDER	U.R. CORNER	1000 T12	141	L. LADDER-TOP-FRAMESIDES
27	6" " " "	" "	AREA 1	750 T12	141	" BOTTOM " US
28	6" " " "	" "	U.L. CORNER	500 T12	141	" " " "
29	6" FRESNEL-LENS SPOTLIGHT	1ST VALANCE-L	" "	500 T20	117	
30	6" " " "	" " "	WASH-COOL	"	119	BARN DOOR-OFF AUDIENCE
31	6" " " "	" " "	" - WARM	"	134	" " " "
32	6" ELLIPS'L REF'R SPOTLIGHT	" " "	AREA 1	750 T12	117	
33	6" " " "	" " "	SOFA	"	117	
34	6" " " "	1ST VALANCE R.	"	"	152	
35	6" FRESNEL-LENS SPOTLIGHT	" " "	BENCH	500 T20	152	
36	6" ELLIPS'L REF'R "	" " "	AREA 1	750 T12	152	FRAME BOTTOM
37	6" FRESNEL-LENS "	" " "	WASH - WARM	500 T20	134	BARN DOOR OFF AUDIENCE
38	6" " " "	" " "	" - COOL	"	119	" " " "
39	6" " " "	" " "	U.R CORNER	"	152	
40	8" ELLIPS'L REF'R SPOTLIGHT	RIGHT LADDER	U.L.	1000 T12	153(2)	R. LADDER -TOP FRAMESIDE
41	6" " " "	" "	AREA 1	750 T12	153(2)	" BOTTOM " US
42	6" " " "	" "	U.R. CORNER	"	153(2)	" " " US
43	6" " " "	GRID. OVER STAGE	BENCH	750 T12	117	SOFT E. FRAME OFF AUDIENCE
44	6" FRESNEL-LENS "	" " "	AREA 3	500 T20	CLEAR	BARNDOOR " "
45	6" ELLIPS'L REF'R "	" " "	LEFT TUNNEL	750 T12	102	FRAME TO TUNNEL
46	6" FRESNEL-LENS "	" " "	AREA 5	500 T20	CLEAR	BARN DOOR OFF AUDIENCE
47	6" ELLIPS'L REF'R "	" " "	RIGHT TUNNEL	750 T12	102	FRAME TO TUNNEL
48	6" FRESNEL-LENS "	" " "	AREA 4	500 T20	CLEAR	BARN DOOR OFF AUDIENCE
49	6" ELLIPS'L REF'R "	" " "	STEPS	750 T12	152	SOFT E. FRAME TO STEPS
50	6" FRESNEL-LENS "	" " "	AREA 2 DS	500 T20	CLEAR	
51	6" ELLIPS'L REF'R "	" " "	ARCHWAY	750 T12	102	FRAME TO ARCHWAY
52	6" FRESNEL-LENS "	" " "	AREA 2 US	500 T20	CLEAR	
53	6" ELLIPS'L REF'R "	" " "	AREA 3	750 T12	"	FRAME L AND TOP
54	6" FRESNEL LENS "	" " "	SOFA	500 T20	"	
55	6" ELLIPS'L REF'R "	" " "	AREA 4	750 T12	117	FRAME R AND TOP
56	6" " " "	" " "	LEFT RAMP	"	103	" OFF R. WALL
57	6" " " "	" " "	RIGHT "	"	103	" " L. "
58	6" " " "	" " "	UL ENTRANCE	"	103	" " R. "
59	6" " " "	" " "	UR "	"	103	" " L. "
60	6" FRESNEL-LENS "	" " "	UL CORNER	500 T20	CLEAR	
61	6" ELLIPS'L REF'R "	" " "	AREA 1	750 T12	"	SOFT EDGE
62	6" FRESNEL-LENS "	" " "	UR CORNER	500 T20	"	
63	6" " " "	" " "	HALL WAY - L	"	104	
64	6" " "	" " "	" R	"	104	
65	6" " " "	" " "	WINDOW SEAT	"	CLEAR	BARN DOOR OFF AUDIENCE

As with arena staging, strong colors are not desirable on the thrust stage, although we can become somewhat bolder because of the one closed side. Spots to hit the stage at the familiar 45-degree angle from the front might use very pale tints, while other instruments on the same area can take stronger shades of the same basic colors, with those coming in directly from the sides using quite deep tones. The down or back lighting is often not far from white light.

The stage floor becomes a major scenic element in most thrust houses because of the steep audience rake. As in the arena, lighting color, texture, and composition will read quite strongly on the floor.

Designing the Lighting

Figure 23-9 shows a sketch of a typical thrust stage with properties and a few scenic pieces set for a play. Also shown are a layout for lighting this production and schedule of the instruments to be used.

Areas • The stage divides itself into five natural areas: the upper platform and archway being #1; the central section as outlined by the carpet, #2; and the margin of the platform surrounding the carpet, #3, #4, and #5. The designer has sought to put five to seven instruments on each area, but the difficulty of focusing to cover an area properly without hitting the audience at the same time has limited this in some instances. The further to the side the instruments are mounted, the deeper the colors they use. For this layout Lee filters are employed.

Area 1 • Because area #1 is so far upstage, it is lit somewhat from the front, proscenium style, by two 6-by-12 ellipsoidal reflector spotlights, #32 and #36, mounted in the inner box. Two 8-inch ellipsoidals, #1 and #23, strike it from the booms placed in the ramp entrances on either side of the stage. Two more 6-inchers, #27 and #41, are on the ladders hung in the upstage entrances. One 6-inch ellipsoidal (#61) works as a back light from above the upstage archway. The colors, working from front to rear on the left side are Lee No. 117 (steel blue), No. 144 (no color blue), and No. 141 (bright blue). On the right side they are No. 152 (pale gold), No. 151 (gold tint), and a double No. 153 (pale salmon). The back light is clear. The other areas use these same colors for instruments working from the same angles.

Area 4 • Figure 23–9 highlights the instruments being used for area #4. Instrument #15, an 8-inch ellipsoidal, strikes the area from the front with Lee No. 152. Instruments #19 and #22 are 6-by-12 ellipsoidals colored in Lee No. 151 and No. 153 doubled, with the more-saturated double salmon (No. 153) coming from the far stage-right side. Instruments #48 and #55 are both quite steep to avoid spill off the stage, and the 6-inch Fresnel has barn doors as well. The back-light ellipsoidal (#55) has no color and the stage-left Fresnel is colored in No. 117, steel blue.

Color Wash • A pair of 8-inch Fresnel spotlights strike the entire set from dead ahead to give it a tonal wash that may be varied by dimming the warm and cool instruments to different readings. Two pairs of 6-inch Fresnels, on either side of the inner box, and two pairs of 6-inch ellipsoidals in the ramp entrances work with the others. For the cool wash a

No. 119 (dark blue) is used, for the warm wash a No. 134 (golden amber). The golden amber will have a warming effect on the rather cool blue, resulting in lavender tones when mixed properly.

Specials • A great many specials have been hung. The extreme up-left and up-right corners, which might almost be considered areas in themselves, are each covered by three spots from front and sides, plus a back light. The tunnel entrances through the audience section (called *vomitory* entrances), the entrances along the ramps left and right, and those at the extreme back, as well as the archway in the center of the backwall, are all lighted. The bench, the window seat, the sofa, and the steps leading up to area #1 have appropriate coverage. Additional specials might be suggested, particularly as we see the development of the director's staging. Actors might, for example, be placed on the steps leading down from the platform, in which case, of course, suitable lighting would have to be provided.

The ellipsoidal reflector spotlights have been used a great deal in this layout because of the good control we have over their beams. When possible they are soft-edged by shifting the lenses to throw the gate out of focus, so as to cut down on sharp beam edges that result in abrupt changes of intensity on the stage and actors. For the same reason Fresnel spotlights are used when their spill light will not be critical, and even then barn doors are suggested on many instruments.

Variations

Our sample lighting layout is designed for a rather light and charming piece of drama with a simple interior setting. Lighting angles are standard for good visibility and the colors are chosen for their pale tints. The arrangements of color (cool on one side and warm on the other) and angle are derived from proscenium lighting and provide good coverage. However, this two-sided color approach allows for very little variety or color interest and may not be desirable for a production with a number of scenes each demanding specific lighting.

With a minimum of five instruments on each acting area and a color arrangement as shown in Figure 23–10, the designer is provided with several more options.

1. The two warms can act as key light with the cools filling.
2. The two cools can act as key with the warms filling.
3. Any one instrument (except the back light neutral) can be lowered in intensity or dropped out completely, causing a color shift as well as compositional change.

If more than the minimum five instruments per area is possible, even greater variety of color and distribution can be achieved.

Side Angle • For more-dramatic productions, the vertical angle of side light can be raised. The following occurs:

1. Higher angle distribution will cause sharper facial and body shadows.
2. Spill into side audience seating is more controllable.
3. Area control can be tighter.

Figure 23-10
A Possible Thrust Color Key

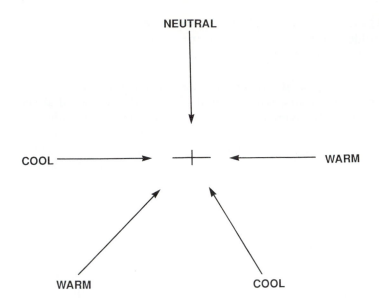

Texture • Texture achieved by patterns or gobos can break up the some-times flat and dull surface of the thrust stage, with high side often being a desirable angle (Plate 23–2).

THE FLEXIBLE STAGE

Another form of performance space which should not go without men-tion is the popular "black box." This flexible space is primarily intended as an actor's performance space rather than a production facility, but lighting nonetheless is often required. Black-box seating can be set up in any number of configurations that will, as a result, define the playing space. Common seating arrangements are:

1. One-sided, or full front—a proscenium-type orientation
2. Two-sided, or corner staging
3. Three-sided, or thrust
4. Four-sided, or arena
5. Aisle—with seats on two sides of a central aisle

Lighting the Black Box

Lighting the flexible space is not very different from lighting one of the several theatre forms previously examined except that the lighting po-sitions are generally closer to the stage. But lighting positions must also be flexible. A cross-pipe grid over the entire space is a fair solution to the problem of flexibility. Such a grid will allow lighting instruments to be hung in any position and focused in any direction. A better solution is the tension wire grid (Figure 23–11). One-eighth-inch wire rope is woven in all directions, forming a weight-bearing surface upon which an electrician can walk. Pipes supported from the ceiling are arranged to allow complete hanging flexibility with a minimum of time and effort. The lighting instruments shoot through the thin wire mesh as shown in the photograph. This grid is ideal for the flexible space as well as ex-tremely useful in arena or over thrust situations.

Figure 23-11
The Tension Wire Grid

(a) View from the grid of the new Keck Theatre at Occidental College in Los Angeles. The woven cable grid is weight-bearing and offers complete access to overhead lighting positions. This full ceiling grid was installed by Hoffend & Son. (b) View from the stage. The Keck is a Courtyard Theatre with a seating capacity of 475. (c) Close-up view of a grid installation over the auditorium of a proscenium theatre. System developed by George Izenour and manufactured by J. R. Clancy. *Photo by Eiseman*

a

b

c

LIGHTING DANCE

At first glance, dance, which is most often performed on a proscenium stage with a formal leg-and-border arrangement, would seem to require the same sort of lighting as do other forms of production. But there is one most-important difference: when we attend a play we are vitally interested in the face of the actor to convey character, thoughts, and emotion. This is not true in dance, particularly ballet, in which the position and movement of the dancer's body tell all. A knowledgeable lover of ballet will scarcely notice a dancer's face and will surely not concentrate on it. The primary concern is movement, which good dance lighting will reveal and emphasize.

Figure 23-12
Dance Patterns

These patterns coincide with the principal movements of the dancers on the stage. (a) *Cross-stage "zones."* Dancers enter from and exit into the wings, working in zones that parallel the apron.
(b) *Up-and-down stage.* Dancers move toward the apron and away again. In ballet the chorus frequently poses along the sides while the principals take center stage. (c) *The diagonals.* An important pattern in modern dance, dancers enter from upstage wings and exit downstage on the opposite side, or vice versa.
(d) *Center stage.* An obvious location for important dancing.
(e) *Special spots.* These may be any place on stage (a few possibilities are indicated) in which a tight movement by principal dancers is performed.

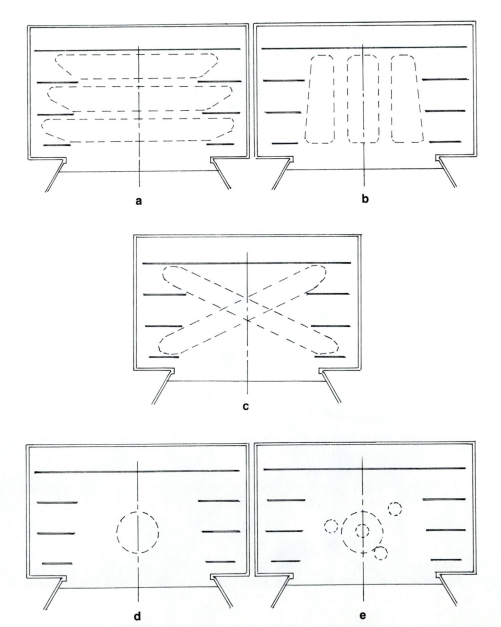

To do this, the axis of the principal light should parallel the axis of the movement. Thus a ballerina spinning in a pirouette should have the light hitting straight down on her or straight up from below. The latter, which has been used for trick effects in modern dance routines, would probably not be appropriate for classical ballet. Although light from directly overhead tends to make the human body appear shortened, it is still a good way to accent the rapid turning of the dance.

Assume that a ballerina faces the audience and raises her arm gracefully from her side to an angle of 45 degrees above her shoulder. This kind of movement is best accented by a light striking her armpit along the center line of the angle through which her arm was raised. A spotlight about 13 feet away at stage level would fulfill the requirement and would be hidden from the view of the audience if the dancer is close to the wings. If farther away, the ideal angle would no longer be possible, but this same location remains the best available position.

Of course it would be quite impractical to attempt to cover every single movement of a dance. A prodigious number of spotlights and an extremely complicated list of cues and light changes would be required. But provision can be made for some of the most significant moments and for more general lighting that will best suit the major movements of the work. The light designer must attend as many rehearsals as possible and take careful notes before sitting down at the drawing board. Fortunately, dances do fall into certain basic patterns of movement which can usually be covered successfully by one or more of the areas suggested in Figure 23–12.

Design Considerations

When lighting a theatrical production, it is probably most natural for the designer to begin with front visibility light and then move on to consideration of side and back light angles. In lighting most dance however, the designer will begin with the side lights: for here is the source of figure-modeling light. While a typical, theatrical lighting plot for the proscenium theatre will have at least one-half of its equipment located front-of-house, the dance plot will probably have three-quarters of its instruments backstage. This fact should be of interest to the lighting design student in terms of stage circuits as well as design technique; many houses have not provided the necessary number of circuits backstage for an average dance plot.

Location of Instruments

The following are the more-usual mounting positions for instruments (almost invariably spotlights).

Low Front • For the low-front position, the lights might be mounted on a low balcony rail. Although light from this angle tends to wash out body form, a little is desirable for the sake of visibility and/or color washing.

Medium Front • These lights would be mounted on a second balcony or a beam position. Again, this does little for the body and accentuates the shadows of the dancers' costumes on their legs. This angle corresponds with the 45-degree visibility light common to theatrical presentation and can be used as such if necessary.

High-Front • Roughly at a 60-degree angle, high-front is much more useful for dramatic presentation than for dance. This angle casts serious costume shadows on the legs of an otherwise beautiful ballerina.

Low-Side • For the low-side position, light would come from the floor of the wings. Although an unnatural angle, it is flattering to dancers, for it tends to lift the body. Low-side lighting instruments are called "shin kickers" or "shin busters" for obvious reasons. They are normally clear or colored with very light tints, and their light can fairly effectively be cut off the floor surface in order to eliminate scallops from the beams.

Medium-Side • For the medium-side position, lights are mounted about 8 or 10 feet above the floor in the wings. This may be regarded as *the* basic dance-lighting angle. It throws a wash across the stage with little important shadowing. It may be desirable to mount one or two additional spotlights a few feet higher to carry across to the far side of the stage. In this case both long- and short-throw spots are focused so that the centers of their beams are parallel. Medium-side should not be confused with high-side, which is described below.

High-Side • Light in the high-side position comes from 15 to 20 feet high in the wings or from the ends of electric battens (such units are called "pipe ends"). If too high an angle is chosen, the light will tend to push the dancers down and make them seem squat. However, a 60-degree high-side can be very effective for a dramatic moment and is particularly useful in modern dance.

Straight-Back • In the straight-back position, light comes from above but also from behind the dancer. This is a very fine position, for it highlights the body in space, separating it from the background, and it does not cause one dancer to throw a shadow on the next one.

Diagonal-Back • Like the straight-back position, light comes from above and behind the dancer but from an angle to the side as well. Frequently this is more desirable than straight-back because more of the dancer's body is lighted.

Down-Light • In the down-light position, lights are mounted directly overhead, an effect that tends to push the body down. They are useful only for specialized moments.

Follow Spots • The follow spot may come from the house or from some onstage location. This must be unobtrusive and should be used with a superior operator who can keep it so. Of course, in musical comedy dancing and the like, the blatant follow spots are all part of the show.

Booms

Low and medium side lighting require floor stands or booms as hanging positions. A dance concert or ballet will almost always call for a boom in each wing on both sides of the stage. This can total twelve booms for a large production. It is traditional to hang lighting instruments to the side of booms in the theatre, but for dance they should be mounted straight out from the boom pipes. In this way, the boom will take up as little wing space as possible, allowing more freedom for dancer entrances and exits (often leaps into the wings). See Figure 23–13 for a typical dance boom layout.

Booms must be clean and safe, with safety ties from the top of the pipe to the grid. Cable to booms will be neatest if run up the boom and onto an electric pipe for circuiting. However, many times floor pockets will have to be used. If this is the case, run the cable straight offstage from the boom and then turn up- or downstage to floor pocket locations. Cover the cable with carpeting and tape it securely.

Caution. Inexperienced dancers may try to use light booms as balance bars to warm up. Discourage this practice without being rude.

Color

For most ballet, strong colors are not desirable, but a basic tint certainly is. Pale lavender is frequently used, but for some ballets tradition may prescribe some other tint. Whatever color is selected becomes the neutral for the particular ballet. The other shades work in relation to it, and when blended together on the stage, approximate the neutral. Thus if lavender is the neutral, a violet next to it will appear quite warm and light blue will appear cool, while the violet and blue together will mix to lavender.

S.R. BOOM #2

Figure 23-13
A Dance Boom Layout

Instruments are hung on-stage from the boom to take up as little wing space as possible. This illustration shows instrument #1 lighting far stage-left in the second zone while instrument #2 lights mid-stage and #3 close. Instrument #4 is a low angle "shin."

An excellent effect is obtained by use of advancing and receding colors, which add apparent depth to the stage. The use of slightly cooler tints on the upstage dancers will make them appear farther away than they would seem otherwise. Likewise, warmer shades on the downstage dancers will bring them even farther forward. Care must be taken in using this technique, however. The tints must not be so far apart that the dancers visibly change color as they move through the zones.

The use of stronger colors for modern dance, especially in the side lights, is a common technique for expressing mood. Double hanging from the sides with a light tint or no color mixing into a more saturated color can offer the designer much variety.

Cueing and Other Considerations

Cue placement for a dramatic piece is often dictated by the rhythm of the work. This is even more true of dance. Movement nearly always corresponds to the music, and cueing should do the same. The cues for a ballet should be called by the stage manager from the score. The lighting designer should become extremely familiar with the music before beginning the design.

Dancers maintain balance by finding their "center." The lighting designer can help them by placing a "spotting light" or "centering light" in the auditorium. This should be a small 7½- or 15-watt red light located dead center at head height from the stage.

The Dance Plot

Figure 23–14 is a ¼-inch scale lighting plot for a production of the classical ballet *La Sylphide,* as well as for a short pas de dix. The ballet is in two acts with the first being an interior and the second a forest exterior. The theatre seats over 3,000 people in a large auditorium with front-of-house lighting positions limited to balcony rail and box booms. Figure 23–15 is a ½-inch scale plot of the overstage hang and Figure 23–16 is a ½-inch scale section. Color Plates 23–3a and 23–3b are photographs from the production.

Color • Three color washes come from the balcony rail: house left is Roscolux No. 18 (flame); center is Roscolux No. 01 (light bastard amber); and house right is Lee No. 161 (slate blue). Side light color coming from the booms was changed between the pas de dix and the two acts of *La Sylphide:* Act I having Roscolux No. 24 from stage right and no color from stage left; and Act II having no color from stage right and Roscolux No. 33 from stage left. Back light comes from medium PAR-64s colored in Roscolux No. 60 (no color blue) and 6-by-12 ERSs colored in Roscolux No. 38 (light rose). Leaf gobos colored with Roscolux No. 87 (pale yellow green) fill the stage for Act II.

Distribution • The normal boom has four instruments on it: a 6-by-12 "shin buster" (at approximately 2'0" above the deck) with no color; a 6-by-9 ERS (at approximately 6'0") to light the close side; a 6-by-12 ERS (at approximately 10'0") to light mid-stage; and a 6-by-16 ERS (at approximately 15'0") to light the far side of the zone. Front light comes from the balcony rail washes (a low angle) or the box booms (a high side angle).

AN OPERA PLOT

Lighting for the opera calls for a heightened theatricality and often will combine the techniques of theatre and dance.

Rape of Lucretia

Figure 23–17 is a light plot designed by Cindy Limauro for the Cincinnati Conservatory of Music's production of *Rape of Lucretia.* Scenery was designed by Paul Shortt. Figure 23–18 is the scene designer's cross section and Figure 23–19 is a part of the designer's hook-up. Color Plates 23–4a and 23–4b are production photographs.

Each of the two acts of this opera has two scenes. Act I, Scene 1 takes place at night in a military camp outside of Rome (Plate 23–4a); the second scene is an evening interior – inside Lucretia's home; Act II, Scene 1 is the rape scene; and Act II, Scene 2 is an exterior garden (Plate 23–4b).

The theatre is a small extended apron with a rather steep audience rake seating approximately 800 people. The control system is a LEE Colortran Prestige 2000.

Scene 1 • A stormy evening is the choice for this scene, with the atmosphere intended to have an aggressive and dirty feel. The flown tent piece, which can just be seen at the top of the production photograph in Plate 23–4a, was lit with down lights from bridge #2 (instruments #22 and #23). A practical brazier is located down-stage left and supported by ambers (R16) from the stage left torm positions. The front light for the scene comes from the first beam and is colored in a combination R60/R55 from house-left and R70 from house-right. A high-side R76 completes the picture. As the scene progresses, several lights located in the pit are brought up to accentuate the eerie and uneasy feeling desired by the designer.

Scene 2 • For this candlelit scene inside Lucretia's house the designer wanted a softer, yet menacing look. Front-of-house instruments in the second beam replaced those of the first beam, providing a less harsh angle and color of light; while still used, the R76 high side light was lowered in intensity.

Scene 3 • The scene in which the rape of Lucretia takes place begins with a very soft and gentle look created by light lavenders isolating the bed and its immediate surroundings. During the rape this shifts to "jagged" lighting angles and colors that emphasize the brutality of the act.

Scene 4 • The final scene in which Lucretia dies takes place in her garden, beautifully textured with break-up leaf gobos colored in R88 (Plate 23–4b). The lighting is gentle, with front sources from the second beam colored in R02.

Figure 23-14
The Dance Plot

A ¼-inch scale light plot for the classical ballet *La Sylphide* as produced by the Richmond Ballet. Staged by Frederic Franklin, lighting design by Craig Wolf. See Plate 23-3.

NOTE: SEE PLATE #3 (½" HANGING PLOT) FOR OVER-STAGE DETAIL.

S.L. BOOM #6

S.L. BOOM #5

S.L. BOOM #4

CALDRON SPECIALS

S.L. BOOM #3

S.L. BOOM #2

S.L. BOOM #1

ORCHESTRA PIT

CABLE TO FLOOR PKT. #4   S.L. BOOM #6
CABLE TO FLOOR POCKET #3   S.L. BOOM #5

CABLE TO FLOOR PKT. #2   S.L. BOOM #4
CABLE TO FLOOR PKT. #1   S.L. BOOM #3

CABLE TO ELEC. #1
CABLE TO TORM LEFT
S.L. BOOM #2   S.L. BOOM #1

H.R. "BOOM"

INSTRUMENT #   INSTRUMENT TYPE
FOCUS AREA   COLOR #
INSTRUMENT ANNOTATION

H.R. BALC. RAIL

CENTER BALC. RAIL

THE RICHMOND BALLET
PRODUCTION OF
PAS DE DIX AND LA SYLPHIDE
LIGHTING PLAN
THE MOSQUE THEATRE; RICHMOND, VA.
DESIGN BY: R. CRAIG WOLF

| DRAWN BY: R.C.W. 10-'82 | SCALE: ¼"=1'-0" | PLATE # 2 of 5 |
| DATE: 10-'82 | | |

Figure 23-15
La Sylphide

The ½-inch over-stage lighting layout to show detail.

#5 ELEC.: REQUIRES 10 CIRCUITS:
2 DROP BOXES = 8 +
2 FLOOR PKT. = 10
NO SPARE

S.L. BOOM #6
3 CIRCUITS TO
FLOOR PKT. #4

CIRCUITS ONLY: R89 + R44   8

REMAINDER CABLE TO TWO
4 - CIRCUIT DROP BOXES. PER ELEC.

#4 ELEC.: REQUIRES 9 CIRCUITS:
2 DROP BOXES = 8 +
1 FLOOR PKT. = 9 +
NO SPARE

S.L. BOOM #5
3 CIRCUITS TO
FLOOR PKT. #3

2 CIRCUITS:
1 TO FLOOR PKT. #3
1 TO FLOOR PKT. #4
CALDRON SPECIALS

S.L. BOOM #4
4 CIRCUITS TO
FLOOR PKT. #2

#2 ELEC.: REQUIRES 15 CIRCUITS:
2 DROP BOXES = 8 +
7 FROM TORMS = 15
LEAVES 1 SPARE

REMAINDER CABLE TO TWO
CIRCUIT DROP BOXES.

CABLE 2 CIRCUITS
TO TORM LEFT

CABLE 2 CIRCUITS
TO TORM LEFT

S.L. BOOM #3
4 CIRCUITS TO
FLOOR PKT. #1

#1 ELEC.: 21 CIRCUITS ON PIPE
6   "   TO #2 BOOMS L+R
1   "   TO FIREPLACE
2   "   SPARE
30 TOTAL CIRCUITS

3 CIRCUIT DROP TO
S.L. BOOM #2

S.L. BOOM #2
3 CIRCUITS TO
#1 ELEC.

CIRCUITS ONLY: R89 + R94   3

NOTE: SEE PLATE #2
FOR BOOM DETAILS.

4 CIRCUITS TO
LEFT TORM

S.L. BOOM #1

INSTRUMENT #   INSTRUMENT TYPE

FOCUS AREA   COLOR #

INSTRUMENT ANNOTATION

THE RICHMOND BALLET PRODUCTION OF
PAS DE DIX AND LA SYLPHIDE
LIGHTING OVER-STAGE HANG PLAN
THE MOSQUE THEATRE; RICHMOND, VA.
DESIGN BY: R. CRAIG WOLF
DRAWN BY: R.C.W.   SCALE: ½" = 1'-0"   PLATE # 3
DATE: 10·'82   OF 5

Figure 23-16
La Sylphide
The ½-inch center line section.

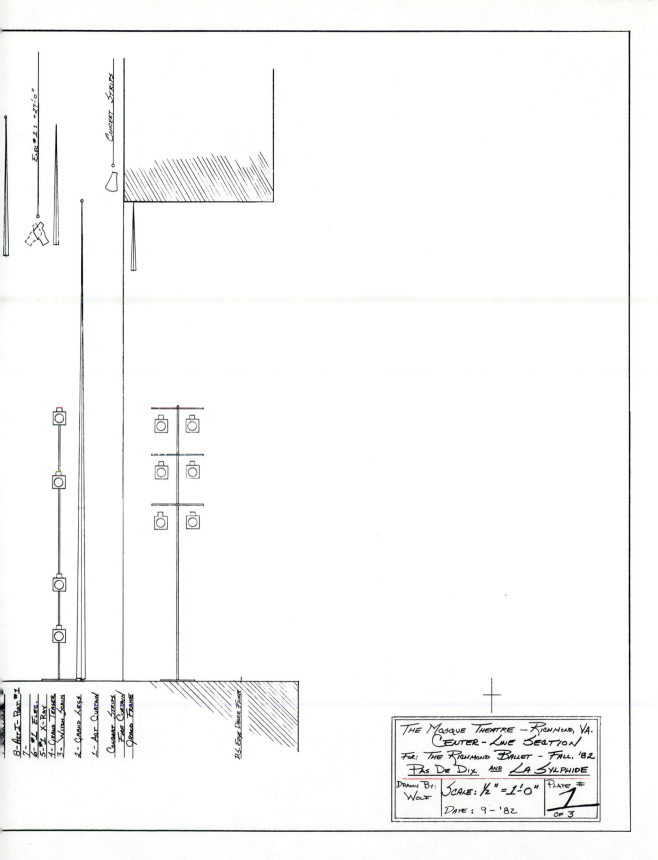

 Elec. #1: +27'-0"

Concert Strips

8 - Act I - Port. #1
7 -
6 - #1 Elec.
5 - #2 X-Ray
4 - Grand Teaser
3 - Witch Scrim

2 - Grand Legs

1 - Act Curtain

Concert Strips
Fire Curtain
Grand Frame

D.S. Edge Dance Floor

The Mosque Theatre — Richmond, VA.
CENTER - LINE SECTION
For: The Richmond Ballet - Fall '82
Pas De Dix and La Sylphide

Drawn By: Wolf

Scale: 1/2" = 1'-0"

Plate # 1 of 3

Date: 9 - '82

Figure 23-17
An Opera Plot

A light plot for *Rape of Lucretia,* produced by the Cincinnati Conservatory of Music, directed by John Eaton, and designed by Cindy Limauro. See Plate 23-4.

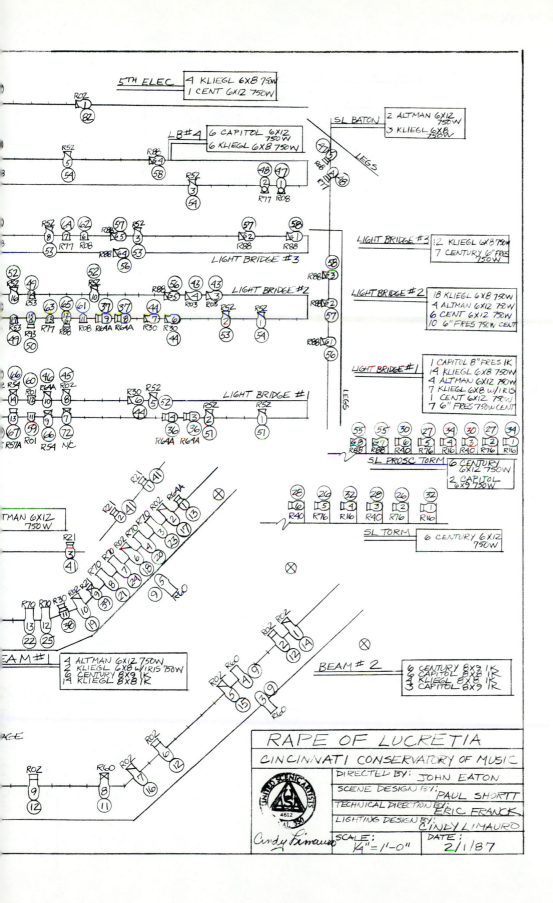

RAPE OF LUCRETIA

CINCINNATI CONSERVATORY OF MUSIC

DIRECTED BY: JOHN EATON
SCENE DESIGN BY: PAUL SHORTT
TECHNICAL DIRECTION BY: ERIC FRANCK
LIGHTING DESIGN BY: CINDY LIMAURO

SCALE: ¼" = 1'-0"   DATE: 2/1/87

Figure 23-18
Rape of Lucretia
The center line section.

Figure 23-19
Rape of Lucretia
The hook-up.

Channel	Position & Unit #	Type	Focus	Color	Circuit	Dimmer
1	SL PLAT CAN DNLTS 1-2-3	PAR 64 NSP 1K	DOWN LIGHT	R60		
2	SR PLAT CAN DNLTS 1-2-3	PAR 64 NSP 1K	DOWN LIGHT	R60		
3	RAKE CAN DNLT 2	PAR 64 NSP 1K	MALE CHORUS DOWNLIGHT	R60		
4	RAKE CAN DNLT 3	PAR 64 NSP 1K	DOWN LIGHT	R60		
5	RAKE CAN DNLTS 4-5-6	PAR 64 NSP 1K	DOWN LIGHT	R60		
6	SL RAMP CANS 1-2 SR RAMP CANS 1-2	PAR 64 NSP 1K	DOWN LIGHT	R60		
7	CENTER RAMP CANS 1-2	PAR 64 NSP 1K	DOWN LIGHT	R60		
8	RAKE CAN DNLT 1	PAR 64 NSP 1K	FEMALE CHORUS DOWNLIGHT	R60		
9	#1 BEAM 5 #2 BEAM 3-4	KLIEGL 8X8 1K	SL PLAT NARRATOR	R60		
10	#1 BEAM 20 #2 BEAM 16-17	KLIEGL 8X8 1K	SR PLAT NARRATOR	R60		
11	#2 BEAM 8-10-12	CAPITOL 8X9 1K	DS DECK WASH	R60		
12	#2 BEAM 2-6-9 11-14-18	CAPITOL 8X8 1K	DS DECK WASH	R02		
13	#1 BEAM 1-26	ALTMAN 6X12 750W	RAKE HPE	R64A		
14	#2 BEAM 1-13	CENTURY 8X9 1K	RAKE DL	R02		
15	#2 BEAM 5-15	CENTURY 8X9 1K	RAKE DC	R02		
16	#2 BEAM 7-19	CENTURY 8X9 1K	RAKE DR	R02		
17	#1 BEAM 2-17	CENTURY 8X9 1K	RAKE UL	R02		
18	#1 BEAM 6-21	CENTURY 8X9 1K	RAKE UC	R02		
19	#1 BEAM 10-24	CENTURY 8X9 1K	RAKE UR	R02		

Glossary

Arc Light A spotlight that has for its source an electric current arcing between two electrodes.

Amperage The rate of flow of an electric current through a conductor. The capacity of an electrical conductor.

Angstrom A unit of length used to specify wavelengths of light.

ANSI American National Standards Institute. The ANSI Code is a three-letter code used to identify lamps.

Asbestos Although asbestos is no longer used in the theatre, the term is sometimes used when referring to the Safety Curtain (see Safety Curtain).

Avista Change of scene or movement of scenery in full view of the audience.

Back Cloth English theatre expression for back drop.

Backstage Much the same as *off-stage* but used generally in reference to stage workers and stage machinery rather than to actors.

Bag Line Pick-up or bull line on a sandbag to lift the weight of the bag while trimming or clewing a line-set.

Barn Doors A device consisting of two or four hinged metal flaps which is placed in front of a spotlight to reduce the beam spread in one or more directions.

Batten (1) Pipe batten. Horizontal pipe hung from a line-set of a flying system. (2) Wooden batten. Top and bottom of roll drop.

Beam Port A front-of-house lighting position located in the ceiling of the theatre.

Blackout The instantaneous killing of all stage lights.

Bleeding Brightly colored undercoat of paint showing a second coat.

Bloom Specular reflection from mirror or highly polished surface.

Boards Slang for stage.

Book Set a two-fold of scenery in an open-book position.

Boom or **Boomerang** A vertical pipe for mounting spotlights.

Bounce Reflected diffuse light off the floor or walls.

Box Booms Lighting booms located in front-of-house box-seat positions.

Break To fold or unfold scenery.

Breakaway Scenery or properties rigged to break on cue.

Breast Line Fixed line to wall or gridiron that drags or breasts a piece of hanging scenery into an eccentric position. Also called a *drag line.*

Bridle Means of dividing the load of each liftline by spreading the pick-up points along the batten.

Bull Line Heavy four-stranded hemp rope used on a winch to lift uncounterweighted scenery.

Bumper (1) Low platform downstage of portal against which castered wagons bump. (2) Metal hoop fastened to a batten carrying lighting instruments to protect them from flying scenery and the scenery from hot instruments.

Bump-up Sudden movement of lights to a higher intensity.

Channel A lighting control path.

Channel replaces the term *dimmer* in modern usage.

Circuit Established paths of electricity.

Clewing Several lines are held together by knots or clew for handling as a single line.

Company Switch A distribution panel with hook-up terminals to supply the power for a traveling company's switchboard. Usually three-wire 220 volts, 600 amps on a side.

Cross Fade To fade from one lighting set-up to another without going through a dimout.

Cue A visual or audible signal from the stage manager to execute a predetermined movement of lights or scenery.

Cyc Short for cyclorama.

Cyc Knuckle Hardware for attaching side arms of a cyc batten to a regular pipe batten.

Dark House No performance or inactive theatre.

Dead Hung A unit of scenery hung directly from the gridiron and not a part of the flying system.

Deck Stage floor.

Diffusion A plastic medium placed in the color holder of a spotlight to break up the light in a variety of ways.

Dim Change the intensity of a light, either brighter or less bright.

Dimmer Apparatus for altering the flow of electric current to cause a light to be more or less bright.

Dimmer-per-Circuit A system in

which an individual dimmer is permanently assigned to each stage circuit.

Disappearance Trap Special counterweighted elevator trap used as a quick exit or disappearance by an actor.

Disconnect *see* Company switch.

Dolly A type of wagon.

Donkey Electric winch.

Douser Mechanical means of putting out a light.

Downstage The area nearest the footlights and curtain.

Draw Line Operating line of a traveler curtain rigging.

Dutchman (1) Condensing lens in a lens projector. (2) Scab or mending cleat. (3) Cloth strip covering a hinged joint.

Edge-up Framed scenery maneuver; raise a flat upright on its edge.

EMF Electromotive force or voltage.

End for End Reverse the position of an object.

ERF Stage jargon for ellipsoidal reflector floodlights.

ERS Stage jargon for ellipsoidal reflector spotlights.

Feel-up Take slack out of lift lines prior to setting the trim.

FEV Short for French Enamel Varnish.

Fill Light Wash or soft light that fills in the light on the face from the direction opposite the key light.

Flag Small piece of cloth inserted into the lay of the purchase line as a trim mark.

Flat In the commercial theatre, the stiffening of two or more hinged wings into a flat plane or wall.

Flipper Jog hinged to a single wing.

Floatdown Kitelike action when a flat is allowed to fall or float to the floor.

Flood Widespread focus on a spotlight. Also, short for floodlight.

Floodlight A lighting instrument that produces a broad spread of light. Often misapplied to other lighting apparatus.

Focus (1) The direction in which a lighting instrument is aimed. (2) Adjustment of the size or shape of a light beam.

FOH Front-of-house. Anything located on the audience side of the proscenium arch.

Follow Cue A cue timed to follow an original cue so quickly it does not warrant a separate cue number.

Follow Spot A high-intensity, long throw spotlight requiring an operator in order to follow action on stage.

Footcandle The measurement of illumination; the amount of light from one candle that will fall on a surface one foot from the candle.

Fresnel (correctly pronounced Fre′ nel) A lens recognized by its concentric rings. The spotlight designed to use this lens.

Front Lighting Illumination on the stage from instruments placed in the auditorium.

Frost *see* Diffusion.

Funnel Also known as a top hat. A short metal cylinder placed in front of a spotlight to reduce the beam spread.

Gobo A metal cutout used with a spotlight to obtain a patterned beam.

Grand Drape Decorative first border in old proscenium-type theatres.

Greek-it Fake lettering that has no meaning; doubletalk.

Grip Stagehand.

Gripping Running scenery on the floor by stagehands or grips.

Ground Row Horizontal profile unit of scenery to mask the bottom of a drop or cyclorama.

Halation Undesirable spreading of light from a spotlight. A halo of light around the beam.

Head Block Multigrooved pulley or multipulley sheave in a lineset.

Head Spot Very narrow beam from a spotlight focused on an actor's head. Also called *pin spot*.

Hook-up A lighting schedule which lists instruments by dimmer number.

House Curtain Main curtain of a proscenium theatre designed to tie in with the house decorations. Also called act curtain.

IA Short for IATSE—International Alliance of Theatrical Stage Employees. The stagehands' union.

In-one Foremost downstage acting position, traditionally in front of oleo.

Interconnect A flexible system allowing the electrical connection of any stage circuit with any dimmer. Also called patch panel.

Iris Mechanical means of closing the aperture of a spotlight.

Jack Framed brace to hold scenery upright.

Jackknife Pivoting wagon movement like the action of blades in a jackknife.

Jog Narrow-width wing.

Juice Commercial slang for electricity.

Jumper Cable connecting two or more lighting instruments.

Key Light Accent or highlight on actor's face, usually from the direction of the motivating light for the scene.

Keystoning Distortion of a projected image when the projector is oblique to the screen.

Klieglight A type of spotlight sold by Kliegl Bros. *Klieg* is often used as a synonym for any bright light.

Knife Steel guide for a tracked wagon.

Ladder Hanging ladderlike frame for mounting spotlights.

Lamp (1) Correctly, the name of what is often called a light bulb. (2) In the commercial theatre the term for any lighting instrument, particularly a spotlight.

Lead Cable from power supply.

Left Stage To the actor's left as he or she faces the audience.

Lekolite A type of spotlight sold by Strand Lighting. *Leko* is often used as a generic term for any ellipsoidal reflector spotlight.

Light Leak Unwanted spill from an instrument or through scenery.

Line Set A group of from three to five lines using the same head block to lift a pipe batten or unit of scenery.

Lip A beveled three-ply strip attached so as to overhang the edge of a framed unit of scenery and thereby conceal the open crack of a joint with an adjacent unit.

Load Lamp or instrument.

Load In When a show's scenery

moves into the theatre. The reverse is *Load Out.*

Loft Block Individual pulley on the gridiron of a line set.

Lumen Intensity measurement of a source of light.

Make-up Put together a setting.

Mask Conceal from the audience, usually by scenic pieces or neutral hangings, any portion of the backstage area or equipment.

Mat Shutter or matting material over the face of a spotlight to change the shape of the beam.

Muling Block Pulley to change the horizontal direction of a moving line.

Offstage Out of sight of the audience. Away from the center of the stage.

Ohm An electrical measurement of resistance in a circuit.

Ohm's Law A statement of the relationship of current, electric potential, and resistance in a circuit. It may be expressed by the equation: $I = \dfrac{E}{R}$.

Oleo Traditionally the in-one backdrop. A decoratively painted addrop from vaudeville.

Olivette Old stand floodlight.

On and Off Referring to scenery sitting parallel to the footlights.

Onstage In sight of the audience. Toward the center of the stage.

P and OP Promp and Opposite Promp. An English and old American method indicating the left and right side of the stage. *Promp* was the side of the prompter or stage manager.

PAR Short for parabolic aluminized reflector lamp.

PAR Head Slang for PAR 64 lighting instrument.

Patch Panel *see* Interconnect.

P-C Plano convex lens or lighting instrument.

Peek Expose the backstage or see past masking.

Picture The general composition of the setting as seen from the average sightline seat.

Pigtail Short length of lead cable.

Pin Spot *see* Head spot.

Plot Short for lighting plot.

Practical Descriptive of something that can be used by the actor, like a window sash that can actually be raised or a light that can be switched on and off.

Pre-set (1) A pre-arranged lighting set-up held in readiness for later use. (2) Prepositioned scenery that will be revealed later in the scene.

Prop Short for *property*. Also refers to anything not real or practical.

Purchase Line Flyman's operating line in a counterweight system.

Quartz-iodine Early name for what is now known as the tungsten-halogen lamp.

Raked Scenery or stage floor angled to the footlights.

Return Element of scenery that returns the downstage edge of the setting offstage to the right or left.

Right Stage To the actor's right as he or she faces the audience.

Roundel A glass color filter for lighting instruments.

RPF Short for Rigid Plastic Foam. Styrofoam.

RUF Short for Rigid (Poly)Urethane Foam.

Safety Curtain Fire-retardant curtain or framed member located directly upstage of the proscenium opening to protect the audience from fire on the stage.

Sandbag Counterweight for pin-and-rail flying system.

Scenography (In European theatre, *scenographie*) Literally, the graphics of scenery, drawing, and painting. In modern usage, combining the design of scenery, lighting, and costumes into a single visual concept.

Scoop Slang for ellipsoidal reflector floodlight.

Sharp Focus Narrow-beam focus of a spotlight.

Shoe (1) Special construction on the end of the toggle rail, the internal framing member of a flat. (2) Framed platform to encase the legs of furniture for protection on tour.

Shop Order A lighting rental equipment list for the purpose of bids.

Short Slang for short circuit, the term for the escape of electricity from its prescribed path.

Show Portal Framed teaser and tormentor designed especially for the show.

Shutter A beam-framing device located at the aperture of an ellipsoidal reflector spotlight.

Sightline Line of sight from an audience seat to a point on stage. In perspective, line of sight to a point on object from observation point.

Slash A diagonal beam of side lighting on a stage drapery or window curtain creating an arbitrary pattern of light.

Snatch Block Pulley block with removable side to permit its insertion into rigging or tackle system without having to rethread all the line.

Snatching To hook and unhook a flown piece of scenery during the shift.

Spike Mark on floor to locate the working position of scenery or properties.

Spot Focus Narrow beam focus.

Spot Line A fixed line spotted on the gridiron directly over its working position.

Spotlight A lighting instrument with a lens that throws an intense light on a defined area. The term is often misapplied to other lighting instruments.

Spot Sheave The special placement of a loft sheave on the gridiron for an additional or single running line.

Stab Low trim or tie-off on the bottom rail of the pin-and-rail flying system.

Stage Left and Stage Right *see* Left stage and Right stage.

Stage Peg and Plug Bolt-threaded peg which fits into an inside threaded plug.

Stage Screw Screw-threaded peg.

Strike Take down a setting. Remove properties or lights.

Sunday Knot used to clew or hold several lines together.

Surround or **Shroud** Carry-off platforms that surround a turntable.

Switchboard Fixed or movable panel with switches, dimmers, and so forth, used to control the stage lights.

Tails Lines dropped from a batten to hang scenery several feet below the batten.

Teaser Top or horizontal member of the adjustable frame downstage of the setting.

Top Hat   *see* Funnel.

Tormentor   Side or vertical members of the adjustable frame downstage of the setting.

Traps   System of openings through the stage floor.

Trick Line   Small line used to trigger a breakaway or trick device.

Trim   Mark designating the height of a line set.   **High Trim** Height of a flown piece when in *out* position.   **Low Trim** Height of flown piece when in an *in* (or working) position.

Tripping   Raising a piece of soft scenery from the bottom as well as from the top.

Tungsten-Halogen   An improved form of the incandescent filament lamp which contains a small quantity of halogen gas in the bulb.

Up and Down   Reference to scenery sitting perpendicular to the footlights.

Upstage   On the stage but away from the audience.

USA   United Scenic Artists. Theatrical union for scenic artists; scenery, costume, and lighting designers; and allied crafts.

Voltage   The pressure behind electrical flow.

Wagon   A platform on casters.

Wattage   An electrical term for the rate of doing work.

Wash   Low angle front-of-house lighting sources which illuminate in a general manner.

Wild   Hinged portion of a setting that is free to move.

Wing   In the commercial theatre the term *single wing* refers to the basic unit of framed scenery, commonly called a *flat* in the noncommercial theatre.

Wings   Area offstage right and left, stemming from the era of wings and backdrops.

X-Rays   Old expression designating the first row of border lights.

Zone   A single stage-left to stage-right lighting area; most often used in dance lighting.

Additional Reading

Scene Design

The following books are recommended as additional reading to increase the reader's understanding of the philosophy and historical background of scene design as part of the art of theatre.

THE DESIGN CONCEPT

Appia, Adolphe. *"Adolphe Appia: A Gospel for Modern Stage."* *Theatre Arts Monthly*, August 1932.
 Entire issue devoted to Appia's influence on present-day scene and lighting design.

Bay, Howard. *Stage Design.* New York: Drama Book 1978.

Brockett, Oscar G. *The Theatre: An Introduction*, 4th ed. New York: Holt, Rinehart and Winston, 1979.

Burian, Jarka. *The Scenography of Josef Svoboda.* Middletown, Conn.: Wesleyan University Press, 1971.

Gorelik, Mordeca. *New Theatres for Old.* New York: Samuel French. 1975.

Izenour, George. *Theatre Design.* New York: McGraw-Hill, 1979.

Jones, Robert E. *The Dramatic Imagination.* New York: Theatre Arts, 1941.

Kernodle, George R. *From Art to Theatre.* Chicago: University of Chicago Press, 1988.

Mielziner, Jo. *Designing for the Theatre.* New York: Atheneum, 1965.

Nicoll, Allardyce. *Theatre and Dramatic Theory.* London: Greenwood, 1978.

Oenslager, Donald M. *The Theatre of Donald Oenslager.* Middletown, Conn.: Wesleyan University Press, 1978.

Pendleton, Ralph. *Theatre of Robert Edmund Jones.* Middletown, Conn.: Wesleyan University Press, 1977.

Welker, David. *Theatrical Set Design.* Boston: Allyn & Bacon, 1979.

DESIGN APPLICATION

The following are recommended to broaden knowledge of the practicable application of design principles to modern theatre practices and related theatrical forms.

Aronson, Arnold. *American Set Design.* New York: Theatre Comm., 1985.

Dean, Alexander and Carra, Lawrence. *Fundamentals of Play Directing*, 3d ed. New York: Holt, Rinehart and Winston, 1974.

Hainaux, René (editor). *Stage Design Throughout the World Since 1970.* New York: Theatre Arts, 1975.

Nagler, Alois. *Source Book in Theatre History.* New York: Dover, 1952.

Good source book still in print.

Payne, Darwin R. *Materials and Crafts of the Scenographic Model.* Carbondale, Ill.: Southern Illinois University Press, 1987.

Payne, Darwin R. *The Sceno-graphic Imagination.* Carbondale, Ill.: Southern Illinois University Press, 1986.

DRAWING AND PAINTING

The following books are recommended to the student scene designer to help develop his skill as a visual artist and draftsman.

Albers, Josef. *The Interaction of Color.* New Haven, Conn.: Yale University Press, 1975.
 Still a classic study of color.

Birren, Faber. *A Grammar of Color*, based on Munsell. New York: Van Nostrand Reinhold, 1984.

Chevreul, M. E. *The Principles of Harmony and Contrast of Colors.* New York: Van Nostrand Reinhold, 1981.

Color Harmony Manual, Ostwald Theory of Color. Chicago: Container Corporation of America, 1948.
 Limited ed., expertly presented.

Itten, Johannes. *The Art of Color.* New York: Van Nostrand Reinhold, 1973.

Jones, Tom Douglas. *The Art of Light and Color.* New York: Van Nostrand Reinhold, 1972.

Parker, W. Oren. *Sceno-Graphic Techniques.* Carbondale, Ill.: Southern Illinois University Press, 1987.

FURNITURE AND DECORATIONS

The following are recommended as general reference material for designing furniture and decorating interiors.

Flanigan, Micheal. *American Furniture from Kaufman Collection.*
Washington: National Gallery of Art, 1987.

Gottshall, Franklin H., *How to Make Colonial Furniture.* New York: Macmillan, 1980.

Grant, Ian (editor). *Great Interiors.* London: Hamlyn, 1971.

Hayward, Helena (editor). *World Furniture.* London: Hamlyn, 1971.

Jones, Bernard E. *The Complete Woodworker.* Berkeley, Calif: Ten Speed Press, 1980.

Meyer, Franz S. *Handbook of Ornament.* New York: Dover, 1957.

Praz, Mario. *An Illustrated History of Interior Decoration.* New York: Thamas Hudson, 1984.

Richter, G. M. *The Furniture of the Greek Etruscan and Roman.* Ithaca, N.Y.: Cornell University Press, 1984.

Strange, T. Arthur. *A Guide to Collectors: English Furniture and Decoration.* London: McCorquodale, 1903.
 In the rare book class, but still an excellent compilation and analysis of seventeenth- and eighteenth-century English and French furniture, interior styles.

Strange, T. Arthur. *Historical Guide to French Interiors.* London: McCorquodale, 1903.

Wilson, Jose, and Leaman Arthur. *Decorating Defined.* New York: Simon and Schuster, 1970.
 A dictionary of decoration and design.

Technical Production

The following books are recommended as additional reading to give the reader a greater insight into scenery construction techniques and general shop practices.

SCENERY CONSTRUCTION

Arnold, Richard L., *Scene Technology.* Englewood Cliffs, N.J.: Prentice Hall, 1985.

Bowman, Ned. *Handbook of Technical Practice for the Performing Arts.* Norwalk, Conn.: Scenographic Media, 1975.

Bryson, Nicholas L. *Thermoplastic Scenery for the Theatre.* New York: Drama Book Publishers, 1970.

Burris-Meyer, Harold, and Cole, Edward C. *Scenery for the Theatre*, rev. ed. Boston: Little, Brown, 1972.

The Complete Woodworker. New York: David McKay Co., n.d.

Daniels, George. *How to Use Hand and Power Tools.* New York: Van Nostrand Reinhold, 1978.

Dykes Lumber Company, *Moulding Catalog*, No. 49. Dykes Lumber Co., 137 West 24th Street, New York, N.Y., 10011, n.d.

Feirer, John, and Hutchings, Gilbert. *Carpentry and Building Construction.* New York: Scribner, 1981.

Finelli, Patrick M. (editor). *Directory of Software for Technical Theatre.* United States Institute of Theatre Technology, 1988.

Krenov, James. *Worker in Wood.* New York: Van Nostrand Reinhold, 1981.

Ramsey, Charles G., and Sleeper, Harold R. *Architectural Graphic Standards*, 7th ed. New York: Wiley, 1981.

Salaman, R. A. *Carpentry Tools.* New York: Scribner, 1976.

Taylor, Douglas C. *Metalworking for the Designer and Technician.* New York: Drama Book Publishers, 1974.

THE HANDLING OF SCENERY

The following provide a more specialized knowledge of the various methods of moving scenery, backstage organization, and rigging techniques.

Gillette, A. S. *Stage Scenery.* New York: Harper & Row. 3rd ed. 1980.

Glerum, Jay O. *Stage Rigging Handbook.* Carbondale, Ill.: Southern Illinois University Press, 1987.

How to Put Rope to Work. Plymouth Cordage Company, North Plymouth, Mass.

Irving, J., and Searl. *Knots, Ties and Splices.* New York: Routledge & Kegan Paul, 1978.

PAINTING AND PROPERTIES

The following are recommended to expand skill in scene-painting techniques and the building of properties.

Kenton, Warren. *Stage Properties and How to Make Them.* New York: Drama Books, 1978.

Motley. *Theatre Props.* New York: Drama Books, 1976.

Pecktal, Lynn. *Designing and Painting for the Theatre.* New York: Holt, Rinehart and Winston, 1975.

Pinnell, Willard. *Theatrical Scene Painting.* Carbondale, Ill.: Southern Illinois University Press, 1985.

Polunin, Vladimir. *The Continental Method of Scene Painting.* Princeton, N.J.: Princeton Book, 1980.

Veaner, Daniel. *Scene Painting, Tools and Techniques.* Englewood Cliffs, N.J.: Prentice Hall, 1984.

GENERAL

The following books are recommended as supplementary reading in the generalized area of scene design, technical production, and stage lighting.

American Theatre Planning Board. *A Theatre Check List.* Middletown, Conn.: Wesleyan University Press, 1983.
Guide to planning and construction of proscenium and open stage.

Bellman, Willard F. *Scene Design, Stage Lighting, Sound, Costume and Makeup.* New York: Harper & Row, 1983.

Rossol, Monona, *Stage Fright.* New York: Center for Occupational Hazards, 1986.
Health and safety in the theatre, a very practical guide.

Selden, Samuel, and Rezzuto, Tom. *Essentials of Stage Scenery.* New York: Appleton-Century-Crofts, 1972.

Theatre Design and Technology.
The official journal of the U.S. Institute of Theatre Technology, 330 West 42nd St., New York, N.Y. 10036.

Theatre Sound

While there are very few books written specifically on theatre sound, the following is a list of those which cover related topics. Under the supplementary heading will be found periodicals and other materials of value to the audio designer and technician.

GENERAL

Ballou, Glen, (editor). *Handbook for Sound Engineers.* Indianapolis: Howard W. Sams, 1987.
The most comprehensive of audio reference books.

Burris-Meyer, Harold; Mallory, Vincent; Goodfriend, Lewis S. *Sound in the Theatre.* Rev. Ed. New York: Theatre Arts Books, 1979.
Fairly outdated, but useful for theatre acoustics.

Collison, David. *Stage Sound,* 2nd Ed. London: Cassell, 1982.
Good reading, but slightly outdated and relates almost exclusively to British practice.

Davis, Don and Carolyn. *Sound System Engineering,* 2nd Ed. Indianapolis: Howard W. Sams, 1987.
Formulas needed to build a sound system.

Davis, Gary and Jones, Ralph. *The Sound Reinforcement Handbook.* Milwaukee: Hal Leonard, 1987.
A Yamaha publication with a great deal of valuable information covering practical material not found in other books.

Eargle, John. *The Microphone Handbook.* Plainview, N.Y.: Elar, 1982.
Good information on stereo microphone techniques.

Huber, David Miles. *Microphone Manual.* Indianapolis: Howard W. Sams, 1988.
An up-to-date volume covering all types of microphones.

Pohlmann, Ken C. *Principles of Digital Audio.* 2nd Ed. Indianapolis: Howard W. Sams, 1989.

Sadie, Stanley (editor). *Norton/Grove Concise Encyclopedia of Music.* London: Macmillan, 1988.
A reference book on classical music.

Sinclair, Ian R. (editor). *Audio Electronics Reference Book.* Oxford: Blackwell Scientific, 1989.
The inner workings of various audio components.

Thom, Randy. *Audio Craft,* 2nd Ed. Washington: National Federation of Community Broadcasters, 1989.
An excellent introductory book, however it is designed primarily for radio production.

Waaser, Carol M. *Sound and Music for the Theatre.* New York: Richards Rosen, 1976.
Probably the best of sound *design* books, but badly outdated.

Woram, John M. *The Recording Studio Handbook.* Plainview, N.Y.: Elar, 1981.

SUPPLEMENTARY

Audio.
A monthly magazine aimed at the consumer with good articles on audio applications.

Audio Engineering Society (AES).
This organization publishes tapes and reprints of papers delivered at their annual conventions in addition to their journal listed below.

db magazine.
A bi-monthly publication containing articles primarily of interest to musicians and small recording studios.

Journal of the Audio Engineering Society.
Published 10 times a year by the AES, often containing highly technical information and papers on new developments.

Mix.
Published monthly, this magazine is intended primarily for audio professionals.

Recording Engineer/Producer.
A magazine aimed at those

working in the recording industry. It is published monthly. *Schwann.*

A quarterly guide to all currently available CDs, LPs, and cassettes.

Stage Lighting

The following books are recommended as supplementary reading in the areas of lighting design and technology. They would form an invaluable nucleus for the private library of anyone genuinely interested in the field.

The general list contains books of broad approach to the whole stage-lighting field, and offers material of value in several facets of theatre lighting. The supplementary titles contain matter related to specific aspects, and also include a few periodicals that frequently carry articles of interest to the lighting designer for the stage.

GENERAL

Bellman, Willard F. *Lighting the Stage: Art and Practice*, 2nd Ed. New York: Crowell, 1974.

Bentham, Frederick. *The Art of Stage Lighting*, 2nd Ed. New York: Theatre Arts Books, 1976.
Covers the field well, but for the American reader the British terminology is sometimes confusing.

Burian, Jarka. *The Scenography of Josef Svoboda.* Middletown, Conn.: Wesleyan University Press, 1971.

Gillette, J. Michael. *Designing with Light*, 2nd Ed. Mountain View, Calif.: Mayfield, 1989.

McCandless, Stanley. *A Method of Lighting the Stage*, 4th Ed. New York: Theatre Arts Books, 1958.
This little book has had more influence on lighting design in the United States than any other.

Moody, James L. *Concert Lighting.* Boston: Focal Press, 1989.
The first book published concerned with the field of concert lighting.

Palmer, Richard H. *The Lighting Art.* Englewood Cliffs, N.J.: Prentice-Hall, 1985.
An interesting book on the aesthetics of stage lighting design.

Pilbrow, Richard. *Stage Lighting*, Rev. Ed. New York: Drama Book Publishers, 1979.
A delightful book covering the theories of this English designer.

Rosenthal, Jean and Wertenbaker, Lael. *The Magic of Light.* Boston: Little, Brown, 1972.

Ruben, Joel E. and Watson, Leland H. *Theatrical Lighting Practice.* New York: Theatre Arts Books, 1954.

Watson, Lee. *Handbook of Lighting Design.* New York: McGraw-Hill, 1990.
Part One of this new volume covers lighting design of all the specialty areas, while Part Two concerns itself with employment and working in the profession.

SUPPLEMENTARY

Bureau of Naval Personnel. *Basic Electricity.* New York: Dover Publications, 1962.
A clear and simple presentation of the fundamentals of electricity.

General Electric Company. Cleveland. *Fundamentals of Light and Lighting.* 1956.
Excellent material on color, sources, and behavior of light.

General Electric Company. Cleveland. *Large Lamp Bulletin.*
Almost a textbook on sources.

GTE Sylvania. *Sylvania Lighting Handbook.* 7th Ed. Danvers, Mass.: GTE Sylvania Lighting Center, 1985.
Very good information on lamps and basic lighting considerations.

Illuminating Engineering Society, New York: *IES Lighting Handbook.*
Pertinent information on color, instruments, equipment, and use.

Jones, Robert Edmond. *The Dramatic Imagination.* New York: Theatre Arts Books, 1941.
Just for the inspiration.

Kliegl Bros., New York: Equipment Catalogues.

Kook, Edward F. *Images in Light for the Living Theatre.* New York: Privately printed, 1963.
An interesting survey on the use of projections in the theatre.

Lee Colortran, Burbank, Calif. Equipment Catalogues.

McCandless, Stanley. *A Syllabus of Stage Lighting.* 11th Ed. New York: Drama Book Publishers, n.d.
A historical reference book and dictionary of stage-lighting terms.

Penzel, Frederick. *Theatre Lighting Before Electricity.* Middletown, Conn.: Wesleyan University Press, 1978.

Strand Lighting, Rancho Dominguez, Calif. Equipment Catalogues.

Warfel, William. *Handbook of Stage Lighting Graphics.* New York: Drama Book Publishers, 1974.
A publication intending to establish a standard for lighting graphics.

Warfel, William B. and Klappert, Walter A. *Color Science for Lighting the Stage.* New Haven, Conn.: Yale University Press, 1981.
Color filter analysis.

Theatre Crafts.
A general theatre technology magazine often containing valuable lighting information.

Lighting Dimensions.
A magazine for lighting designers and technicians published by the same company as *Theatre Crafts.*

Theatre Design and Technology.
A publication of the United States Institute of Theatre Technology.

Index